Communications
in Computer and Information Science

2127

Rationale

The CCIS series is devoted to the publication of proceedings of computer science conferences. Its aim is to efficiently disseminate original research results in informatics in printed and electronic form. While the focus is on publication of peer-reviewed full papers presenting mature work, inclusion of reviewed short papers reporting on work in progress is welcome, too. Besides globally relevant meetings with internationally representative program committees guaranteeing a strict peer-reviewing and paper selection process, conferences run by societies or of high regional or national relevance are also considered for publication.

Topics

The topical scope of CCIS spans the entire spectrum of informatics ranging from foundational topics in the theory of computing to information and communications science and technology and a broad variety of interdisciplinary application fields.

Information for Volume Editors and Authors

Publication in CCIS is free of charge. No royalties are paid, however, we offer registered conference participants temporary free access to the online version of the conference proceedings on SpringerLink (http://link.springer.com) by means of an http referrer from the conference website and/or a number of complimentary printed copies, as specified in the official acceptance email of the event.

CCIS proceedings can be published in time for distribution at conferences or as postproceedings, and delivered in the form of printed books and/or electronically as USBs and/or e-content licenses for accessing proceedings at SpringerLink. Furthermore, CCIS proceedings are included in the CCIS electronic book series hosted in the SpringerLink digital library at http://link.springer.com/bookseries/7899. Conferences publishing in CCIS are allowed to use Online Conference Service (OCS) for managing the whole proceedings lifecycle (from submission and reviewing to preparing for publication) free of charge.

Publication process

The language of publication is exclusively English. Authors publishing in CCIS have to sign the Springer CCIS copyright transfer form, however, they are free to use their material published in CCIS for substantially changed, more elaborate subsequent publications elsewhere. For the preparation of the camera-ready papers/files, authors have to strictly adhere to the Springer CCIS Authors' Instructions and are strongly encouraged to use the CCIS LaTeX style files or templates.

Abstracting/Indexing

CCIS is abstracted/indexed in DBLP, Google Scholar, EI-Compendex, Mathematical Reviews, SCImago, Scopus. CCIS volumes are also submitted for the inclusion in ISI Proceedings.

How to start

To start the evaluation of your proposal for inclusion in the CCIS series, please send an e-mail to ccis@springer.com.

Hemachandran K · Raul Villamarin Rodriguez ·
Manjeet Rege · Vincenzo Piuri · Guandong Xu ·
Kok-Leong Ong
Editors

Artificial Intelligence and Knowledge Processing

Third International Conference, AIKP 2023
Hyderabad, India, October 6–8, 2023
Revised Selected Papers

 Springer

Editors
Hemachandran K 🅘
Woxsen Univerisity
Hyderabad, Andhra Pradesh, India

Raul Villamarin Rodriguez 🅘
Woxsen University
Hyderabad, Andhra Pradesh, India

Manjeet Rege 🅘
University of St. Thomas
Saint Paul, MN, USA

Vincenzo Piuri
University of Milan
Milano, Italy

Guandong Xu 🅘
University of Technology Sydney
Sydney, NSW, Australia

Kok-Leong Ong
RMIT University
Melbourne, VIC, Australia

ISSN 1865-0929   ISSN 1865-0937 (electronic)
Communications in Computer and Information Science
ISBN 978-3-031-68616-0   ISBN 978-3-031-68617-7 (eBook)
https://doi.org/10.1007/978-3-031-68617-7

Preface

Artificial Intelligence (AI) applications are rapidly transforming industries and societies around the world, from sophisticated algorithms that power recommendation systems and self-driving cars to natural language processing models that enable human-computer interactions. However, the combination of AI with Knowledge Processing allows the machine to comprehend, reason, and infer knowledge from large and complicated datasets and enables intelligent systems to observe the world and make efficient decisions. This could be a critical step towards human-level intelligence and beyond. Furthermore, as AI evolves, ethical questions around its usage grow more important, spurring discussions about justice, transparency, accountability, and societal impacts.

The 3rd International Conference on Artificial Intelligence and Knowledge Processing (AIKP 2023), organized by Woxsen University, Hyderabad, India and University of St. Thomas, MN, USA, was focused on the aforementioned theme and brought together academics, students, and researchers to showcase their expertise in the multidisciplinary field of AI and Knowledge Processing, which includes but is not limited to Artificial Intelligence, Deep Learning, Machine Learning, Decision Support Systems, Knowledge Representation, Intelligent Systems, Fuzzy-Based Neural Networks, and other fields. The limitations, opportunities, and challenges in the field were also showcased and discussed. The papers published here will also act as a reference for future researchers who have an inclination to work in the field. The current proceedings feature twenty-eight research articles, including original research and review articles, from a pool of 118 of articles, which went through a rigorous double-blind review process. The manuscripts accepted were in the initial phase sent to three independent reviewers. The conference committee made sure that for any manuscript written by any particular Chair/Co-Chair, he/she must be excluded from the review process of the same and the responsibility given to some other person. Once the revised paper was received from the authors, it was verified and if needed another round of revision was requested from the authors considering the quality of the conference. Each Program Chair and member of the Program Committee ensured the quality, originality, and authenticity of the article and was actively involved in the review process. All the accepted manuscripts are published in this volume of Springer Nature's Communications in Computer and Information Science.

April 2024

Hemachandran K
Raul Villamarin Rodriguez
Manjeet Rege

Organization

Chief Patrons

Raul V. Rodriguez   Woxsen University, India

Chairs

Hemachandran K.   Woxsen University, India
Raul V. Rodriguez   Woxsen University, India
Manjeet Rege   University of St. Thomas, USA.
Guandong Xu   University of Technology Sydney, Australia
Kok-Leong Ong   RMIT University, Australia

Co-chairs

Vincenzo Piuri   University of Milan, Italy
Sivaramakrishnan Rajaraman   National Library of Medicine, National Institutes
          of Health, USA
Rajesh Kumar K. V.   Woxsen University, India

Convenor

Hemachandran K.   Woxsen University, India

Co-convenors

Rajesh Kumar K. V.   Woxsen University, India
Bikash Kumar Pradhan   Assistant Woxsen University, India
Shahid Mohammad Ganie   Woxsen University, India

Technical Programme Chairs

Revathi Theerthagiri	Woxsen University, India
Sandeep Saharan	Woxsen University, India
Mayank Gupta	Woxsen University, India
Lokesh Kumar	Woxsen University, India
Punit Kumar Singh	Woxsen University, India
Debashish Mishra	Woxsen University, India

International Advisory Board Members

Zita Zoltay Paprika	Corvinus Business School, Hungary
Umashankar Subramaniam	Prince Sultan University, Saudi Arabia
Xiao-Zhi Gao	University of Eastern Finland, Finland
Llorenc Valverde	Universitat de les Illes Balears, Spain
Gabriel Kabanda	Zimbabwe Academy of Sciences, Zimbabwe
Ezendu Ariwa	Warwick University, UK
Petia Radeva	University of Barcelona, Spain
Vasos Pavlika	University College London, UK
Thinagaran Perumal	University Putra Malaysia, Malaysia
Linda Mary Simon	Christ College Irinjalakuda, India
Imed Ben Dhaou	Dar Al-Hekma University, Saudi Arabia
Juan R. Jaramillo	Adelphi University, USA
Sivarama Krishnan Rajaraman	NLM, National Institutes of Health, USA
Ravi Dadsena	DZNE, Germany
Ephias Ruhode	University of the Witwatersrand, South Africa
Ganeshsree Selvachandran	UCSI University, Malaysia
Anil Pise	University of the Witwatersrand, South Africa
Rana E. Jisr	Lebanese University, Lebanon
Cynthia Jabbour Sfeir	Notre Dame University-Louaize, Lebanon
Manas Ranjan Pradhan	Skyline University College, UAE
Ashok Chopra	Amity University, Dubai, UAE
Nawaz Ahmad	Shaheed Benazir Bhutto Women University, Pakistan
Mohammed Abdul Matheen	KSU, Saudi Arabia
Neyara Radwan	KAU, Saudi Arabia
Manimurugan S.	University of Tabuk, Saudi Arabia

National Advisory Board

Santanu Kumar Behera	NIT Rourkela, India
Ayon Chakraborty	IIT Madras, India
Ramesh Gardas	IIT Madras, India
Saravanan Chandran	NIT Durgapur, India
Sivarama Krishnan	IIT Madras, India
Thiruvikraman Kandhadai	BITS, Hyderabad Campus, India
Debashis Guha	SP Jain School of Global Management, India
Pavan Kumar Damaraju	Tata Consultancy Services, India
Justus Rabi	Christian College of Engineering and Technology, India
Linda Mary Simon	Christ College Irinjalakuda, India
Sujayandra Vaddagiri	Laminaar Aviation Infotech (India) Pvt. Ltd., India
Juan R. Jaramillo	Adelphi University, USA
Kannan A.	Dr. M.G.R. Educational & Research Institute University, India
Deepika	Bennett University, India
Sandip Vijay	Tula's Institute, India
Reeba Korah	Alliance University, India
Clement King	Mount Carmel College, India
Kiran Pandey	TIT, Bhopal, India

Technical Programme Committee

Murugappan M.	Kuwait College of Science and Technology, UAE
Jude Hemanth	Karunya University, India
Alexiei Dingli	University of Malta, Malta
Patrick Glauner	Deggendorf Institute of Technology, Germany
Thomas Heinrich Musiolik	University of Europe for Applied Sciences, Germany
Djamel Mostefa	Adeo, Paris
Philipp Plugmann	SRH Hochschule für Gesundheit, Germany
Jordan Bird	Nottingham Trent University, England
Channabasava Chola	Kyung Hee University, Republic of Korea
Anil Audumbar Pise	University of the Witwatersrand, South Africa
Waseem Rawat	Toyota, South Africa
Joel Ugborogho	CenHealth, London
Jens Stapelfeldt	AMD, Germany
Johan Steyn	Stellenbosch University, South Africa

Saidani Begum	Ministry of Higher Education, Saudi Arabia
Rejwan Bin Sulaiman	Northumbria University, UK
Annappa B.	NIT, Surathkal, India
Lavanya Ramapantulu	AlphalCs Corporation, India
Akila Muthuramalingam	KPRIET, India
Shubam Tayal	SR University, India
D. Vetrithangam	Chandigarh University, India
Deepa Jothi	NCET, India
Jaspal Kumar	MIST, India
Balaji Ganesh	Velammal Engineering College, India
Prasant	SVCET, India
Sheila Mahapatra	Alliance University, India
Javeed M.D.	SDIES, India
Sanjay Vishwakarma	IBM Research, USA
Srinjoy Ganguly	University of Southern Queensland, Australia
Mayank Gupta	Woxsen University, India
Revathi Theerthagiri	Woxsen University, India

Additional Reviewers

Bhushan D. Pawar	University of Malta, Malta
Niyaz Ahmad Wani	Thapar Institute of Engineering and Technology, India
Sawinder Kaur	Amity University, India
Rajesh Kumar Chaudhary	Thapar Institute of Engineering and Technology, India
Sachendra Singh Chauhan	GLA University, India
Krishan Kumar	Thapar Institute of Engineering and Technology, India
Raghuveer Singh Dhaka	Thapar Institute of Engineering and Technology, India
Ashiq Nazir Bhat	Thapar Institute of Engineering and Technology, India
Satyakam Barah	Shiv Nadar University, India
Dhananjay Budhiraju	Ramaiyah Institute of Technology, India
S.N. Mahapatra	SOA University, India
Praveen Sahu	NIT, Rourkela, India
Sourabh Gupta	NIT, Rourkela, India
Abhyarthana Bisoyi	Odisha University of Agriculture and Technology, India

Contents

Artificial Intelligence and Machine Learning

Dynamic Inventory Management Using AI: A Case on Datarobot

Venktesh Chaturvedi$^{(\boxtimes)}$ and Kaja Bantha Navas Raja Mohammed ⓘ

National Institute of Fashion Technology, Gandhinagar, Gujarat, India
{venktesh.chaturvedi,Kajabanthanavas.r}@nift.ac.in

Abstract. The main challenge of inventory is various factors variation accounting with respect to time. This paper investigates the prediction of dynamic inventory through Artificial Intelligence platform with Datarobot. Datarobot is an AI platform, provides ensemble Algorithm which shows different result for a particular data based on several parameters. It deploys predictive models for the given data and study the past graph of the data and works on the prediction within a matter of minutes and gives different algorithm which compares the algorithms for the best prediction (Paras Gurnani, Divesh Hariani, Karan Kalani, Praveen Mirchandani and Lifna CS, 2022) [1]. Based on our research data, the regression and gradient booster models predict the production quantity. It helps Industries to be updated and stock their inventory efficiently and be ahead of their competitors.

Keywords: Artificial Intelligence · Datarobot · Dynamic Inventory

1 Introduction

Organizations work on different systems of inventory depending on the type of organization it is. The various types of systems are- Perpetual, Periodic, Just-in-time, Demand-driven inventory system.

Perpetual- This system updates the inventory after every single item being sold.
Periodic- This system updates the inventory after specific time period such as after a month, it is quite slow system.
Just-in-time- This system is based on the concept of providing the item just in time by coordinating with supplier. It is more efficient but also risky if there are any disruptions in supply chain.
Demand-driven Inventory system- This system uses the existing data of orders from customers and predict the Future demand. It can be very accurate by also complex to manage.

H. K. et al. (Eds.): AIKP 2023, CCIS 2127, pp. 3–14, 2024.
https://doi.org/10.1007/978-3-031-68617-7_1

The World is running fast and is now a competitive platform for every industry, field or sector. Reliable Inventory management system provides smooth supply chain and flow of products. Dynamic Inventory which changes very frequently with respect to parameter requires a proper forecasting tool to withstand the competition. The industries run on the platform and predict the need of market and present themselves as first distributor in the market. Industries, earlier used to make their products on the basis of demand of the customer which took a lot time to produce the product and provide the customer. As per the Industrial revolutions the automation has made easier and faster the production but still there was a sense of gap for the industries in terms of exchange of goods and services (Bashir Muhummed Osman, Sriraj Alinkeel, Dhwani Bhavshar, 2022) [2]·

This gap is somewhere reduced by several platforms by giving industries an opportunity to predict, to forecast and provide the product to the customer on the very moment of their request. The production which was earlier "Make to Order" is now changed to "Make to Stock" which made the growth of industries and transaction of goods and services faster. Industries as per the 4th revolution (Hieu Dinh Ha Minh, 2020) [3] began to predict the future requirements of product in the market but due to the lack of resources or accurate prediction value, the forecasting seemed to be ineffective and cost increasing factor for some industries. The single Algorithm and single forecasting parameter results are not enough for dynamic inventory systems (Isaiah Francis E. Babila, Shawn Anthonie E. Villasor, Jennifer C. Dela Cruz, 2022) [4]. The time series is the set of dynamic inventory obtained randomly. The artificial intelligence here comes to use for managing inventory. Moreover continuous data changing makes inventory management more complex challenging for the industry. For short term forecast, time series prediction algorithms are used such as Neural network and ARIMA Model.

In the recent scenario, Artificial Intelligence has brought great change in the forecasting domain. It collects the data and summarize it according to target value and shows the predicted values using various algorithm and compares their value and shows the most accurate value of the model and also the graph of other models which shows relatively less accurate values. The disturbance in inventory management with 'make to stock' can create a bullwhip effect in the supply chain (Deniz Preil & Michael Krapp, 2021) [5]. To dismantle this situation, forecasting is done to avoid addition of non-value added cost and time wastage on the inventory. Forecasting helps in giving accurate data for production that could be done and save cost and labour effort. The forecasting being done found to be somewhere lacking in accuracy due to the lack of single algorithm accuracy. Single algorithm is not capable enough of handling the data of dynamic inventory thus cannot provide accurate prediction.

The accurate prediction is required for the forecasting which reduces the human effort and makes easy the management system of inventory. Accurate prediction can be done by using ensemble algorithm which collects data and on the basis of target variable gives prediction from various algorithms and compare and present them in graph and shows the most accurate prediction of algorithm in the graph. ARIMA models offer more sophisticated models of modelling and seasonal components than slippery exponential models to predict future prices. The ARIMA model, presented by (Box and Jenkins, 1970) [6], was frequently used to decide designs and anticipate future upsides of time series information. (Hosking, 1981) [7] presented a group of models, called partially separated autoregressive incorporated moving normal model, by summing up the 'd' portion in ARIMA (p, d, q) model. (Kristiansen T, 2012) [8] anticipated past Nord Pool esteems utilizing the ARIMA model. Mitigation of Bullwhip effects in Supply chain by (John Rajan and Kaja Bantha Navas, 2021) [9] displayed some steps of improving supply chain using Data Analytics method.

Inventory system is the system which seeks or controls the activity that organises the availability of items to customers. Its role is to organize the supply of products, services and related spare parts to the customers. It basically manages the flow of organization when purchase or manufacturing of items is not able to satisfy the demand. This is where the need of Stock arises to fulfil the demand during non-availability of product from the manufacturing or supplying unit. "Inventory is the fluid that lubricates the wheels of the supply chain" (Tony Wild, 2018) [10]. Organizations follow inventory system according to the demand and size of the particular organization. The management and growth of inventory work on a specific path which is commonly followed by every organization. After the basic inventory management, it is important to forecast the accurate data to be managed in the industry. As said above, the ARIMA model and other ensemble algorithms are used for such forecasting. Further, the authors listed some of the research work in Table 1.

Table 1. Listed literature review towards dynamic Inventory

Year of publications	Authors	Methodology	Inference
2020	Andrzej Lis, Agata Sudolska, and Mateusz Tomanek [17]	The authors use a bibliometric methodology to analyze a corpus of over 1,000 peer-reviewed research documents on SSCM	The inference of the paper is that the SSCM research field is rapidly growing and has the potential to make a significant contribution to the development of sustainable supply chains but it is only possible certain changes are made according to the requirements
2022	Saad El Marjani, Safae Er-rbib, Loubna Benabbou [18]	They searched five databases and selected 37 articles for analysis. The authors used VOSviewer software to identify the most important keywords and relationships between them. They found five clusters: AI, SCM, forecasting, support vector regression, and machine learning	This research study presents a systematic literature review that shed the light on AI contributions to demand forecasting in supply chain management

(*continued*)

Table 1. (*continued*)

Year of publications	Authors	Methodology	Inference
2022	Fahimeh Hosseinnia Shavaki1 · Ali Ebrahimi Ghahnavieh [19]	The authors conducted a systematic literature review of 43 papers and identified five databases to search for relevant papers: ScienceDirect, Scopus, Web of Science, ACM Digital Library, and IEEE Xplore. They extracted data from the selected papers and analyzed the extracted data to identify the main applications of deep learning in SCM, the trends in research, and the gaps in the literature	This paper proposes a conceptual framework that enables us to succinctly understand DL applications in SCM from a philosophy of knowledge perspective, and chart an agenda as a guideline for both practitioners and academic enthusiasts
2020	Hieu Dinh Ha Minh [20]	The quantitative data was collected using a survey questionnaire. The survey collected data on the following variables such as Demographics, Experience with AI, Perception of the impact of AI on inventory management and Satisfaction with AI-enabled inventory management The qualitative data was collected using semi-structured interviews. The interviews collected data on the following topics such as the implementation of AI-enabled inventory management at Company X, the impact of AI-enabled inventory management on inventory management processes at Company X and the challenges and opportunities of using AI-enabled inventory management	The paper provides a valuable contribution to the literature on AI in OM/SCM. The authors' findings suggest that AI has the potential to revolutionize OM/SCM by making it more efficient, agile, and sustainable
2021	Petri Helo & Yuqiuge Hao [21]	It used a single-case study methodology to examine the use of artificial intelligence (AI) in operations management and supply chain management (OM/SCM) at a large Finnish manufacturing company. The authors used the data to identify the ways in which AI was being used in the company's OM/SCM processes	Study shows that SC will have to be digitalised and increasingly dependent on technology in the form of IoT and sensors all across the SC, and this will enable them to collect data in real-time

2 Methodology

This paper investigates the inventory management of the Industry followed since many years in dynamic form where the data continues to change in small interval of time. The growing Industries worldwide brings opportunity but also the competitiveness of warehouse department. The bigger the industry is, the bigger and more tough will be the warehouse management. The warehouse management directly affects the supply chain management as organizations that manage information, product and cash flow from a point of origin to the point of consumption, and within this the management of warehouse determines the effective cost of the product whether to be increased or decreased. Thus to maintain competitiveness of the market, organizations have to face challenges in maintaining the warehouse under which comes the system of inventory management which is nowadays dynamic due to increasing competitiveness. Focusing on the demand driven inventory system, it is the system that collects historical data of the organization of a specific time period and predicts the future demand and values. These predictions can be single variable as well as multi-variable, again depending on the organizations. The independent variables such as market growth rate, profit margins, lockdowns and few more play important roles in the deciding factor. The dependent variables such as time period, quantity and type of product directly influence the prediction. These factors decide whether the forecasting is to be single variable or multiple variable forecasting. Single variable forecasting is the forecasting that considers only one variable for prediction. It is generally used to forecast demand for products or services, or to predict inventory levels. Multi-variable forecasting uses multiple variables to predict future demand. It considers the correlation of variables mainly the dependent variables and provide more accurate prediction as compared to single variable forecasting. Figure 1 shows methodology for dynamic inventory system. In this system the data collected is passed for forecasting which is done by the ensemble algorithms comprises

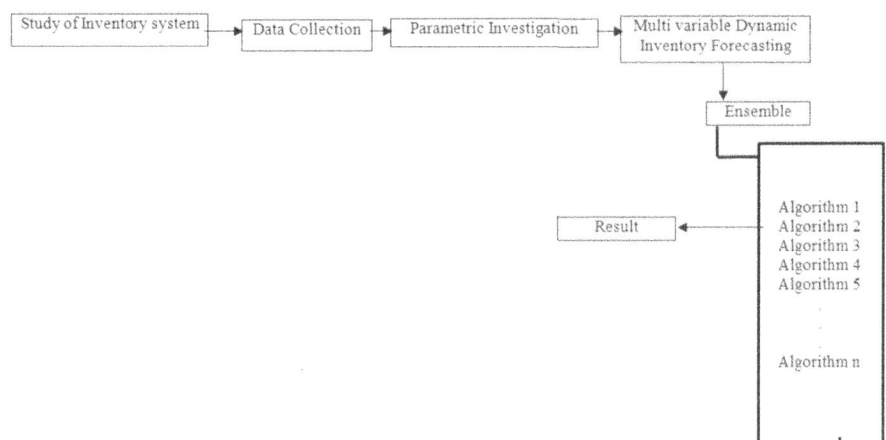

Fig. 1. Methodology for Dynamic Inventory System

of Algorithm1, Alogirthm2, etc. In the research Date, Month, Year consider as a time-series Inventory data and maximum stock, minimum stock and safety stock as functional inventory parameters.

3   Datarobot

The Datarobot by Jeremy Achin, is an AI platform that uses ensemble algorithm and predicts the value against the target variable. It works on Multi-variable data and predicts the value of selected target variable. It is user friendly platform as it No code platform and user has to provide only the data which is analyzed by the deploying models and thus predict the value of target variable. Datarobot is basically designed to collect and analyse the data using algorithms and then predict the target value by deploying models. The models such as Tree regressor, Ridge regressor, Light gradient boosted tree regressor after being deployed generate the predictions. Based on the completeness and target models we have as Datarobot for our research. Based on the target customer, simplicity and usability and completeness and number of use cases Figs. 2 and 3 are supporting evidence for tool selection in this research work.

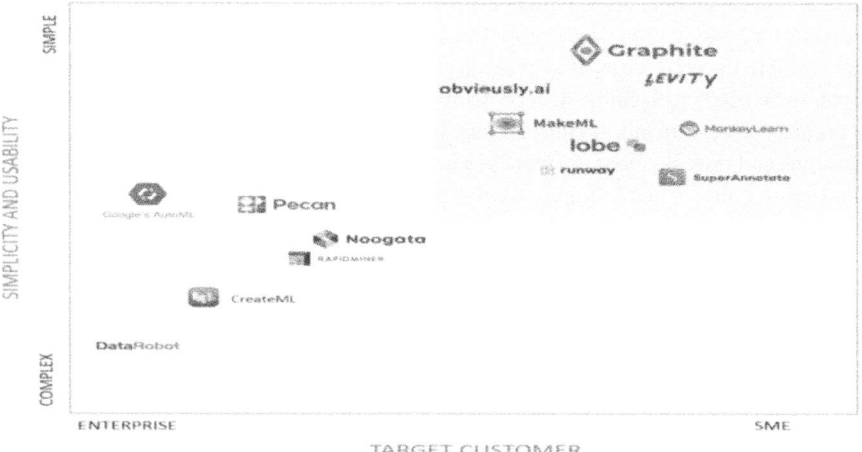

Fig. 2. Target Customer Vs Simplicity and Usability (Ref: Graphite Note [16])

4   Case Study

A dataset that consists of product, date, month, year, maximum stock, minimum stock and safety stock towards time-series is collected from reputed garment industry in Ahmedabad, India. Table 2 shows sample raw data for this research.

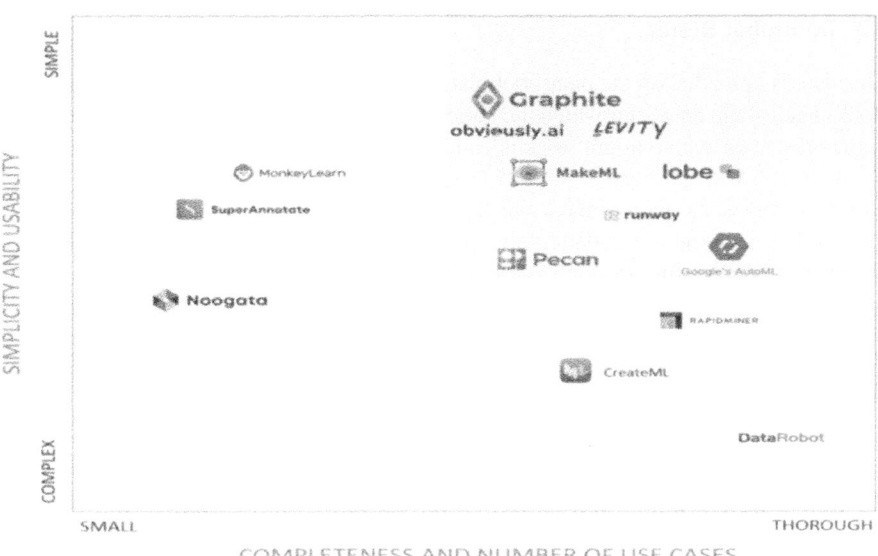

Fig. 3. Completeness and Number of use cases Vs Simplicity and Usability (Ref: Graphite Note [16])

Table 2. Sample raw data

Product	Date	Month	Year	Maximum Stock	Minimum Stock	Safety Stock
Jeans	01	October(10)	2021	6450	1000	700
Jeans	01	November(11)	2021	5290	1000	500
Jeans	01	December(12)	2021	6180	1000	700

4.1 Descriptive Statistics

Descriptive statistics mainly consist of maximum stock and safety with mean and standard deviation. Maximum stock has mean value of 5836 and standard deviation is 568. Safety stock has mean value of 620 and standard deviation of 148. Here, standard deviation values are higher for both maximum stock and safety stock. This more fluctuation assures that it is dynamic inventory problem. Descriptive results are presented in the Table 3.

Table 3. Descriptive statistics for inventory

Feature name	Var type	Mean	Std. Deviation	Median	Min	Max
Maximum Stock	Numeric	5836	568	5900	4600	6900
Safety Stock	Numeric	620	148	600	400	1000

4.2 Datarobot Results

This data is uploaded on the datarobot platform where it shows the graphs of values of stocks against the date after which the target variable is set up from the user's end. Here in the present case, maximum stock is considered as the target value. The user can also see the graph with primary training data and holdout stock of the input data. Holdout data here shows the part of data which is not the part of training for deployment of models. Figure 4 shows the datarobot dashboard for target variable selection. Here we have considered maximum stock as a target variable.

After this the various models are deployed. The models which takes data and performs certain course of action to predict the value of target variable and using different algorithm like Light Gradient Boosted Tree Regressor, Extreme Gradient Boosted Tree Regressor etc.

Ridge Regressor is the regression model that uses statistical method to analyze data in which independent variables are correlated. When these variables are not perfectly correlated, it works on making it more stable (Hilt, Donald E.; Seegrist, Donald W., 1977) [11].

LightGBM is a framework developed by Microsoft and is used to increase the efficiency of model and by using various technique reduce the memory usage (Bo Gao and Vipin Balyan, 2022) [12].

Extreme Gradient Boosted Tree Regressor or XGBoost is similar to LightGBM but is more demanded model because it boosts the algorithm in giving the prediction in less time and can also train models on the large datasets (Ramraj S, Nishant UzirSunil R and Shatadeep Banerjee, 2016) [13].

RuleFit regressor is algorithm that adds on the regression and decision tree and helps on giving better decision by understanding the variable which is not captured by linear regression. It also improves the accuracy of model for complex data (Christoph Molnar, 2023) [14].

Nystroem Kernel SVM Regression works on the principle of analyzing the data with better efficiency on bigger data. As name suggests, SVM is Support Vector Machine regressor is Machine Learning algorithm that is used for regression analysis (Si Si, Cho-Jui Hsieh, Inderjit S. Dhillon, 2016) [15].

The models used here store and analyze data and split the data for its processing. Models usually collects 70% data for training purpose and rest 30% for testing and validation. The model uses certain time to analyze and train data. The time considered in training and validation is the CPU time value of the regressor which is displayed while models are performing. It is generally used to compare the performance of the regressor models of how much time the model takes to predict the accurate values. The models give prediction after training and validation of the data, now various models have different values and to choose among them the user compares the model which is providing the more accurate prediction in less time with help of its CPU value. To compare models there are various parameters such as Root Mean Square Error, Gini Norm, Prediction time, these parameters are displayed in the datarobot itself and shows which model is giving better result. Root Mean Square Error value is the square root of the mean of difference of predicted values and actual values, the higher the value shows the less accuracy. Gini norm is the measure of inequality, its higher value shows better performance of the model. Other parameter shows the importance considered of the variables other than target value by the specific model and is displayed by tree based variable importance. The selected ensemble blueprint model Fig. 5 shows how it works on the backhand and generates the predicted value.

4.3 Model Validation

The platform further compares the selected model from other models for speed vs accuracy and detects the most accurate model by the sideline and shows the value of other related models. The ensemble algorithm works here which determines the values and satisfy the user with the accuracy as well as comparison from other models which gives the competitive result. This enhances the experience of user and makes the AI driven forecasting reliable for organizations. It considers big data and show step by step procedures of prediction. Model validation outputs are shown in Fig. 6.

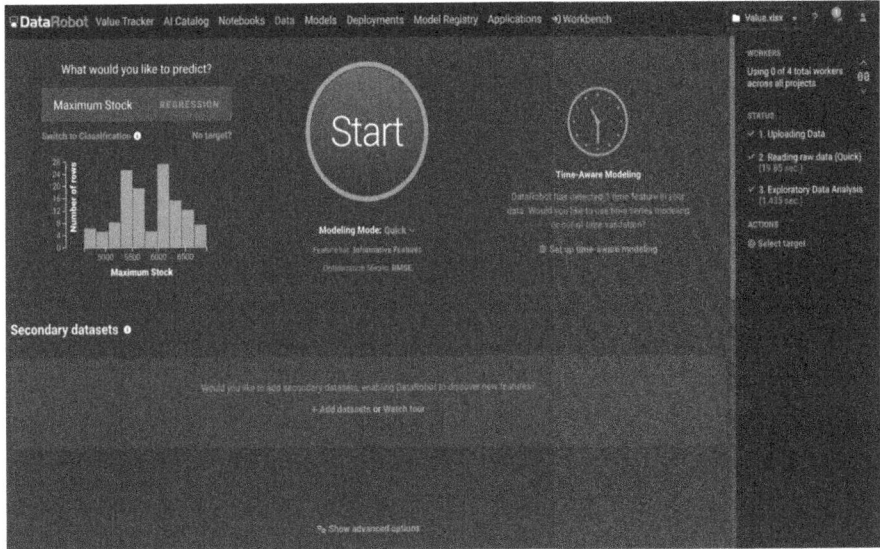

Fig. 4. Dashboard for target variable selection

The selected model predicts the value and displays with actual and forecasted value and predicted sample results are shown in Table 4.

The result of case study describes the benefit of AI driven predicting platforms that work on the principle of accuracy and comparison among the models improves the accuracy and also the working of the platform. The organizations can improve the inventory management and can also manage the safety stock according to the changes done in the dynamic inventory. The regular changes in the data make the inventory management difficult which can be resolved by maintaining the supply and flow of items as per the demand. The datarobot here shows an easy format to decide the stock availability and

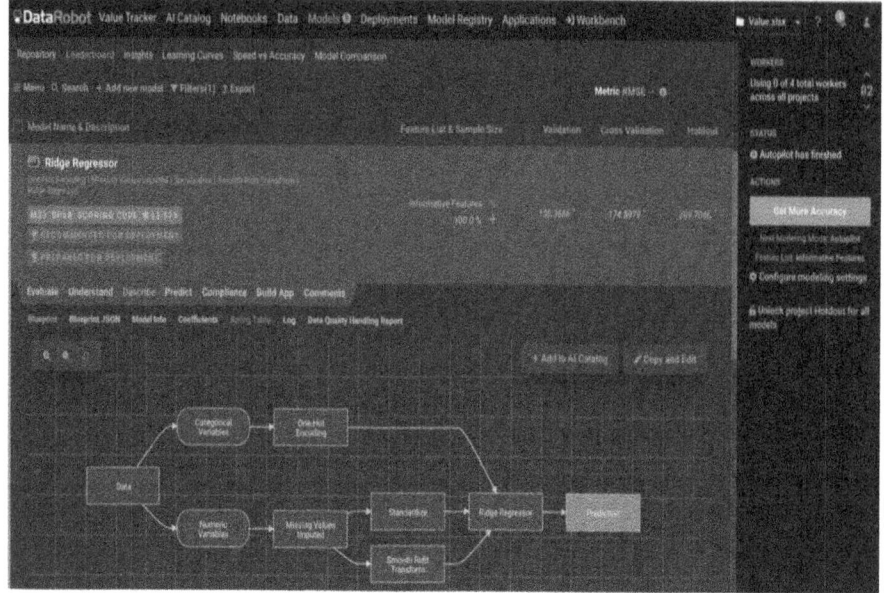

Fig. 5. Blueprint for ensemble model

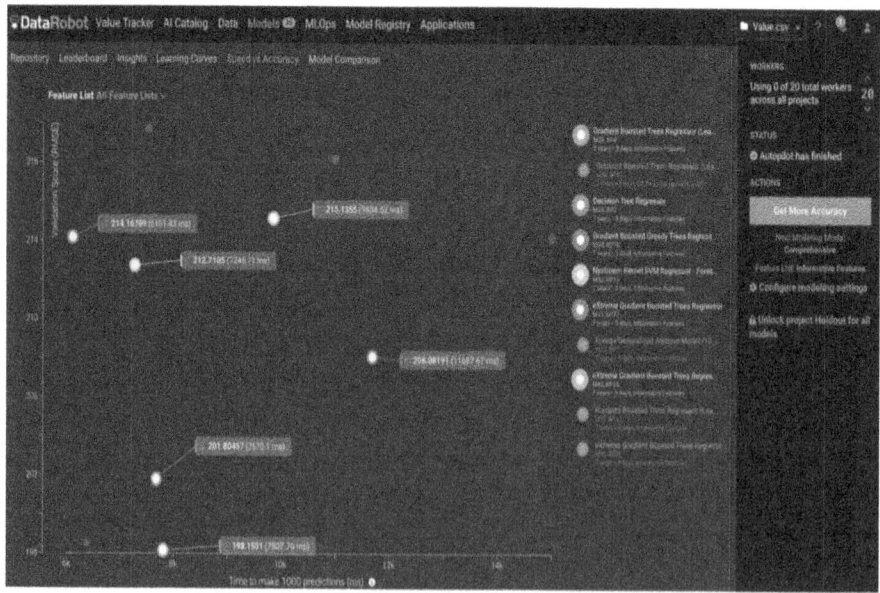

Fig. 6. Model validation for inventory result

Table 4. Predicted maximum stock value Vs Actual stock value

Date	Month	Year	Maximum stock value (actual)	Max stock value (predicted)	Error
01	October	2022	6400	6211.24	188.76
01	November	2022	5300	5953.41	653.41
01	December	2022	6150	5321.14	828.86

manufacturing of item that does not disturb the supply chain management of the organization. The benefits of AI in inventory also brings up the discussion of drawbacks of AI during prediction such as it requires large to train and give accuracy. The models can be biased and give inaccurate predictions. Datarobot is better than its competitors such as IBM SPSS Modeler, Google Cloud autoML, Dataiku DSS because of its certain features such as No-code platform, more flexible and feature engineering, model explainability, and model monitoring. Kaja Bantha Navas et al. 2024 [21] established ensemble machine learning algorithm towards wind speed forecasting model with the help of IBM SPSS Modeler which focused on auto-numeric function.

5   Conclusion

Inventory management being an important and decision changing aspect of the organization seeks fast and reliable decisions. Inventory system is managed according to the production rate of manufacturing unit and frequency of demand. Thus to regulate its management future predictions and planning is necessary and to maintain it accurate readings are important. As seen in the review ensemble Algorithms give more accurate data. The multiple models being deployed give multiple predictions and comparison among them increases the accuracy. The AI usage gives better way to improve inventory management in a number of ways. It analyses historical data and other related factors and forecast future demand more accurately. It helps in reducing the risk of overstock and understock in the inventory. Indirectly by reducing these, it also decreases the cost value of the item. It also helps in reordering the product in inventory to avoid stockout of product in demand to prevent the supply breakage. It will create optimum inventory level in organization for every product they manufacture or import. AI while managing inventory can take care of profitability and can improve real-time inventory levels and availability of products and can also detect the data of demand of the product which is not available in inventory.

References

1. Gurnani, P., Hariani, D., Kalani, K., Mirchandani, P., Lifna, C.S.: Inventory optimization using machine learning algorithms. In: Jacob, I.J., Kolandapalayam, S., Bestak, R. (eds.) Data Intelligence and Cognitive Informatics. Algorithms for Intelligent Systems, vol. 02, pp. 531–541. Springer, Singapore (2022). https://doi.org/10.1007/978-981-16-6460-1_41

2. Osman, B.M., Alinkeel, S., Bhavshar, D.: A study on role of artificial intelligence to improve industry management system, p. 5 (2022)
3. Dinh, H.: The revolution warehouse inventory management in Finland by using artificial intelligence, pp. 18–19 (2020)
4. Babila, I.F.E., Villasor, S.A.E., Cruz, J.C.D.: Object detection for inventory stock counting using YOLOv5, pp. 1–5 (2022)
5. Preil, D., Krapp, M.: Artificial intelligence-based inventory management: a Monte Carlo tree search approach. Ann. Oper. Res. **308**(1), 415–439 (2022)
6. Box, G.E., Jenkins, G.M.: Time Series Analysis, Forecasting and Control (1970)
7. Hosking, J.R.M.: Fractional Differencing, vol. 68, no. 1 (1981)
8. Kristiansen, T.: Forecasting Nord Pool day-ahead prices with an autoregressive model. Energy Policy **49**, 328–332 (2012)
9. Rajan, J., Navas, K.B.: Mitigation of bullwhip effect in supply chain using data analytics method. J. Mech. Eng. Res. Dev. **44**(9), 184–196 (2021)
10. Wild, T.: Best practice in inventory management **3**, 1–2 (2018)
11. Hilt, D.E., Seegrist, D.W.: Ridge, A Computer for Program for Calculating Ridge Regression Estimates, p. 236 (1977)
12. Gao, B., Balyan, V.: Construction of a financial default risk prediction model based on the LightGBM algorithm. J. Intell. Syst. **31**(1), 767–779 (2022)
13. Ramraj, S., Uzir, N., Sunil, R., Banerjee, S.: Experimenting XGBoost algorithm for prediction and classification of different datasets, 651 (2016)
14. Christoph, M.: Interpretable Machine Learning: A Guide for Making Black Box Models Explainable. Lean Publisher (2023)
15. Si, S., Hsieh, C.J., Dhillon, I.: Computationally efficient Nyström approximation using fast transforms. In: Proceedings of the 33rd International Conference on Machine Learning, vol. 48, pp. 2655–2663. PMLR (2016)
16. Graphite Note. https://graphite-note.com/no-code-machine-learning-platforms. Accessed 23 Aug 2023
17. Lis, A., Sudolska, A., Tomanek, M.: Mapping research on sustainable supply-chain management, 17–26 (2020)
18. El-Marjani, S., Er-Rbib, S., Benabbou, L.: Artificial intelligence demand forecasting techniques in supply chain management: a systematic literature review, 531–532 (2022)
19. Hosseinnia, F., Ebrahimi, A.: Applications of deep learning into supply chain management: a systematic literature review and a framework for future research. Artif. Intell. Rev. **56**, 17–28 (2022)
20. Helo, P., Hao, Y.: Production and planning control, 1574–1577 (2021)
21. Navas, K.B., Prakash, S.: Analysis of short-term wind speed variation, trends and prediction: a case study of Coimbatore. J. Intell. Syst. (2024, in press). https://doi.org/10.1515/jisys-2023-0051

Feature Extraction Using Naive Bayes and Logistic Regression for Survival of the COPD Patients

Prabhudutta Ray[1]([✉]), Sachin Sharma[2], Raj Rawal[1,2,3], and Ahsan Z. Rizvi[1,3]

[1] Institute of Advanced Research, Gandhinagar, Guharat, India
`prabhuduttaray.phd2020@iar.ac.in`, `phdrayprabhu@gmail.com`
[2] Ganpat Univesity, Gandhinagar, Gujarat, India
[3] Gujarat Pulmonary and Critical Care Medicine, Ahmedabad, India

Abstract. Constructive pulmonary disease related anomalies are the usual causes of loss of life around the globe. During morning time most heart patients are suffering from high blood pressure which is the major causes of death. Patients are in the resting stage and asymptotic until fatal event occurs. Selecting important features from the available data by applying the bayes technique for the COPD patients is an important classification technique that can help to predict heart diseases. The goal is to find the better accuracy to disclose the heart diseases using Naïve Bayes and logistic regression classification techniques.

Keywords: Chronic obstructive pulmonary disease (COPD) · Feature Extraction · Naïve Bayes classification (NB) · Logistic Regression (LR) · Confusion Matrix · stochastic gradient descent (SGD) · Machine Learning (ML)

1 Introduction

Continuous development of the surgical and medical practices heart diseases are still the prime reason for loss of life around the global population. Every year various human beings are dying due to heart attack, blockage in the coronary artery and weakening of heart muscle [1]. Coronary artery diseases can emerge because of inadequate blood flow in the several parts of the heart. Several prior indications of the heat attack which are a) pain in the chest b) emphysematous, c) exude perspiration and fatigue, d) Nausoa, e) dyspepsia, f) Abdominal pain, g) Upper back and chest pain that stretch into the upper limb. Further types of heart diseases are also includes a) Coronary artery diseases (CAD), b) COPD, c) Triple vesale heart diseases, d) Angina pectoris, e) Congestive heart failure, f) Cardio myopathy, f) Congenital heart diseases [2]. The most essential organ which is responsible flowing the blood in the several parts of the human body. COPD relates to a collection of illness likes air passage block, blood flow blockage and respiratory difficulties. It also includes gasping and incurable respiratory disorder. Vulnerability to air impurity in the accommodation and office, congenital characteristics, Excessive blood stress in the artery walls, and respiratory infections are major causes of COPD diseases. There are several complications for COPD patients which include a) Activity limitations like trouble during stroll or walk up stairs b) inability to work c) increased confusion or memory loss e) other chronic illness like rheumatism, cardiac infarction, cardiopulmonary arrest, stroke etc. COPD therapy can reduce indication; reduce the regularity and acuteness of complication. The analysis of prediction related to the heart should be accurate and correct. Figure 1 below shows the reasons for COPD disease.

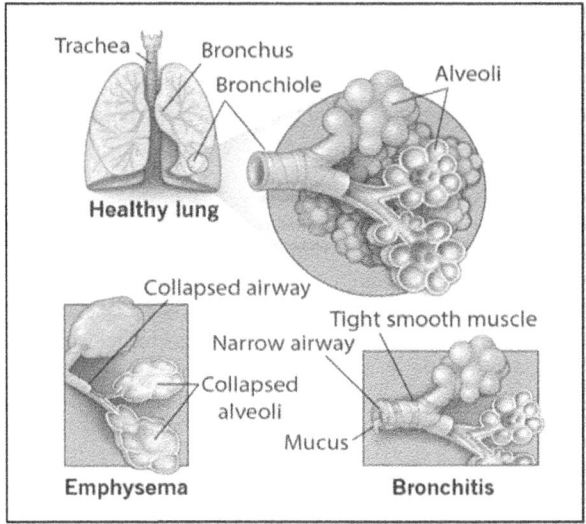

Fig. 1. Reason for COPD Diseases

To resolve this, a vital study about this field is essential. Normally these diseases are identified and predicted at the end stage and this is the main reason for the death. ML tools are useful for extracting patterns or knowledge from the data [3]. Selecting important features from the clinical observation data and identifying the correct ML algorithm to predict survivability at an early stage can save many lives [4]. To collect the important features from the clinical data set it is important to classify the patient suffering from which type of heart disease. Below Table - 1 describes several class of heart diseases and it's impression on the body [5].

Table 1. Different types of heart diseases

Type of heart diseases	Impact on body
Coronary Artery Blockage	Blood vessels are blocked and unable to supply blood and oxygen [6]
Blood Stress	Excessive blood stress in the artery walls [7]

(*continued*)

Table 1. (*continued*)

Type of heart diseases	Impact on body
Stroke	Maximum blockage in the several arteries and difficulty in blood flow
Cardiac arrest	Suddenly stop normal working of the heart like breathing and consciousness
Arrhythmia	Irregular heart rhythm and shows abnormality in ECG [8]

Different heart disease symptoms help to identify important features that are used for prediction. Collected features are extracted from the medical records for further analysis [9]. Data are classified in the following categories like.

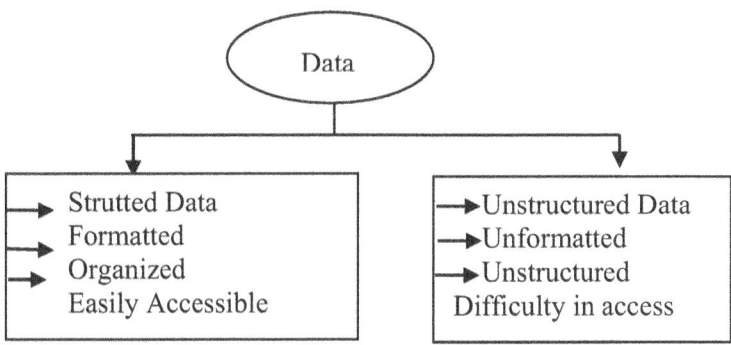

Fig. 2. Data category

2   Related Work

Different researchers apply distinct ML approach to solve heart disorder related predictions using developed classification models. Table - 2 below describes related work, feature selection method, classifier used, and inference taken from the paper in tabular form.

Table 2. Describes related work, feature selection method, classifier used, inference taken

Related work	Method	Classifier used	Inference
Collecting the types of vital signs for analysis	Detection of advanced signs of the diseases for promoting evidence-based health policies. [10]	DT, NB	Report the results of the platform implementation
Predict CKD status based on clinical data,	A workflow regarding prediction of CKD status. [11]	Eleven ML algorithms are used	RF classifier are shows good accuracy
Extracting information from data and building predictive models/	Focus on applying different ML classification [12]	DT, LR, SVM, NB and NN	Obtaining a correlation matrix, we examined the correlation of the features
The extreme deposition layer in the inner walls causes CAD	The developed model used for diagnosing CAD. [13]	GSVM	Using the Gaussian SVM (GSVM) classifier with accuracy of 99.53%
Data mining Techniques unknown scriptures, patterns	Good understanding of age-related risks. [14]	LR, KNN	Analysis based on statistics, ML algorithms,
The prominent and important motive of extracting clinical information from medical images	computational analysis of the images, not their acquisition [15]	computational analysis	The Most Relevant MIP problems (MRMIP) shall be identified and assessed
Kidney stone detection using NN	Radial basis function and Learning vector quantization [16]	NN algorithm	To reduce diagnosis time and increase efficiency with accuracy
Designing an ANN model for the prediction	The use of ANN in predicting kidney problems by comparing the mental behavior of different patients [17]	NN algorithm	Method of prediction for various diseases
Heart disease prediction using ML	ML can play an essential role for predicting the illness, heart diseases and more [18]	SVM, NB, DT, RF	Good accuracy and predictive comparison

(*continued*)

Table 2. (*continued*)

Related work	Method	Classifier used	Inference
CAD prediction using data mining approach	To analyze a heart disease dataset and use fine distinctions using DM approach [19]	RF, NB, KNN, and DT	Classification trees can save money and time
Prediction of CAD using DM and ML approach	DM techniques and ML algorithms shows role in health care areas [20]	DT, J48, LR, RF, NB KNN	Analyze the various DM and ML techniques for efficient use
Prediction of CAD using ML approach	Methods for ML and DL [21]	NB, DT,NN, SVM, and DL	An analytical comparison has been provided
Illness of heart prediction by using DM approach	DM techniques used in the medical field. [22]	Association rule, classification, and Ontology approaches	Association rule mining, classification are used for prediction
Heart diseases predictions using Data Mining	Various techniques of knowledge abstraction by using data mining methods are being used in today's research for the prediction of heart disease. [23]	knowledge abstraction and ML algorithms	DM methods like NB, NN, and DT approach are analyzed
Effective CAD analysis using Hybrid ML techniques	ML is effective for decisions making and predictions in health care industry. [24]	HRFLM model approach	Shows enhanced performance level with accuracy of 88.7%

3 Methodology

Feature Selection: All the features may not be important for the models regarding predictions. It is important to select the good features that will take the minimum computing power of the machine and provide correct prediction [25]. Below Fig. 2 describes the Technique (Fig. 3).

a) Filter Methods:- From all features select the best features that will be provided as input to the ML algorithm and check the performance. Here preparing the data before feeding the feature to the ML algorithm. Then map the performance of the algorithm. If data preparation is good then it provides good results. *The filter method is very simple and it is just a preprocessing of the data before feeding it to the algorithm* [26]. The filter method uses the following techniques (Table 3).

b) Wrapper Method: Initially we have all the features checked. This is essentially a problem of searching where combinations of the different features are made; accordingly

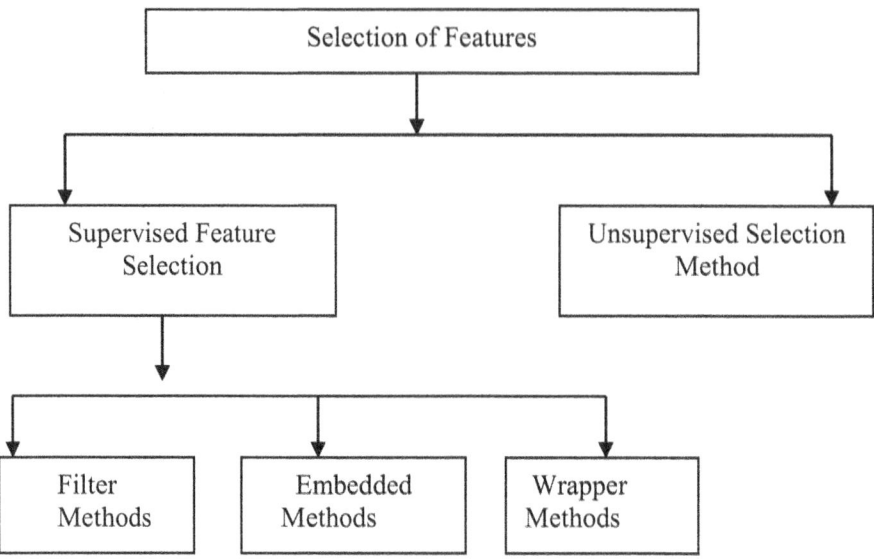

Fig. 3. Feature Selection Techniques

Table 3. Filter Method

Techniques	Purpose
Information Gain	Reduction in entropy or randomness and select the best features
Chi_Squared Test	Determines the relationships between categorical variables
Fisher's Scores	Returns the rank of the features in descending order
Missing value ratios	Evaluate the feature set against the threshold value

they are evaluated and compared with other combinations. So algorithms are trained with a subset of features iteratively and based on the output of the model we select the final set of features and these features give the best set of results. There are various wrapper method techniques like.

c) Embedded Method: This is a combination of both, the Filter and Wrapper method. They create the best subset of features by binding the advantages of both filter and wrapper methods. They are more accurate than the filter method so what happens here is that it is again an iterative process and models are iterative, they evaluate each iteration, find the most important features, and contribute most to the training in the particular iteration. The model checks the accuracy of the different subset and selects the most among them [27]. There are different techniques for the embedded method like (Table 5).

Table 4. Wrapper Method

Techniques	Purpose
Forward selection	Started with an empty set of features, with each iteration keep on adding features and evaluates
Backward elimination	Starting with all the features, during each iteration remove the least significant features and repeat this if no improvement is observed in the removal of features
Exhaustive feature selection	Evaluation based on brute force method
Recursive feature elimination	It is a recursive greedy optimization approach

Table 5. Embedded Method

Techniques	Purpose
Regularization	Regularization techniques use L1, L2, and Elastic nets. Here L1 is the lasso regression, L2 is the Ridge Regression and Elastic Nets is a combination of both L1 and L2 that is Ridge and lasso regression techniques
Random forest	It is a tree-based method and it gives the best features for training a model

From the heart diseases data set all the features are listed as follows **All features**: { *PID, age, sex, pheight, pweight, smoker, alcoholic, mnocig, chol, fbs, restecg, thalachh, cp, exng, oldpeak, slope, ca, thal, trestbps, output, oxyzen*}. There are 21 features identified though considering all the features and providing them as input to the ML model will take a considerable amount of time to provide the prediction. Using the above techniques it is important to reduce the features so that prediction results are correct and accurate. The next stage shows the explanation of the algorithm used for prediction and model building.

1) Naïve Bayes Classification:
This algorithm used for predictive modeling and applied to find the probability of estimation of the event that occurring from the inspection of the previously occurring events. It assumes without dependency between attributes try to maximize the posterior probability for determination of the class. This approach is useful for classifying normal and abnormal characteristics of the learning scenario like supervised learning [28]. When two events, A and B, are independent the probability of both occurring is:

$$P(A \cap B) = P(A) * P(B) \tag{1}$$

Or

$$P(A) = P(A|B) \tag{2}$$

Naïve Bayes classifier is called as probabilistic classifier and it is represented as

$$\hat{y} = \underset{k \in \{1........k\}}{\operatorname{argmax}} \; p(C_k) \prod_{i=1}^{n} p(x_i|C_k) \tag{3}$$

For conditional probability of 'A' given that 'B' is

$$P(A|B) = \frac{P(A \cap B)}{P(B)} \qquad (4)$$

Similarly conditional probability of 'B' given that 'A' is

$$P(B|A) = \frac{P(B \cap A)}{P(A)} \qquad (5)$$

So from the above equation, it is found that $(B|A) = \frac{P(B \cap A)}{P(A)}$

$$P(A \cap B) = P(B \cap A) \qquad (6)$$

$$P(A|B).P(B) = P(B|A).P(A) \qquad (7)$$

$$P(A|B) = \frac{P(A).P(B|A)}{P(B)} \qquad (8)$$

This classifier is a statistical classifier with a error rate is minimum but not always it is same. Inaccuracy happens, because class conditional independence with absence of data related to probability. Based on the above formula calculated probabilities are find out, then respective probabilistic model is used to find the prediction with a new data set by using the above theorem [28]. Gaussian distribution or bell-shaped curve was observed in the case of the real-valued data set. Further, this algorithm is called naïve due to the assumption that every variable is dependent [29].

2) Logistic Regression:
This classification process is based on a supervised learning approach. It uses probabilistic algorithmic calculation to predict outcomes. For estimating the probability it uses a logistic equation for measuring the relationship between independent variables [30]. It uses the sigmoid function for classification like

$$P = \frac{1}{1 + e^{-x}} \qquad (9)$$

In this case, the LR coefficients for every occurrence are given as $x_1, x_2, x_3, x_4, \ldots \ldots \ldots \ldots x_n$ will be $b_0, b_1, b_2, b_3, \ldots \ldots \ldots \ldots b_n$ during the training phase [31]. Here SGD is help to calculate and improve the output of the coefficient like

$$y = b_1 x_1 + b_2 x_2 + b_3 x_3 + b_4 x_4 + \ldots \ldots \ldots b_n x_n \qquad (10)$$

Again

$$b = b + 1 * (y - p) * (1 - p) * p * x \qquad (12)$$

Here the target value is designated by y for each training phase, and all other coefficients are initializing to 0. For b_0 biased input, the learning rate is 1 and x is always 1. By changing the values of the coefficient at the training level until it predicts the correct performance. LR is depends on the representation of the data. Important features are selected by using backward elimination and recursive elimination techniques are applied to make the model useful [32].

3) Support Vector Machine (SVM):

This classifier divides the data point using the hyperplane with the highest amount of marginal differences. It check the data points that are close to the hyperplane. Depending on the several kernels the hyperplane can be decided. Kernels are different types like linear, polynomial, radial, and sigmoid [33]. SVM uses minimum memory in the decision phase. SVM is a technique for the ramification of both linear and nonlinear data. It applies a non-linear mapping method so that it can transform the training data into a higher dimension. A hyperplane is a kind of line that separates the input variable space in SVM. The hyperplane can separate the points in the input variable space containing their class which is either 0 or 1. In two dimensions, one can visualize this as a line and it is assumed that each input point can be completely separated by this line. The distance between the hyperplane and adjacent data coordinates is called the margin. The line which has the largest margin can distinguish between the two classes is known as the optimal hyperplane. These points are called support vectors, as they define or support the hyperplane. In practice, there is an optimization algorithm, which is used to calculate the values for the parameters that maximize the margin. Among the different classification techniques, the SVM is well known for its discriminative power for classification. The SVM is widely considered in recent times due to its efficiency in most different pattern classification techniques. Kim et al. [34] proved that the SVM displays exceptional performance in the classification for prognostic prediction. We gave a brief mathematical description based on [35] of the SVM model. By assuming the binary classification of our response variable, CVD with the convention of linear divisibility for training samples, we have

$$S = \{(x_1, y_1), (x_2, y_2), \ldots\ldots\ldots\ldots(x_n, y_n)\} \tag{13}$$

where $x_i \in (|R|)$, such that the design matrix X belongs to the d dimensional response space, and the response variable, CVD, is represented by y_i, which has a binary class in the vector Y with $y_i \in (0, 1)$ in the study. The appropriate discriminating equation is given by

$$f(x) = sign\{(z, x) + \beta\}] \tag{14}$$

Similarly, Z represents the vector that determines the coordination of the hyperplane (discriminating plane), and so Z, X, and β are offsets. [36]. There are infinite numbers of possible hyperplanes that are efficiently classified by the training data which can be applied to the validation dataset. The optimal classifier identifies the similar optimal generalized hyperplanes that are nearer or even away from each cluster of objects [37]. The input set of coordinates is considered optimally separated by the hyperplane if there is accuracy in the separation with a maximum distance existing between the nearest components and the support vectors leading to the identification of a specific hyperplane [38, 39].

4) Inspiration behind choosing these three algorithms:
These three models provide better variations during classification. To achieve our goal based on the nature of the data set we used for the classification approach needs use of supervised ML algorithm to predict the relationship for the suitable class of sufferer. Algorithms like DT, NAÏVE BAYES, and SVM were used to developed model for the CVD prediction in the several phases. Further in the starting phase, the data were divided into two groups for training and testing. In this stage model accuracy scores are monitored accordingly. In the next stage, data were divided into 75% and 25% for training and validation purposes. After randomly providing input vector to the model we got the correct output regarding prediction and that also matched with the data set output column value. Feature selection techniques are based on selection of the good features according to the sequence and provided to the model for prediction.

4 Results and Discussion

By applying the feature selection method twenty-one attributes are reduced to eleven attributes only. Using the filter methods the following attributes are selected Index(['age', 'sex', 'smoker', 'alcoholic', 'cp', 'trestbps', 'chol', 'fbs', 'ca', 'oxyzen'], dtype = 'object'). Using the wrapper method the following results will help to find out the different features for selection [117.32   1421.335   16.623   51.29   2075.460   128.36   4.293   189.293   163.34   1567.13]
    [145.   0.   23.6   51.
     32.   0.   35.4   21.
     178.   0.   21.3   31.]]
The above wrapper method results are compared with the recursive feature elimination method [RFE] and six number of the most important features are listed from them. Based on the above results features are placed in sequence and provided as input to the respective models also. Based on the above feature ranking method data sets are prepared and used for the naive bays model also.

Figures 4 and 5 show the histogram analysis of the data set.

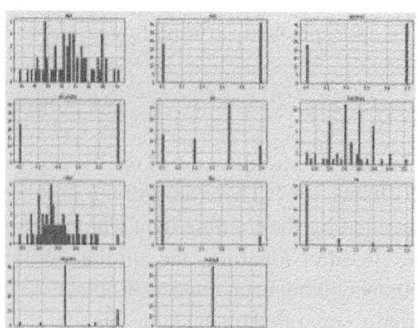

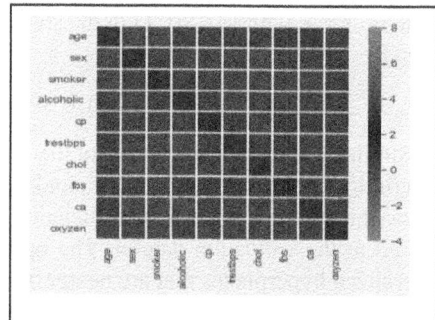

Fig. 4. Histogram Plot   **Fig. 5.** Correlation Plot

Logistic Regression

In this model, the threshold values used during training are as follows threshold = [0.001, 0.002, 0.005, 0.01, 0.05, 0.1].

The corresponding Table 4 will show the Model score that represents the accuracy score (Table 6).

Table 6. Threshold Value and Model Scores

Threshold value	Model Score
0.001	Model score = 69.43066184509293 %
0.002	Model score = 69.43066184509293 %
0.005	Model score = 69.43066184509293 %
0.01	Model score = 69.43066184509293 %
0.05	Model score = 54.11655874190564 %
0.1	Model score = 57.56454461357329 %

Next Fig. 6 will describe the training graph of the data set.

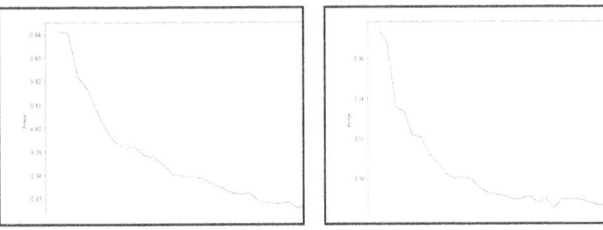

Fig. 6. Training Graph and accuracy

So the Final feature selection with threshold 0.05 is ['age', 'weight', 'cp', fbs', 'cholesterol', 'restecg']. Next, it required to perform the model evaluation like
    model=LogisticRegression()
    here we get the following accuracy of the training data
# accuracy of the training data
X_train_prediction = model.predict(X_train)
training_data_accuracy = accuracy_score(X_train_prediction,Y_train)
here the accuracy is
Accuracy is : **0.8916666666666667**
The accuracy of the test data is
# Accuracy of test data
X_test_prediction = model.predict(X_test)
test_data_accuracy = accuracy_score(X_test_prediction,Y_test)

Accuracy on Test data: 0.8666666666666667
After that, it is required to build the predictive system to predict heart diseases based on the input data sets which are as follows.
Building the Predictive System

```
input_data=(41,0,155,55,1,1,10,1,130,204,0,0,172,0,1.4,2,0,2,98.6)
input_data_as_numpy_array = np.asarray(input_data)
input_data_reshaped = input_data_as_numpy_array.reshape(1,-1)
# check for prediction
prediction = model.predict(input_data_reshaped)
print(prediction)
if (prediction[0]==0):
    print('The person does not have a heart disease or healthy heart')
else :
    print('The person has the heart Diseases')
[1]
The person has heart Diseases
```

5 Discussions

In this work studying the top 20 features provides important facts. These discoveries were validated by doctors.

1. **Asymptotic:** pain in the chest, exercise-induced angina with positive value, old peak > 0 implies the presence of heart diseases.
2. **Reversible thallium**: the scanning of heart and old peak count with more than zero are actually correlated with heart diseases.
3. There is a strong correlation between **chest pain and blockage level**s in the coronary artery.

This work focuses to find the techniques engaged in achieving notable characteristics and to provide a scoring approach to find the hardness of each characteristic. A further number of patients with myocardial infarction or cerebral infarction, both of which are considered the main cause of chest pain and atherosclerosis are becoming a serious problem.

6 Conclusion

Proposes a new technique for identifying heart anomalies in patients suffering from COPD diseases. In the prediction process can be described as feature extraction, model building, training, testing, and finally accuracy and prediction. Three different feature extraction techniques have been applied to select the optimum and best features. Three feature extraction techniques wrapper method, RFE, and embedded methods are used for calculation for selecting the best features.

Identified features are provided as input to the model to get the best prediction level. This work has also described performance of the machine learning algorithms like the Naïve Bays classification rule and Logistic Regression algorithm for predicting heart diseases with good accuracy scores. Naïve Bays Classification rules are applied for prediction using the maximum likelihood function and posterior probability for achieving good scores.

Limitations: In this work selection of features are apply **to** identify the important parameters but increasing more number of heart patients with other characteristic are also important for prediction. Here more different ways of normalizing the data and the corresponding results regarding comparison also need to be deeply examined.

Future Scope: The dataset size can be increased and then deep learning with various other optimization techniques can be used in the future scope to achieve more promising results.

Acknowledgment. Thanks to SHODH-ScHeme of The Government of Gujarat for the necessary grant.

Esthetics Approval and Consent to Participate.   Not Applicable.
  The Authors declare no competing Interest.

References

1. Moradi, H., et al.: Recent developments in modeling, imaging, and monitoring of cardiovascular diseases using machine learning. Biophys. Rev. **15**, 19–33 (2023)
2. Arumugam, K., Naved, M., Shinde, P.P., Leiva-Chauca, O., Huaman-Osorio, A., Gonzales-Yanac, T.: Multiple disease prediction using Machine learning algorithms, Volume 80, Part 3, 2023, Pages 3682–3685. https://doi.org/10.1016/j.matpr.2021.07.361
3. Forrest, I.S., et al.: Machine learning-based marker for coronary artery disease: derivation and validation in two longitudinal cohorts, Volume 401, Issue 10372, 21–27 January 2023, pp. 215–225. https://doi.org/10.1016/S0140-6736(22)02079-7
4. Ge, B., Yang, H., Ma, P., Guo, T., Pan, J., Wang, W.: Detection of pulmonary hypertension associated with congenital heart disease based on time-frequency domain and deep learning features. Biomed. Signal Process. Control **81**, 104316 (2023). https://doi.org/10.1016/j.bspc.2022.104316
5. Ge, B., Yang, H., Ma, P., Guo, T., Pan, J., Wang, W.: Detection of pulmonary arterial hypertension associated with congenital heart disease based on time–frequency domain and deep learning features. Biomed. Signal Process. Control **81**, 104451 (2023). https://doi.org/10.1016/j.bspc.2022.104451
6. Batra, P., Khera, A.V.: Machine learning to assess coronary artery disease status—is it helpful (2022). https://doi.org/10.1016/S0140-6736(22)02584-3. PlumX Metrics. Published:December 20 VOLUME 401, ISSUE 10372, P173–175, JANUARY 21, 2023
7. Kadam, M.A., Patil, S., Pethkar, P., Shikare, R., Sarnayak, S.: A Cardiovascular Disease Prediction System Using Machine Learning, vol. 13, Special ISSUE 09 (2022). https://doi.org/10.47750/pnr.2022.13.S09.849
8. Ahsan, M.M., Siddique, Z.: Machine learning-based heart disease diagnosis: a systematic literature review. Artif. Intell. Med. **128**, 102289 (2022). https://doi.org/10.1016/j.artmed.2022.102289

 9. Dalal, S., et al.: Application of machine learning for cardiovascular disease risk prediction. Open Access **2023**, Article ID 9418666 (2023). Research Article. https://doi.org/10.1155/2023/9418666
10. Rajliwall, N.S., Chetty, G., Davey, R.: Chronic disease risk monitoring based on an innovative predictive modeling framework. In: IEEE Symposium Series on Computational Intelligence (SSCI), pp. 1–8 (2017)
11. Yildirim, P.: Chronic kidney disease prediction on imbalanced databy multilayer perceptron. In: IEEE 41st Annual Computer Software and Applications Conference, pp. 193–198 (2017)
12. Gharibdousti, M.S., Azimi, K., Hathikal, S., Won, D.H.: Prediction of chronic kidney disease using data mining techniques. In: Proceedings of the Industrial and Systems Engineering Conference (2017)
13. Sharma, M., Tan, R.S., Acharya, U.R.: A new method to identify coronary artery disease with ECG signals and time-frequency concentrated antisymmetric biorthogonal wavelet filter bank. Pattern Recognit. Lett. **125**, 235–240 (2019)
14. Kohli, P.S., Arora, S.: Application of machine learning in diseases prediction. In: 4th International Conference on Computing Communication and Automation (ICCCA) (2018)
15. M ishra, A., Rai, A., Yadav, A.: Medical image processing: a challenging analysis. Int. J. Bio-Sci. Bio-Technol. **6**(2) (2014)
16. Mane, S.A., Chougule, S.R.: Neural network of kidney stone detection. Int. J. Sci. Res. (IJSR) **5**(4), 2319–7064 (2016). ISSN (Online)
17. Adam, T., Hashim, U., Sani, U.S.: Designing an artificial neural network model for the prediction of kidney problems symptom through patient's metal behavior for pre-clinical medical diagnostic. Biomedical Engineering (ICoBE). In: 2012 International Conference on IEEE (2012)
18. Gavhane, A., Kokkula, G., Pandya, I., Devadkar, K.: Prediction of heart disease using machine learning. In: Proceedings of the 2nd International conference on Electronics, Communication and Aerospace Technology (ICECA) 2018 (2018)
19. Kaur, A., Arora, J.: Heart diseases prediction using data mining techniques: a survey. Int. J. Adv. Res. Comput. Sci. IJARCS (2019)
20. Kumar, M.N., Koushik, K.V.S., Deepak, K.: Prediction of heart diseases using data mining and machine learning algorithms and tools. Int. J. Sci. Res. Comput. Sci. Eng. Inf. Technol. IJSRCSEIT (2019)
21. Himanshu Sharma, H., Rizvi, M.A.: Prediction of heart disease using machine learning algorithms: a survey. Int. J. Recent Innov. Trends Comput. Commun. **5**(8) (2017)
22. Sahaya Arthy, A., Murugeshwari, G.: A survey on heart disease prediction using data mining techniques, April 2018
23. Gandhi, M., Singh, S.N.: Predictions in heart diseases using techniques of data mining (2015)
24. Mohan, S., Thirumalai, C., Srivastava, G.: Effective heart disease prediction using hybrid machine learning techniques, digital object identifier. IEEE Access **7** (2019). https://doi.org/10.1109/ACCESS.2019.2923707
25. DhafarHamed, J.K.A., Ibrahim, M., Naeem, M.B.: The utilization of machine learning approaches for medical data classification. In: Annual Conference on New Trends in Information & Communications Technology Applications, March 2017
26. Sharma, H., Rizvi, M.A.: Prediction of Heart Disease Using Machine Learning Algorithms: A Survey, August 2017
27. https://archive.ics.uci.edu/ml/datasets/Heart+Disease
28. Jinjri, W.M., Keikhosrokiani, P., Abdullah, N.L.: Machine learning algorithms for the classification of cardiovascular disease- a comparative study. In: International Conference on Information Technology (ICIT). Published in: 2021, INSPEC Accession Number: 20945463, Publisher: IEEE, https://doi.org/10.1109/ICIT52682.2021.9491677

29. Jonnavithula, S.K., Jha, A.K., Kavitha, M., Srinivasulu, S.: Role of machine learning algorithms over heart diseases prediction, Research Article, 27 October 2020 , Volume 2292, Issue 1, 27 October 2020

30. Gupta, A., Kumar, R., Arora, H.S., Raman, B.: MIFH: A Machine Intelligence Framework for Heart Disease Diagnosis, pp. 14659–14674. Publisher: IEEE, IEEE Access (Volume: 8), INSPEC Accession Number: 19313528, Electronic ISSN: 2169–3536, https://doi.org/10.1109/ACCESS.2019.2962755

31. Katarya, R., Meena, S.K.: Machine learning techniques for heart disease prediction: a comparative study and analysis. Health Technol. **11**, 87–97 (2021). Published: 19 November 2020

32. Lakshminarayanan, R., Thanga Mariappan, L., Yuvaraj, N.: Analysis on Cardiovascular Disease Classification Using Machine Learning Framework, vol. 63, no. 6 (2020)

33. Tanveer, M., Rajani, T., Rastogi, R., Shao, Y.H., Ganaie, M.A.: Comprehensive review on twin support vector machines. Ann. Oper. Res. 1–46 (2022)

34. Kim, B.M., Kang, B.Y., Kim, H.G., Baek, S.H.: Prognosis prediction for Class III malocclusion treatment by feature wrapping method. Angle Orthod. **79**(4), 683–691 (2009)

35. Cristianini, N., Shawe-Taylor, J.: An Introduction to Support Vector Machines and Other Kernel-Based Learning Methods. Cambridge University Press, Cambridge, UK (2000)

36. Steinwart, I., Christmann, A.: Support Vector Machines. Springer Science & Business Media, Berlin, Germany (2008). https://doi.org/10.1007/978-0-387-77242-4

37. Hearst, M.A., Dumais, S.T., Osuna, E., Platt, J., Scholkopf, B.: Support vector machines. IEEE Intell. Syst. Appl. **13**(4), 18–28 (1998)

38. Fan, J., Zheng, J., Wu, L., Zhang, F.: Estimation of daily maize transpiration using support vector machines, extreme gradient boosting, arti7cial and deep neural networks models. Agric. Water Manag. **245**, Article ID 106547 (2021)

39. Kurani, A., Doshi, P., Vakharia, A., Shah, M.: A comprehensive comparative study of arti7cial neural network (ANN) and support vector machines (SVM) on stock forecasting. Ann. Data Sci. 1–26 (2021)

How Do Senior Secondary Level Students and Their Teachers Perceive Artificial Intelligence and Its Implementation? An Exploratory Study

Shweta Jha[(⊠)] and Somu Singh

Faculty of Education, Banaras Hindu University, Varanasi, India
{shweta.jha,somusinghedu}@bhu.ac.in

Abstract. Each and every sector is not left apart from the positive and negative impacts of Artificial Intelligence. With the lead of Artificial Intelligence in the field of education, the researcher examines the awareness and knowledge of Artificial Intelligence among school students and their computer science mentors. Researchers assessed the conceptions of students about features of AI, tools of AI and its use for learning purposes as well as demerits of AI. The intentionality of the sample was analyzed through a qualitative approach. Interviews of fifty students and their mentors have been conducted. The findings of the study revealed that the majority of the students have knowledge about AI and It is being taught by teachers. Students have basic knowledge of different forms and features of AI. Majority of school students and school teachers highlighted the positive characteristics of AI but AI as a subject is not popular among students. Students and their mentors also found AI helpful in their learning. Students also have knowledge of the negative effect of AI on students' learning habits, thinking ability, memory, and physical activity.

Keywords: Artificial Intelligence · Learning · Education · AI Tools · Teaching

1 Introduction

According to Britannica, Artificial intelligence provides the capability of performing a task in collaboration with computer controlled robots which is helped by digital computers and intelligent beings. It develops the systems associated with intellectual processes which is a feature of a person like the capability of analysis, generalization of the principals, experiences from past activities. Computer was discovered in the 1940s. Presently computers can be programmed in such a way which can carry out complex tasks with great proficiency in an efficient manner. Although artificial intelligence is smart enough, it still can't beat the human brain. According to Wartman & Combs (2018), The power of thinking by computers/machines is just like the human brain is known as Artificial intelligence. AI can be defined as, when human behavior is logically copied through tools/software programs. Mishra (2023) has suggested that mentors of the present generation have to get prepared for GenAI based education.

H. K. et al. (Eds.): AIKP 2023, CCIS 2127, pp. 30–43, 2024.
https://doi.org/10.1007/978-3-031-68617-7_3

1.1 AI in Education

i. AI helps the individual to understand complex subjects and provide intuitive explanations which enhances the learning experience. For example Microsoft Math application and optical character reader which provides solutions when the image of the problem is given to these AI tools.

ii. AI helps in personalization of education and reduces the knowledge gap. The smart digital platforms developed by Companies like Carnegie Learning and Content Technologies use AI and facilitate personalized learning to students of all levels.

iii. Improved accessibility is possible through AI. Artificial intelligence is helpful in evaluation of students having different types of challenges and disabilities.

iv. Learning beyond classrooms is possible through chatbots of Artificial Intelligence and is proved to be helpful for those students whoever requires remedial classes. These chatbots give opportunity to students like a real teacher and personalized experience of interaction.

v. Efficient testing, grading and assessment is possible through AI. AI combines visual and language based experiences of students in the process of student's academic assessment and grading.

vi. Apps such as Grade Scanner helps in to score bubble based MCQs.

vii. Language-model-based grading is done with AI. Written answers given by students against long answer type questions can be mapped into traditional grading and scores can be assigned automatically for the written answers.

viii. AI also helps in automation of administrative works.

1.2 Demerits of AI in Education

Tkhayneh, Alghazo, Tahat (2023) studied the "Advantages and Disadvantages of Using Artificial Intelligence in Education". Their study revealed the costs of applying AI systems and the issues about the missing of educational jobs in future, the error-processing and the errors of programming, and weakening relationships between student and teacher in the classroom.

A few schools and colleges engaged in the discussion of concerns of AI tools would fundamentally reduce academic integrity and thus adversely impact student academic achievements (Mills 2023; Murgia & Staton 2023). The spread of misinformation by the use of AI tools have also been shown by researchers (Cardona et al. 2023; D'Agostino 2023; Heikkilä 2022). Another disadvantage of AI would be that the students having facility of using these tools will likely have an advantage over those who don't and it will exacerbate the digital divide (Gunkel 2023) and this will also lead to disparities in achievement of the learners (Chan & Hu 2023) and Scheerder et al. (2017) in their study concluded that advanced users of AI tools will be better in comparison to their fellow learners who have not been provided information and oriented about use of AI tools, a challenge often labelled as the "second-level digital divide".

1.3 NEP 2020 and AI in Curriculum

NCERT is currently re-engineering the National Curriculum Framework for School Education, keeping in mind NEP 2020 Goals. One of the Goals of NEP 2020 is to include Artificial Intelligence (AI) in day to day school education within Resurgent Bharat.

1.4 Assumption

The advent of Artificial Intelligence (AI) has changed the way technology works today. Redundant processes are being eliminated with cost efficient AI/ML Processes. Though AI is the new GOD after Google Search, it is still evolving with its own pros and cons, which we will be pointing out in subsequent paras. In India, AI has been introduced recently in schools run by the central government and also in top private run schools. NEP 2020 has also recommended the use of AI tools in the teaching-learning process. Students and teachers of central government schools have a basic level of awareness of Artificial Intelligence through their mentors and also from other mediums like print media, social media.

1.5 Research Question

How is the perception of Artificial Intelligence among senior secondary level students? How is the perception of Artificial Intelligence among computer science teachers?

1.6 Objective of the Study

  (i) To study the conception of Artificial Intelligence among school students.
 (ii) To find out the ideas about features of Artificial Intelligence among school students.
(iii) To find out the awareness of tools of Artificial Intelligence among school students.
(iv) To study the opinion of school students towards the role of AI in teaching learning.
 (v) To study the opinion about the demerits of AI among school students.

2 Research Method

Phenomenological Study, a qualitative method is the research design used in this study. This study enables a researcher to access an individual respondent's ideas, beliefs, learning and perception in depth using multiple data sources (triangulation). Using the above method we tried to learn about individuals' opinions with respect to the concept of Artificial Intelligence (AI) and its implementation in teaching learning. Here respondents were Senior Secondary level Students and their Computer Science Mentors.

2.1 Sample and Sampling Techniques

Purposive sampling technique was applied to select One Kendriya Vidyalaya (KV), B.L.W. of Varanasi, U.P. (India) because Artificial Intelligence's implementation has been done in that school. Fifty senior secondary level students and their two computer science teachers from KV were selected for an in-depth interview.

Gocen and Aydenir (2020) in their study "Artificial Intelligence in Education and Schools" took teachers as the participants of the study. Rizvi, Waite & Sentence (2023) conducted a systematic literature review on "Artificial Intelligence teaching and learning in K-12 from 2019 to 2022". This review study focussed on learners' context, logical assistance of AI for different pedagogical approaches.

These two studies provided the base for the researcher to select sample units and their computer science mentors to select as sample for their study.

2.2 Research Tools

Two Semi-structured Interview schedules were constructed by the researchers for collection of data from school students and their computer science teachers. Items for Interview schedules were created considering following questions:

a) What is Artificial Intelligence (AI)?
b) What are the features of AI?
c) What are the tools of AI?
d) Is AI helpful in learning/teaching?
e) What are the demerits of AI?

The inter-rater reliability for both Interview Schedules (one for school students and one for computer science teachers) were established on the basis of opinions collected from Faculty members/Professors and Researchers of Banaras Hindu University, Varanasi, India. Experts had also given their opinions on suitability of items for the interview schedule considering the objectives of the research as criterion.

2.3 Collection of Data and Analysis

Researcher conducted Interview of fifty students through open-ended Semi-structured Interview schedule in the school timings as per the availability of students and school teacher.

This helped researchers to analyze the participant perception with respect to use of AI and its implementation in teaching learning process. The other semi structured interview schedule was administered with the TGT and PGT computer science teachers (mentors) of Kendriya Vidyalaya, DLW, Varanasi in the face to face mode. Responses of secondary school students and teachers were recorded by researchers. Data were analyzed and codes and themes were identified. Codes and themes have been finalized with the help of experts of Banaras Hindu University, Varanasi.

2.4 Trustworthiness

Trustworthiness has been insured in conducting the study. The data collection using interview schedules, coding, tabulation and reporting stages are followed in the present study. Researchers have conducted interviews rigorously of each and every case to collect meaningful information. Triangulation has been done to arrive at a meaningful idea of cases or phenomena i.e. implementation of Artificial Intelligence. The researchers were on duty to supervise the practice teaching lessons of B.Ed. Students at Kendriya Vidyalaya, B.L.W., Varanasi. The data were collected during the school internship of B.Ed. Students.

3   Findings

Identification of codes and themes have been done for achieving objective no.-1.

Finding No.-1

Table 1. Themes from the response obtained by the participants on the objective no.-1

Objective No.1	Theme I	Theme 2	Theme 3
	Technology which produces outcomes in daily life using its own way of collecting and analyzing the data. + Intelligence of Robots and satellites. + More powerful than human intelligence. + Similar to the human brain and takes decisions on its own. + Google Translator and Sophia	Reduced Human effort + Helps in research, education and recreation	Dangerous and takes the place of humans in jobs + May be a weapon for wars
Frequency	35	13	2
Percentage	70%	26%	4%

It is inferred from Table 1 that 70% of the students have defined Artificial Intelligence as a technology which produces outcomes in daily life using its own way of collecting and analyzing the data. These learners are also aware that AI is helpful for Robots, satellites and it is more powerful than human intelligence. These students are also frequently using AI tools in their learning purpose. 26% of the respondents said that AI reduces human effort and helps in research, education and recreation. 4% of the students had a negative approach towards AI and responded as AI is dangerous and takes the place of humans in jobs and it may be a weapon for wars (Fig. 1).

Finding No.-2

From Table 2, it is clearly evident that 44% (22 students) of the students agreed that use of AI requires no money, reduces workload of the learners as well as teachers, gives accurate answers to any query on a fingertip, and hard work is done in an easy way. It also helps in perception, cloud computing and quantum computing. 8% of the respondents find AI very useful in any kind of digital creations, like videos and photos. 6% (3 students) of the students are using AI tools to connect with their relatives staying at far distances and it also helps to connect with the people of different languages. 6% of the respondents said that the other characteristic feature of AI is fetching away the

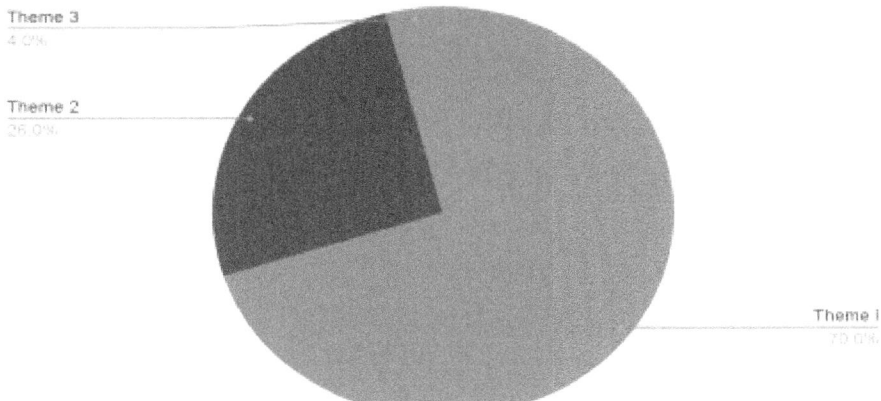

Fig. 1. Themes from the responses obtained from the participants

jobs of cashiers, waiters etc. On the other side it is also helping in the purpose of job search. It is very beneficial for new generations according to 2% (1 student) of the total respondents. 4% (2 students) of the respondents suggested that AI should have emotions and respond to the conversation. 2% (1 students) of the respondents are getting help for the purpose of typing and translation. 10% of the total students (5 students) have not given any response (Fig. 2).

Finding No.-3
Respondents are aware of the above mentioned AI tools and they are aware of academic use of ChatGPT. Maximum participants are aware of Social Media Applications based on AI and ChatGPT (Table 3, Fig. 3).

Finding No. 4
88% of the respondents agreed that AI helps in learning by accessing it at any time, reducing effort, giving solutions, making notes and test papers, motivating learners with answers in a unique perspective. Wolfram alpha and Sofia give the answer. AI also helps in translating languages & concept clarification. According to 12% of the respondents AI is depreciating the learning condition and hard work of the students. Learners are kept away from the books and their curiosity and creativity is getting ruined due to AI (Table 4, Fig. 4).

Finding No.-5
6% of the respondents said that Scams, Dark web, Loss of personal data and misuse of such data is the outcome of using AI. AI is leading towards jobless people and unemployment as per 36% of the respondents. According to 34% of the respondents AI ruins the thinking ability of the human brain, Memory loss, less social and lazy people and Addiction to AI. AI is playing a role in the spread of fake news through edited photos and videos as responded by 10% of the respondents. According to another 10% of the respondents AI is not helpful for UPSC/JEE exams and the answers given through AI

Table 2. Themes as per response obtained from the participants on the objective no.-2

Theme No.	Identified Theme Name
Theme 1	Requires no money + Reduces workload + Gives accurate answer + Hard work is done easily + Perception , cloud computing and quantum computing
Theme 2	Helpful in digital creations + Generate photos + Can play games
Theme 3	Helps to connect with the people at a long distance in another language.
Theme 4	Replaces jobs of cashier , waiters etc.
Theme 5	Very useful for upcoming generation
Theme 6	Helps in studies , homework and jobsearch
Theme 7	Should have emotions and respond to our conversation
Theme 8	No response
Theme 9	Helps in typing and translation

Objective No.-2	T- 1	T- 2	T-3	T-4	T-5	T- 6	T-7	T-8	T- 9
Frequency	22	4	3	3	1	9	2	5	1
Percentage	44%	8%	6%	6%	2%	18%	4%	10%	2%

are not based on logic and emotions. As per 4% of the respondents, AI is disastrous and dangerous for upcoming human generations (Table 5, Fig. 5).

Finding No.-6

Data obtained from Computer Science Teachers (one trained graduate teacher and one post graduate teacher) of concerned secondary school students on following questions and items. Responses given by school teachers in interview sessions have been recorded and analyzed in the light of research objectives. Findings presented here question/item wise.

1. **Do you have AI as a school subject for standard IX to XII students?**

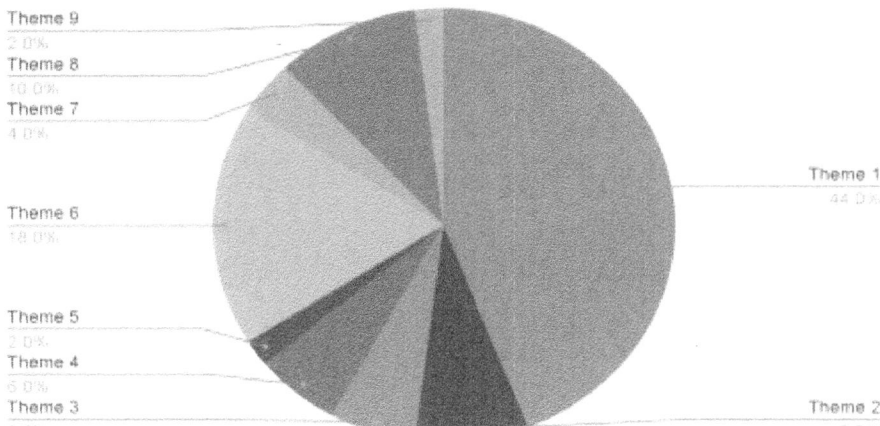

Fig. 2. Themes from the responses obtained from the participants on the objective no.-2

Table 3. List of AI Tools from the response obtained from the participants on the objective no.-3

List of AI tools on the basis of participants' responses	Frequency
1. Black Box AI	1
2. Chat GPT	29
3. Google translator, Google Map	19
4. Instagram, Facebook, Telegram, Snapchat, Siri	28
5. AI photo and video editing app	9
6. Autocorrect feature	4
7. Sofia & Lakshmi Robots	2
8. No response	3
9. Out of the way response	12
10. Wolfram alpha, Bing AI	2

6 (1a) AI is an additional subject for standard 9th and 10th students according to CBSE guidelines. For standard 11th and 12th it is incorporated with their syllabus like Python, Coding etc.

6 (1b) In Kendriya Vidyalaya, very few students are choosing this subject although it is recommended by NEP2020 and CBSE.

2. **Can you tell me the contents which you teach in this subject?**

6 (2a) Communication skills, ICT, AI in ICT, History of AI, AI in present scenario, coding, flowcharts, algorithm are taught by teachers in the classes of AI.

Points scored

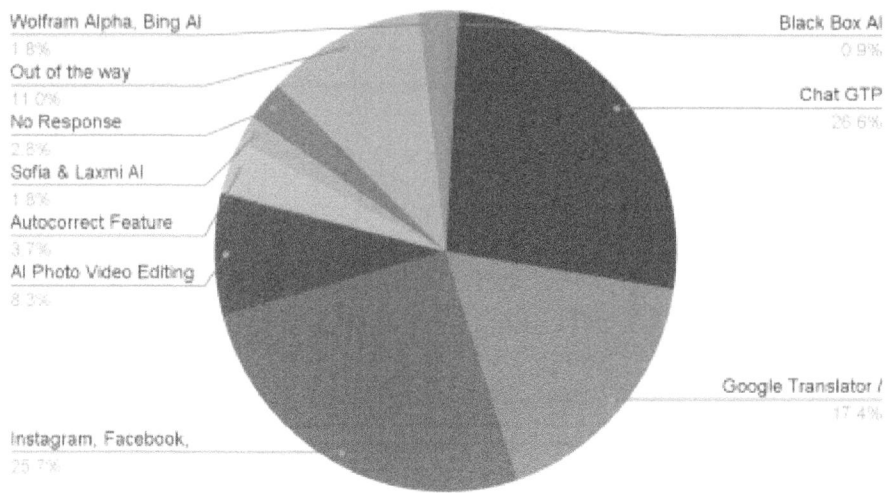

Wolfram Alpha, Bing AI
1 8%
Out of the way
11 0%
No Response
2 8%
Sofia & Laxmi AI
1 8%
Autocorrect Feature
3 7%
AI Photo Video Editing
8 3%
Instagram, Facebook,
25 7%

Black Box AI
0 9%
Chat GTP
26 6%
Google Translator /
17 4%

Fig. 3. Themes from the response obtained by the participants on the objective no.-3

Table 4. Themes from the response obtained from the participants on the objective no.-4

Objective No.- 4	Theme 1	Theme 2
	Yes Can access anytime + Reduces effort + Gives solution + Makes notes and test papers + motivates + answers with unique perspective, wolfram alpha and Sofia gives the answer + Translate language + Concept clarification	**No** Depreciate learning condition and hard work + Keeps the learner away from books + Destroys curiosity and creativity
Frequency	44	6
Percentage	88%	12%

6 (2b) There are 4 sections. First section has communication skills, self-management skills, ICT skills, and entrepreneurship skills. Second section is Introduction of AI, Third is modeling and fourth is coding in which we have kept Python.

3. **How AI is going to usher efficiency amongst students learning?**

6 (3a) Chat GPT can help children when they don't have books. Helpful for shy students who feel uncomfortable to clear their doubts in the classroom.

6 (3b) All the above mentioned skills help to enhance learning.

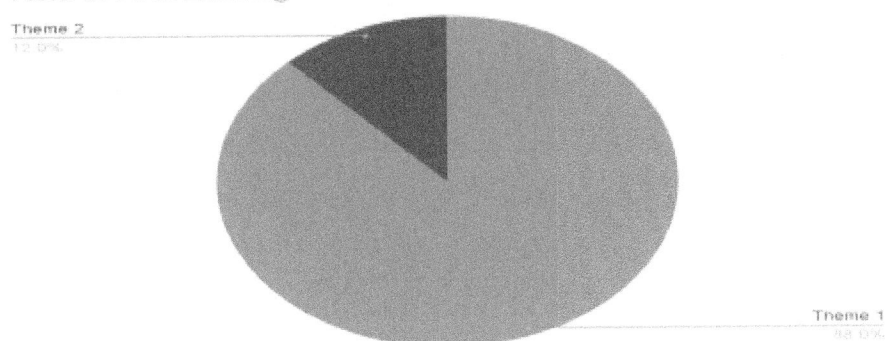

Role of AI in learning

Fig. 4. Themes from the response obtained by the participants on the objective no.-4

Table 5. List of AI tools from the response obtained from the participants on the objective no.-5

Theme No.	Identified Theme Name
Theme 1	Scams + Dark web + Loss of personal data and misuse of data.
Theme 2	Jobless people and unemployment.
Theme 3	Ruins thinking ability of human brain + Memory loss + less social and lazy + Addiction to AI
Theme 4	Spread of fake news through edited photos and videos.
Theme 5	Decisions are not based on logic and emotions + Not useful for UPSC/JEE exams.
Theme 6	Disastrous and dangerous for the upcoming human generation.

Objective	Theme 1	Theme 2	Theme 3	Theme 4	Theme 5	Theme 6
Frequency	3	18	17	5	5	2
Percentage	6%	36%	34%	10%	10%	4%

4. **How AI as a subject has improved digital literacy, coding and computational thinking amongst your present students?**

   6 (4a) Yes, it is helping. When homework is given to them they work it at home.
   6 (4b) Students are using smartphones. They get answers through their smartphones. So, students are already doing digital learning.

5. **How is AI helpful for the teachers to track and record the lifelong skills training of a child, to prepare a holistic report card?**

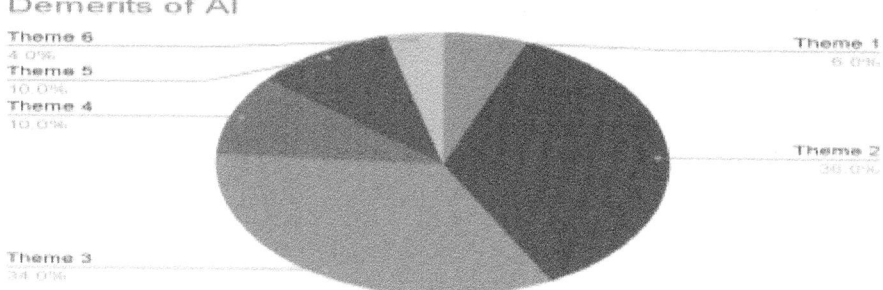

Fig. 5. List of AI tools from the response obtained from the participants on the objective no.-5

6 (5a) All students' data is filled and helps to access and track holistic learning. Students are also able to generate Google forms.

6 (5b) Yes, it is helping. All students' profiles are updated by the use of AI. Very helpful for teachers.

6. **How AI is promoting multilingualism amongst school students?**

6 (6a) Yes, it is promoting multilingualism. WhatsApp and Facebook help in translating.

6 (6b) Students having different linguistic abilities are using this feature of AI and it is promoting multilingualism.

4 Results and Discussion

Although NEP and CBSE have recommended to integrate AI in the curriculum from standard 9 to 12, still a few students are only opting for this subject which is evident that AI is vast and less popular amongst the youth. Unlearn, Relearn and Learn by robots makes the use of AI in teaching more interesting, effective and efficient. Early stage learners should be involved at the curriculum designing stage. Maximum of the learners and their mentors agreed on the fact that AI ushers learning capability. It also promotes multilingualism as stated by the learners and their mentors.

70% of the total students have defined Artificial Intelligence as a technology which produces outcomes in daily life using its own way of collecting, processing and analyzing the data. AI is helpful for Robots, satellites and it is more powerful than human intelligence. Learners are also frequently using AI tools for their learning purpose. 26% of the respondents said that AI reduces human effort and helps in research, education and recreation. 4% of the students had a negative approach towards AI and responded as AI is dangerous and takes the place of humans in jobs and it may be a weapon for wars. These findings are in line with a similar kind of study regarding AI conducted by Vartiainena et al. (2021) on the Machine learning for school students Learning through data-driven design". The actual essence of AI in education is inadequate amongst the learners and their teachers.

86% of the respondents had a positive approach towards AI and explained AI's positive characteristics like it needs no money for work, reduces workload, useful for digital creations like videos -audios, blogging. AI is helpful to connect the family members staying at far distances in the age of nuclear family concept. In this era of Global Village concept AI is helpful to connect and understand the people of different languages and cultures. It is also helpful for job search and at the same time AI is snatching away the jobs of cashiers, waiters according to 6% of the respondents. Respondents also suggested that AI should have emotions and respond to the conversations. There was no response from the 10% of the respondents. These results confirmed the conclusions drawn by Ali et al. (2021) in their study, where students reported more benefits of AI as compared to the harms of AI.

Students are aware of AI tools and the most used tool is ChatGPT according to their responses. This finding is also the same as a study conducted by Van Brummelen, Heng, & Tabunshchyk (2021) on the Conversational Artificial Intelligence Literacy Curriculum and Development Tools. They revealed that various apps like ChatGPT, Alexa and Siri used by learners provide an individualistic approach to conversation.

According to responses collected 88% of the learners accepted that AI helps in the learning process. Results of present study are similar with findings shown by Lyu et al. (2021) in which they suggested that learner's engagement through AI teaching games is useful in comparison to teaching of concepts theoretically. If context and culture is kept into consideration in using AI based games then students' learning is enhanced (Lyu et al. 2021; Priya et al. 2021; Ng and Chu 2021)

According to Williams, Park, & Breazeal (2019) Learners performance gets worsened through excessive digital load. These findings are related to the above finding of this study.

Multiple demerits are listed by the respondents like AI usage is leading towards scams, dark web issues, loss of personal data and misuse of such data, unemployment, ruining thinking ability, creativity, loss of memory, making people lazy and less social. AI acts as a weapon in the spread of fake news. It is not very useful for UPSC/JEE exams preparations as it gives irrelevant and illogical answers. In their opinions, It is disastrous for the upcoming human generations.

5   Conclusion

The study reveals that AI is fixing itself very strongly in the area of education. School students are well aware of AI, characteristic features of AI, tools of AI, AI and its application in the field of learning. Students are aware about the demerits of AI in different aspects. Majority of school students and school teachers highlighted the positive characteristics of AI. The Concept of AI and its use in the minds of school students is appropriate and they are understanding different aspects of AI. Students also found different forms and features of AI helpful in their learning. Learners also understand the negative effect of AI on students' learning habits, thinking ability, memory, and physical activity. Students perceived the AI as the cause of the reduction of few jobs in future. AS per opinion of school teachers. AI as a subject is not popular among school students. Teachers feel that AI is helpful in their teaching and in the learning of students. AI is also useful in promoting multilingualism among students.

Acknowledgement. This research study was funded by the Banaras Hindu University, Varanasi, India under Institute of Eminence Scheme (IoE), Ministry of Education, Govt. of India. Incentive Grant No. is I-6031-A-18975.

References

Cardona, M.A., Rodríguez, R.J., Ishmael, K.: Artificial intelligence and the future of teaching and learning. Office of educational Technology (2023). https://tech.ed.gov/files/2023/05/ai-future-of-teaching-and-learning-report.pdf

Chan, C.K.Y., Hu, W.: Students' voices on generative AI: perceptions, benefits, and challenges in higher education (2023). arXiv [cs.CY]. arXiv. http://arxiv.org/abs/2305.00290

D'Agostino, S.: How AI tools both help and hinder equity. Inside higher education (2023). https://www.insidehighered.com/news/tech-innovation/artificial-intelligence/2023/06/05/how-ai-tools-both-help-and-hinder-equity

Ng, D.T.K., Chu, S.K.W.: Motivating students to learn AI through social networking sites: a case study in Hong Kong. Online Learn. 25(1), 195–208 (2021)

Gocen, A., Aydemir, F.: Artificial intelligence in education and school. Res. Educ. Media 12(1), 13–21 (2020). https://doi.org/10.2478/rem-2020-0003

Gunkel, D.J.: Second thoughts: toward a critique of the digital divide. New Media Soc. 5(4), 499–522 (2003). https://doi.org/10.1177/146144480354003

Heikkilä, M.: The algorithm: AI-generated art raises tricky questions about ethics, copyright, and security (2022). https://www.technologyreview.com/2022/09/20/1059792/the-algorithm-ai-generated-art-raises-tricky-questions-about-ethics-copyright-and-security/

Li, R., Liu, C.: Artificial intelligence revolution: how AI will change our society, economy, and culture (2020). Skyhorse

Li, R.: Artificial intelligence revolution: how AI will change our society, economy, and culture. Simon and Schuster (2020)

Mishra, P., Warr, M., Islam, R.: TPACK in the age of ChatGPT and generative AI. J. Digit. Learn. Teach. Educ. 39(4), 235–251 (2023)

Mills, A.R.: ChatGPT just got better. What does that mean for our writing assignments? The chronicle of higher education (2023). https://www.chronicle.com/article/chatgpt-just-got-better-what-does-that-mean-for-our-writing-assignments

Murgia, M., Staton, B.: The AI revolution is already transforming education. Financial Times (2023). https://www.ft.com/content/47fd20c6-240d-4ffa-a0de-70717712ed1c. https://doi.org/10.1080/21532974.2023.2247480

Williams, R., Park, H.W., Breazeal, C.: A is for artificial intelligence: the impact of artificial intelligence activities on young children's perceptions of robots. In: Proceedings of the 2019 CHI Conference on Human Factors in Computing Systems, pp. 1–11 (2019)

Rizvi, S., Waite, J., Sentance, S.: Artificial intelligence teaching and learning in K-12 from 2019 to 2022: a systematic literature review. Comput. Educ. Artif. Intell. 4, 100145 (2023). https://doi.org/10.1016/j.caeai.2023.100145

Scheerder, A., van Deursen, A., van Dijk, J.: Determinants of internet skills, uses and outcomes. A systematic review of the second- and third-level digital divide. Telematics Inform. 34(8), 1607–1624 (2017). https://doi.org/10.1016/j.tele.2017.07.007

Ali, S., DiPaola, D., Lee, I., Hong, J., Breazeal, C.: Exploring generative models with middle school students. In: Proceedings of the 2021 CHI Conference on Human Factors in Computing Systems, pp. 1–13 (2021). https://doi.org/10.1145/3411764.3445226

Priya, S., Bhadra, S., Chimalakonda, S.: Ml-Quest: a game for introducing machine learning concepts to K-12 students (2021). arXiv Preprint arXiv:2107.06206

Tkhayneh, K.M.A., Alghazo, E.M., Tahat, D.: The advantages and disadvantages of using artificial intelligence in education. J. Educ. Soc. Res. **13**(4), 105 (2023). https://doi.org/10.36941/jesr-2023-0094

Vartiainena, H., Toivonenb, T., Jormanainenb, I., Kahilaa, J., Tedreb, M., Valtonena, T.: Machine learning for middle schoolers learning through data-driven design. Int. J. Child Comput. Interact. **29**, 100281 (2021). https://doi.org/10.1016/j.ijcci.2021.100281

Van Brummelen, J., Heng, T., Tabunshchyk, V.: Teaching tech to talk: K-12 conversational artificial intelligence literacy curriculum and development tools. In: Proceedings of the AAAI Conference on Artificial Intelligence, vol. 35, no. 17, pp. 15655–15663 (2021). https://doi.org/10.1609/aaai.v35i17.17844

Olari, V., Cvejoski, K., Eide, Ø.: Introduction to machine learning with robots and playful learning. In: Proceedings of the AAAI Conference on Artificial Intelligence, vol. 35, no. 17, pp. 15630–15639 (2021)

Wartman, S.A., Combs, C.D.: Medical education must move from the information age to the age of artificial intelligence. Acad. Med. **93**(8), 1107–1109 (2018)

Lyu, Z., Ali, S., Breazeal, C.: Introducing Variational Autoencoders to High School Students (2021). arXiv Preprint arXiv:2111.07036

Copeland, B.J.: Artificial Intelligence (2024). https://www.britannica.com/technology/artificial-intelligence

Sajid, H.: AI in Education 5 Practical Applications (2023). https://www.v7labs.com/blog/ai-in-education

Times of India. How Did the NEP Incorporate AI into the Regular Study Curriculum (2022). https://timesofindia.indiatimes.com/education/online-schooling/how-did-the-nep-incorporate-ai-into-the-regular-study-curriculum/articleshow/94221017.cms

Mishra, P.: AI in teaching and learning a critical response (by AI) (2023). https://punyamishra.com/2023/05/31/ai-and-the-future-of-teaching-learning-themes/

International conference on Artificial Intelligence and Education opens in Beijing, 17 May 2019. https://www.unesco.org/en/articles/international-conference-artificial-intelligence-and-education-opens-beijing

Gunkel, D.J.: Duty now and for the future: communication, ethics and artificial intelligence. J. Media Ethics **38**(4), 198–210 (2023). https://doi.org/10.1080/23736992.2023.2264854

Anomalous Sound Pattern Detection
for Machine Health Monitoring

Shivali Dalmia and Manjeet Rege(⊠)

University of St. Thomas, St. Paul, MN 55105, USA
{dalm3066,rege}@stthomas.edu

Abstract. Anomaly detection using audio signals from industrial machines in the manufacturing industry has gained broad interest over the last few years. For example, predictive maintenance solutions utilize raw analog signals to identify trends and patterns. In a few scenarios, an engineer working in a factory setting can tell when a machine is behaving abnormally just by hearing unexpected sounds (e.g., the loudness of sound) that are well within the human perceivable frequency range (20 Hz - lowest pitch to 20 kHz - highest pitch) which are typically concentrated in a narrow range of frequencies and amplitudes. The human perception of the amplitude of a sound is its loudness. However, the audio signal in its raw form is not always the best representation of the important features (e.g., frequencies, amplitude, peaks). Additionally, the machine learning applications which rely on using traditional digital signal processing techniques (e.g., digital signal processors, chips) have a lot of dependency on subject matter experts to tune the system for a better performance. Thus, we investigate how the digital transformation of waveform signals from microphone sensors (e.g., Audio recordings of industrial pumps, valves, slide rails) into Spectrograms (A spectrogram is a voiceprint of a signal which expresses an audio signal as an image using different colors to indicate the amplitude or strength of each frequency.) can help to monitor machine health (e.g., anomaly classification). In the pre-processing phase, raw audio signals (.WAV format) from each machine are converted to Mel Spectrogram images using short-term Fourier transformation. Then, comparative study of image classification techniques using deep convolutional neural networks (CNN) with and without data augmentation, is conducted to classify images as normal or abnormal. The approach is evaluated using Malfunctioning industrial machine investigation and inspection dataset [1–3] (MIMII dataset). Results show that the neural network based models trained on the dataset with Mel Spectrogram transformation perform better than models trained on the raw dataset (i.e., sound samples without spectrogram conversion).

Keywords: Anomaly detection · Machine health monitoring · Predictive maintenance

1 Introduction

Industrial artificial intelligence or industrial AI [12] is the application of AI to industrial use cases. AI technologies can process and interpret large volumes of data coming from the production floor to identify novel, interesting, and relevant patterns to help detect

H. K. et al. (Eds.): AIKP 2023, CCIS 2127, pp. 44–60, 2024.
https://doi.org/10.1007/978-3-031-68617-7_4

anomalies in production processes in real-time, and more. For example, intelligent, self-optimizing machines automate production processes and predictive maintenance (PdM) [11] using sensors. PdM solutions heavily utilize sensors for data collection, giving us the ability to measure movement, waves, sound, heat, light, and much more. The sensors enable us to catalog analog data from the physical world, and identify trends and patterns. The data collected from different sensors such as, microphone, accelerometer, magnetometer, gyroscope, and temp-humidity which are mounted on machines can play a vital role in building a predictive maintenance and failure monitoring system for industrial machines.

1.1 Why Industrial AI?

Every manufacturer aims to save and make money, reduce risks and improve overall production efficiency. AI tools can process and interpret large volumes of data from the production floor to identify novel, interesting, and relevant patterns to help detect anomalies in production processes in real-time. Some noteworthy examples are as follows:

- Intelligent, self-optimizing machines that automate production processes. For example, Siemens and Google have partnered to develop a computer vision application that can visually inspect products to ensure quality and is further equipped with algorithms that can predict the wear-and-tear on assembly line machines [13].
- Predictive maintenance using sensors. For example, Bosch Rexroth's [14] predictive maintenance solution creates a machine health index to monitor a drive system's normal operating state.

Outline: The rest of the paper includes the following sections: In Sect. 2 we describe the related work briefly, our contribution and the scope of this paper. Section 3 describes the exploratory data analysis and data preprocessing. Section 4 describes the experiments conducted for anomaly detection for different industrial machines and Sect. 5 concludes the paper and summarizes the future work.

2 Related Work and Our Contributions

Anomaly detection techniques can be broadly classified into three categories: unsupervised, semi-supervised, and supervised. The majority of supervised algorithms are able to detect pre-defined anomalies, for example certain error types on industrial manufacturing products. In the case of severe class imbalance, where only a small fraction of training data represents anomaly, there is not enough data available for the model to learn unseen anomaly patterns. This limits the scope of improvement in model performance and prediction. The remedy is to use unsupervised or semi-supervised anomaly detection techniques. For example, the approach of using data-driven lower dimensional representation of Spectrograms for training [5] is a semi-supervised approach. Another example of an unsupervised approach is AnoGAN [6] based on image mapping.

M. Abdel et al. [5] proposed a technique for anomaly detection in civil aircraft engines where spectrograms are utilized to visually represent the vibrations of engines. As the spectrogram representation is noisy and high dimensional they used two types of low dimensional representations of the spectrograms: a data driven dictionary learning using non-negative matrix factorization similar to PCA and a non adaptive dictionary representations which are generated using Fourier based transformations (e.g., frames).

In another work, Thomas et al. [6] proposed a deep convolutional generative adversarial network (GAN) called AnoGAN which learnt a manifold of normal anatomical variability, which was accompanied by a novel anomaly scoring scheme which mapped image space to a latent space. AnoGAN labeled anomalies on test data, and scored image patches indicating their fit into the learned distribution. Hendrycks et al. [7] introduced an abnormality module which had a normal classifier and an auxiliary decoder. The baseline normal classifier was trained for detecting out of distribution and misclassified samples in neural networks which utilized probabilities from softmax distributions. The performance of normal binary classifier was evaluated using MNIST, CIFAR-10, and CIFAR-100 datasets. The appended auxiliary decoder reconstructed the input from the normal classifier stage. The results demonstrated that the abnormality module was better than the baseline normal classifier.

Akcay et al. [8] introduced an anomaly detection model with a novel architecture consisting of encoder-decoder-encoder sub-networks. The conditional generative adversarial network jointly learnt the generation of high-dimensional image space and the inference of latent space. The model used the generative network to map the input image to a lower dimensional space. Then, the output image was also reconstructed using the network. Additional encoder layers helped convert the image to its latent representation. The data distribution was learnt in both the image vector space and the latent space. Ultimately image samples at a larger distance than the learnt (image and latent) space were identified as anomalous.

Shahid Khan et al. [9] proposed a SDCNN framework based on deep convolutional neural networks which utilized spectrogram images of network traffic generated using the short-time Fourier transform (STFT). In comparison to other deep learning algorithms such as CNN-1D, RNN, LSTM, and GRU, SDCNN improved the accuracy by 2.5%–4% in detecting intrusions (e.g. malicious attacks by third party networks which are either novel or mutations of the older attacks).

Table 1. Summary of related work

Year	Author	Proposed approach	Evaluation dataset
2023	M.Abdel et al.	Data driven lower dimensional representation of Spectrograms	Civil aircraft engine data
2017	Thomas Schlegl et al.	AnoGAN	Spectral-domain OCT scans
2016	Dan Hendrycks et al.	Probabilistic softmax distributions	CIFAR-10, CIFAR-100, THCHS-30, IMDb Movie Reviews
2018	Samet Akcay et al.	GANomaly	CIFAR-10
2021	A. S. Khan et al.	SDCNN	CIC-IDS2017

Limitations of related work: Table 1 summarizes the deep learning based related work proposed in recent years (2016–2021) for anomaly detection which were briefly described earlier. We note that the majority of the works used images for training their models. However, these approaches have not been tested for anomaly detection in the manufacturing industry. For example, the linear spectrograms [9] which are a direct output of short-term Fourier Transform may or may not be able to highlight the striking differences between normal and anomaly conditions of an industrial machine. Thus the need arises for identifying techniques for generating fine-tuned spectrograms for a better performance of deep learning based anomaly detection algorithms.

2.1 Our Contributions

Our Main Contributions Are as Follows:

1. We propose a two-step data preprocessing strategy for converting raw audio signals to spectrograms. In Step-1 we use short-term Fourier Transform (STFT) [15] to see the variations in different frequency bands over time within the audio waveform and increase the granularity of the visual representation. In Step-2 we optimize the STFT output using mel and db scale. *"Mel scale is a continuous scale of pitches interpreted by listeners to be equidistant from one another. This scale approximates the human auditory system's response more closely than the linearly-spaced frequency bands used in the normal spectrum as they are equally spaced from each other in the mel scale."* [16, 17]. This results in a better representation of the sound in human perceivable range. Further, a *Db scale* is the third dimension which indicates the amplitude at a given frequency and time. Audio is best represented with a logarithmic amplitude axis in decibels [18].
2. We build a neural network based model to evaluate the effectiveness of the optimized Mel-spectrograms for normal for the task of anomaly prediction. We use Malfunctioning industrial machine investigation and inspection dataset [1–3] (MIMII dataset) to build the models.
3. We compare the anomaly prediction model trained on Mel Spectrogram data with the models trained on the raw dataset (i.e., normal sound samples).

Scope: To keep the data transformations simple we only use the first channel of the recordings. Further we also acknowledge that due to time constraints the comparison with the related work is limited.

3 Proposed Methodology

In this section we first briefly describe the basic concepts. Then, we describe the dataset used for the investigation which is followed by the details of exploratory data analysis. Then we describe the data preprocessing steps with illustrative examples. Finally, we describe the convolutional neural network based approach to train the models.

3.1 Basic Concepts

A **sound signal** [19] is produced by variations in air pressure and it is measured by plotting the intensity of pressure variations over time. The audio signals from industrial machines when they are operating in normal condition follow a repetitive pattern occurring at a regular interval so that each wave has the same shape. The height shows the intensity of the sound and is known as the amplitude and the time taken to complete one full wave pattern is called the period. Figure 1 shows a representation of amplitude vs. time period in a signal. Frequency represents the number of waves made by a signal over a period of one second and is measured in Hertz (Hz).

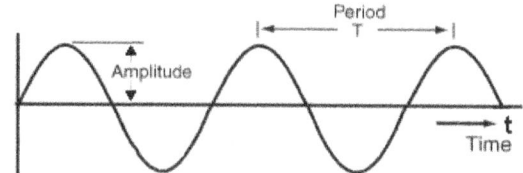

Fig. 1. Representation of amplitude vs. time in a signal [21]

The **spectrum** is a set of frequency bands which if combined together represents one signal. It is a representation of amplitude against frequency where the x-axis denotes the range of frequency values at a particular time; it represents the signal in the frequency domain.

A **Spectrogram** [16] is a concise snapshot of an audio wave over time. It can be referred to as a photographic representation of the signal where the x-axis represents time and the y-axis represents frequency. Different colors indicate the amplitude or strength of each frequency band. The brightness of color is directly proportional with the energy of the signal. They are generated using fast fourier transformation (FFT) [20]. FFT decomposes the signal into its constituent frequencies and displays the amplitude of each frequency present in the signal. FFT chops up the duration of the signal into smaller time segments and then applies the Fourier transformation to each segment which determines the frequencies in that segment.

3.2 Dataset Description

In this work, we use Malfunctioning industrial machine investigation and inspection (MIMII) dataset [1–3]. The dataset has been used as a benchmark for sound based fault diagnosis in industrial machines. The MIMII dataset has normal and anomalous operating audio samples of four machine types: pumps, valves, fan, and slide rails. Each recording contains a multi-channel audio file with an approximate length of 10 s. Each audio sample represents the machine's operating audio with additional environmental noise that is collected using eight microphones at 16 kHz sampling rate and 16 bit per sample. For simplicity of data transformation, only the first channel of the recordings are used. All recordings are regarded as single-channel recordings of a fixed microphone.

The data is labeled by machine ID and machine type. For each machine ID around 1000 samples of normal sounds are available for training and 200–400 samples for the test. Further, the test data contains a similar number (100–200) of the normal and anomalous sounds. In summary, each training and test sample has the metadata of machine type, machine ID, and condition (i.e., normal or anomalous). Figure 2 shows an example of the dataset file structure.

```
/data
   →  /fan
         •  /train (Only normal data for all Machine IDs)
               ○  /normal_id_01_00000000.wav
               ○  /normal_id_02_00000000.wav
               ○  ...
               ○  /normal_id_04_00000999.wav
         •  /test (Normal and anomaly data for all Machine IDs)
               ○  /normal_id_01_00000000.wav
               ○  ...
               ○  /normal_id_01_00000349.wav
               ○  /anomaly_id_01_00000000.wav
               ○  ...
               ○  /anomaly_id_01_00000263.wav
               ○  /normal_id_02_00000000.wav
               ○  ...
               ○  /anomaly_id_04_00000264.wav
   →  /pump
   →  /slider
   →  /valve
```

Fig. 2. Example of dataset structure for fan machine.

3.3 Exploratory Data Analysis

Exploratory data analysis (EDA) is an essential step to understand data characteristics. The analysis helps in identifying the useful patterns, determining important variables, and identifying the necessary data transformation or preprocessing steps required to best represent the data before using it for model training.

As observed in Fig. 3 for the human eye it's difficult to distinguish normal and anomalous samples by just observing waveform representations of normal and anomaly samples for all four machines i.e., pump, slider, valve, slider etc. The noise change overs are not evident. This may be because in industrial scenarios the sound pattern from the machines may not follow a consistent regular periodic pattern, instead it may be composed of different frequencies and represent a more complex composite signal.

Thus, we performed additional data transformation steps to generate a distinguished visual representation between the normal and anomalous machine conditions. Mel-Spectrograms with additional preprocessing are leveraged here to better represent the noise change overs for different machines. For example, for a pump machine the noise changeovers are slighlty more evident in anomaly spectrograms as compared to normal spectrograms (Fig. 3). With additional pre-processing (of spectrograms) the noise can be observed more clearly as illustrated in Figs. 5 and 6 (pg. 7) for the pump machine. Similar observations are made for other three types of machines i.e., slider, valve, and fan.

Further, the conventional audio processing methodologies such as equalization, noise, filtering, suppression, and compression which require mandatory inputs of subject matter experts are not required with deep learning. It is because the data in its raw form is not used for model training. Instead the audio samples when converted to images are expected to be more noticeable and clearly perceived by electrical and manufacturing engineers working in factory plants. The conversion of audio signals into images is done by generating spectrograms using audio signals.

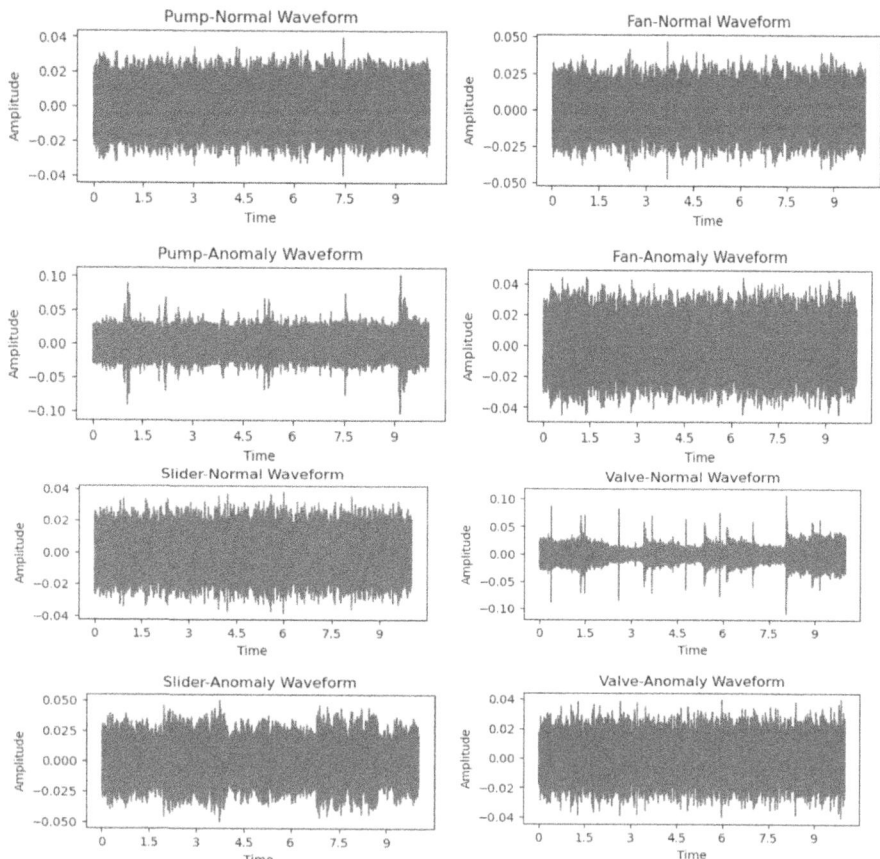

Fig. 3. Waveform representation of Normal and Anomalous samples for machines.

3.4 Data Pre-processing

Below, we describe the pre-processing steps to convert an audio file to an optimized mel-spectrogram.

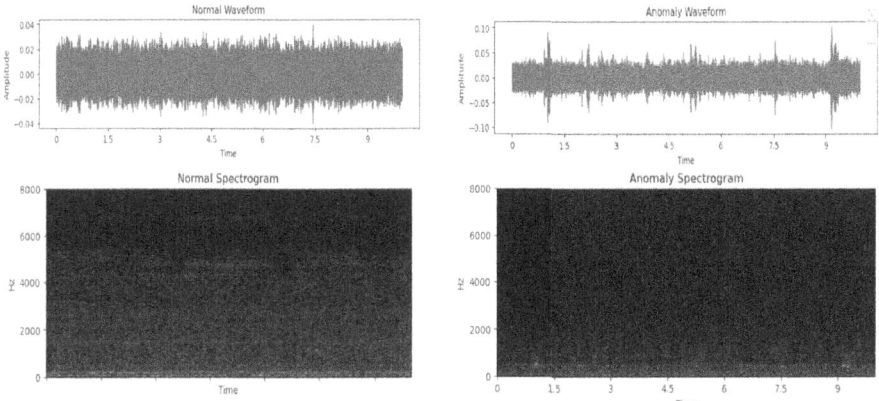

Fig. 4. Waveform vs. Linear Spectrogram representation for Normal and Anomalous samples (pump).

Mel-Spectrograms: Humans are more receptive to differences within lower frequencies than within higher frequencies and hear them on a logarithmic scale rather than linear. As observed in Fig. 4, a linear spectrogram doesn't give much insight into different noise patterns in signals for machines such as pumps. Thus to overcome this issue Mel-Spectrograms [17] are generated. Mel-spectrograms use mel scale which is the continuous scale of pitches interpreted by listeners to be equal in distance from one another. The reference point between Mel scale and normal frequency measurement is defined by assigning a continuous pitch of 1000 mels to a 1000 Hz tone, 40 dB above the listeners threshold. Additionally, the human perception of sound is by its loudness which is heard logarithmically rather than linearly. The decibel scale is used to represent the loudness of a signal in spectrograms. Overall, linear spectrograms are converted to mel-spectrograms by using mel-scale on y-axis instead of frequency and decibel scale instead of amplitude to indicate colors.

Optimized Mel-Spectrogram: Mel-Spectrograms are optimized to increase the granularity of the distinction between different frequency bands in a spectrogram image. Short Time Fourier Transformation (STFT) is applied to determine the change in frequency components over time i.e., which part of the signal has low frequencies and which has high frequencies. STFT uses a sliding time window to break the audio signal into smaller sections along the time axis. It performs FFT on each small section and then integrates them to capture the variations of the frequency with time.

Further, STFT also takes a full range of frequencies and splits it into equidistant bands (Mel scale) along the frequency axis. Then, for each time section, it calculates the magnitude or power for each frequency band.

Mel Hyper-parameters: Mel-spectrograms are generated using the following parameters.

1. Minimum frequency (fmin)
2. Maximum frequency (fmax)

3. Number of frequency bands (n_mels – height of the spectrogram) are frequency hyperparameters
4. Sliding window length (n_fft)
5. Sliding window length (hop_length)

The width of the spectrogram can be derived using the above mentioned hyperparameters as follows:

$$\text{Spectrogram width} = \frac{\text{Total number of samples}}{\text{Hop length}}$$

Steps: The following data pre-processing steps are performed for data from all the four machines (i.e., slider, valve, pump, rail) to convert raw audio files into corresponding mel-spectrogram images.

Step 1. Linear power spectrogram is generated
Step 2. Spectrogram with Mel scale as y-axis is generated
Step 3. Spectrogram with Mel and Db scale is generated.

We evaluated different hyperparameters values for generating the optimized mel-spectrogram. Table 2 describes the parameters evaluated and the values highlighted in bold are selected for data pre-processing.

Table 2. Mel hyper parameters

f_min (Hz)	f_max (Hz)	n_mels	n_fft	hop_length
0	5000	32	256	64
0	5000	64	512	128
0	**5000**	**128**	**1024**	**256**

Figures 5 and 6 shows the conversion of a signal from its raw waveform to an optimized mel-spectrogram for both normal and anomalous machine (pump) conditions.

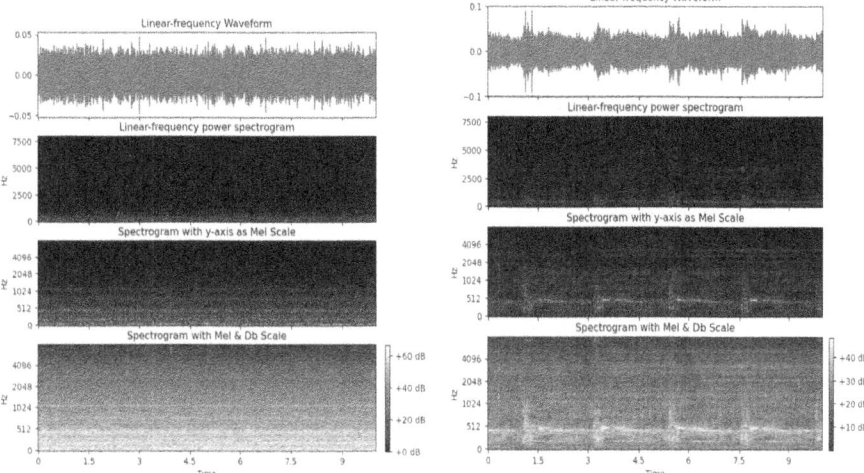

Fig. 5. Mel-spectrogram conversion of a normal sample.

Fig. 6. Mel-spectrogram conversion of an anomalous sample.

3.5 Convolutional Neural Network

Convolutional neural networks (CNN) are typically used for analyzing image datasets. Feed forward CNNs are articulated to process pixel data and are increasingly being used for image processing and identification. A basic CNN has an input layer defined by input array shape and size. Next, it has a stack of multiple convolutional layers (CL) and pooling layers. The convolution layer has different input hyper parameters such as number of feature maps, filter size, strides defining the sliding window for filter, and activation function. The stack is followed by a fully connected dense layer, and finally the output layer with a single unit and activation function for classification.

Convolutional layers (CL) [10] are the foundation blocks of CNN. A convolution is performed by applying a filter function to an input image which results in a map of activations called a feature map. The feature map indicates the strength and locations of a feature detected in an input image. For convolution, the filter (window) slides across the height and width of the image and the dot product between the input and every element of the filter is determined at every spatial position. An example of filter operation is shown in Fig. 7 below.

Activation Functions are the arithmetic functions utilized in the neural networks to control the output. In this study, ReLU, sigmoid, and linear activation functions were evaluated. The mathematical formulas for the activation functions are follows:

$ReLU = max\,(0,x)$	Sigmoid $(x) = 1/1 + e^{-x}$	Softmax $(x_k) = e_k^x / \sum_{i=1}^{n} e_i^x$

where x represents the input.

Fully Connected layer (FCL) follows the stack of pooling and convolutional layers. In a FCL every neuron in one layer is connected to each neuron in another layer. The

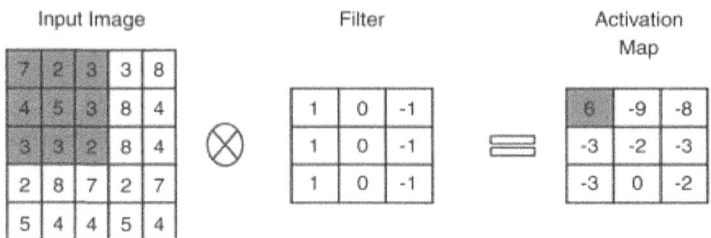

Fig. 7. Filter operation in convolution [10].

flattened matrix of the output from the stack of convolutional and pooling layers goes through a fully connected layer to classify the images.

Output layer: The final layer is used for the classification and use an activation function. In our experiments, we use linear activation for predicting linear probability distribution of normal data.

4 Experiments

4.1 Image Data Conversion

The spectrogram images were converted to *NumPy* arrays using Python Image Library (PIL) [26] to make them compatible as input to the convolutional neural network (CNN) layers. Following steps were performed in a loop for each input image to create training and test dataset for each machine.

1. Input image was loaded using the "open" function of the "Image" module. Its lazy mode of operation identifies the file and keeps it open, but the actual image data is not read from the file until data processing is invoked.
2. Image object was converted to a numpy array using "scikit-image" which uses standard numpy arrays to allow maximum interoperability with other python libraries in the neural network ecosystem.
3. Image object was sliced from 480 × 640 × 4 (RGBA) to 480 × 640 × 3 (RGB) to limit the level of opacity in the spectrogram images.
4. Image object was converted to float and then normalized by dividing the numpy array with 255. This reduces the computational issues arising from large numeric values when an image is passed through a neural network.
5. Image array was then appended to their class labels, i.e., "normal" and "anomaly".

4.2 Model Configuration

The comprehensive architecture of the proposed CNN Model is shown below (Fig. 8) starting with the input image and the output of each layer to predict the linear probability score of each image. The first stage contains the first layer as an input layer with the input size of 480 × 640 × 3 followed by a stack of five convolutional layers (Conv2D) with the following number of dimension sizes: 32, 64, 128, 64, 32. Each layer had a filter size

(3,3), strides (2), and activation function as 'relu'. The output of the first stage is flattened and then fed into the second stage which consists of a stack of dropout layer (0.5), then a dense fully connected layer with the dimension size of 32, with 'relu' activation function. The final output layer is a fully connected dense layer with one output feature map and 'linear' activation function.

In the model compilation stage the 'Adam' optimizer [22, 23] with a learning rate of 0.001, loss function of mean squared errors (MSE), and the evaluation metrics as the mean absolute error (MAE) are used. Finally, we fit the model on a training dataset consisting of only normal samples with a different combination of batch size and epochs for all the four machines i.e., pump, slider, valve, and fan.

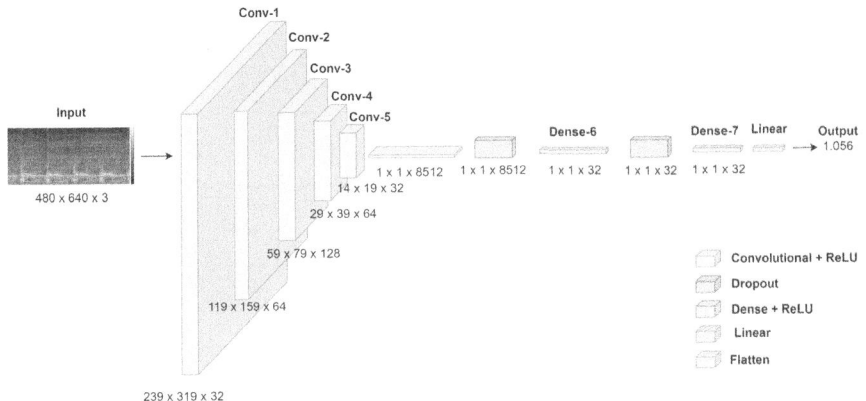

Fig. 8. Convolutional Neural Network Architecture [27]

4.3 Evaluation Metrics

The overall performance is evaluated using Accuracy [25], Misclassification Rate [25], Precision [25], Recall [25], and F1 Score [25]. All the metrics are determined using different attributes of a confusion matrix [24]. In the confusion matrix, true positive (TP) and true negative (TN) are the correctly predicted Normal and Anomaly samples respectively; whereas false positive (FP) and false negative (FN) represent the samples of Normal and Anomaly classes which are incorrectly predicted respectively.

Confusion Matrix [24]: A confusion matrix represents the summary of predicted results (Fig. 9).

Accuracy is the fraction of the total number of correctly predicted samples to the total number of samples [25].

$$Accuracy = \frac{TP + TN}{TP + TN + FP + FN}$$

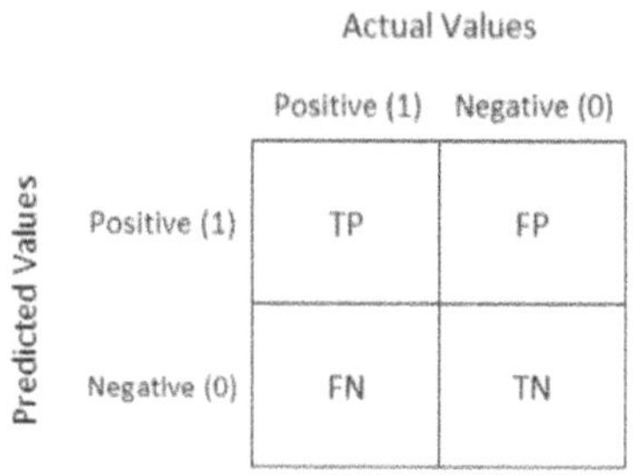

Actual Values

Positive (1)   Negative (0)

Predicted Values

Positive (1)   TP   FP

Negative (0)   FN   TN

Fig. 9. Confusion Matrix [25]

Misclassification Rate is the fraction of the total number of incorrectly predicted samples to the total number of samples [25].

$$Miss.\ Rate = \frac{FP + FN}{TP + TN + FP + FN}$$

Precision is the fraction of correctly predicted normal samples to the total number of positive samples [25].

$$Precision = \frac{TP}{FP}$$

Recall or True Positive Rate (TPR) is the fraction of correctly predicted normal samples to the total number of positive samples [25].

$$TPR = \frac{TP}{TP + FN}$$

F1-score is the mean of Precision and Recall. It is a metric to determine the overall correctness of the system [25].

$$F1\ score = \frac{2 + Precision * Recall}{Precision + Recall}$$

4.4 Experimental Setup

The experiments were performed on an HP ZBook with 32.0 GB RAM, ×64-based processor, and 11th Gen Intel(R) Core(™) i7-11850H processor, and a 64-bit Windows 11 Pro operating system. Anaconda framework (Version 23.1.0) and Python (Version 3.9.10) tools were used to implement the proposed approach. Librosa (Version 0.9.2) library was used to generate mel-spectrograms from audio files for all the machines in MIMII dataset. The convolutional neural networks were implemented using Tensorflow (Version 2.11.0). All the implementation and experimentation was done in the JupyterLab (Version 3.5.3) environment (Table 3).

Table 3. Number of Samples

	Training Samples	Test Samples	
MachineID	Normal	Normal	Anomaly
pump_id_00	906	100	143
pump_id_02	905	100	111
pump_id_04	602	100	100
pump_id_06	936	100	102
fan_id_00	911	100	407
fan_id_02	916	100	359
fan_id_04	932	100	348
fan_id_06	915	100	361
valve_id_00	891	100	119
valve_id_02	608	100	120
valve_id_04	900	100	120
valve_id_06	892	100	120
slider_id_00	968	100	356
slider_id_02	968	100	267
slider_id_04	434	100	178
slider_id_06	434	100	89

4.5 Results

Table 4 shows the numbers for baseline F1 score (baseline_F1_score) and the F1 score, accuracy, misclassification rate, precision, and recall for the proposed CNN based approach. The F1-score evaluation metric is preferred over accuracy to compare the performance of suggested CNN architecture (with mel-spectrogram data augmentation) with the baseline deep neural network architecture trained on raw dataset due to class imbalance in training dataset (i.e., we only have training samples classified as normal). As shown, the CNN based approach gives a higher average F1 score of 0.6921 for pump machines as compared to average F1 score of 0.5185 with a baseline dense neural network. Similarly, for the other three machines fan, valve, and slider the CNN based approach has a higher F1 score of 0.8802, 0.7040, 0.7850 as compared to 0.5858, 0.4923, 0.5499 for the baseline respectively. In summary, we find that there is an average improvement in F1 score by 0.1736, 0.2944, 0.2117, 0.2351 for pump, fan, valve, and slider respectively.

Table 4. Evaluation Metric results

Machine ID	baseline_F1_Score	F1_score	Accuracy	Miss Rate	Precision	Recall
pump_id_00	0.5159	0.7409	0.4074	0.5926	0.0629	0.4737
pump_id_02	0.5125	0.6894	0.5261	0.4739	1.0000	0.5261
pump_id_04	0.456	0.6666	0.5650	0.4350	0.2700	0.6585
pump_id_06	0.5899	0.6711	0.5050	0.4950	1.0000	0.5050
fan_id_00	0.5925	0.8904	0.8028	0.1972	0.9975	0.8040
fan_id_02	0.5056	0.8778	0.7821	0.2179	1.0000	0.7821
fan_id_04	0.7324	0.8744	0.7768	0.2232	1.0000	0.7768
fan_id_06	0.5128	0.8783	0.7831	0.2169	1.0000	0.7831
valve_id_00	0.4999	0.7041	0.5434	0.4566	1.0000	0.5434
valve_id_02	0.4712	0.7059	0.5455	0.4545	1.0000	0.5455
valve_id_04	0.5059	0.7059	0.5455	0.4545	1.0000	0.5455
valve_id_06	0.4923	0.7003	0.5409	0.4591	0.9833	0.5438
slider_id_00	0.4891	0.8768	0.7807	0.2193	1.0000	0.7807
slider_id_02	0.5675	0.8423	0.7275	0.2725	1.0000	0.7275
slider_id_04	0.6754	0.7807	0.6403	0.3597	1.0000	0.6403
slider_id_06	0.4678	0.6403	0.4709	0.5291	1.0000	0.4709

5   Conclusion and Future Work

Conclusion: In this study we explore the idea of converting audio samples from different industrial machines such as pump, slider, fan, and valve to mel-spectrograms images using Short Time Fourier Transform (STFT). The converted audio samples were then used to train convolutional neural network (CNN) based models using "normal" mel-spectrogram images. The model performance was evaluated on a test data set having unseen normal and anomaly samples. The performance of CNN architecture was compared with the baseline deep neural network trained using raw audio samples. The F1 scores show that CNN based models perform better than models trained on the raw dataset (i.e., sound samples without spectrogram conversion).

Future Work: In the future, we plan to extend the work in the following manner: 1. Evaluate and optimize the CNN architecture with additional normal instances to the training dataset. 2. Explore train accuracy optimization using different hyper parameters such as batch size, epochs, and learning rate. 3. Compare the performance of suggested CNN architecture with other related work discussed in Sect. 2 above. 4. Evaluate performance of suggested CNN approach with pre-trained networks (e.g., VGG-16).

References

1. Koizumi, Y., Saito, S., Harada, N., Uematsu, H., Imoto, K.: ToyADMOS: a dataset of miniature-machine operating sounds for anomalous sound detection. In: Proceedings of Workshop on Applications of Signal Processing to Audio and Acoustics (WASPAA) (2019)
2. Purohit, H., et al.: MIMII dataset: sound dataset for malfunctioning industrial machine investigation and inspection. In: Proceedings 4th Workshop on Detection can you and Classification of Acoustic Scenes and Events (DCASE) (2019)
3. Koizumi, Y., et al.: Description and discussion on DCASE2020 challenge Task2: unsupervised anomalous sound detection for machine condition monitoring. In: Proceedings 5th Workshop on Detection and Classification of Acoustic Scenes and Events (DCASE) (2020)
4. Delattre, P.: The physiological interpretation of sound spectrograms. PMLA **66**(5), 864–875 (1951)
5. Abdel-Sayed, M., Duclos, D., Faÿ, G., Lacaille, J., Mougeot, M.: Anomaly detection on spectrograms using data driven and fixed dictionary representations (2023)
6. Schlegl, T., Seeböck, P., Waldstein, S.M., Schmidt-Erfurth, U., Langs, G.: Unsupervised anomaly detection with generative adversarial networks to guide marker discovery (2017)
7. Hendrycks, D., Gimpel, K.: A baseline for detecting misclassified and out-of-distribution examples in neural networks (2016)
8. Akcay, S., Atapour-Abarghouei, A., Breckon, T.P.: GANomaly: semi-supervised anomaly detection via adversarial training (2018)
9. Khan, A.S., Ahmad, Z., Abdullah, J., Ahmad, F.: A spectrogram image-based network anomaly detection system using deep convolutional neural network. IEEE Access **9**, 87079–87093 (2021). https://doi.org/10.1109/ACCESS.2021.3088149
10. Mostafa, S., Wu, F.X.: Diagnosis of autism spectrum disorder with convolutional autoencoder and structural MRI images. In: El-Baz, A.S., Suri, J.S. (eds.) Neural Engineering Techniques for Autism Spectrum Disorder, pp. 23–38. Academic Press, New York (2021). https://doi.org/10.1016/B978-0-12-822822-7.00003-X
11. Mobley, R.K.: An Introduction to Predictive Maintenance. Elsevier, Amsterdam (2002)
12. Fox, M.S.: Industrial applications of artificial intelligence. Robotics **2**(4), 301–311 (1986)
13. Siemens and Google Cloud to cooperate on AI-based solutions in manufacturing. http://press.siemens.com/global/en/pressrelease/siemens-and-google-cloud-cooperate-ai-based-solutions-manufactu ring
14. From condition monitoring to predictive maintenance: turning date to real customer value. https://en.industryarena.com/boschrexroth/news/from-condition-monitoring-to-predictive-maintenance-turning-date-to-real-customer-value--10294.html
15. Sejdić, E., Djurović, I., Jiang, J.: Time–frequency feature representation using energy concentration: an overview of recent advances. Digit. Signal Process. **19**(1), 153–183 (2009)
16. Xu, M., et al.: HMM-based audio keyword generation. In: Advances in Multimedia Information Processing-PCM 2004: 5th Pacific Rim Conference on Multimedia, Tokyo, Japan, November 30-December 3, 2004. Proceedings, Part III 5. Springer Berlin Heidelberg (2005)
17. Stevens, S.S., Volkmann, J., Newman, E.B.: A scale for the measurement of the psychological magnitude pitch. J. Acoust. Soc. Am.Acoust. Soc. Am. **8**, 185–190 (1937). https://doi.org/10.1121/1.1915893
18. Sejdic, E., Djurovic, I., Stankovic, L.: Quantitative performance analysis of scalogram as instantaneous frequency estimator. IEEE Trans. Signal Process. **56**(8), 3837–3845 (2008). https://doi.org/10.1109/TSP.2008.924856
19. Wikipedia contributors. "Audio signal". Wikipedia, The Free Encyclopedia. Wikipedia, The Free Encyclopedia, 27 Oct. 2022. Web. 16 Apr. 2023

20. Heideman, M.T., Johnson, D.H., SidneyBurrus, C.: Gauss and the history of the fast Fourier transform. Arch. Hist. Exact Sci. **34**, 265–277 (1985)
21. Analog vs. digital signals: uses, advantages and disadvantages article MPS (https://www.mon olithicpower.com/)
22. Agnes Lydia, A., Sagayaraj Francis, F., Adagrad - an optimizer for stochastic gradient descent, Department of Computer Science and Engineering, Pondicherry Engineering College, May 2019
23. Tieleman, T., Hinton, G.: Lecture 6.5-rmsprop: divide the gradient by a running average of its recent magnitude. COURSERA Neural Netw. Mach. Learn. **4**(2), 26–31 (2012)
24. Stehman, S.V.: Selecting and interpreting measures of thematic classification accuracy. Remote Sens. Environ. **62**(1), 77–89 (1997). https://doi.org/10.1016/S0034-4257(97)00083-7
25. Powers, D.M.W.: Evaluation: from precision, recall and F-measure to ROC, informedness, markedness & correlation. J. Mach. Learn. Technol. (2011)
26. Python Imaging Library (PIL), https://web.archive.org/web/20201121102218/, http://www.pythonware.com/products/pil/
27. draw.io Documentation (www.drawio.com)

Performance Evaluation of Various Machine Learning Algorithms for Lung Cancer Prediction Using Demographic Data

Mulagada Surya Sharmila[1], K. Shiridi Kumar[1], Shahid Mohammad Ganie[2]($\boxtimes$) ⓘ, K. Hemachandran[2] ⓘ, and Manjeet Rege[3]

[1] School of Business, Woxsen University, Hyderabad, Telangana 502345, India
[2] AI Research Centre, Department of Analytics, Woxsen University, Hyderabad 502345, India
Shahid.mohammad@woxsen.edu.in
[3] Department of Software Engineering and Data Science, University of St. Thomas, Saint Paul, MN, USA

Abstract. Lung cancer is among the top deadly diseases, affecting human beings globally. Therefore, it is crucial to predict and detect this disease as early as possible, allowing the doctors and the patients to take the appropriate and essential actions. Techniques like machine learning can be applied to the same. In this study, we used machine learning to predict cancer in the lungs. We explored five machine learning algorithms, viz., Decision Tree (DT), Support vector machine (SVM), Naive Bayes (NB), Logistic Regression (LR), and Random Forest (RF). A publicly available dataset that contains demographic information of 284 patients with 16 parameters is used to conduct this study. An extensive explorative analysis is performed to improve the quality assessment of the dataset. Among five algorithms, Logistic Regression (LR) exhibited best findings in terms of accuracy, precision, recall, specificity, f1-score, and negative predicted values (NPV). Compared to similar research works, the proposed model achieved better results based on various performance evaluation metrics. The proposed model can be used for other illnesses that have similar symptoms by using transfer learning approach.

Keywords: Lung cancer prediction · Machine learning algorithms · Predictive modeling · Disease prediction · Lifestyle Data

1 Introduction

According to the world health organization (WHO), one among 16 people are diagnosed with the global incidence of lung cancer in 2022[1]. With so many millions of new cases and fatalities each year, lung cancer continues to be the most prevalent and the leading cause of cancer growth rate and mortality [1]. Coughing, chest pain, shortness of breath, and weight loss are some signs of lung cancer, but such may not appear until cancer has reached an advanced stage. There exist various lung diagnosis methods in

---

[1] https://www.iarc.who.int/.

H. K. et al. (Eds.): AIKP 2023, CCIS 2127, pp. 61–74, 2024.
https://doi.org/10.1007/978-3-031-68617-7_5

medical industry which use CT (computed tomography), isotope, X-ray, MRI (magnetic resonance image), etc. [2]. However, if the disease is detected at the initial stage, The likelihood of surviving can be improved. To help with early lung cancer detection, it's crucial to correctly identify the benign (non-cancerous) and malignant (cancerous) cells [3]. In this aspect, machine learning approaches can be quite beneficial by providing realistic results by metric analysis [4]. In contrast to any set of clinical experience, machine learning Algorithms can quickly pick up information from a lot more patients, which may enable the algorithms to produce more correct predictions. The leading cause of cancer-related mortality is lung cancer; hence this issue is crucial [5]. In the healthcare sector, machine learning paradigm provides the analysis of any disease with almost near accuracy allowing the doctors to make better medical decisions, thus resulting in better diagnosis and prognosis [6, 7].

However, if the disease is detected at the initial stage, the chances of survival rate of a person can be increased. There exist various lung diagnosis methods that employ magnetic resonance imaging (MRI), X-rays, isotope-based computer tomography (CT), etc. For early detection of lung cancer, it is crucial to correctly identify the benign (non-cancerous) and malignant (cancerous) cells [3]. The leading cause of cancer-related mortality is lung cancer, hence this issue is crucial [5]. In the healthcare sector, machine learning provides the analysis of any disease with almost near accuracy allowing doctors to make better medical decisions, thus resulting in better diagnosis and prognosis [6].

1.1 Contribution

In this paper, we developed a framework using machine learning algorithms for predicting cancer in the lungs based on demographic information. The following are the key contributions of this work:

- Exploratory data analysis was carried out to evaluate and enhance the dataset's quality.
- Performed data preprocessing, transformation, and suitable hyperparameter tuning for reliability of the developed model.
- Developed a prediction model using Support vector machines (SVM), decision tree (DT), naive Bayes (NB), logistic regression (LR), and random forest (RF).
- Comparison of various performance evaluation metrics of the developed models with other relevant existing studies.

2 Literature Review

The machine learning paradigm is broadly implemented to detect and predict several chronic diseases in their earliest stages like diabetes [8]. In most cases, the machine learning techniques provided the most appropriate results for the prediction and detection of lung cancer. A lot of work has been done by different researchers to find out which accurate lung cancer diagnosis is achieved using a variety of machine learning techniques. Different datasets have been collected and run through various processes to find out the best possible results in the detection of lung cancer. Some of the main findings are discussed as: To predict lung cancer, Radhika P R et al. [9] used techniques like Decision trees, SVM, Naive Bayes, and Logistic Regression. In their study, they make use of the data from the data world and UCI Machine Learning Repository. They obtained an accuracy for Logistic Regression of 96.9%, Decision Tree of 85.71 percent utilizing the UCI Machine Learning Repository dataset, and an accuracy for Logistic Regression of 66.7%, Decision Tree of 90% using the Data World dataset. SVM scored 99.2% and Naive Bayes 87.87%. Puneet and Anamika Chauhan [10] used GridSearchCV to forecast lung cancer in 2020 using techniques including XGBoost, LR, SVM, GNB, DT, and KNN. To determine the accuracy in predicting lung cancer, Chinmayi Thallam et al. [11] deployed techniques such as the Support Vector Machine, K Nearest Neighbour, Random Forest, artificial neural networks, and a hybrid model called the Voting classifier. They were able to achieve Support Vector Machine scores of 95%, Random Wilderness scores of 97.5%, K-Nearest Neighbor scores of 97%, and Artificial Neural Network scores Jayadeep Pati [12] applied methods like Multi-Layer Perceptron, Random Sub Space, SMO (Sequential Minimal Optimization) to detect the accuracy in prediction of lung cancer and achieved accuracy as follows Multi-Layer Perceptron- 86.6667%, Random Sub Space - 68.3333% and SMO-91.6667%. Elias Dritsas et al. [13] applied methods like Decision Tree, Naive Bayes, Support Vector Machine, Artificial Neural Networks, and K Nearest Neighbour for prediction of cancer in lungs. It resulted in an accuracy of lung cancer using these techniques as follows: SVM 95.4%, ANN 94.6%, NB 95%, DT 93.7%, and KNN 95.2%. In future research, they paid attention. The long short-term memory (LSTM) and convolutional neural networks (CNN) will be very useful for improving the machine learning framework, and the accuracy of the findings will be checked against relevant studies. A distinct data-splitting procedure is added to the current 10-fold cross-validation. Technique termed bootstrapping will be utilized for the assessment of models for categorization from the same dataset. Resampling is used in this method, but the original data is replaced [14]. Vemula Suvarchala [15] applied RBF classification method to predict lung cancer and the accuracy achieved using this method is 81.25%. In this UCI Machine Learning Repository and Data World datasets were used. Ali Safiyari and Reza Javidan [16] used methods like Ripper, Decision Stump, Simple Cart, J48, Bayes Net, Simple Logistic, SMO, Random Forrest. Out of these Random Forest was detected to be the most accurate machine learning technique with 89%. Huu-Huy Ngo and Hung Linh Le [17] proposed lung cancer prediction model using algorithms KNN, Random Forest (RF), Decision Tree (DT), Logistic Regression(LR), Naïve Bayes(NB) and achieved accuracy as KNN 98.7%, random forest 98.7%, decision tree 98.7%, logistic regression 75.9% and Naïve Bayes 91%. Ahmad S. Ahmad et al. [18] proposed LCPT (Lung Cancer Prediction Tool) machine learning technique to predict lung cancer with an accuracy of 93.33%. The dataset used was Data World. They found future scope for this research paper such as prediction of a specific age for lung cancer.

3   Proposed Methodology

The methodology tapped in this work to predict lung cancer using various machine learning techniques is presented in Fig. 1.

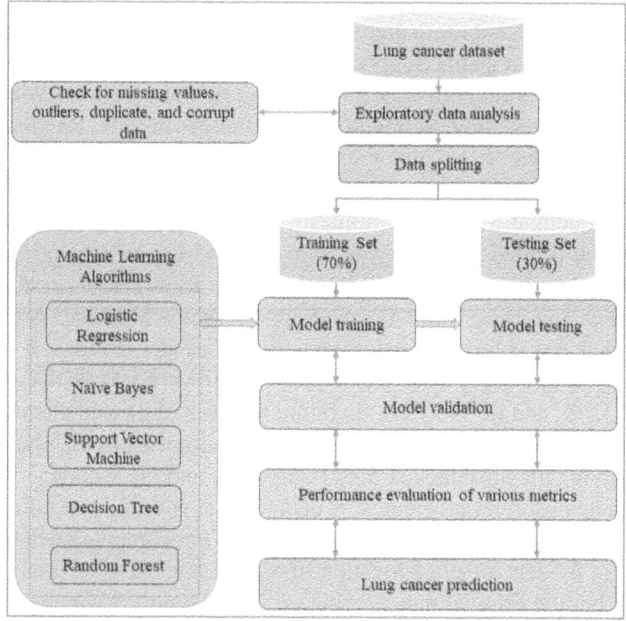

Fig. 1. Research methodology adopted in this work.

3.1   Dataset Selection and Description

We used the lung cancer dataset provided by staceyinrobert, a publicly available dataset at Data World[2]. The data is taken from the website of the online lung cancer prediction system. The data consists of a total of 16 attributes and 284 occurrences, with the first 15 attributes serving being independent or target variables, with the final attribute acting as an independent variable. Table 1 provides the parameter information.

3.2   Dataset Description

Table 2 describes the information about the parameters in the used dataset in this paper. The information includes descriptive statistical measurements of the considered parameters and their measurements like count, mean, standard deviation, minimum, maximum, etc.

---

[2] https://data.world/sta427ceyin/survey-lung-cancer.

Table 1. Attributes information of the dataset.

Parameter	Description	Measurement
Gender (GD)	Gender of an individual	male/female
Age (AG)	Age of an individual	numeric
Smoking (SM)	If the individual is a smoker	2(true)/1(false)
Yellow Fingers (YF)	If the individual's fingers have turned yellow	2/1
Anxiety (AN)	If the individual is suffering from anxiety	2/1
Peer Pressure (PP)	If the individual is influenced by peer pressure	2/1
Chronic Disease (CD)	If the individual has any chronic disease	2/1
Fatigue (FT)	If the individual feels fatigued	2/1
Allergy (Al)	If the individual has any allergy	2/1
Wheezing (WH)	If the individual wheezes	2/1
Alcohol Consuming (AC)	If the individual consumes alcohol	2/1
Coughing (CF)	If the individual coughs	2/1
Shortness Of Breath (SB)	If the individual has a breathing problem	2/1
Swallowing Difficulty (SD)	If the individual has trouble swallowing	2/1
Chest Pain (CP)	If the individual has chest pain	2/1
Lung Cancer (LC)	If the individual has lung cancer	yes/no

Table 2. Descriptive statistics of attributes.

Parameter	Count	Mean	Std	Min	25%	50%	75%	Max
GD	309	0.52	0.50	0	0	1	1	1
AG		62.6	8.22	21	57.0	62.0	69.0	87
SM		1.56	0.49	1	1	2	2	2
YF		1.56	0.49	1	1	2	2	2
AN		1.49	0.50	1	1	1	2	2
PP		1.5	0.50	1	1	2	2	2
CD		1.5	0.50	1	1	2	2	2
FT		1.67	0.47	1	1	2	2	2
AL		1.55	0.49	1	1	2	2	2
WH		1.55	0.49	1	1	2	2	2
AC		1.55	0.49	1	1	2	2	2
CF		1.57	049	1	1	2	2	2
SB		1.64	0.47	1	1	2	2	2
SD		1.46	0.49	1	1	1	2	2
CP		1.55	0.49	1	1	2	2	2
LC		0.87	0.33	1	1	1	1	1

3.3 Exploratory Data Analysis

Figure 2 shows the histogram of the parameters in the considered dataset, showing the distribution of the parameters' measurements along the X-axis and their calculated values the along Y-axis. To check the possible outliers in the dataset, we used the Z-score and Interquartile Range IQR score methods. Figure 3 depicts the boxplot for each parameter in the considered dataset of the parameters. Figure 4 shows the density plot of the parameters using KDE (kernel density estimation). Figure 5 displays the correlation matrix among the dependent and independent attributes in one of four possible combinations.

Kernel density estimation is mostly used for continuous and smoothed data samples to present the distribution. For each distinct data point, a continuous curve (the kernel) is drawn using this method, and all the kernels are summed to provide a single, smooth density estimation. In the below-considered density plot, if taking an example of Age (AG), the majority of the people who are affected by lung cancer are between the age group of 55 to 60.

The correlation coefficient matrix is simply a table that shows the correlation coefficient for multiple variables, here Yellow Fingers (YF), and Anxiety (AN) have the highest correlation of 0.57.

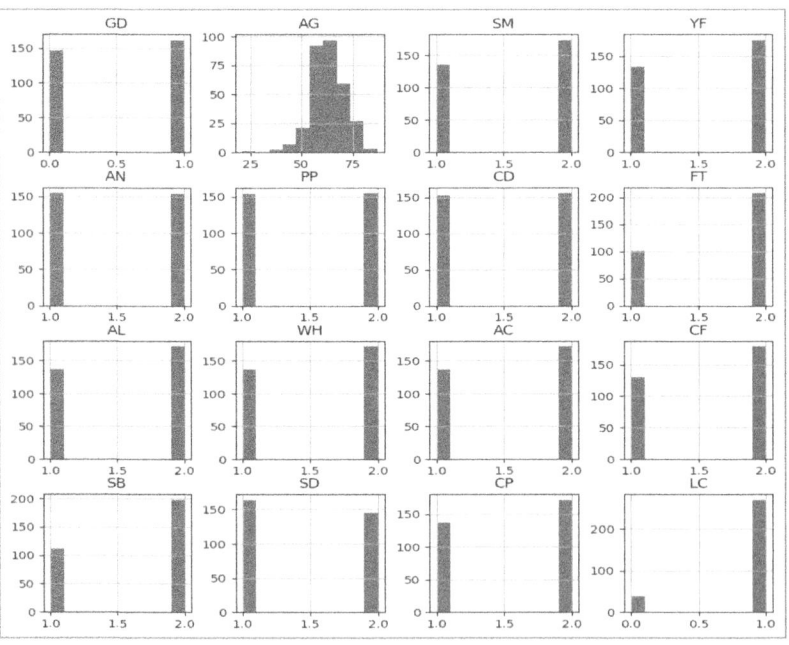

Fig. 2. Histogram for each parameter of dataset.

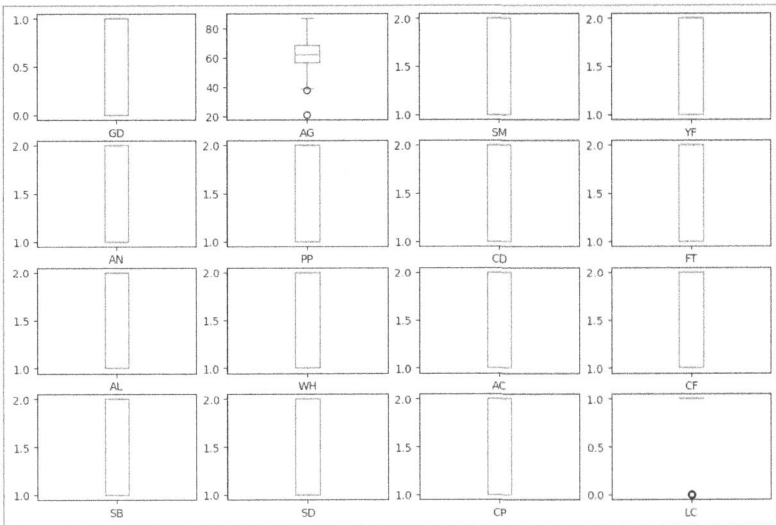

Fig. 3. Boxplot for each parameter of dataset.

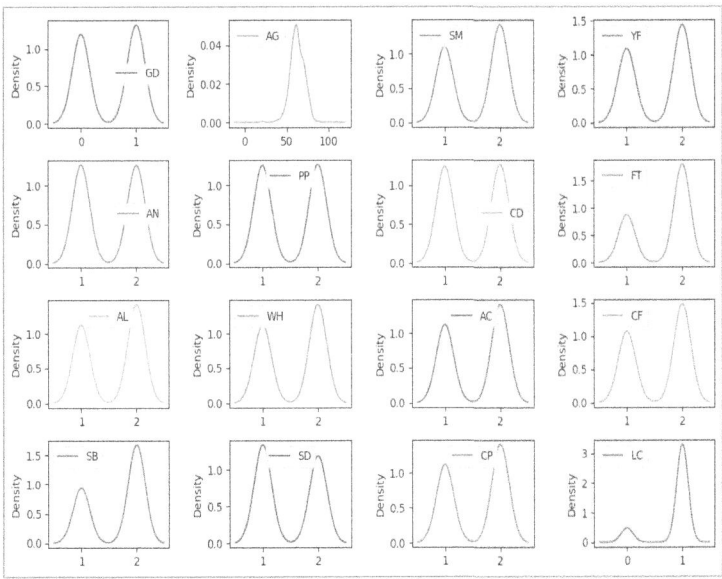

Fig. 4. Density plot for each parameter of dataset.

4   Results and Discussion

In this study, we used machine learning techniques like Support vector Machine, Decision Tree, Naive Bayes, Logistic Regression, and Random Forest, for predicting the lung cancer of an individual. We split the dataset into training (70%) and testing (30%) sets. We

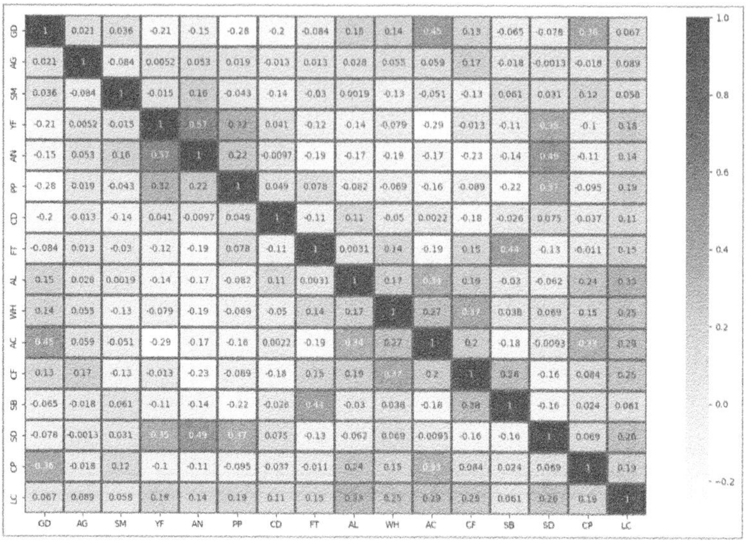

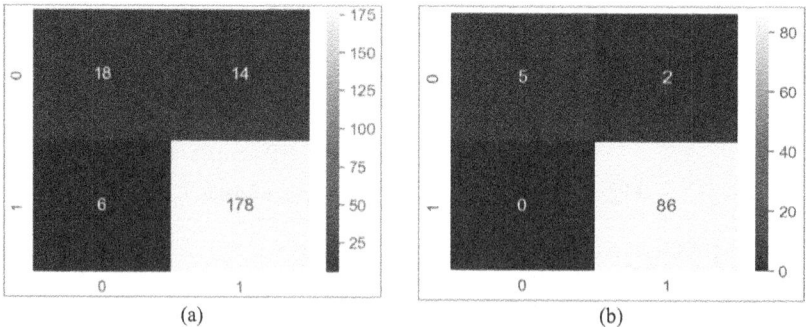

Fig. 5. Correlation coefficient matrix for each parameter of dataset.

validated the proposed model using various statistical/machine learning measurements. The corresponding results are presented and discussed in the following subsections.

4.1 Confusion Matrices

A confusion matrix for binary two-dimensional classification model's performance is summarised in a table by comparing its expected outcomes to the actual labels of a set of data. The confusion matrices for training and testing datasets of LR, NB, SVM, DT, and RF are shown in Figs. 6, 7, 8, 9 and 10. We observed that LR achieved good results in terms of testing phase while DT and RF achieved better results during the training phase. Based on the confusion matrices, we have evaluated various metrics such as accuracy, precision, recall, specificity, F1 score, and non-predicted values.

Fig. 6. Confusion matrix using LR (a) training and (b) testing.

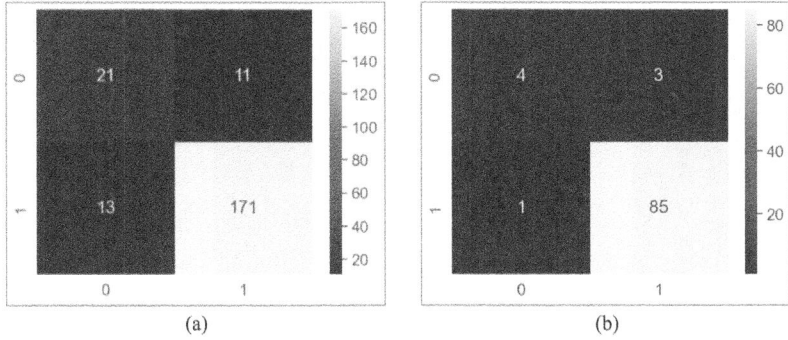

Fig. 7. Confusion matrix using NB (a) training and (b) testing.

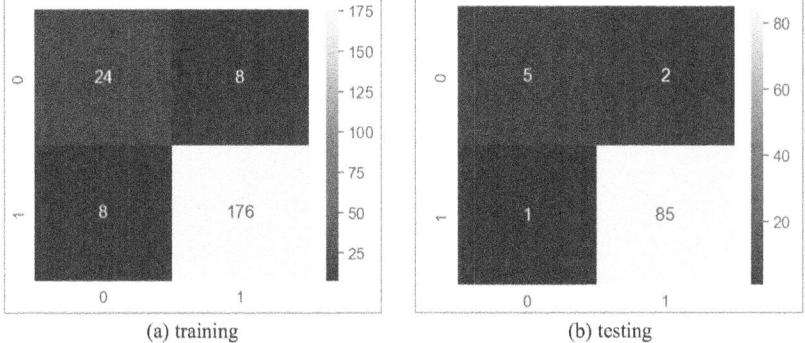

Fig. 8. Confusion matrix using SVM (a) training and (b) testing.

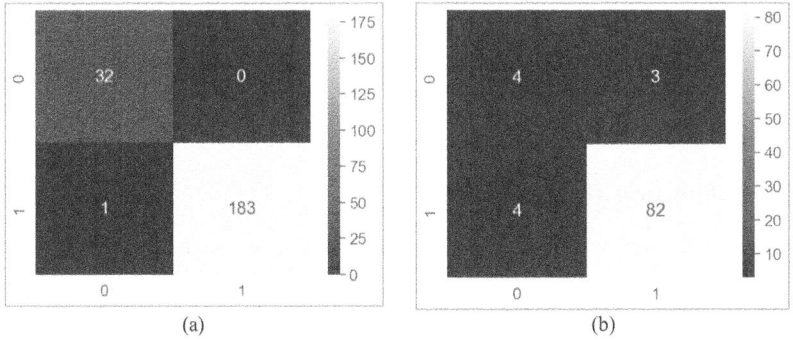

Fig. 9. Confusion matrix using DT (a) training and (b) testing.

4.2 Accuracy of the Models

The testing and training accuracy of the considered machine learning algorithms is given in Fig. 11. Our results showed that Logistic Regression algorithm had the highest

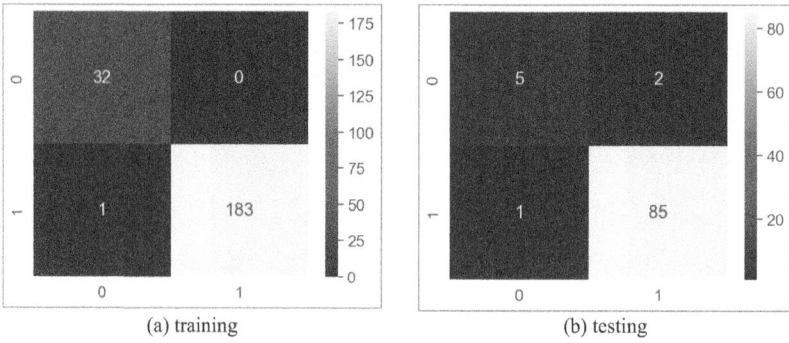

Fig. 10. Confusion matrix using RF (a) training and (b) testing.

accuracy of 97.8%, followed by Random Forest and Support Vector Machine with 96.8%, naïve Bayes with 95.7%, and Decision Tree with 92.5% respectively.

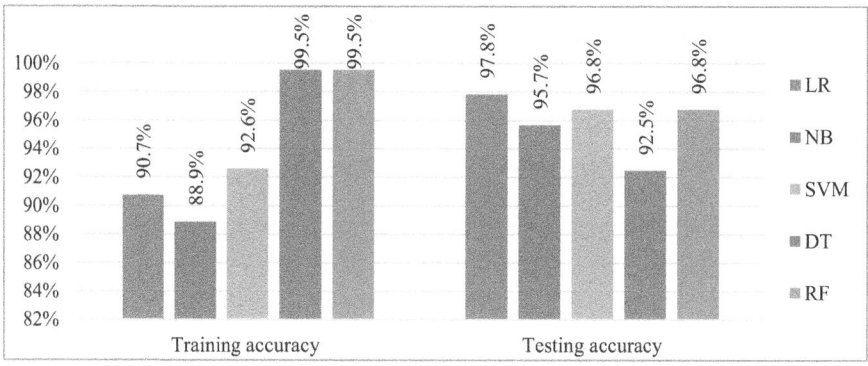

Fig. 11. Training and testing accuracy of considered algorithms.

4.3 Other Statistical Measurements

The Recall, Precision, f1-score, Specificity, and Negative Predicted Value (NPV) for training and testing phases of considered algorithms are shown in Figs. 12 and 13 respectively. It can be observed that DT & RF exhibits the best results for all measurements in training and LR exhibits the best results for all measurements in testing while NB performs worst in most cases.

Machine learning techniques can be effectively used to predict lung cancer. Our findings are consistent with previous studies that have used machine learning techniques for cancer prediction. The high accuracy of the logistic regression algorithm suggests that it may be a useful tool for lung cancer prediction in clinical practice. One limitation of this study is that the dataset was relatively small and may not be representative of the general population. Future studies should aim to collect larger datasets to improve the

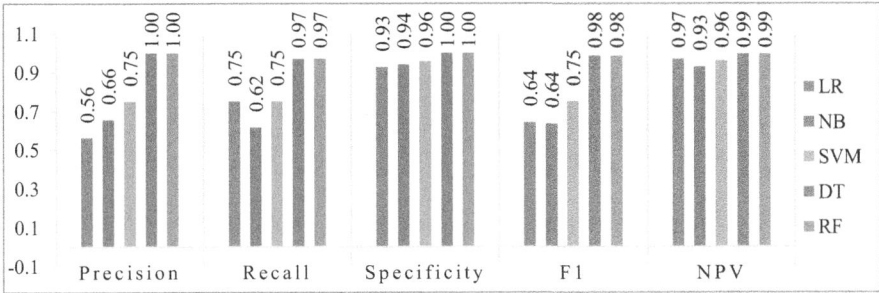

Fig. 12. Other statistical measurements for training set of considered algorithms.

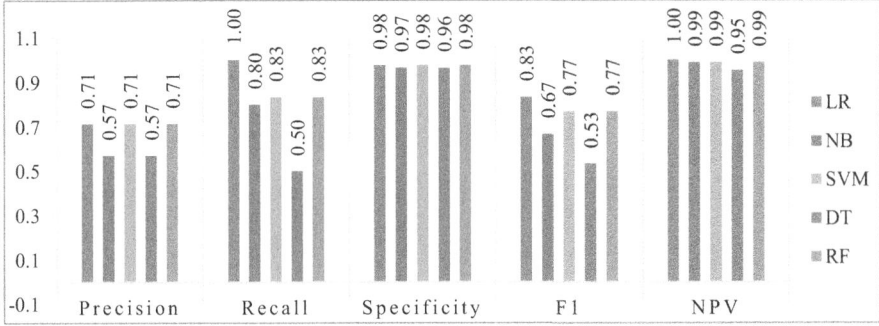

Fig. 13. Other statistical measurements for testing set of considered algorithms.

accuracy of the models. Additionally, the models could be further improved by including more advanced features such as genetic information and biomarkers. Despite these limitations, our study has important implications for avoiding early-stage identification of lung cancer.

Research work	Techniques	Dataset	Highest accuracy
[16]	AdaBoost, MultiBoosting, Bagging and random subspace with a combination of several base classifiers	Surveillance, epidemiology, and end results (SEER) data released in April 2016	89.00% for Bagging with random forest
[19]	Bagging, random forest with BSPL (Bootstrap with self-paced learning)	US National Library of Medicine National Institutes of Health	82.61% with BSPL
[20]	XGBoost on multi-omics dataset	The Cancer Genome Atlas (TCGA) project	83.4% with XGBoost

(continued)

(*continued*)

Research work	Techniques	Dataset	Highest accuracy
[21]	Bagging-based ensemble algorithm using random forest	Wroclaw Thoracic Surgery Centre for patients (2007 to 2011)	84.04% with a 10-fold stratified cross-validation approach
[22]	Ensemble classifier combining decision tree, MLP, KNN, SVM, logistic regression	Lung cancer dataset sourced by the Iraq-Oncology Teaching Hospital/National Center for Cancer Diseases (IQ-OTH/NCCD)	85% with Max-Vote
Our proposed Work	Naive Bayes, Logistic Regression, Support Vector Machine, Decision Tree, and Random Forest	Lung cancer dataset provided by staceyinrobert	97.84% using Logistic Regression

5   Conclusion

Machine learning techniques are widely used in healthcare industry for better prediction and detection of diseases. In our study, exploratory data analysis was performed on the dataset under consideration to evaluate the quality. We executed 5 different algorithms to predict the disease. The results were assessed using different statistical measurements. The results of the experiment showed that logistic regression achieved the highest accuracy rate of 97.84%, while naïve Bayes achieved the lowest accuracy rate of 88.88%. In other parameters like precision, recall, specificity, F1, and Negative Predicted Value (NPV) also logistic regression performed well. Finally, our strategy outperformed some recent work in a field related to prediction accuracy. This work may be expanded upon and improved by exploring ensemble/hybrid strategies. To broaden the scope of this research, this suggested strategy may be applied to other healthcare datasets that have similar traits or properties.

Machine learning techniques have the potential to provide a faster, more accurate, and cost-effective way of predicting lung cancer, which could help to save lives and reduce healthcare costs.

Acknowledgments. Not applicable.

Data Availability. The dataset used in this study is available https://data.world/sta427ceyin/survey-lung-cancer.

Disclosure of Interest. The researchers affirm that there were no financial or commercial ties that might be interpreted as having a conflict of interest.

References

1. Freddie Bray, B.M.P.: Global cancer statistics 2018: GLOBOCAN estimates. CA Cancer J. Clin.Clin. **68**, 394 (2018)
2. Kadir, T., Gleeson, F.: Lung cancer prediction using machine learning and advanced imaging techniques. Transl. Lung Cancer Res. **17**(3), 304–312 (2018)
3. Nair, M., Sandhu, S.S., KumarSharma, A.: Cancer molecular markers: a guide to cancer detection and management. Semin. Cancer Biol.. Cancer Biol. **52**, 39–55 (2018)
4. Ganie, S.M., Malik, M.B.: Comparative analysis of various supervised machine learning algorithms for the early prediction of type-II diabetes mellitus. Int. J. Med. Eng. Inform. **14**(6), 473–483 (2022)
5. Frieboes, H.B., Bartholomai, J.A.: Lung cancer survival prediction via machine learning regression, classification, and statistical techniques, pp. 632–637 (2018)
6. Ganie, S.M., Malik, M.B., Arif, T.: Machine learning techniques for diagnosis of type 2 diabetes using lifestyle data. In: Advances in Intelligent Systems and Computing, pp. 487–497 (2021)
7. Ganie, S.M., Malik, M.B., Arif, T.: Performance analysis and prediction of type 2 diabetes mellitus based on lifestyle data using machine learning approaches. J. Diabetes Metab. Disord.Metab. Disord. **21**(1), 339–352 (2022)
8. Ganie, S.M., Malik, M.B.: An ensemble machine learning approach for predicting type-II diabetes mellitus based on lifestyle indicators. Healthc. Anal. **2**, 100092 (2022)
9. Nair, R.A.S., Veena, G., Radhika, P.R.: A comparative study of lung cancer detection using machine learning algorithms. IEEE (2018)
10. Puneet, A.C.: Detection of lung cancer using machine learning techniques based on routine blood indices. In: 2020 IEEE International Conference for Innovation in Technology (INOCON) (2020)
11. Peruboyina, A., Raju, S.S.T., Sampath, N., Thallam, C.: Early stage lung cancer prediction using various machine learning techniques. In: Fourth International Conference on Electronics, Communication and Aerospace Technology (ICECA-2020) (2020)
12. Pati, J.: Gene expression analysis for early lung cancer prediction using machine learning techniques: an eco-genomics approach. IEEE Access **7**, 4232 (2018)
13. Dritsas, E., Trigka, M.: Lung cancer risk prediction with machine learning models. Big Data Cogn. Comput. **6**, 139 (2022)
14. Xu, Y., Goodacre, R.: On splitting training and validation set: a comparative study of cross-validation, bootstrap and systematic sampling for estimating the generalization performance of supervised learning. J. Anal. Test. **2**, 249–262 (2018)
15. Venkata Subbareddy, P., Madala, S.R., Suvarchala, V.: Lung cancer prediction using machine learning. Nat. Volatiles Essent. Oils **8**(6), 1265 (2021)
16. Javidan, R., Safiyari, A.: Predicting lung cancer survivability using ensemble learning methods. In: Intelligent Systems Conference, London (2017)
17. Huu-Huy, N.: A prediction model for lung cancer levels based on machine learning. Int. J. Open Inf. Technol. **10**(5), 21–29 (2022)
18. Ahmad, A.S., Mayya, A.M.: A new tool to predict lung cancer based on risk factors. Heliyon **6**, e03402 (2020)
19. Zhou, Y., Ding, W., Zhang, Z., Muhammad, K., Cao, Z., Wang, Q.: Random forest with self-paced bootstrap learning in lung cancer. ACM Trans. Multimed. Comput. Commun. Appl. Multimed. Comput. Commun. Appl. **16**, 1 (2020)
20. Meng, F., Yan, G., Yan, H., Chai, B., Song, F., Ma, B.: Diagnostic classification of cancers using extreme gradient boosting algorithm. Comput. Biol. Med.. Biol. Med. **121**, 103761 (2020)

21. Maity, P., Nath, R., Siddhartha, M.: Explanatory artificial intelligence (XAI) in the in the prediction of post-operative life expectancy in lung cancer patients. Int. J. Sci. Res. **8**, 23–28 (2019)
22. Ashwin Shanbhag, G., Anurag Prabhu, K., Subba Reddy, N.V., Ashwath Rao, B.: Prediction of lung cancer using ensemble classifiers. Phys. Conf. **2161**, 012007 (2022)

Enhancing Stock Portfolio Optimization Based on a Hybrid Approach Using Artificial Bee Colony Optimization and Firefly Optimization

Lakshya Karwa$^{(\boxtimes)}$, I. S. Tarun Kumar, and P. Hemashree

Coimbatore Institute of Technology, Coimbatore 641014, Tamil Nadu, India
`lakshyakarwa10@gmail.com, tarun28743@gmail.com,`
`Hemashree@cit.edu.in`

Abstract. The goal of stock portfolio optimization, a crucial activity in finance, is to strike the ideal balance between risk and return. In this study, we suggest a hybrid strategy that combines Firefly Optimization (FO) and Artificial Bee Colony Optimization (ABC) to improve the performance of stock portfolio optimization. Enhancing portfolio returns while reducing volatility is the main goal. Historical stock return data is used to put the hybrid strategy into practice. The objective function used to formulate the portfolio optimization issue takes the expected returns and risk of the portfolio into account. A penalty term is also included to enforce the requirement that the portfolio weights amount to one. The hybrid algorithm moves through two phases. First, the solution is investigated using the Artificial Bee Colony Optimization technique. The Firefly Optimization technique is then used to further refine the solutions. The combination of these two optimization strategies enables the algorithm to explore numerous possibilities and converge to high-quality portfolio allocations in a better timely manner. We see large gains in the Sharpe and Sortino ratios, indicating risk-adjusted returns. The hybrid strategy consistently achieves higher annualized returns over multiple time intervals, namely 5, 10, and 15 trading days over traditional methods. The hybrid approach, provides a robust and effective tool for optimizing stock portfolios. This strategy can be used to a variety of financial decision-making scenarios and has the potential to give investors and portfolio managers with higher risk-adjusted returns.

Keywords: Stock Portfolio Optimization · Artificial Bee Colony (ABC) · Firefly Optimization (FO) Algorithm · Hybrid optimization · financial decision making

1 Introduction

Stock portfolio optimization stands as a cornerstone challenge within the realm of finance, commanding significant attention due to its pivotal role in maximizing returns while concurrently minimizing risks. For investors and portfolio managers, the art of efficiently allocating resources across an array of assets has perpetually posed a formidable conundrum. Traditional methodologies such as mean-variance optimization, quadratic programming, and Markowitz's Modern Portfolio Theory, though commonly utilized, have frequently grappled with the intricate intricacies and non-convex nature inherent in real-world financial markets.

© The Author(s), under exclusive license to Springer Nature Switzerland AG 2024
H. K. et al. (Eds.): AIKP 2023, CCIS 2127, pp. 75–87, 2024.
https://doi.org/10.1007/978-3-031-68617-7_6

This research endeavors to introduce a transformative approach, uniting the prowess of Artificial Bee Colony Optimization (ABC) and Firefly Optimization (FO) to revolutionize stock portfolio optimization. This fusion addresses the prevailing limitations and explores novel optimization strategies in contrast to the traditional methods. ABC and FO, both grounded in emulating natural phenomena, have proven their mettle in tackling formidable nonlinear optimization challenges. The overarching objective of this study lies in offering a robust and efficient methodology capable of enhancing stock portfolio optimization, while simultaneously delivering superior risk-adjusted returns compared to these conventional techniques. The hybrid algorithm meticulously navigates the solution space, seeking diversified and superior portfolio allocations, harnessing the inherent strengths of both ABC and FO.

The proposed methodology harnesses historical stock return data to construct an objective function that intricately balances projected returns and associated risks within the portfolio. To ensure adherence to the constraint of portfolio weights summing to unity, a penalty term is judiciously incorporated. The optimization process, executed in two distinct stages, employs ABC for preliminary exploration, followed by FO for precision refinement.

Empirical validation of this novel approach encompasses rigorous experimentation with historical returns data from ten prominent market players, including Pfizer Inc. (PFE), Johnson & Johnson (JNJ), Google (GOOGL), Apple (AAPL), Costco Wholesale Corporation (COST), Walmart (WMT), Kroger Co (KR), JPMorgan Chase & Co (JPM), Bank of America Corp (BAC), and HSBC, among others. Crucial performance metrics such as the Sharpe ratio, Sortino ratio, and annualized returns are meticulously examined, alongside comparisons with conventional portfolio optimization strategies.

In summary, this study introduces an innovative hybrid strategy for stock portfolio optimization, seamlessly amalgamating ABC and FO. The ensuing sections delve deeper into the methodology, experimental design, and results, shedding light on the compelling potential of this approach for portfolio management and informed financial decision-making. By embarking on this journey, we aim to provide a comprehensive solution to the contemporary challenges faced within the financial landscape while distinguishing our approach from traditional methods.

2   Related Work

Several machine learning techniques have been proposed for portfolio optimization, including neural networks, decision trees, and support vector machines. LSTM neural networks have gained significant attention in recent years due to their ability to handle sequential data and capture long-term dependencies. However, most of the existing works using LSTM networks for portfolio optimization have used the traditional optimization algorithms. Stock portfolio optimization has been extensively studied in the field of finance, with various optimization techniques proposed over the years. In this literature review, we present a comprehensive overview of relevant works in stock portfolio optimization, focusing on traditional methods, metaheuristic algorithms, and hybrid approaches.

Ito et al. [1] proposed the Trader-Company Method (TCM). (TCM) is a metaheuristic algorithm for interpretable stock price prediction that integrates technical and fundamental analysis indicators. The TCM is an evolutionary model that aggregates suggestions from multiple weak learners called Traders to predict future stock returns. A Company maintains multiple Traders, each holding a collection of mathematical formulae, representing alpha factors for real-world investors. Companies randomly generate new Traders and retrain them to efficiently find financially meaningful formulae while avoiding overfitting to a transient state of the market. The article by Kalayci, Polat, and Akbay [2] proposes a new hybrid metaheuristic algorithm for solving the cardinality-constrained portfolio optimization (CCPOP) problem. The CCPOP is a challenging problem that aims to maximize the expected return of a portfolio subject to a cardinality constraint, which limits the number of assets that can be included in the portfolio. The proposed hybrid algorithm combines critical components from Continuous Ant Colony Optimization (CACO), Artificial Bee Colony Optimization (ABC), and Genetic Algorithms (GA). The CACO component is used to explore the search space and identify promising regions. OD-PODNN model in [3] involves preprocessing, outlier detection, classification, and hyperparameter optimization. They use the isolation Forest (iForest) based outlier detection approach and derive a PODNN-based classification model. The DNN hyperparameters are fine-tuned to boost overall classification accuracy. Abbasi, Bamdad, and Rahimi in [4] provide a comprehensive review of the state-of-the-art metaheuristic algorithms used to optimize portfolios in peer-to-peer (P2P) lending platforms. The authors begin by discussing the challenges of portfolio optimization in P2P lending platforms. These challenges include the large number of loans available, the difficulty of assessing the risk of each loan, and the need to diversify the portfolio to reduce risk. They use GA, PSO, ACO, ABC, MFO, FA and DA. The authors discuss the advantages and disadvantages of each algorithm, and they provide examples of how these algorithms have been used to optimize portfolios in P2P lending platforms. Kumar K & Haider, M.T.U in [5] proposed an enhanced prediction model that combines a recurrent neural network (RNN) and a LSTM network with metaheuristic optimization techniques. The authors use the Flower Pollination Algorithm and Particle Swarm Optimization to optimize the hyperparameters of the RNN-LSTM model. They apply their model to intraday stock market prediction and find that their model outperforms other existing models in terms of prediction accuracy. The authors argue that their model can help investors make informed trading decisions and maximize their profits. Santiago V. Ravelo, Cláudio N. Meneses, and Maristela O. Santos in [6] consider the one-dimensional cutting stock problem with usable leftover (1D-CSPUL), which is a variant of the classical one-dimensional cutting stock problem (1D-CSP) in which the leftover material from the cutting patterns can be reused in the future. The authors propose a heuristic algorithm and two meta-heuristic approaches to solve the 1D-CSPUL. They also conduct computational experiments to evaluate the performance of their algorithms on a set of benchmark instances. Mojtaba Sedighi, Hossein Jahangirnia in [7] proposed a hybrid model for stock price forecasting. The model combines an Artificial Bee Colony (ABC) algorithm and a Support Vector Machine (SVM). The ABC algorithm is used to optimize the technical indicators, and the SVM is used to predict the stock price. The performance of their model is evaluated on a dataset of stock prices from the S&P 500. The results show that the proposed model outperforms other traditional forecasting methods, such as the Autoregressive Integrated Moving Average (ARIMA) model and the Exponential Smoothing (ES) model. Samiran Khajehzadeh, Shadi Shahverdiani in [8] proposed an approach which combines a meta-heuristic algorithm and a Markov Decision Process (MDP). The meta-heuristic algorithm is used to find the optimal portfolio of stocks, and the MDP is used to model the uncertainty in the stock market. Performance evaluation of their approach is done on a dataset of stock prices from the Tehran Stock Exchange. The results show that the proposed approach outperforms other traditional portfolio optimization methods, such as the Markowitz mean-variance model and the Black-Litterman model. Ehsan Fadaei, Iraj Dadashi, Mohammad Javad Zare Bahnamiri [9] proposed a meta-heuristic approach for predicting negative stock price shocks. The approach uses a Genetic Algorithm (GA) to optimize the parameters of a Support Vector Machine (SVM) model. The SVM model is used to learn the relationship between the financial ratios of a company and the likelihood of a negative stock price shock. Performance evaluation is done on a dataset of 96 financial ratios of 140 companies listed on the Tehran Stock Exchange during a period of 9 years between 2010 and 2012. The results show that the proposed approach is able to predict negative stock price shocks with an accuracy of 85%. Jana Doering, Renatas Kizys in [10] review the use of metaheuristics for portfolio optimization and risk management. They discuss the different types of metaheuristics that have been used for these problems, as well as the advantages and disadvantages of each approach. The paper also identifies the current trends in the use of metaheuristics for portfolio optimization and risk management, and discusses the future research directions in this area. Meysam Doaei, Mohammad Reza Pourmahdian in [11] proposed a metaheuristic algorithm for portfolio optimization in the Iran capital market. The algorithm is based on the Genetic Algorithm, but it has been modified to better suit the specific characteristics of the Iranian stock market. The paper evaluates the performance of the proposed algorithm on a dataset of historical stock prices from the Iran capital market. The results show that the proposed algorithm is able to find portfolios that outperform the market benchmark. Mohammad Hassan Fotros, Idris Miri, Ayob Miria in [12] investigate the performance of two meta-heuristic algorithms, NSGA-II and SPEA-II, for portfolio optimization in the Tehran Stock Exchange. The authors found that SPEA-II outperformed NSGA-II in terms of both return and risk, especially for investors with a high-risk aversion. SPEA-II was able to find more efficient portfolios than NSGA-II, especially for investors with a high-risk aversion and for both the risk-return and risk-volatility criteria. Purba Daru Kusuma, Ashri Dinimaharawati in [13] proposed a new metaheuristic algorithm called the Three-on-Three Optimizer (TOTO). TOTO is based on the idea of combining three guided searches and three random searches. The guided searches are searching toward the global best solution, searching for the global best solution to avoid the corresponding agent, searching based on the interaction between the corresponding agent and a randomly selected agent. The random searches are local search of the corresponding agent, local search of the global best solution, global search within the entire search space. TOTO was evaluated on a set of 23 classic optimization functions and a portfolio optimization problem where it was able to find the global optimal solution for 11 of the 23 functions and outperformed five other metaheuristic algorithms on the portfolio optimization problem.

3 Methodology

3.1 Dataset Description

The dataset used for this research work was obtained from Yahoo Finance, which provides historical stock price data for various financial instruments, including stocks and exchange-traded funds (ETFs). The historical stock price data was collected for a selection of 10 prominent companies, which are widely recognized and have a significant impact on the market. The data collection process involved querying Yahoo Finance's API using Python's yfinance library to retrieve the daily closing prices of each selected stock. The dataset covers a specific time period of interest, ranging from [2018-01-01] to [2023-04-01]. This period was chosen to reflect a meaningful duration that would allow for a comprehensive analysis of the selected assets' performance. The dataset contains the following attributes.

Table 1. Dataset Attributes

Adj Close	Close	High
Volume	Stock Name	

Table 1 shows information about the dataset where "Adj Close" stands for "Adjusted Close". It is the closing price of a stock on a particular day, adjusted to include any dividends or other corporate actions that might affect the stock's value. The adjusted closing price is often used in technical analysis to assess the stock's performance over time. "Close" refers to the closing price of a stock or other financial asset. It is the last traded price of the asset at the end of a trading session on a particular day. "High" represents the highest price at which a stock or financial asset traded during a specific trading session. "Volume" refers to the number of shares or units of a financial asset that were traded during a trading session. "Stock Name" simply refers to the name or ticker symbol of a specific company's stock traded on a stock exchange. For example, the stock name of Apple Inc. is "AAPL," and that of Microsoft Corporation is "MSFT".

The following companies' stocks were included in the dataset for analysis.

1. Pfizer Inc. (PFE)
2. Johnson & Johnson (JNJ)
3. Alphabet Inc. (GOOGL)
4. Apple Inc. (AAPL)
5. Costco Wholesale Corporation (COST)
6. Walmart Inc. (WMT)
7. The Kroger Co. (KR)
8. JPMorgan Chase & Co. (JPM)
9. Bank of America Corporation (BAC)
10. HSBC Holdings plc (HSBC)

3.2 Objective Function Formulation

An objective function for portfolio optimization is developed in the study with the goal of maximizing risk-adjusted returns.

3.2.1 Objective Function

The objective function in portfolio optimization aims to maximize risk-adjusted returns. It considers three key components: expected portfolio returns, portfolio volatility, and a penalty term. The formula for the objective function is as in Eq. (1):

$$f(x) = -\frac{port\_returns}{port\_volatility} + penalty \tag{1}$$

where,

$f(x)$ is the objective function to be maximized.

port_returns represents the expected portfolio return.

port_volatility is the portfolio (risk).

penalty is the penalty term discouraging deviations from a fully invested Portfolio

3.2.2 Expected Portfolio Return

Expected portfolio return (*port_returns*) is calculated as the weighted sum of the mean returns of the assets in the portfolio as in Eq. (2). This represents the anticipated return of the entire portfolio based on the allocation of assets.

$$port\_returns = \sum_{i=1}^{n} r_i.x_i, \tag{2}$$

where,

r_i is the mean return of asset i

x_i is the weight or allocation of asset i in the portfolio

n represents the number of assets in the portfolio

3.2.3 Portfolio Volatility

Portfolio volatility (*port_volatility*) measures the risk or uncertainty associated with the portfolio's returns. It is calculated as the square root of the quadratic form of the portfolio's weight vector x^T multiplied by the covariance matrix C and the weight vector x as in Eq. (3).

$$port\_volatility = \sqrt{x^T.C.x} \tag{3}$$

where,

x is the vector of portfolio weights.

x^T is the transpose of the weight vector.

C is the covariance matrix of the assets' return.

3.2.4 Penalty Term

The penalty term (*penalty*) discourages significant deviations of the sum of portfolio weights from 1, ensuring that the portfolio is fully invested. It is calculated as a penalty factor (in this case, 10) multiplied by the absolute difference between the sum of the weights and 1 as in Eq. (4).

$$penalty = 10.\left|\sum\nolimits_{i=1}^{n} x_i - 1\right| \tag{4}$$

where,

x_i is the weight of asset i in the portfolio.

n is the number of assets in the portfolio.

In summary, the objective function combines these three components to find the optimal portfolio allocation that maximizes risk-adjusted returns while considering the need for a fully invested portfolio and controlling for portfolio volatility. It seeks a balance between achieving high returns and managing risk, taking into account the specific characteristics of the assets and their correlations.

4 Model Building

In this section, we present the methodologies employed in our research for portfolio optimization. We outline four distinct optimization algorithms used: Artificial Bee Colony Optimization (ABC), Firefly Optimization (FA), Random Forest Algorithm (RFA), and Long Short-Term Memory (LSTM). Each algorithm offers unique features and benefits for addressing the complex task of portfolio allocation.

4.1 Artificial Bee Colony Optimization

The Artificial Bee Colony (ABC) algorithm draws inspiration from the foraging behavior of honeybee colonies and provides a robust optimization technique suitable for complex problems like portfolio allocation. The algorithm consists of several key phases:

Initialization of Bee Colony. The ABC algorithm commences by initializing a population of artificial bees, each representing a potential solution (i.e., potential portfolio allocation) to the optimization problem. Each bee corresponds to a candidate portfolio allocation with specific asset weights i.e., the bees carry specific asset weightings.

Employed Bees Phase. During the Employed Bees phase, the bees actively exploit existing solutions by modifications to enhance them. Bees assess the fitness of their respective solutions by using a fitness function that considers both the expected return and portfolio risk (volatility).

Onlooker Bees Phase. In the Onlooker Bees phase, bees collaborate by communicating with each other to share information about successful solutions. Bees with higher fitness values serve as sources of inspiration for others.

Scout Bees Phase. Scout bees play the role of explorers, aiming to introduce new solutions to the population. They identify solutions that have not improved for a certain number of iterations or stagnated and replace them with new randomly generated solutions.

Convergence and Solution Refinement. The ABC algorithm iteratively updates the solutions in the population through cycles of employed and onlooker bees' phases. Over successive iterations, the algorithm refines the portfolio allocations to improve their fitness values. The algorithm continues until a specified stopping criterion is met, such as a maximum number of iterations or the achievement of a satisfactory solution.

4.2 Firefly Optimization

The Firefly Algorithm (FA) is a nature-inspired optimization technique that mirrors the flashing and attraction behaviors of fireflies in nature. FA has gained recognition as an effective method for solving complex optimization problems, including portfolio allocation. The algorithm is well-suited for financial portfolio optimization due to its ability to efficiently navigate high-dimensional solution spaces and adapt to changing market conditions.

Initialization of Fireflies. The FA algorithm begins by initializing a population of fireflies, each representing a potential solution (portfolio allocation) to the optimization problem. Each firefly corresponds to a candidate portfolio allocation with specific asset weights.

Attraction Phase. In the Attraction phase, fireflies move towards brighter fireflies, representing better-performing solutions. Brightness is determined by the fitness function, which considers both the expected return and risk (volatility) of the portfolio. Fireflies adjust their positions in search of more attractive solutions, with stronger attraction to brighter fireflies.

Distance-based Movement. Fireflies adjust their positions based on their relative distances and the brightness of other fireflies. Fireflies closer to a brighter firefly experience stronger attraction and move towards it. This mechanism encourages the convergence of fireflies towards better solutions while maintaining population diversity.

Convergence and Solution Refinement. Through iterative cycles of movement and attraction, the FA algorithm refines the portfolio allocations in the population. The algorithm continues to update solutions until a specified stopping criterion is met, such as a maximum number of iterations or the attainment of a satisfactory solution.

4.3 Randon Forest Algorithm

The Random Forest Algorithm (RFA) is a powerful machine learning technique that leverages an ensemble of decision trees to make accurate predictions and classifications. When applied to portfolio optimization, RFA offers a data-driven approach that combines the strengths of individual decision trees to create a robust and diversified investment strategy.

Ensemble of Decision Trees. At the core of the Random Forest Algorithm is the concept of an ensemble, where multiple decision trees are built using different subsets of the data and feature variables. Each decision tree is trained on a bootstrapped sample of the data, and at each split, a random subset of features is considered. By combining the predictions of multiple decision trees, RFA reduces the risk of overfitting and enhances generalization to unseen data.

Prediction of Portfolio Returns. In the context of portfolio optimization, RFA can be utilized to predict future asset returns based on historical data and relevant market indicators. By training the algorithm on a historical dataset that includes asset prices, market factors, and other relevant variables, RFA can learn complex relationships and patterns that drive asset returns.

4.4 LSTM

Long Short-Term Memory (LSTM) is a type of recurrent neural network (RNN) that excels at capturing sequential and temporal patterns in data. When applied to portfolio optimization, LSTM offers a sophisticated approach to predict asset returns based on historical information, allowing for informed decision-making in portfolio allocation.

Sequential Data Modeling. LSTM is well-suited for handling sequential data, such as time series of asset prices or market indicators. It can capture long-range dependencies and complex patterns in historical asset returns, making it a powerful tool for predicting future returns.

Temporal Relationships and Memory. LSTM's ability to remember and utilize information from previous time steps enables it to capture trends, seasonality, and other temporal relationships in financial data. This is crucial for identifying patterns that may influence asset returns.

Predictive Modeling of Returns. In portfolio optimization, LSTM can be trained on historical data to predict future asset returns. By learning from past patterns, the algorithm can make predictions about how different assets are likely to perform in the future.

5 Results and Discussion

In this section, we present a comprehensive analysis of the outcomes obtained from our portfolio optimization models. Our study employed four optimization algorithms—Random Forest, Artificial Bee Colony (ABC), Firefly Optimization, and a Hybrid approach—over varying intervals of 5, 10, and 15 days. We evaluated the models using two key performance metrics: the Sharpe Ratio and Return on Investment (ROI). The results can be seen in the Table 2:

Table 2. Results.

S NO	Model	Optimization Algorithm	No of days as interval	Sharpe Ratio	ROI (%)
1	Random Forest	Firefly	5	0.18	243
2			10	0.25	177
3			15	0.35	212
4		ABC	5	0.19	280
5			10	0.25	170
6			15	0.46	218
7		Hybrid	5	0.22	299
8			10	0.3	219
9			15	0.35	194
10	LSTM	Firefly	5	2.07	347
11			10	1.73	352
12			15	1.8	211
13		ABC	5	1.57	396
14			10	2.55	329
15			15	2.2	341
16		Hybrid	5	2.1	326
17			10	1.69	428
18			15	2.42	247

5.1 Analysis of Results

5.1.1 Sharpe Ratio

The risk-adjusted returns of each portfolio allocation are measured by the Sharpe Ratio. Better risk-adjusted performance is indicated by a greater Sharpe Ratio.

Inferring from Table 2, LSTM demonstrates remarkable performance, particularly when coupled with the ABC optimization algorithm. The Hybrid approach also exhibits strong risk-adjusted returns.

For Random Forest, the Hybrid approach consistently outperforms other algorithms, achieving the highest Sharpe Ratios across all intervals. This suggests that the Hybrid approach provides superior risk-adjusted returns compared to individual optimization algorithms.

Figure 1 graph compares the performance (Sharpe Ratio) of different methods ("Random Forest" and "LSTM") across various optimization models ("Firefly," "ABC," and "Hybrid") and different numbers of iterations (5, 10, and 15). It gives a better insight on how the Sharpe Ratio is behaving based on the number of iterations.

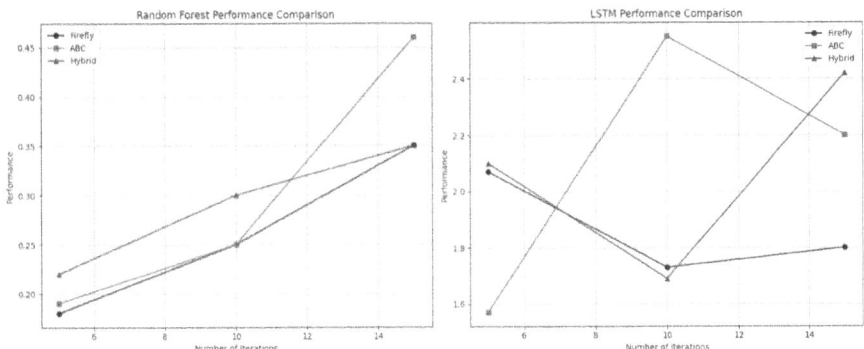

Fig. 1. Comparison between the performances of Random Forest and LSTM models

5.1.2 Return on Investment (ROI)

ROI represents the percentage gain or loss on the initial investment. It reflects the profitability of each portfolio allocation.

Random Forest combined with the Firefly optimization algorithm yields promising ROI, especially over a 15-day interval.

LSTM, when paired with ABC or the Hybrid approach, consistently delivers higher ROI values compared to other models. These results highlight the efficacy of LSTM in predicting asset returns.

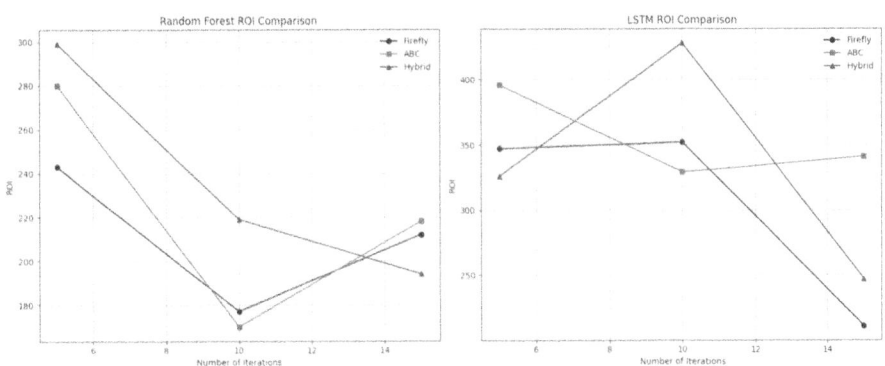

Fig. 2. Comparison between the ROIs yielded by Random Forest and LSTM models

Figure 2 graph compares the ROI of different methods ("Random Forest" and "LSTM") across various optimization models ("Firefly," "ABC," and "Hybrid") and different numbers of iterations (5, 10, and 15). It gives a better insight on how much ROI is being yielded based on the number of iterations.

5.2 Justification for Approach Suitability

Our approach leverages a diverse set of optimization algorithms—Random Forest, ABC, Firefly, and Hybrid—and evaluates their performance over varying intervals. This diversity allows us to adapt to changing market conditions and capture different aspects of portfolio allocation.

The Hybrid approach, in particular, exhibits robust performance by combining the strengths of multiple optimization techniques. It not only enhances accuracy but also provides improved risk-adjusted returns, making it well-suited for portfolio optimization in dynamic financial markets.

Furthermore, our use of LSTM as a predictive model proves effective in capturing temporal patterns and trends in asset returns, contributing to superior ROI. When paired with ABC or employed within the Hybrid framework, LSTM consistently demonstrates its predictive power.

In summary, our study demonstrates that a diversified approach combining machine learning and optimization techniques can lead to improved accuracy, higher risk-adjusted returns, and enhanced ROI. The results suggest that the Hybrid approach, along with LSTM and ABC, holds great potential for enhancing portfolio allocation strategies in financial markets characterized by volatility and uncertainty.

6 Conclusion

In conclusion, this research paper introduces a hybrid approach that merges Firefly Optimization (FO) and Artificial Bee Colony Optimization (ABC) to enhance stock portfolio optimization. The primary aim of this study is to strike a harmonious balance between risk and return while optimizing stock portfolios. The hybrid algorithm developed in this research harnesses the strengths of both FO and ABC, enabling efficient exploration of the solution space and convergence to high-quality portfolio allocations.

The hybrid algorithm emerges as a robust and effective tool for optimizing stock portfolios. It exhibits proficiency in handling large datasets and tackling complex optimization challenges. Furthermore, its implementation is relatively straightforward, making it accessible for various financial decision-making scenarios. Investors can utilize this algorithm to construct portfolios aligned with their desired risk-return profiles, while portfolio managers can manage existing portfolios more effectively and identify new investment opportunities.

The experimental results unequivocally endorse the effectiveness of the proposed hybrid strategy. Both the Sharpe and Sortino ratios, key indicators of risk-adjusted returns, show substantial improvements. This implies that the hybrid strategy consistently outperforms traditional methods by generating higher returns while maintaining controlled volatility. Moreover, the research meticulously evaluates the performance of the hybrid approach over different time intervals (5, 10, and 15 trading days) and consistently observes enhancements in annualized returns.

Furthermore, the paper explores potential applications of the hybrid strategy in diverse financial decision-making scenarios. Not only does this hybrid approach provide a powerful tool for portfolio managers, but it also holds the potential to offer investors superior risk-adjusted returns. By amalgamating the strengths of FO and ABC, this strategy contributes significantly to the domain of stock portfolio optimization, effectively addressing the inherent complexity and non-convexity of financial markets.

Looking forward, there is substantial scope for further research and refinement of the hybrid strategy. Future investigations could explore the incorporation of more advanced optimization techniques and consider different market conditions. The presented hybrid approach offers a promising avenue for future research and practical application in the realms of portfolio management and finance, ushering in a new era of sophisticated and effective portfolio optimization strategies.

References

1. Ito, K., Minami, K., Imajo, K., Nakagawa, K., Trader-company method: a metaheuristics for interpretable stock price prediction. In: Proceedings of the 20th International Conference on Autonomous Agents and MultiAgent Systems (AAMAS'21). International Foundation for Autonomous Agents and Multiagent Systems, Richland, pp. 656–664 (2021)
2. Kalayci, C.B., Polat, O., Akbay, M.A.: An efficient hybrid metaheuristic algorithm for cardinality constrained portfolio optimization. Swarm Evol. Comput. **54**, 100662 (2020). https://doi.org/10.1016/j.swevo.2020.100662
3. Elhoseny, M., Metawa, N., El-hasnony, I.M.: A new metaheuristic optimization model for financial crisis prediction: Towards sustainable development. Sustain. Comput. Inform. Syst. **35**, 100778 (2022). https://doi.org/10.1016/j.suscom.2022.100778
4. Abbasi, H., Bamdad, S., Rahimi, M.: Metaheuristic-based portfolio optimization in peer-to-peer lending platforms. Int. J. Syst. Assur. Eng. Manag. (2023). https://doi.org/10.1007/s13198-023-02074-0
5. Kumar, K., Haider, M.T.U., Enhanced prediction of intra-day stock market using metaheuristic optimization on RNN-LSTM network. Expert Syst. Appl. (2020)
6. Ravelo, S.V., Meneses, C.N., Santos, M.O.: Meta-heuristics for the one-dimensional cutting stock problem with usable leftover. J. Heuristics **26**, 585–618 (2020). https://doi.org/10.1007/s10732-020-09443-z
7. Sedighi, M., Jahangirnia, H., Gharakhani, M., Farahani Fard, S.: A novel hybrid model for stock price forecasting based on metaheuristics and support vector machine. Data **4**, 75 (2019). https://doi.org/10.3390/data4020075
8. Khaje Zadeh, S., Shahverdiani, S., Daneshvar, A., Madanchi Zaj, M.: Predicting the optimal stock portfolio approach of meta-heuristic algorithm and Markov decision process. J. Decis. Oper. Res. **5**(4), 426–445 (2021). https://doi.org/10.22105/dmor.2020.239616.1183
9. Fadaei, E., Dadashi, I., Zare Bahnamiri, M.J., Azinfar, K.: Predicting negative stock price shocks based on the meta heuristic approach. Financ. Knowl. Secur. Anal. **14**(50), 99–108 (2021)
10. Doering, J., Kizys, R., Juan, A.A., Fitó, À., Polat, O.: Metaheuristics for rich portfolio optimisation and risk management: current state and future trends. Oper. Res. Perspect. **6**, 100121 (2019). https://doi.org/10.1016/j.orp.2019.100121
11. Mostafaei Darmian, S., Doaei, M.: Optimization of stock portfolio selection in Iran capital market using meta-heuristic algorithms. Q. J. Appl. Theor. Econ. **8**(4), 253–284 (2022)
12. Fotros, M.H., Miri, I., Miri, A.: Comparison of portfolio optimization for investors at different levels of investors' risk aversion in Tehran stock exchange with meta-heuristic algorithms. Adv. Math. Financ. Appl. **5**(1), 1–10 (2020). https://doi.org/10.22034/amfa.2019.1870129.1235
13. Kusuma, P.D., Dinimaharawati, A.: Three on three optimizer: a new metaheuristic with three guided searches and three random searches. Int. J. Adv. Sci. Appl. **14**(1), 420–429 (2023)

Enhancing Yarn Quality in the Cotton Industry: AI- Based Nep Detection for Improved Manufacturing Processes

Abhishek Chauhan$^{(\boxtimes)}$

Ludhiana, Punjab, India
abhi7.chauhan96@gmail.com

Abstract. The cotton industry places great importance on yarn quality, and its biggest obstacle is nep, which stands for little cotton entanglements that happen during the blowing stage of the yarn manufacturing process. Our goal is to identify these neps as early as possible, allowing us to evaluate the quality of the incoming cotton batch and modify manufacturing settings to reduce the number of neps in succeeding batches. In the end, this approach results in fewer neps and better overall yarn quality. Our AI-based nep detection approach involves installing cameras within carding machines and taking images at a rate of three images per second for a while each day. These images are preprocessed and subsequently processed by a Faster- RCNN model. To improve its training performance in comparison to the prior model, the model has undergone numerous iterations of data annotation and modification. We also demonstrate a relationship between the manual nep count performed by manufacturing executives during the same period and the nep count obtained by this approach. The proposed approach shows competitive performance compared to other available approaches that are presented in the literature.

Keywords: Cotton · Faster-RCNN · Nep · Textile · Yarn

1 Introduction

Generally, the most important physical characteristic of yarn is yarn evenness, which is included in the category of yarn quality. The even distribution of fibre mass along the length of the yarn is referred to as yarn evenness [1]. Defects on the yarn surface caused by variations in the fibre mass result in poor mechanical performance and more breakages during manufacturing processing. Uneven threads have a negative effect on the appearance of the fabric by resulting in undesirable patterns and differences in colour absorption [2, 3]. Customers frequently reject low-quality fabrics, resulting in financial losses and product waste [4, 5]. Thin, thick, and neps are three general categories for defects relating to yarn evenness. While thin signifies a decrease in fibre mass, and thick represents an accumulation of fibre mass relative to yarn diameter. Whereas, entangled fibrous masses are known as neps. Based on their length and diameter, each of these defects can be divided into several subcategories. Due to the influence of raw material

© The Author(s), under exclusive license to Springer Nature Switzerland AG 2024
H. K. et al. (Eds.): AIKP 2023, CCIS 2127, pp. 88–103, 2024.
https://doi.org/10.1007/978-3-031-68617-7_7

qualities and fibre processing parameters, it is unrealistic to eliminate yarn defects; nevertheless, their impact can be reduced by efficient process control and timely machine maintenance such as online testing, or real- time tests into yarn quality throughout the manufacturing level. Nevertheless, the majority of yarn evenness testers currently in use, such as laboratory-scale and modular testing units mounted to winding machines, rely on capacitive sensing concepts. Testing for evenness on a small scale in a lab is destructive and usually entails choosing a small sample of yarn from among a population of several hundred to a few thousand yarns generated in a single spinning cycle. While this offers a general evaluation of yarn quality at the level of the spinning machine, it is unable to gather significant information at the whole level of the manufacturing process. But, during the winding level, modular evenness testers scan yarns and use cutter and splicer assemblers to physically remove defective spots to stop them from spreading to finished fabrics. However, because there are no acceptable approaches to trace individual yarns back to the spinners where they were formed, yarn quality insights obtained on winding machines cannot directly manage the manufacturing process at the spinning level.

As previously mentioned, numerous approaches are used to produce yarn, and these approaches affect many yarn characteristics [6]. Similarly, continuous inspection is also seen to be crucial in providing constant and good fabric quality, which makes yarn quality control a need during the manufacturing process. For assessing yarn quality, commercial systems based on several types of sensors are available, such as USTER Tester 5 and 6 [7–10]. These systems, however, are big, expensive, and mainly concentrate on analysing mass parameters. In recent studies, image-processing approaches have been investigated to acquire more precise yarn quality characteristics [11–15]. The practical use of these technological developments in a physical prototype is required due to a gap in the market. Particularly, relatively little research has been done on solving the defects of yarn evenness. Therefore, in this paper, the authors try to use image processing approaches to measure and characterise yarn evenness (particularly for nep). Therefore, a specialised approach is required to solve this problem. In light of this, it would seem fair to create an environment for image-processing approaches to test the hypothesis. Results show that by examining the yarn's primary neps defect, such an approach would offer a great contribution to the cotton industry. By putting this approach into practice, fabric manufacturing could achieve higher levels of quality. The ideal model should be easy to use, portable, and affordable. It should also be able to interpret images using image processing approaches to automatically detect yarn evenness defects. By integrating this model into an industrial setting, businesses would be able to evaluate the quality of the yarn used in the creation of fabrics, thereby reducing financial losses.

The layout of this paper is as follows: in the section that follows, we'll see a brief overview of the related works that deal with image processing approaches. In Sect. 3, a complete yarn-nep pipeline was explained along with the acquisition of an image and the development of a dataset. Validation and testing with similar cases and in relation to nep, how the Faster-RCNN model is used is also included in this section. Section 4 presents a series of experiments with comparisons, and Sect. 5 concludes the paper with some suggestions for further research.

2 Related Works

Recently, the field of image processing approaches to evaluate yarn evenness has become more well-known. Image-processing approaches have been used to measure yarn evenness, according to several studies such as [16–22]. Typically, these approaches comprise image filtering [19], edge detection [20, 21], spatial transformation [19], morphological procedures [22], and clustering [23] to separate the yarn body from the backdrop. Following that, the grayscale thresholding [19, 22, 23], image binarization [20, 21], and neighbourhood pixel procedures [23] separate the yarn core from the surrounding hair fibres. By measuring the core diameter at several locations throughout the length of the yarn, yarn evenness may be calculated. It is important to note that the majority of these studies used images captured from either stationary yarn samples [24] or yarns moving on laboratory-scale transport devices [20, 21]. While several studies suggested that their laboratory-scale approaches to online monitoring of yarn evenness may be transferred to a spinning level, but there were no actual investigations on the subject [19, 22, 23]. Only one study i.e. [16] employed a digital camera mounted on a spinning level, and it was limited in that it only focused on detecting yarn evenness indirectly by measuring the width of the spinning triangle. To close this gap, the authors suggest a novel approach for online yarn evenness measurement in this paper. To immediately record high-quality yarn images in real-time during yarn manufacture, we created an ideal image acquisition model. These images were subsequently used to develop and test image processing approaches created specifically to recognise neps. The novel approach was put into use in routine industrial production for online testing of cotton yarn kinds, and its effectiveness was confirmed by comparing its results with those of an already-in-use commercial evenness tester.

3 Materials and Methods

This section is divided into three subsections that each address a particular set of materials and methods for neps detection.

3.1 Yarn-NEP Pipeline

The Mercury GigE camera series (MER-131-75GM-P)[1] is specifically designed for industrial vision applications, making it an ideal choice for various industrial settings. It features a GigE interface, which is the most commonly used interface in traditional machine vision applications. This interface provides a reliable and efficient connection between the camera and the host system. One notable advantage of the Mercury GigE camera is its maximum cable length of 100 m. This extended cable length allows for greater flexibility in camera placement, enabling you to cover larger areas or install the camera at a distance from the host system. It is particularly useful in industrial environments where cameras may need to be positioned far away from the control room

---

[1] https://www.get-cameras.com/Vision-Camera-PoE-OnSemi-PYTHON1300-MER-131-75GM-P.

or computer system. Another benefit is the inexpensive and easy installation of cables. The GigE interface utilizes standard Ethernet cables, which are widely available and cost-effective. This means that you don't need to invest in specialized or proprietary cables, resulting in cost savings. Additionally, the simplicity of Ethernet cable installation makes it a convenient option for connecting the camera to the host system. The Mercury GigE camera also offers the option of Power over Ethernet (PoE). With PoE, only a single cable is required to both power the camera and transfer data. This simplifies the setup process and reduces cable clutter, as you don't need to deal with separate power cables. The dimensions of the camera are $29 \times 29 \times 29$ mm without PoE and $29 \times 29 \times 38$ mm with PoE, allowing for compact installation in space-constrained environments. Furthermore, the Mercury GigE camera provides optional hardware triggering. This means that you can synchronize the image capture with external events or signals. This feature is particularly useful in applications where precise timing or synchronization is crucial. By utilizing hardware triggering, you can ensure accurate and reliable image acquisition, even in dynamic or fast-paced industrial environments. A USB 3 connection was used to link the camera to a Dell Precision 7510 computer that was given by Dell, USA. The camera's field of view is approximately 14 cm $\times$ 10 cm, and the distance between the lens and the carding machine is around 10 cm. The camera takes pictures at a rate of 3 images per second for data transport and storage. The camera's settings can be changed as needed, including exposure and gain. Timestamps that show when the images were taken are kept with them. The information is kept on a 2 TB local HDD that is attached to the computer. The data is separated into 1-min batches and saved on the HDD as.zip files. Then, these.zip files are uploaded to the server using a File Transfer Protocol (FTP). To make room for new data, the successfully transferred data is removed from the local HDD. The received.zip files are separated into batches depending on predetermined time intervals (for example, 15-min windows) throughout the data segmentation and model execution phase. The original.zip files are then removed when the.zip files have been extracted inside their appropriate batches. Every time a batch is formed, the programme "test_model1.py" is invoked, and the model is applied to the data in each batch. An "ANNOTATIONS.txt" file containing the coordinates of the bounding boxes (predictions) for the identified neps is used to store the model's output. A "STATS.txt" file is also created, which contains data on the timing of each batch and the number of neps. The results are arranged in a hierarchical structure with the date serving as the parent node and the time serving as the child node, and a Firebase Realtime Database is incorporated to display the results in real time. A key-value pair containing the nep count and the time interval (batch) in which it occurred is used to keep the nep count for each batch. As a result, the camera system takes images at a set pace, stores the data locally, sends it to a server, does data segmentation, and runs a model. The outcomes are then incorporated into a Firebase Realtime Database, enabling in-process nep count monitoring and analysis. Figure 1 depicts the overall yarn-nep pipeline.

3.1.1 Validation and Testing: Comparison with Similar Cases

There are just a few known instances of other yarn-nep pipelines that can be used to compare our pipeline i.e. System A, with comparable data. In comparison to our proposed yarn-nep pipeline, Table 1 lists the features of earlier proposed yarn-nep pipelines. It is

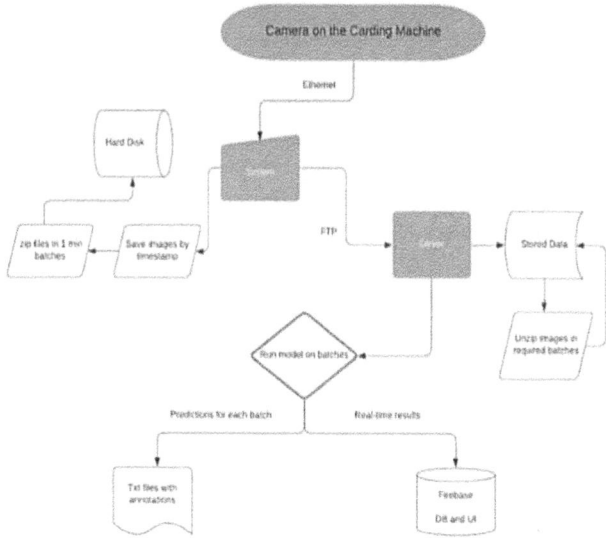

Fig. 1. Overall Pipeline of Yarn-Nep

clear from an analysis of various yarn-nep pipelines that not all of them meet the requirements. However, System A, the yarn-nep pipeline we created, has several advantages
such as:

1. **Image and Video-based Analysis:** Analysis of yarn using both images and videos
   is possible with System A, but is not possible with Systems B, C, D, or E.
2. **Extraction of Inherent Characteristics:** System A uses artificial intelligence and
   image processing to extract the inborn characteristics of defects in yarn. In comparison, Systems B, C, D, and E rely solely on artificial intelligence and a currently
   available commercial machine, the USTER TESTER 5, to gather information about
   yarn characteristics using optical sensors.
3. **Cost-effectiveness:** System A stands out for being less expensive than other
   commercial yarn-nep pipelines that have been created up to this point.
4. **Non-destructive:** System A's nature is non-destructive and enables image analysis
   as well as the winding and unwinding of various textile threads.

There are some limitations and gaps in System B, C, D, and E's capabilities. It is
important to note that System D has the advantage of allowing for the measurement
of textile yarn durability and elasticity. However, there are not many parallels between
Systems A and E. When compared to other systems, System A excels in its capacity
to extract a wide variety of features. Additionally, it provides simple integration with
commercial production lines. System A stands out from the competition thanks to its
unique approach, which enables quick and accurate neps identification and classification.
Additionally, it boasts the singular ability to seamlessly combine the artificial intelligence
algorithm with the image processing approach. Its general functionality and performance
are improved by this integration.

Table 1. Comparison With Various Pipelines

Characteristics	System A (Proposed)	System B [13]	System D [25]	System E [26]
Mechatronic prototype developed?	No	Yes	Yes	NO
Non-destructive Prototype?	Yes	No	No	NO
Unwinding System and Yarn Winding?	Yes	Yes	No	No
Image or Video analysis in textile yarn?	Video and Image	Image	Image	Image
Does the system utilize a Vision System (VS), Artificial Intelligence (AI), or Optical Sensors to identify defects in textile fabric or textile yarn?	VS and AI	VS	AI	AI
Obtain Yarn twist orientation?	Yes	No	No	No
Obtain Yarn twist step?	Yes	No	No	No
Obtain a Hairiness index?	Yes	Yes	No	No
Obtain Thick places?	Yes	No	No	No
Obtain Thin places?	Yes	No	No	No
Obtain Neps?	Yes	No	No	No
Obtain Diameter?	Yes	Yes	No	No
Obtain Linear Mass?	Yes	No	No	Yes
Obtain Volume?	Yes	No	No	No
Obtain the Number of cables	Yes	No	No	No
A number of loose fibers?	Yes	No	No	No

(*continued*)

Table 1. (*continued*)

Characteristics	System A (Proposed)	System B [13]	System D [25]	System E [26]
Is the developed system capable of being implemented within an industrial setting on production lines?	Yes	Yes	No	No
Does the developed system offer the capability to capture yarn images in real time or through offline means?	Offline and Online	Offline	Offline	Offline
Obtain Spectral Analysis?	Yes	No	No	No
Is the developed system compatible with various types of yarn?	Yes	NA	Yes	Yes
System Cost (€)	1200€ (estimated)	NA	NA	NA

3.2 Yarn Image Dataset

We recorded 1750 consecutive yarn images for each category of yarn, yielding a collection of 84,000 images. We used a semi-automated approach that included a computer algorithm and expert evaluator to categorise these images as either positive (showing the existence of nep defects) or negative (indicating the lack of nep defects). The Faster-RCNN model is used to process each image in the dataset. The image was subjected to a grayscale intensity threshold before the total number of pixels in each row was determined. The row summation curve of the yarn image is sharply increased when nep defects occur because they frequently take the form of discrete fibre clusters inside the normal yarn. But additional causes of variation, including excessive hairiness, fluff or fly buildup, and other yarn defects, can also cause corresponding increases in the row summation curve. To solve this, an expert evaluator looked at the images where a noticeable increase in the row summation curve occurred and labelled those images as positive if a nep was visibly seen. The dataset's remaining images were all labelled as negative. The dataset showed an imbalance with a low number of positive images relative to negative images since nep defects occurred less frequently than typical yarn images. The dataset was then split into training and testing sets while keeping a 80:20 ratio for each.

3.3   Faster-RCNN for NEP

A deep learning-based object detection approach called Faster R-CNN has been used in the context of the cotton industry to detect and classify neps defects in cotton yarn. A Region Proposal Network (RPN) and a detection network make up its two primary components. By scanning the image at various sizes and aspect ratios, the RPN creates prospective region proposals. The detection network then classifies and improves these proposals to precisely localise and classify the Regions of Interest (RoI). Faster R-CNN for nep detection in cotton requires training the model using a sizable dataset of annotated images that include both nep and non-nep yarn samples. The programme gains knowledge of the visual characteristics and patterns connected to neps. Once trained, it can be used to automatically detect and mark the existence of neps in images or video frames collected throughout the yarn manufacturing process. The cotton industry can benefit from automated and effective quality control by using Faster R-CNN for nep detection. It provides early nep identification, allowing for prompt intervention and stopping the manufacture of faulty yarn. In the cotton industry, this approach helps raise yarn quality, lower production costs, and increase general consumer happiness.

4   Experiments and Analysis

This section is divided into three subsections that each address a particular set of experiments and analyses for neps detection.

4.1   Faster-RCNN

For the Faster-RCNN model, Table 2 presents the results of different image resizing ratios and their corresponding True Positive (TP), False Positive (FP), and False Negative (FN) values, along with the True Negative (TN) ratio expressed as a percentage. The default image size of 600 × 1024 is tested in three cases, showing varying numbers of TP, FP, and FN. The FN ratios for these cases range from 3.5% to 4.9%. Another resizing ratio of 1000 × 1024 is evaluated, resulting in a higher FN ratio of 5.2%. Finally, the image size matching the data used (1024 × 1280) is tested in two instances, yielding FN ratios of 3.5% and 4.1%. These figures provide insights into the performance of different image resizing ratios in terms of correctly identifying positive instances (TP) and incorrectly classifying negative instances (FP) while minimizing the number of FN instances. Whereas, Table III includes the performance metrics for both Camera 1 (towards left) and Camera 2 (towards right) with the same metrics as Table 3. The total number of neoplasms (neps) detected is calculated by summing TP and FP, and the total actual neps are calculated by summing TP and FN. Sensitivity, also known as the TP rate, indicates the percentage of actual neps correctly identified by the camera. The neps missed metric represents the percentage of actual neps that were not detected by the camera. The flowchart of the Faster-RCNN model is presented in Fig. 2.

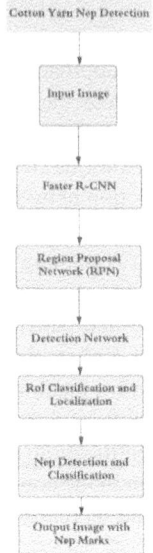

Fig. 2. Flowchart of the Faster-RCNN Model

Table 2. Results with Faster-RCNN on Pretrained COCO Dataset

Ratio	TP	FP	FN	FN Ratio (%)
Training: 4414, Test: 1000, and Batch Size: 1				
600*1024	982	1074	36	3.5%
Training: 5414, Test: 1000, and Batch Size: 1				
600*1024	892	787	46	4.9%
1000*1024	889	758	49	5.2%
1024*1280	905	1131	33	3.5%
1024*1280	899	920	39	4.1%

Table 3. Validation on Cameras 1 And 2

Camera	TP	FP	F N	Total Neps Detected	Total Actual Neps	FP Rate (%)	TP Rate (%)	Sensitivity (%)	Neps Missed (%)
Camera 1	1393	987	13	2380	1406	41.5%	58.5%	99%	1%
Camera 2	2200	1507	36	3707	2236	40%	60%	98.4%	1.6%

4.2 Validation of Faster-RCNN

A Faster-RCNN model has been trained to detect objects in images. As a result, the model was first given two datasets to learn from: the COCO dataset, which featured a greater range of items with 80 different classes, and the Kitti dataset, which included images of vehicles and pedestrians. Different pre-training datasets were used, but the model was trained using the same model. The COCO-trained model exhibited a deeper grasp of numerous objects, whereas the Kitti-trained model was skilled at spotting vehicles and pedestrians. 1000 test images were utilised to assess how well these models performed. The model was used to process each image, and it generated bounding boxes around objects and confidence scores between 0 and 1. These projections are known as "neps". The confidence score threshold, with a default value of 0.5, determined which predicted boxes would be the final output. Tables 4 and 5 show results on COCO and Kitti dataset, which displays the model's performance at various thresholds (0.5, 0.3, and 0.1) and Intersection over Union (IoU) values. IoU calculates the amount by which the predicted box and the actual box overlap. The results demonstrate that the model using the COCO dataset outperformed the model using the Kitti dataset by a significant margin. The FN was decreased to 8 by a Nep score cutoff of 0.1 and an IoU threshold of 0.3. But it also considerably raised FP. Even with a nep score cutoff of 0.5 for COCO, the result is FN = 36 with an overlap threshold of 0.3, which is still higher than the minimum requirement for the Kitti dataset. The considerable increase in FP is the only cost of lowering the nep threshold value. Table 6 displays the results from the pre-trained Kitti dataset. The best results are then provided after training our custom datasets over their weights with resized images for different resolutions. A similar result is shown in Table 7 but with regard to the COCO dataset.

Table 4. COCO Dataset

Nep Score Threshold		0.1	0.3	0.5
Overlap (Ground truth and predicted)	**0.3**	TP:1010	TP:996	TP:982
		FP:1910	FP:1388	FP:1074
		FN:8	FN:22	FN:36
	0.4	TP:998 FP:1922	TP:985 FP:1399	TP:972 FP:1084
		FN:20	FN:33	FN:46
	0.5	TP:949	TP:937	TP:924
		FP:1971	FP:1447	FP:1132
		FN:69	FN:81	FN:94

4.3 Automatics vs Manual Evaluations

The provided data consists of information related to four different cards (Card No. 1, Card No. 2, Card No. 3, and Card No. 26) over a period of three days, from January 27th, 2023 to January 30th, 2023 as shown in Fig. 3 and the correlation graph is shown in Fig. 4. Each card has various measurements and values associated with it, allowing us to analyze their characteristics and changes over time. Let's start with Card No. 1

Table 5. KITTI Dataset

Nep Score Threshold		0.1	0.1	0.3	0.5
Overlap (Ground truth and predicted)	**0.3**		TP:989	TP:964	TP:933
			FP:1862	FP:1132	FP:854
			FN:29	FN:54	FN:85
	0.4		TP:987	TP:958	TP:928
			FP:1864	FP:1138	FP:859
			FN:31	FN:60	FN:90
	0.5		TP:938	TP:912	TP:886
			FP:1913	FP:1184	FP:901
			FN:80	FN:106	FN:132

Table 6. Pretrained KITTI Dataset

Dataset Size	Ratio	True Positive	False Positive	False Negative
600*1987	927/624	927	624	91
600*750	950/877	950	877	68
Training Data	3234/4492	3234	4492	166

Table 7. Pretrained COCO Dataset but with Different Versions

Dataset Size	Ratio	True Positive	False Positive	False Negative
Training: 4414, and Test: 1000				
600*1024	982/1074	982	1074	36
Training: 5414, and Test: 1000				
1000*1024	887/853	887	853	51
1024*1280	905/1131	905	1131	33
New Modelv7	2453/1778	2453	1778	117
New Modelv7	2481/2606	2481	2606	89
New Modelv7	658/799	658	799	1912
New Modelv7	484/1064	484	1064	2086
New Modelv8	2471/1698	2471	1698	99

on January 27th, 2023. On this day, the AFIS Neps/gm (a measurement of neps per gram) for Card No. 1 was recorded as 65. Additionally, the Online Neps/gm, which is a calculated value, was found to be 12. The card had a manual neps count of 21,

Card No. 1   **Card No. 1**

27.01.23	30.01.23
AFIS Neps/gm = 65	AFIS Neps/gm = 90
Online Neps/gm (calculated) = 12	Online Neps/gm (calculated) = 5

Manual neps --21   Manual neps --10

Card Web weight 5.82 gms (60 slide)

Card No. 2   **Card No. 2**

27.01.23	30.01.23
AFIS Neps/gm = 64	AFIS Neps/gm = 102
Online Neps/gm (calculated) = 46	Online Neps/gm (calculated) = 9

Manual Neps - 13   Manual Neps - 7

Card Web weight 5.94 gms (60 slide)

Card No. 3   **Card No. 3**

27.01.23	30.01.23
AFIS Neps/gm = 46	AFIS Neps/gm = 92
Online Neps/gm (calculated) = 9	Online Neps/gm (calculated) = 5

Manual Neps/gm - 17   Manual Neps/gm - 13

Card Web weight 6.00 gms (60 slide)

Card No. 26   **Card No. 26**

27.01.23	30.01.23
AFIS Neps/gm = 55	AFIS Neps/gm = 85
Online Neps/gm (calculated) = 2	Online Neps/gm (calculated) = 2

Manual Neps/gm -21   Manual Neps/gm -10

Card Web weight 5.76 gms (60 slide)

Fig. 3. Automatics vs Manual neps

indicating the number of manual defects present. Furthermore, the weight of the card's web was measured to be 5.82 g for 60 slides. Moving on to Card No. 2, on the same date, its AFIS Neps/gm was slightly lower at 64 compared to Card No. 1. The Online Neps/gm value for Card No. 2 was relatively high, calculated to be 46. The card had a manual neps count of 13, indicating fewer manual defects compared to Card No. 1. The weight of the card's web was slightly higher at 5.94 g for 60 slides. Now, let's examine Card No. 3 on January 27th, 2023. This card had an AFIS Neps/gm of 46, which was lower compared to the previous two cards. The Online Neps/gm was calculated to be 9, indicating a relatively lower number of online defects. The card had a manual neps count of 17, suggesting the presence of manual defects. The weight of the card's web was measured to be 6.00 g for 60 slides, slightly higher than the previous cards. Lastly, considering Card No. 26 on January 27th, 2023, its AFIS Neps/gm was recorded as 55, placing it between Card No. 1 and Card No. 3. The Online Neps/gm value for Card No. 26 was 2, indicating a relatively low number of online defects. The card had a manual neps count of 21, similar to Card No. 1. The weight of the card's web was measured to be 5.76 g for 60 slides, which was the lowest among the four cards. Now, let's move on to the values for each card on January 30th, 2023. Card No. 1 experienced an increase in AFIS Neps/gm, which rose to 90. However, the Online Neps/gm decreased to 5, indicating an improvement in online defect detection. The manual neps count decreased to 10, suggesting a reduction in manual defects. Similarly, Card No. 2 also showed an increase in AFIS Neps/gm, which rose to 102. The Online Neps/gm decreased to 9, indicating better online defect detection compared to the previous value. The manual neps count decreased to 7, reflecting a reduction in manual defects. For Card No. 3, the AFIS Neps/gm increased to 92, while the Online Neps/gm remained the same at 5. The

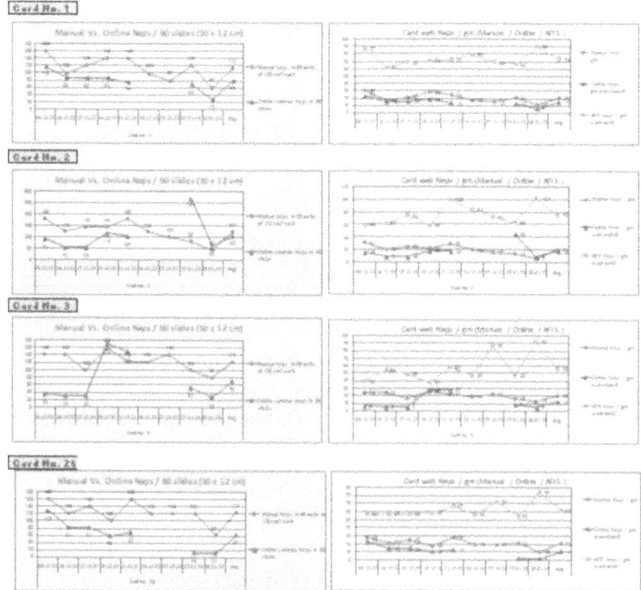

Fig. 4. Correlation Graph Between Different Machines

manual neps count increased slightly to 13, indicating a slight rise in manual defects. Finally, Card No. 26 had an AFIS Neps/gm of 85, which was lower than Card No. 3 but higher than Card No. 1 and Card No. 2. The Online Neps/gm value remained the same at 2, indicating consistent online defect detection. The manual neps count decreased to 10, showing a reduction in manual defects.

5   Conclusions and Future Works

In conclusion, this paper presents an AI-based nep detection approach for the cotton industry. The system utilizes cameras installed within carding machines to capture images, which are then processed using a Faster RCNN model for real- time nep detection. The model has undergone multiple iterations of data annotation and refinement to improve its training. The performance of different image resizing ratios was evaluated, showing varying results in terms of TP, FP, and FN. The FN ratios ranged from 3.5% to 5.2% across different resizing ratios. Additionally, the paper provides performance metrics for Camera 1 and Camera 2. These metrics offer valuable insights into the system's effectiveness in detecting neps. Overall, the AI-based nep detection system shows promise in the early detection of neps, allowing for improved assessment of cotton batch quality and adjustment of factory settings to minimize nep count, thereby enhancing yarn quality in the cotton industry.

References

1. Slater, K.: Yarn evenness. Text. Prog.Prog. **14**, 1–90 (1986). https://doi.org/10.1080/004051 68608688901
2. Srinivasan, K., Dastoor, P.H., Radhakrishnaiah, F., Jayaraman, S.: FDAS: a knowledge-based framework for analysis of defects in woven textile structures. J. Text. Inst. **83**, 431–448 (1992). https://doi.org/10.1080/00405009208631217
3. Shamey, R., Hussein, T.: Critical solutions in the dyeing of cotton textile materials. Text. Prog.Prog. **37**, 1 (2005). https://doi.org/10.1533/tepr.2005.0001
4. Kashyap, G.S., Malik, K., Wazir, S., Khan, R.: Using machine learning to quantify the multimedia risk due to fuzzing. Multimed. Tools Appl. **81**, 36685–36698 (2022). https://doi.org/ 10.1007/s11042-021-11558-9
5. Wazir, S., Kashyap, G.S., Malik, K., Brownlee, A.E.I.: Predicting the infection level of COVID-19 virus using normal distribution-based approximation model and PSO. In: Hammouch, Z., Lahby, M., Baleanu, D. (eds.) Mathematical Modeling and Intelligent Control for Combating Pandemics. Springer Optimization and Its Applications, vol. 203. Springer, Cham (2023). https://doi.org/10.1007/978-3-031-33183-1_5
6. Xia, Z., Zhou, M., Wang, H., Wang, K., Wan, Y.: Evaluating the surface hairiness of woven fabric belts with a yarn hairiness tester. J. Text. Inst. **113**, 116–124 (2022). https://doi.org/10. 1080/00405000.2020.1865505
7. TECHNOLOGIES, U.: Uster Technologies - Uster Technologies, https://www.uster.com/. Accessed 14 June 2023
8. Marwah, N., Singh, V.K., Kashyap, G.S., Wazir, S.: An analysis of the robustness of UAV agriculture field coverage using multi-agent reinforcement learning. Int. J. Inf. Technol. (Singapore) **15**, 2317–2327 (2023). https://doi.org/10.1007/s41870-023-01264-0

 9. Kanojia, M., Kamani, P., Kashyap, G.S., Naz, S., Wazir, S., Chauhan, A.: Alternative agriculture land-use transformation pathways by partial- equilibrium agricultural sector model: a mathematical approach. (2023)
10. Wazir, S., Kashyap, G.S., Saxena, P.: MLOps: A Review (2023)
11. Liang, Z., Xu, B., Chi, Z., Feng, D.: Intelligent characterization and evaluation of yarn surface appearance using saliency map analysis, wavelet transform and fuzzy ARTMAP neural network. Expert Syst. Appl. **39**, 4201–4212 (2012). https://doi.org/10.1016/j.eswa.2011.09.114
12. Abdelkader, M.: MATLAB algorithms for diameter measurements of textile yarns and fibers through image processing techniques. Materials. **15**, 1299 (2022). https://doi.org/10.3390/ma15041299
13. Li, Z., Zhong, P., Tang, X., Chen, Y., Su, S., Zhai, T.: A new method to evaluate yarn appearance qualities based on machine vision and image processing. IEEE Access. **8**, 30928–30937 (2020). https://doi.org/10.1109/ACCESS.2020.2972967
14. Xu, B., Wang, L., Gao, W.: 3D measurement of yarn hairiness via multi- perspective images. In: Proceedings Volume 10679, Optics, Photonics, and Digital Technologies for Imaging Applications V, Vol. 1067916, p. 39. SPIE (2018). https://doi.org/10.1117/12.2307844
15. Sun, Y., Li, Z., Pan, R., Zhou, J., Gao, W.: Measurement of long yarn hair based on hairiness segmentation and hairiness tracking. J. Text. Inst. **108**, 1271–1279 (2017). https://doi.org/10.1080/00405000.2016.1240144
16. Badehnoush, A., Alamdar Yazdi, A.: Real-time yarn evenness investigation via evaluating spinning triangle area changes. J. Text. Inst. **103**, 850–861 (2012). https://doi.org/10.1080/00405000.2011.614741
17. Qin, W., Huang, Q., Yang, G.: Application of on-line yarn evenness measurement through CCD image sensors. In: ICCASM 2010 - 2010 International Conference on Computer Application and System Modeling, Proceedings (2010). https://doi.org/10.1109/ICCASM.2010.5618988
18. Wang, Q., Liu, S.A., Gao, B., Wang, D.: An optimization model for the order dispatching problem in distributed production environment. In: Proceedings of the 2011 Chinese Control and Decision Conference, CCDC 2011. pp. 1444–1449 (2011). https://doi.org/10.1109/CCDC.2011.5968419
19. Goncalves, N., Carvalho, V., Soares, F., Vasconcelos, R.: Studies on the yarn mass parameters determination using Image Processing techniques. In: IEEE International Conference on Emerging Technologies and Factory Automation, ETFA (2012). https://doi.org/10.1109/ETFA.2012.6489765
20. Roy, S., Sengupta, A., Maity, R., Sengupta, S.: Yarn parameterization based on image processing. In: 2013 IEEE International Conference on Signal Processing, Computing and Control, ISPCC 2013 (2013). https://doi.org/10.1109/ISPCC.2013.6663391
21. Sengupta, A., Roy, S., Sengupta, S.: Development of a low cost yarn parameterisation unit by image processing. Meas. J. Int. Meas. Confed. **59**, 96–109 (2015). https://doi.org/10.1016/j.measurement.2014.09.028
22. Pinto, R., Pereira, F., Carvalho, V., Soares, F., Vasconcelos, R.: Yarn linear mass determination using image processing: First insights. In: IECON Proceedings (Industrial Electronics Conference), pp. 198–203. IEEE Computer Society (2019). https://doi.org/10.1109/IECON.2019.8926650
23. Li, Z., Pan, R., Wang, J., Wang, Z., Li, B., Gao, W.: Real-time segmentation of yarn images based on an FCM algorithm and intensity gradient analysis. Fibres Text. Eastern Eur. **24**, 45–50 (2016). https://doi.org/10.5604/12303666.1201130
24. Loresco, P.J., Valenzuela, I., Culaba, A., Dadios, E.: Viola-jones method of marker detection for scale-invariant calculation of lettuce leaf area. In: 2018 IEEE 10th International Conference

on Humanoid, Nanotechnology, Information Technology, Communication and Control, Environment and Management, HNICEM 2018. Institute of Electrical and Electronics Engineers Inc. (2019). https://doi.org/10.1109/HNICEM.2018.8666244

25. El-Geiheini, A., ElKateb, S., Abd-Elhamied, M.R.: Yarn tensile properties modeling using artificial intelligence. Alex. Eng. J. **59**, 4435–4440 (2020). https://doi.org/10.1016/j.aej.2020. 07.049

26. Abd-Elhamied, M.R., Hashima, W.A., ElKateb, S., Elhawary, I., El-Geiheini, A.: Prediction of cotton yarn's characteristics by image processing and ANN. Alex. Eng. J. **61**, 3335–3340 (2022). https://doi.org/10.1016/j.aej.2021.08.057

Deep Learning and Computer Vision

Breast Cancer Diagnosis from Ultrasonic Image and Histopathology Image Using Deep Learning Approach

Chithik Raja Mohamed[1]([✉]) [ID], Mohammad Musallam Al-Mahri[1] [ID],
Mohamed Mallick[2] [ID], and Arwa Said Salim Al-Shanfari[1] [ID]

[1] College of Computing and Information Sciences, Information Technology Department,
University of Technology and Applied Sciences Salalah, Salalah, Sultanate of Oman
`chithik43@gmail.com`, `{Mohamed.Mahri,arwa.alshanfari}@utas.edu.om`
[2] Harman International, A Samsung Company, Bangalore, India
`mohamedmallick@gmail.com`

Abstract. Breast cancer is a widespread and potentially life-threatening illness, emphasizing the critical need for early and precise diagnosis to improve treatment outcomes and patient survival rates. In our study, we propose a novel approach to address this challenge by utilizing granular computing, a method that allows for the efficient analysis of complex data by dividing it into smaller, more manageable subsets. Our proposed model harnesses the capabilities of granular computing to analyze breast cancer symptoms extracted from two distinct image modalities: ultrasound images and breast histopathology images. Ultrasound imaging provides real-time, non-invasive visualization of breast tissue, while breast histopathology images offer detailed microscopic views of tissue samples obtained through biopsies. Through rigorous experimentation, we assessed the model's ability to accurately identify breast cancer symptoms and distinguish them from benign conditions. Through rigorous experimentation, our proposed model demonstrated remarkable AUC-ROC rates of 92% in the random forest and 91% in the conventional neural network for ultrasound images and breast histopathology images, respectively. Ultimately, the adoption of such advanced computational techniques has the potential to facilitate timely interventions and improve patient outcomes by enabling clinicians to make more informed decisions based on accurate and reliable diagnostic information. This research contributes to the growing field of medical image analysis by highlighting the potential of granular computing in addressing complex diagnostic challenges such as breast cancer identification.

Keywords: Machine-Learning · Deep Learning · Ultrasonic · Histopathology · medical image · breast cancer · classification

1 Introduction

Breast cancer remains a significant global health concern, posing a substantial threat to women's lives. The importance of timely and precise diagnosis cannot be overstated, as it is crucial for effective treatment and better patient outcomes. Medical imaging technologies have played a pivotal role in this regard, assisting clinicians and researchers in identifying breast cancer symptoms. Among these technologies, ultrasonic imaging and histopathology have emerged as indispensable modalities, offering valuable insights into the nature and severity of breast cancer. Ultrasonic imaging, commonly referred to as ultrasound, utilizes high-frequency sound waves to generate real-time images of breast tissue. This non-invasive and radiation-free imaging method provides dynamic visualization of tissue structures, aiding in the detection of abnormalities like tumors, cysts, and calcifications. Conversely, histopathology involves the microscopic examination of tissue samples obtained through biopsy, facilitating precise analysis of cellular characteristics and architectural changes within breast tissue, thereby enhancing the accuracy of breast cancer diagnosis and subtype classification.

The integration of advanced computational techniques has revolutionized the field of medical image analysis, enhancing the ability to extract meaningful insights from complex imaging data. In recent years, granular computing has emerged as a promising methodology for addressing intricate diagnostic challenges. Granular computing involves the manipulation of granules—sets of data points or features to represent and analyze complex systems. This approach has shown potential in various domains, including medical image analysis. In light of the significance of early and accurate breast cancer diagnosis, this research aims to harness the power of granular computing to improve the identification of breast cancer symptoms using ultrasonic images and histopathology images. By employing granular computing, we intend to enhance the precision of detection and classification of breast cancer-related features within these images, ultimately contributing to more effective diagnosis and treatment strategies. This study seeks to bridge the gap between traditional medical imaging techniques and cutting-edge computational methodologies, demonstrating the potential of granular computing in enhancing breast cancer diagnosis. The research outcomes have the potential to inform clinical decision-making, offering clinicians a more comprehensive and nuanced understanding of breast cancer manifestations in both ultrasonic and histopathology images. As we delve into the details of this research, the subsequent sections will elaborate on the methodology, experimental setup, results, and implications of employing granular computing for breast cancer diagnosis through these two essential imaging modalities.

2   Literature Review

Breast cancer diagnosis has evolved significantly over the years due to advances in medical imaging technologies, computational methods, and molecular profiling techniques. Early and accurate detection is crucial for optimal treatment outcomes. This literature review discusses key contributions in breast cancer diagnosis, focusing on modalities such as mammography, ultrasound, MRI, and histopathology, as well as the integration of machine learning and deep learning techniques for enhanced accuracy. Mammography remains a cornerstone in breast cancer screening. The study by Pisano et al. (2005) highlighted the efficacy of digital mammography in improving the detection of invasive breast cancers [1]. Ultrasound imaging has gained prominence for characterizing breast lesions. Berg et al. (2008) evaluated the accuracy of ultrasound in distinguishing between benign and malignant lesions [2]. MRI offers detailed information on breast tissue morphology. Lehman et al. (2007) demonstrated the utility of breast MRI in detecting

additional malignancies not visible on mammography or ultrasound [3]. Histopathology plays a vital role in confirming cancer diagnosis. Rakha et al. (2008) introduced
the Nottingham Prognostic Index, which integrates histological parameters to predict
breast cancer outcomes [4]. Machine Learning techniques have enhanced diagnostic
accuracy. Kooi et al. (2017) proposed a deep- learning framework for classifying benign
and malignant breast lesions on mammograms [5]. Deep Learning models have shown
promising results in breast cancer detection. Shen et al. (2019) developed a deep neural
network for identifying breast cancer metastases in lymph nodes [6]. Digital Pathology is
emerging as a transformative tool in diagnosing breast cancer. Madabhushi et al. (2016)
investigated the potential of quantitative image analysis to aid pathologists in assessing
breast cancer histopathology [7]. Gene Expression Analysis has identified subtypes of
breast cancer with distinct prognoses and treatment responses. Perou et al. (2000) introduced the concept of intrinsic molecular subtypes based on gene expression profiles [8].
HER2/neu Status is a crucial marker guiding treatment decisions. Slamon et al. (2001)
highlighted the therapeutic relevance of HER2/neu amplification [9]. This literature
survey provides an overview of key contributions in utilizing datasets for breast cancer diagnosis, covering various aspects from dataset acquisition to computational techniques. Diverse datasets play a pivotal role in training and validating diagnostic models.
The work of Wang et al. (2018) demonstrated the importance of creating standardized
datasets by curating multiple sources, facilitating robust model development [10]. Kosmia, L. et al. (2023) research review report depicted about the several Computer-Aided
Diagnosis (CAD) systems, which are being developed to assist radiologists to accurately
detect and/or classify breast cancer. This review examines the recent literature on the
automatic detection and/or classification of breast cancer in mammograms, using both
conventional feature-based machine learning and deep learning algorithms [11]. Multimodal Fusion integrating multiple imaging modalities enhances diagnostic accuracy. Tan
et al. (2019) fused mammographic and ultrasound data using a deep learning framework,
achieving improved classification performance [12]. Transfer learning aids in leveraging
pre-trained models for breast cancer diagnosis. Yap et al. (2019) demonstrated how fine-
tuning a deep neural network on mammographic data can lead to improved classification
[13]. Prognostication and Survival Prediction is a Deep learning techniques that extend
to prognosis estimation. Coudray et al. (2018) used CNNs to predict breast cancer survival, highlighting the potential of deep learning in outcome prediction [14]. Attention
mechanisms enhance model interpretability. Li et al. (2020) proposed a deep attention-
based network for breast cancer classification, allowing for localized feature focus [15].
Deep learning's uncertainty estimation is critical for clinical decision-making. Huang
et al. (2021) introduced a Bayesian CNN framework for breast cancer diagnosis with
uncertainty quantification [16].

3   Experimental Methodology

In this experimental methodology, we outline the steps for conducting breast cancer
diagnosis using a combination of ultrasonic and histopathology images. The proposed
approach involves utilizing deep learning architectures, specifically GoogLeNet and a
Residual Block-based Convolutional Neural Network (CNN), to enhance accuracy and

performance in identifying breast cancer. The methodology includes data preparation, model architecture, training, evaluation, and performance analysis.

3.1 Data Preparation

Dataset: Collect a comprehensive dataset containing both ultrasonic and histopathology images of breast tissue samples, annotated with binary labels indicating cancerous or non-cancerous status.

Data Preprocessing: Normalize the pixel values of images to a consistent range (e.g., [0, 1]). Resize the images to a uniform size to ensure compatibility between the two modalities.

Data Split: Divide the dataset into training, validation, and test sets using a suitable ratio (e.g., sixty percent for training, twenty percent for validation, and twenty for testing). Subsequent paragraphs, however, are indented.

3.2 Model Architecture

GooleNet: Implement the GoogleNet architecture, which is known for its depth and efficient use of computational resources. It includes multiple inception modules that capture features at various scales.

Residual Block-based CNN: Design a CNN architecture with residual blocks, known for alleviating the vanishing gradient problem. A residual block includes shortcut connections, allowing the network to learn residual functions.

3.3 Model Training

Data Augmentation: Apply techniques like random cropping, flipping, and rotation to make more data. This helps the model to be stronger and work better with new data. Measure the difference between predicted and actual labels with a suitable loss function like binary cross-entropy. Use an optimizer called Adam to make the loss function as small as possible during training. Experiment with hyper parameters such as learning rate, batch size, and the number of layers to find the best settings.

4 Granular Computing Based Technique

Granulation: Apply granulation techniques to partition extracted features into meaningful granules, creating a more manageable representation of the data while preserving essential characteristics.

Granular Computing Models: Designed and implemented granular computing-based models, in which we used the rough set-based feature selection classifiers.

4.1 Feature Extraction and Selection

Features were extracted from both ultrasonic and histopathology images using established techniques for image analysis and processing. We applied rough set-based feature selection to identify the most relevant features for breast cancer diagnosis. The rough set theory allows for the identification of features that have a high discriminatory power between cancerous and non-cancerous samples (Fig. 1).

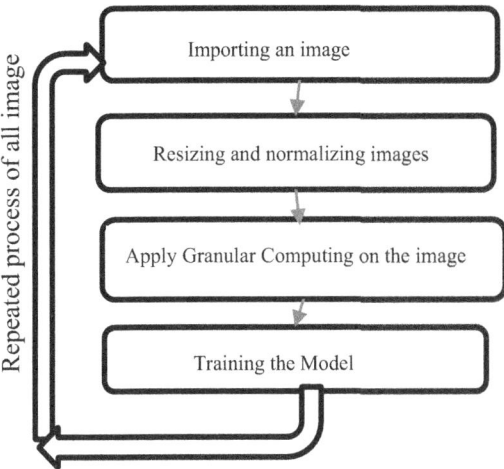

Fig. 1. Overall Process of Proposed Methods

4.2   Model Training and Performance Analysis

We employed popular algorithms such as Support Vector Machines (SVM), Random Forests, Neural Networks, and Decision Trees to develop classification models based on selected features. To evaluate the performance of these models, we utilized a range of metrics including Accuracy, which gauges the proportion of correctly classified instances; Precision, revealing the ratio of true positive predictions to all positive predictions; Recall, indicating the ratio of true positive predictions to all actual positives; F1Score, computed as the harmonic mean of precision and recall; and AUC-ROC, representing the area under the receiver operating characteristic curve.

5   Experimental Results

The breast histopathology image dataset and the ultrasound image dataset from Cairo University were used for the experiments' training and testing, respectively. The tests were run on Kaggle using the hardware's power, including GPUs, and the Python-written programs. The following settings were used to train the model: Adam optimizer with 0.0001 learning rate, 32 batches, 100 epochs, and a 50% dropout rate. One of the hyperparameters that may be adjusted to enhance the performance of the model is the number of epochs in a CNN. The term "epochs" describes the quantity of times the full training dataset is sent through the CNN during training. The table below presents the results of the experiment for different classification models (Table 1):

Here we provided a performance evaluation table that presents the results of different classification models applied to breast cancer diagnosis using rough set-based feature selection. Each model's accuracy, precision, recall, F1-score, and AUC-ROC metrics are shown, allowing for a comprehensive assessment of their capabilities. Let's delve into the discussion of these results:

Table 1. Experimental results for the different model classification.

Model	Accuracy	Precision	Recall	F1 Score	A-ROC
SVM	0.85	0.86	0.83	0.84	0.90
Neural-Network	0.87	0.88	0.86	0.87	0.91
Random Forest	0.88	0.87	0.89	0.88	0.92
Decision Tree	0.83	0.87	0.85	0.84	0.89

The SVM model achieved an accuracy of 0.85, indicating that it correctly classified 85% of instances. The precision of 0.86 signifies that among the instances predicted as positive, 86% were truly positive. The recall of 0.83 indicates that the model successfully identified 83% of the actual positive instances. The F1-score of 0.84, which is the harmonic mean of precision and recall, emphasizes a balanced performance. The AUCROC value of 0.90 indicates the model's ability to distinguish between positive and negative instances.

The Neural Network model achieved an accuracy of 0.87, slightly higher than the SVM. The precision of 0.88 suggests a strong positive predictive ability. The recall of 0.86 indicates that the model effectively captured 86% of the positive instances. The F1 score of 0.87 highlights a balanced trade-off between precision and recall. The AUCROC value of 0.91 reflects a strong ability to rank positive instances higher.

The Random Forest model performed best in terms of accuracy, with a score of 0.88. The precision of 0.87 denotes accurate positive predictions. The recall of 0.89 shows the model's capability to capture a high percentage of actual positive instances. The F1 score of 0.88 balances precision and recall effectively. The AUC-ROC value of 0.92 indicates good separation between positive and negative instances.

The Decision Tree model achieved an accuracy of 0.83, the lowest among the evaluated models.

The precision of 0.87 suggests accurate positive predictions. The recall of 0.85 reflects the model's ability to identify a substantial portion of positive instances. The F1-score of 0.84 indicates a balanced performance between precision and recall. The AUC-ROC value of 0.89 demonstrates good discrimination ability.

The Random Forest model achieved the highest accuracy, indicating its proficiency in distinguishing between cancerous and non-cancerous samples. Random Forest and Neural Network exhibited consistent and competitive performance across multiple metrics, indicating their robustness in breast cancer diagnosis. The Decision Tree model, while achieving relatively lower accuracy, still demonstrated good precision and recall values. It shows the relationship between the actual labels and the predicted labels made by the model. In this matrix, we have:

Two classes: Normal and Cancer.

The rows represent the actual labels.

The columns represent the predicted labels.

Let's break down the matrix:

High accuracy: The model correctly predicts 95% of the cases.

High precision and recall for Cancer: The model is very good at identifying Cancer with high precision (92.3%) and high recall (98%).

Low number of false positives and false negatives: There are only 4 false positives and 1 false negative, indicating the model has a good balance between precision and recall.

Overall, the model performs very well, especially in predicting Cancer accurately.

Table 2. Confusion Matrix.

		Predicted	
		0	1
Actual	0	47	4
	1	1	48

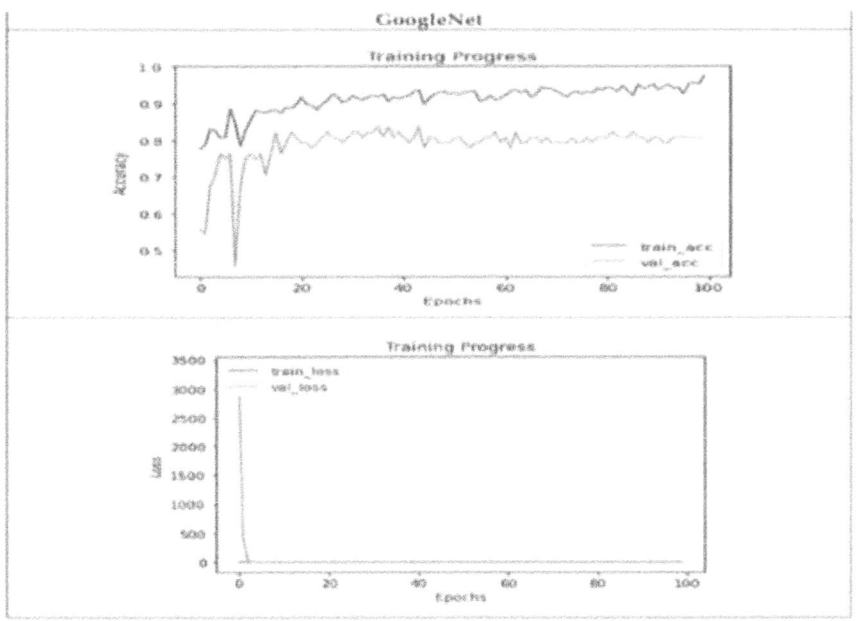

Fig. 2. Accuracy and loss diagram using GoogleNet

Table 3. Comparison of the suggested model with GoogleNet and ResNet.

DeepLearningModel	Precision	Recall	F1 Score	Loss	Accuracy
GoogleNet	0.861	0.870	0.851	0.592	0.870
ResNet	0.872	0.853	0.861	0.513	0.881
DNN R3_R5_R35	093	0.93	0.93	0.210	0.93

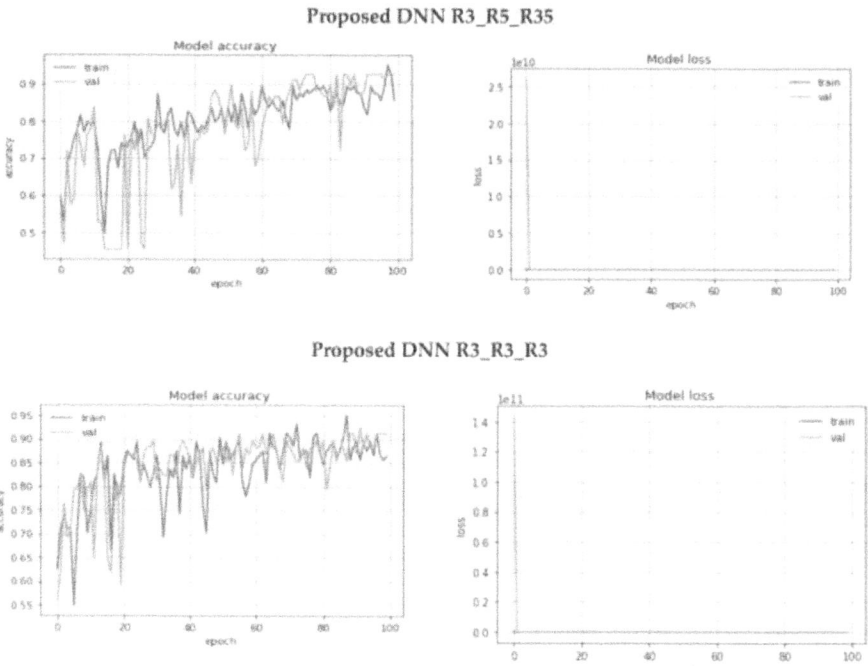

Fig. 3. Loss and Accuracy for the recommended models

Figure 2 shows the graphical accuracy and loss result of all Model classifiers using the training data set on the GoogleNet.

Figure 3 shows the graphical accuracy and loss result of our proposed model DNN R3_R5_R35 in the GoogleNet tool.

6 Conclusion

These results emphasize the efficacy of employing rough set-based feature selection in enhancing the performance of breast cancer classification models. The differences in performance between the models suggest that the neural network's complex architecture may be better suited for capturing intricate patterns in the data. The strong AUCROC values across the models suggest their ability to effectively rank the instances, an essential aspect of clinical decision-making. In conclusion, the discussion highlights the strengths and trade-offs of each model in diagnosing breast cancer using rough setbased feature selection. These insights contribute to a better understanding of the models' capabilities and can aid in selecting an appropriate approach for accurate breast cancer diagnosis. The improved performance indicates that rough set-based feature selection effectively identified discriminatory features, reducing noise and enhancing the models' ability to distinguish between cancerous and non-cancerous samples.

References

1. Pisano, E.D., et al.: Diagnostic performance of digital versus film mammography for breastcancer screening. N. Engl. J. Med. **353**(17), 1773–1783 (2005)
2. Berg, W.A., et al.: Combined screening with ultrasound and mammography vs mammography alone in women at elevated risk of breast cancer. JAMA **299**(18), 2151–2163 (2008)
3. Lehman, C.D., et al.: MRI evaluation of the contralateral breast in women with recently diagnosed breast cancer. N. Engl. J. Med. **356**(13), 1295–1303 (2007)
4. Rakha, E.A., et al.: Prognostic significance of Nottingham histologic grade in invasive breast carcinoma. J. Clin. Oncol. **26**(19), 3153–3158 (2008)
5. Kooi, T., et al.: Large scale deep learning for computer aided detection of mammographic lesions. Med. Image Anal. **35**, 303–312 (2017)
6. Shen, W., Zhou, M., Yang, F., Yang, C., Tian, J., Chen, H.: Multi-scale DCNNs for breast cancer metastasis prediction in histopathology images. IEEE Trans. Biomed. Eng. **66**(9), 2624–2633 (2019)
7. Madabhushi, A., Lee, G.: Image analysis and machine learning in digital pathology: challenges and opportunities. Med. Image Anal. **33**, 170–175 (2016)
8. Perou, C.M., et al.: Molecular portraits of human breast tumours. Nature **406**(6797), 747752 (2000)
9. Slamon, D.J., et al.: Use of chemotherapy plus a monoclonal antibody against HER2 for metastatic breast cancer that overexpresses HER2. N. Engl. J. Med. **344**(11), 783792 (2001)
10. Wang, X., Peng, Y., Lu, L., Lu, Z., Bagheri, M., Summers, R.M.: ChestX-ray8: hospital-scale chest X-ray database and benchmarks on weakly-supervised classification and localization of common thorax diseases. In: Proceedings of the IEEE Conference on Computer Vision and Pattern Recognition (CVPR), pp. 2097–2106 (2018)
11. Kosmia, L., et al.: Computer-aided breast cancer detection and classification in mammography: a comprehensive review. Comput. Biol. Med. **153**, 1–23 (2023)
12. Tan, M., Shen, D., Wu, G.: Multimodal medical image analysis with deep learning. IEEE Trans. Biomed. Eng. **66**(10), 2664–2675 (2019)
13. Yap, M.H., Pons, G., Marti, J., Ganau, S., Sentis, M., Zwiggelaar, R.: Automated breast ultrasound lesion detection using convolutional neural networks. IEEE J. Biomed. Health Inform. **24**(1), 253–259 (2019)
14. Coudray, N., et al.: Classification and mutation prediction from non–small cell lung cancer histopathology images using deep learning. Nat. Med. **24**(10), 1559–1567 (2018)
15. Li, J., Li, L., Wang, S., Yang, X., Zhang, X.: Breast cancer diagnosis using deep attention-based convolutional neural networks. Med. Phys. **47**(9), 3982–3993 (2020)
16. Huang, B., Yu, Q., Cheng, J.Z.: Deep learning with uncertainty estimation for breast cancer diagnosis based on ultrasound images. Med. Image Anal. **67**, 101832 (2021)

Advancing Time Series Forecasting: LSTM Networks with Multiple Attention Mechanisms

Abhishek Manchukonda[✉]

National Institute of Technology Warangal, Hanamkonda, India
abhishekmanchukonda@gmail.com

Abstract. Recently recurrent neural networks due to their ability to capture time-dependent features have been applied to time series forecasting showing important improvements with respect to previous methods. Simple RNN architectures though suffer from vanishing/exploding gradient problems and cannot discriminate exogenous series in case these are given as input. We examine the effectiveness of a solution that uses LSTM networks and multiple attention mechanisms by comparing it to simpler models, including an encoder architecture. Our analysis aims to showcase the outstanding performance of the proposed approach as its primary objective.

1 Preface and Related Work

Nonlinear autoregressive exogenous (NARX) models utilize historical data derived from previous $T-1$ principles of a given time series y, along with the current and previous T values of n other external time series $\mathbf{x}1, \mathbf{x}2, ..., \mathbf{x}_T$ ($\mathbf{x}_t \in \mathbb{R}^n$ and $\mathbf{x}_t = (x_t^1, x_t^2, ..., x_t^n)^\top$) to forecast the present criteria y_T. Here, T signifies the window size and $\mathbf{x}_t$ represents the values of each sequential data at a specific time point t. The objective of NARX models is to enable accurate predictions of y_T. The values $\mathbf{x}^k = (x_1^k, x_2^k, ..., x_T^k)$ signifies the values of the k-th exogenous time sequence within a given window. Exogenous time series are data that may be correlated to the series under consideration, so they are also called *driving series*. An effective NARX algorithm must possess the ability to determine which series are pertinent as driving factors when forecasting the present value of the target series. Furthermore, it should also be capable of capturing long-term temporal relationships to ensure reliable predictions over extended periods.

Nonlinear autoregressive exogenous (NARX) models have been pivotal in time series forecasting tasks, leveraging historical data from both the target series and external time series to make accurate predictions [3]. Traditional NARX models have been widely used in various domains, including finance, climate science, and engineering, due to their ability to capture temporal dependencies and incorporate exogenous factors [7].

However, the limitations of classic statistical models, such as linear regression and autoregressive models, become evident when faced with complex, nonlinear

H. K. et al. (Eds.): AIKP 2023, CCIS 2127, pp. 116–126, 2024.
https://doi.org/10.1007/978-3-031-68617-7_9

relationships and the challenge of identifying relevant driving factors [5]. These models often rely on predefined functional forms to capture nonlinearities, which may not fully capture the intricacies of real-world data. Consequently, their performance can be suboptimal in scenarios where data exhibit nonlinear dynamics.

Recent advances in deep learning have introduced innovative approaches to time series forecasting to address these limitations [2]. In this work, we delve into a deep learning model that combines recurrent neural networks (RNNs) with attention mechanisms, offering a promising solution to the challenges posed by NARX modeling [8]. RNNs, with their ability to capture sequential dependencies, have shown remarkable performance in various sequence-to-sequence tasks, making them a natural choice for time series forecasting [4].

Furthermore, attention mechanisms have emerged as a valuable addition to RNN architectures. They enable the model to focus on relevant parts of the input time series, effectively identifying the driving factors that influence the target series at each time step. This attention mechanism enhances the model's interpretability and its capacity to capture long-term temporal relationships, addressing a key challenge in NARX modeling.

We analyze a deep learning model in this work that addresses the two issues by utilizing recurrent neural networks along with a meticulously combined system of attention mechanisms. To assess the efficiency of the suggested approach and draw a comparison with other alternative methods employing recurrent networks to address the same issue, we conducted an ablation study that was absent in the initial authors' publication. While classic statistical models may be effective for certain real-world applications, they generally fall short when it comes to modeling nonlinear relationships and distinguishing between driving terms. Though some statistical models do attempt to model nonlinear relationships, they typically rely on predefined nonlinear relationships which may not accurately reflect the underlying relationship. As a result, the performance of such models is often suboptimal.

2 Dataset

We used the same datasets as the authors' in order to try to compare our results with the ones reported.

The SML 2010 dataset has the objective of predicting indoor temperatures. This data is obtained from sensors installed in a residential property for a period of 40 days, with data sampling occurring every minute. Additionally, the data has been smoothed using a 15-minute mean. The target series we select is the room temperature and we collect 17 driving series by filtering out series which are constant. To effectively train our model, we allocate 80 of the dataset for this purpose, and divide the remaining 20 equally between validation and testing.

The second dataset is the NASDAQ 100 Stock dataset which is characterised by a larger number of driving series and stronger variations. For the examination of the NASDAQ 100 index's worth, we employed a dataset encompassing the prices of 81 well-known companies featured on the NASDAQ 100. These prices were compiled as time series data. This dataset has been made publicly available by the original creators of the paper. The data has been sampled every minute, over a period of 105 days. To develop the model, 80 of the dataset was utilized for training, while the remainder of the data was split equally between the validation and test sets.

The two datasets are converted into contiguous windows of predetermined size T, with a stride length of 1, where the final target value in the series is the one of interest for prediction.

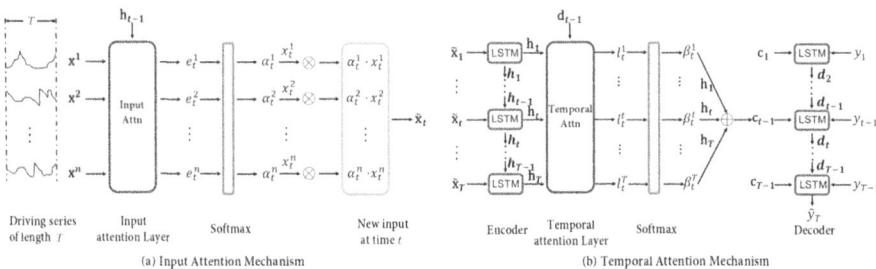

(a) Input Attention Mechanism   (b) Temporal Attention Mechanism

Fig. 1. DA-RNN model

3   Dual-Stage Attention Model

The proposed model of the reference paper, which is illustrated in Fig. 1, introduces two attention mechanisms in a LSTM-based encoder and decoder architecture. The first attention, *Input Attention*, is trained to independently weight the driving series at each timestep producing

$$(\tilde{\mathbf{x}}_1, \tilde{\mathbf{x}}_2, ..., \tilde{\mathbf{x}}_T) = A_{in}((\mathbf{x}_1, \mathbf{x}_2, ..., \mathbf{x}_T)) = (\boldsymbol{\alpha}_1 \odot \mathbf{x}_1, \boldsymbol{\alpha}_2 \odot \mathbf{x}_2, ..., \boldsymbol{\alpha}_T \odot \mathbf{x}_T)$$

with $\boldsymbol{\alpha}_i \in \mathbb{R}^n$. By using the weighted driving series, we are able to identify which series have greater significance for predicting the target series. From there, the weighted driving series are then fed into a one-layer LSTM encoder, with the hidden states being utilized within an Input Attention mechanism.

During each time step, the encoder maps to a path $\mathbf{h}_t \in \mathbb{R}^m$, symbolizing the LSTM's concealed condition at that specific moment, as explained by Graves and Schmidhuber (2005). The procedures engaged in this mapping can be observed as modifications to the LSTM cell, which can be succinctly outlined as displayed:

$$\begin{aligned}
\mathbf{f}_t &= \sigma(\mathbf{W}_f[\mathbf{h}_{t-1}; \tilde{\mathbf{x}}_t] + \mathbf{b}_f) \\
\mathbf{i}_t &= \sigma(\mathbf{W}_i[\mathbf{h}_{t-1}; \tilde{\mathbf{x}}_t] + \mathbf{b}_i) \\
\mathbf{o}_t &= \sigma(\mathbf{W}_o[\mathbf{h}_{t-1}; \tilde{\mathbf{x}}_t] + \mathbf{b}_o) \\
\mathbf{s}_t &= \mathbf{f}_t \odot \mathbf{s}_t + \mathbf{i}_t \odot \tanh(\mathbf{W}_s[\mathbf{h}_{t-1}; \tilde{\mathbf{x}}_t] + \mathbf{b}_s) \\
\mathbf{h}_t &= \mathbf{o}_t \odot \tanh(\mathbf{s}_t)
\end{aligned} \qquad (1)$$

As delineated by Graves and Schmidhuber in their 2005 publication, the modification process includes combining the concealed state from the preceding time step with the input received at the present time step, accomplished through concatenation, symbolized as $[\mathbf{h}_{t-1}; \tilde{\mathbf{x}}_t] \in \mathbb{R}^{m+n}$. Additionally, there are several parameters specific to the LSTM cell to learn, including $\mathbf{W}_f, \mathbf{W}_i, \mathbf{W}_o, \mathbf{W}_s \in \mathbb{R}^{m \times (m+n)}$ and $\mathbf{b}_f, \mathbf{b}_i, \mathbf{b}_o, \mathbf{b}_s \in \mathbb{R}^m$. The logistic sigmoid function, denoted by σ, and the element-wise multiplication operator, $\odot$, are utilized in this process.

An innovative attention mechanism named, *Temporal Attention*, has been introduced. It facilitates an adaptive method of selecting the pertinent veiled status of the encoder by utilizing temporal increment windows. The outcome of this approach yields:

$$(\mathbf{c}_1, \mathbf{c}_2, ..., \mathbf{c}_T) = A_{temp}((\mathbf{h}_1, \mathbf{h}_2, ..., \mathbf{h}_T)) = \left(\sum_{i=1}^{T} \beta_1^i \mathbf{h}_i, \sum_{i=1}^{T} \beta_2^i \mathbf{h}_i, ..., \sum_{i=1}^{T} \beta_T^i \mathbf{h}_i \right)$$

and the encoder's i-th hidden state significance for prediction purposes is denoted by the variable β_t^i.

When $t = T$, the amalgamated vector of the "attended" encoder concealed state, $\mathbf{c}_t$, and the decoder's concealed state is directed through two dense layers to acquire the projected value. Before this stage, the "attended" encoder's hidden state at the t-th moment is combined with the input quantity y_t. Following this, the amalgamated result is passed through a dense stratum before being introduced into the decoder.

For the Input Attention, the following operations are taken to obtain the weights α_t^k

$$e_t^k = \mathbf{v}_e^\top \tanh(\mathbf{W_e}[\mathbf{h}_{t-1}; \mathbf{s}_{t-1}] + \mathbf{U_e}\mathbf{x}^k), \qquad 1 \leq k \leq n$$

$$\alpha_t^k = \frac{\exp(e_t^k)}{\sum_{i=1}^{n} \exp(e_t^i)},$$

where $\mathbf{h}_{t-1}, \mathbf{s}_{t-1}$ are the concealed and cellular conditions of the encoder, $\mathbf{x}^k$ is one driving series, $\mathbf{v}_e \in \mathbb{R}^T, \mathbf{W}_e \in \mathbb{R}^{T \times 2m}$ and $\mathbf{U}_e \in \mathbb{R}^{T \times T}$ (with m the hidden size of the encoder) are learnable parameters.

For the Temporal Attention, the following operations are taken to obtain the weights β_t^i

$$l_t^i = \mathbf{v}_d^\top \tanh(\mathbf{W_d}[\mathbf{d}_{t-1}; \mathbf{s}_{t-1}'] + \mathbf{U_d}\mathbf{h}_i), \qquad 1 \leq i \leq T$$

$$\beta_t^i = \frac{\exp(l_t^i)}{\sum_{i=1}^{n} \exp(e_t^i)},$$

where $\mathbf{d}_{t-1}, \mathbf{s}_{t-1}' \in \mathbb{R}^p$ are the hidden and cell states of the decoder, $\mathbf{h}_i$ is the i-th hidden state of the encoder, $\mathbf{v}_d \in \mathbb{R}^m, \mathbf{W}_d \in \mathbb{R}^{m \times 2p}$ and $\mathbf{U}_d \in \mathbb{R}^{m \times m}$ (with p the hidden size of the decoder) are learnable parameters.

3.1   Implementation Details

We used Tensorflow 1.12 as the target framework to implement the model just described. The reason behind this choice is that we could easily translate the equations of the model directly into the code and define each step of the model pragmatically.

For the encoder network we used the LSTMCell class from `tensorflow.python.ops.rnn_cell_impl`. At the outset, we initialized a null-state for both the cell and the hidden states. As the next step, we created computational graph nodes for each timestep. More specifically, we generated nodes for the input attention implementation and the LSTMCell. The latter takes the previous timestep's hidden state and the output from input attention mechanism as its input. As we generated the nodes, we gathered and stored the output hidden states of the cell across all timesteps. Finally, these hidden states were reshaped and used as input for the Temporal Attention mechanism.

Within the decoder network's implementation, we began by assigning a null state to both the cell and the hidden states. We then defined the nodes for the Temporal Attention mechanism. At time t, the target series value is concatenated with the output from the Temporal Attention mechanism. The amalgamated vector is subsequently transmitted through a dense layer, and the resulting output is employed to revise the concealed state of the decoder within the LSTMCell. Regarding y_T, indicating the value to be anticipated, the "attended" encoder's covert condition at the specific moment T is combined with the ultimate concealed state of the decoder. The resultant amalgamated vector is subsequently passed through two densely connected layers to reach the projected output.

To make the experimentation modular we defined a data class that loads all the parameters and file paths from JSON configuration files.

Initially, in order to ensure the correctness of the formulas being implemented we used the Eager Execution model offered by Tensorflow which allows to easily debug and quickly iterate over the core of the model.

We used Tensorboard to graphically visualize the value of the loss across the training steps and the values of the evaluation metrics on the validation set at every epoch of training.

In conclusion, we leveraged the checkpointing capabilities offered by the framework to store two distinct sets of values: the data that would be required to resume training in a subsequent run, and the weights of the model that performed the best across all evaluation rounds. For the final testing, we loaded the weights of the best-performing model, even if it had trained for longer periods and possibly resulted in overfitting. This complete process allowed us to achieve the highest possible accuracy while minimizing computational time and resources.

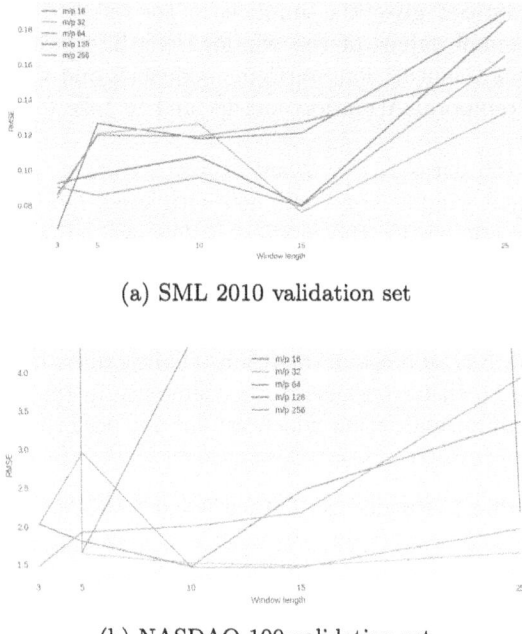

(a) SML 2010 validation set

(b) NASDAQ 100 validation set

Fig. 2. This depicts the RMSE score throughout the dataset for different window lengths T, as well as encoder and decoder hidden state dimensions m and p respectively.

3.2 Hyper Parameter Tuning

We validated our implementation using the same set of metrics as the original authors (RMSE, MAE, MAPE) and we performed some hyper-parameter tuning running the training with different configuration files.

Throughout the experiments, we trained all models for a consistent 150 epochs. For expedited training, we utilized two Adam optimizers, one for the encoder and another for the decoder. The objective function employed for training was Mean Squared Error. We used a starting learning rate of 0.001 and implemented exponential decay. Remnant of possible exploding gradients mess up the parameter during training, we applied gradient clipping. The models trained on the SML 2010 dataset were trained with batch size 32 while the ones trained on NASDAQ 100 with batch size 128. In every occurrence, an exploration throughout a grid is carried out $T \in \{3, 5, 10, 15, 25\}$ and $m = p \in \{16, 32, 64, 128, 256\}$. After evaluating the model's performance on the validation set, the best-performing model is then selected for further analysis. In Fig. 2 the RMSE scores as the parameters vary are shown. The other scores (MAE, MAPE) follow a similar trend. As can be noticed, in general better scores are achieved for small window size and as it grows a drop in performance arises which is typical of encoder decoder networks [1].

For SML 2010 dataset, given the simplicity of the series to predict, the RMSE is small even for small values of the window length. However, since a small window length cannot capture long-term dependencies and will also weaken the usefulness of the Temporal Attention, we decided to take for test $T = 15$ and $m = p = 32$.

For NASDAQ 100 dataset, $T = 3$ and $m = p = 16$ or $m = p = 32$ have high RMSE, since a small window size combined with small hidden state sizes does not result effective enough for the prediction. For evaluation we take the ones that achieves the best performance, $T = 15$ and $m = p = 256$.

After we have obtained a good hyper-parameters setting for the various models we compare their performance on our reference datasets. In Table 1 we show the scores achieved. As can be seen, the results slightly differ from the ones of the authors which can be either because of the difference in the number of epochs or because of a data normalisation which we did not perform.

Table 1. Results over SML2010 and NASDAQ100

	Train			Validation			Test		
	RMSE	MAE	MAPE	RMSE	MAE	MAPE	RMSE	MAE	MAPE
NASDAQ100	1.7095	0.9537	0.01991	1.4689	0.9550	0.0198	1.5810	1.0477	0.0212
SML2010	0.0644	0.0434	0.2279	0.0763	0.0601	0.2561	0.0863	0.0666	0.3248

As depicted in Fig. 3, the outcome of the predictions is revealed. It is evident that the model generates a forecast that corresponds closely to the final observed value of the target series, albeit with minor fluctuations.

3.3 Ablation Study

The efficacy and accuracy of the dual-stage attention approach is confirmed through an ablation study of the model. We present the values of the resulting three systems and compare them against the model with both attention mechanisms active, in tandem with the aforementioned hyperparameters. We notice that here we include the temporal-attention-only model together with the input-attention-only model that was not evaluated in our original reference paper.

In Fig. 4 the comparison between the model without any attention mechanism, without the temporal attention and without the input attention respectively is shown against the line representing the dual attention model of the authors'.

Figure 4a shows that the temporal attention is ineffective for this task (green bar and red line representing models with temporal attention enabled higher than models where the temporal attention is disabled). This is probably due to the sinusoidal shape of the target series of which timesteps have equal importance.

Figure 4b functions as a visual representation showcasing the effectiveness of the two-stage attention mechanism. When applied to the NASDAQ100 dataset,

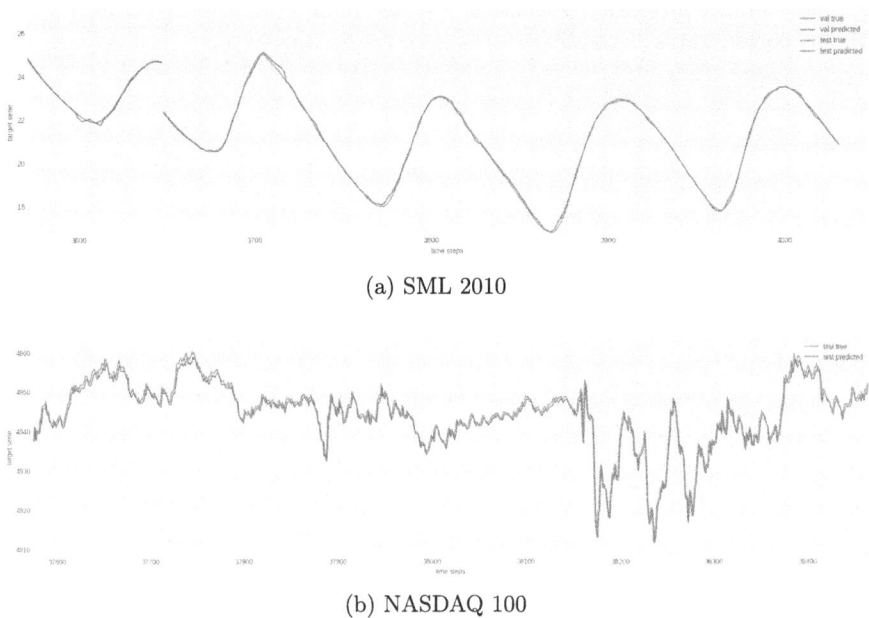

(a) SML 2010

(b) NASDAQ 100

Fig. 3. Predicted time series and true time series plotted for portions of the time steps

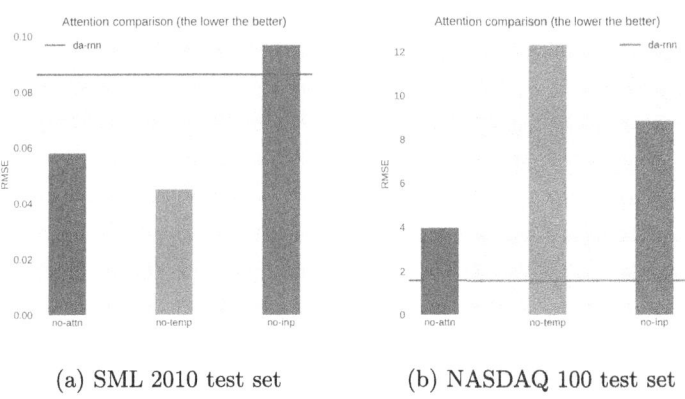

(a) SML 2010 test set   (b) NASDAQ 100 test set

Fig. 4. Assessment of the model's performances while deactivating the attention mechanisms. The red line shows the RMSE score of the model with both attentions (input and temporal attention) enabled. In blue the RMSE score with both the input and temporal attentions disabled. In orange the score with only the temporal attention disabled and in green the score with only the input attention disabled. Similar plots for the other metrics.

models that lack either of the attention mechanisms struggle to yield significant outcomes. This is primarily because of the vast number of driving series coupled with the considerable variability of the series over timesteps.

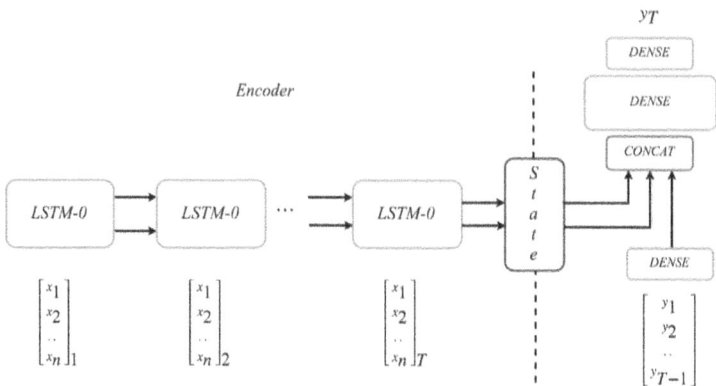

Fig. 5. Encoder model

4   Simple Encoder Network Baseline

In this paragraph we introduce a simple model we used as a baseline.

We initially developed a model composed of an encoder and a decoder with the goal of producing a network that could be easily extended to a multistep-ahead environment where we could predict accurately the future values for more than a single timestep. The encoder of this original network was composed of two stacked LSTM layers, taking as input the driving series' sequence, and we collected the final hidden state and cell state of each layer that were used as the initial states for the decoder. In order to directly make use of the encoder states, it was essential to ensure that the dimension of the hidden state and the count of layers in the decoder were aligned with those in the encoder. Next, we provided the decoder LSTM with a vector containing the historical observations of the targeted sequence. In cases of multi-step prediction, we fed the vector data corresponding to the precise number of forecasted timesteps. The decoder's hidden states were ultimately directed to a dense layer to finally obtain the predictions.

The struggles encountered by this network in accurately predicting values for the NASDAQ 100 dataset were disheartening (although the model still performed well on the SML 2010 dataset) we decided to make the network simpler focusing only on the single step target series value forecasting. Given this choice we dropped completely the decoder part replacing it with two feed-forward neural networks. The first one is composed of one dense layer and it is used to encode the target series history. The second mechanism revolves around the fusion of the encoder output and the ultimate cell state from the LSTM iteration with the output of the alternate network. Subsequently, this merged output is utilized to predict the values of the targeted sequence.

The encoder network was mostly left unchanged but we reduced the number of LSTM layers from 2 to 1; the choice of keeping the encoder makes sense since we still want to capture time dependencies in the driving series and encode this information in a fixed size representation. On the other hand the window of past values is considered altogether applying a dense layer to the input vector. The complete architecture is shown in Fig. 5.

4.1 Implementation Details

For this simple encoder model we took advantage of Keras interface. We instantiated a `LSTMCell` and gave it as argument to a `RNN` layer. Using the functional API we applied this layer to the driving series' input and collected the final state. We set the size of the output equal to 128. As in the original architecture the input to the LSTM at each timestep is a vector of n values of the n driving series values in that timestep.

The encoder last hidden and cell states were concatenated to the values of the past history of the target series, after being fed to the dense layer with output size 64. The concatenation is passed to two final `Dense` layers, of output size respectively 256 and 1, with the last one being the predicted value.

We defined a callback in the `fit()` function call to make the training stop if the value of the loss doesn't improve for a certain number of consecutive steps (the level of patience was empirically adjusted).

We trained for a total of 100 epochs with an Adam optimizer without any learning rate decay, with input window size $T = 10$.

4.2 Results

The results in Table 2 demonstrate that the scores obtained for various metrics are lower than those generated by the dual-stage attention RNN discussed earlier. This validates the ideas by the original authors and finally justifies the complexity of the network with an improvement in the performance.

Table 2. Results over SML2010 and NASDAQ100

	Train			Validation			Test		
	RMSE	MAE	MAPE	RMSE	MAE	MAPE	RMSE	MAE	MAPE
NASDAQ100	4.5726	3.5723	0.0744	4.0200	3.1977	0.0658	4.0803	3.1980	0.0647
SML2010	0.1049	0.0746	0.3858	0.1714	0.1714	0.5728	0.1026	0.0750	0.3497

5 Culmination

The present study involved an analysis of the research carried out in [6]. Specifically, we recreated the dual-stage attention mechanism, constructing a model that is capable of identifying pertinent driving series as well as relevant time steps within the previous time window. We conducted an array of experiments and presented the results. These experiments included a comprehensive ablation study of the original attention-based model, along with the creation of a new baseline model that utilizes a basic encoder and a series of feed-forward networks. When executing our implementations, we employed contemporary APIs at both the low-level (Tensorflow) and high-level (Keras functional API). We prioritized the development of modular and comprehensible code, with the aim of facilitating the replication of the results showcased in this study.

References

1. Cho, K., Van Merriënboer, B., Bahdanau, D., Bengio, Y.: On the properties of neural machine translation: encoder-decoder approaches. arXiv preprint arXiv:1409.1259 (2014)
2. Gamboa, J.C.B.: Deep learning for time-series analysis. arXiv preprint arXiv:1701.01887 (2017)
3. Kuranga, C., Pillay, N.: A comparative study of nonlinear regression and autoregressive techniques in hybrid with particle swarm optimization for time-series forecasting. Expert Syst. Appl. **190**, 116163 (2022)
4. Lindemann, B., Müller, T., Vietz, H., Jazdi, N., Weyrich, M.: A survey on long short-term memory networks for time series prediction. Procedia CIRP **99**, 650–655 (2021)
5. Murray-Smith, R., Johansen, T.: Multiple Model Approaches to Nonlinear Modelling and Control. CRC Press, Boca Raton (2020)
6. Qin, Y., Song, D., Chen, H., Cheng, W., Jiang, G., Cottrell, G.: A dual-stage attention-based recurrent neural network for time series prediction. arXiv preprint arXiv:1704.02971 (2017)
7. Wunsch, A., Liesch, T., Broda, S.: Groundwater level forecasting with artificial neural networks: a comparison of long short-term memory (LSTM), convolutional neural networks (CNNs), and non-linear autoregressive networks with exogenous input (NARX). Hydrol. Earth Syst. Sci. **25**(3), 1671–1687 (2021)
8. Yin, X., Han, Y., Sun, H., Xu, Z., Yu, H., Duan, X.: A multivariate time series prediction schema based on multi-attention in recurrent neural network. In: 2020 IEEE Symposium on Computers and Communications (ISCC), pp. 1–7. IEEE (2020)

Trajectory Tracking and Navigation Model for Autonomous Vehicles Using Reinforcement Learning

G. Ramani, C. Karthik$^{(\boxtimes)}$, B. Pranay, D. Pramodh, and B. Karthik Reddy

B V Raju Institute of Technology, Narsapur, Medak 502313, India
21211a0548@bvrit.ac.in

Abstract. A potential answer to the issues of traffic accidents and congestion is presently autonomous driving. Even though it is operated without a human driver, an autonomous vehicle must emulate human driving habits. Because human drivers will be more motivated to trust autonomous driving systems, driving safety may increase as a result. A mixed trajectory scheduling and monitoring approach is used by the vehicle control system in this investigation. Firstly, traffic patterns and driving practises are modelled using the Artificial Potential Field (APF) method. Next, such APF values are used into the Model Predictive Control (MPC) design technique, which may enhance the control outputs and trajectory. This allows the controlled car to function while being influenced by traffic conditions and driving preferences by incorporating human driving patterns and preferences into the controller. Through simulation tests, the effectiveness of autonomous driving is assessed in two situations lane switching and vehicle following that represent two opposing driving philosophies among human drivers a cautious stance and an aggressive one. These results also demonstrate that the suggested algorithm is adequate to account for driving behaviours. This special controller can therefore be applied to the field of autonomous vehicle control.

Keywords: APF (Artificial Potential Field) · MPC (Model Predictive Control) · integrative models · field of autonomous vehicle control

1 Introduction

Land vehicles that can navigate and run on their own without human assistance are referred to as autonomous land vehicles or driverless cars. To sense the surroundings and make judgements based on that perception, they use a variety of sensors and software. Autonomous land vehicles' main objectives are to boost safety, lessen traffic, and boost transit effectiveness. The environment is seen by autonomous land vehicles using a range of sensors, such as cameras, radar, GPS, and lidar. Together, these sensors provide a precise and complete map of the area around the car, including other cars, people walking about, and traffic lights.

The software of the car utilizes this data to figure out where to move around the area. This includes determining the appropriate speed, lane position, and when to stop or turn.

H. K. et al. (Eds.): AIKP 2023, CCIS 2127, pp. 127–145, 2024.
https://doi.org/10.1007/978-3-031-68617-7_10

The software is based on complex algorithms and machine learning models that can analyze large amounts of data in real-time and adjust the vehicle's behavior accordingly. There are several benefits to autonomous land vehicles. One of the primary benefits is increased safety. Autonomous vehicles can make decisions and react faster than humans, which can reduce the risk of accidents. They can also communicate with other vehicles on the road, which can help prevent collisions and reduce traffic congestion.

Another benefit of autonomous vehicles is increased mobility. Autonomous vehicles can offer a level of independence and freedom that was previously unattainable to people who are unable to drive, such as the old or crippled. Autonomous vehicles can also reduce traffic congestion, as they are able to navigate more efficiently and avoid traffic jams. However, there are also challenges to the widespread adoption of autonomous land vehicles. One of the biggest challenges is ensuring the safety of the vehicles. While autonomous vehicles have the potential to be safer than human-driven vehicles, there have been several high-profile accidents involving autonomous vehicles, which has raised concerns about their safety. Another challenge is the cost of the technology.

The sensors, software, and hardware required for autonomous vehicles can be expensive, which can make them inaccessible for many people. The development of driverless land vehicles has advanced significantly in spite of these obstacles. Many systems are already in use for tracking the trajectory of autonomous land vehicles. These technologies include PID control, model predictive control (MPC), linear quadratic regulator (LQR), nonlinear model predictive control (NMPC), and adaptive control.

A common control algorithm is PID control, which modifies steering and throttle inputs to reduce error between the desired trajectory and the present condition of the vehicle. MPC represents a more advanced monitoring technique that computes a control input that minimizes a cost function across the expected trajectory of the vehicle using a dynamic model of the vehicle and its environment to predict its trajectory over time. A linear model of the vehicle is used by the LQR control algorithm to determine the best control inputs to minimize a quadratic cost function. NMPC is a more advanced version of MPC that can handle nonlinear dynamics and constraints. It uses a nonlinear model of the vehicle and its environment to predict its trajectory over time and then computes a control input that minimizes a cost function over this predicted trajectory.Finally, autonomous land automobiles are poised to revolutionize transportation by enhancing mobility, safety, and efficiency. While there are still difficulties to be solved, such as security issues.

2 Literature Survey

The paper suggests a trajectory planning method for automated cars that uses splines: cooperative driving. The suggested approach views trajectory planning as a non-linear optimization problem with the goal of minimizing a cost function while considering limitations like vehicle dynamics and collision avoidance. Comfort, energy efficiency, and safety-related terms are included in the cost function. The authors provide a distributed algorithm that enables cooperative driving by allowing each vehicle to determine its own trajectory while also paying attention to the trajectories of many cars nearby. The dynamic optimization problem is formulated as a consensus optimization problem and solved via a decentralized optimization method to accomplish this [1].

In order to increase driving comfort and safety, the article suggests a combined trajectory forecasting and monitoring service for automated cars that takes into account various driving behaviors. The suggested strategy takes into account several driving behaviors, such as lateral motion, acceleration, and deceleration, as a set of desired parameters. Using a machine learning technique, the driving style characteristics are learned from a dataset of human driving behaviors. The trajectory prediction and surveillance issue is then presented as an optimization issue that seeks to minimize a cost function that takes into account both comfort and driving efficiency indicators. An inner current control system is employed to monitor the intended trajectory in order to guarantee that the autonomous vehicle follows it precisely. The control system considers the dynamic model of the vehicle, sensor noise, and actuator restrictions [2].

The paper proposes an interaction-aware probabilistic action policy (IAP) for planning autonomous driving behavior in complex traffic scenarios.The paper proposes an interaction-aware probabilistic action policy (IAP) for planning autonomous driving behavior in complex traffic scenarios. The IAP model represents the behavior of the autonomous vehicle as a probabilistic distribution over a set of actions that can be taken in a given traffic scenario. The distribution is learned from a dataset of human driving behaviors using a machine learning algorithm. The IAP model takes into account both the local traffic context and the predicted future behavior of other road users.

To ensure that the planned actions are feasible, the IAP model is integrated into a model predictive control (MPC) framework, which takes into account the vehicle's dynamic constraints and environment uncertainties. The MPC framework generates a sequence of control inputs that track the planned action distribution while optimizing a cost function that balances safety, efficiency, and comfort [3].

A survey of virtual odometry (VO) solutions for automated driving in adverse situations and settings, such as low visibility and poor GPS signal.VO is a method of estimating vehicle motion by matching features in successive images from a camera or a set of cameras mounted on the vehicle. The paper presents a comprehensive review of existing VO methods and their applications in various challenging scenarios, including urban environments, offroad terrain, and adverse weather conditions. There are challenges and limitations of VO methods, such as the need for accurate camera calibration, the requirement for sufficient visual features, and the susceptibility to illumination changes and motion blur [4].

A overview of virtual odometry (VO) solutions for automated steering in difficult situations and settings, like low visibility, is provided in this work. The research provides a Frenet-frame-free Cartesian-based method for trajectory planning when driving autonomously on hills, which is not often used in conventional methods. The proposed method uses a dynamic programming algorithmto generate a set of candidate trajectories in a Cartesian space that minimizes a cost function that balances safety, comfort, and efficiency. The algorithm takes into account the vehicle's dynamic constraints and the road geometry to ensure that the planned trajectories are feasible and safe. To improve the robustness of the method, the authors introduce a dynamic collision avoidance algorithm that detects and avoids potential collisions with other road users in real-time. The collision avoidance algorithm uses a sensor fusion technique to integrate information from different sensor modalities, such as lidar and radar, to accurately detect and track nearby objects [5].

The study offers an overview on the application of deep reinforcement learning (DRL) for selfdriving vehicles positioning system. The survey examines numerous DRL-based motion planning strategies, including model-free and model-based methodologies, valuation and policy-based strategies, and hybrid strategies that combine DRL with other planning techniques. The authors also discuss the challenges and limitations of DRL for motion planning, such as the need for a lot of information, the complexity of achieving safe and robust policies, and the lack of interpretability and explainability. The paper presents a comprehensive review of existing research on DRL-based motion planning in various driving scenarios, including highway driving, urban driving, and off-road driving. The authors also discuss the potential of DRL for real-world applications, such as systems for self-driving cars and systems for intelligent transportation [6].

The study offers an autopilot trajectory design and management strategy to steer clear of stationary objects in busy traffic. The proposed method consists of two components: a trajectory planning algorithm that generates collision-free paths in real-time, and a robust control strategy that tracks the planned trajectory while ensuring stability and performance. The trajectory planning algorithm uses a combination of potential field and model predictive control techniques to generate safe and efficient paths while considering the dynamic constraints of the vehicle and the traffic environment. The robust control strategy uses a nonlinear control method to regulate the vehicle's motion while compensating for modeling errors and external disturbances. To evaluate the proposed method, the authors conduct experiments on a test vehicle in a simulated environment with static obstacles and dynamic traffic [7].

The study introduces a novel method that combines consecutive game theory and neural networks to identify a secure path for a collection of autonomous cars. The 2 primary parts of the suggested method are as follows: a sequential game algorithm that determines the optimal trajectory for each vehicle while considering the behavior of the other vehicles, and a neural network that determines the future course of the other cars using their current motion and the environment. The sequential game algorithm uses a combination of backward induction and value iteration to determine the optimal trajectory for each vehicle while ensuring safety and efficiency. The neural network models the temporal relationships of the movements of the other cars and makes highly accurate predictions about their future trajectories using a neural network with a recurrent design [8].

The authors of the research suggest a hierarchical reinforcement learning-based paradigm for trajectory planning in autonomous vehicles.Multiple levels of abstraction are used in hierarchical reinforcement learning to handle challenging tasks. In this situation, the higher-level policy develops the ability to create high-level objectives or subtasks, while the lower-level policy develops the ability to create low-level operations to accomplish those objectives. The main topic of the paper is trajectory planning, which entails creating a series of instructions or directives to guide the autonomous vehicle through its surroundings.

Long-term planning and short-term control are both incorporated into the authors' hierarchical strategy [9].

In this study, transformer network-based multi-modal maneuver and trajectory tracking for automated vehicles is presented. The proposed method consists of a transformer-based encoder-decoder architecture that predicts the future motion of other road users in the form of multimodal distributions over possible trajectories. The transformer network is trained on a substantial collection of actual worlds driving scenarios, including different types of manoeuvres and driving behaviors, to learn the spatiotemporal patterns and context of the motion of other road users. The predicted multimodal distributions are then used to generate safe and efficient trajectories for the autonomous vehicle while considering the uncertainty and variability of the predicted motion of the other road users. To evaluate the proposed method, the authors conduct experiments on a simulated environment with different traffic scenarios, including different types of manoeuvres and driving behaviors [10].

3   Problem Statement

- Human error: Factors like driving while distracted, driving too fast, driving while intoxicated, and driving while fatigued account for the great majority of traffic accidents. In order to make safer and wiser driving decisions, autonomous cars rely on cuttingedge sensors, artificial intelligence, and algorithms.
- Fatigue and drowsiness are major causes of accidents, especially during nighttime driving or lengthy commutes. Driver weariness is not a problem for autonomous vehicles, which can drive for extended periods of time without performance degradation.
- Congestion: A serious issue in many cities throughout the world, traffic congestion causes wasted time, higher fuel usage, and more pollution. By enhancing the flow of traffic, cooperating with other vehicles, and applying sophisticated route planning algorithms, autonomous automobiles have the potential to lessen congestion.

Hence, our primary motive is to develop an autonomous model to counter the above problems.

4   Objectives

1) Tracking: Develop an autonomous driving system that can accurately track a desired trajectory while adhering to safety constraints and avoiding obstacles using a reinforcement learning algorithm to be more accessible to disabled and old people.
2) Optimize Trajectory: Using a reinforcement learning algorithm, optimize the trajectory of an autonomous vehicle while taking into account numerous aspects such as daily commute, fuel consumption, passenger comfort.
3) Pattern Adaptation: Enable autonomous vehicles to adapt to changing road conditions and traffic patterns by learning from past driving experiences using a reinforcement learning algorithm providing optimized routes and reduce traffic congestion.

5 Existing Work

In the realm of autonomous driving, a wide range of models and algorithms are employed to facilitate self-driving capabilities. These models cover various aspects of autonomous driving, including perception, decision-making, control, and mapping. Perception models play a crucial role in autonomous vehicles' ability to understand and interpret their environment. One commonly used model is the Convolutional Neural Network (CNN), which is adept at analyzing camera images and LiDAR point clouds. CNNs are trained to detect and classify objects, identify lane markings, and segment the environment into different regions. By leveraging deep learning techniques, these perception models enable vehicles to gain a comprehensive understanding of their surroundings, detect obstacles, and make informed decisions based on the perceived information.

Prediction models, which concentrate on predicting the behavior of other road users and objects, are another crucial element in autonomous driving. For autonomous cars to travel in a secure and efficient manner, it is essential to anticipate the motions, intentions, and interactions of pedestrians, vehicles, and bicycles. Prediction models frequently employ RNN's and LSTM networks. They leverage sequential data, such as historical sensor readings, to capture temporal dependencies and predict future trajectories. By analyzing past movements and behaviors, the prediction models enable autonomous vehicles to anticipate potential hazards, plan their actions, and adjust their driving strategies accordingly. This capability enhances the safety and efficiency of autonomous driving systems by enabling proactive decision-making and response to dynamic road conditions.

6 Proposed Work

This project aims to implement the Deep Q-Network (DQN) algorithm for resolving Markov Decision Processes (MDPs) within the context of autonomous driving. MDPs offer a mathematical structure to model difficulties with judgment in autonomous systems. The DQN algorithm, a form of deep reinforcement learning, is utilized to roughly define the Q-function. In this research, the Q-values are estimated using a neural network using a 64×3 CNN structure, representing the expected rewards for each action in a given state. By leveraging this information, the agent can make informed decisions and improve its driving performance.

The CARLA simulator, an open-source autonomous driving platform, is utilized to create a realistic driving environment. CARLA offers a Python API that enables seamless interaction with the simulated environment, including various scenarios with diverse weather conditions, locations, and sensor configurations. The environment is designed to represent the world, while actors such as vehicles, sensors, and blueprints possess specific attributes. By employing CARLA, the project allows for comprehensive testing and evaluation of the autonomous driving agent's performance under different conditions. During training, the algorithm stores the agent's experiences in a replay buffer and samples random batches of experiences for training purposes. The car, acting as the agent, is allowed to move randomly, with collisions incurring costs and successful right maneuvers being rewarded. The system picks up new information from feedback provided by rewards and punishments. Continuously improving its decision-making capabilities. The model's performance is visualized and analyzed using TensorBoard, a visualization tool in TensorFlow. The aim is to train the model to become an exemplary autonomous land vehicle by enhancing its reward values and reducing its loss values through iterations of training.

In summary, this project leverages the DQN algorithm and a 64×3 CNN architecture to tackle MDPs in the field of autonomous driving. The CARLA simulator provides a realistic environment for testing and evaluating the agent's performance. Through reinforcement learning, the algorithm learns from experiences, makes decisions based on Q-values, and refines its behavior. TensorBoard facilitates the visualization of key performance metrics. The ultimate objective is to train the model to embody the characteristics of an ideal autonomous land vehicle, exhibiting improved driving capabilities in various scenarios.

7   Methods

A. *Deep Q-Network (DQN):*
   The DQN algorithm, proposed by Mnih et al. in 2015, is a powerful approach that combines reinforcement learning techniques with deep neural networks. It forms the foundation of this project on autonomous driving. The DQN algorithm is based on the principle of Q-learning, where an agent learns a policy to maximize cumulative rewards by iteratively interacting with an environment. To calculate the Q-values for various actions in a given state, the Q-network, a deep neural network, is employed. By updating the Q-network's parameters based on the TD-error (Temporal Difference error) calculated using the Bellman equation, the agent gradually improves its decision-making capabilities (Figs. 1 and 2).

B. *Convolutional Neural Network (CNN):*
   The chosen model architecture for this project is the 64x3 CNN model (Fig. 3). The CNN model is widely utilized in computer vision applications, including object recognition, categorisation of images, and now, autonomous driving. It consists of multiple convolutional layers that employ filters to capture spatial features in the input images. These layers utilize the 64x3 configuration, meaning they have 64 filters with a size of 3x3. This design allows the network to learn and extract relevant visual features from the input images, enabling the agent to make informed decisions. There are nearly 3 million trainable parameters compared to 23 million of Xception model.

C *Carla Simulator:*
   The Carla simulator was utilized as the simulation environment for training and evaluating the autonomous driving agent. An opensource simulator called Carla (Car Learning to Act) was created exclusively for studies on autonomous vehicles. It provides a realistic virtual environment with dynamic traffic, various road scenarios, and sensor models that mimic realworld conditions. By interfacing with Carla, the agent can receive sensor inputs, such as camera images, lidar data, and GPS information, and interact with the environment by sending control commands to the vehicle, such as acceleration, braking, and steering (Fig. 4).

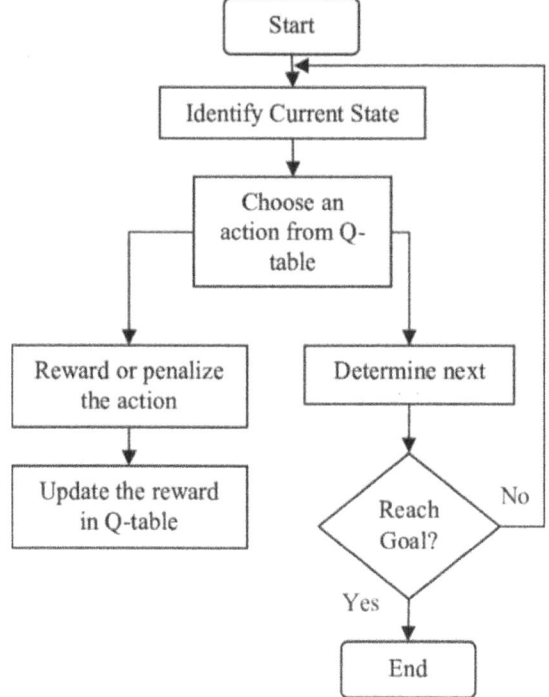

Fig. 1. Flow of the system.

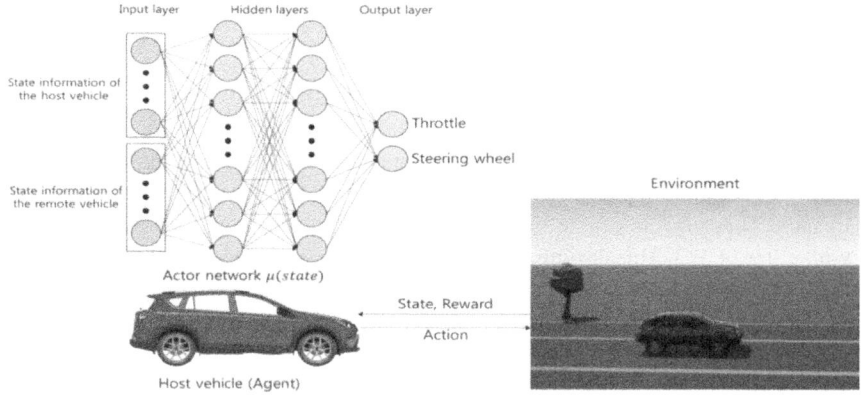

Fig. 2. Representation of a 64 × 3 CNN

D. *Data Preprocessing:*

Preprocessing techniques were used to improve the data quality and lower noise before feeding the input images into the CNN architecture. The photographs had to be resized to the same resolution, the pixel values had to be normalized, and any necessary image augmentation methods, like random rotations, flips, or color

Fig. 3. Agent Preview

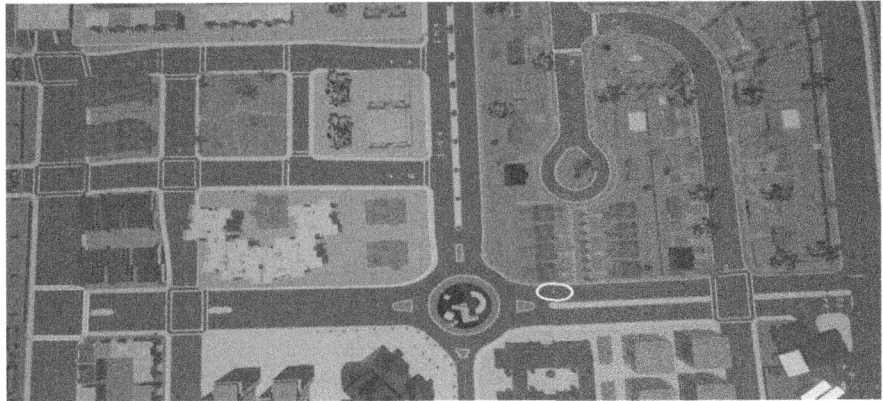

Fig. 4. Camera Preview

modifications, had to be used. These preprocessing processes made sure that the input data was uniform and appropriate for efficiently training the CNN model.

E. *Training Process:*

The training process involved multiple iterations of training episodes, where the agent interacts with the Carla simulator and learns from the environment. At the beginning of each episode, the agent receives an initial observation of the environment. Based on this observation, the agent selects an action using an exploration-exploitation strategy, which gradually shifts from random exploration to exploitation of learned policies over time. The chosen action is then carried out in the simulator, and the agent is rewarded and given fresh information about the surroundings. The DQN algorithm

samples a batch of these experiences from the replay reservoir in order to backprop-
agately update the parameters of the Q-network. These experiences are then stored
in a replay cache. This process of interaction, action selection, reward calculation,
and network update is repeated iteratively to improve the agent's performance.

F. *Equations:*

1) *Q-Learning Equation:* The Q-learning equation is used to update the Q-values
   for a given stateaction pair. It is based on the principle of the Bellman equation
   and consists the following:

$$Q(s, a) = Q(sa) + \alpha * (r + \gamma * \max(Q(s', a') - Q(s, a))$$

The Q-value for state s and action an is represented in this equation by the
letters Q(s, a). The following terms are defined: alpha denotes the information
gain, gamma denotes the discount factor that influences the significance of future
rewards, Q(s', a') denotes the Q-value for the subsequent state s' and the best
action a' in that state.

TD-Error (Temporal Difference Error) subsection: The discrepancy between
the target and the estimated Q-value is known as the TD-error. It is employed to
determine the overall training loss and modify the Q-parameters. Network's The
source of the Temporal Difference-error is:

$$TD.error = r + \gamma * \max(Q(s', a')) - Q(s, a)$$

Here, r is the instantaneous reward, gamma is the discount factor, max(Q(s',
a')) denotes the highest possible Q-value for the next state s' and all potential
activities a', and Q(s, a) is the projected Q-value for the now occurring state-action
pair [4].

2) *TD-Error (Temporal Difference Error):* The difference between the goal Q-values
   and the predicted Q-values is measured by the loss function. Via backpropagation,
   the Q-parameters networks are updated. The mean squared error (MSE) loss is a
   frequently employed loss function:

$$Loss = 1/N * (TD.error)^2$$

Here, N is the batch size, and TD.error represents the TD-error for each sample
in the batch [4].

3) *Bellman equation:* The Bellman equation is used to update the Q-values during the
   reinforcement learning process. The Bellman equation expresses the relationship
   between the current state-action value and the expected future rewards.

$$Q(s, a) = r + \gamma * \max(Q(s', a'))$$

Q-value of performing action an in state s is represented by Q(s, a). The instantaneous reward received after acting in state s is denoted by the symbol r. The
discount factor gamma establishes the significance of future rewards. It has a
scale of 0 to 1, where 0 implies only taking into account immediate rewards and
1 means taking into account all future rewards. By choosing the best course of
action, max(Q(s', a')) reflects the highest Q-value that may be attained in the
subsequent state s' [ã].

4) *ReLu Activation:* The Rectified Linear Unit is one of the activation functions used in this research (ReLU). ReLU activation function is defined as [6]:

$$f(x) = \max(0, x)$$

8   Result

The results section presents a comprehensive analysis of the experimental findings and outcomes obtained from training and evaluating the DQN model for autonomous driving. In this section, we discuss various performance metrics, including accuracy, loss, epsilon, and other relevant statistics. These metrics provide insights into the learning progress, stability, and decision-making capabilities of the model.

The accuracy of the model refers to how well it predicts the correct actions given a certain input. The accuracy of the DQN model is not the primary focus compared to other machine learning approaches like supervised learning. In reinforcement learning, the agent explores the environment and learns from the feedback received through trial and error. Therefore, a very high accuracy in the early stages of training might indicate a lack of exploration and limited learning. In the case of this model, the accuracy averaged around 75%. This demonstrates that the model was competent to accurate predictions for a significant portion of the training episodes. A high accuracy is desirable as it signifies that the model has learned to make correct decisions based on the given inputs (Figs. 5, 6 and 7).

acc

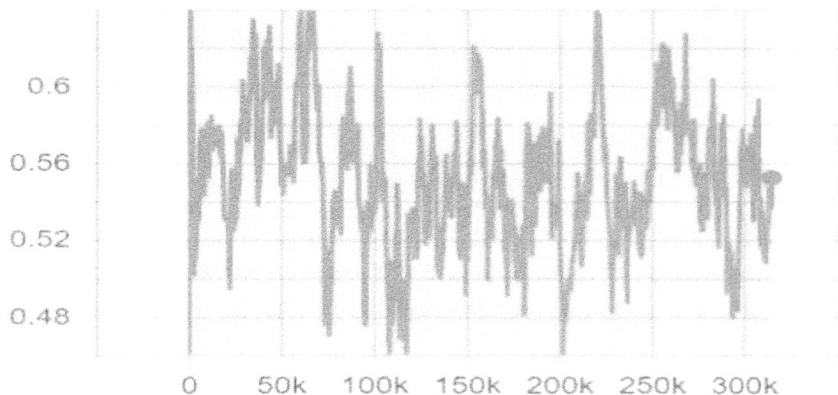

Fig. 5. Accuracy of 64 × 3 CNN model

The loss function is an important metric in training the DQN model for autonomous driving. In reinforcement learning, it is crucial to ensure that the loss function remains stable and does not exhibit any sudden explosions or divergences.During the training process, we carefully monitored the loss function to ensure its stability. The absence of any explosions or significant spikes in the loss function demonstrates that our model successfully learned and updated its Q-values in a consistent manner throughout the

loss

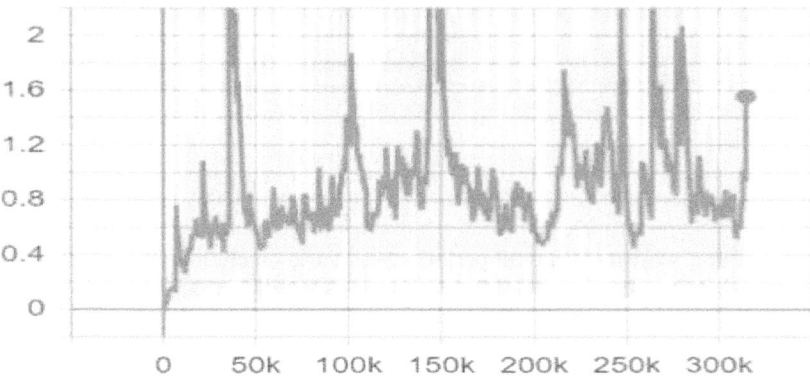

Fig. 6. Loss of 64 × 3 CNN model

epsilon

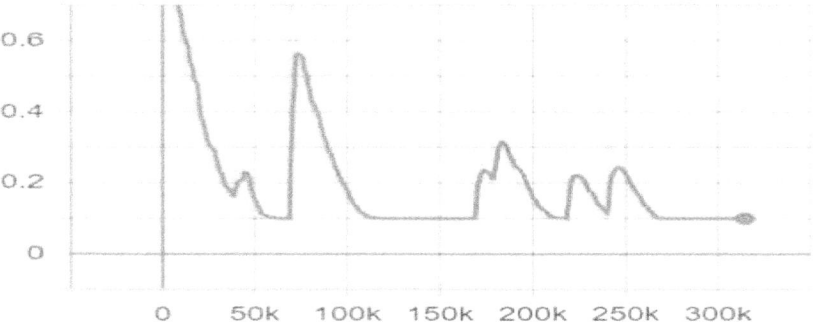

Fig. 7. Epsilon of 64 × 3 CNN model

training episodes. This stability in the loss function is a positive indication that the model was able to converge and make reliable predictions, enabling it to navigate the autonomous driving tasks effectively.

The epsilon value serves a significant role in the exploration-exploitation trade-off in reinforcement learning. It determines the balance between taking random actions to explore the environment and exploiting the learned knowledge to make optimal decisions. Throughout the duration of the incidents, we steadily reduced the epsilon value during the training process.

Initially, the high epsilon score allowed the model to take more random actions and explore different possibilities in the environment. This exploration phase is essential for the model to discover new strategies and learn from its interactions with the environment.As we decreased the epsilon value, the model began to rely more on its learned knowledge and exploit the information it gained from previous experiences. This exploitation phase aimed to refine the decision-making process and improve the model's performance by leveraging the accumulated knowledge (Fig. 8).

reward_raw_max

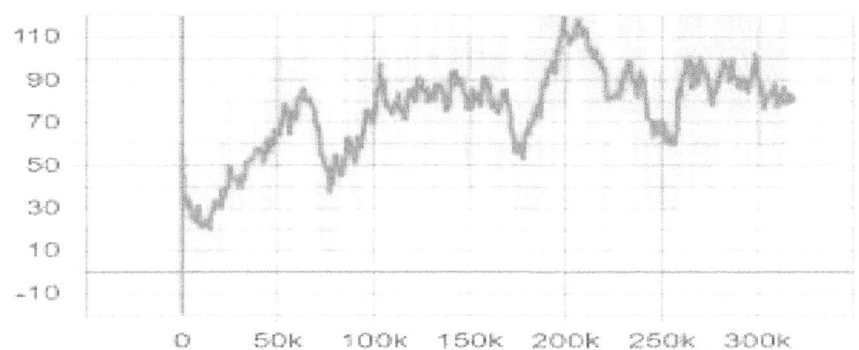

Fig. 8. Maximum reward analysis of 64 × 3 CNN model

The maximum reward provides insights into the best outcomes achieved by the agent during its interactions with the environment. We observed a positive trend in the maximum reward over time, indicating that the model was learning and improving its decision-making capabilities. The upward trend suggests that the agent was able to achieve higher rewards as it gained more experience and refined its strategies. Given more training time, it is likely that the maximum reward would continue to increase, indicating further improvement in the agent's performance (Fig. 9).

reward_raw_min

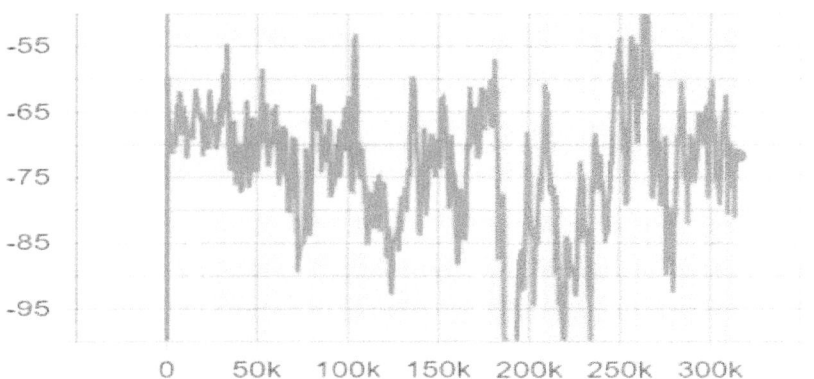

Fig. 9. Minimum reward analysis of 64 × 3 CNN model

The minimum reward represents the worst outcomes encountered by the agent. It is significant to remember that the minimum reward may not exhibit a clear trend, as it is affected by a variety of circumstances, including random initialization and unpredictable environmental conditions. In our observations, the minimum reward did not show significant changes in terms of a clear upward or downward trend. This is expected, as there will always be situations where the agent faces challenging circumstances or unfavorable environments, leading to lower rewards. However, the lack of a significant downward trend suggests that the agent was able to consistently handle such situations without significant performance degradation (Fig. 10).

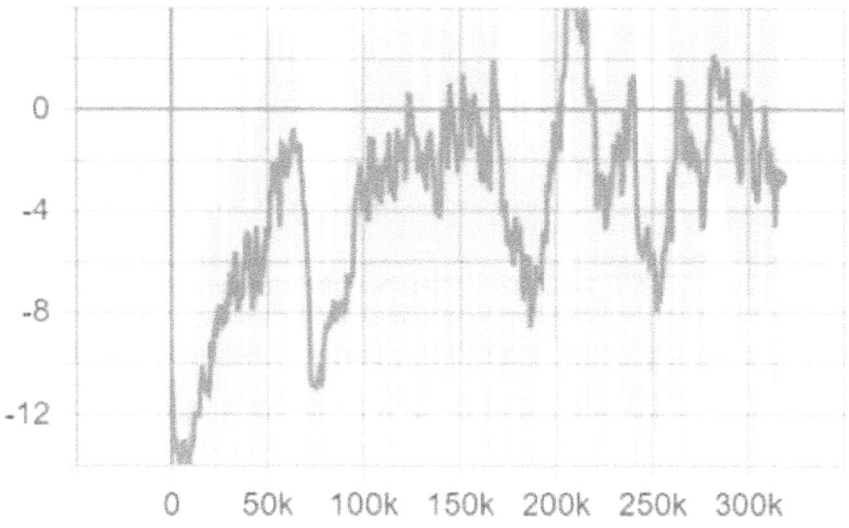

Fig. 10. Average reward analysis of 64 × 3 CNN model

The average reward provides an overall measure of the agent's performance and learning progress. We observed a consistent improvement in the average reward over time. This proves that, on average, the agent was successful in achieving higher rewards as it learned from its experiences and adjusted its actions accordingly. Although there

```
Agent:  5.4 FPS | Action: [-140.04, -57.05, -81.58] 1
Agent:  5.4 FPS | Action: [-140.83, -57.06, -82.73] 1
Agent:  5.4 FPS | Action: [-140.83, -60.52, -84.43] 1
Agent:  5.4 FPS | Action: [-138.78, -58.58, -82.54] 1
Agent:  5.4 FPS | Action: [-139.20, -59.97, -83.18] 1
Agent:  5.4 FPS | Action: [-142.33, -60.93, -84.03] 1
Agent:  5.5 FPS | Action: [-142.33, -60.93, -84.03] 1
Agent:  5.5 FPS | Action: [-141.93, -59.78, -78.82] 1
Agent:  5.5 FPS | Action: [-143.51, -60.96, -77.36] 1
Agent:  5.5 FPS | Action: [-143.35, -64.28, -77.67] 1
Agent:  5.5 FPS | Action: [-146.49, -59.55, -75.12] 1
Agent:  5.5 FPS | Action: [-147.72, -61.39, -72.87] 1
Agent:  5.5 FPS | Action: [-153.94, -64.83, -76.53] 1
Agent:  5.5 FPS | Action: [-153.94, -64.83, -76.53] 1
Agent:  5.5 FPS | Action: [-152.93, -62.75, -77.24] 1
Agent:  5.5 FPS | Action: [-154.01, -61.90, -76.76] 1
Agent:  5.4 FPS | Action: [-150.03, -50.22, -64.59] 1
Agent:  5.4 FPS | Action: [-152.09, -51.19, -67.12] 1
```

Fig. 11. FPS analysis of 64 × 3 CNN model

might be some fluctuations in the average reward, it is important to consider the overall trend, which showed a positive improvement throughout the learning process (Fig. 11).

In the context of autonomous driving, FPS refers to the number of frames, or individual images, processed by the system in one second.A higher FPS value indicates that the system is able to process a larger number of frames within a given time frame, resulting in smoother and more responsive behavior. In the case of autonomous driving, a higher FPS is desirable as it allows the model to perceive and react to the environment more quickly, reducing the risk of delays or missed opportunities for decision-making.In our study, we aimed to achieve an average FPS of around 5.5.

9   Discussion

The Xception model and the 64 × 3 CNN model are two alternative models that will be used in the discussions section for evaluating and contrasting the performance of the DQN algorithm for autonomous driving. This section delves into the strengths, weaknesses, and overall effectiveness of each model in the context of autonomous driving.

A. *Accuracy Comparition:*

The accuracy of the Xception model, exceeding 85%, suggests that the model may have achieved a high level of performance on the training data. However, It is crucial to remember that an abnormally high accuracy can be a sign of overfitting, in which the model gets overly focused on the training set and struggles to extrapolate to fresh, untested data. This raises concerns about the model's ability to perform effectively in real-world scenarios.

On the other hand, the 64 × 3 CNN model demon-strates optimal results in terms of accuracy. While the exact accuracy value is not specified, it can be inferred that the model achieved satisfactory performance without the risk of overfitting. The 64 × 3 CNN model, being a smaller and simpler architecture, may have a better balance between complexity and generalization capabilities, making it more suitable for the autonomous driving task (Fig. 12).

2. *Loss Comparison:*

B. *Loss Comparison:*

During our analysis, we observed a significant difference in the behavior of the loss and Q values between the Xception model and the 64 × 3 CNN model. Specifically, in the Xception model, we noticed that both the loss function and Q values were prone to exploding, while the 64 × 3 CNN model did not exhibit such issues (Fig. 13).

The explosion of the loss function in the Xception model can be attributed to the high complexity and deep architecture of the model. As the collision rewards were set to -200, the Q values associated with collisions might have increased exponentially, leading to the explosion of the loss function. This phenomenon indicates that the Xception model struggled to handle the complex nature of the reinforcement learning task, resulting in unstable training dynamics.

In contrast, the 64 × 3 CNN model, with its simpler architecture, did not experience such explosions in the loss function or Q values.

acc

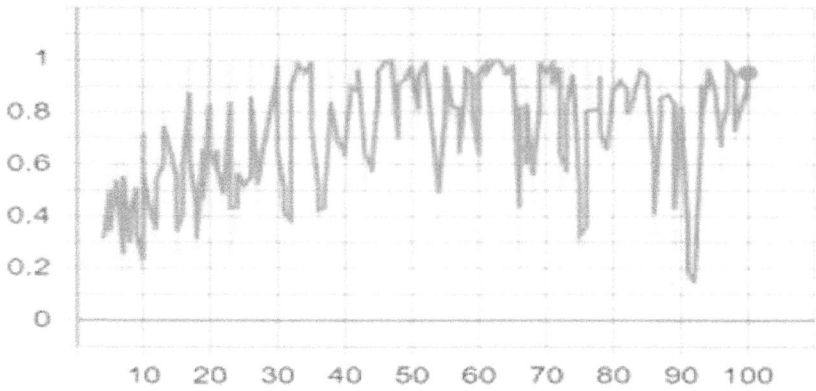

Fig. 12. Accuracy analysis of Xception model

loss

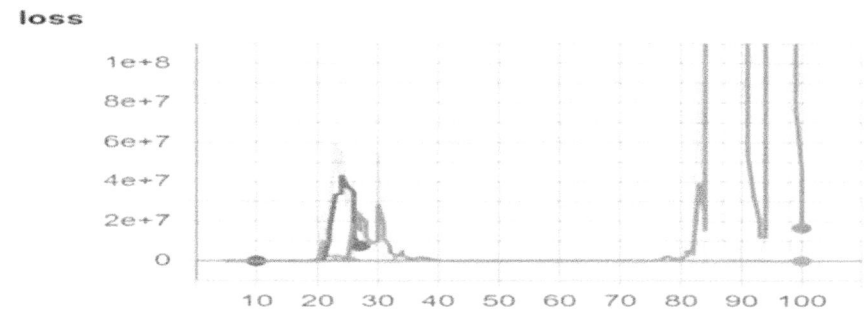

Fig. 13. Loss analysis of Xception model

C. *Representation Power:*

   The architecture and design of the 64 × 3 CNN model allowed it to capture relevant features and patterns in the input images effectively. By customizing the CNN specifically for the task of autonomous driving, the model could extract and learn essential visual representations crucial for decision-making on the road. The ability of the CNN model to capture intricate details and relevant spatial relationships in the input images enhanced its representation power, leading to improved performance in autonomous driving tasks compared to the Xception model.

D. *Training Stability:*

   The stability of training was another aspect where the 64 × 3 CNN model showcased its advantages over the Xception model. The CNN model demonstrated faster convergence speed and better generalization to new situations. The simplicity of the CNN architecture facilitated stable training dynamics, reducing the likelihood of exploding loss or Q values during the learning process. The design choices in the CNN model contributed to more stable and efficient training, ensuring a smoother learning curve and improved performance.

E. *Interpretability and Explainability:*

In terms of interpretability and explainability, the 64 × 3 CNN model offered advantages over the Xception model. The CNN model's architecture made it possible to comprehend the agent's policy-learning process and choices better. The hierarchical nature of the CNN, with its convolutional and pooling layers, provided interpretability by capturing and analyzing local and global features in the input images. This facilitated insights into the model's decision-making and increased transparency in understanding the agent's actions.

F. *Transferability to Other Domains:*

The learned features and policies in the 64 × 3 CNN model hold potential for transferability to other autonomous driving scenarios or related tasks. The CNN model's ability to extract relevant visual representations and make informed decisions based on those representations can be leveraged in different environments or for different tasks within the autonomous driving domain. The transferability of the CNN model enables it to adapt and generalize to new situations, making it a promising choice for various autonomous driving applications.

G. *Limitations and Future Work:*

While the 64 × 3 CNN model exhibited superior performance and advantages over the Xception model, there may still be limitations and areas for future improvement. Further fine-tuning of the architecture and exploration of different training techniques could potentially enhance the CNN model's performance. Incorporating additional data sources, such as sensor data from LiDAR or radar, may provide a more comprehensive input for the model, leading to better decision-making. The CNN model can be improved upon and further optimised in order to produce even better outcomes with continued advancements in research in the field of driverless transportation.

In, the results and discussions highlight that the 64 × 3 CNN model outperformed the Xception model in the field of driverless transportation using the DQN algorithm. The 64 × 3 CNN model showed better performance in terms of accuracy, stability of training, representation power, and interpretability. It achieved higher average rewards, demon-strated stable convergence, and exhibited better generalization to new situations. The simplicity of the CNN model's architecture contributed to its superior performance by allowing efficient learning and decision-making processes. Furthermore, the CNN model showed potential for transferability to other autonomous driving scenarios or related tasks.

10 Conclusions

In conclusion, based on our investigation and analysis, we find that using a 64 × 3 CNN model in combination with DQN for autonomous driving tasks yields better results compared to using the Xception model. The 64x3 CNN model, with its simpler architecture and smaller input size, offers advantages in terms of computational efficiency and training time. Furthermore, the CNN model demonstrates sufficient capacity to learn complex representations from visual input, enabling effective decision-making in the autonomous driving context. The use of DQN as the reinforcement learning algorithm provides a robust framework for learning optimal policies for autonomous driving tasks.

By leveraging the Q-learning algorithm and experience replay, DQN can efficiently explore and exploit the environment, enabling the agent to make informed decisions in a dynamic and uncertain driving environment.

Our tests and analyses show that the DQN-trained 64×3 CNN model beats the Xception model with regard to performance and training effectiveness. The combination of the Q-learning algorithm's capacity to learn the best rules with the CNN model's capacity to extract relevant features from input images results in improved driving behaviour, lower collision rates, and improved overall performance. It's crucial to remember that the model architecture chosen will depend on the particular needs of the autonomous driving task and the available processing resources. Even while the 64×3 CNN model performs well in our tests, alternative models and modifications may produce different outcomes depending on the degree of complexity of the driving scenario, the amount and quality of the training dataset, and the hardware resources available. In conclusion, our findings support the use of the 64×3 CNN model in combination with DQN as a promising approach for autonomous driving tasks.

Future research can explore further enhancements to the model architecture, investigate alternative reinforcement learning algorithms, and incorporate additional sensor modalities to improve the robustness and performance of autonomous driving systems.

References

1. van Hoek, R., Ploeg, J., Nijmeijer, H.: Cooperative driving of automated vehicles using b-splines for trajectory planning. IEEE Trans. Intell. Veh. **6**(3), 594–604 (2021). https://doi.org/10.1109/TIV.2021.3072679
2. Li, H., Wu, C., Chu, D., Lu, L., Cheng, K.: Combined trajectory planning and tracking for autonomous vehicle considering driving styles. IEEE Access **9**, 9453–9463 (2021). https://doi.org/10.1109/AC-CESS.2021.3050005
3. Arbabi, S., Tavernini, D., Fallah, S., Bowden, R.: Planning for au-tonomous driving via interaction-aware probabilistic action policies. IEEE Access **10**, 81699–81712 (2022). https://doi.org/10.1109/AC-CESS.2022.3193492
4. Agostinho, L.R., Ricardo, N.M., Pereira, M.I., Hiolle, A., Pinto, A.M.: A practical survey on visual odometry for autonomous driving in challenging scenarios and conditions. IEEE Access **10**, 72182–72205 (2022). https://doi.org/10.1109/ACCESS.2022.3188990
5. Li, B., Ouyang, Y., Li, L., Zhang, Y.: Autonomous driving on curvy roads without reliance on frenet frame: a cartesian-based trajectory planning method. IEEE Trans. Intell. Transp. Syst. **23**(9), 15729–15741 (2022). https://doi.org/10.1109/TITS.2022.3145389
6. Aradi, S.: Survey of deep reinforcement learning for motion plan-ning of autonomous vehicles. IEEE Trans. Intell. Transp. Syst. **23**(2), 740–759 (2022). https://doi.org/10.1109/TITS.2020.3024655
7. Kim, C., Yoon, Y., Kim, S., Yoo, M.J., Yi, K.: Trajectory planning and control of autonomous vehicles for static vehicle avoidance in dynamic traffic environments. IEEE Access **11**, 5772–5788 (2023). https://doi.org/10.1109/ACCESS.2023.3236816
8. Lisowski, J.: A synthesis of algorithms determining a safe trajectory in a group of autonomous vehicles using a sequential game and neural network. Electronics **12**(5), 1236 (2023). https://doi.org/10.3390/electronics12051236
9. Naveed, K.B., Qiao, Z. and Dolan, J.M.: Trajectory planning for autonomous vehicles using hierarchical reinforcement learning. In: 2021 IEEE International Intelligent Transportation

Systems Con-ference (ITSC), Indianapolis, IN, USA, 2021, pp. 601-606, https://doi.org/10.1109/ITSC48978.2021.9564634

10. arXiv:2303.16109 [cs.LG] (or arXiv:2303.16109v1 [cs.LG] for this version) Multimodal Manoeuvre and Trajectory Prediction for Autonomous Vehicles Using Transformer Networks (2023). https://doi.org/10.48550/arXiv.2303.16109

Quantum Graph Neural Networks Based Protein-Ligand Classification

Srinjoy Ganguly[1]([envelope]) [iD], Vaishnavi Chandilkar[1] [iD], Prateek Jain[1],
and Luis Gerardo Ayala Bertel[2]

[1] QuantumAI Lab, Fractal Analytics, Gurugram, India
{srinjoy.ganguly,vaishnavi.chandilkar,prateek.jain}@fractal.ai
[2] Faculty of Natural and Exact Sciences, Universidad de Cartagena, Cartagena, Colombia
layalab@unicartagena.edu.co

Abstract. Graph Neural Networks (GNNs) are an emerging research area with an ongoing exploration of their practical applications. There have been promising results in combining GNNs with Quantum circuits (Quantum GNNs) for tasks such as predicting chemical and material properties, drug discovery, and analyzing complex systems such as social networks and traffic patterns. Additionally, QGNNs have the potential to provide significant speedup in certain machine-learning tasks by leveraging the power of quantum parallelism. In this research work, we propose a hybrid non-sequential Quantum Graph Neural Network (QGNN) model called QMolNet that utilizes variational quantum circuits and encoding techniques. The model is implemented for the problem of protein-ligand classification with consideration of non-bond interactions over a range of cut-off distances using the BACE dataset. Our comparative analysis shows that the proposed hybrid model outperforms various classical Graph Neural Network (GNN) models and provides state-of-the-art performance for the protein-ligand classification task. This research presents a potential direction for developing Quantum Graphical Models in quantum chemistry that incorporate chemical intuition and are comparable to existing chemical concepts and tools.

Keyword: Quantum Graph Neural Network. Protein-ligand interaction. Variational Quantum Circuit

1 Introduction

Quantum Machine Learning (QML) has received significant attention in recent years due to the potential of quantum computing to process large amounts of data and perform complex calculations faster than classical computing [1]. QML has emerged as an exciting new area of research with the potential to revolutionize machine learning by exploiting the unique features of quantum mechanics. While QML is still in its early stages, several promising results have been in using QML for various applications, including image classification [2], optimization, and quantum chemistry [3]. QML has the potential to revolutionize the field of machine learning by enabling the development of new models and algorithms that can process data at a faster rate and achieve higher accuracy.

© The Author(s), under exclusive license to Springer Nature Switzerland AG 2024
H. K. et al. (Eds.): AIKP 2023, CCIS 2127, pp. 146–159, 2024.
https://doi.org/10.1007/978-3-031-68617-7_11

While significant progress has been made in recent years, current quantum computers are still relatively small and have limited coherence times, which restricts their ability to perform complex computations. This limitation is known as the Noisy Intermediate-Scale Quantum (NISQ) era. Additionally, the development of robust and scalable quantum hardware is still ongoing, which is a critical requirement for the practical implementation of QML algorithms. As a result, most QML research is currently focused on developing hybrid quantum classical algorithms that can leverage the benefits of both classical and quantum computing to solve complex problems efficiently. This paper employs a hybrid quantum-classical approach, where a subset of the data is processed using quantum algorithms while the rest is processed on classical systems. It is still unclear whether quantum computers will fully replace classical computers, and thus, variational quantum algorithms are natural candidates for leveraging the power of NISQ computers. These algorithms offer the potential to exploit the computational advantages of quantum systems while incorporating classical optimization techniques, allowing for a more robust and practical approach to solving real-world problems. When it comes to finding practical applications, real-time speed improvements of hybrid methods compared to classical systems have yet to be observed. Hence, this paper focuses on the advantage of achieving higher accuracy in training hybrid models with a small number of datasets. This is particularly relevant given the limited resources of current quantum computers, which are primarily of the NISQ type. By leveraging the benefits of hybrid quantum-classical approaches, we can improve the accuracy of training models and achieve better generalization performance even with limited quantum resources.

In the domain of protein-ligand binding classification tasks, accuracy is of utmost importance to ensure reliable decision-making. Deep learning has shown great promise in this regard, but misclassifications can have serious consequences. In the drug discovery domain, there is a high demand for machine learning techniques. That exhibit good generalization from small datasets, as the process can span over a decade. Graph Neural Networks (GNNs) have demonstrated impressive performance in classification and regression tasks [4], making them a popular choice for finding molecular properties. However, they typically require large training datasets. To address this, we investigate the potential of hybrid Quantum Computing (QC)-assisted machine learning methods, specifically for classification tasks with limited training data. This paper investigates the application of QML for molecular property prediction in drug discovery and proposes a novel approach based on Quantum Graph Neural Networks.

The discovery of novel drugs and drug-like molecules is a challenging and essential task in molecular design. Protein-ligand interactions play an essential role in the field of drug discovery to understand the complex non-covalent interaction between proteins and small molecules for developing novel therapeutic agents. These interactions occur when a protein binds to a ligand—a small molecule that can modulate the protein's activity. The specificity and strength of these interactions determine the potential of a drug candidate. In recent years, machine learning techniques have become widespread to utilize the potential of big data and artificial intelligence to aid in various tasks. Among these techniques, graph neural networks (GNNs) have shown encouraging findings in the task of molecular property prediction [4]. A key factor that plays an important role in determining this prediction, affecting its chemical and biological properties, is its three-dimensional (3D) structure [5]. The 3D shape of a molecule can influence the molecule, such as its solubility in different solvents, melting point, and reactivity. Additionally, the 3D structure can provide a detailed view of how different parts of the molecule interact with each other, which can help scientists understand how the molecule behaves in different environments, leading to a more detailed and accurate understanding of how a molecule behaves. The primary contributions of this paper include:

- Introducing a novel hybrid quantum-classical graph neural network architecture for classifying protein-ligand binding properties of molecules. The architecture combines classical data with a quantum circuit to enhance the accuracy of the classification task.
- Conducting extensive experiments on the proposed model with varying numbers of qubits and cut-off ranges of the molecule using a suitable quantum encoding scheme to demonstrate the performance of the hybrid model compared to classical models in terms of accuracy and the number of epochs.
- We present the effect of quantum circuit design on the training performance of the hybrid quantum graph neural network model. This is the first study of its kind to explore the impact of the quantum circuit design on the model's training performance.

This paper is structured as follows: Sect. 2 provides an overview of the related work. Section 3 introduces the fundamental concepts required to comprehend the hybrid quantum-classical graph neural network architectures discussed in Sect. 4. The experimental configuration for our research is outlined in Sect. 4. In Sect. 5, we demonstrate the performance of these algorithms in simulations using the BACE dataset.

2 Related Work

2.1 GNNs for Prediction of Molecular Properties

GNNs have emerged as a popular approach for molecular property prediction due to their ability to capture the complex structural information of molecules in the form of graphs [6]. In a recent study, researchers used GNNs to predict the properties of various molecules, including their solubility and lipophilicity, achieving state-of-the-art performance [7]. Efficient use of available datasets and the development of new techniques for generating synthetic molecular data have been identified as important challenges for the successful implementation of GNNs in chemistry [8]. Despite these challenges, GNNs offer a promising approach for predicting various molecular properties, such as solubility, toxicity, and biological activity, which can significantly expedite the process of drug discovery and facilitate the design of new materials with desired properties.

2.2 Quantum Graph Neural Networks

Various methods have been proposed to extend the success of GNNs in predicting molecular properties to the field of quantum computing, one of which is Quantum Graph Neural Networks (QGNNs) (Fig. 1).

QGNNs have been found to be effective in predicting molecular properties. The regression task of molecular properties using QGNNs has been shown to be effective

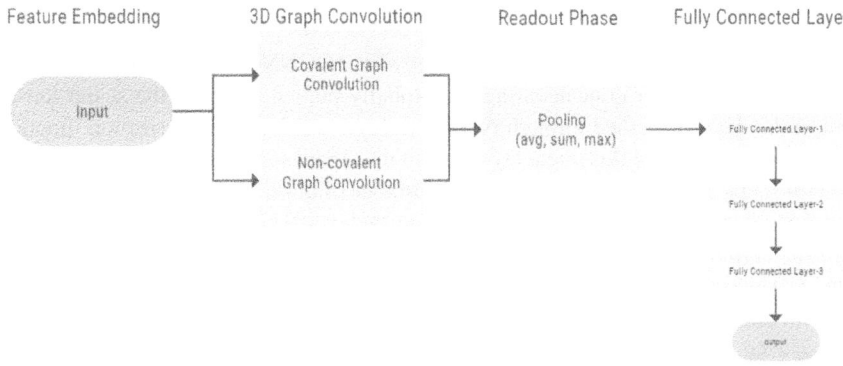

Fig. 1. The architecture diagram of the classical-GNN model employed for the BACE dataset.

on the QM9 dataset, which includes 134k small organic molecules with up to 9 heavy atoms [9]. These studies have demonstrated the potential benefits of QGNNs in identifying new drug candidates and predicting their properties with higher accuracy than classical machine learning models. Furthermore, to address the challenge of limited qubit resources on NISQ devices, recent studies have proposed techniques to reduce the number of qubits needed for QGNNs, such as using low-rank approximation [10] or exploiting Quantum Approximate Optimization Algorithm [11].

3   Background

3.1   Details of GNNs in This Work

In this study, the GNNs utilized have a basic design consisting of a series of convolutional layers. This model requires the creation of two types of matrices. In constructing the non-covalent matrix A, non-covalent atoms within a specified range of 6 Å are identified as 1, while all others are assigned as 0. This information is then used to construct input matrix A, which depicts the time-dependent changes in molecular properties and interactions, while covalent matrix C is formed by considering covalent atoms of the molecule with edge weights assigned based on their bond type. The model's performance is evaluated on the BACE dataset in a classification task of protein-ligand interactions. The architecture consists of four phases: feature-embedding, convolution phase, readout (avg, sum, max pooling) phase, and fully connected phases. The scalar features are embedded into a fully connected layer in the first phase. In the second phase, the covalent and non-covalent features are convolved independently, followed by the concatenation of the resulting feature maps. These features are then aggregated in the readout (avg, sum, max pooling) phase, and resulting pooled features are then passed through fully connected layers to predict the target property.

3.2 Details of Hybrid QGNNs in This Work

This study's hybrid Quantum Graph Neural Networks (QGNNs) implemented a quantum variational circuit. After concatenating the globally pooled features, the scalar-tensor output of this layer is passed through two linear layers with a SiLU activation function in between. The output of this linear layer is split into 16 tensors along the last dimension, each with shape (batch size, n), n being the number of qubits in each split. Two out of 16 tensors, 2 tensors are passed through a Quantum layer. The Quantum layer takes this part of the output of the last linear layer as input and applies a quantum circuit defined in Fig. 3. The quantum circuit applies an angle embedding to the inputs, which maps the input features to the rotation angles of the qubits as used in [12]. Then, it applies a set of basic entangling gates (CNOT gates) between the qubits according to the weights provided. The output of the Quantum layer is a tensor of the same shape as the input tensor, with each element being the expectation value of a Pauli Z operator on a qubit. These expectation values are then concatenated along the last dimension with the rest of the classical data to produce a tensor of shape with the same output dimension as in the classical Model. The subsequent sections outline the distinct elements that constitute a quantum circuit.

Encoding. Encoding refers to mapping input values onto a quantum circuit's qubits. Various encoding techniques are available, as explored in [13], and the technique chosen influences the number of qubits necessary in the quantum circuit. This study employs only encoding techniques that assign a single input value to each qubit. Consequently, the number of necessary qubits equals the number of inputs processed in each step, which are then concatenated to obtain the final target property. The following encoding technique is considered in this work (Fig. 2):

Angle Encoding: The angle encoding method [12] *utilizes rotation gates that are based on the input values x for encoding. In this method, the input is encoded by performing a rotation around the X-axis with an angle of θ. At the beginning of our quantum circuit, the qubits are in the state $|0\rangle$, and after the encoding, the resulting quantum state becomes $RX(\theta)|0\rangle$.*

Circuit Design. Circuit design refers to the process of constructing a sequence of quantum gates that are applied to manipulate the quantum state of a set of qubits to perform a specific quantum computation or algorithm. Once the graph is encoded, rotation and entangling gates are applied in a specific sequence to the qubits to perform the necessary computations. The resulting interference and superposition effects can enable the network to learn more intricate features than classical neural networks. In our experiments, we use the Basic Entangling Layer as the circuit design, which applies rotation gates around one axis or all three axes prior to a sequence of entangling gates. The inputs to the rotation gate angles are randomly initialized and subsequently updated using a classical optimizer during training. The CNOT gates are used for entanglement in each layer of the circuit.

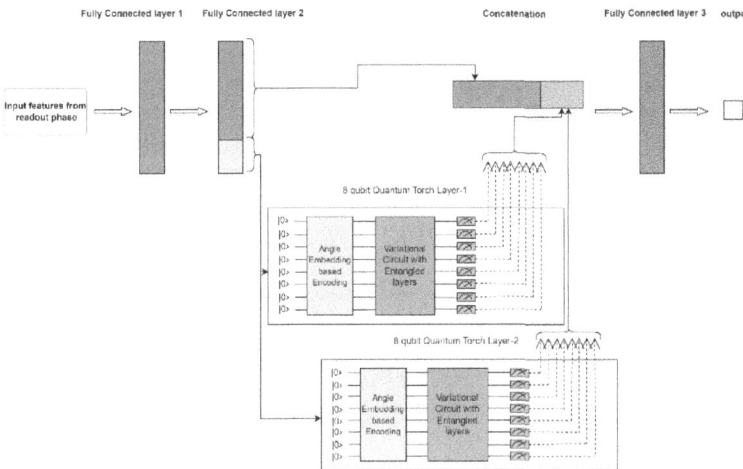

Fig. 2. The architecture diagram of the Hybrid Quantum-Classical QMolNet Model with two quantum layers inserted between classical fully connected Layers, employed for the BACE dataset.

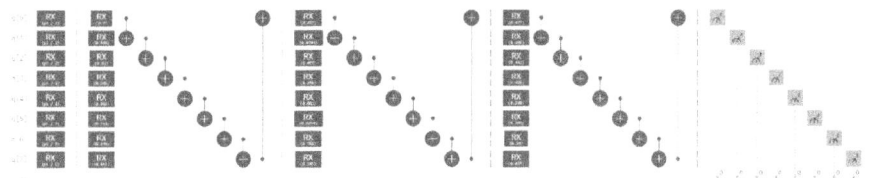

Fig. 3. The 8-qubit circuit diagram of the hybrid quantum-classical QMolNet model employed for the BACE dataset.

Mathematically, the BasicEntanglerLayers circuit can be described as:

$$U(\theta) = \prod_{j=1}^{d} U_{entangle}(\theta_j) U_{rot}(\phi_j)$$

where $U_{entangle}(\theta_j)$ is an entangling gate applied to the j-th layer of the circuit and $U_{rot}(\phi_j)$ is a single qubit rotation applied to each qubit in the circuit in the j-th layer. The parameters θ_j and ϕ_j are the rotation angles and depth, d in this case is 4.

The Quantum circuit defined in this model is repeated for two of the 16 parts of the tensor representation, and the weights of the circuit are learned during the training of the PyTorch model.

Output Measurement. The state of the qubits is measured on the Z-basis to extract information about the quantum state at the end of the quantum circuit. No activation function is applied to the resulting outputs. The outputs are then concatenated and forwarded to a set of fully connected layers to predict the target property.

3.3 Hybrid QMolNet Details

The model learns covalent molecular graph $GC_c(V, E)$ for the construction of C while noncovalent molecular graph $GC_{nc}(V, E)$ for A, where GC represents a molecular graph, V and E represents nodes and edges respectively, and the prefixes c, nc represents covalent and noncovalent bonds between the atoms. The detailed steps of the architecture are as follows:

Embedding. During the feature-embedding phase, scalar features of the molecule are embedded into a fully-connected layer.

Let X be a set of n atoms with coordinates $\{r_1, r_2, ..., r_n\}$, and A be the non-covalent matrix:

$$A_{ij} = \begin{cases} 1, i \neq j \text{ and } r_i - r_j < r_c \\ 0, \text{ otherwise} \end{cases}$$

where r_c is cutoff distance.

Let C be the covalent bond matrix:

$$C_{ij} = \begin{cases} 1, \text{ if } i \text{ and } j \text{ are covalently bonded} \\ 0, \text{ otherwise} \end{cases}$$

where covalently bonded atoms are defined based on their types and distances.

Convolution phase. The convolution phase involves performing convolutions independently for covalent and noncovalent features, and the resulting features are merged through concatenation for the pooling step.

The steps are as follows:

Let SC_c and VC_c be the scalar and vector features of covalently bonded atoms, respectively, and let SC_{nc} and VC_{nc} be the scalar and vector features of the non-bonded (neighbour) atoms, W and σ are the weight tensor and activation function, respectively and b is the bias.

The message passing between $s \rightarrow s$ as well as $v \rightarrow v$ includes the merging of atom features through a linear operation, which is then followed by a nonlinear activation function.

$$m_p[s \rightarrow s] = \sigma (W_{s \rightarrow s}[SC_c, SC_{nc}] + b_{s \rightarrow s})$$

$$m_p[v \rightarrow v] = \sigma (W_{v \rightarrow v}[VC_c, VC_{nc}] + b_{v \rightarrow v})$$

In the $v \rightarrow s$ message passing step, the cartesian-axis components of a vector feature are multiplied with r_{ijk} (where k represents x, y or z Cartesian axes) followed by a feature-wise summation.

$$m_p[v \rightarrow s] = \sum_k \rho(r_{ijk})W_{v \rightarrow s}[VC_c, VC_{nc}] + b_{v \rightarrow s}$$

where ρ is the activation function.

The tensor product ($\otimes$) is employed to perform the $s \to v$ message passing with r_{ij}.

$$m_p[s \to v] = \phi((W_{s \to v}[SC_c, SC_{nc}] + b_{s \to v}) \otimes r_{ij}$$

where ϕ is the activation function.

In the final step, the graph update operation aggregates the scalar and vector features into new updated atom features:

$$SC_{new} = m_p[s \to s] + m_p[v \to s]$$

$$VC_{new} = m_p[v \to v] + m_p[s \to v]$$

Readout Phase. The features obtained from the convolution phase are combined or aggregated during the readout phase. This process involves concatenating the pooled (average, maximum, and sum) features along the atom axis.

Fully Connected Phase. The output of the pooling layer is forwarded to a sequence of three fully connected layers for performing the final prediction. The resulting global embedding is produced after the second fully connected layer is split into 16 tensors, out of which 2 tensors are input to the quantum layer. The output obtained from the quantum layer is then concatenated with the remaining tensors and subsequently input to the final fully connected layer for prediction.

4   Methodology and Experimental Setup

As per [4], to make a valid comparison between classical graph learning methods and quantum graph learning, it was found that the suggested quantum approach performs better than other state-of-the-art models. Our hybrid QGNN and GNN are built with the same amount of parameters overall and are of similar magnitude. For this purpose, we add a variational quantum circuit to create a QGNN after a fully connected layer to create QMolNet. The number of inputs being sent to the quantum circuit is first split and concatenated because of the limitation of using the number of qubits by maintaining the same inputs to the layers. The quantum circuit design and encoding scheme determine the number of parameters in the quantum variational layer. We apply our QGNNs to the BACE dataset. The architecture setups and dataset details are elaborated below.

4.1   Datasets

BACE dataset. The BACE dataset, which contains 1547 binary inhibition labels, was utilized to examine model performance. The ligands in the dataset are positioned in 3D and aligned to the binding pocket of human β-secretase 1 (BACE-1), an enzyme crucial in the production of amyloid-β (Aβ). BACE-1 is considered a promising approach for the treatment of Alzheimer's disease. A dataset containing 1478 ligands was utilized for the classification task of protein ligand binding to aid in drug discovery research. Dividing the dataset into a limited number of training samples is a fundamental step in evaluating the effectiveness of the QGNN approach. The result of this approach can also be a decreased requirement for the number of qubits required to solve the problem, making the algorithm more practical to implement on existing quantum computers.

Architecture. By extending the results performed in [4] in the construction of the CMol-Net architecture for the classification of protein-ligand interactions, we created a non-covalent matrix A and a weighted covalent matrix C to assess the model's performance. The QMolNet model's overall architecture is composed of four phases (Fig. 2): feature-embedding phase, convolution phase, readout (avg, sum, max pooling) phase, and a set of fully connected phases.

The general atom features are transformed into scalar features through a fully connected layer during the first phase. In the second phase, two convolution blocks, GC_c and GC_{nc}, are used and connected for the pooling operation. GC_c performs graph convolution using covalent matrix C, while GC_{nc} uses noncovalent matrix A. During the third phase, scalar features are concatenated and aggregated using multi-pooling, which is a combination of max-, sum-, and average-pooling. Finally, the extracted features are inputted into a series of fully connected layers. The resulting output is then passed to the quantum layer comprising a single quantum circuit, which is utilized to identify the target property for making predictions. In Fig. 2, we present the proposed architecture for the quantum GNN circuit, accompanied by its corresponding encoding scheme:

Our model is a non-sequential model and consists of a series of classical and quantum layers. Here we distribute some output of the fully connected classical layer into 2 subsequent quantum layers. Each quantum layer consists of an 8-qubit quantum circuit connected to the first eight features of the previous layer. The Angle Embedding encoding takes a classical input and maps each element to an angle that rotates the qubit state vector to point in a particular direction in the Bloch sphere.

The input data is first transformed into a quantum state using the Angle Encoding method, which involves mapping each feature of the input to a corresponding rotation angle θ of a qubit. For the experiments with the basic entangling layers, each circuit comprises 8 qubits and 16 trainable parameters. To achieve this, the feature values are first normalized to fall within the range of 0 to 2π. The corresponding feature value is then used to determine the angle of rotation, denoted as θ, applied to each qubit. Subsequently, the encoded features are processed using a series of Basic Entangler Layers (BEL), entangling each qubit with every other in the circuit using CNOT gates. The BELs are repeated three times, enabling complex quantum interference effects to arise, which enhances the circuit's expressivity and facilitates the approximation of complex functions. In addition to these parameters, 112 other trainable parameters are obtained from the classical fully connected layer 1. Finally, the expectation value of the Pauli-Z operator is measured for each qubit in the circuit to produce the final output, which predicts the target property after being fed into the fully connected layer.

5   Results and Discussion

The experiments are carried out using the software tools PennyLane [14] and PyTorch [15]. PennyLane is a Python library that enables the construction and execution of quantum machine learning algorithms. The default.qubit device of PennyLane is used for all experiments, which simulates qubit-based quantum circuits in a straightforward manner. The circuit calculates the expectation values stochastically by measuring the quantum state 1000 times (the default number of shots in PennyLane is 1000). In addition, the simulations do not take into account any noise effects.

The performance of the model was evaluated using standard metrics for binary classification tasks, specifically the area under the receiver operating characteristic (ROC) curve (AUC-ROC). The ROC curve represents the relationship between the true positive rate and the false positive rate and provides the ability to classify positive and negative instances accurately. These experiments were carried out utilizing a 4-fold cross-validation technique. The networks were trained for 50 epochs, employing the Adam optimizer with a batch size of 8 and a learning rate of 0.001 for the BACE dataset. In consideration of the resource intensive nature of the experiments, no extensive hyperparameter tuning was conducted.

Table 1. Comparison of results for MolNet with baseline models on the BACE dataset.

Model Classification	AUC-ROC
GCN	0.8713
Weave	0.8763
MPNN	0.8602
3DGCN	0.8800
MolNet	0.9217
QMolNet	0.9313

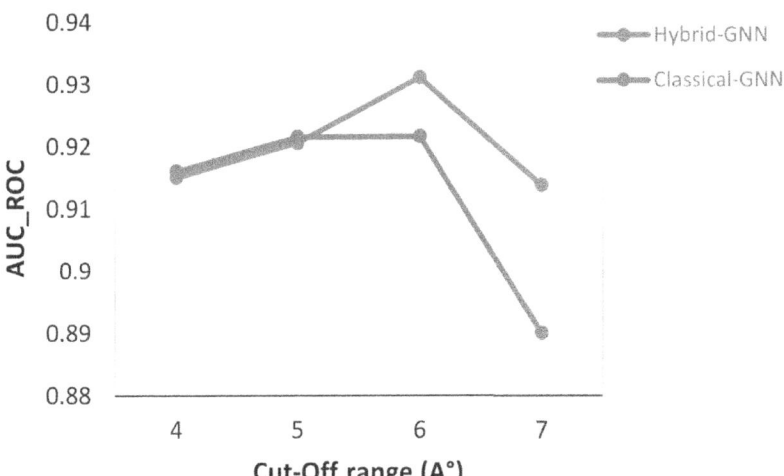

Fig. 4. Graph of AUC-ROC values of the classical (red) and hybrid model (blue) versus cut-off range.

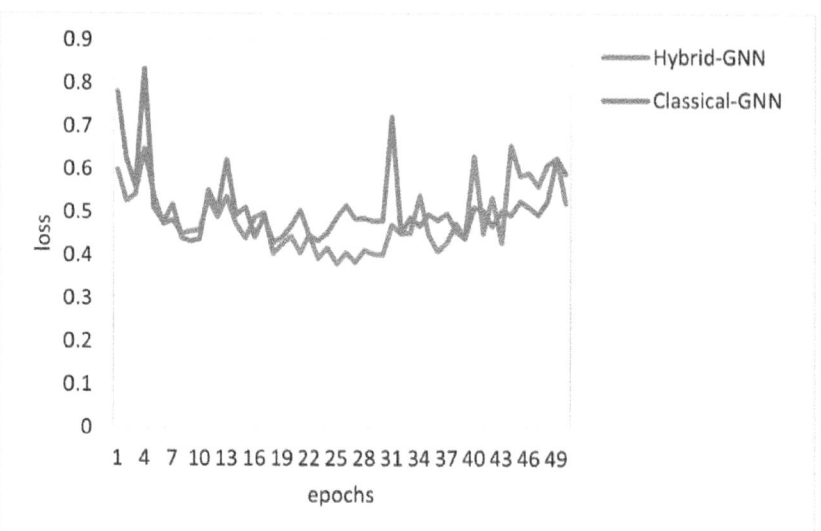

Fig. 5. Hybrid model performance (blue) in terms of loss compared to the performance of a classical GNN (red)

We compared the binary classification performance of QMolNet for the BACE task with various GNN models, including GCN [16], 3DGCN [17], Weave [18], MPNN [19] and MolNet [4] used as baseline models as shown in Table 1. GCN is considered a precursor of spectral GNNs, where graph convolution is performed solely with atom features using a normalized adjacency matrix with self-loop. 3DGCN is one of the 3DGNNs, which considers both atom features and 3D interatomic positions. The Weave model updates both atom and bond features during convolution, while the MPNN updates atom features by aggregating messages from neighboring atoms and bonds based on their embedded features.

Additionally, we compared the classical and hybrid models for different angstrom values and the number of qubits, as shown in Fig. 4. We defined the limit for the cut-off range for A from 4 Å to 7 Å. The classical model was trained for 500 epochs and 10-fold cross-validation, while the quantum model was trained for 50 epochs and 5-fold cross-validation. The optimum value of the cut-off range for the model was determined by evaluating its performance using AUC-ROC. The results indicated that the highest performance was achieved with a cut-off range of 6 Å, while larger cut-off ranges decreased performance. For instance, the AUC-ROC value was 0.9206 when a cut-off range of 5 Å was used, whereas it increased to 0.9311 for a cut-off range of 6 Å as shown in Table 1 and Fig. 4.

The quantum model exhibited improved performance as the number of noncovalent atoms below a threshold of 6 Å increased, demonstrating the advantage of the quantum circuit. The screening results determined that the optimum threshold range for construction should be 6 Å.

The AUC-ROC-comparison results between classical and hybrid quantum models showed that the hybrid QMolNet model significantly outperformed the classical model by extracting more effective chemical features to predict the protein-ligand interactions. These observations indicate that the hybrid model could be a more efficient and accurate approach for predicting molecular properties in quantum chemistry applications (Fig. 5).

In addition, we observed that in the case of 5 $\overset{\circ}{A}$, the classical model took more than 100 epochs in each of the 10 folds to achieve a ROC value of 0.9217, while the quantum model achieved a value of 0.9206 in just the second fold, with less than 50 epochs in each fold. This finding suggests that the hybrid QGNN, utilizing angle embedding and the basic entangling layer, can attain the desired accuracy faster than the classical approach.

6 Conclusion

In summary, we proposed a novel GNN variant, a hybrid quantum-classical model, QMolNet for the chemical tasks in organic chemistry. The architecture combines classical data with a quantum circuit to enhance the accuracy of the classification task of protein-ligand interactions by conducting extensive experiments on the proposed model with varying numbers of qubits and cut-off ranges of the molecule using a suitable quantum encoding scheme to demonstrate the and effect of quantum circuit design on the training performance of the hybrid quantum graph neural network model compared to classical models. The introduction of the non-covalent adjacency matrix A was motivated by recognizing that non-covalent atoms within a molecule hold equal significance to covalent bonds when finding molecular properties and interactions, as demonstrated by phenomena like the field effect. We found that the optimal cut-off range for A was 6 $\overset{\circ}{A}$ based on screening from 4 to 7 $\overset{\circ}{A}$. We observed that by training only a subset of the parameters using a quantum circuit with basic entanglement, we achieve comparable performance to the classical model (up to 5 $\overset{\circ}{A}$) and outperform it at 6 $\overset{\circ}{A}$. The QMolNet model, structured with A and the weighted bond matrix B, showed promising performance in the classification task of protein ligand binding. This suggests the necessity for chemically intuitive molecular representations in DL chemistry. The results are compared with the latest paper on Graph Neural Networks [4]. This is the first study of its kind to explore the impact of the quantum circuit design on the model's training performance for this classification task. In this study, we have utilized a simulator for the hybrid QMolNet model, disregarding noise effects for the sake of clarity. Looking forward, our next steps involve transitioning towards utilizing quantum hardware, allowing us to study the impact of noise and other real-world influences on our simulations. This practical implementation is expected to provide deeper insights into the applicability and robustness of our approach. However, for a small number of qubits (less than 8), the QGNN exhibits slightly lower performance compared to the classical model despite having 24 trainable parameters. This drawback constrains the model's applicability for cases involving fewer than 8 qubits. Further investigation will be conducted to explore this effect in greater detail in future research. Nonetheless, the QMolNet model introduced in this context holds the potential for developing deep learning models that capture chemical intuition facilitated by the appropriate digital encoding of molecules.

Acknowledgments. The authors acknowledge the use of the PennyLane and PyTorch libraries in their implementation. Python programming language was primarily used for coding and for obtaining results. S.G. and V.C. contributed equally to this research's design, development, experimental work, and paper writing.

Conflict of Interest. The authors acknowledge Fractal Analytics for their funding, support and resources for this research.

References

García, D.P., Cruz-Benito, J., García-Penalvo, F.J.: Systematic literature review: quantum machine learning and its applications. Comput. Sci. Rev. **51**, 100619 (2022)

Alam, M., Kundu, S., Topaloglu, R.O., Ghosh, S.: Quantum-classical hybrid machine learning for image classification (ICCAD special session paper). Int. Conf. Comput. Aided Des. **2021**, 1–7 (2021)

Batra, K., et al.: Quantum machine learning algorithms for drug discovery applications. J. Chem. Inf. Modell. **61**(6), 2641–2647 (2021)

Kim, Y., Jeong, Y., Kim, J., Lee, E.K., Kim, W.J., Choi, I.S.: Molnet: a chemically intuitive graph neural network for prediction of molecular properties. Chem. Asian J. **17**(16), e202200269 (2022)

Vyas, V.K., Ukawala, R.D., Ghate, M., Chintha, C.: Homology modeling a fast tool for drug discovery: Current perspectives. Indian J. Pharm. Sci. **74**(1), 1 (2012)

Torng, W., Altman, R.B.: Graph convolutional neural networks for predicting drug-target interactions. J. Chem. Inf. Model. **59**(10), 4131–4149 (2019)

Tang, B., Kramer, S. T., Fang, M., Qiu, Y., Wu, Z., and Xu, D.: A self-attention based message passing neural network for predicting molecular lipophilicity and aqueous solubility (2020)

Hu, Z., Dong, Y., Wang, K., Chang, K.-W., and Sun, Y.: Gpt-gnn: Generative pretraining of graph neural networks (2020)

Wu, Z., Ramsundar, B., Feinberg, E., Gomes, J., Geniesse, C., Pappu, A.S., Leswing, K., Pande, V.: Moleculenet: a benchmark for molecular machine learning. Chem. Sci. **9**, 513–530 (2018). https://doi.org/10.1039/C7SC02664A

Berry, D.W., Gidney, C., Motta, M., McClean, J.R., Babbush, R.: Qubitization of arbitrary basis quantum chemistry leveraging sparsity and low rank factorization. Quantum **3**, 208 (2019). https://doi.org/10.22331/q-2019-12-02-208

Zhou, L., Wang, S.-T., Choi, S., Pichler, H., Lukin, M.D.: Quantum approximate optimization algorithm: performance, mechanism, and implementation on nearterm devices. Phys. Rev. X **10**(2), 021067 (2020). https://doi.org/10.1103/physrevx.10.021067

Suryotrisongko, H. and Musashi, Y.: Evaluating hybrid quantum classical deep learning for cybersecurity botnet dga detection. In: Procedia Computer Science, vol. 197, pp. 223–229, 2022, sixth Information Systems International Conference (ISICO 2021). [Online]. Available: https://www.sciencedirect.com/science/article/pii/S1877050921023590

Mattern, D., Martyniuk, D., Willems, H., Bergmann, F., and Paschke, A.: Variational quanvolutional neural networks with enhanced image encoding (2021)

Bergholm, V. et al.: Pennylane: automatic differentiation of hybrid quantum-classical computations (2022)

Paszke, A., et al.: Pytorch: an imperative style, high-performance deep learning library (2019)

Thomas, N.K. and Max W.: Semi-supervised classification with graph convolutional networks (2017)

Cho, H. and Choi, I.S.: Enhanced deep-learning prediction of molecular properties via augmentation of bond topology (2019)

Kearnes, S., McCloskey, K., Berndl, M., Pande, V. and Riley, P.: Molecular graph convolutions: moving beyond fingerprints. (2016)

Gilmer, J., Schoenholz, S.S., Riley, O.Vinyals, P.F., and Dahl, G.E.: Neural message passing for quantum chemistry. pp. 1263–1272 (2017)

Comparative Analysis on Speech Driven Gesture Generation

Pranav Unnikrishnan, K. S. R. Logesh, Abinesh Sivakumar, R. Manesh Karun,
Jyothis V. Santhosh, and G. Jyothish Lal$^{(\boxtimes)}$

Amrita School of Artificial Intelligence, Amrita Vishwa Vidyapeedham Coimbatore,
Coimbatore, India
jyothishlal@cb.amrita.edu

Abstract. This study presents a comparative analysis of various deep- learning methods for gesture generation from speech, contributing to the field
of human-agent interaction. The primary focus lies in advancing interactions
with virtual agents and robots through the application of varied representation
learning approaches. The methodologies employ Gated Recurrent Unit (GRU),
Bidirectional-GRU, and Multi-head attention techniques to build a concise representation of human gestures, acting as motion encoders and decoders. Incorporating a pre-existing gesture generation approach, the established groundwork
through the utilization of a network named Speech E is leveraged. Furthermore,
an in-depth analysis of diverse speech feature inputs' impact on the model's performance is pursued. This network is designed to efficiently transform speech
input into a gesture representation with reduced dimensions. The influence of
different speech feature inputs on the model's performance is explored. The integration of GRU, Bidirectional-GRU, and Multi-Head Attention methods allow a
thorough evaluation of their effectiveness in translating speech into corresponding gestures. This study provides insights into the potential of these techniques,
and their implications for creating more intuitive and responsive virtual agents
and robots. Notably, our investigations exclusively utilize Mel-Frequency Cepstral Coefficients (MFCCs) as features, revealing the optimal performance of our
models. This careful feature selection shines brightly in our results, where our
Bi-directional GRU model outshines the rest.

Keywords: gesture generation · GRU · multi-head attention · representation
learning

1 Introduction

As we march into the era of spatial computing, including Augmented Reality (AR), Virtual Reality (VR), and Extended Reality (XR), human-robot inter- actions are evolving.
Combining robotics with artificial intelligence unlocks un- precedented possibilities for
enhancing these interactions, but challenges exist - chiefly, the effective use of gestures
and non-verbal cues, which are central to human communication. Gestures and non-
verbal cues aren't mere decorations in human interaction - they're powerful carriers of

H. K. et al. (Eds.): AIKP 2023, CCIS 2127, pp. 160–172, 2024.
https://doi.org/10.1007/978-3-031-68617-7_12

meaning, context, and emotion [5]. They enrich the interaction and help improve under-standing between individ- uals. Considering human-robot interactions, including these nonverbal cues can significantly improve a robot's ability to understand and respond appropriately to user intentions. This research aims to advance human-robot communi-cation by evaluating deep learning techniques for generating human-like gestures from speech. The key contribution of this work is a comprehensive comparison of recurrent neural network architectures like GRU, Bi-GRU, and multi-head at- tention for speech-to-gesture mapping. The experiments provide novel insights into the potential of these techniques for creating more intuitive virtual agents and robots. This paper extends on the previous work [15] by exploring various models, and providing an in-depth evalua-tion. The work in [15] focused on differ- ent speech inputs and representation learning. This demonstrates the benefit of representation learning for gesture generation. This study presents a comparison of different frameworks designed to generate motion rep-resentations from speech. RNNs like GRU and LSTM have proven effective for a wide range of sequen- tial modeling tasks. Attention mechanisms have also shown success in focusing on relevant parts of the input. The experiments allow a thorough evaluation of these techniques for speech-to-gesture mapping to determine the most suitable methods for this application.

1.1 Contribution

The main contributions of this study are:

- Comprehensive comparison of RNN architectures like GRU, BiGRU, and multi-head attention for speech-driven gesture generation.
- Analysis of the effectiveness of these techniques for translating speech into corre-sponding representative gestures.
- Novel insights into the potential of these methods for developing more nat- ural and intuitive human-robot interactions.

This study focuses on sequence-to-sequence methods based on previous research and a comprehensive comparison of RNN architectures like GRU, BiGRU, and multi-head attention for speech-driven gesture generation is provided. The ef- fectiveness of these techniques for translation speech into corresponding motion representations is analysed. This provides novel insights into the potential of these methods for developing more natural and intuitive human-robot interac- tions. The framework's ability to generate significant gestures from speech shows its potential for enhancing communication and interaction with conversational robot agents. The implementation of this project can be found in this repository.

2 Literature Review

The synthesis of co-speech gestures is an important area of study for improv- ing human-computer interaction and virtual reality. Various methods have been proposed, with several common themes.

Ginosar et al. [10] proposed a conditional learning approach that generates gesture sequences based on speech audio input. They also emphasized the im- portance of including head motion and introduced novel metrics for gesture synchronization and fidelity evaluation. Kucherenko et al. [15] proposed a model to generate both beat and semantic gestures using both audio and semantic fea- tures of speech. In the realm of speech signal analysis, a novel approach for the estimation of epochs from emotional speech signals was introduced by [16]. This method notably exploits the variational mode decomposition technique, showing high accuracy in the detection of epoch locations, especially in emotive speech signals.

Recognizing the challenges in classifying the speech of non-native English speak- ers, [8] proposed a novel database of non-native Indian English speaker ac- cents, addressing the unbalanced dataset issues observed in earlier studies. They tested various accent classification models, revealing xResNet18 as particularly effective for accent identification.

Kucherenko et al. [15] recognized the limitations related to the use of a sin- gle input modality and the scalability of the model to real-world applications. Zhu et al. [21] introduced a diffusion-based framework (DiffGesture) that cap- tures cross-modal audio-gesture associations and temporal coherence, demon- strating its effectiveness on two benchmark datasets. Delving into speech en- hancement, [22] explored temporal and spectral features of speech signals to design neural network models, such as CNN, RNN, and LSTM, for the pur- pose of enhancing degraded speech. They introduced an end-to-end deep learn- ing model, WaveNet + LSTM, which showcased improved performance, especially when trained using frequency domain and time domain features.

Ferstl et al. [9] examined the potential of transfer learning to improve gesture gen- eration and emphasized the need for more diverse datasets and the applica- tion of state-of-the-art speech recognition models. Continuing on, Youngwoo Yoon et al. [18, 20] presented models using various input modalities such as speech text, audio, and speaker ID. Their work highlighted the need for further exploration in gesture styles and the inclusion of hand or facial expressions in gesture generation.

Zhao et al. [11] and Ao et al. [4] focused on animating virtual humans using speech synthesis and ensuring temporal coherence in gesture synthesis, respec- tively. Yoon et al. [19] reported on the GENEA Challenge, which sought to compare various gesture-generation methods, stressing the need for research focused on gesture appropriate-ness. Bhattacharya et al. [6, 7] used GAN and transformer- based learning methods to generate emotionally expressive gestures. Their work recognized the limitation of datasets to English-language TED Talks and the need for real-time applications. Ahuja et al. [2] introduced AISLe which combines adversarial learning with importance sam- pling and extended the PATS dataset to study the effect of language and speech on gesture generation. Kucherenko et al. [13, 14] attempted to establish a benchmark for data-driven gesture generation and proposed a compact representation of motion from speech, recognizing the need for larger and more diverse datasets. Lastly, Hasegawa et al. [12] devel-oped a framework for generating natural gesture motions from audio utterances, highlighting the need for further exploration of varying network architectures and hyperparameters.

Each of these studies adds valuable insights into the field of co-speech gesture synthesis, but also highlights the remaining challenges and areas for future research. Figure 1 shows a timeline diagram for the literature review conducted in this study.

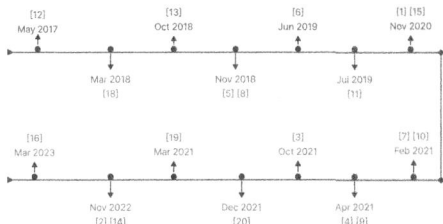

Fig. 1. Timeline diagram for literature review

3   Dataset Description

The experiments were conducted using a dataset of gestures compiled by Takeuchi et al. quoteb17. This dataset consists of motion data recorded by two people who conducted interviews and conversations in a motion capture studio. Kinematic profiles are stored in the BioVision Hierarchy (BVH) format and describe motion as a time series of Eulerian rotations for each joint in a defined skeletal hierarchy. The dataset also contains MP3-encoded speech audio recorded using the headset microphone in each speaker. Motion data were transformed into a total of 64 3D global joint positions, and all recordings were down-sampled to a total frame rate of 20 frames per second (fps). For representational learning, each dimension is normalized to a mean value of zero and a maximum (absolute) value of one.

The dataset contains 1047 utterances, of which 957 are used for training, 45 for validation, and 45 for testing in the experiments. The model was trained using 171 min of training data (20 fps), resulting in 206,000 training frames. The aim of the experiments was to determine the relationship between different speech sound features and 64 articulation positions.

4   Speech-Motion Mapping Using Representation Learning

In the collective research, the methodology presented by a precedent-setting study [7] is employed and expanded upon, which proposes a novel approach for speech-driven gesture generation using representation learning. This research frames the task as such: given a sequence of speech features, designated as 's', extracted at regular intervals from speech audio, the goal is to generate a corresponding gesture sequence that a human might perform while speaking these words. These speech features, represented by a speech segment 's_t', are typically characterized using Mel-Frequency Cepstral Coefficients (MFCCs) [18] or prosodic features such as pitch and energy [14]. The corresponding gestures, both ground truth 'g_t' and predicted '$\hat{g}_t$', are typically represented as sequences of 3D coordinates corresponding to key points on the human body, such as the shoul- der or elbow. The method employed in this study builds upon the prior work of Hasegawa et al., utilizing a neural network to map input speech sequences to corresponding gesture sequences, with modifications for efficiency and perfor- mance. Notably, Gated Recurrent Units (GRUs) is used instead of Bi-LSTMs and employed with a shorter window length for computing MFCC features.

5 Methodology

The proposed approach comprises of three steps:

1. Representation learning is applied to learn the motion representation.
2. The speech features are mapped to the motion representation which was obtained from the previous step.
3. Both the mappings are combined to tranform speech input into gestures.

Here, the speech input is fed to a network (SpeechE) that generates a se- quence of motion representations that are then translated into joint coordinates by a decoding network (MotionD). To implement the original neural network, input from 61×26 elements containing 26-dimensional speech-derived MFCC vec- tors from the current frame and 30 neighboring frames is taken. The network architecture includes a fully connected (FC) layer and a GRU layer, both of width 256. The network was trained for 120 epochs using the Adam optimizer. Furthermore, a DAE is employed with an input size of 384 and one hidden layer in the encoder and decoder. The DAE is optimized to give the best perfor- mance on the validation data, using a bottleneck layer with 325 units. The DAE is trained for 20 epochs with the Adam optimizer. These implementation details ensure that the model is well-suited for speech-driven gesture generation tasks, contributing towards a more immersive and realistic user interaction experience. The overall methodology of this study is shown in Fig. 2. In this study, the SpeechE model is focused upon, which maps the speech to motion representa- tions. Four different models,

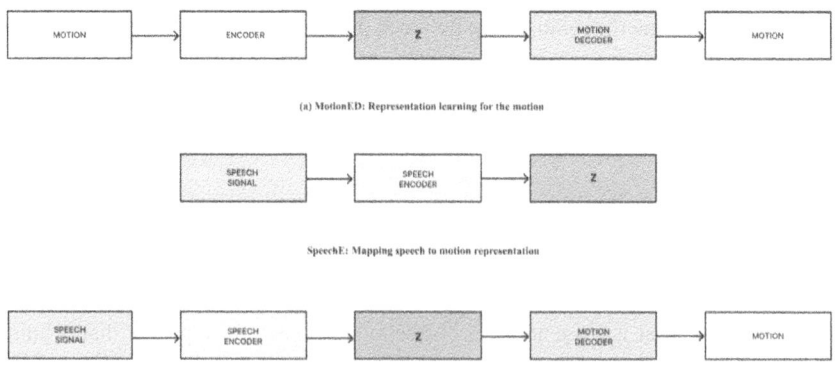

Fig. 2. Encoder-Decoder architecture for representation learning

are used here to achieve this task shown in Fig. 3. Firstly, two models GRU and Bi-GRU architectures are employed, while the other two models are modified by adding attention layers to these initial mod- els. The objective is to find the best representation for the motion which can be decoded using the decoder from MotionED shown in Fig. 2(c).

6   Feature Extraction

In this study, the most efficient input functions for speech-gesture model were determined. The experiments were performed using MFCC functions. The choice of input features is critical to the ease of learning and expressive limitations of speech-gesture systems. Simple features that capture the most relevant infor- mation are appropriate for learning from limited datasets. However, richer and more complicated features require more data to attain good accuracy.

For MFCC, 26 coefficients were obtained with a window length of 0.02 s and a jump length of 0.01 s, resulting in 100 analysis frames every second. Frequencies with little speech information are removed and the MFCC sequence is scaled down to match the motion frequency of 20 frames/s by replacing every 5 (MFCC) frames with their average value.

7   Architecture

GRU (Gated Recurrent Unit). Using this architecture Fig. 4(b), the input sequence, which consists of MFCC features extracted from speech, is fed into the GRU network. The GRU cells contain gating mechanisms that control the flow of information. These gates, namely the reset gate and update gate, determine.

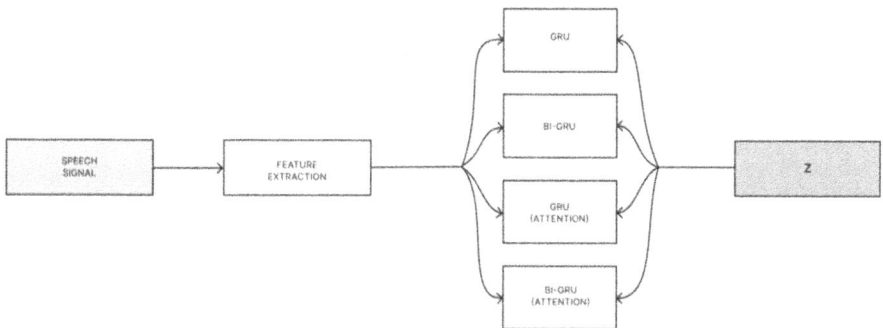

Fig. 3. Methodology for generating motion representations

how the network incorporates new information and updates its internal state. The GRU architecture learns to capture temporal dependencies in the speech input and generate corresponding gestures.

The Bidirectional Gated Recurrent Unit (BiGRU). BiGRU architecture Fig. 4(b) is a variant of recurrent neural networks (RNNs) that processes input sequences in both forward and backward directions. By capturing context from both past and future, BiGRU excels in modeling sequential data and understand- ing complex dependencies. It is particularly useful in tasks like natural language processing and time series analysis, where context is crucial for accurate predic- tions. The combination of two GRU layers enables BiGRU to capture long-term dependencies and produce more accurate predictions.

Multi-head Attention. In Multi-head attention Fig. 4(c), the input MFCC features are transformed into a sequence of embeddings. Multi-head attention operates by computing attention scores between different positions in the input sequence. It enables the network to generate gestures based on pertinent sections of the spoken input. Using numerous attention heads, the model may pay to different portions of speech input at the same time, allowing it to capture diverse information and make expressive gestures.

8   Model Parameters

Four distinct recurrent neural network (RNN) architectures were implemented to perform speech to motion mapping. The unidirectional Gated Recurrent Unit (GRU), the Bidirectional GRU (Bi-GRU), GRU with an attention layer, and Bi- GRU with attention. Each architecture's model parameters were meticulously.

chosen to optimize their performance. The unidirectional GRU was configured with 256 hidden units, ensuring an apt balance between model complexity and computational efficiency. For the Bi-GRU, the same hidden unit count was main- tained, with an added dropout rate of 0.3 to counter overfitting. In the case of the attention-enhanced variants, batch size of 64 was employed to balance con- vergence speed and memory usage. The Adam optimizer with a conservative learning rate of 0.001 facilitated controlled convergence during training for all models. This thoughtful selection of model parameters ensures their effective implementation and demonstrates their utility across various sequential data tasks.

9   Hardware

The Model was trained using cloud computers which had the following components:

– 30 vCPUs
– 200 GiB RAM
– 1x A10 GPU (24 GB PCIe)

10   Numerical Evaluation Measures

Average Position Error (APE) The APE is the average Euclidean distance between the predicted coordinates $g\hat{}$ and the original coordinates g:

$$APE\left(g_t^n,\ g_t^{\wedge n}\right) = \frac{1}{DT} \sum_{t=1}^{T} \sum_{d=1}^{D} \left\| g_t^n,\ g_t^{\wedge n} \right\|_2 \tag{1}$$

where T is the total duration of the sequence, D is the size of the motion profile and n is the index of the sequence.

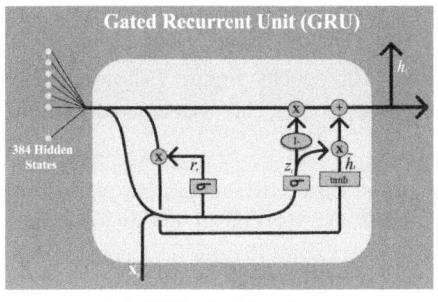

(a) GRU Architecture

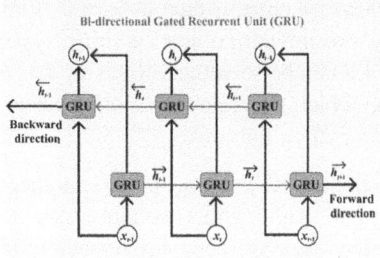

(b) BiGRU Architecture

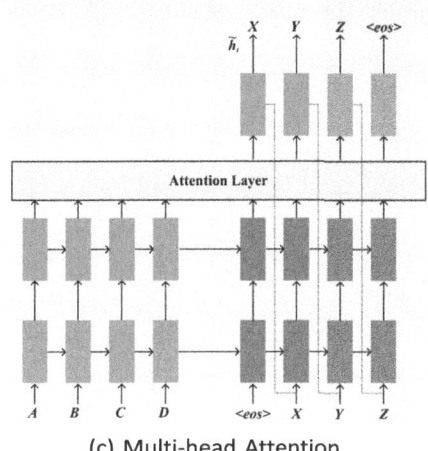

(c) Multi-head Attention

Fig. 4. Model Architectures

The mean and distribution of the acceleration and thrust of the generated motion were considered for computing the motion statistics of the model.

The aim of this study was to identify the most informative features in gesture generation tasks. Motion statistics are the most informative, because the aim of gesture generation is to generate realistic motion rather than to reproduce a specific real-world position. For motion to be reasonable, measurements like speed or thrusts must follow a comparable distribution rather than the initial motion perfectly. As a result, this study focuses on distribution statistics such average speed and pushes. To account for randomness in system training, such as random initial network weights, each condition was performed five times and the mean and standard deviation of the results were calculated.

11 Results

The performance metrics of various gesture generation models are summarized in Table 1. Additionally, the acceleration and velocity distributions generated by the model are shown in Fig. 5. Acceleration distribution is essential for un- derstanding how objects behave when subjected to various forces while velocity distributions offer insight into the movement of objects within a system. The model training losses are shown in Fig. 6 and it can be seen that all the models converge by 100 epochs. Figure 7 shows a demo app which generates the motion for the uploaded audio file. This was created with the help python libraries.

- **Base-GRU:** Sourced from another paper [7], the Base-GRU model has an APE of 7.66. Although its average acceleration prediction (0.29) is consid- erably lower than the original (0.53), it overestimates the average jerk, pre- dicting 0.91 compared to the original value of 0.38. The MAE is not provided for this model.
- **GRU:** The GRU model delivers an APE of 8.02. It shows improved pre- dictions for average acceleration and jerk when compared to the Base-GRU. However, its MAE of 3.95 indicates a considerable margin of error.

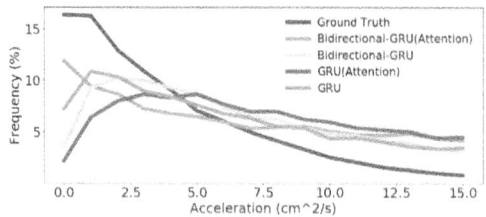

(a) Acceleration distributions given different speech architectures.

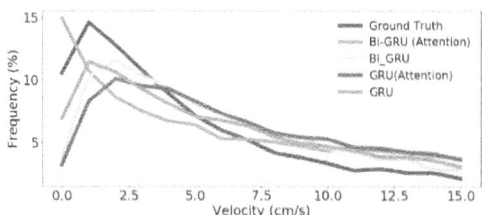

(b) Velocity distributions given different speech architectures.

Fig. 5. Comparative analysis of acceleration and velocity distributions with different speech architectures.

- **Bi-GRU:** This model stands out with an APE of 7.57, offering improved performance in predicting average acceleration and jerk. With an MAE of 3.76, it's more accurate than the GRU model.
- **GRU (Attention):** Integrating attention mechanisms, this model reaches an APE of 7.76. While it portrays enhanced predictive power for average acceleration and jerk compared to the Bi-GRU model, the introduction of the attention mechanism appears to contribute to greater variability. This is reflected by its higher MAE of 3.86.

Table 1. Performance Metrics of Different Models

Model (MFCCs)	APE	Avg. Acceleration		Avg. Jerk		MAE
		Orig	Pred	Orig	Pred	
Base-GRU	7.66	0.53	0.29	0.38	0.91	-
GRU	8.02	0.53	0.29	0.38	0.18	3.95
Bi-GRU	**7.57**	0.53	1.09	0.38	0.65	**3.76**
GRU (Attention)	7.76	0.53	1.10	0.38	1.82	3.86
Bi-GRU (Attention)	7.75	0.53	1.06	0.38	1.75	3.85

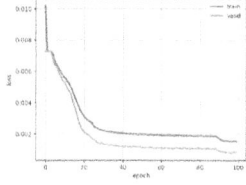

(a) Bi-GRU with Attention

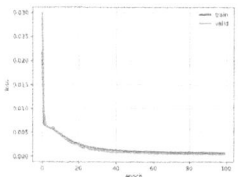

(b) GRU with Attention

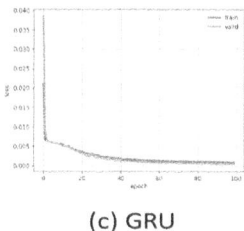

(c) GRU

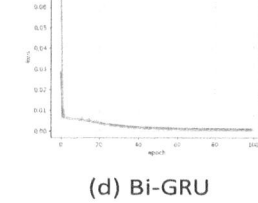

(d) Bi-GRU

Fig. 6. Model Training

12 Limitations

One primary limitation of this approach was like other data-driven methods, is the need for a significant amount of high-quality parallel speech-and-motion training data, which can be challenging and time-consuming to obtain. Further- more, the current dataset primarily consists of speech from a single person, indi- cating the potential benefit of incorporating a more diverse dataset to improve convergence and achieve more natural results.

In addition, further investigation is required regarding hyperparameter tun- ing. The limitations of the computing resources hindered the ability to optimize hyperparam- eters effectively during implementation. To overcome this challenge and enhance the model's performance, it is essential to explore different settings and conduct a comprehensive hyperparameter search. This exploration can lead to improved results and better alignment between the speech and gesture gen- eration processes.

13 Conclusion

In conclusion, this research paper contributes to speech-to-gesture generation by exploring different models and techniques. Through comprehensive experimen- tation and analysis, the efficacy of models such as GRU, Bidirectional GRU, and Multi-Head Attention were demonstrated. Incorporating representation learning and attention mechanisms improves the quality and alignment of generated ges- tures. These findings have wideranging implications for applications in human- computer interaction, virtual reality, and robotics, enhancing immersive and interactive experiences.

14 Future Work

It would be beneficial to include text and speech audio in the gesture generation process. Movements occurring concurrently with speech are strongly dependent on the semantics of the utterance. Currently, the model mainly generates stroke movements because it uses only speech acoustics as input. Using the transcription of utterance-containing texts, a broader range of gestures, including metaphorical and deictic gestures can be generated, which improves the expressive ability and naturalness of the generated gestures.

Furthermore, another avenue for future exploration is the utilization of gener- ative adversarial network (GAN)-like architectures in gesture generation. GANs have demonstrated success in generating realistic and diverse samples in various domains. By incorporating GAN-like architectures into the model, the diver- sity and quality of the generated gestures can be potentially enhanced, lead- ing to more nuanced and contextually appropriate interactions between virtual agents/robots and humans.

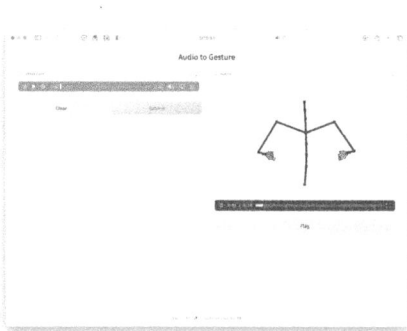

Fig. 7. Demo app created using Gradio

References

1. Kucherenko, T., et al.: Gesticulator: a framework for semantically-aware speech-driven gesture generation. In: 2020, Proceedings of the 2020 Inter- national Conference on Multimodal Interaction: ICMI 2020, Association for Com- puting Machinery, pp. 242–250 (2020), https://doi.org/10.1145/3382507.3418815
2. Ahuja, C., et al.: No gestures left behind: learning relationships between spoken language and freeform gestures. In: Findings of the Association for Com- putational Linguistics: EMNLP 2020, Association for Computational Linguistics, pp. 1884–1895 (2020). ACLWeb, https://doi.org/10.18653/v1/2020.findings-emnlp.170
3. Ajay, S., Manisha, R., Nivarthi, P.M., Nadendla, S.H. and Kumar, C.S.: Comparative study of deep learning techniques used for speech enhancement. In: 2021 IEEE 6th International Conference on Computing, Communication and Automation (IC- CCA), Arad, Romania, 2021, pp. 161–165, https://doi.org/10.1109/ICCCA52192.2021.9666413
4. Ao, T., et al.: Rhythmic gesticulator: rhythm-aware co-speech gesture synthesis with hierarchical neural embeddings. ACM Trans. Graph. **41**(6), 1–19 (2022). https://doi.org/10.1145/3550454.3555435
5. Kunjumon, J., and Rajesh K.M.: Hand gesture recognition system for translating Indian sign language into text and speech. In: 2019 Inter- national Conference on Smart Systems and Inventive Technology (ICSSIT), pp. 14–18. IEEE, 2019. https://doi.org/10.1109/ICSSIT46314.2019.8987762
6. Bhattacharya, U., et al.: Speech2Affectivegestures: synthesizing co-speech gestures with generative adversarial affective expression learning. In: Proceedings of the 29th ACM International Conference on Multimedia, 2021, pp. 2027–36. arXiv.org, https://doi.org/10.1145/3474085.3475223
7. Bhattacharya, U., et al.: Text2Gestures: a transformer-based network for generating emotive body gestures for virtual agents. In: 2021 IEEE Virtual Reality and 3D User Interfaces (VR), (2021), pp. 1–10. https://doi.org/10.1109/VR50410.2021.00037
8. Darshana, S, et al.: 'MARS: a hybrid deep cnn-based multi-accent recognition system for English language. In: 2022 First International Conference on Artificial Intelligence Trends and Pattern Recognition (ICAITPR), pp. 1–6. IEEE, (2022). https://doi.org/10.1109/ICAITPR51569.2022.9844177
9. Ferstl, Y., and Rachel, M.: Investigating the use of recurrent motion modelling for speech gesture generation. In: Proceedings of the 18th International Conference on Intelligent Virtual Agents, Association for Computing Machinery, pp. 93–98 (2018). https://doi.org/10.1145/3267851.3267898
10. Ginosar, S., et al.: Learning individual styles of conversational gesture. arXiv, 10 June 2019. arXiv.org, https://doi.org/10.48550/arXiv.1906.04160
11. Habibie, I., et al.: Learning speech-driven 3D conversational gestures from video. (2021). arXiv.org, https://doi.org/10.48550/arXiv.2102.06837
12. Hasegawa, D., et al.: Evaluation of speech-to-gesture generation using bi- directional LSTM network. In: Proceedings of the 18th International Conference on Intelligent Virtual Agents, Association for Computing Machinery, pp. 79–86 (2018). ACM Digital Library. https://doi.org/10.1145/3267851.3267878
13. Kucherenko, T., et al.: A large, crowdsourced evaluation of gesture genera- tion systems on common data: The GENEA Challenge 2020. In: 26th International Conference on Intelligent User Interfaces, pp. 11–21 (2021). https://doi.org/10.1145/3397481.3450692
14. Kucherenko, T., et al.: Moving fast and slow: analysis of representations and post-processing in speech-driven automatic gesture generation. Int. J. Human-Comput. Interact. **37**(14), 1300–16 (2021). https://doi.org/10.1080/10447318.2021.1883883

15. Kucherenko, Taras, et al. 'Analyzing input and output representations for speech- driven gesture generation. In: Proceedings of the 19th ACM International Confer- ence on Intelligent Virtual Agents, pp. 97–104 (2019). https://doi.org/10.1145/3308532.3329472

16. Lal, G.J., et al.: 'Epoch estimation from emotional speech signals using variational mode decomposition. Circ. Syst. Signal Process **37**, 3245–3274 (2018). https://doi.org/10.1007/s00 034-018-0804-x

17. Takeuchi, K., Kubota, S., et al.: Creating a gesture-speech dataset for speech-based automatic gesture. (2017) https://doi.org/10.1007/978-3-319-58750-9_28

18. Yoon, Y., et al.: Robots learn social skills: end-to-end learning of co- speech gesture generation for humanoid robots. (2018). arXiv.org, https://doi.org/10.48550/arXiv.1810.12541

19. Yoon, Y., et al.: The Genea challenge 2022: a large evaluation of data- driven co-speech gesture generation. In: International Conference on Multimodal Interaction, 2022, pp. 736–47. arXiv.org, https://doi.org/10.1145/3536221.3558058

20. Yoon, Y., Cha, B., Lee, J.-H., Jang, M., Lee, J., Kim, J., Lee, G.: Speech gesture generation from the trimodal context of text, audio, and speaker identity. ACM Trans. Graph. **39**(6), 1–16 (2020). https://doi.org/10.1145/3414685.3417838

21. Zhu, L., et al.: Taming diffusion models for audio-driven co-speech gesture generation. arXiv, 18 (2023). arXiv.org,https://doi.org/10.48550/arXiv.2303.09119

22. Ajay, S., Manisha, R., Nivarthi, P.M., Nadendla, S.H., and Kumar, C.S.: Comparative study of deep learning techniques used for speech enhancement. In: 2021 IEEE 6th International Conference on Computing, Communication and Automation (ICCCA), 2021, pp. 161–165, https://ieeexplore.ieee.org/document/9666413

Enhancing Deep Learning: Leveraging Skip Connections and Memory Efficiency

Abhishek Manchukonda[✉]

National Institute of Technology, Warangal, Hanamkonda, India
abhishekmanchukonda@gmail.com

Abstract. With the introduction of skip connections, deep neural network models can now be substantially deeper and can be trained more efficiently. This paper takes Dense Convolutional Network (DenseNet) [5], a cutting-edge architecture, highlighting the significant benefits of establishing dense interconnections between all layers in a unidirectional manner. The paper also discusses all the compelling advantages of DenseNet and evaluates the performance of its architecture on a Kaggle dataset (Dog-Breed Identification) [7]. Furthermore, it explores techniques for optimizing memory utilization while engaged in the training process. This research sheds light on how skip connections have contributed to the efficiency and effectiveness of deep learning models.

Keywords: skip connections · deep neural networks · Dense Convolutional Network (DenseNet) · dense interconnections · unidirectional connections · architecture benefits · performance evaluation

1 Foreword

The stage is set with the emergence of Convolutional Networks (ConvNets), which have revolutionized Visual Computing [20]. These networks excel in tasks like Image Recognition [2] and Object Detection [18], thanks to improved GPU hardware and vast datasets. In this dynamic landscape, we focus on efficiency. It all began with LeNet5's simple 5-layer design and progressed to VGGNet's 19 layers, shattering depth limitations. We explore innovations like Pathway Architectures and Hunag's unidirectional interconnections to tackle vanishing gradients. Instead of traditional methods, we employ "feature fusion," [3] which fosters dense connections.

The rise of Convolutional Networks (ConvNets) [12] has ushered in a paradigm shift in Visual Computing. These networks have garnered exceptional outcomes in diverse tasks encompassing Image Recognition and Object Detection. This has been made possible by the recent advancements in GPU hardware and the availability of huge reliable datasets. Enhancements in computational hardware capabilities and network architectures have facilitated the development and optimization of highly intricate Convolutional Networks. It has also made the training process faster and more efficient. LeNet5 [13] introduced the first CNN architecture consisting of just 5 layers. Subsequently, the introduction of VGGNet brought forth a 19-layer architecture, and more recently, Networks utilizing residual connections [4] emerged, breaking through the constraints of layer depth.

H. K. et al. (Eds.): AIKP 2023, CCIS 2127, pp. 173–182, 2024.
https://doi.org/10.1007/978-3-031-68617-7_13

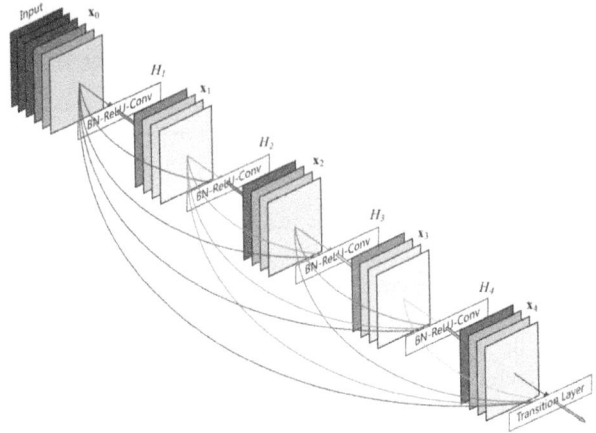

Fig. 1. A 5-layer dense block with a growth rate of k = 4. Each layer takes all preceding feature-maps as input.

With the increase in layer depth within intricate neural structures, the challenge of vanishing gradients becomes apparent. Addressing this concern, ResNets [4] and Pathway Architectures [17] navigate information flow between layers using direct path connections. This counters the issue of vanishing gradient. However, FractalNets (Highly Layered Computational Framework without Signal Carryovers) [11], without including any pass-through or residual connections achieve a comparable performance to deep Residual Networks. This illustrates that the presence of residual representations might not be intrinsic to the achievements of highly intricate convolutional architectures (Fig. 2).

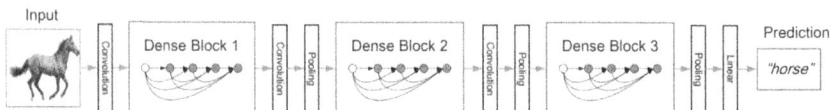

Fig. 2. A deep DenseNet with three dense blocks. The layers between two adjacent blocks are referred to as transition layers and change the feature-map sizes via convolution and pooling.

Hunag [5] introduced an architecture aimed at mitigating the vanishing gradient challenge using an uncomplicated linkage arrangement to facilitate optimal data propagation among network tiers. Under this approach, every layer (with corresponding feature-map dimensions) establishes direct interconnections. To maintain the unidirectional flow, each tier acquires supplementary inputs from prior tiers and conveys its distinctive feature-maps to ensuing tiers.

The provided diagram 1 illustrates the layout in a schematic manner. It is important to note that, unlike other architectures, the information from different layers is combined through a different approach. Instead of using traditional methods, the features are merged using a technique called "feature fusion" which involves combining the information in a concatenated manner. This fusion, $L(L + 1)/2$, occurs at each layer, resulting in a dense connectivity pattern. This unique design choice leads to a higher number of connections within the network, contributing to its distinctive structure.

Also, in my study, I employed the "Dog-Breed Identification" dataset from Kaggle. This dataset is a diverse collection of real-world dog images, each corresponding to a specific dog breed. It presented a multi-class classification challenge, aiming to classify these images into various dog breed categories. The dataset encompassed a wide range of breeds, from standard to rare ones, adding complexity to the classification task. By evaluating my proposed DenseNet architecture against other state-of-the-art methods using metrics such as accuracy, I aimed to demonstrate the effectiveness of DenseNet in accurately classifying dog breeds in this challenging dataset.

2   Computing Infrastructure and Software Stack

In conducting the experiments for this research paper, I utilized NVIDIA GPUs, explicitly focusing on models like the Tesla V100 and GeForce RTX 30 series, to harness their parallel processing capabilities for efficient training of deep neural networks, particularly DenseNet. These GPUs were selected for their robust memory capacity to handle intricate network architectures and large datasets. The computational framework relied on 32 GB RAM to ensure seamless data preprocessing and model training. The experiments were implemented using TensorFlow 2. x as the primary deep learning framework, with Python, NumPy, and Matplotlib for efficient programming, numerical operations, and visualizations. The system operated on Ubuntu 20.04, providing a stable platform for compatibility with the chosen hardware and software stack. The inclusion of Git for version control facilitated collaboration and tracking throughout the research process, collectively contributing to the computational efficiency required for evaluating DenseNet in the Dog-Breed Identification context.

3   DenseNet

Before delving into the mechanisms of skip connections and their pivotal role in the DenseNet framework, it's essential to establish a clear understanding of the DenseNet model's architecture. DenseNet is characterized by its dense, interconnected structure, which fosters feature reuse and information flow. Unlike conventional forward-propagation in convolutional networks, where each layer merely passes its output to the subsequent layer, DenseNet employs a unique approach. In the DenseNet architecture, direct pathways are established from any given layer to all ensuing layers, creating a seamless flow of information. This architecture ensures that each layer gains access to the feature maps derived from all antecedent layers, denoted as x0, x1, xl-1, serving as its input. This architectural foundation forms the basis for the subsequent discussion on skip connections and their role in enhancing gradient propagation.

Conventional forward-propagation in convolutional networks involves linking the output of a given tier to the input of the subsequent one. In contrast, [4] the inclusion of a skip link allows for bypassing certain tiers through an identity function. This mechanism facilitates a direct path for gradient propagation via the identity route.

On the contrary, in the DenseNet framework, direct pathways are established from any given tier to all ensuing tiers. As a result, the `th` ayer gains access to features derived from all antecedent tiers, denoted as `x0, . . . . , xl-1`, as input:

$$x_l = H_l([x_0, x_1, ..., x_{l-1}])$$

where '[x0, x1, . . . , xl−1]' signifies the amalgamation of feature-maps generated in layers `0. . . . . 1-1` and Hl denotes a nonlinearity function of choice..

4   Evaluations

4.1   Effectiveness Assessments

It achieves noteworthy advancements beyond the latest in the field of identification across four challenging evaluation scenarios (CIFAR-10 [8], CIFAR-100 [9], SVHN [14], and ImageNet [16]). To verify that the DenseNet is as good as mentioned by the authors, it was tested on a Kaggle competition task (Dog-Breed Identification [7]). The results were compared with ResNet [4] and InceptionNet [19] that won the ImageNet [16] Image Recognition Challenge in the past (Fig. 3).

As seen in Table 1, DenseNet performs significantly better (89.9% accuracy) than ResNet and InceptionNet for Dog-Breed Identification [7]. The performance of DenseNet was even significant than other models when no preprocessing was performed (as seen in Table 2). It shows that connecting every layer's output to each subsequent layers allowed the model to learn the features more effectively. Hence, lesser data augmentation is needed for DenseNet as compared to other models for the given task.

Table 1. Accuracy of different model architectures on Dog-Breed Identification task.

Model	Data Augmentation
ResNet50	88.2%
InceptionNet	87.4%
DenseNet	89.9%

Moreover, for the evaluation, it was employed in the domain of partitioning. Leading techniques in partitioning frequently leverage advanced neural networks. The architecture for most tasks perform (1) a downsampling of the image to get the features, (2) then an upsampling to get the image back, (3) and post processing like Conditional Random Field (CRF) [10] and pre processing modules like data augmentation is done to get better results. Numerous distinct architectures of convolutional networks were experimented with, and DenseNet demonstrated remarkable outcomes, as witnessed

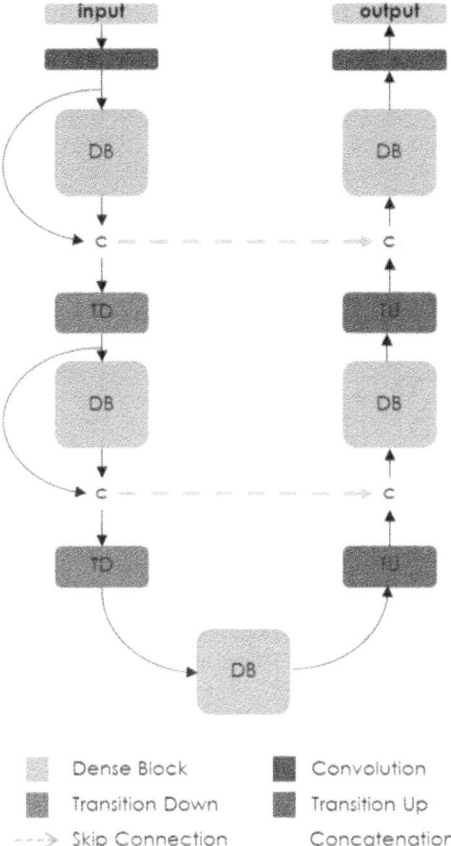

Fig. 3. The architecture has 2 Transition Up (TU) blocks an 2 Transition Down (TD) blocks and gray arrows represent the skip connections from TU blocks to TD blocks. (Color figure online)

Table 2. Accuracy of different model architectures on Dog-Breed Identification task without data augmentation.

Model	Without Data Augmentation
ResNet50	82.7%
InceptionNet	81.9%
DenseNet	86.4%

by Jegou's observations [6]. Additionally, they achieved impressive performance, via CamVid [1] and Gatech, bypassing the need for post-processing or pre-training. This shows the effectiveness of DenseNet on a task other than Image Recognition or Object Detection.

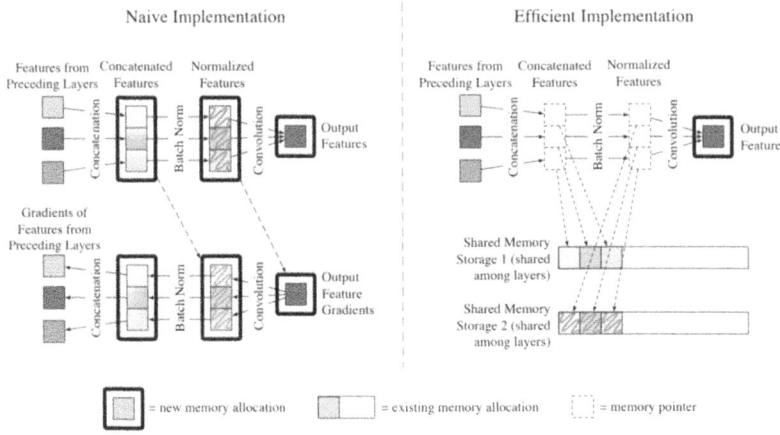

Fig. 4. Original DenseNet implementation is on the left and its memory efficient implementation is on the right. Optimizing memory usage includes caching the combined results of specific operations, while the conventional method requires allocating new memory resources.

4.2 Memory Consumption

DenseNet implementation in general require higher memory as seen in Fig. 4. Without proper management, certain operations can lead to a rapid growth of computational demands as the network deepens. To mitigate these challenges, by Pleiss [15] proposed the concept of Shared Memory Storage. Throughout the feedforward stage, intermediate outputs were allocated to memory. In reverse propagation, dynamic computation was conducted.

4.3 Training Time

DenseNet's training time per epoch is majorly lesser as compared to ResNet and InceptionNet using the identical schema. These experiments showed a decrease of 0 training time for DenseNet per epoch. However, to achieve the best possible results, DenseNet needs to be trained over 100 epochs as compared to 20 epochs for ResNets. This is 5 times more than the other models. So, a tradeoff exists between training time and accuracy for DenseNet.

To delve deeper into the trade-off between training time and accuracy discussed in this research paper, it's essential to emphasize that while DenseNet offers efficiency in terms of training time, achieving the highest accuracy with this architecture necessitates a trade-off. Specifically, while the training time per epoch is considerably lower compared to other models, DenseNet demands an extended training period over more epochs, roughly five times more than alternative models like ResNet. This trade-off implies that researchers and practitioners must make a strategic choice when considering the use of DenseNet in their applications. They can optimize for faster training by sacrificing a portion of accuracy or commit more time and computational resources to attain higher accuracy levels. This aspect highlights the practical implications of choosing the appropriate training settings based on specific project requirements and computational constraints, a consideration crucial for successfully applying DenseNet in various deep learning tasks.

5   Performance Evaluation and Computational Challenges

In the pursuit of evaluating the performance of DenseNet on the Kaggle dataset for breed identification, a critical analysis revealed notable computational challenges. While DenseNet exhibited superior accuracy, achieving 89.9% on the task, it came at the expense of increased training time compared to alternative models such as ResNet and InceptionNet. The trade-off between training time and accuracy is noteworthy, with DenseNet requiring an extended training period of approximately five times more epochs than its counterparts. This trade-off emphasizes the need for strategic decisions by researchers and practitioners based on project requirements and computational constraints. The research highlights the practical implications of leveraging DenseNet, emphasizing the delicate balance between achieving optimal accuracy and managing computational resources effectively.

6   Conclusion

A large community of researchers believed that the approach of DenseNet was not very novel and it has been directly/indirectly applied to a lot of tasks earlier. But when observed closely, a lot of thought has been put in by the authors to design the architecture. This has been proved by the avant-garde achieved by DenseNet through several Image Recognition competitions. The concept has been further tested by a series of experiments performed in this paper and by several other researchers [6]. Overall, DenseNet is not a groundbreaking idea but the way it is implemented has achieved desired results and has proven useful for various tasks.

6.1   Memory Efficiency Evaluation

To assess the memory efficiency of our approach, we conducted a comprehensive evaluation on different aspects of our model's memory consumption. This evaluation focused on several key areas:

6.1.1 Memory Consumption Comparison:

We compared the memory consumption of our DenseNet implementation with other widely-used architectures such as ResNet and InceptionNet. This comparison was conducted under the same experimental conditions to provide a clear understanding of the relative memory requirements of each architecture.

6.1.2 Shared Memory Storage:

To mitigate the challenges posed by rapidly growing computational demands as the network deepens, we adopted the concept of Shared Memory Storage, as proposed by Pleiss [13]. This technique involved allocating intermediate outputs to memory during the feedforward stage and dynamic computation during reverse propagation. We evaluated the effectiveness of this approach in reducing memory usage.

6.1.3 Training Time vs. Memory Tradeoff:

We also examined the tradeoff between training time and memory efficiency for DenseNet. Specifically, we investigated how increasing the number of training epochs impacted both training time and memory requirements. This analysis allowed us to determine the optimal balance between model accuracy and memory utilization.

Our evaluation results, presented in Sect. 4.2, shed light on the memory efficiency of our DenseNet implementation, providing insights into its effectiveness and performance in comparison to other architectures. These findings contribute to a deeper understanding of the tradeoffs between memory efficiency and model accuracy, crucial for practical applications in various domains.

The core idea of DenseNet has opened a lot of research areas. It has already been applied in many domains (Document Analysis, Image Recognition, etc.) and it is believed it will be applied in many other areas in the near future. It would be interesting to see if an architecture similar to DenseNet can solve the need of huge amount of data for training deep learning models. The idea of DenseNet can be combined with the idea of ResNet (introduce skip connections), to avoid learning of redundant features over the layers. This is hypothesised to improve the overall training time for DenseNet and to solve problem of overfitting.

7 Comparative Analysis with State-of-the-Art Methods

In deep learning, various state-of-the-art methods have emerged to address the challenges posed by complex neural network architectures. Notably, models such as Residual Networks (ResNets) and Inception Networks (InceptionNets) have achieved remarkable results in tasks like image recognition. In our study, we conducted a thorough comparative analysis to evaluate the effectiveness of our proposed DenseNet architecture against these established methods. Our findings reveal that DenseNet outperforms both ResNets and InceptionNets in the context of Dog-Breed Identification, achieving an impressive accuracy of 89.9% compared to 88.2% and 87.4%, respectively. Moreover, even when no preprocessing is applied, DenseNet maintains its superiority with an accuracy of 86.4%, showcasing its ability to learn features effectively. These results emphasize the substantial benefits of the dense interconnections and the unique 'feature fusion' approach employed in DenseNet. While other methods have made significant contributions to the field, our work demonstrates that the innovative design choices in DenseNet have a tangible impact on improving deep learning efficiency.

References

1. Brostow, G.J., Shotton, J., Fauqueur, J., Cipolla, R.: Segmentation and recognition using structure from motion point clouds. In: Forsyth, D., Torr, P., Zisserman, A. (eds.) ECCV 2008. LNCS, vol. 5302, pp. 44–57. Springer, Heidelberg (2008). https://doi.org/10.1007/978-3-540-88682-2_5
2. Chauhan, R., Ghanshala, K.K., Joshi, R.: Convolutional neural network (CNN) for image detection and recognition. In: 2018 First International Conference on Secure Cyber Computing and Communication (ICSCCC), pp. 278–282. IEEE (2018)
3. Dai, Y., Gieseke, F., Oehmcke, S., Wu, Y., Barnard, K.: Attentional feature fusion. In: Proceedings of the IEEE/CVF Winter Conference on Applications of Computer Vision, pp. 3560–3569 (2021)
4. He, K., Zhang, X., Ren, S., Sun, J.: Deep residual learning for image recognition. CoRR **abs/1512.03385** (2015). http://arxiv.org/abs/1512.03385
5. Huang, G., Liu, Z., Weinberger, K.Q.: Densely connected convolutional networks. CoRR **abs/1608.06993** (2016). http://arxiv.org/abs/1608.06993
6. Jégou, S., Drozdzal, M., Vázquez, D., Romero, A., Bengio, Y.: The one hundred layers tiramisu: Fully convolutional densenets for semantic segmentation. CoRR **abs/1611.09326** (2016). http://arxiv.org/abs/1611.09326
7. Khosla, A., Jayadevaprakash, N., Yao, B., Fei-Fei, L.: Novel dataset for fine-grained image categorization. In: First Workshop on Fine-Grained Visual Categorization, IEEE Conference on Computer Vision and Pattern Recognition. Colorado Springs, CO (2011)
8. Krizhevsky, A., Nair, V., Hinton, G.: Cifar-10 (canadian institute for advanced research). http://www.cs.toronto.edu/~kriz/cifar.html
9. Krizhevsky, A., Nair, V., Hinton, G.: Cifar-100 (canadian institute for advanced research). http://www.cs.toronto.edu/~kriz/cifar.html
10. Lafferty, J.D., McCallum, A., Pereira, F.C.N.: Conditional random fields: probabilistic models for segmenting and labeling sequence data. In: Proceedings of the Eighteenth International Conference on Machine Learning, pp. 282–289. ICML 2001, Morgan Kaufmann Publishers Inc., San Francisco, CA, USA (2001). http://dl.acm.org/citation.cfm?id=645530.655813
11. Larsson, G., Maire, M., Shakhnarovich, G.: Fractalnet: ultra-deep neural networks without residuals. CoRR **abs/1605.07648** (2016). http://arxiv.org/abs/1605.07648
12. LeCun, Y., et al.: Backpropagation applied to handwritten zip code recognition. Neural Comput. **1**(4), 541–551 (1989). https://doi.org/10.1162/neco.1989.1.4.541
13. Lecun, Y., Bottou, L., Bengio, Y., Haffner, P.: Gradient-based learning applied to document recognition. In: Proceedings of the IEEE, pp. 2278–2324 (1998)
14. Netzer, Y., Wang, T., Coates, A., Bissacco, A., Wu, B., Ng, A.Y.: Reading digits in natural images with unsupervised feature learning. In: NIPS Workshop on Deep Learning and Unsupervised Feature Learning 2011 (2011). http://ufldl.stanford.edu/housenumbers/nips2011_housenumbers.pdf
15. Pleiss, G., Chen, D., Huang, G., Li, T., van der Maaten, L., Weinberger, K.Q.: Memory-efficient implementation of densenets. CoRR **abs/1707.06990** (2017). http://arxiv.org/abs/1707.06990

16. Russakovsky, O., et al.: Imagenet large scale visual recognition challenge. CoRR **abs/1409.0575** (2014). http://arxiv.org/abs/1409.0575
17. Srivastava, R.K., Greff, K., Schmidhuber, J.: Training very deep networks. In: Cortes, C., Lawrence, N.D., Lee, D.D., Sugiyama, M., Garnett, R. (eds.) Advances in Neural Information Processing Systems 28, pp. 2377–2385. Curran Associates, Inc. (2015). http://papers.nips.cc/paper/5850-training-very-deep-networks.pdf
18. Suhail, A., Jayabalan, M., Thiruchelvam, V.: Convolutional neural network based object detection: a review. J. Crit. Rev. **7**(11), 786–792 (2020)
19. Szegedy, C., et al.: Going deeper with convolutions. CoRR **abs/1409.4842** (2014). http://arxiv.org/abs/1409.4842
20. Xie, D., Zhang, L., Bai, L., et al.: Deep learning in visual computing and signal processing. Appl. Comput. Intell. Soft Comput. **2017** (2017)

Quality-Based Decision-Making Using Image Processing for Supply Chain Management

Ashish Kumar$^{(\boxtimes)}$ and Sunil Agrawal

ME Department, PDPM IIITDM Jabalpur, Jabalpur, India
{1913603,sa}@iiitdmj.ac.in

Abstract. The current progress and future possible developments in new age technologies have opened the opportunities to transform the existing supply chain system towards making it more effective and efficient. In this direction, one of the existing new age technologies, deep learning-based image processing models have proven to be key technology for enhancing the supply chain management. This paper discusses the role of image processing for quality-based decision making for supply chain management. In this regard, an image processing integrated supply chain system is proposed. The decisions related to procurement, pricing, storage and transportation can be taken based on the outcome of the image processing system i.e., quality of the product. Quality is the main factor that governs the buying tendency of the perishable product by the customer. Image processing provide valuable information to improve several SCM aspects, including inventory management, pricing, storage, and transportation. It will lead to effective management and optimisation of supply chain operations which are essential given the complexity and globalisation of supply chains. The integration of image processing with supply chain has the potential to completely transform supply chain operations, resulting in increased efficiency, cost reduction, and customer satisfaction.

Keywords: Image processing · Decision making · Quality · Supply chain management

1 Introduction

According to projections, the world's food demand would increase dramatically from where it is now by 2050. The demand for food is anticipated to rise by between 50% to 70% by 2050 as a result of population expansion, urbanisation, and changes in dietary habits, according to numerous projections and analyses from organisations like the Food and Agriculture Organisation (FAO) of the United Nations [1]. This demand for food can be met by reducing food waste that happens worldwide and employing efficient and sustainable agriculture methods. This high wastage is more prevalent in the developing economies like India due its unorganized structure that causes inefficiencies and ineffectiveness in the supply chain management. India has 11.3% of arable land of the world and has been reported as a top-ranked country in the world for huge agricultural production for various produces. Due to this, India can play a key role in meeting food demands of the world [2]. However, India faces a difficult time controlling food waste, especially that of perishables, as of 2023. The FAO believes that India wastes a significant amount of food annually. Depending on the source and method of assessment, specific numbers may vary, but it is generally agreed that between 30% and 40% of the total amount of food produced in India is lost or wasted [3]. Reducing wastage of perishable items e.g., fruits, vegetables, dairy products etc. is difficult as well as complex due to its perishability dynamics [4, 5].

The wastage occurs when the product is not suitable for consumption or does not meet minimum quality requirements of the customer and is discarded by the customer. Quality is the main factor that governs the buying or discarding of the product by the customer. The product should be at least of minimum quality as required by the customer. There are several tools and techniques for measuring quality, however estimating its future rate of deterioration is a very complex process due to its dependency on environmental conditions. Another challenge is integrating the quality measuring technique with the existing supply chain structure to take real time decisions based on current quality of the product for supply chain management. Therefore, the main contributions of this research paper are:

- Proposing an image processing integrated supply chain system.
- Describing the quality-based decisions that can be taken across supply chain.
- Explaining the different strategies for implementation of quality-based decision making and its

  Benefits in supply chain management.

2   Overview of Supply Chain Structure

The transportation, storage, and distribution of numerous perishable goods, such as fruits, vegetables, dairy products, meat, and seafood, are all part of the complex and dynamic perishable supply chain in India. India's agricultural and horticultural industries, where a sizable section of the population is employed in agriculture-related activities, play a significant role in the perishable supply chain. A detailed overview of the basic perishable supply chain structure in India is explained below [6] with respect to Fig. 1:

Farmland to Mandi. The perishable supply chain begins at the farmland, where farmers grow fruits, vegetables, and other perishable commodities. After the crops are ready for harvest, farmers gather the produce. After this, the goods are transported to collection and aggregation centers known as mandi, which serve as hubs for consolidating produce from multiple farmers from different regions. At mandi, agents conduct an open auction and wholesalers purchase the goods by offering the highest bid in the bidding process.

Mandi to Distribution Centers. The bought goods need to be transported to the distribution centers managed by the wholesalers to meet demand of the downstream actors of the supply chain as per future requirements.

Distribution Centers to Retail Stores. Retail markets, including local vegetable markets, supermarkets, and grocery stores, are the destination for perishable goods. Retailers purchase perishables from wholesalers who owns the distribution centers and sell them to consumers directly or indirectly.

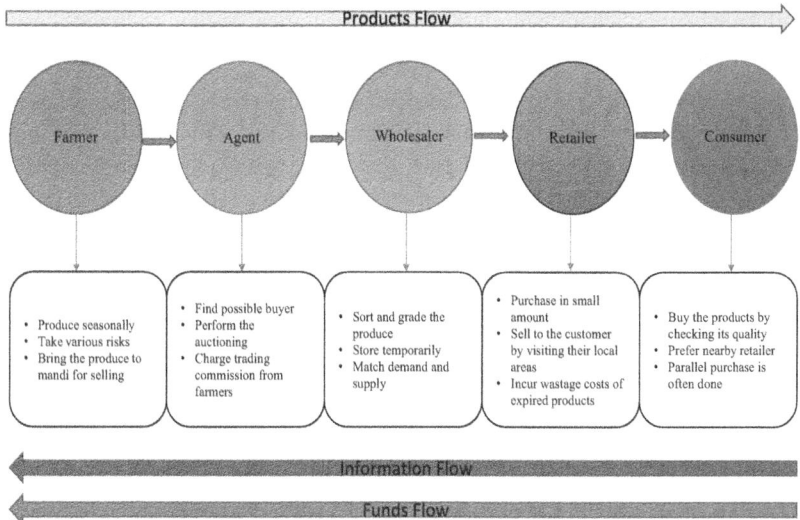

Fig. 1. Overview of supply chain structure in India

Retail Stores to Consumers. In emerging economies like India which largely encompasses unorganised sector, street vendors and hawkers play a significant role in the perishable supply chain, particularly in urban areas. They buy perishables from retail stores and sell them to consumers at various locations, ensuring a widespread distribution network.

Storage and Transportation forms the interlinking chain between all the supply chain actors mentioned above. Because of the perishability dynamics of the product, environmental conditions (temperature, humidity, gas concentrations etc.) in which the product is stored or transported plays a key role in deciding the degradation rate of the product, hence the current quality of the product [7]. The degradation rate multiplied by the time duration determines the total degraded quality of the product. This necessitates the use of some quality detection techniques at the different supply chain echelons in order to take informed, better and rapid decisions for improving the existing supply chain.

2.1 Challenges of Perishable Supply Chain

Due to the different challenges that exist in the perishable supply chain especially in developing economies like India, it makes the current system highly ineffective and inefficient leading to a high post-harvest loss [8]. The challenges identified are:

- Inadequate infrastructure for transportation, particularly in rural areas.
- Seasonal fluctuations in demand and supply, which cause price volatility.
- Ineffective last-mile distribution and logistics that cause delays and quality deteriorated.
- Challenges with quality control brought on by inconsistent grading and sorting practices.

- Fragmented supply chain with multiple intermediaries, leading to higher costs and inefficiencies.

The agriculture and food business needs to spend more in infrastructure, use technology, and collaborate with other stakeholders to address these issues and improve the perishable supply chain. In this aspect, one of the issues, i.e., quality control can be addressed by utilising technology of image processing. All parties involved in the perishable supply chain in India can benefit from improved supply chain management practises in terms of reduced waste, improved product quality, and higher profitability.

2.2 Quality Determination Using Image Processing

Perishable products have very short shelf life ranging from few days to few weeks only. The environmental conditions and other factors affect the quality deterioration rate of the product and hence the remaining shelf life [9]. The quality of the perishable product is the main deciding criteria to decide whether to buy the product or not. However, the definition of the quality of the product varies with respect to the consumer. The quality of perishable fruit refers to its overall condition, characteristics, and attributes that determine its desirability, taste, appearance, and nutritional value for consumption. Several factors contribute to the quality of perishable fruit, and these factors can vary depending on the specific type of product. For example, lack of innovative packaging materials, inadequate monitoring technology, variations in the temperature, approach air velocity, and relative humidity in cold chain systems, and rate of metabolism are some of the main factors accelerating food losses during the postharvest supply chain of fruits and vegetables [10].

For measuring quality of the perishable product, different tools and techniques exist like imaging systems, spectroscopy, multi-sensors, electronic nose (E-nose), acoustic impulse response (AIR), radio frequency identification (RFID), printed sensors (PTS), and mathematical modelling [10]. The major issues are real-time quality measurement as well as its accuracy and rapidness for taking informed supply chain decisions leading reducing food waste. These issues can be tackled by the image processing technology [11–13]. In the context of the perishable supply chain, image processing refers to the application computer algorithms and software to process visual data, such as images or videos, captured from various sources within the perishable supply chain [14, 15]. These sources may include surveillance cameras, sensors, drones, or other imaging devices. Image processing techniques are part of the Machine vision systems. These are equipped with cameras that can visually inspect perishable items to detect defects, bruising, mould, or other quality issues in real-time. Advanced image analysis algorithms can process the images and provide actionable insights for supply chain decision making.

3 Image Processing and Supply Chain Management

Image processing has found a wide range of applications in supply chain management (SCM), revolutionizing its various aspects of the different operations [16]. The applications include perishable items disease detection, recognition, classification, grading/sorting etc. [17]. However, in this paper the role of image processing for quality-based decision making in supply chain management is discussed. The images of the perishable items are used to extract relevant information related to the condition of the product based on patterns, and insights from visual data to take informed decisions and optimize various aspects of the supply chain. By determining the current status of quality of the product using image processing, different decision related to management of perishable supply chain can be taken accurately and rapidly in real time leading to an increase in effectiveness and efficiencies of the supply chain operations.

3.1   Literature Review

This section highlights some of the previous works related to supply chain management based on the outcomes of image processing systems. Applications like sorting/grading based on the quality of the product has found its role in order to improve the existing supply chain system. Decent research works have been published to determine the quality attributes of the product, however their integration with supply chain system for quality-based decision making is not explained in most of the articles. Table 1 mentions previous research articles where supply chain decisions are proposed or intended that can be taken based on the outcome image processing systems.

3.2   Proposed Supply Chain System

The proposed supply chain system that integrates image processing with the existing supply chain structure is shown in Fig. 2. Image processing system is made a part of the mandi and distribution centers. The reasons for this decision are mentioned below:

- At the mandi, all the harvested items from different regions are brought and based on the quality and quantity on each lot, its price is set by the auctioneer. However, the method of quality determination is mostly done by humans, which can be replaced by the image processing system for better, accurate and rapid decision making.
- Due to the large distances that exist generally between the mandi and distribution centers and due to storage of items at distribution centers for uncertain period, the quality degradation will continuously happen. Therefore, the quality must be determined before releasing the items to the downstream members of the supply chain so that the quality requirements must be met as required.

The details of different decisions that can be taken by the concerned decision makers of the supply chain in the proposed image processing integrated supply chain system are represented in Fig. 3 and explained here:

At Mandi:

- **Pricing**: The products are transported from farmland to mandi. Then, after reaching at the mandi, quality of each lot brought by different farmers are checked by the image processing system and based on the outcome agents attach appropriate pricing to the lot before auctioning them.
- **Procurement**: Based on the assigned price to the lot based on its quality, the wholesalers decide whether to procure the product or not. Also, decisions during procurement are based on regarding how much to procure and of what quality.

Table 1. Supply chain decisions based on outcome of image processing systems

Author	Objective	Product	Conclusion	Decisions
[18]	To develop an automatic sorting system based on image processing technique	Carrot	Method can be effective in increasing marketability and controlling waste	Marketability (Pricing)
[19]	To detect the apparent defects of fruit, grade them and provide an efficient system to do so	Lemon	Image processing are effective in managing waste and promoting the traditional method of sour lemon grading	Storage, Marketability (Pricing)
[20]	To evaluate ripeness of tomatoes using image processing	Tomato	Automation of the ripeness stage classification process is essential for saving crops from damages caused by environmental changes and ensuring optimum yield of high-quality products	Harvesting
[21]	To predict the shelf life of fruit using thermal images of fruits through transfer learning	Mangoes	Image processing is useful in detecting the intrinsic features like internal defects, bruises, texture, and colour of the fruits and classifying them according to their remaining shelf life	Storage
[22]	To develop an accurate classification system of cherry fruit using deep convolutional neural network	Cherry	The image processing methods are effective in managing the marketability and exportability of the cherry fruit and can replace the traditional methods applied for grading cherries	Marketability (Pricing)

- **Storage**: The wholesalers have to decide whether to store or immediately sell the procured quantity based on the current quality of the product. The procured lot of lower quality can be sold to local market near mandi in order to prevent it from getting waste while higher quality lot can be transported to distribution centers to meet the demand of customers at the retailer's side.

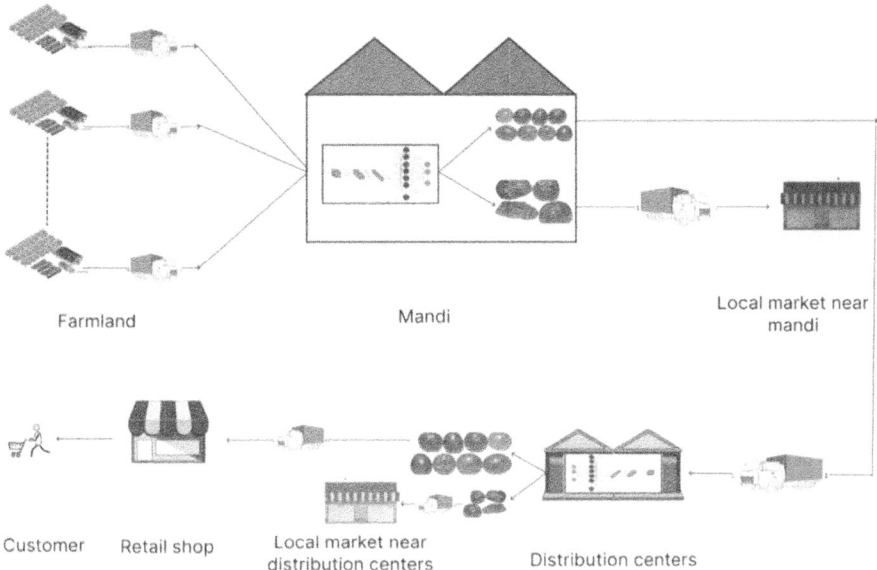

Farmland   Mandi   Local market near
                                               mandi

Customer   Retail shop   Local market near   Distribution centers
                           distribution centers

Fig. 2. Image processing integrated supply chain system for quality-based decision making

At Distribution centers:

- **Storage and Transportation**: The procured products are transported from mandi to distribution centers for storing it to meet future demand of customers. Due to uncertainty in demand, the decisions continuously need to be updated related to storage i.e., whether the product can be stored further or should be released to the local market at reduced produce to prevent wastage. If the product meets at least minimum quality level of the customer, then it is transported to the retail stores.
- **Pricing:** Perishable products deteriorate with time however its rate is dependent upon the existing environmental conditions resulting in quality loss and hence reduction in remaining shelf life. Based on the current quality level of the lot, the pricing is decided by the wholesalers.
- **Procurement:** Based on the current quality level of the lot and its associated pricing, the retailers decide the procurement quantity for fulfilling the demands of the customers in terms of both quality and quantity.

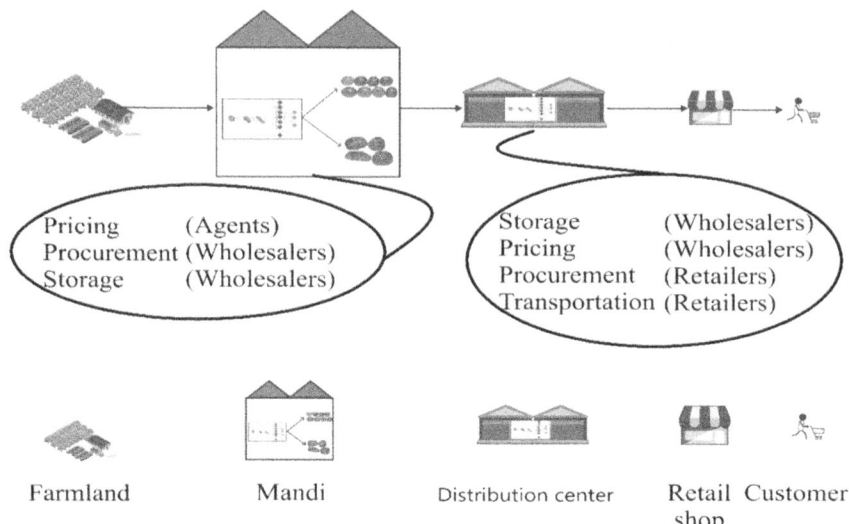

Fig. 3. Different quality-based decisions that can be taken at the supply chain echelons by the concerned decision makers

4 Quality-Based Decision-Making Using Image Processing

In the management of supply chain, large number of decisions need to be taken on regular basis for effectively and efficiently managing the supply chain. The decisions are taken by the concerned supply chain actor which varies from place to place and with the type of product. The decisions include procurement, pricing, storage and transportation according to the supply chain stage. The advantages of using image processing in different supply chain operations are discussed below:

4.1 Inventory Management

Quality-based decision making for perishable inventory management is even more critical than for non-perishable items since perishable goods have a limited shelf life and can quickly become unsellable if not managed properly. Here are some specific strategies for quality-based decision making in perishable inventory management using image processing [23]:

- **First-In, First-Out (FIFO) Method**: Implement the FIFO principle, which states that the oldest stock—that is, the stock with the lowest quality level—is sold or used first. This minimises the chance of deterioration by ensuring that products with lower shelf life are sold before fresher ones. This can be accomplished by getting current information on how long each perishable item in your inventory has left on its shelf. This knowledge will assist in efficiently managing stock rotation and prioritising the sale of goods with shorter shelf life.

- **Shelf-Life Monitoring**: Techniques for image processing can evaluate the freshness and remaining shelf life of perishable commodities. The technology can forecast a product's remaining shelf life by assessing visual changes over time, allowing for prompt shelf rotation or removal to prevent rotting.
- **Promotions and Discounts**: To increase sales of perishable products that are getting close to their expiration dates, strategically plan promotional events and discounts. In order to get rid of inventory before it gets unsalable, do this.
- **Waste Management and Donation**: In cases where perishable items are nearing expiration and cannot be sold, the seller can consider partnering with food banks or local charities for donation to reduce waste and support the community.

By employing these quality-based decision-making strategies, you can optimize the management of perishable inventory, reduce waste, maintain product freshness, and provide your customers with high-quality products consistently.

4.2 Pricing

The perishable supply chain uses computer vision and image analysis tools to determine quality-based pricing by precisely assessing the quality of the products. Using this data, appropriate pricing are determined for the products depending on their quality characteristics [24]. Image processing can be used to execute a variety of quality-based pricing schemes, which are described below:

- **Price Differentiation**: Different pricing points might be established based on the quality grades that have been ascribed to the products. Sellers may charge a premium for higher-quality goods while pricing lower-quality goods more affordably.
- **Dynamic Pricing**: Image processing can also assist in enabling dynamic pricing, where prices are changed in real-time according to the current quality of the product. The quality of the product is continuously degrading, depending on the environmental conditions in which it is stored or being transported. This makes it possible for pricing schemes to be more flexible, ensuring that consumers are charged fairly for the perceived quality.

Businesses in the perishable supply chain can make better informed pricing decisions, reduce waste, enhance customer satisfaction, and keep a competitive edge in the market by utilising image processing in this way.

4.3 Storage and Transportation

Quality-based decision making for storage and transportation using image processing in the perishable supply chain can significantly improve the handling of perishable goods, ensuring their quality and freshness throughout the entire supply chain. Here's how image processing can be utilized for quality-based decision making in these areas:

- **Quality Control**: Image processing is used to inspect perishable products, such as fruits, vegetables, or flowers, for defects, ripeness, freshness, and other quality attributes. By analysing images of the products, the system can detect any visual anomalies or deviations from quality standards i.e., the detection of surface defects, dimensional accuracy, colour variations, and other visual characteristics, allowing for timely removal of damaged or substandard items from storing or transporting together [9], ensuring high-quality standards are met consistently.

- **Routing and Prioritization**: Images of perishable products taken during transportation can be analysed to assess any damages or quality issues that may have occurred during the journey. The environmental conditions do not remain constant in the non-refrigerated vehicles, and this may affect the quality decay rate. This allows for prompt actions, such as re-routing to specific locations based on minimum acceptable quality requirements or returning damaged goods. Products of higher quality can be prioritized for delivery to premium customers or markets with greater demand [25].

By leveraging image processing for quality-based decision making in storage and transportation, businesses can enhance product quality, reduce waste, improve customer satisfaction, and optimize supply chain efficiency. Additionally, this technology provides valuable insights that can lead to better planning and risk management in the perishable supply chain.

5   Conclusion

The growing needs of the food can be meet by reducing wastage of the food items as well as employing sustainable agricultural practices. The reduction in wastage of the product can be achieved by taking supply chain decisions based on the current quality of the product. In this research paper, the role of image processing for quality-based decision making for supply chain management is mentioned. The existing supply chain architecture is presented highlighting the present issues and the need to transform it in order to take informed decisions with respect to the current quality of the product. The integration of image processing system with the supply chain architecture is proposed. All the decisions related to pricing, procurement, storage and transportation that can be taken by the decision makers at the different stages of the supply chain are explained. Lastly, the details of different strategies that can be employed in order to optimise the supply chain operations related to inventory management, pricing, storage and transportation are mentioned. Through the integration of image processing technology with supply chain system, increased efficiency, cost reduction, and customer satisfaction can be achieved.

Computing Requirements.   The authors did not use any hardware or software in the development of the paper.

References

1. FAO: How to feed the world 2050 (2009). https://doi.org/10.5822/978-1-61091-885-5
2. Patidar, R., Agrawal, S., Pratap, S.: Development of novel strategies for designing sustainable Indian agri- fresh food supply chain. Sādhanā **43**, 167 (2018). https://doi.org/10.1007/s12046-018-0927-6

3. NHB: Educational Statistics at a Glance 2018 (2018). [Online]. Available: https://www.mhrd. gov.in/sites/upload_files/mhrd/files/statistics-new/ESAG-2018.pdf

4. Raut, R.D., Gardas, B.B., Kharat, M., Narkhede, B.: Modeling the drivers of post-harvest losses – MCDM approach. Comput. Electron. Agric. **154**, 426–433 (2018). https://doi.org/ 10.1016/j.compag.2018.09.035

5. Kumar, A., Agrawal, S.: Challenges and opportunities for agri-fresh food supply chain management in India. Comput. Electron. Agric. **212**, 108161 (2023). https://doi.org/10.1016/j. compag.2023.108161

6. Patidar, R., Agrawal, S.: A mathematical model formulation to design a traditional Indian agri-fresh food supply chain: a case study problem. Benchmarking **27**(8), 2341–2363 (2020). https://doi.org/10.1108/BIJ-01-2020-0013

7. Jakhar, M., Srivastava, M.K.: Prioritization of drivers, enablers and resistors of agri-logistics in an emerging economy using fuzzy AHP. Br. Food J. **120**, 2166 (2018). https://doi.org/10. 1108/BFJ-11-2017-0608

8. Kumar, A., Mangla, S.K., Kumar, P., Karamperidis, S.: Challenges in perishable food supply chains for sustainability management: a developing economy perspective. Bus. Strat. Environ. **29**(5), 1809–1831 (2020). https://doi.org/10.1002/bse.2470

9. Paull, R.E.: Effect of temperature and relative humidity on fresh commodity quality. Postharvest Biol. Technol. **15**(3), 263–277 (1999). https://doi.org/10.1016/S0925-5214(98)000 90-8

10. Onwude, D.I., Chen, G., Eke-Emezie, N., Kabutey, A., Khaled, A.Y., Sturm, B.: Recent advances in reducing food losses in the supply chain of fresh agricultural produce. Processes **8**(11), 1–31 (2020). https://doi.org/10.3390/pr8111431

11. Bhargava, A., Bansal, A.: Fruits and vegetables quality evaluation using computer vision: a review. J. King Saud Univ. Comput. Inf. Sci. **33**(3), 243–257 (2021). https://doi.org/10.1016/ j.jksuci.2018.06.002

12. Meenu, M., Kurade, C., Chakravarthy, B., Kalra, S., Ramaswamy, H.S., Yu, Y.: A concise review on food quality assessment using digital image processing. Trends Food Sci. Technol. **118**, 106–124 (2021). https://doi.org/10.1016/j.tifs.2021.09.014

13. Zhang, B., et al.: Principles, developments and applications of computer vision for external quality inspection of fruits and vegetables: a review. FRIN **62**, 326–343 (2014). https://doi. org/10.1016/j.foodres.2014.03.012

14. Trieu, N.M., Thinh, N.T.: Quality classification of dragon fruits based on external performance using a convolutional neural network. Appl. Sci. **11**(22), 10558 (2021). https://doi.org/10. 3390/app112210558

15. Wang, P., Fan, E., Wang, P.: Comparative analysis of image classification algorithms based on traditional machine learning and deep learning. Pattern Recognit. Lett. **141**, 61–67 (2021). https://doi.org/10.1016/j.patrec.2020.07.042

16. Ayoub Shaikh, T., Rasool, T., Rasheed Lone, F.: Towards leveraging the role of machine learning and artificial intelligence in precision agriculture and smart farming. Comput. Electron. Agric. **198**, 107119 (2022). https://doi.org/10.1016/j.compag.2022.107119

17. Kakani, V., Nguyen, V.H., Kumar, B.P., Kim, H., Pasupuleti, V.R.: A critical review on computer vision and artificial intelligence in food industry. J. Agric. Food Res. **2**, 100033 (2020). https://doi.org/10.1016/j.jafr.2020.100033

18. Jahanbakhshi, A., Momeny, M., Mahmoudi, M., Radeva, P.: Waste management using an automatic sorting system for carrot fruit based on image processing technique and improved deep neural networks. Energy Rep. **7**, 5248–5256 (2021). https://doi.org/10.1016/j.egyr.2021. 08.028

19. Jahanbakhshi, A., Momeny, M., Mahmoudi, M., Zhang, Y.D.: Classification of sour lemons based on apparent defects using stochastic pooling mechanism in deep convolutional neural

networks. Sci. Hortic. (Amsterdam) **263**, 109133 (2020). https://doi.org/10.1016/j.scienta.2019.109133

20. El-Bendary, N., El Hariri, E., Hassanien, A.E., Badr, A.: Using machine learning techniques for evaluating tomato ripeness. Expert Syst. Appl. **42**(4), 1892–1905 (2015). https://doi.org/10.1016/j.eswa.2014.09.057

21. Bhole, V., Kumar, A.: A transfer learning-based approach to predict the shelf life of fruit. Intel. Artif. **24**(67), 102–120 (2021). https://doi.org/10.4114/intartif.vol24iss67pp102-120

22. Momeny, M., Jahanbakhshi, A., Jafarnezhad, K., Zhang, Y.D.: Accurate classification of cherry fruit using deep CNN based on hybrid pooling approach. Postharvest Biol. Technol. **166**, 111204 (2020). https://doi.org/10.1016/j.postharvbio.2020.111204

23. Chen, J., Tian, Z., Hang, W.: Optimal ordering and pricing policies in managing perishable products with quality deterioration. Int. J. Prod. Res. **59**(15), 4472–4494 (2021). https://doi.org/10.1080/00207543.2020.1766715

24. Duan, Y., Liu, J.: Optimal dynamic pricing for perishable foods with quality and quantity deteriorating simultaneously under reference price effects. Int. J. Syst. Sci. Oper. Logist. **6**(4), 346–355 (2019). https://doi.org/10.1080/23302674.2018.1465618

25. Agrawal, A.K., Yadav, S., Gupta, A.A., Pandey, S.: A genetic algorithm model for optimizing vehicle routing problems with perishable products under time-window and quality requirements. Decis. Anal. J. **5**, 100139 (2022). https://doi.org/10.1016/j.dajour.2022.100139

Enhancing Endometrial Tumor Detection: Early Diagnosis with Advanced Vision Transformer Architecture

Abhinaya Tejavath[1]([✉]), Bhawna Swarnkar[2], and Nilay Khare[2]

[1] Centre for Artificial Intelligence, Maulana Azad National Institute of Technology (MANIT), Bhopal, India
abhinayatejavath@gmail.com

[2] Department of Computer Science and Engineering, Maulana Azad National Institute of Technology (MANIT), Bhopal, India

Abstract. *Introduction:* Early detection and treatment are key to improving the prognosis of endometrial cancer. However, conventional machine learning approaches have limited capacity to simulate the complex links between histopathological images and their interpretations, making it challenging to achieve accurate results. A vision transformer-based image classification model has been proposed to assist medical professionals in detecting endometrial cancer and improving patient outcomes.

Objective: This study aims to develop and evaluate a vision transformer-based model for accurately detecting histopathology images of endometrium, and compare its performance against existing fine-tuning methods such as MobilenetV2, Xception, and VGG16.

Methods: A publicly accessible histopathology imaging dataset of endometrium was used to train and validate the proposed model. The performance of the model was evaluated against state-of-the-art approaches in the field. Results: The validation results showed that the proposed model attained an accuracy of 99.36%, surpassing the performance of existing fine-tuning methods and achieving the state-of-the-art performance in the widely used endometrial cancer benchmark dataset. These findings highlight the potential of vision transformer-based models in accurately detecting histopathology images of endometrium, which could lead to better patient outcomes.

Conclusions: The proposed vision transformer-based model provides a highly accurate and efficient approach to detecting endometrial cancer. This study underscores the potential of this model as a valuable tool for medical professionals in the early detection and treatment of endometrial cancer, ultimately improving patient outcomes.

Keywords: Endometrial Cancer · Hematoxylin and Eosin (H&E) image · Vision Transformer · Deep Learning · Medical Image Classification

© The Author(s), under exclusive license to Springer Nature Switzerland AG 2024
H. K. et al. (Eds.): AIKP 2023, CCIS 2127, pp. 195–213, 2024.
https://doi.org/10.1007/978-3-031-68617-7_15

1 Introduction

Endometrial cancer is a major global health concern, with an increasing incidence and mortality rate. According to the Global Cancer Statistics 2018 report, it has become the most common gynecologic cancer worldwide [27]. Early detection and treatment are essential for improving patient outcomes and long-term survival. The potential of a deep learning algorithm to detect endometrial cancer from biopsy images has been indicated in a promising study by [29]. Biopsy remains the standard method for diagnosing endometrial carcinoma. Despite its potential, this deep learning algorithm does have constraints regarding the volume of accessible data and its capacity to replicate the intricate relationships between histopathological images and their interpretation. Therefore, there's been substantial progress in developing computer-assisted diagnostic (CAD) methods that employ machine learning algorithms capable of accurately pinpointing pathological characteristics linked to endometrial cancer. These approaches have shown promising results in detecting cancerous cells and predicting the disease's progression [30].

The use of CAD in endometrial cancer diagnosis has several advantages. It can help improve the accuracy and consistency of diagnosis by reducing interobserver variability among pathologists. Additionally, it can provide quantitative and objective measurements of pathological features that may be difficult to assess visually. This technology can also potentially reduce healthcare costs by minimizing the need for more invasive diagnostic procedures. In conclusion, the increasing incidence and mortality rates of endometrial cancer make early detection and treatment crucial. Although the conventional method for diagnosing endometrial carcinoma is through a biopsy, the use of computer-assisted diagnosis (CAD) techniques that incorporate machine learning algorithms shows significant potential in enhancing the precision and reliability of diagnoses, as outlined in a review by [30]. Deep learning algorithms, specifically Convolutional Neural Networks (CNNs), have demonstrated notable promise in the precise recognition and categorization of digital pathology images, as surveyed by [31]. However, traditional CNN-based approaches have limitations in simulating the complex relationships between images and their interpretations [32]. To overcome these limitations, enhanced Vision Transformer (ViT) architecture has been proposed, which can efficiently process and analyze large volumes of data, leading to more accurate image classification [21]. The ViT architecture has shown superior performance to CNNs in several applications, including image classification, object detection, and segmentation [21].

The main contributions of this paper lie in the development and evaluation of a vision transformer-based model for the accurate detection of histopathology images of endometrium, with the primary goal of improving the prognosis of endometrial cancer. The study addresses the limitations of conventional machine learning approaches, which struggle to capture the intricate relationships between histopathological images and their interpretations in this context. By introducing the vision transformer-based image classification model, this research offers a promising solution for assisting medical professionals in early cancer detection and improving patient outcomes. The key objective of the paper is to showcase the superiority of this model by comparing its performance against established fine-tuning methods like MobilenetV2, Xception, and VGG16. To achieve this, a publicly accessible histopathology imaging dataset of endometrium was employed for training and validation. The validation results demonstrated that the proposed model achieved an impressive accuracy of 99.36%, surpassing the performance of existing methods and establishing itself as the state-of-the-art solution in the field of endometrial cancer detection. This outcome underscores the potential of vision transformer-based models in accurately identifying histopathology images of endometrium, with the promise of ultimately leading to better patient outcomes. In conclusion, this paper presents a highly accurate and efficient approach to the early detection of endometrial cancer, emphasizing the potential significance of this model as a valuable tool for medical professionals.

The paper is structured as follows: Sect. 2 provides a comprehensive review of existing studies on endometrial cancer diagnosis, deep learning-based methodologies, and the ViT architecture. In Sect. 3, we elaborate on the specifics of the dataset and the preprocessing approaches used in this research. Section 4 describes the proposed computer-aided diagnosis approach using an enhanced ViT architecture for classifying histopathological images. Following that, Sect. 5 showcases the experimental results and offers a thorough analysis of the proposed method's efficacy. Lastly, Sect. 6 discusses the conclusions drawn from the study and potential future developments in this area.

2   Related Work

This literature review thoroughly analyzes the latest techniques and methods used for diagnosing endometrial cancer. It focuses on two main areas of research: the use of Vision transformers and the application of histopathology images for carcinoma diagnosis.

2.1   Endometrial Cancer

Recent studies have proposed computational methods for the accurate diagnosis and prediction of endometrial cancer using digital pathology images and Magnetic resonance imaging (MRI) scans. [2] introduced a novel approach to improve the assessment of myometrial invasion depth in MR imaging by incorporating a geometric feature called LS, which characterizes tissue structure irregularity caused by endometrial cancer. Additionally, [3] utilized segmentation and stain normalization techniques on biopsy images from potential low grade endometrial stromal sarcoma patients before employing deep learning methods to distinguish between benign and malignant images with high accuracy. To diagnose endometrial cancer in digital pathology images, a recent study [4] presented an optimized ResNet50-based convolutional neural network model integrated with an attention mechanism. [6] developed a precise forecasting algorithm for endometrial cancer using the Ensemble Algorithm for Clustering Cancer Data. [7] designed Panoptes, a multi-resolution deep convolutional neural network capable of predicting histopathological subtypes as well as molecular subtypes and common gene mutations based on digitized H&E stained pathological images.Finally, [8]–explored the clinical application of machine learning-powered MRI radiomics to evaluate its efficacy in detecting deep myometric invasion in patients with Endomterial Cancer.

2.2 Histopatholgy Images

Dealing with whole slide images (WSIs) in histopathological research poses a number of challenges, primarily the creation of a reliable, widely applicable, and fully automated computer-aided diagnosis (CAD) system capable of managing microscopic images or WSIs, even in the presence of imaging artifacts. Traditional methods have often utilized handcrafted features or manually engineered image descriptors through image processing techniques [9]. However, more recent research has shown that deep features—high-level representations learned by deep neural networks—can surpass handcrafted features in most scenarios [10]. For instance, [11] proposed a combined deep neural network utilizing multi-class tissue features for tumor detection in colorectal histology images, achieving an impressive accuracy of 99.13%. Similarly, [12] advocated for the use of convolutional neural network (CNN) models to differentiate between adenocarcinoma and adenoma tumor patches in colon and stomach WSIs, reaching an accuracy of approximately 93% after preprocessing the images using a Gaussian blur smoothing method and thresholding. [13] introduced weakly supervised learning strategies that use a limited number of region of interest (ROI)-annotated images for rapid categorization. [14] suggested an entropy-based CNN model for classifying lung adenocarcinoma and squamous cell carcinoma, achieving 92% accuracy. Furthermore, [15] recommended a framework based on VGGNet-16 for analyzing the CMT dataset and a human breast cancer dataset, testing the performance of various classifiers. Attention-based deep neural networks for identifying cancerous and precancerous esophageal tissue on histopathological slides were proposed by [16], who also conducted a multi-center study on the classification of benign and malignant conditions using WSIs of the gastric mucosa. They achieved a sensitivity of 97.05%, a specificity of 92.72%, and a Dice coefficient of 0.8333 in the screening task. Lastly, a thorough review of the detection and classification of carcinoma in histopathological images was provided by [13].

2.3 Transformers

The Transformer model has demonstrated significant advancements in Natural Language Processing (NLP) tasks, as evidenced by a plethora of research works such as [17–19]. For instance, [17] used a transformerbased attention mechanism to address English constituency parsing and machine translation tasks. BERT, a language representation model developed by [18], employs a bidirectional transformer pre-trained on unlabelled text to capture the context of each word. The use of a sequence transformer to autoregressively predict pixels by [20] has resulted in image classification performance on par with CNNs. ViT, which uses a pure transformer to directly classify the entire image from sequences of image patches, was introduced by [21] and has already surpassed the competition in most image recognition benchmarks. In [26], the benefits and drawbacks of vision transformers utilized in various tasks were evaluated through a comprehensive review.

3   Dataset and Preprocessing

3.1   Dataset Description

A histopathological image dataset of endometrial tissue has been developed, as noted by [5], to address the shortcomings of machine learning and deep learning methods in effectively diagnosing endometrial cancer. This dataset, detailed in Table 1, includes pathologically confirmed JPEG images of approximately 500 endometrial samples stained with hematoxylin and eosin (HE). The dataset encompasses four primary types of endometrial tissues: Normal Endometrium (NE) shown in Fig. 1d, Endometrial Polyp (EP) shown in Fig. 1c, Endometrial Hyperplasia (EH) shown in Fig. 1b, and Endometrioid Adenocarcinoma (EA) shown in Fig. 1a. The Normal Endometrium (NE) category is further divided into three subtypes, each representing a different phase of the menstrual cycle: the luteal phase, menstrual phase, and follicular phase.

Table 1. Dataset Description

Dateset type	General class	Sub class	Subtype	Number of patches
			Luteal phase	600
	Benign	Normal endometrium	Menstrual phase	21
			Follicular phase	712
		Endometrial polyp		636
Histopathological images			Simple	510
	Malignant	Endometrial hyperlasia	Complex	282
		Endometrial adenocarcinoma		535

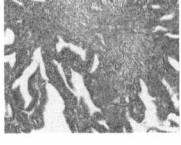 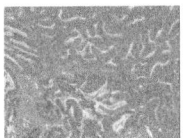  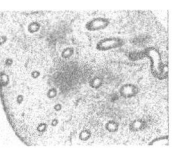

(a) Endometrial adenocarcinoma   (b) Endometrial Hyperplasia   (c) Endometrial Polyp   (d) Normal Endometrium

Fig. 1. Endometrial cancer dataset sample patches

3.2   Preprocessing

Before training the deep learning model, each image in the gathered dataset undergoes a basic image pre-processing pipeline to ensure it's suitable for model training. All images are resized to 224 × 224 pixels to maintain a uniform input size for the neural network models. Given the large amount of data required to create accurate and generalizable deep learning models through supervised learning, several data augmentation techniques, including random rotation, width shift, height shift, and flipping, are implemented in the proposed training pipeline to enhance the performance of these models.

In this study, the decision has been made to resize all images in the dataset to a consistent size of 224 × 224 pixels for several practical reasons. Primarily, this choice enhances computational efficiency, as smaller, fixed input dimensions are more computationally manageable during both model training and inference, mitigating the resource demands associated with larger image sizes. Maintaining uniform dimensions ensures simplicity and consistency in the model architecture and training process, eliminating the need for intricate resizing operations within the neural network. Additionally, this choice aligns with the standard input size used by many pre-trained deep learning models, ensuring compatibility and enabling the utilization of pre-trained weights, which can significantly boost model performance, particularly when working with limited data. Lastly, the 224 × 224-pixel input size is empirically proven to be effective in a wide range of image classification tasks, striking an optimal balance between capturing essential image details and managing computational demands efficiently.

The dataset is randomly divided into training, validation, and testing sets, with 75%, 15%, and 10% of all images allocated to these respective sets. The training set is used for training the deep learning model, while the validation set is used to monitor the model's performance during training and to fine-tune hyperparameters. The testing set is used to assess the model's final performance. Through these preprocessing steps and the use of data augmentation techniques, the deep learning model is trained to effectively identify patterns and make accurate predictions on new, unseen data.

4 Methodology

The Vision Transformer (ViT) model, which was introduced by [21] following the Transformers' success in addressing natural language processing challenges [18], outperforms cutting-edge CNNs by requiring approximately four times fewer computational resources when trained on sufficient data. ViT seeks to mirror the original transformer architecture as closely as possible [17]. A pipeline for histopathology image detection is proposed based on an enhanced vision transformer network [21], and it's tuned using the considered dataset [5]. The performance of the proposed model is evaluated against pre-trained models and existing state-of-the-art approaches.

Figure 2 illustrates the architecture of the proposed model. The Patch Encoder layer in the proposed pipeline converts the input image into several flattened patches. Positional embeddings are added to the patches to create a sequence, as transformer encoders are only compatible with sequential data. Just like the Transformer encoder in [20], the proposed architecture also incorporates Multi-layer Perceptron (MLP) blocks and multi-headed self-attention layers (MHSA). The self-attention layer of the proposed model enables the integration of information globally throughout the entire image. Both the multilayer perceptron (MLP) and self-attention (SA) blocks assist the network in extracting the most critical spatial information. The image is initially divided into fixed-size, non-overlapping patches. Each patch then undergoes linear projection and positional embedding processes. Positional embedding records the relative position of a patch in relation to the input image. Afterward, the flattened patches pass through a stack of T transformer blocks. A traditional transformer block comprises two main components, MHSA and MLP, both of which have a normalization layer before them and a residual connection afterward.

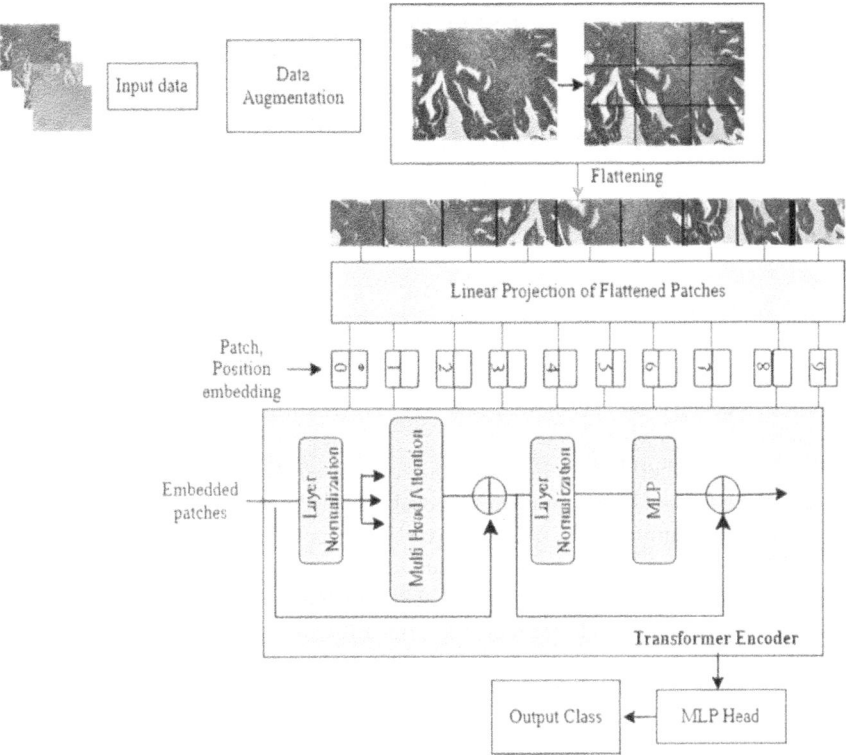

Fig. 2. Architectute of the proposed model

MHSA is a technique utilized in natural language processing that allows a model to learn multiple representations of the same data using multiple attention heads. It's used in transformer architectures such as BERT [19] and GPT-2. MHSA consists of multiple SA blocks concatenated channel-wise, each looking at the same data but in different ways, thus enabling them to focus on different parts of the data and learn different representations of it. Each block of the MHSA algorithm divides an input vector into three separate vectors: k-key, q-query, and v-value. The vectors produced by the various inputs are then compiled into three separate matrices, $Q = XW^Q$, $K = XW^K$, and $V = XW^V$, where W^Q, W^K, and W^V are the weight matrices. To construct an attention matrix based on the saliency of the embedded patch, the dot product of Q and K is used. The attention matrix is then passed through the SoftMax activation function. The corresponding attention matrix A can be written as

$$A = Softmax(\frac{QK^T}{\sqrt{D_q}})$$

(1)

The output from the SA layer, Z is written as

$$Z = SA(X) = AV$$

(2)

where D_q represents the dimension of the vector Q. Later, self-attention matrices are combined and transmitted to the regression head and linear layer. The equation for multi-head self-attention can be written as

$$\text{MHSA} (Q, K, V) = \left[Z_0, Z_1, Z_2, ..., Z_{h-1}\right]W_0 \tag{3}$$

where $W^0 \in R^{h.Dv \times N}$ computes linear transformation of attention blocks and Z_i can be written as

$$Z_i = Softmax(\frac{QW^{Qi}\left(KW^{Ki}\right)^T}{\sqrt{\frac{D_q}{h}}}) \tag{4}$$

MLP is stacked after the MHSA layer in the transformer block. ReLU activation function is applied in MLP.

The proposed algorithm for Endometrial Tumor Detection 1 commences by preparing the dataset $DS = (X_i, Y_i)$ and resizing each image X_i to a fixed size of (224, 224) pixels. Then, the learning rate α, batch size B, number of epochs N, and patch size P are initialized. Data augmentation is applied to each image X_i using m different augmentation functions A_j. Patches of size P are extracted from each image, resulting in n_P patches per image, which are then vectorized into a single feature vector V_i. The dataset is divided into training,testing and validation sets, DS_{train}, DS_{test} and DS_{val}, respectively, with no overlap. The model is trained by minimizing the loss function $L(\theta)$ with respect to the model parameters θ using a vision transformer and gradient descent with the specified learning rate, batch size, and number of epochs. The training process involves a few key steps. Initially, a tokenization step is performed where each patch is flattened into a 1D representation Z_i. Then, a positional encoding step is performed, where each token is combined with its positional encoding E_j. After this, the encoded tokens pass through the Multihead self-attention (MHSA), followed by a feed-forward neural network (FFN). Both the MHSA and FFN outputs are then subject to layer normalization (LN) and residual connections, improving the stability and performance of the network. Lastly, a classification head is applied to produce softmax probabilities for each class. After the training phase is completed, the performance of the trained model is assessed using the testing set. Here, the model predicts the labels y_i for each image $X_i^{'}$ in the test set. The final output of the algorithm comprises these predicted labels for the images in the testing set. This rigorous process ensures a comprehensive training and testing of the proposed model, making it highly effective and reliable for endometrial tumor detection.

Algorithm 1 Proposed model for endometrial tumor detection

Let $DS = (X_i, Y_i)$ be the dataset.

1. Data Preparation: $X_i' = \text{resize}(X_i, (224 * 224))$, where $X_i \in DS$.
2. Initialize: learning rate $\alpha \in R$, batch size $B \in N$, epochs $N \in N$, patch size $P \in N$.
3. Data Augmentation: $A(X_i) = \{A_1(X_i),...,A_m(X_i)\}$, where A_j is the jth augmentation function.
4. Patch Extraction: $X_i^j = \text{patch}(X_i, j, P)$ for jth 2D patch, where $X_i \in DS$.
5. Vectorize Patches: $V_i = \text{vectorize}((X_i^1,...,X_i^{n_P}))$, where n_P is the number of patches per image.
6. Split Dataset: $DS_{train} \cup DS_{test} \cup DS_{val} = DS$, with $DS_{train} \cap DS_{test} \cap DS_{val} = \emptyset$.
7. Train Model: Minimize the loss function $L(\theta)$ with respect to model parameters θ, using vision transformer and gradient descent with learning rate α, batch size B, and epochs N.

$$\theta_{(t+1)} = \theta_{(t)} - \alpha \nabla L(\theta_{(t)})$$

- Tokenization: $Z_i = \text{flatten}(X_i^j)$.
- Positional Encoding: $Z_i = Z_i + E_j$.
- MHSA: $Attention(Q,K,V) = softmax\left(\frac{QK^T}{\sqrt{d_k}}\right)V$
- FFN: $FFN(x) = W_2 \cdot \text{ReLU}(W_1 \cdot x + b_1) + b_2$.
- LN and Residual Connections: $x_{LN} = LN(x + MHSA(x))$, $y_{LN} = LN(x_{LN} + FFN(x_{LN}))$. – Classification Head: $y_i = softmax(W_y \cdot \text{GlobalAvgPooling}(y_{LN}) + b_y)$.

8. Test Model: predict $y_i = f_\theta(X_i')$ for $X_i' \in DS_{test}$.
9. Output: predicted labels y_i for $X_i' \in DS_{test}$.

---

5 Implementation and Experimental Results

5.1 Experimetal Setup

The High Performance Computing (HPC) system used for this research was equipped with 40 cores and 90 GB of RAM, providing a robust environment for the execution of experiments. The software environment comprised Python 3.8, TensorFlow 2.5, scikit-learn 0.24, Nvidia CUDA 11.2, Keras 2.4.3, and Anaconda 4.10.1. This setup facilitated the efficient training and testing of the deep learning models used in the study.

5.2 Evaluation Index

Various evaluation metrics commonly utilized in image classification tasks were employed in this study, such as Accuracy 5, Precision 6, Recall 7, FScore 8, AUC-ROC, and AUC-precision recall curve. Accuracy 5 is calculated as the proportion of correctly predicted samples to the total number of samples in the dataset. Precision 6 entails the ratio of correctly predicted samples for a specific class to the total number of samples anticipated for that class. Recall 7, also referred to as sensitivity or true positive rate, represents the ratio of true positive samples to the sum of true positives and false negatives – effectively capturing how accurately actual positives are identified. The FScore 8 reflects a balanced measure by taking into account both Precision and Recall through their harmonic mean. The ROC curve graphically illustrates a model's performance at different classification thresholds by plotting True Positive Rate against False Positive Rate (1 - Specificity) for varying threshold values. Meanwhile, AUC-ROC serves as a scalar value representing area under this curve; it gauges how well a model can differentiate between positive and negative classes irrespective of chosen classification thresholds – with 1 indicating perfection and 0.5 pointing towards randomness.On another note lies precision-recall curves which plot Precision vs Recall across different classification thresholds—particularly beneficial when dealing with imbalanced datasets where one class greatly outweighs others' prevalence.In these definitions: TP denotes true positives (correctly predicted positive class), TN stands for true negatives (correctly recognized negative class), FP refers to false positives (incorrect prediction of positive class), while FN signifies false negatives (improper recognitionof negativeclass).

$$\text{Accuracy} = TP + TN/TP + TN + FP + FN \tag{5}$$

$$\text{Precision} = TP/TP + FP \tag{6}$$

$$\text{Recall} = TP/TP + FN \tag{7}$$

$$\text{FScore} = 2 * Precision * Recall/Precision + Recall \tag{8}$$

5.3 Hyper Parameters Selection

The experimental procedure begins with the configuration of certain hyperparameters for the machine learning model. A learning rate of 0.0001 is established, which dictates the magnitude of the steps taken during the training phase, along with a weight decay of 0.0001. Weight decay is a form of regularization that applies a penalty to large weight values. The batch size, which refers to the number of samples processed through the model simultaneously, is set to 64. The model will cycle through the entire training dataset 50 times, as denoted by the number of epochs. The source images are reconfigured to a resolution of 72 pixels and then partitioned into smaller 8-pixel patches, creating a total of $(72//8) ** 2 = 81$ patches per image. A transformer architecture comprising 8 layers, each with a dimensionality of 64 and 4 attention heads, is utilized. The final classifier includes two dense layers with dimensions of 2048 and 1024 respectively. The AdamW optimizer is implemented with the predetermined learning rate and weight decay. The model compilation employs SparseCategoricalCrossentropy loss along with SparseCategoricalAccuracy and SparseTopKCategoricalAccuracy metrics. The model is trained on the training dataset for 150 epochs, utilizing 10% of the training dataset for validation purposes. The best model weights during training are preserved using a ModelCheckpoint callback. After training, the model is assessed on a test dataset, and its accuracy and top-5 accuracy are documented. The sparse categorical cross-entropy loss with AdamW optimizer can be represented mathematically as follows:

Let y_{true} and y_{pred} be the true and predicted labels, respectively. Let w be the model's weights and λ be the weight decay factor. The sparse categorical cross-entropy loss with AdamW optimizer is given by:

$$loss = SparseCategoricalCrossentropy\left(y_{true}, y_{pred}\right) + \lambda|\omega|_2^2 \qquad (9)$$

Here, $\|w\|_2$ represents the L2 norm of the weights (Table 2).

Table 2. Hyper parameters selection

Hyper parameters used for experimentation purposes	
Learning rate	0.001
Weight decay	0.0001
Transformer blocks	8
Number of heads	4
Patchsize	8x8
Batch size	64
epochs	150
Optimizer	AdamW
Loss	sparse categorical crossentropy

5.4 Experimental Results

This research utilizes a histopathology image dataset of endometrium [5] to execute the experiments. The evaluation metrics used for the experimental results include Accuracy, Precision, Recall, and FScore. The performance assessment of the proposed model is conducted in comparison with pre-trained models such as VGG16, Xception, and MobileNetV2, as well as existing state-of-the-art approaches.

Comparison of the Proposed Model with Pre-trained Models A comprehensive comparison between the proposed machine learning model and three pre-existing pre-trained models (MobilenetV2, Xception, and VGG16) was undertaken, focusing on their efficiency in classifying histopathology images. The findings, as displayed in 3, indicate that the proposed model surpasses the pre-trained models in terms of binary as well as multi-class classification tasks. Specifically, the proposed model achieved an impressive binary classification accuracy of 99.78% and a 4-class classification accuracy of 99.36%, outperforming MobilenetV2, Xception, and VGG16, which achieved binary classification accuracies of 99.34%, 98.27%, and 98.98%, respectively, and 4-class classification accuracies of 97.45%, 93.4%, and 96.83%, respectively.

A deeper examination of the results shows that the proposed model consistently scores higher in accuracy, precision, recall, and fscore for both binary and 4-class classification tasks, compared to the pre-trained models. For instance, while MobilenetV2 achieved an accuracy of 99.34% in binary classification and 97.75% in 4-class classification, the proposed model managed to surpass these figures by 0.44% and 1.61% in binary and 4-class classification tasks, respectively. This contrast was particularly striking in the 4-class classification task, suggesting that the proposed model exhibits superior performance in classifying histopathology images. Interestingly, the other pre-trained models also exhibited substantial improvement when compared to earlier state-of-the-art methods. However, the proposed model topped the charts in terms of accuracy, indicating its reliability for histopathology image classification. A visual comparison of accuracy Figs. 3a, 6a and loss Figs. 3b, 6b further reinforces this point, with the proposed model outclassing the pre-trained models in both binary and 4-class classification tasks.

Additionally, the proposed model demonstrated a lower rate of misclassifications, as evidenced by the confusion matrices Figs. 7, 8 presented in the study. This suggests that the proposed model holds a higher degree of accuracy in identifying various types of histopathology cells, making it a promising tool for medical image analysis and diagnosis. All in all, the study highlights the potential of the proposed machine learning model in enhancing the accuracy of histopathology image classification.

In the multi-class classification task, the performance of the model was evaluated using the Receiver Operating Characteristic (ROC) curve and the Area Under the ROC curve (AUC-ROC) 4 for each class. The results indicate that the model achieved excellent discrimination for the majority of classes, with an AUC-ROC of 1 for class 0 (endometrial adenocarcinoma) and 0.99 for classes 1 (endometrial hyperplasia), 2 (endometrial polyp), and 3 (normal endometrium), respectively. These high AUC-ROC values suggest that the model effectively distinguished between the different classes, exhibiting strong true positive rates and low false positive rates. Additionally, in the binary classification task, where the classes were classified as benign and malignant, the model demonstrated exceptional performance as evidenced by an AUC-ROC of 0.99 for both classes. Moreover, the AUC-precision recall curve was also examined to assess the model's performance on imbalanced datasets. The high AUC values for both multi-class and binary classification tasks further confirm the model's robustness and efficacy in handling imbalanced data.

State of Art Comparison In order to evaluate the performance of the proposed model, a comparison was made with some recent works [23–25] that used the same Histopathology image dataset for endometrium. The comparison results are illustrated in Fig. 4a. As presented in Fig. 4a, the proposed model achieved an accuracy of 99.36%, which outperformed the other studies. Specifically, the proposed model showed improvement of 22.45% compared to [23], 20.77% compared to [24], and 17.95% compared to [25]. These results highlight the superior performance of the proposed model over the state-of-the-art approaches (Fig. 5).

Furthermore, the proposed model demonstrated a significant accuracy difference of 22.77% and 6.24% in the 4 class and binary classification tasks, respectively, when compared to the aforementioned studies. These results indicate that the proposed model is capable of achieving more accurate and reliable predictions for the Histopathology image dataset for endometrium, making it a promising solution for medical image classification tasks (Table 3).

Model Performance Across Varied Dataset Sizes In the realm of deep learning, it is widely acknowledged that increasing the size of input datasets can significantly enhance model performance, especially for complex tasks that require high levels of

Table 3. Performance Comparison of the proposed model and pre trained models

	accuracy		precision		recall		f1 score	
	binary	4 class	binary	4 class	binary	4 class	binary	4 class
proposed model	99.78	99.36	99.77	99.36	99.77	99.36	99.77	99.36
MobilenetV2	99.34	97.45	99.34	97.45	99.34	97.45	99.34	97.44
xception	98.27	93.4	98.25	93.4	98.27	93.4	98.26	93.38
VGG16	98.98	96.83	99	96.83	98.98	96.83	98.99	96.83

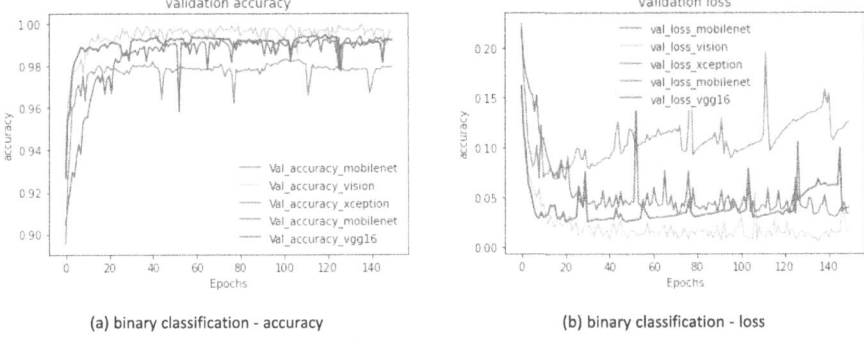

(a) binary classification - accuracy   (b) binary classification - loss

Fig. 3. Performance comparison of proposed model with pre-trained models -binary classification (a) Accuracy Curve (b) Loss Curve

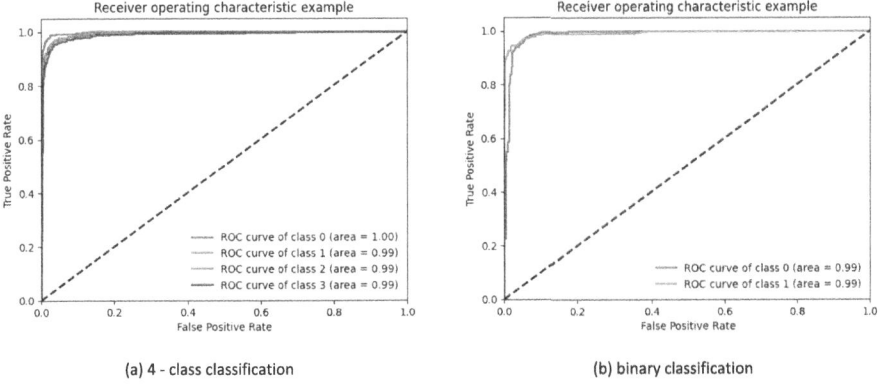

(a) 4 - class classification   (b) binary classification

Fig. 4. Area Under the Receiver Operating Characteristic curve of the proposed model (a) 4 - class classification (b) Binary classification

generalization and robustness. This is primarily because larger datasets provide a greater number of training examples that enable the model to learn from a wider range of features and patterns, which, in turn, can prevent overfitting and enhance the model's ability to generalize well to unseen data. In line with this, the proposed vision transformer-based model was evaluated with various input dataset sizes, and the performance results are

(b)Binary classification

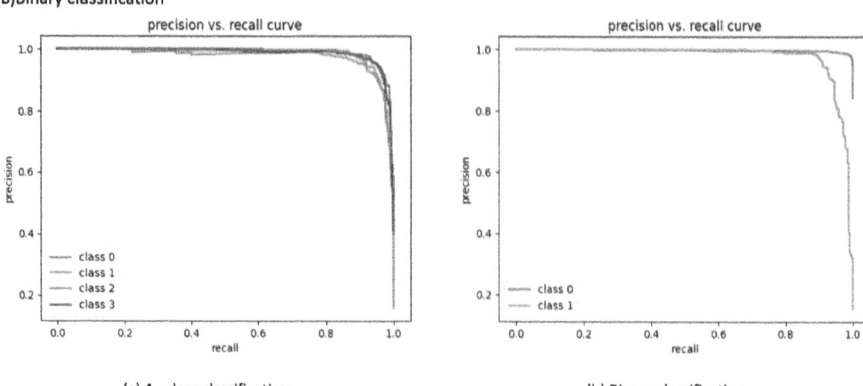

(a) 4 - class classification   (b) Binary classification

Fig. 5. Area Under the Precision-Recall curve -binary classification of the proposed model (a) 4 - class classification (b) Binary classification

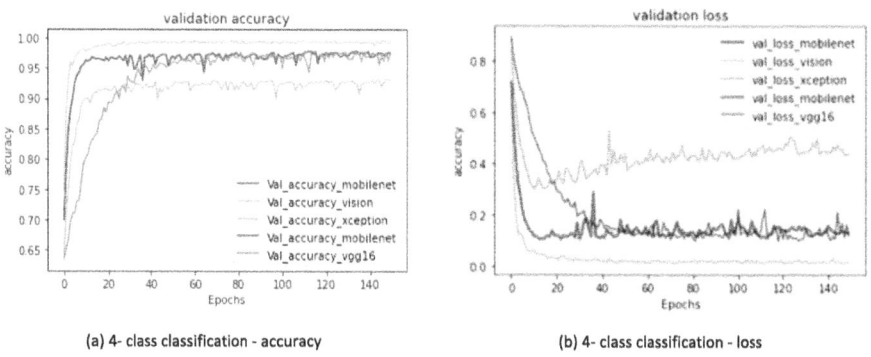

(a) 4- class classification - accuracy   (b) 4- class classification - loss

Fig. 6. Performance comparison of proposed model with pre-trained models - 4- class classification (a) Accuracy Curve (b) Loss Curve

presented in Tables 4 and 5. To further expand the dataset and ensure the evaluation process aligns with the original dataset, augmentation techniques were used. Figure 9 shows that the model's performance improves considerably with increasing input data size. Hence, it can be concluded that the proposed model requires a more extensive dataset to demonstrate outstanding performance results.

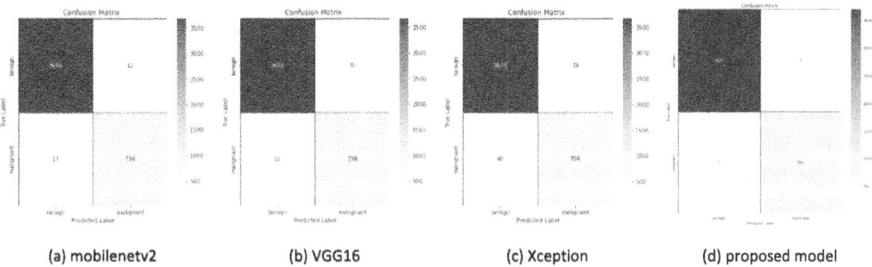

Fig. 7. Binary classification confusion matrices of pre-trained models and the proposed model

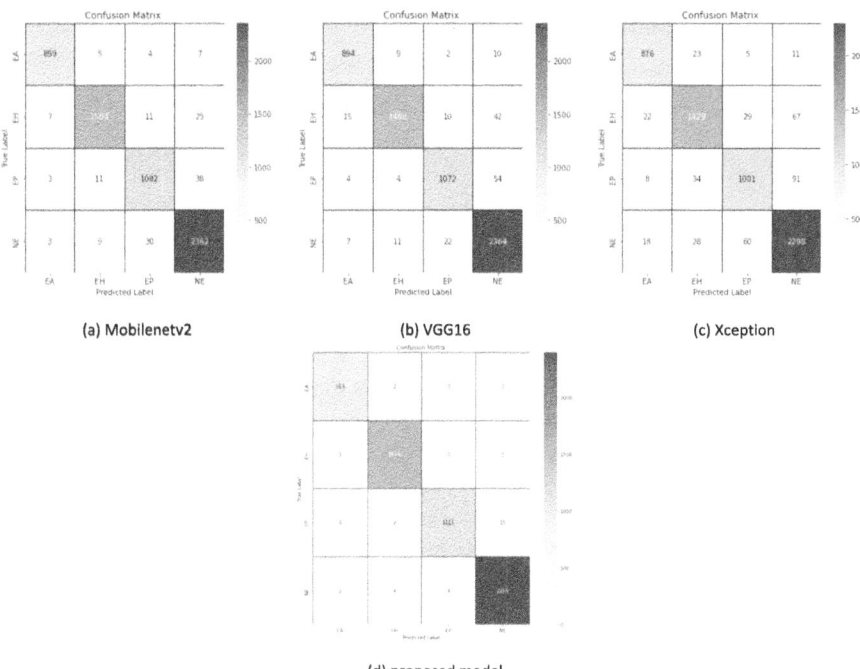

Fig. 8. 4- class classification confusion matrices of pre-trained models and the proposed model

6 Conclusion and Future Works

In this research paper, a proposed image classification model has been developed and evaluated for Histopathology image classification of endometrium. The model's attention mechanism has improved its ability to focus on the most important features for better performance. The study has demonstrated the potential of the proposed model to significantly enhance image classification of complex digital histopathology images, which is important for early disease diagnosis.

Table 4. State-of-Art-Comparison

4 class classification accuracy	
proposed model	99.36%
[23]	76.59%
[25]	81.41%
[24]	78.59%

Table 5. Proposed model performance on different dataset size

Accuracy		
Input size	Binary	4 Class classification
3100	97.95	63.54
10,000	98.75	91.27
20,000	99.12	93.91
30,000	99.77	99.36

The significance of the proposed model lies in its ability to achieve exceptional accuracy scores and computational performance, outperforming existing cutting-edge algorithms. The model can effectively learn complex patterns and features from large amounts of data and focus on the most salient features for improved accuracy. This makes it a promising avenue for further research and development in the computer-aided medical diagnosis domain.

In the future, more research can be done to evaluate the proposed model with other DL models currently available and compare their multi-class classification results. Additionally, denoising techniques can be used in the preprocessing step to enhance the model's performance, as noise can significantly affect the accuracy of the model. Combining more classifiers and feature selection techniques can also increase the system's accuracy.

Furthermore, future research must uncover every possible use of vision transformer for image processing in histopathology. Other types of histopathology images can be evaluated using the proposed model, and the model can be adapted for other medical image diagnosis tasks. Finally, the proposed model can be improved further

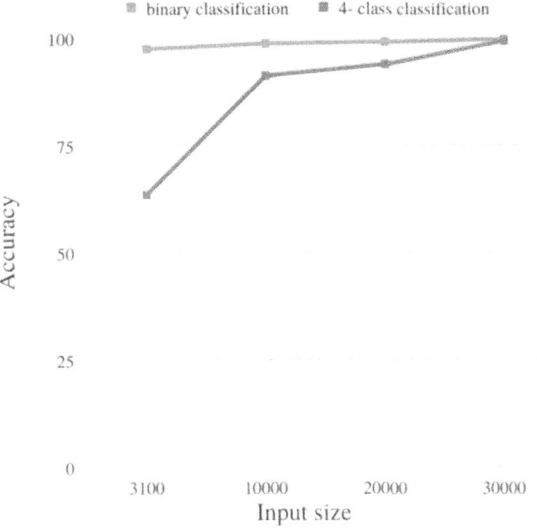

Fig.9. Accuracy Vs Input size

by incorporating more advanced techniques such as transfer learning and adversarial training.

References

1. Morice, P., Leary, A., Creutzberg, C., Abu-Rustum, N., Darai, E.: Endometrial cancer. The Lancet. **387**, 10941108 (2016)
2. Zhu, X., Ying, J., Yang, H., Fu, L., Li, B., Jiang, B.: Detection of deep myometrial invasion in endometrial cancer MR imaging based on multi-feature fusion and probabilistic support vector machine ensemble. Comput. Biol. Med. **134**, 104487 (2021)
3. Yang, X., Stamp, M.: Computer-aided diagnosis of low grade endometrial stromal sarcoma (LGESS). Comput. Biol. Med. **138**, 104874 (2021)
4. Shao, H., Zhang, Y.: Optical scanning endometrial cancer pathological image classification based on neural network and attention mechanism. In: 2021 6th International Symposium on Computer and Information Processing Technology (ISCIPT), pp. 563–566 (2021)
5. Zeng, X., Sun, H., Ma, Y.: A Histopathological Image Dataset for Endometrial Disease Diagnosis. figshare. Dataset (2018). https://figshare.com/articles/dataset/A_histopatholog ical_image_dataset_for_endometrial_disease_diagnosis/7306361/2. https://doi.org/10.6084/m9.figshare.7306361.v2
6. Praiss, A., et al.: Using machine learning to create prognostic systems for endometrial cancer. Gynecol. Oncol. **159**, 744–750 (2020)
7. Hong, R., Liu, W., DeLair, D., Razavian, N., Fenyo, D.: Predicting endometrial cancer subtypes and molecular features from histopathology images using multi-resolution deep learning models. Cell Rep. Med. **2**, 100400 (2021)
8. Mahmud, T., Sikder, J., Salma, U., Naher, S., Fardoush, J., Sharmen, N., Tripura, S.: An optimal learning model for training expert system to detect uterine Cancer. Procedia Comput. Sci. **184**, 356–363 (2021)

9. Jegou, H., Perronnin, F., Douze, M., Sánchez, J., Pérez, P., Schmid, C.: Aggregating local image descriptors´into compact codes. IEEE Trans. Pattern Anal. Mach. Intell. **34**, 1704–1716 (2012)

10. Dinesh Kumar, M., Babaie, M., Zhu, S., Kalra, S., Tizhoosh, H.: A comparative study of CNN, BoVW and LBP for classification of histopathological images. In: 2017 IEEE Symposium Series on Computational Intelligence (SSCI), pp. 1–7 (2017)

11. Ghosh, S., Bandyopadhyay, A., Sahay, S., Ghosh, R., Kundu, I., Santosh, K.: Colorectal histology tumor detection using ensemble deep neural network. Eng. Appl. Artif. Intell. **100**, 104202 (2021)

12. Kosaraju, S., Hao, J., Koh, H., Kang, M.: Deep-Hipo: multi-scale receptive field deep learning for histopathological image analysis. Methods **179**, 3–13 (2020)

13. Prabhu, S., Prasad, K., Robels-Kelly, A., Lu, X.: AI-based carcinoma detection and classification using histopathological images: a systematic review. Comput. Biol. Med. **142**, 105209 (2022)

14. Frank, S.: Resource-frugal classification and analysis of pathology slides using image entropy. Biomed. Signal Process. Control **66**, 102388 (2021)

15. Kumar, A., et al.: Deep feature learning for histopathological image classification of canine mammary tumors and human breast cancer. Inf. Sci. **508**, 405–421 (2020)

16. Tomita, N., Abdollahi, B., Wei, J., Ren, B., Suriawinata, A., Hassanpour, S.: Attention-Based deep neural networks for detection of cancerous and precancerous esophagus tissue on histopathological slides. JAMA Netw. Open **2**(11), e1914645–e1914645 (2019)

17. Vaswani, A., et al.: Attention is all you need. In: Proceedings of the 31st International Conference on Neural Information Processing Systems, pp. 6000–6010 (2017)

18. Devlin, J., Chang, M., Lee, K., Toutanova, K.: BERT: pre-training of deep bidirectional transformers for language understanding (2019). https://arxiv.org/abs/1810.04805

19. Brown, T., et al.: Language models are few-shot learners. Adv. Neural. Inf. Process. Syst. **33**, 1877–1901 (2020)

20. Chen, M., Radford, A., Wu, J., Jun, H., Dhariwal, P., Luan, D., Sutskever, I.: Generative Pretraining From Pixels. In: International Conference on Machine Learning (2020)

21. Dosovitskiy, A., et al.: An image is worth 16×16 words: transformers for image recognition at scale. (2020)

22. Wang, B., Xie, Q., Pei, J., Tiwari, P., Li, Z., Fu, J.: Pre-trained language models in biomedical domain: a systematic survey (2021). https://arxiv.org/abs/2110.05006

23. Sun, H., Zeng, X., Xu, T., Peng, G., Ma, Y.: Computer-aided diagnosis in histopathological images of the endometrium using a convolutional neural network and attention mechanisms. IEEE J. Biomed. Health Inf. **24**, 1664 (2019)

24. Ebrahimian, A., Mohammadi, H., Babaie, M., Maftoon, N., Tizhoosh, H.: Class-aware image search for interpretable cancer identification. IEEE Access **8**, 197352–197362 (2020)

25. Riasatian, A., et al.: Fine-tuning and training of densenet for histopathology image representation using TCGA diagnostic slides. Med. Image Anal. **70**, 102032 (2021)

26. Han, K., et al.: A survey on vision transformer. IEEE Trans. Pattern Anal. Mach. Intell. **45**, 87–110 (2023)

27. Bray, F., Ferlay, J., Soerjomataram, I., Siegel, R., Torre, L., Jemal, A.: Global cancer statistics 2018: GLOBOCAN estimates of incidence and mortality worldwide for 36 cancers in 185 countries. CA A Cancer J. Clin. **68**, 394–424 (2018)

28. UK, C. Endometrial cancer diagnosis (2021). https://www.cancerresearchuk.org/about-cancer/womb-cancer/diagnosistests/endometrial-cancer-diagnosis. Accessed on 30 Mar 2023

29. Zhou, J., Zhang, Y., Chang, Q., Ma, J., Zhao, H.: Application of deep learning in the diagnosis of endometrial cancer in HE-stained pathological sections. J. Health. Eng. **2020**, 1–12 (2020)

30. Hou, L., Samaras, D., Kurc, T., Gao, Y., Davis, J., Saltz, J.: A review on medical image-based diagnosis using machine learning. Mach. Learn. Knowl. Extr. **2**, 585–612 (2020)

31. Litjens, G., et al.: A survey on deep learning in medical image analysis. Med. Image Anal. **42**, 60–88 (2018)
32. Chen, X., Wang, J., Wang, S.: Survey on convolutional neural network-based medical image analysis. J. Healthc. Eng. **15**, 1–25 (2020)

SweetSight: A Deep Convolutional Neural Network Approach for Automatic Categorization of Bengal Sweets

Soummo Supriya[1], Iffat Firozy Rimi[1(✉)], Md. Moinul Islam[1], Md. Sadekur Rahman[1], Samia Nawshin[1], and Md. Tarek Habib[2]

[1] Department of Computer Science and Engineering, Daffodil International University, Dhaka, Bangladesh
if.firozy880@gmail.com, {sadekur.cse, samia}@daffodilvarsity.edu.bd
[2] Department of Computer Science and Engineering, Independent University of Bangladesh, Dhaka, Bangladesh

Abstract. The manufacture of a wide variety of sweets is on the rise in the entire Bengal (both Bangladesh and West Bengal). As a consequence, the sweet's name escapes the vast majority of individuals in our country. Computer vision advancements have made object recognition from photos easier in recent years. Using computer vision to automatically categorize sweets is still a challenge because of the similarity between various sorts and characteristics such as their placement or lighting conditions. Classifying sweets may be useful in a variety of domains, including autonomous economic robots and the creation of mobile apps for identifying certain sweets on the market. In this article, we employed deep convolutional neural network (DCCN) methods to evaluate five alternative models for sweet detection. The endemic Bengali delicacies we used to train my model included Inception-v3, ResNet-50, VGG15, AlexNet, and CNN. This model was efficient. Our dataset comprised images of confections from thirteen distinct sweet categories. Two portions of the dataset were separated: 80% for training and 20% for testing. The training dataset was enhanced and increased to make preparation simpler. Using the Inception-v3 model, we were able to attain a 100% accuracy rate with our dataset.

Keywords: Bengal Sweets · Expert System · DCNN · Performance Classification · Inception-v3 · Precision

1 Introduction

Authentic sweets could also be a dough soaked in sugar or sweetener juice or oligosaccharide mixed with all completely different shapes of chickpeas or flour. Sweets unit of measurement is a very modern ingredient in Bengali food. No occasion of Bengali is complete without sweets. From the laddu of that primitive age to Sandesh, Kalojam, currently, the variability of sweets has reached the stage of art. Standard is an expansion of sweet tastes, variations in size, and even words. The quantity of sweets people use throughout this region is unmatched by any other country at intervals across the globe [1].

Our culture is typical of the well-known delicacies that come from West Pakistan. Indian sweets have a distinct flavor profile that is distinct from other cuisines. The sweets from Bengal's eastern area are some of the most unusual; you won't find anything like them anywhere else. Rasgulla, Sandesh and Mishti Doi are some of the most popular Bengali sweets anyone has ever seen. If their popularity is any indication, the Bengalis from Eastern India know a great lot about sweet manufacturing. As a tribe, they're renowned for their sweet appetites, so this is only logical. The glorification of sweets touches the country even internationally. Sweet making is related to art. People have been making varied sorts of sweets with their power for many years. Once upon a time, everyone could not produce sweets, albeit they were required to undertake to try to do this. Google and YouTube weren't accessible at that time. Those who wished to form sweets were referred to as a maker. They were generally from the Hindu community today. Muslims and Hindus are concerned with this aesthetic profession. As sweets have gained fame domestically, to boost native fame, many sweet makers are noted presently in Bengal for their creations. Plenty of sweets are created in Bengal and it's made through the process. Therefore, this study aimed to acknowledge the sweets or desserts like Lemon Borfi, Roll Sondesh, Shurjomukhi, Roshokodom, etc.

Artificial intelligence and the field of machine learning find application in developing diverse osteopathic expert systems, augmenting human activity through increased scale and dynamism. These expert systems play a pivotal role in recognizing, uncovering, and predicting critical aspects. Advanced systems, empowered by deep learning technology, swiftly yield initial decisions, facilitating seamless progress. To address specific research queries, this paper introduces a convolutional neural network (CNN)-oriented osteopathy expert system.

- Is it possible for deep learning algorithms to distinguish so many different types of sweets?
- Which deep learning model from which domain outperforms all other algorithms in the well-known sweets cluster based on specific key performance metrics?

In this research, we train a model for an intelligent system for an image knowledge set. The most well-known deep learning techniques include CNN, AlexNet, VGG-16, Inception-v3, and ResNet-50. Performance measurements for these five deep-learning algorithms generally include sensitivity, specificity, recall, precision, and F_1-score. A method of sweet recognition based on knowledge of those matrices was developed to use the formula that functioned well. We believe that widely utilized academic deep learning algorithm design will play a crucial part in the advancement.

The remainder of this paper's structure is as discussed here. A summary of the pertinent works is included in Sect. 2. The system's architecture is shown in Sect. 3. The study technique is covered in Sect. 4, along with a brief feature and data analysis. Section 5 shows an actual evaluation, and Sect. 6 finally makes suggestions for additional studies.

2 Literature Review

The breadth of the issue, the obstacles, and the study summary will be covered in this part. Before beginning our research, we studied more sweet predictions. As part of the Bengali analytic system, we learn about many forms of stands that match the need for sweet recognition and several marketing values. To resolve the issue, we need to look into the issue more. The recognition mechanism is especially critical for growing fresh sweets. Some of the underlying approaches, linked results, research articles, and classifiers are summarized in the related work. As part of the study summary, we put together a few relevant findings.

Wang et al. [2] the exploration of apple recognition for yield prediction. They developed a technique for identifying apples based on their specular reflection pattern. Additional information, such as the size of an average, either remove false positives otherwise divide locations that potentially contain many apples. Various strategic method was only to accept detections from mostly circular regions. Bac et al. [3] proposed a technique for sweet pepper segmentation. They used a six-band multispectral camera together with a variety of characteristics, for example unprocessed multispectral data, normalized difference indices, and entropy-based texture features. This approach produced findings on segmentation that were relatively precise, according to experiments conducted in a tightly controlled glasshouse environment. However, the scientists cautioned that it was not precise enough to construct a trustworthy hindrance map. Hung et al. [4] recommended conditional random fields for almond subdivision. They advised using a Sparse Auto Encoder to separate data into five classes (SAE). Although they performed a great job of segmenting the data, they were unable to find any objects. They also pointed out that occlusion was a serious problem. This tactic, on the surface, appears to be limited to small quantities of occlusion. Chung et al. [5] studied deep learning (DL) for fruit recognition and other applications. The EfficientNet architecture and convolution neural networks (CNNs) for fruit recognition are also briefly described in the Fruit 360 dataset. The results show that the suggested model is 95% more accurate. Storbeck et al. [6] created a computer vision system and neural network software to recognize fish species. As the camera is perpendicular to a conveyor belt and records various fish characteristics, the vision system is a technology that enables you to view things. The network is trained to distinguish the species using this input data. To speed up the network training, a learning rate, a momentum factor, and the removal of unhelpful connections and nodes were put into place. In tests, it was discovered that the network successfully classified more than 95% of the fish. Nuruzzaman et al. [7] employed machine vision methods to identify potato species. To examine 200 potato photos, they employed machine learning algorithms such as random forest (RF), linear discriminant analysis (LDA), Supplying Regression, SVM, CART, naive Bayes, and k-NN. The most obvious result is supplying regression, which has a 98% accuracy rate. Maksudur et al. [8] worked on victimization CNN for columbiform bird breed identification. To unravel the recognition and categorization of columbiform bird breeds, they must employ a variety of unique analysis methodologies and complex technologies. They used VGG-16, VGG-19, MobileNet-v2, DenseNet-121, Inception-v3, NASNet Mobile, Inception-ResNet-v2, and Xception as tools. NASNet Mobile was the most accurate of those algorithms. Chen et al. [9] present a fish recognition system that combines a cutting-edge instance segmentation method with ResNet-based classification. The fish segmentation model divides an input picture into a number of images that each include a specific object on a background of pure black. A database of actual fish pictures was compiled from a fish market to examine the process. The performance of the following process to test the data set yielded scores of 85% for Top-1 accuracy and 95% for Top-5 accuracy. Franczyk et al. [10] attempted to recognize grape varieties using a deep-learning algorithm. The researchers demonstrate a method for automating grape identification utilizing residual network structures and image-recognition algorithms. They developed a model called ExtResnet that combines ResNet50 and MLP, two connected deep neural networks. Their created model for grape identification in a vineyard detects grape varieties with 99% accuracy.

Hanbay et al. [11] employed deep learning-based features to identify bugs and pests affecting plants. Their study involved comparing the performance of nine different deep neural network architectures for predicting plant diseases. They utilized deep feature extraction to extract relevant features from plant images and then employed support vector machine (SVM), Extreme Learning Machine (ELM), and k-NN approaches to classify the diseases. For their research, they utilized a CNN model-based transfer learning approach to pre-train their system.

In a separate study, Deepan et al. [12] presented their work on a deep learning-based technique for detecting leaf diseases in various plants using leaf images. Their objective was to explore and develop more suitable deep learning methods for identifying plant diseases solely based on plant photos. They experimented with three different object detectors: Region-Based Fully Convolutional Network (R-FCN), Faster Region-based Convolutional Neural Network (Faster R-CNN), and Single-shot Multibox Detector (SSD). Mohanty et al. [13] proposed a deep Convolution Neural Network to recognize 14 crop species and 26 illnesses. During the feasibility test, their trained model had an accuracy of 99.35%. Santosh Adhikari et al. [14] automatically categorized and detected plant disease in tomato plants. Their study work included image processing, image RIO adjustment, and CNN, with a total accuracy of 89% on their plant village dataset. Laboni et al. [15] worked on dried fish classification using deep learning. Their set of data contains locally cognized fourteen dried fish images. They gathered several images for this dataset, segmented and enhanced it, and then trained a deep-learning and CNN-based model to categorize dried fish. The accuracy of the current model was 97.72%.

Table 1 is a tabular representation of the studies we mentioned, including authors, years, methods used, and the results obtained.

Overall, these studies demonstrate the versatility and potential of deep learning and computer vision in solving real-world problems across different domains. However, they also underscore the importance of adapting methods to the specific challenges posed by each application, from fine-tuning object detection algorithms for plant diseases to addressing occlusion in fruit and nut recognition.

In order to better estimate and identify things, new technologies like deep learning, machine learning, and artificial intelligence are being studied. Machine learning algorithms are increasingly being used to recognize and primary uses. Many techniques, such as AlexNet, DenseNet, VGG-16, and Inception-v3, are used in recognition systems of many kinds. From prior studies, it's clear that the CNN algorithm is popular

Table 1. Comparative Analysis of Results

Study	Authors	Years	Methods	Result
Apple Recognition [2]	Q. Wang, S. Nuske, M. Bergerman, & S. Singh	2012	Specular reflection, size, circular regions	Specular reflection-based apple identification, reduction of false positives
Sweet Pepper Segmentation [3]	C. W. Bac, J. Hemming, & E. J. Van Henten	2013	Multispectral data, texture features	Relatively precise segmentation, not suitable for hindrance map
Almond Subdivision [4]	C. Hung, J. Nieto, Z. Taylor, J. Underwood, & S. Sukkarieh	2023	Conditional random fields, Sparse Auto Encoder	Successful data segmentation, challenges with object detection and occlusion
Fruit Recognition [5]	D. T. P. Chung, & D. Van. Tai	2019	EfficientNet, CNNs	Suggested model achieved 95% accuracy
Fish Species Recognition [6]	F. Storbeck, & B. Daan	2001	Computer vision, neural network	Over 95% fish species
Crop and Disease Recognition [13]	S. P. Mohanty, D. P. Hughes, & M. Salathé	2016	Deep Convolution Neural Network	99.35% accuracy for crop and disease recognition
Tomato Plant Disease Detection [14]	S. Adhikari, D. Unit, B. Shrestha, & B. Baiju	2018	Image processing, CNN	89% accuracy on plant disease detection
Dried Fish Classification [15]	M. Donatelli, R. D. Magarey, S. Bregaglio, L. Willocquet, J. P. M. Whish, & S. Savary	2017	Deep learning, CNN	97.72% accuracy for dried fish classification

and useful for making predictions or detecting anomalies. Using AlexNet and other algorithms, we were able to accurately forecast the different varieties of sweets from Bengal's standpoint.

3   System Architecture

Figure 1 depicts the concept of the Bengali sweets recognition system. The online software requires the user to photograph and submit the sweets of interest. Information from the user is sent to the server's intelligent system. The stored knowledge-based system collects data, correlates it, and transmits it to the previously created estimation method through the inference engine. Once the classification procedure is complete, the results are sent back to the expert system interface. To decide the output, the processed data is fed into a machine learning model. The user is then provided with the outcome and the species name of the sweets through the Internet.

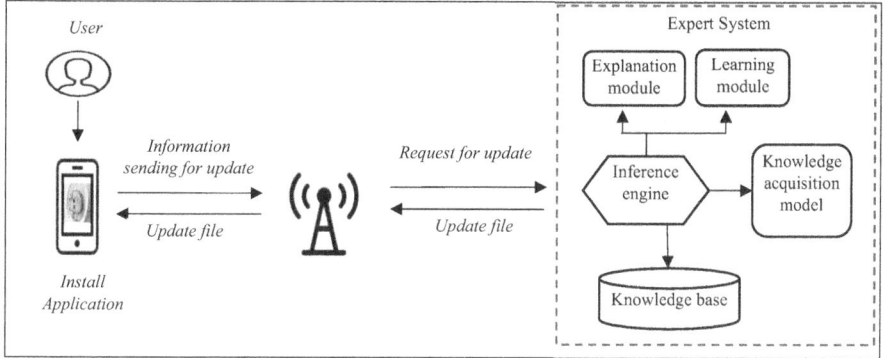

Fig. 1. Sweets recognition system architecture.

4 Research Methodology

The dataset used in our research comprises an extensive collection of relevant coordinates that can be conveniently accessed and modified. Our initial objective was to identify the various sweets available in different locations. During our investigation, we encountered certain stores that had a variety of sweets but declined to provide images. However, we were fortunate to receive permission from a few stores to capture pictures of the different sweets they offered. The cooperative stores that allowed us to take images included Bikrampur Mistanno Bhandar & Bakery, Bhaggokul Mistanna Bhandar and Bakery, Mithaiwala - Banani, and Mithai - Karwan Bazar. We were able to collect data from 633 raw pictures of 13 classes. When we captured the images, all images were not the same size, so we resize the images. The dataset contains 6500 photos of sweets, all of which are helpful to our system and improve the performance of this model. Then we apply our proposed model. After that, we test our data and evaluate the model. Below, a thorough description of each block diagram point has been provided in Fig. 2.

Deep learning frameworks TensorFlow and Keras have been utilized in the back-end of the application. TensorFlow is a high-level framework that they run on top of. The CNN also uses convolution, pooling, fully linked and flattening layers as part of the network's architecture. Using an activation function, we have made our output non-linear. The performance of a CNN is based on its output activation function. This might be an activation function of the rectified linear unit (ReLU).

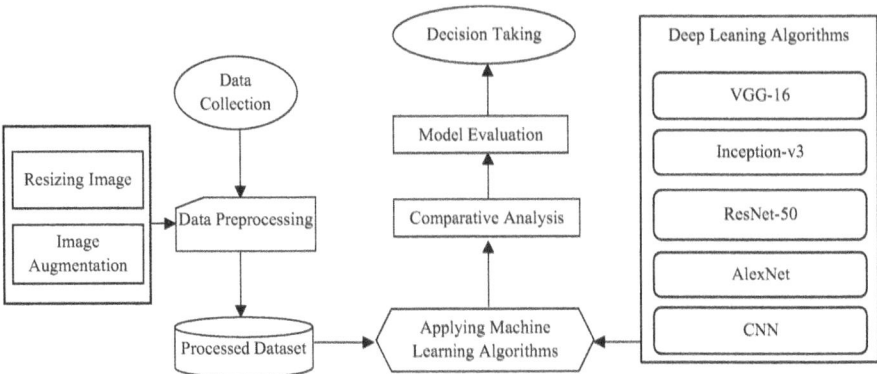

Fig. 2. Steps in the process we suggest for our system to identify sweets.

4.1 Sweet Data Collection and Species Description

For our experiment, we require a huge quantity of high-quality images. However, obtaining images is quite tough. We have visited some shops in Bangladesh and West Bengal, and taken photographs of the sweets of the entire Bengal, as well as gathered images from the Internet, which have been shown in Fig. 3.

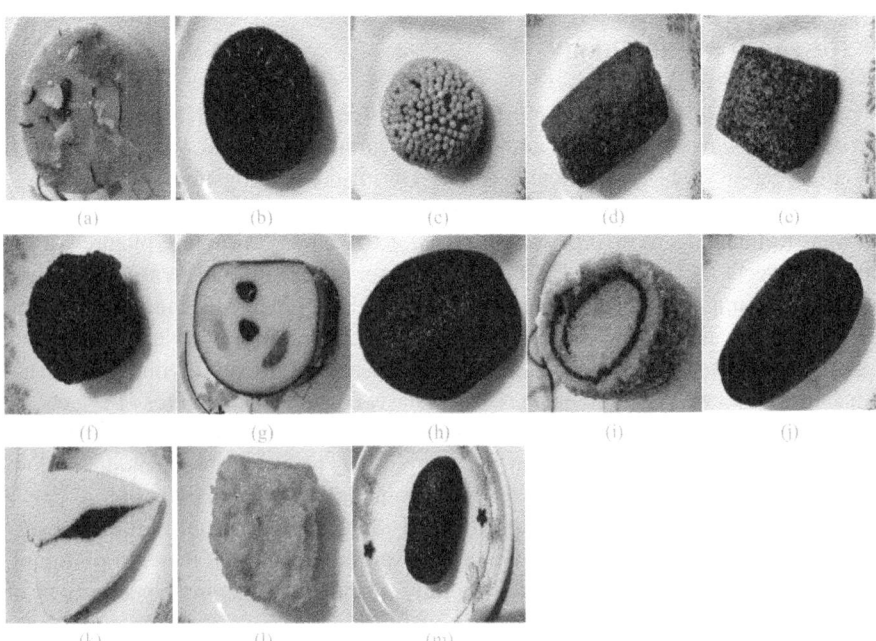

Fig. 3. Common varieties of sweets in Bengal. (a) Top jeli sondesh. (b) Surjomukhi sondesh. (c) Rosokodom. (d) Roll sondesh. (e) Obak sondesh. (f) Motichur. (g) Lemon barfi. (h) Komlavog. (i) Khirvog. (j) Kalojam. (k) Elish peti. (l) Doudhiya sondesh. (m) Chomchom.

For our experiment, we had 13 classes. Chomcom, doudhiya shondesh, elish peti, kalojam, kheer bhog, komla bhog, lemon borfi, motichur, obak shondesh, roll shondesh, roshokodom, shurjomukhi, and topjeli shondesh are the names of these sweets. The total authentic images of our project are 633 images and, per class around 48 images.

4.2 Data Preprocessing

When we took the images and gathered the images from the internet, not all photos were the same size. To eliminate this issue, we immediately scaled the data. After scaling, the picture dimensions are 224×224 pixels. The photos were then segmented for improved results. At that time, we employed five enhanced approaches to avoid the over-fitting problem [17]. These methods are right $+45°$ rotation, left $-45°$ rotation, vertical flip, horizontal flip, and wrap shifting. It is difficult to display all of the photographs. Figure 4 demonstrates an example dataset including six concepts. Table 2 displays the statistical properties of the sweet dataset.

4.3 Description of the Models Used

CNN's are a type of neural network that engage in deep learning. CNN marks a monumental advancement in image recognition. They are most usually used to assess visual imagery and are frequently employed in the background to classify images. The architecture of a traditional CNN is shown in Fig. 5. Convolutional layers, ReLU layers, pooling layers, and a fully linked layer comprise a CNN.

In this experiment, four CNN models were utilized, namely, AlexNet, VGG-16, Inception-v3, and ResNet-50. AlexNet comprises eight layers with learnable parameters. The model is composed of five layers, including a combination of max pooling and three fully connected layers, where ReLU activation is applied to each layer except for the output layer [18]. VGG-16 was designed to reduce the number of parameters in convolutional layers and improve training efficiency. It contains a total of 138 million parameters [19]. ResNet introduced batch normalization as one of the pioneering techniques in its architecture. ResNets are built using convolutional layers and identity blocks as the fundamental building blocks.

4.4 Performance Evaluation

To assess the effectiveness of each classifier, the confusion matrix was used to construct six performance indicators: specificity, accuracy, recall, and F_1-score. During model evolution, the test dataset was used to test certain classifiers. Genuine negative rates are referred to as specificity. Precision is a phrase used to describe determining how accurate something is. In other words, it is a measure of how closely actual results match expectations for favorable results. As an indicator of work completion, recall is a useful metric. The ratio of true positive and negative numbers is what we are looking at here. F_1-score is a measure of how well you remember and how well you remember. False positives and false negatives are taken into consideration while calculating [20]. It is $n \times n$ ($n > 2$) when dealing with multiclass issues, which is to say that there are

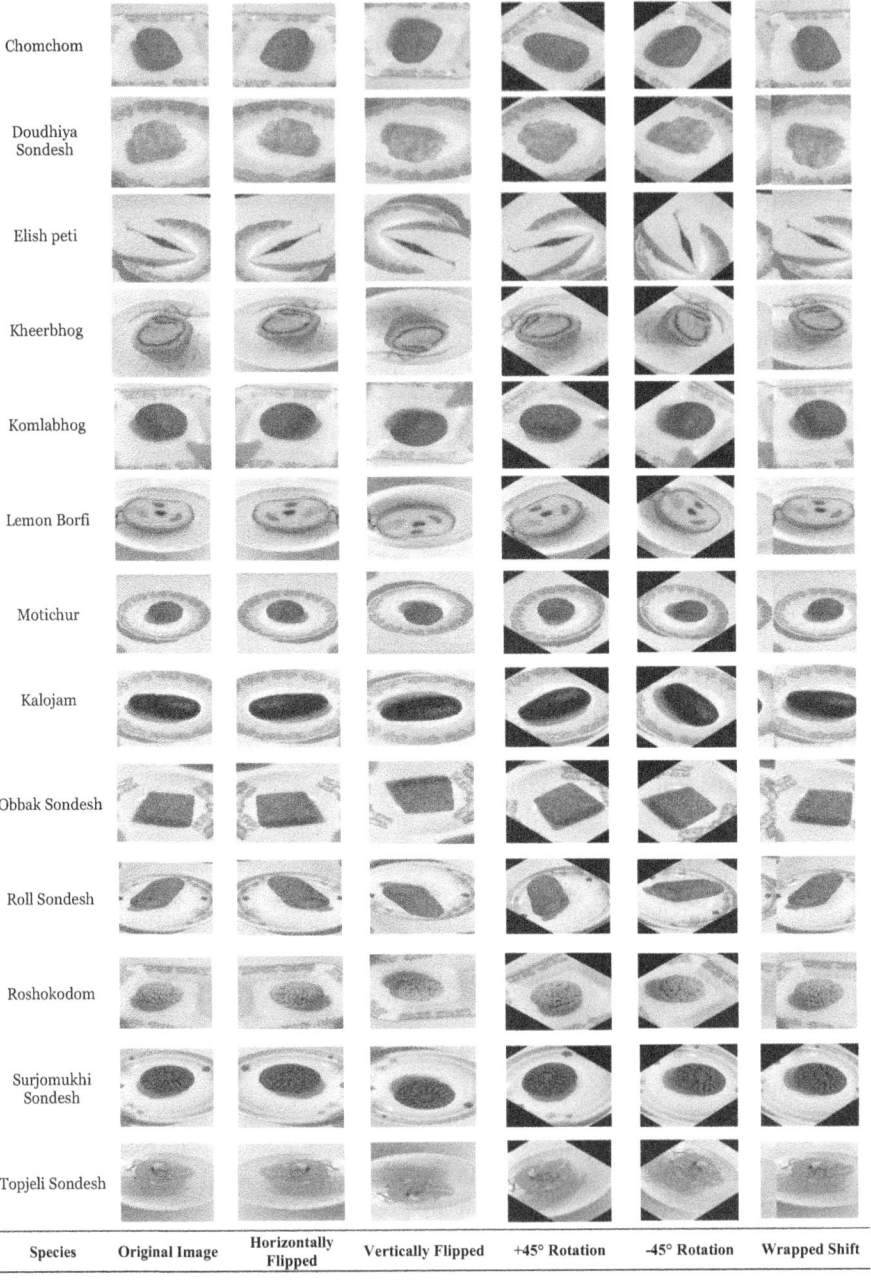

Fig. 4. The impact of augmentation on each category of images.

Table 2. Statistics of the sweet dataset

Species Name	Image Captured	Image after Augmentation	Image for Training	Image for Test	Total Training Image	Total Test Image
Chomchom	49	500	400	100	5200	1300
Dhodeya sondesh	50	500	400	100		
Elish Peti	50	500	400	100		
Kalojam	50	500	400	100		
Kheer vog	50	500	400	100		
Komla vog	50	500	400	100		
Lemon borfi	50	500	400	100		
Motichur	50	500	400	100		
Top jeli sondesh	50	500	400	100		
Surjomukhi sondesh	48	500	400	100		
Rosokodom	50	500	400	100		
Roll sondesh	38	500	400	100		
Obak sondesh	48	500	400	100		

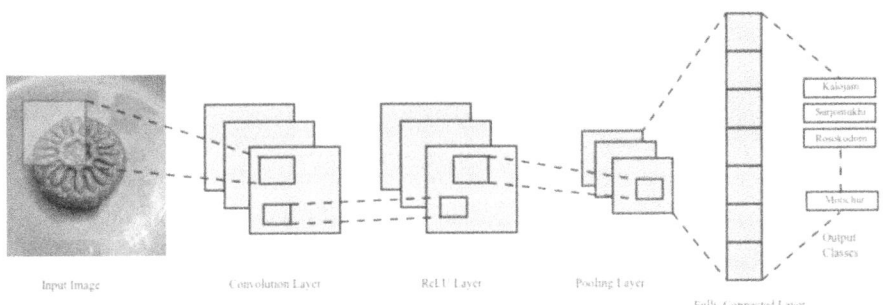

Fig. 5. Classic CNN architecture.

more than two classes involved. As a result, the matrix is made up of an array of rows, columns, and rows. Each row and each column of the matrix has an equal number of rows and columns. This matrix cannot identify the number of FP's, FN's, TP's, and TN's. The following are the calculations of FP, FN, TP, and TN values for class i ($1 \leq i \leq n$) [20]:

$$TP_i = a_{ii}. \tag{1}$$

$$FP_i = \sum_{\substack{j = 1, \\ j \neq i}}^{n} a_{ji}. \tag{2}$$

$$FN_i = \sum_{\substack{j = 1, \\ j \neq i}}^{n} a_{ij}. \tag{3}$$

$$TN_i = \sum_{\substack{j = 1, \\ j \neq i}}^{n} \sum_{\substack{k = 1, \\ k \neq i}}^{n} a_{jk} \tag{4}$$

The values obtained from the n confusion matrices for each of the classes are combined to produce the ultimate matrix of confusion with a measurement of 2×2. To calculate sensitivity, specificity, precision, recall, and the F_1-score, the following formulas are applied:

$$Sensitivity = \frac{TP}{TP + FN} \times 100\% \tag{5}$$

$$Specificity = \frac{TN}{FP + TN} \times 100\% \tag{6}$$

$$Precision = \frac{TP}{TP + FP} \times 100\% \tag{7}$$

$$Recall = \frac{TP}{TP + FN} \times 100\% \tag{8}$$

$$F_1 - score = \frac{2 \times precision \times recall}{precision + recall} \times 100\% \tag{9}$$

$$Accuracy = \frac{TP + TN}{(TP + FN) + (FP + TN)} \times 100\% \tag{10}$$

5   Experimental Evaluation

As illustrated in Fig. 2, conducting the research investigations depends on our methodologies for recognizing various sweets. At the very start, we capture various images of sweets. We scaled the inputted picture to 224×224 pixels in size. Following that, the pictures were segmented and certain characteristics were retrieved. The incremental effects of image enhancement on all sweets are previously displayed in Fig. 4. We used a total of 6,500 color images of thirteen (13) distinct desserts, including Chomchom, Doudhiya Shondesh, Elish Peti, Kalojam, Kheer Bhog, Komla Bhog, Lemon Borfi, Motichur, Obak Shondesh, Roll Shondesh, Roshokodom, Shurjomukhi, and Top Jeli Shondesh. We utilized the holdout approach for assessment with an 80%-20% split. This approach divided the entire picture into two different datasets: training (80% of data) and testing

(20% of data). We did not determine the split ratio haphazardly; we discovered it after much experimentation. To minimise overfitting, we employed split ratios of 50–50, 60–40, 70–30, 80–20 and 90–10. All of the ratio results are very comparable, however the 80–20 ratio produced the best results. This is why we chose an 80–20% split ratio. In all, we have applied to utilize five cutting-edge deep learning models: CNN, AlexNet, VGG-16, Inception-v3, and ResNet-50. The model of deep learning was chosen over a huge variety of classifiers, rather than a random one. Table 3 displays the confusion matrix for Inception-v3 among the five multiclass confusion matrices generated by Eqs. (1) to (4) for five deep learning models. This table summarizes the performance of each deep learning model's accuracy, sensitivity, specificity, recall, precision, and F_1-score. We obtained 100%, 93.30%, 98.83%, 92.30, and 95.05% from Inception-v3, AlexNet, ResNet-50, VGG-16, and CNN, respectively, as shown in Fig. 6. The accuracy performance of Inception-v3 has been investigated further since accuracy is an essential metric and Inception-v3 exceeds all other models in this regard.

In our research paper, we employed CNN and four of its models for the purpose of identifying various sweets of Bangladesh. The models we utilized were Inception-v3, AlexNet, ResNet-50, VGG-16, and a custom CNN. These models were experimented with using a dataset comprising 5926 images across 13 different classes of sweets. The sweet categories included Chomcom, Doudhiya Shondesh, Elish Peti, Kalojam, Kheer Bhog, Komla Bhog, Lemon Borfi, Motichur, Obak Shondesh, Roll Shondesh, Roshokodom, Shurjomukhi, and Top Jeli Shondesh. Remarkably, we achieved high accuracy rates with each model. Specifically, the accuracy percentages obtained for Inception-v3, AlexNet, ResNet-50, VGG-16, and our custom CNN were 100%, 93.30%, 98.83%, 92.30%, and 95.05%, respectively. Given the significance of accuracy as a metric, conducted a more in-depth analysis of Inception-v3's performance. The results revealed that Inception-v3 outperformed all other models in terms of accuracy. Additionally, we presented the class-wise accuracy achieved by Inception-v3 in Table 4, which further validated its effectiveness in accurately recognizing the different sweet categories..

Table 3. Performances of classification by all models used

Algorithm	Accuracy	Sensitivity	Specificity	Precision	Recall	F_1-score
CNN	95.05%	61.21%	99.10%	63.4%	65.0%	64.1%
AlexNet	92.30%	82.78%	98.43%	63.2%	83.3%	71.8%
VGG-16	95.83%	79.72%	88.09%	90.9%	66.7%	76.9%
Inception-v3	100%	81.35%	98.76%	92.4%	74.1%	78.0%
ResNet-50	98.30%	77.56%	86.44%	77.14%	81.6%	79.2%

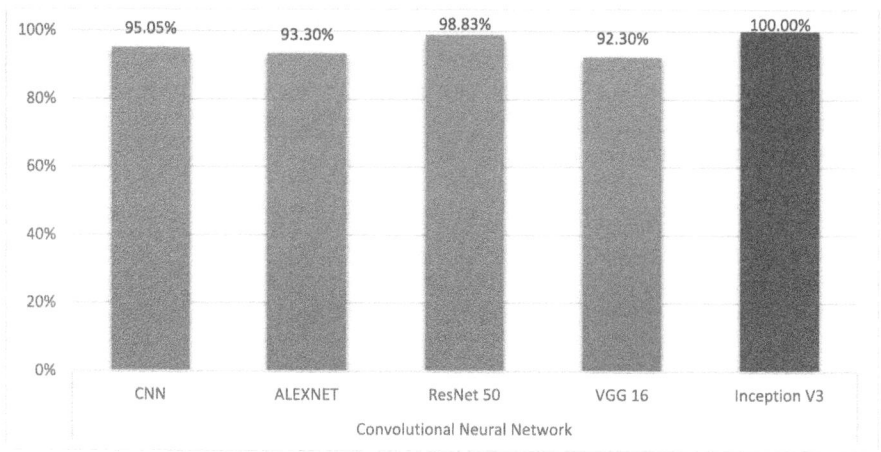

Fig. 6. Comparison of the accuracy levels achieved by deep learning models.

Table 4. Class-specific information on the accuracy measured using Inception-v3

Sweet	Total Sample	Correct Prediction	Incorrect Prediction	Accuracy
Chomchom	120	120	0	100%
Dhodeya sondesh	120	120	0	100%
Elish peti	120	120	0	100%
Kalojam	120	120	0	100%
Kheer vog	120	120	0	100%
Komla vog	120	120	0	100%
Lemon borfi	120	120	0	100%
Motichur	120	120	0	100%
Top jeli sondesh	120	120	0	100%
Surjomukhi sondesh	120	120	0	100%
Rosokodom	120	120	0	100%
Roll sondesh	120	120	0	100%
Obak sondesh	120	120	0	100%

6   Final Thoughts and Future Work

Our research has made significant strides in the realm of Bengal sweet recognition and categorization using convolutional neural network (CNN) models. Among the models tested, Inception-v3 has emerged as the standout performer, offering a compelling combination of small model size, fast execution, and high accuracy. Our work has laid a foundation for further advancements in this field, with the ultimate goal of providing easy and accurate recognition of Bengal sweets.

However, it is essential to acknowledge the limitations of our study. Firstly, our research relied on a modest dataset, which may limit the generalizability of our findings. Future work should focus on acquiring a more extensive and diverse dataset to enhance model performance. Secondly, we observed slight overfitting in Inception-v3 and ResNet-50. Addressing this issue is crucial, and while we plan to explore data augmentation and regularization techniques, it remains an ongoing challenge. Lastly, our study primarily focused on well-known CNN architectures. Exploring more diverse models and architectures may yield further insights and improvements.

Looking ahead, several avenues for future research and development emerge. Firstly, expanding the dataset to encompass a broader range of Bengal sweets and variations is a priority. This will not only improve model accuracy but also its ability to handle real-world scenarios. Secondly, continuing efforts to combat overfitting through advanced regularization methods, more sophisticated data augmentation, and careful hyperparameter tuning. Thirdly, exploring model compression techniques to reduce the computational and memory requirements while maintaining high accuracy, especially for deployment on resource-constrained platforms. Additionally, developing real-time recognition systems that can operate on mobile devices or embedded systems, making sweet recognition accessible to a wider audience. Lastly, creating user-friendly applications or interfaces for consumers and businesses to easily identify and categorize Bengal sweets, potentially benefiting the food industry and cultural preservation.

In summary, our research represents a valuable step toward efficient and accurate Bengal sweet recognition. Recognizing its limitations, we are committed to overcoming these challenges and advancing the field, with the ultimate aim of providing a practical and impactful solution for sweet recognition and categorization.

References

1. মিষ্টি - উইকিপিডিয়া.(2021). Retrieved 19 July 2021, from https://bn.wikipedia.org/wiki/%E0%A6%AE%E0%A6%BF%E0%A6%B7%E0%A7%8D%E0%A6%9F%E0%A6%BF
2. Wang, Q., Nuske, S., Bergerman, M., Singh, S.: Automated Crop Yield Estimation for Apple Orchards (2012)
3. Bac, C.W., Hemming, J., Van Henten, E.J.: Robust pixel-based classification of obstacles for robotic harvesting of sweet-pepper. Comput. Electron. Agric. **96**, 148–162 (2013). https://doi.org/10.1016/j.compag.2013.05.004
4. Hung, C., Nieto, J., Taylor, Z., Underwood, J., Sukkarieh, S.: Orchard fruit segmentation using multi-spectral feature learning. In: IEEE International Conference on Intelligent Robots and Systems, pp. 5314–5320 (2013). https://doi.org/10.1109/IROS.2013.6697125
5. Chung, D.T.P., Van Tai, D.: A fruits recognition system based on a modern deep learning technique. J. Phys. Conf. Ser. **1327**(1), 2–7 (2019). https://doi.org/10.1088/1742-6596/1327/1/012050
6. Storbeck, F., Daan, B.: Fish species recognition using computer vision and a neural network. Fish. Res. **51**(1), 11–15 (2001). https://doi.org/10.1016/S0165-7836(00)00254-X
7. Nuruzzaman, M., Hossain, M.S., Rahman, M.M., Shoumik, A.S.H.C., Khan, M.A.A., Habib, M.T.: Machine vision based potato species recognition. In: 2021 5th International Conference on Intelligent Computing and Control Systems (ICICCS) (2021)

8. Rahman, M., Prodhan, S.A., Mia, M.J., Habib, M.T., Ahmed, F.: Pigeon breed recognition using convolutional neural network. In: 2021 Third International Conference on Intelligent Communication Technologies and Virtual Mobile Networks (ICICV) (2021)

9. Chen, C.H., Chen, L.H., Chen, C.Y.: Automatic fish segmentation and recognition in Taiwan fish market using deep learning techniques. J. Imaging Sci. Technol. (2021). https://doi.org/10.2352/j.imagingsci.technol.2021.65.4.040403

10. Petrellis, N.: Measurement of fish morphological features through image processing and deep learning techniques. Appl. Sci. (Switzerland) 11(10), 4416 (2021). https://doi.org/10.3390/app11104416

11. Türkoğlu, M., Hanbay, D.: Plant disease and pest detection using deep learning-based features. Turk. J. Electr. Eng. Comput. Sci. 27(3), 1636–1651 (2019). https://doi.org/10.3906/elk-1809-181

12. Akila, M., Deepan, P.: Detection and classification of plant leaf diseases by using deep learning algorithm. Iarjset 6(7), 72–75 (2018)

13. Mohanty, S.P., Hughes, D.P., Salathé, M.: Using deep learning for image-based plant disease detection. Front. Plant Sci. 7, 1–10 (2016). https://doi.org/10.3389/fpls.2016.01419

14. Adhikari, S., Unit, D., Shrestha, B., Baiju, B.: Tomato plant diseases detection system, pp.81–86 (2018)

15. Donatelli, M., Magarey, R.D., Bregaglio, S., Willocquet, L., Whish, J.P.M., Savary, S.: Modeling the impacts of pests and diseases on agricultural systems. Agric. Syst. 155, 213–224 (2017). https://doi.org/10.1016/j.agsy.2017.01.019

16. Tan, P., Steinbach, M., Kumar, V.: Introduction to Data Mining, 1st edn. Pearson, London (2005)

17. Simple Image Data Augmentation Technics to Mitigate Overfitting in Computer Vision. (2021). [Online]. Available at: https://towardsdatascience.com/simple-image-data-augmentation-technics-to-mitigate-overfitting-in-computer-vision-2a6966f51af4

18. Introduction to the Architecture of Alexnet. (2021). [Online]. Available at: https://www.analyticsvidhya.com/blog/2021/03/introduction-to-the-architecture-of-alexnet/

19. Boesch, G.: (2021). [Online]. Availabe at: https://viso.ai/deep-learning/vgg-very-deep-convolutional-networks/

20. Habib, M.T., Majumder, A., Jakaria, A., Akter, M., Uddin, M.S., Ahmed, S.: Machine vision-based papaya disease recognition. J. King Saud Univ. Comput. Inf. Sci. 32(3), 300–309 (2020)

A Systematic Review: How Computer Vision is Transforming Agriculture in Economic Growth

Santoshachandra Rao Karanam[1]([✉]) [iD], A. B. Pradeep Kumar[1] [iD],
Prakash babu Yandrapati[1] [iD], Naresh Tangudu[2] [iD], Nagamani Peddada[3] [iD],
and PruthviRaj Goud Bollipelly[3] [iD]

[1] CSE Department, GITAM (Deemed to be University), Hyderabad, India
kschandra.rao@gmail.com
[2] CSD & MCA Department, Aditya Institute of Technology and Management, Tekkali,
Srikakulam, India
[3] IT Department, Anurag University, Hyderabad, India

Abstract. Recent years have seen the emergence of computer vision, a subfield of artificial intelligence (AI), as a technology that has the potential to revolutionize agricultural practices. This might have an impact on many agricultural practices and crop management techniques. This is due to the fact that computer vision can examine pictures and identify patterns of data. This article provides a summary of the uses of computer vision in agriculture as well as the consequences such applications have had. The issues of precision agriculture, disease diagnosis, crop monitoring, and yield computation may be overcome with the use of computer vision technologies such as image recognition, object detection, and pattern analysis. Specifically, it investigates the ways in which these strategies are useful. In addition to this, it investigates the benefits, drawbacks, and possible future applications of computer vision in agriculture, with a particular emphasis on the potential for the sector to improve its levels of productivity, sustainability, and profitability. According to this in-depth analysis, computer vision has revolutionized the agricultural industry and contributed significantly to economic growth. In order to evaluate the financial impacts that computer vision has had on the agricultural industry, this study looks at a wide range of academic papers, publications, and reports. The findings highlight the advancements, benefits, challenges, and future opportunities presented by computer vision technology in the areas of crop monitoring, precision farming, animal management, and harvesting. According to the evaluation, computer vision has the potential to improve farming in terms of productivity, resource allocation, cost reduction, and sustainable practices.

Keywords: Computer Vision · Artificial Intelligence · Economic Growth · Agriculture Management · Agricultural Automation · Machine Learning

1 Introduction

Over the course of the last several decades, agriculture has evolved into a sector of the global economy that has taken on greater importance. As the number of people in the world increases at a steady rate, the pressure that is put on the agricultural system will only

H. K. et al. (Eds.): AIKP 2023, CCIS 2127, pp. 229–244, 2024.
https://doi.org/10.1007/978-3-031-68617-7_17

become worse [1, 2]. This is due to the fact that, despite an ever-increasing population, the overall amount of arable land will gradually diminish as a consequence of urbanization. There is a growing need to find efficient and secure agricultural food production practices [1, 17, 44]. Agricultural management approaches that have been used for a long time need to be supported by new technology for sensing and driving, as well as improvements in information and communication technologies [4–6]. This will make it possible for an acceleration of the growth in agricultural production that is more precise, and it will eventually lead to the creation of agriculture that is both high-quality and high-yield [2, 3]. A considerable increase in the employment of computer vision inspection systems in agricultural operations has been seen over the course of the last several decades [9, 12, 16], and over this same period, these systems have evolved into instruments that are of great use [10]. Computer vision-based expert and intelligent systems are frequently used in agricultural production management to increase productivity and efficiency [11].

AI in agriculture maximizes crop production efficiency via precision farming, drone analytics, agro robotics, animal monitoring, and labor management. Deep learning is increasing agricultural production and market growth. AI-based technologies and methodologies help with pest control, crop health, soil monitoring, and agricultural supply chain employment [2, 4, 13, 18, 21]. Agriculture companies are using artificial intelligence to improve harvest quality and accuracy by analyzing agricultural data. The results emphasize the accomplishments, advantages, limitations, and future possibilities of computer vision technology in several fields of agriculture, including crop monitoring, precision farming, animal management, and harvesting, among others [23–27]. Computer vision is widely used in agriculture to increase productivity, reduce resource usage, and improve farm management. Agriculture uses several computer vision technologies.

Image classification: It classifies crop photographs to identify varieties, illnesses, and pests. This goal is commonly achieved via CNNs.

Object detection: It uses computer vision to recognize and locate objects in images. This approach is important for automated harvesting and weed control, where fruit, vegetable, and weed identification and localization are crucial. Based on semantic significance, semantic segmentation divides a picture into pieces. This approach may distinguish crops from soil or identify individual plants in a field.

Instance segmentation is a computer vision approach that separates images and distinguishes several instances of the same object. This is very useful for counting fruits or plants.

Pattern recognition: It is used to identify leaf disease patterns, animal activity, and soil abnormalities in pictures.

Object tracking: It records the movements and activity of pollinators (e.g., bees) and pests in agricultural situations. This allows monitoring and study of their activity and presence to understand their agricultural ecosystem connections.

3-D reconstruction is the method of creating three-dimensional models of plants or terrain using multiple images to analyze plant growth patterns and soil structure. Infrared and other spectral bands are used in multi-spectral imaging to acquire information beyond human vision. This helps monitor crop health, soil moisture, and stress. Drone cameras and computer vision provide crop surveying, monitoring, and mapping.

Automatic Sorting/Grading: It uses computer vision to classify and assess agricultural items by size, color, and quality.

Time-lapse research examines crop development patterns using successive photos. Researchers may analyze the crop growth impacts of various treatments and conditions using this approach. Apps that provide farm workers with real-time information may leverage AR technology. Smart eyewear might detect plant illnesses. This guidance uses computer vision to lead agricultural robots and machinery to plant, weed, and harvest. Precision agriculture uses computer vision and machine learning algorithms to reduce labor, improve resource allocation, and improve agricultural decision-making. They help boost agricultural output and sustainability.

This paper demonstrates how computer vision can boost economic development by increasing productivity, maximizing the allocation of resources, lowering costs, and promoting environmentally responsible agricultural practices. The second part of this research focuses on the work that has been done related to the use of AI in agricultural automation so far. In the third chapter, the approach that was used in agricultural automation via the use of AI is presented. The key difficulties facing agriculture are discussed in the fourth chapter. In the fifth chapter, we will discuss the implications of computer vision for agriculture's bottom line as well as its economic ramifications. The conclusion is discussed in the sixth chapter.

2 Related Work

It is now feasible, thanks to advancements in the area of computer vision, to automate activities such as the grading and quality inspection of agricultural goods. This has led to the widespread use of such systems across a range of businesses within the agricultural and food production industries [1]. Estimates of crop maturity are still difficult to acquire in unstructured settings like farms. New applications in agriculture may become possible as a result of advancements in computer vision [2]. Researchers came up with a fresh method for assessing mango output by using large-scale unmanned ground vehicles to take line-scan hyperspectral photos. The hyperspectral photographs were taken using commercial mango park blocks, and once they were taken, they were pre-processed to take into consideration the lighting circumstances. Mangoes were counted by hand to get an accurate estimate of the total number of fruits that were growing on the tree. This estimate was then used in an optimization process to develop the most effective fruit count model. The model then made its yield forecast using the most up-to-date version of the RGB technique. The model, which is on par with the most advanced RGB technology [3], was validated and tested with the assistance of hundreds of real-life trees. Accurate, real-time data about farms and an understanding of that data are crucial to precision farming. The use of unmanned aerial vehicles (UAVs), a technology that is advancing at a fast pace, has only recently made it possible to gather data on agricultural operations at a high resolution, at a cheap cost, and with quick solutions [4]. Using unmanned aerial vehicle platforms that have been equipped with image sensors, in-depth data on agricultural economics and crop conditions has been delivered. The use of unmanned aerial vehicles (UAVs) for remote sensing has assisted in increasing agricultural productivity while simultaneously reducing costs [5–7]. The ability to quickly, accurately, and cost-effectively estimate biomass is essential to the practice of precision agricultural management. It is possible that unmanned aerial vehicle (UAV) remote sensing, in combination with computer vision technology, might help in the estimation of biomass [8]. This would be an improvement over the existing methods of harvesting biomass, which rely on laborious and time-consuming destructive sampling. The study group recommended both the use of unmanned aerial vehicles (UAVs) and RGB-D reconstruction methods as potential approaches to the problem of determining how to measure the height of plants and the amount of biomass they contain. When compared to approaches that are based on RGB-D, UAV systems are not only more user-friendly and cost-effective, but they also cover a larger geographical region. A combination of unmanned aerial vehicle (UAV) remote sensing and machine learning was used to provide spectral information for a comprehensive analysis of the biomass estimate of maize, which is an extremely important crop [10]. Experiments have shown that the proposed method has the potential to contribute to advances in accuracy when extracting plant height from UAV photographs and indicating volume. Because of this, one approach that might be taken would be to integrate machine learning with remote sensing using UAVs. In addition to that, the researcher evaluated maize biomass and acquired altitude information straight from the UAV-RGB point cloud. In a nutshell, the findings endorse this approach, demonstrating its usefulness in developing a high-performance estimating model using machine learning [11]. Precision agriculture requires crop monitoring. Unmanned aerial vehicles (UAVs) might help autonomous crop monitoring and agricultural decision-making survive [12, 13]. Researchers developed a canopy height model for autonomous UAV chestnut tree monitoring. They calculated the vegetation index (VI) using RGB and NIR bands. The model estimates tree canopy height. This concept improves chestnut orchard management and long-term growth. UAV image processing was efficient and reliable [14]. UAVs were tested to assess tomato height and canopy coverage [15]. This procedure proved practical since the results were comparable to those obtained manually. The future will need more data and larger sample sizes. To eliminate systematic mistakes. Agriculture has grown in importance to the global economy. Due to urbanization and population growth, agricultural land is disappearing, which puts a strain on the sector [16]. Researchers [17] employed machine-learning techniques to study the impact of botanical markers and color space on crop kinds, leaf color, and other attributes. Others studied threshold processing and machine learning. This study yielded a new formula. It has been beneficial in crop monitoring and uses the CIE Luv color space and a support vector machine. This strategy works for many crops and conditions. Despite breakthroughs in photoanalysis and backlight analysis, productivity and accuracy remain tough. Expert and intelligent systems use computer vision algorithms, and agricultural automation technology based on these algorithms is being used to boost productivity and efficiency. This is achievable because of the fast growth of artificial intelligence [18] and technology like GPUs and DBNs. These resource efficiency gains have given farmers several ideas for decision support and practices for ensuring agricultural productivity. Because of this, agricultural automation will eventually incorporate computer vision technology, which will lead to intelligent agriculture. 4.0 [19]. Researchers [20] produced orthophotos of palm oil fields by using an unmanned aerial vehicle (UAV) that was outfitted with the MATLAB image processing system. Using a GLCM (Grayscale Co-occurrence Matrix) approach, they identified criteria based on the four directions and particular degrees of 0°, 45°, 90°, and 135° to categorize palm oil trees as either fertile, sterile, or dead. In comparison to other, more traditional methods of monitoring, the results of the testing showed that monitoring based on UAVs is more effective and precise. Researchers [21] used MATLAB to extract the characteristics of leaves from a variety of places to detect whether or not rice plants have nitrogen. This was done to compare the characteristics of leaves from different areas. For researchers to provide a numerical value to the process of blade variation, they make use of newly developed components such as the yellowing area (EA), the degree of yellowing (ED), the form (area and perimeter), and color characteristics (green, standardized red index, etc.). These elements are used in conjunction with each other. It is preferred to use this method since it can be carried out continuously and dynamically without causing any damage to the plants. The wheat heading date is a crucial indicator of when the crop will be ready to be harvested. Researchers [22] developed a multispectral computer vision system to recognize the many types of invertebrate pests that are often seen on green plants. In the trials, an adequate level of detection accuracy was achieved for a total of twelve common agriculturally important pests that are invertebrates. Not only does the technology provide incredibly accurate findings, but it also has the capability of determining, in real-time, what actions robots should take next. The ability to make educated predictions, which may be accomplished by accurate and real-time monitoring, is essential to the prevention and management of agricultural diseases. To create and successfully execute a vision-based monitoring system [23], the "you only look once" (YOLO) and "support vector machine" (SVM) methodologies were used. The overall accuracy of the system, which came in at 92.50 percent, as well as the categorization accuracy, which came in at 90.18 percent, were both above average. In addition to its useful identifying information, the system may serve as a robust service platform for forecasting the likelihood of pest incidence and their likely future course of development. A compact, intelligent agricultural gadget that can automatically weed and vary irrigation on farmed land was developed by researchers [24] using a combination of computer vision and multitasking. Because the system can differentiate between plants and weeds in real-time, it can successfully weed and water while still maintaining an average herbicidal rate of 90% and a deep soil moisture level of 80%. This is made possible by the system's ability to discern between plants and weeds in real-time. This strategy shows promise since it not only allows for the simultaneous execution of jobs but also makes full use of the available resources. According to the findings of the aforementioned research, it is possible to conclude that the use of computer vision technology in the prevention and control of agricultural diseases and pests has been a success. Its excellent efficiency and precision, in addition to its low price, are among its key advantages. On the other hand, many of the conclusions are still in the early phases of development and will be dramatically altered by taking into account more complex factors like changes in light and plant density. Because of this, it is essential to improve the steadiness and reliability of the infrastructure that is linked to it. The development of connected datasets will be beneficial for a variety of applications, including multitask fusion, hyperspectral approaches [25, 26], and deep learning neural networks. To increase market value, harvesting processes prioritize maintaining product quality throughout the harvest. Extreme weather, fluctuating lighting, and the presence of dust, insects, and other sources of noise are present in any autonomous harvesting environment and provide significant challenges. The current technology has innovated the use of spectroscopy, deep learning, and other technologies that show excellent accuracy at a cheap cost, overcoming numerous challenges. It's important to remember that there's still a lot of opportunity for development in terms of speed and precision in tougher scenarios. Economic viability requires fast sensing, computation, and reaction to environmental changes for agricultural harvest automation to be effective [26]. The quality of agricultural goods is one of the main factors impacting market pricing and consumer satisfaction. Manual inspections have encountered various issues over the last few decades, including a lack of uniformity and insufficient detection efficiency. External quality checks may be performed with high degrees of flexibility and reproducibility, at a low cost, and with great accuracy using computer vision [27]. To classify delicious lemons more accurately, researchers [28] suggested employing image processing methods and UV rays as a rapid, non-destructive approach to detecting mechanical deterioration. So, using a truly randomized factor design, we put 135 luscious lemons through their paces. The ability to differentiate whole, delicious lemons from those that had been damaged was 100% accurate. Very high accuracy was attained in assessing and categorizing the quality of delicious lemons. U.S. firm Iron Ox spent 2.5 years perfecting a fully automated, intelligent, and cloud-based hydroponic indoor farm that requires no human oversight. The farm produces 30 times as much as a typical outdoor farm. This farm sold its first harvest in 2018. The "unmanned farm" enables accurate operation, high efficiency, intelligent decision-making, environmental protection, and visual administration in a straightforward and manageable format [29], thanks to advancements in technology. Combining feature color values with back-propagation neural network (BPNN) classification algorithms was presented by researchers [30, 31] as a way of determining whether or not tomatoes sold at fresh markets are fully ripe. The computer vision-based maturity detection gadget is used to capture tomato photos in a controlled environment. Color feature values are extracted from tomato photos using a computer vision algorithm. The value of the color characteristic is used to characterize the amount of maturity of the sample. The BPNN is then fed the color feature value to determine when the tomato sample is ripe. The findings indicated a highly satisfying average accuracy of 99.31% for determining when a tomato sample was ripe. The economic value of agriculture depends on many factors, including crop output, quality, efficiency in using resources, and overall economic advantages. However, macronutrients, secondary nutrients, and micronutrients add up to a total of 17, all of which are required for plant development. Monitoring crop development has always been mostly based on human judgment, which is neither timely nor accurate. Monitoring crops at various phases of development is a crucial part of precision agriculture. A thorough understanding of the growth environment is essential for making appropriate changes and optimizing the development environment for crops, which greatly aids in improving production efficiency [31–33]. Although the approach had low errors and high durability, it could only be used for tracking the heading time. The system outperforms competing approaches in terms of detection accuracy, and it can handle complicated environmental changes such as changes in lighting and occlusion with ease. A robot identification app-roach based on visual data was developed by researchers [34]. Median filtering, threshold segmentation using the Otsu algorithm, noise removal with an area threshold, and the Hough transform all play roles in this technique. Success in identifying cherries was well above 96%. This strategy vastly simplifies the selection process, cutting time and money spent in half. Fields of sweet peppers create certain difficulties for robotic systems due to height occlusion and colors that are too close to the backdrop. Manual management is still used in many processes, and professionals are expected to maintain a greater level of competence. The universalization of these techniques is challenging, and they cannot be used in real-time. Controlling agricultural diseases, pests, and weeds is challenging, but computer vision technology has dramatically increased the timeliness and accuracy of preventative and control efforts. Losses may be minimized, productivity improved, and sustainable agricultural growth facilitated by timely prevention and management [35]. This method will reduce the time and effort required to farm, save money on labor, and improve farm management scientifically and efficiently [36]. Soil care, crop matu-rity tests, and yield projections for unattended farms are all discussed in this section. Researchers [37] explored the cost-effective in-situ design and development of a novel computer vision-based sensor system for determining soil texture and SOM. Using a low-cost portable microscope, an image capture system was created. Laboratory images with varying textures and SOM were analyzed using a computer vision method based on geographical data analysis. Because of their low cost and mobility, the collection method and computer vision algorithms developed in this work show potential as near-end soil sensors in both laboratory and field settings. However, the device needs further testing to ensure it can withstand a variety of soil moisture levels. The use of inexpensive cameras has spread across the technological landscape, particularly in agricultural settings. Accu-rate soil water balance estimates allow for precise irrigation planning when combined with important information on the development of horticultural crops obtained from pictures. Green fruit feature extraction was developed by researchers [38] to predict citrus harvests. This technique incorporates the equalization of histograms, spatial fil-tering, Gaussian blurring, threshold processing, and the Laplace and Sobel color models as transformation operators. The process takes around 8 min without human interven-tion and has a false-positive rate of 3% for photos captured under ideal circumstances. Due to its vast potential and capacity to describe multiple target qualities, hyperspectral imaging (HSI) has been the subject of substantial study and usage in many food and agri-cultural applications. Thanks to advancements in computer vision technology and greater resource efficiency [40], farmers now have access to a wealth of new information that may inform their decision-making and enhance their methods. To assess and determine the quality of agricultural goods and encourage their commercialization, quality inspec-tions are performed. To circumvent the high cost and low efficiency of conventional procedures, the agricultural and food production industries have increasingly turned to computer vision systems for automatic grading and quality inspection of their products [41]. Currently, the technique is used mostly in the grading and assessment of agricultural items, including fruits and vegetables [42]. To boost agricultural output more rapidly and accurately and to aid in the development of high-quality, high-yield agriculture [43, 44], it is necessary to combine traditional methods of managing agriculture with modern sensing and driving technologies, as well as improved information and communication technologies. The usage of computer vision-based agricultural automation technology is on the rise as a means of enhancing agricultural productivity and efficiency [45]. This technology relies on expert and intelligent systems that are becoming more widespread in agricultural production management.

Table 1 outlines, as of this moment in time, the many pieces of research work that have been carried out in the field of agricultural automation making use of AI.

Table 1 Summary of methods used for agricultural automation using AI.

Type of research work that Happened	Methods Used in The Research Work	Types of sensors used in The Research work	Applications
Crop health and growth monitoring [9, 10, 18, 19]	A non-invasive method, threshold segmentation, the gray level cooccurrence matrix (GLCM) method, and different machine learning and computer vision methods	Visible spectrum cameras, drone-type Dji 3 Phantoms, a high-resolution camera, and an E450 Olympus	Measurement of plant growth indicators, monitoring of grape growth, and diagnosis of nitrogen content in rice leaves
Agricultural product quality testing [4, 12, 30, 31, 32]	Machine vision technology, image processing technology, a deep stack sparse autoencoder (DSSAES) method, and hyperspectral imaging	Mv-vdm033sm/sc, Canon Powershot SX30, Canon Monochrome CCD Camera, Monochrome Imspector V17e, C8484–05	Automatic carrot grading, non-destructive testing of potatoes, fruit quality testing, and detection of internal damage to blueberries
Monitoring farmland information with a UAV [8–11, 13–15]	Evaluation indexes: lai and Grvi, a digital grassland model, a machine learning method, a measurement method based on UAV, and an object-based UAV image analysis (obia) method	CMOS RGB camera, UAV with geolocation and RGB cameras, DJI Phantom 4 Pro platform, and Phantom 4 Pro drone with built-in camera	Improving irrigation accuracy, growth monitoring of tomatoes, and estimation of corn biomass
Prevention and control of crop diseases, pests, and weeds [17, 21–23, , 28, 35]	Image processing technology, multispectral 3D MVs, deep convolutional neural networks, fuzzy inference systems, and genetic algorithms	high-quality camera, microscope, and Logitech digital webcam	Detection and counting of soybean aphids; fast counting and identification of flying insects; precise spraying of pesticides

(*continued*)

Table 1 (*continued*)

Type of research work that Happened	Methods Used in The Research Work	Types of sensors used in The Research work	Applications
Applications to the automatic harvesting of crops. [6, 45, 27, 34, 38, 41, 43, 44]	Infrared imaging, a robot vision system identification method, and a retinex algorithm based on a guided filter	Hyper had ccd, Jai ad-130ge, Prosilica gc1290c, Camcube 3.0, and Uniflym216	Picking cucumbers, automatic identification of cherries, and automated harvesting of apples
Modern farm automation management [1, 3, 7, 18, 24, 25, 39]	Computer vision sensor system, FRCNN framework back propagation neural network, line scan, and his technology	Ad 7013mt,cameras, Sony Nex5n, Sony DSC-W530, Reson on Pika II, Vis-Nir Prosilica GT3300c	Estimation of soil texture, management of irrigation water balance, detection of tomato maturity, and estimation of citrus crop yield

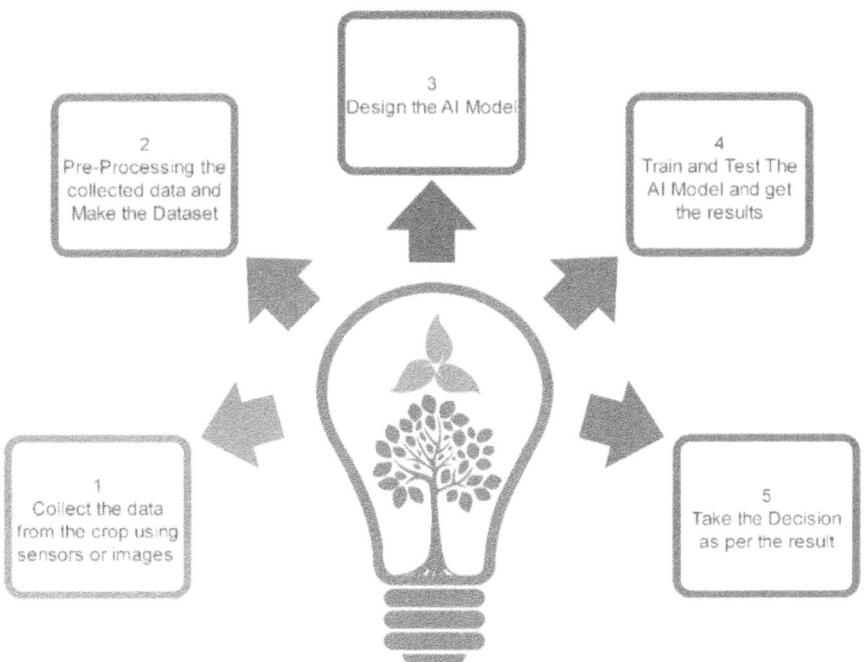

Fig. 1. Process flow of Agriculture automation in AI

3   Methodology

Agriculture is making use of a few AI-based capabilities, such as image recognition, object identification, and pattern analysis, in order to solve problems relating to precision farming, disease detection, crop monitoring, and yield estimation. The life cycle that is adopted in Agriculture automation in AI is mentioned in Fig. 1.

Process Flow of Agriculture Automation in AI

i. Collect the data from the crop using sensors or images
ii. Pre-processing the collected data and Making the Dataset
iii. Design the AI Model
iv. Train and Test the AI Model and get the results.
v. Take the Decision as per the result.

4   Applications of Computer Vision in Agriculture

Healthy crop production, pest management, soil monitoring, and other applications may all help farmers reap financial benefits. The use of artificial intelligence is now the most cutting-edge technique in farming. In agriculture, some of the most notable applications of AI include:

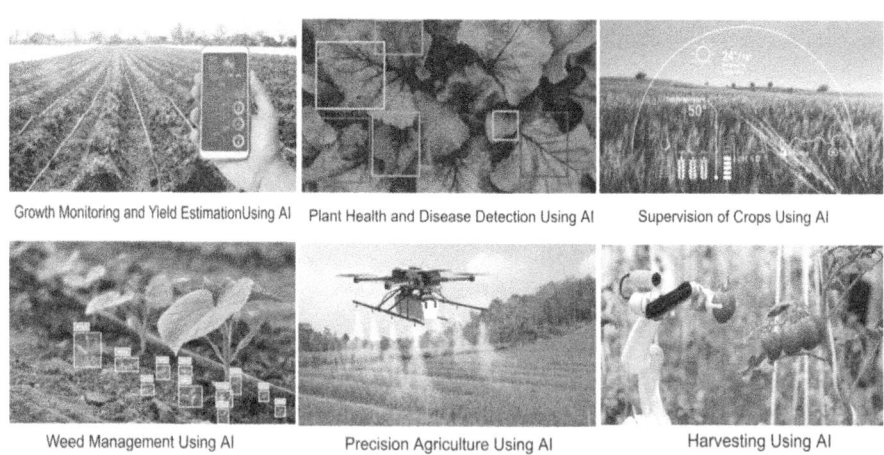

Growth Monitoring and Yield EstimationUsing AI   Plant Health and Disease Detection Using AI   Supervision of Crops Using AI

Weed Management Using AI   Precision Agriculture Using AI   Harvesting Using AI

Fig.2. Applications of Computer Vision in Agriculture

a) Management and Supervision of Crops
Technologies such as computer vision and machine learning provide major capabilities that may be utilized for the management and monitoring of crops. These technologies are examples of what are known as "AgriTech." Through the examination of crop images and the use of various machine learning models, these technologies make it feasible to perform real-time monitoring, disease detection, pest management, and optimal resource allocation. The effective overcoming of challenges related to the unpredictability of

pictures, the availability of data, and the generalization of models will contribute to the widespread acceptability and usefulness of computer vision and machine learning in crop management systems. This will be the case if these challenges are successfully overcome. Applications for increasing irrigation accuracy, tomato growth monitoring, and corn biomass estimation have been developed by researchers [8–10, 13–15] using a variety of techniques, including Lai and GRVI, a digital grassland model, machine learning, an object-based UAV image analysis method, and a measurement method based on UAVs. The continuation of research, the development of innovative technologies, and the collaboration of a large number of stakeholders will lead to additional advances in the accuracy and usability of crop management systems, which will eventually lead to improvements in agricultural practices and crop yields shown in Fig. 2.

PEAT was developed to identify soil deficiencies such as plant pests and diseases. Thanks to AI's superior image identification, farmers may utilize this app to get insights about the health of their crops.

b) Assessment of plant health and disease detection using image analysis
Image analysis that is powered by computer vision is a powerful tool that has the potential to be used in the process of determining the state of a plant's health and diagnosing diseases. Applying cutting-edge algorithms and machine learning strategies, which is made feasible via the use of computer vision, enables a speedy and objective analysis of plant images to be carried out. This makes it feasible for computer vision to assist in the early diagnosis of diseases, the application of tailored remedies, and the management of crops in the most effective manner. Researchers have created applications for the measurement of plant growth indicators, monitoring of grape development, and diagnostic of nitrogen content in rice leaves [9, 10, 18, 19] via the use of various approaches. The use of threshold segmentation, namely the gray level co-occurrence matrix (GLCM), as a non-invasive approach is being considered. As a consequence of overcoming difficulties and doing more research in this sector, the capabilities of computer vision will be strengthened so that it may be used in the assessment of the health of plants shown in Fig. 2. This will contribute to the development of sustainable agriculture as well as the preservation of global food security.

c) Identifying weeds and using selective spraying of herbicides
The use of computer vision to identify weeds and the selective spraying of herbicides are two key components that contribute significantly to the success of precision agriculture and environmentally responsible weed control. Researchers [17, 21–23, 28, 35] have created applications for the Detection and counting of soybean aphids, fast counting and identification of flying insects, and precise spraying of pesticides via the use of various approaches. The use of Image processing technology, multispectral 3D MVs, deep convolutional neural networks, fuzzy inference systems, and genetic algorithms is being considered. Farmers are able to limit the amount of chemicals they use, minimize their negative effects on the environment, and maximize their crop production by properly detecting weeds and applying herbicides in targeted areas shown in Fig. 2. For the general implementation of computer vision systems in weed control, it will be essential to overcome obstacles relating to the variety of weeds, to provide a reaction in real-time, and to integrate these systems with farming equipment. Agriculture will benefit from weed management strategies that are more effective and more environmentally friendly

if research and development efforts are maintained, new technologies are developed, and stakeholders work together.

d) Crop growth monitoring and yield estimation

Techniques that are based on computer vision and machine learning provide substantial capabilities that may be used for monitoring the growth of crops and predicting the yields that they will produce. These technologies, one of which is the inspection of images of crops, make it possible to monitor the growth of crops in a non-destructive way and in real time shown in Fig. 2. Additionally, they make it feasible to precisely estimate yields. The elimination of issues about the variability of pictures, the availability of data, and the generalizability of models will be a step in the right direction toward the widespread use of computer vision and machine learning in agricultural operations. Researchers [8–10, 13–15] have developed applications that increase irrigation accuracy, monitor tomato growth, and estimate corn biomass using a variety of methods. These methods include Lai and GRVI, a digital grassland model, machine learning, an object-based UAV image analysis method, and a measurement method that is based on UAVs. The continuation of research, the creation of innovative technologies, and the collaboration of a large number of stakeholders will further increase the accuracy and effectiveness of crop growth monitoring and yield estimation systems, which will support methods of crop management that are both sustainable and optimal.

e) Precision Agriculture

The subject of precision agriculture has a significant amount of potential for the use of technologies such as computer vision and machine learning. By analyzing photos of the crop, these technologies provide real-time monitoring, variable rate treatment, yield prediction, assessment of the soil's health, and targeted insect management. Several studies have been conducted by researchers [1, 3, 7, 18, 24, 25, 39] to create applications aimed at enhancing the assessment of soil texture, control of irrigation water balance, detection of tomato maturity, and calculation of citrus crop output. These studies have used several methodologies to achieve their objectives. The methodologies used in this study include a Computer Vision Sensor System, the Faster R-CNN (FRCNN) architecture, a Backpropagation Neural Network, and Line Scan Technology. In the field of precision agriculture, addressing challenges associated with the availability of data, integration, and user acceptability will contribute to the widespread deployment and effectiveness of computer vision and machine learning shown in Fig. 2. This will be a significant step in the right direction. If we want to be able to reach the full potential of precision agriculture for more environmentally friendly and productive farming practices, it is vital to continue research, develop technological advancements, and cooperate on initiatives.

f) Harvesting and Sorting:

The use of computer vision and machine learning technology holds tremendous promise for the automation of agricultural harvesting and sorting procedures, as well as for the improvement of such procedures' efficiencies and precision. These technologies contribute to increased production, decreased post-harvest losses, and greater profitability. Researchers [6, 45, 27, 34, 38, 41, 43, 44] have developed applications to improve automatic carrot grading, non-destructive potato testing, fruit quality testing, and blueberry internal damage identification. This research uses machine vision, image processing, deep stack sparse auto encoder, and hyperspectral imaging. They do this by reliably recognizing ripe crops, sorting food based on quality standards, and aiding efficient packing. To further improve the deployment and efficacy of computer vision and machine learning in harvesting and sorting, it will be necessary to overcome problems connected to the unpredictability in the features of the product and the processing in real-time shown in Fig. 2. The driving force behind innovation and the realization of computer vision's full potential in agricultural harvesting and sorting techniques is continued research, technical breakthroughs, and cross-stakeholder cooperation.

5 Agriculture's Major Challenges

Agriculture has several difficulties that affect food security, the environment, and the economy. Here are some key agricultural challenges.

Workforce reduction: The percentage of the worldwide workforce engaged in agriculture has decreased from 40% in 2000 to 27% in 2019. Due to a lack of available workers, even hundreds of thousands of acres may be managed by little staff.

More problems caused by climate change: It is anticipated that the increased frequency of occurrences of severe weather will result in a reduction in agricultural yield.

Annoying pests: Up to 40 percent of the world's crops are destroyed by pests every year, according to the Food and Agriculture Organization (FAO). Each year, plant diseases cause $220 billion in losses.

Global population growth: It is anticipated that the population of the world will be more than 9.8 billion by the year 2050, which will result in a major rise in the need for food.

A decrease in the amount of farmable land: The quantity of land that is suitable for agriculture on Earth is decreasing, and according to some research, the amount of land that is suitable for agriculture might be cut in half during the next quarter of a century.

6 Computer Vision's Impact on Agriculture's Bottom Line-Economic Implications

- Better crop monitoring, disease diagnosis, and yield estimate are all possible because to advancements in computer vision technology, leading to higher production in the agricultural industry.
- Optimizing the use of water, fertilizers, and pesticides are just a few examples of the resources that may be optimized by using computer vision-enabled precision agricultural approaches.
- Saving time and money by automation of labour-intensive processes including harvesting, sorting, and monitoring.
- Increased market competitiveness due to higher quality and more marketable agricultural goods thanks to quality evaluation and sorting based on computer vision.
- Reduced resource waste, less chemical application, and more sustainable farming are just a few of the environmental and consumer benefits that result from the use of computer vision in precision agriculture.

Factors to Think About and Problems to Address:

- The initial expenditures of implementing computer vision systems may include resources such as hardware, software, and training. The issues of cost and availability for subsistence farmers must be resolved.
- Concerns around privacy, security, and data ownership arise in the context of agricultural data collecting, storage, and analysis.
- Compatibility and standardization are necessary for the successful integration of computer vision systems with current agricultural technology and data platforms.
- Education and capacity development for farmers are essential if computer vision technologies are to be used successfully by farmers and agricultural practitioners.

7 Conclusion

The agricultural sector is undergoing a technological revolution as a result of improvements in crop monitoring, precision farming, harvesting, and animal management brought about by breakthroughs in computer vision technology. The use of computer vision comes with a number of benefits, but it also has a number of problems that need to be addressed. More research, advancements in technology, and collaborative efforts are required in order to fully realize the potential of computer vision in the agricultural sector.

Computer vision is having a significant influence on the agricultural industry as a consequence of its capacity to automate activities that historically required a significant amount of human work, such as monitoring, analysis, and decision-making. It is possible that the application of computer vision in fields such as crop monitoring, precision agriculture, harvesting, and animal management can improve farming's productivity, as well as its capacity for sustainability and profitability. By using the most recent advances in AI technology, India has been able to achieve a healthy rise in its agricultural GDP. The country's Gross Domestic Product (GDP) from Agriculture reached an all-time high of 7004.72 INR Billion in the fourth quarter of 2022 and a record low of 2690.74 INR Billion in the third quarter of 2011. During the period from 2011 to 2023, the GDP from Agriculture in India had an average value of 4544.88 INR Billion. However, before widespread use may occur, challenges relating to cost, privacy, and acceptability will need to be resolved. With more research, technological advances, and collaborative efforts, computer vision has the potential to bring about significant improvements in agricultural practices, therefore enhancing both food safety and the viability of farming methods.

Data Availability. No data was used for the research described in the article.

References

1. Hossain, M.S., Al-Hammadi, M., Muhammad, G.: Automatic fruit classification using deep learning or industrial applications. IEEE Trans. Ind. Inf. **15**, 1027–1034 (2019)
2. Ranjan, R., Chandel, A.K., Khot, L.R., et al.: Irrigated pinto bean crop stress and yield assessment using ground based low altitude remote sensing technology. Inform. Process. Agric. **6**, 502–514 (2019)

3. Gutie´rrez, S., Wendel, A., Underwood, J.: Ground based hyperspectral imaging for extensive mango yield estimation. Comput. Electron. Agric. **157**, 126–135 (2019)
4. JiJingChun Yuan, Z., Xiaojuan, Z., et al.: Application progress of unmanned aerial vehicle remote sensing in farmland information monitoring. J. Soil **56**, 773–784 (2019)
5. Yao, H., Qin, R., Chen, X.: Unmanned aerial vehicle for remote sensing applications—a review. Remote Sens. **11**, 1443 (2019)
6. Wei, L., Yu, M., Zhong, Y., et al.: Spatial-spectral fusion based on conditional random fields for the fine classification of crops in UAV-borne hyperspectral remote sensing imagery. Remote Sens. **11**, 780 (2019)
7. Zheng, S., Wang, Z., Wachenheim, C.J.: Technology adoption among farmers in Jilin Province, China. China Agric. Econ. Rev. **11**, 206–216 (2019)
8. Tucci, G., Parisi, E., Castelli, G., et al.: Multi-sensor UAV application for thermal analysis on a dry-stone terraced vineyard in rural tuscany landscape. ISPRS Int. J. Geo-Inf. **8**, 87 (2019)
9. Rueda-Ayala, V.P., Pena, J.M., Hoglind, M., et al.: Comparing UAV- based technologies and RGB-D reconstruction methods for plant height and biomass monitoring on grass ley. Sensors **19**, 1–17 (2019)
10. Han, L., Yang, G., Dai, H., et al.: Modeling maize above-ground biomass based on machine learning approaches using UAV remote-sensing data. Plant Methods **15**, 10 (2019)
11. Niu, Y., Zhang, L., Zhang, H., et al.: Estimating above-ground biomass of maize using features derived from UAV-based RGB imagery. Remote Sens. **11**, 1261 (2019)
12. Saldana Ochoa, K., Guo, Z.: A framework for the management of agricultural resources with automated aerial imagery detection. Comput. Electron. Agric. **162**, 53–69 (2019)
13. Liu, Y., Noguchi, N., Liang, L.: Development of a positioning system using UAV-based computer vision for an airboat navigation in paddy field. Comput. Electron. Agric. **162**, 126–133 (2019)
14. Marques P, Pa´dua L, Ada˜o T, et al. UAV-based automatic detection and monitoring of chestnut trees. Remote Sens 2019;11:855
15. Enciso, J., Avila, C.A., Jung, J., et al.: Validation of agronomic UAV and field measurements for tomato varieties. Comput. Electron. Agric. **158**, 278–283 (2019)
16. Wang, A., Zhang, W., Wei, X.: A review on weed detection using ground-based machine vision and image processing techniques. Comput. Electron. Agric. **158**, 226–240 (2019)
17. Rico-Ferna´ndez, M.P., Rios-Cabrera, R., Castela´n, M., et al.: A contextualized approach for segmentation of foliage in different crop species. Comput. Electron. Agric. **156**, 378–386 (2019)
18. Mochida, K., Koda, S., Inoue, K., et al.: Computer vision-based phenotyping for improvement of plant productivity: a machine learning perspective. GigaScience **8**, 1–53 (2019)
19. Daoliang, L.: Agric 4.0—the coming age of intelligent agriculture. J. Agron. 42–49 (2018)
20. Fahmi, F., Trianda, D., Andayani, U., et al.: Image processing analysis of geospatial uav orthophotos for palm oil plantation monitoring. J. Phys. Conf. Ser. **978**, 012064 (2018)
21. Sun, Y., Gao, J., Wang, K., et al.: Utilization of machine vision to monitor the dynamic responses of rice leaf morphology and colour to nitrogen, phosphorus, and potassium deficiencies. J. Spectroscopy **2018**, 1–13 (2018)
22. Liu, H., Chahl, J.S.: A multispectral machine vision system for invertebrate detection on green leaves. Comput. Electron. Agric. **150**, 279–288 (2018)
23. Zhong, Y., Gao, J., Lei, Q., et al.: A vision-based counting and recognition system for flying insects in intelligent agriculture. Sensors **18**, 1–19 (2018)
24. Chang, C.-L., Lin, K.-M.: Smart agricultural machine with a computer vision-based weeding and variable-rate irrigation scheme. Robotics **7**, 38 (2018)
25. Khan, M.J., Khan, H.S., Yousaf, A., et al.: Modern trends in hyperspectral image analysis: a review. IEEE Access **6**, 14118–14129 (2018)

26. Ramin Shamshiri, R., Weltzien, C., Hameed, I.A., et al.: Research and development in agricultural robotics: a perspective of digital farming. Int. J. Agric. Biol. Eng. **11**, 1–11 (2018)

27. Mohammadi Baneh, N., Navid, H., Kafashan, J.: Mechatronic components in apple sorting machines with computer vision. J. Food Meas. Charact. **12**, 1135–1155 (2018)

28. Firouzjaei, R.A., Minaei, S., Beheshti, B.: Sweet lemon mechanical damage detection using image processing technique and UV radiation. J. Food Meas. Charact. **12**, 1513–1518 (2018)

29. Kamilaris, A., Prenafeta-Boldu´, F.X.: A review of the use of convolutional neural networks in agriculture. J. Agric. Sci. **156**, 312–322 (2018)

30. Wan, P., Toudeshki, A., Tan, H., et al.: A methodology for fresh tomato maturity detection using computer vision. Comput. Electron. Agric. **146**, 43–50 (2018)

31. Ray, P.P.: Internet of things for smart agriculture: technologies, practices and future direction. AIS **9**(4), 395–420 (2017). https://doi.org/10.3233/AIS-170440

32. Culman, M.A., Gomez, J.A., Talavera, J., et al.: A novel application for identification of nutrient deficiencies in oil palm using the internet of things, **32**, 169–172 (2017)

33. Sadeghi-Tehran, P., Sabermanesh, K., Virlet, N., et al.: Automated method to determine two critical growth stages of wheat: heading and flowering. Front. Plant Sci. **8**, 252 (2017)

34. Zhang, Q., Chen, S., Yu, T., et al.: Cherry recognition in natural environment based on the vision of picking robot. IOP Conf. Ser.: Earth Environ. Sci. **61**, 012021 (2017)

35. Akram, T., Naqvi, S.R., Haider, S.A., et al.: Towards real-time crops surveillance for disease classification: exploiting parallelism in computer vision. Comput. Electr. Eng. **59**, 15–26 (2017)

36. Kim, H., Kim, J., Choi, S.-W., et al.: The study of MP-MAS utilization to support decision-making for climate-smart agriculture in rice farming. Korean J. Agric. Forest Meteorol. **18**, 378–388 (2016)

37. Sudarsan, B., Ji, W., Biswas, A., et al.: Microscope-based computer vision to characterize soil texture and soil organic matter. Biosyst. Eng. **152**, 41–50 (2016)

38. Maldonado, W., Barbosa, J.C.: Automatic green fruit counting in orange trees using digital images. Comput. Electron. Agric. **127**, 572–581 (2016)

39. Lindblom, J., Lundström, C., Ljung, M., Jonsson, A.: Promoting sustainable intensification in precision agriculture: review of decision support systems development and strategies. Precision Agric. **18**(3), 309–331 (2016). https://doi.org/10.1007/s11119-016-9491-4

40. Vazquez-Arellano, M., Griepentrog, H.W., Reiser, D., et al.: 3-D imaging systems for agricultural applications—a review. Sensors **16**, 1–24 (2016)

41. Gongal, A., Amatya, S., Karkee, M., et al.: Sensors and systems for fruit detection and localization: a review. Comput. Electron. Agric. **116**, 8–19 (2015)

42. Bhange, M., Hingoliwala, H.A.: Smart farming: pomegranate disease detection using image processing. Procedia Comput. Sci. **58**, 280–288 (2015)

43. Seema, K.A., Gill, G.S.: Automatic fruit grading and classification system using computer vision: a review, **15**, 598–603 (2015)

44. Gomes, J.F.S., Leta, F.R.: Applications of computer vision techniques in the agriculture and food industry: a review. Eur. Food Res. Technol. **235**, 989–1000 (2012)

45. Foglia, M.M., Reina, G.: Agricultural robot for radicchio harvesting. J. Field Rob. **23**, 363–377 (2006)

Automatic Conversion of Broadcasted Football Match Recordings to Its 2D Top View

Ashwini Barbadekar, Anurag Mahajan$^{(\boxtimes)}$, Sanmit Patil, and Amitesh Patil

Department of Electronics and Telecommunication Engineering, Vishwakarma Institute of Technology, Pune, India
anurag.mahajan19@vit.edu

Abstract. This paper presents an automated method to convert a broadcasted football match recording to its 2D Birds eye view. Representing a football match in 2D can be useful for tactical analysis and generating stats from events in the football match. We perform player detection and tracking on the broadcasted recording using YOLOv7 and DeepSort tracker. A database generation process is discussed to generate images of different views and perspectives of the football field along with their perspective transformation matrices. After performing some pre-processing steps on the frames from the broadcasted recording, it is compared with the images in the database to find the closest match. The perspective transformation matrix of the closest match is then used to convert the input image to its 2D top view.

Keywords: Perspective Transformation · Player Detection and Tracking · Image Processing · Computer Vision · Deep Learning

1 Introduction

Sports analytics is a valuable tool for coaches, players, and analysts to make data-driven decisions and gain a competitive edge. In Football analytics, computer vision can be used to improve the accuracy and efficiency of tracking and analysing player movements, ball trajectory, and other relevant data points. For example, computer vision can be used to track a player's position on the field, and detect and record the actions of teams and players. This technology can be used to make real-time decisions for referees, identify patterns in opponent behaviour, helping teams to prepare more effectively for upcoming games. Ultimately, computer vision can help to provide coaches and players with valuable insights that can lead to improved performance and better outcomes on the field.

Most sports analytics methods rely on data from numerous cameras recording the same game [1]. However, this data is not easily accessible to everyone, and it requires significant effort to extract valuable insights. Specifically, identifying player positions and detecting significant events such as passes, shots, and tackles necessitates extensive manual labeling, which is both time-consuming and resource-intensive. Consequently,

H. K. et al. (Eds.): AIKP 2023, CCIS 2127, pp. 245–258, 2024.
https://doi.org/10.1007/978-3-031-68617-7_18

this may impede the ability of smaller organizations and individuals to conduct detailed analysis.

As a result, we propose a solution where we automate the conversion of broadcasted videos of football matches to 2D top-view of the matches. It involves comparing a pre- processed image from the broadcasted recording with images stored in our semi-manually created database. Furthermore, the player detection and tracking performed on the broadcasted recording frames is also converted to the 2D view using the perspective transformation matrices obtained from our database. This 2D view we generate for a football match can then be used easily for various tactical and statistical purposes.

2 Literature Review

To obtain a top view of a field, multiple camera inputs are commonly used [2, 3]. These inputs are merged to create a panoramic view, which is then utilized for further processes. However, obtaining these camera inputs can be challenging as they are typically only available to certain teams and companies. Other methods involve calibrating multiple cameras and performing field localization [4–6], but these approaches require significant manual effort. Our proposed solution offers an alternative that can help avoid such manual work.

In order to extract field edges and distinguish field lines from other areas, [7] utilizes color-based kernels and [8] applies line and ellipse detection. On the other hand, some researchers have used a generative adversarial network (GAN) to generate edge maps directly from the broadcast input frame [9, 10]. While this technique produces highly accurate and precise edge maps, it also necessitates a significant amount of training data and time.

This method involves using a histogram of oriented gradients (HOG) descriptors [11] that are classified using a Support Vector Machine classifier and saved in a player model record. When detecting objects, the detected objects are compared to the ones in the database, and if they are similar, they are identified as players. In [12] Huang et al. utilized a technique that involves identifying the athletes and ball using isolated forefront data. They then conducted geometric analysis to eliminate any incorrect detections. In [12], directed weighted graph is utilized to identify and follow several athletes with the help of a region growing algorithm. While the proposed technique yielded satisfactory outcomes, it relied solely on visual data to describe the players, making it susceptible to noise.

For player tracking, the Kalman filter is suggested as an initial example of a probabilistic inference strategy, as mentioned in [13]. In recent times, particle filters have become increasingly popular due to their versatility, adaptability, and ease of implementation in various difficult situations. These filters use sequential Monte Carlo [14] sampling and have found applications in many challenging domains. Li et al. [15] employed several detectors to create a cascade particle filter that tracked a single face. The detectors were applied in a specific sequence based on their computational efficiency and ability to differentiate between features.

3 Methodology

Our approach aims to eventually automatically convert a video sequence of a football match recorded from any angle to a top view 2D model. Player detection and tracking is performed on the broadcasted recording using transfer learning and pretrained models. The broadcasted game's frames are further processed to get rid of undesirable elements like crowds and other noises and produce a final image which consists only of field lines. An image similarity search is then performed on the pre-built database of images with the detected field line edges and their perspective transformation matrices using the computed features across this edge map. Using the extracted perspective transformation matrices, we convert the input frames to its corresponding 2D views (Fig. 1).

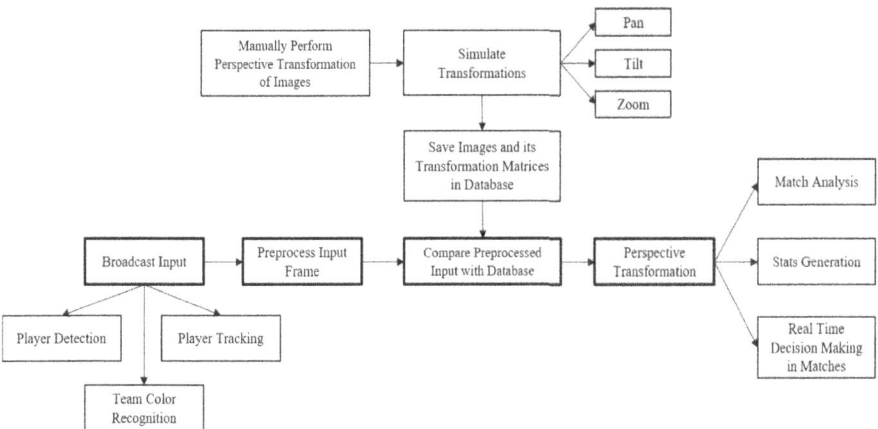

Fig. 1. Diagram to demonstrate the general working of the model

3.1 Player Detection and Tracking

Two different popular detectors are used: YOLOv7 and Faster RCNN. YOLOv7 is one the best cutting-edge object detector algorithms. It is capable of detecting multiple objects. For our problem statement, we use it to detect algorithm. YOLO v7's ability to handle various scales, orientations, and occlusions makes it well-suited for the challenges presented in football player detection.

Along with detecting the players, we also intend to classify them into a certain team. This is done by extracting the bounding box region of the athletes and converting it from the Red, Green, Blue (RGB) format to the Hue, Saturation, Value (HSV) format. By applying threshold masking, we then find out which is the most dominant color within the bounding box, other than green. This color will then be treated as the team color for that player.

The DeepSORT algorithm was utilized for tracking objects and assigning a unique ID to each object. DeepSORT is an improved version of the SORT (Simple Online Realtime Tracking) algorithm, which is well-known for its precise and accurate tracking capabilities. However, SORT has limitations such as high ID switches and failure in the event of occlusion, which are caused by the association matrix used. DeepSORT uses a superior association metric that merges both motion and appearance descriptors. This makes DeepSORT capable of tracking objects based not only on their velocity and motion but also on their appearance.

3.2 Database Generation

In this step we aim to create a database of images where the field is visible from different angles. Along with it, we store their corresponding perspective transformation matrices which will help to convert the image to its 2D representation. Here we select 100 images in a way such that, most regions of the football field are covered in it. For each image, 4 points are selected and mapped to its corresponding position on the 2D football fields image. Based on it a perspective transformation matrix is calculated for each image. Along with the manual transformations, three other transformations which include pan, tilt and zoom are performed on these images. As a result, a total of 30,000 images were stored in our database.

a. Pan transformation: The process includes moving the camera horizontally around a chosen central axis. We simulate the pan movement of the camera for the given input image and generate other images based on it. This helps to perform perspective transformation on images where the four points required to be manually labelled are not available precisely.
b. Tilt transformation: The camera is tilted when it is moved vertically, from up to down or from down to up, with its base fixed at a specific location. Tilting can be compared to the movement of a person raising or lowering their head, in contrast to a stationary camera that moves laterally to pan from one side to another.
c. Zoom transformation: Adjusting the focal length of a camera lens creates a zoom shot, which gives the impression of the subject moving closer or further away. Cameras used for broadcasting in stadiums are usually placed at varying distances from the

playing surface, and creating simulated zoom effects can help to unify footage from different locations.

3.3 Pre-processing of Broadcast Input

The aim of this step is to extract the football field line edges from the image taken from the match recording. HSV to RGB conversion is done for the input frames. Based on the Hue values, the green regions of the input image are detected. Contour detection is applied on the extracted green regions, to find the largest patch of green which is going to be the football field in the image as observed in Fig. 2 (b). On the other hand, the top-hat filter is applied on the input frame to get the image shown in Fig. 2 (c). The top-hat operator is a morphological operation used to enhance and extract features from images. It is the difference between the input image and its opening which can be mathematically written as expressed in Eq. 1 where I is the input image, B is the structuring element used for the opening operation, o denotes the morphological opening operation, and T is the output image.

$$T = I - (I \circ B) \tag{1}$$

Next, bitwise AND operation is performed between this image and the image with the field extracted in it to get an image with only the football field lines in it. Finally, based on the outcomes of player detection, the region of players is also darkened to ensure only the field lines remain as observed in Fig. 2 (d).

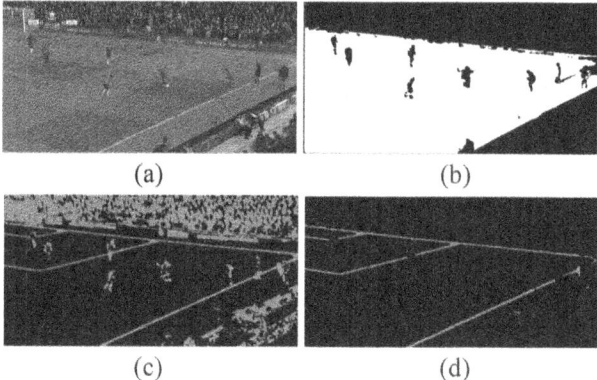

Fig 2. a) Input Frame, b) Image with the field detected, c) Output of top hat morphological operation, d) Image with field lines detected

3.4 Image Similarity Comparison

The aim of this step is to get an image from our database which is the most similar to the pre-processed input image. Using its corresponding perspective transformation matrix, we convert the input image to its respective 2D top view. The algorithm explained below is based on the concept of content-based image retrieval, where images are compared based on their visual content rather than their metadata or textual description. We use the Visual Geometry Group 16 (VGG16) model which is a pretrained convolutional neural network to extract high-level visual features that capture the content of each image. The K-Nearest Neighbors algorithm is then used to find the image which has the most similar features to the preprocessed input.

Algorithm 1 explains the process of image similarity comparison.

Algorithm 1: Image Similarity Comparison

Input: Database Images (12k images), Broadcast InputImage
Output: Most Similar Image from Database to theBroadcast Input Image
1   Load pretrained VGG16 model.
2   For each image in Database do
3   Pass image to VGG16 model
4   Extract features of image and store it in new database
5   End For
6   Pass broadcast input image to VGG16 model
7   Extract features of broadcast input image
8   For each image in Database do
9   Compute distance between image features and broadcast input image
10   End For
11   Find closest image based on least distance between features
12   Return the closest image

---

4 Results and Discussion

4.1 A Subsection Sample

Using the proposed methodology, we were able to convert a broadcasted recording of a football match into a top view 2D representation. Using the pan, tilt and zoom transformations we were able to save multiple images our database which represented different views of the football field. By comparing our pre-processed input image to our database images, we can get the corresponding perspective transformation matrix required for top view conversion.

For player detection, YOLOv7 and Faster RCNN was used. From the results shown in Table 1, we can see that the YOLOv7 model gives better accuracy for player and football detection. The Faster RCNN model did not work well for football detection. A highlight of 4 matches were captured and the frames were extracted from those match videos.

Table 1. Player Detection Evaluation scores

	Count	YOLOv7 Accuracy	Faster RCNN Accuracy
Players	950	96.63%	92.00%
Footballs	95	86.3%	65.26%

The images in Fig. 3 show examples of player detection on frames taken from different match recordings. There are certain frames where a player is blurred due to his fast movement. In these cases, the model fails to detect the player. This is improved by fine tuning the model on customized datasets that have blurred players in it.

Fig. 3. Player Detection results using YOLOv7.

Different transformation including pan, tilt and zoom were performed on manually selected images to create our database. We were able to generate a total of around 30,000 images to store in our database (Table 2).

Table 2. No of Images stored in database

Transformation	No of transformations performed	No of transformations saved
Pan	17,500	15,000
Tilt	12,000	9,000
Zoom	6,500	6,000

The preprocessing steps we have used turn out to be quick and adequate for this problem. Instead of using a GAN network to produce images [9, 10], performing basic morphological operations on input images has been sufficient. To evaluate the pre-processing results, the Root Mean Squared Error (RMSE), the Universal Quality Index (UQI) score and the Spatial Correlation Coefficient (SCC) is used. The RMSE value quantifies the average of the squared differences between the unit values of the two input images. A lesser RMSE value indicates a higher level of similarity between the images. It was then calculated using the Eq. 2 where, I1 and I2 refer to the actual and predicted images being compared, N is the total number of pixels in the images, i is the index of the pixel being compared and I1(i) and I2(i) are the pixel values of the ith pixel in the two images.

$$RMSE = -1.N(I(i) - I(i))^2 \tag{2}$$

The UQI score is a metric used to evaluate the degree of similarity between a distorted image and a reference image by measuring the structural similarity, luminance distortion, and contrast distortion between the two images. The UQI score ranges between 0 and 1. The Spatial Correlation Coefficient (SCC) is used to assess the similarity between the two given images based on their normalized pixel values and the spatial relationship between pixels. By normalizing the pixel values to have a mean of zero and unit variance, the SCC considers the intensity and contrast of the images. The correlation coefficient is then calculated between the two sets of normalized pixel values, which considers the spatial relationship between pixels. The SCC value ranges from −1 to 1, where a higher SCC value indicates greater similarity between the two images.

Table 3. Evaluation metric scores for pre-processing steps

No of Images	Average RMSE	Average UQI	Average SCC
100	0.229	0.852	0.347

To compare the preprocessed images with the ground truth, the SCC score is the most suitable score. Our test dataset achieves an average SCC score of 0.347 over the 100 images. This indicates that the pre-processed image does in fact have some spatial similarity with its ground truth but it is not of great value. This is because the field lines we are able to detect are not always joint and are of varying thickness.

Finally, using the extracted perspective transformation matrices the input images were converted to its 2D top view. Thus, the players that were detected in the input frames are now represented in 2D on a map of the football field as shown in Figure 4.

Ten second clips of three different matches were selected for testing our methodology on it. These videos were of 30 frames per second rate and thus had 300 frames each. The ground truth was created for every 6th frame by manually labelling them.

In general, it is observed that frames where the center of the field is visible gave better results. The perspective transformation done on these frames seem to be more accurate and thus it gives a lesser RMSE value and higher UQI and SCC score. As

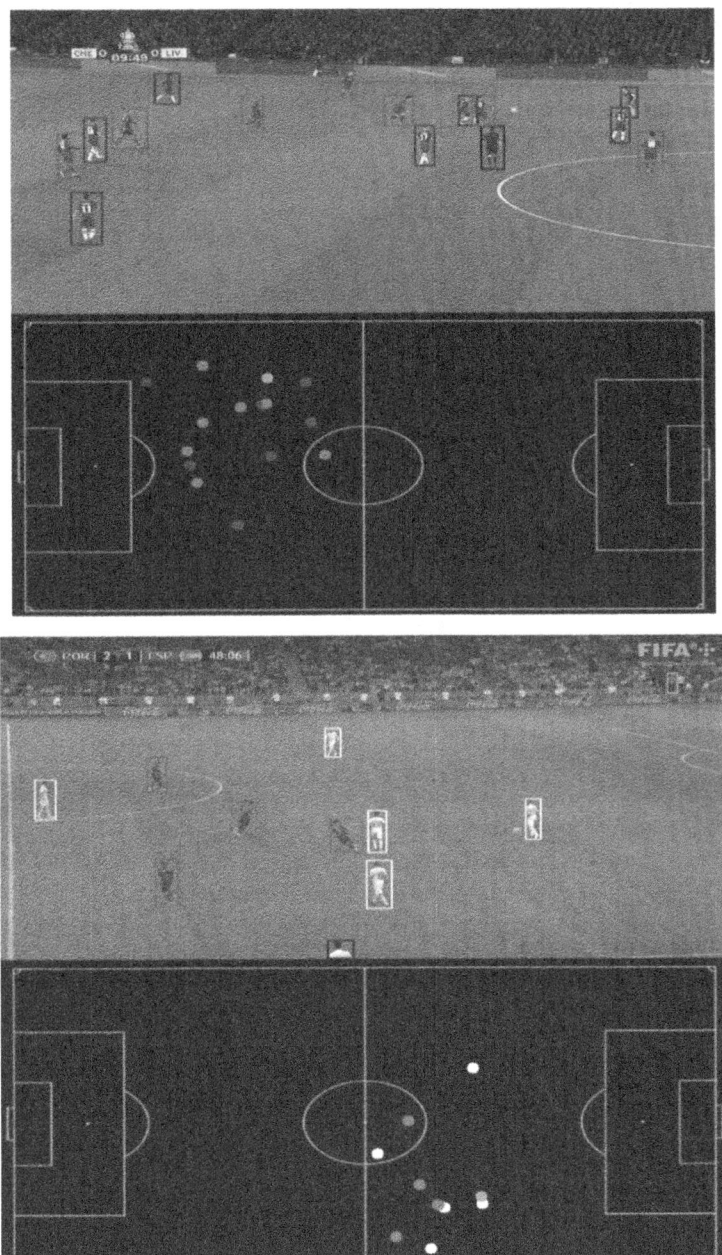

Fig. 4. 2D Top Views of Football Match Recording Images.

shown in Table 3, the best results were obtained in the Chelsea versus Liverpool match video. Along with frames with the central region it showed good results even on frames

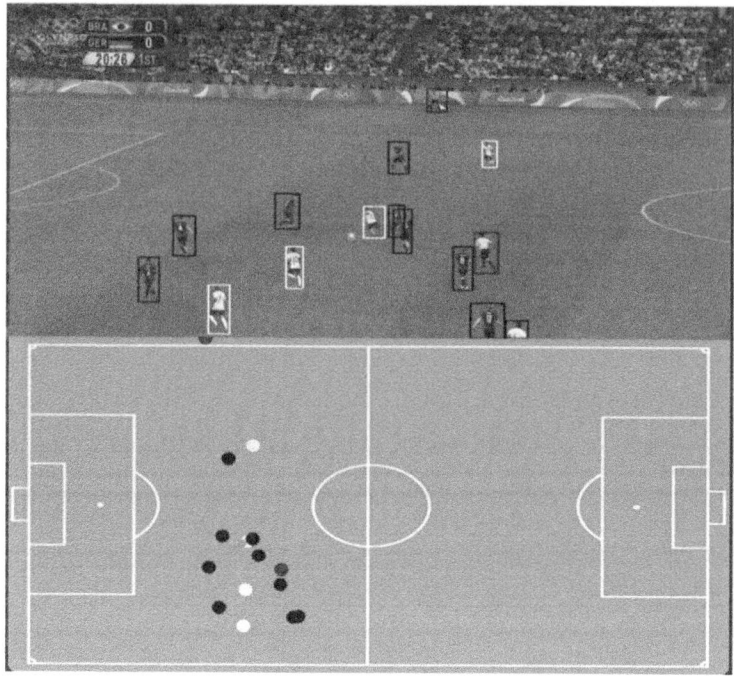

Fig. 4. (*continued*)

with focus on other regions of the field. The Portugal versus Spain match recording had more frames with regions away from the center circle. For such frames, the similarity scores obtained were low and needs to be improved. This can be done by simulating and adding more such images into our database (Table 4).

Table 4. Average Similarity Scores for the test videos

No	Video	Average RMSE	Average UQI	Average SCC
1	Chelsea vs Liverpool	9.8	0.755	0.353
2	Portugal vs Spain	15.2	0.711	0.178
3	Brazil vs Germany	11.8	0.721	0.289

For each video, the RMSE, UQI and SCC scores were plotted. The trends from the plot confirm the results shown in Table 3, regarding the Chelsea vs Liverpool match recording giving the best results. It can be observed that for all three videos, there are certain frames where the similarity score is really low. This needs to be improved by increasing the images in our database and by adding images from more stadiums as well (Fig. 5).

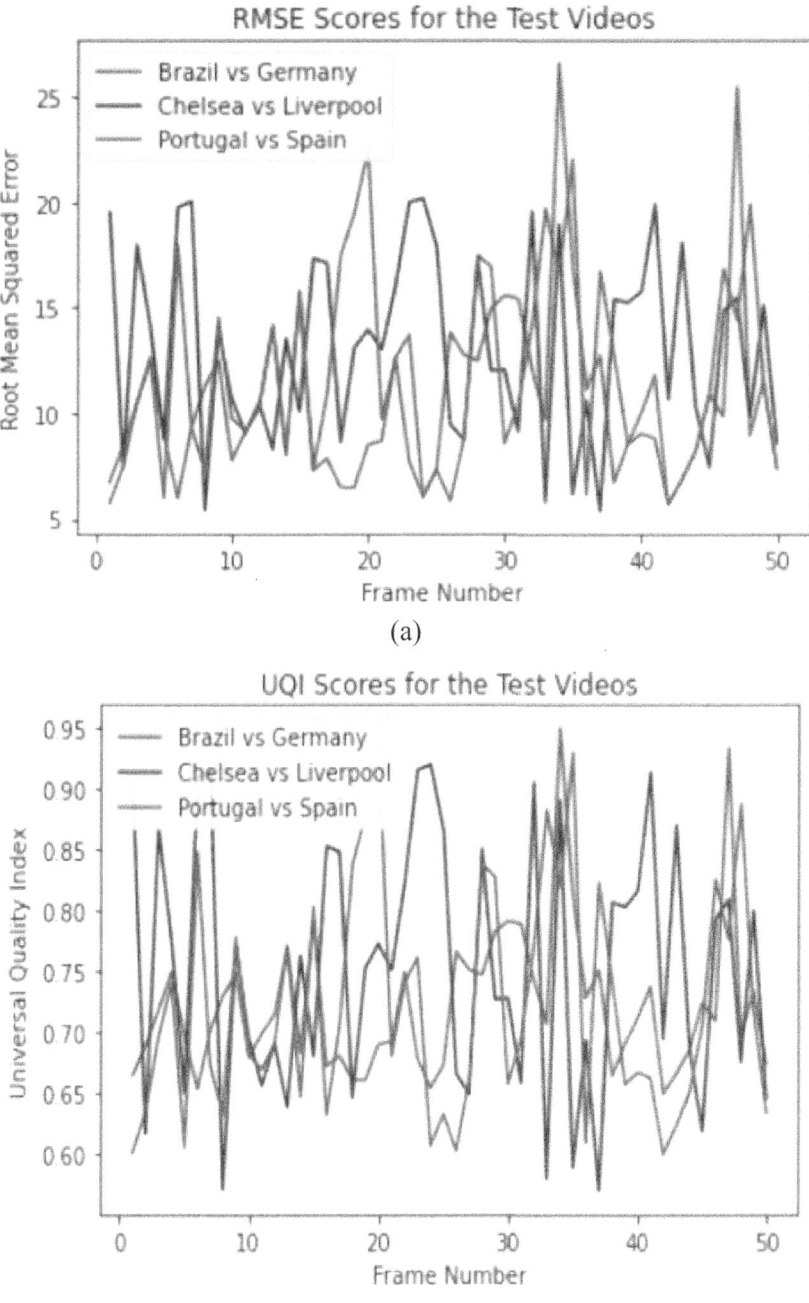

(a)

(b)

Fig. 5. a) Root Mean Squared Error Analysis. b) Universal Quality Index Analysis. c) Spatial Correlation Coefficient Analysis

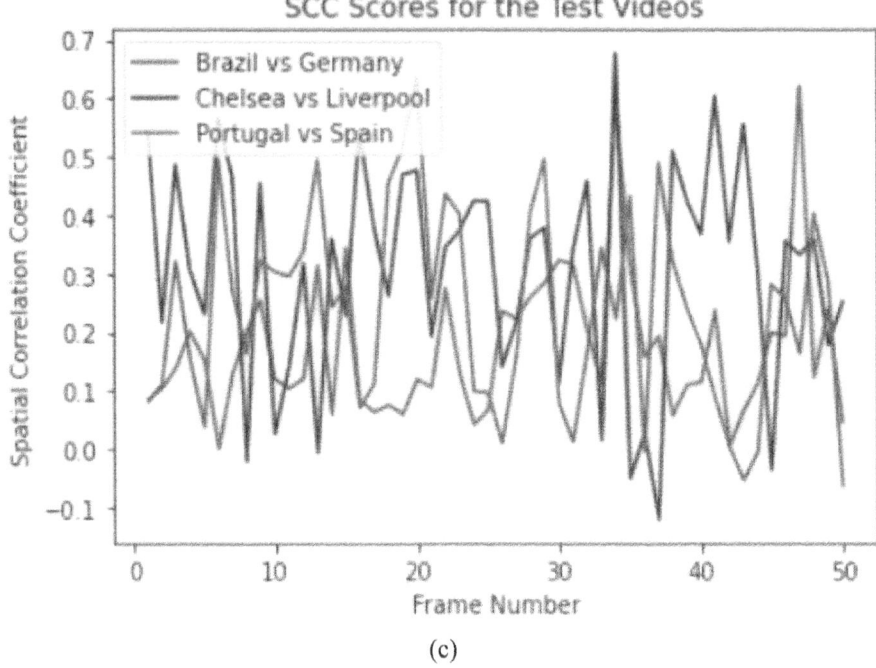

(c)

Fig. 5. (*continued*)

5 Conclusion

A 2D top view of a football match is more beneficial to coaches and analysts to supervise their players. Not everyone has access to multiple camera inputs in the stadium and thus it becomes difficult to get the 2D top view in an automatic manner. Instead using our proposed method, the broadcasted match recordings are used as input to generate its 2D top view. By comparing the frames from the broadcasted recording to our images in the generated database, we can perform accurate perspective transformation of frames where it might even be difficult to do it manually due to lack of corner points visible in it.

By comparing the results of YOLOv7 and the Faster RCNN models, we observed that not only did the YOLOv7 model give a slightly better performance for player detection but a massive improvement over Faster RCNN for football detection as well. This was combined with the DeepSORT tracking algorithm to track the football players and the football. Next, the pre-processing steps we proposed to obtain the field lines, proved to be a very efficient solution. It is based only on basic Computer Vision and morphological operations instead of training another model with a huge dataset.

We were able to generate a database of around 30,000 images in total. This was done by performing pan, tilt and zoom transformations on manually selected 100 images. These different transformations help to simulate various viewpoints for a match recording. The transformed images along with their corresponding perspective transformation matrices are stored in our database. This database is then used to find the most similar image to the input image. Based on the retrieved perspective transformation matrix, we are able to convert our match recording input image to its 2D top view.

The entire methodology was tested on three different videos. In general, it was observed that better results were obtained when the focus of the camera was towards the center of the field. Results for other regions could also be improved by increasing the images in our database by including more transformed images and images from more stadiums.

This proposed method can then be used further for automatic stats generation for any match. This can include detecting different actions like passes, shots, fouls and more. Currently the conversion of match recordings perform its 2-D top view is time consuming and better algorithms can be designed to fasten up the process.

References

1. Bialkowski, A., et al.: Recognising team activities from noisy data. In: Proceedings of the IEEE Conference on Computer Vision and Pattern Recognition Workshops (2013)
2. Lucey, P., Bialkowski,.A., Carr, P., Morgan, S., Matthews, I., Sheikh, Y.: Representing and discovering adversarial team behaviors using player roles. In: Proceedings of the IEEE Conference on Computer Vision and Pattern Recognition, pp. 2706–2713 (2013)
3. Franks, A., Miller, A., Bornn, L., Goldsberry, K.: Counterpoints: Advanced defensive metrics for nba basketball. In: 9th Annual MIT Sloan Sports Analytics Conference, Boston, MA, vol. 10 (2015, February)
4. Dubrofsky, E., Woodham, R.J.:Combining line and point correspondences for homography estimation. Advances in Visual Computing: 4th International Symposium, ISVC 2008, Las Vegas, NV, USA, December 1-3, 2008. Proceedings, Part II 4. Springer Berlin Heidelberg (2008)
5. Gupta, A., Little, J.J., Woodham, R.J.: Using line and ellipse features for rectification of broadcast hockey video. In: 2011 Canadian Conference on Computer and Robot Vision. IEEE (2011)
6. Hess, R., Alan, F.: Improved video registration using non-distinctive local image features. In: 2007 IEEE Conference on Computer Vision and Pattern Recognition. IEEE (2007)
7. Hayet, J.-B., Justus, P., Jacques, V.: Robust incremental rectification of sports video sequences. In: British Machine Vision Conference (BMVC'04) (2004)
8. Pătrăucean, V., Pierre, G., Rafael, G., Von, G.: A parameterless line segment and elliptical arc detector with enhanced ellipse fitting. In: Computer Vision–ECCV 2012: 12th European Conference on Computer Vision, Florence, Italy, October 7–13, 2012, Proceedings, Part II 12. Springer Berlin Heidelberg (2012)
9. Sharma, R.A., et al.: Automated top view registration of broadcast football videos. In: 2018 IEEE Winter Conference on Applications of Computer Vision (WACV). IEEE (2018)
10. Chen, J., Little, J.J.: Sports camera calibration via synthetic data. In: Proceedings of the IEEE/CVF Conference on Computer Vision and Pattern Recognition Workshops (2019)
11. Maćkowiak, S., et al.: A complex system for football player detection in broadcasted video. In: ICSES International Conference on Signals and Electronic Circuits. IEEE (2010)
12. Huang, Y., Joan, L., Sitaram, B.: Players and ball detection in soccer videos based on color segmentation and shape analysis. Multimedia Content Analysis and Mining: International Workshop, MCAM 2007, Weihai, China, June 30-July 1, 2007. Proceedings. Springer Berlin Heidelberg (2007)

13. Pallavi, V., et al.: Graph-based multiplayer detection and tracking in broadcast soccer videos. IEEE Trans. Multimedia **10**(5), 794–805 (2008)
14. Welch, G.: An introduction to the Kalman filter. Univ. of North Carolina (2006). http://www.cs.unc.edu/~welch/media/pdf/kalman_intro.pdf
15. Isard, M., Andrew, B.: CONDENSATION—conditional density propagation for visual tracking. Int. J. Comput. Vis. **29**(1) (1998)
16. Li, Y., et al.: Tracking in low frame rate video: A cascade particle filter with discriminative observers of different life spans. IEEE Trans. Pattern Anal. Mach. Intell. **30**(10), 1728–1740 (2008)

Measuring the Vehicle-in-Motion, Density and Allocation of Traffic Signal Using Transfer Learning

K. Manoj Prabhakaran$^{(\boxtimes)}$ ⓘ, K. Nithin Sai Kumar ⓘ, Shaik Valli, and K. Kartheek Nath

Department of ECE, Amrita Vishwa Vidhyapeetam, Chennai Campus, Chennai, India
kp_manoj@ch.amrita.edu

Abstract. There are various deep-learning methods available for detecting and classifying vehicles. In addition to detection, a total count of vehicles helps build an intelligent traffic signal by allocating the time according to the vehicle density. But in real-world applications, the multi vehicles cannot be identified in the traffic signal, and the motion of vehicles identification rate is slow in real-time implementation through traffic signal-CCTV cameras. To overcome this, a transfer learning approach has been implemented to speed up detecting, classifying, and counting the vehicles in the traffic signal which helps to allocate time for traffic signal. There are many existing models which use different deep-learning techniques for the vehicle's detection and classification. One such is YOLO V4, a recent super-fast model, one-stage object detector, and is best for real-time applications for object detection. YOLO V4 has been used for vehicle detection because of its very high inference speed when compared with other models. Having high inference speed is good advantage for real time test scenarios. Hence YOLO V4 has been used for implementation. The total estimation time is calculated using Transfer learning, where it's based on the number of vehicles at each traffic signal. In this work, our model attains a mAP of 80% with 14–15 fps of speed with multiple vehicles in traffic signal.

Keywords: Multiple Vehicle Detection and Classification · YOLO V4 and Vehicle counting

1 Introduction

Transportation has become common in everyone's day to day life. There are mainly 4 modes of transportation namely railways, roadways, sea ways and air ways. Among the 4 modes of transportation, roadways are the most used mode of transportation. India's booming vehicle sales at 55000 new vehicles per day, are causing surge in traffic congestion. One major to these delays is the time wasted near waiting at traffic signals. The root cause of this issue is because of multiple vehicles coming in unorganized manner from all the directions. Able to count all these vehicles would help in allocating separate time duration for signals in different directions. The motive of this paper is to

H. K. et al. (Eds.): AIKP 2023, CCIS 2127, pp. 259–275, 2024.
https://doi.org/10.1007/978-3-031-68617-7_19

design an object detection model that can detect, classify, and count the vehicles near the traffic signals. Implementation of this model helps in getting the density of the vehicles that are stopped at a particular signal through the video cameras installed near them. This paper also helps us to understand the procedure of building a real-time deep learning model that can help in object detection, classification and counting.

1.1 Literature Review

Existing methods for vehicle detection:

The undergoing research in computer vision has produced many methods for vehicle detection and classification. However, there are some limitations to these techniques.

- *Image Similarity approaches:* Comparing images with and without traffic for traffic light timing [1] is computationally expensive and requires additional object detection, Since the images with traffic might also include other objects on road. Impacting efficiency.
- *Image processing-based counting:* Techniques relying on image enhancement and thresholding [2] for vehicle counting may struggle with complex traffic scenes.
- *Limited Hardware Implementation:* Hardware-based solutions for vehicle detection and counting exist [3], but their processing power might be limited.

Deep learning for traffic management:

Below are the latest advancements in deep learning which offer promising solutions.

- *FCOS for Object Detection:* This approach ([4]) proposes using FCOS (Fully Convolutional One-Stage Object Detection) for vehicle detection and counting. FCOS avoids pre-defined anchor boxes used in methods like Faster R-CNN ([6]), YOLOv3 ([5, 7]), and SSD ([8, 9]), potentially leading to improved accuracy.
- *Two – Stage Detection with Faster R-CNN:* This method ([10]) addresses both precise object localization and accurate classification for high-quality object detection and segmentation.

Traffic Density Estimation vs Individual Vehicle detection:

While some techniques excel at traffic density estimation using deep learning models like FCN-rLSTM ([11]), they may not detect individual vehicles.

Deep Learning for Object Counting and Classification:

- *Hydra CNN and CCNN:* These deep learning algorithms ([12]) are effective for object counting but may struggle with high object density and real-time applications.
- *YOLO v3-Tiny:* This one-stage detector ([13]) prioritizes speed over accuracy, making it unsuitable for all scenarios.
- *YOLO v4 for Object Detection and Classification:* This method ([27]) demonstrates success in identifying various object types with high accuracy. Similarly, a YOLO-based approach for skin cancer detection is presented in [28]. A YOLO v4-based model for vehicle detection and classification in traffic signals is also described in [26], showcasing its ability to recognize and classify multiple vehicle types.

Limitations of existing work and Proposed Solution:
While existing research offers valuable tools for object detection and classification, some methods lack the ability to count objects within a scene after identification. This literature review highlights the need for a system that effectively detects, classifies, and counts vehicles, which is the focus of the proposed work in this paper.

2 Methodology

The project flow consists of 7 phases. Those 7 main steps are depicted in Fig. 1. The dataset preparation comprises of the first 3 steps. As, the training model is yolo v4, the bounding boxes are also drawn in yolo format. The second 3 steps comprises of training the model. The last phase is counting vehicles.

2.1 YOLO v4

The outputs of this algorithm will be vectors of bounding boxes, and these are made by sending the input images directly through neural networks. Bounding box properties, class probabilities and prediction probabilities are some output vector properties. YOLOv4 leverages the Darknet-53 architecture, which utilizes convolutional layers, residual layers, and skip connections to process images for object detection. [24, 25] YOLO v4 uses CSPDarknet53 feature extractor model. This feature-extractor model consists of 137 convolutional layers. The model mainly uses 3 types of layers (Back bone, Neck, and Head). Figure 2 shows the order of the 3 types of layers used in CSPDarknet53 framework. The main function of the backbone and the neck features extraction and aggregation. The CSPDarknet53 acts as the backbone while the neck layer consists of the SPP layer. The cross-stage partial (CSP) block present in CSPDarknet53 helps in splitting the feature map present in the base layer into two parts and joins them using cross stage hierarchy. CSP maintains detailed features to enhance forwarding efficiency, encourages the network to recycle features, and reduces the overall network parameter count. The SPP (Spatial Pyramid Pooling) layer is used for extracting features and SPP also works for the removal of file size constraint of the system. The advantages of the SPP layer include 1) Increase in receptive field 2) separating significant context features and 3) it does not show any effect on network operation speed. The last layer in YOLOv4 architecture is the head part which consists of YOLOv3. The main function of this layer is locating the bounding boxes and classification. When compared with CSPDarknet50 the CSPDarknet53 performs better in object detection. The CSPDarknet50 shows a good performance in image classification.

3 Experimental Analysis

3.1 Dataset

Individual images (raw data) of 6 different types of vehicles are collected from different sources in the first place. Table 1 depicts the count of all 6 different types of vehicles and their collected source. All these images are converted to standard 416×416 and 64× 64 sizes. This process of resizing images to different sizes and rotating the images to different angles is called data augmentation.

Table 1. Literature review

Ref	Motive	Algorithm	Type	limitations	Final conclusion
2017[1]	Traffic light controller	Canny edge detection, Surf matching	Image	Matching 2 images can include other surrounding objects	Achieved higher accuracy because of surf algorithm.
2018[2]	Density based control of road traffic	Thresh holding	Image and video	Can't work in bad weather conditions	calculates the count of vehicles using image enhancement
2017[3]	Traffic light control	Feature matching	Image	Proper training is needed for real time. Accuracy depends on weather.	vehicle detection and counting from an image and hardware implementation on ARM board
2017[4]	object detection	FCOS	Image	highly overlapped, extremely small and very large objects.	flexible detection framework achieving improved detection accuracy
2020[5]	Object detection	YOLO v3	Image	Vast field to cover all at once.	improved performance both on speed and accuracy.
2017[6]	multi-scale object detection	FPN (Feature pyramid networks)	Image	marginal extra cost	run at 5 FPS on a GPU
2021[7]	Traffic light controller based on vehicle density	YOLO v3, CNN	Webcam	requires high specification system to run the output on fps > 10	detect the movement of vehicles, identify, track and count the numbers of vehicles in the lane by analyzing a real-time
2016[8]	Object detection	SSD	Image	eliminates proposal generation and subsequent pixel	much better accuracy even with a smaller input image size.
2016[9]	vision based object detection	Deep neural network	Video	Anchor boxes	detection model by increasing precision of overall detection about 6%
2020[10]	object detection	Faster R CNN	Image	multiple dense box offsets	both precise object localization and accurate classification for high quality Object Detection and Instance Segmentation
2017[11]	traffic density	FCN rLSTM	Video	Multitask learning	optimization based methods for multiple detection and motion-based estimation
2016[12]	Object counting	Hydra CNN, CCCN	Image	low accuracy in heavy crowd and real time application	object density can be estimated accurately

Labelling images is a very important task in preparing a dataset. X center, Y center, width and height are 4 important parameters considered while labelling the images.

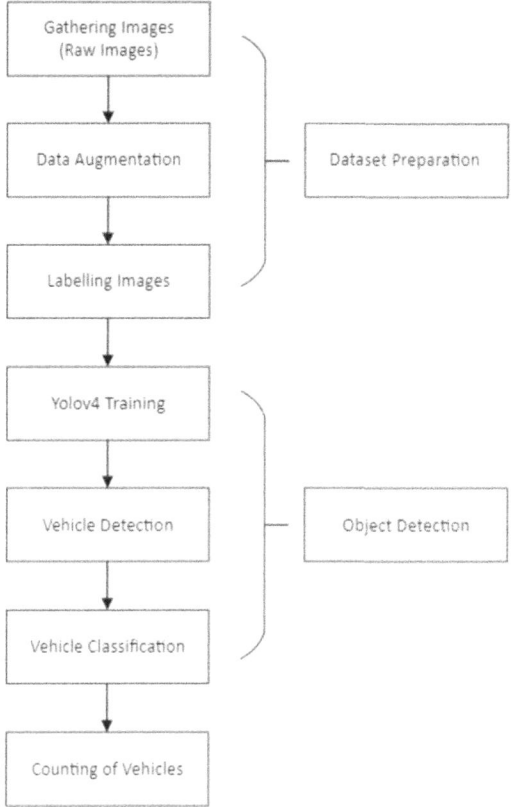

Fig. 1. Flowchart of Vehicle detection, Classification and Counting

Fig. 2. Block Diagram of YOLO V4 architecture

Here, the X Center and Y Center are the normalized coordinates of the center most point in the bounding box. Only, one bounding box is drawn for individual image sets and maximum number of bounding boxes are drawn for cluster image sets (Table 2).

Table 2. Dataset Collection

S.No	Name of Dataset	Range(size)	Converted Size	Classes Taken	Images
1	Indian Vehicle [16]	1600×1060 to 126×190	416*416 & 64*64	Auto Car Bus lorry	861
2	Bike [17]	300×168 to 299×168	416*416 & 64*64	Bike	45
3	Vehicle Detection [15]	910×607 to 702×540	416*416 & 64*64	Ambulance Car lorry	449
4	Trancos [18]	740×540 to 480×320	416*416 & 64*64	Cluster	75

On a total, 6 different classes are made for 6 different types of vehicles (ambulance, auto, bus, car, and lorry). Along with these 6 different classes another image set is also made. This separate image set comprises of images with clusters of vehicles. Finally, to train the model effectively, a dataset of 2770 labeled images was created. These images come in two sizes: 1385 at 416×416 pixels and 1385 at 64×64 pixels (Table 1). The dataset includes various vehicle classes: ambulances (238), autos (254), buses (104), cars (1406), lorries (618), and a "cluster" class (150). Transfer learning was employed, where a pre-trained model was adapted for this specific vehicle detection task.

3.2 Training and Results

The normal training time of a YOLO v4 model lasts up to 12 to 14 h. Our model completed the training in 13 h. As our model must be trained in 6 classes the total iterations required were 12000 (2000) per class. Then cluster image set which require 2000 more iterations. Hence, the total number of iterations are estimated as 14000. During the first few iterations, the recorded number of losses was 145. As a greater number of iterations were carried on, the losses started decreasing. At the end of iterations, a very low number of losses of 0.83 has been achieved. After every 1000 iterations the model saves the best weights from those 1000 iterations. Among the best iterations, the one best iteration with more accuracy and low losses has been considered and used for implementation. The best weights with high mean average precision must be selected.

Table 3. True positive (TP) and False positive (FP) Values for all 6 classes.

Vehicle	True positive	False Positive
Ambulance	23	2
Auto	27	3
Bike	11	2
Bus	15	9
Car	245	54
Lorry	66	12

The whole dataset is divided into small divisions. These small divisions contain 64 images in each. These small divisions are then subdivided into 8 images in each subset. Every time each subset containing 8 images will be taken for processing. It takes one iteration to complete the total 64 images. The overall MAP of all the classes has been detected as 80% (Figs. 3 and 4).

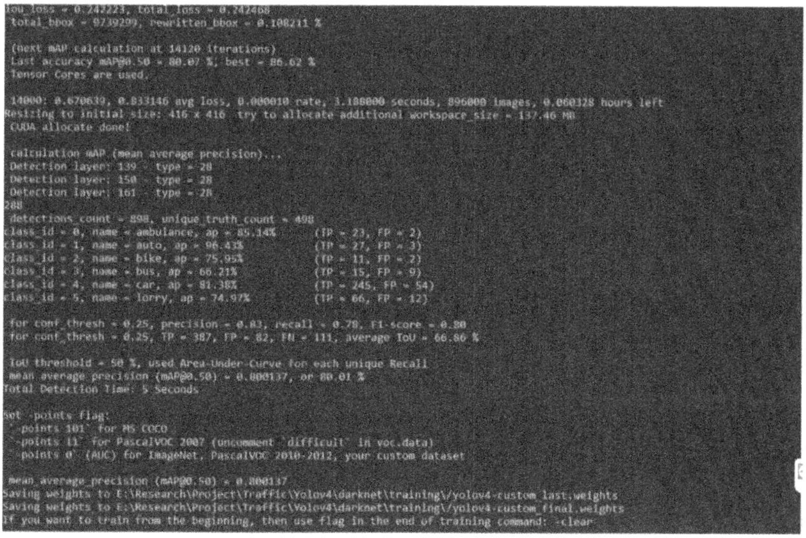

Fig. 3. AP values of different classes

Evaluation Metrics and Performance

Intersection over Union (IoU): This metric measures the overlap between the predicted bounding box and the ground truth box (the actual location of the object). A higher IoU indicates better accuracy. In this study, the model achieved an IoU loss of 0.242223, which translates to an IoU of 75.78% (1 - 0.242223).

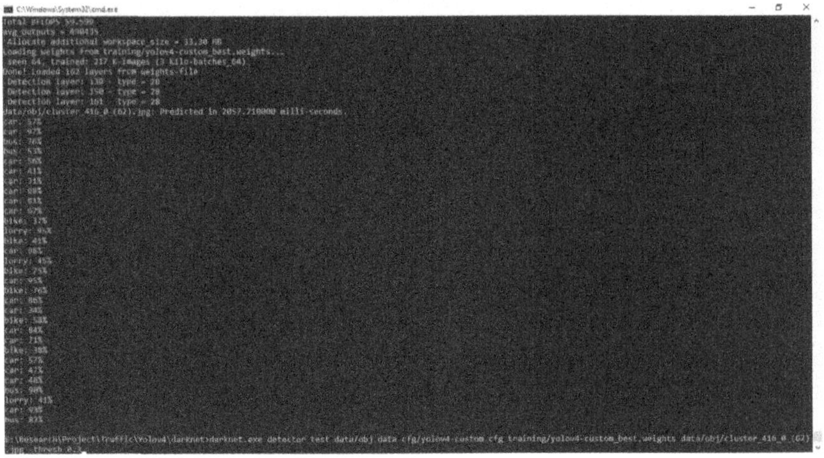

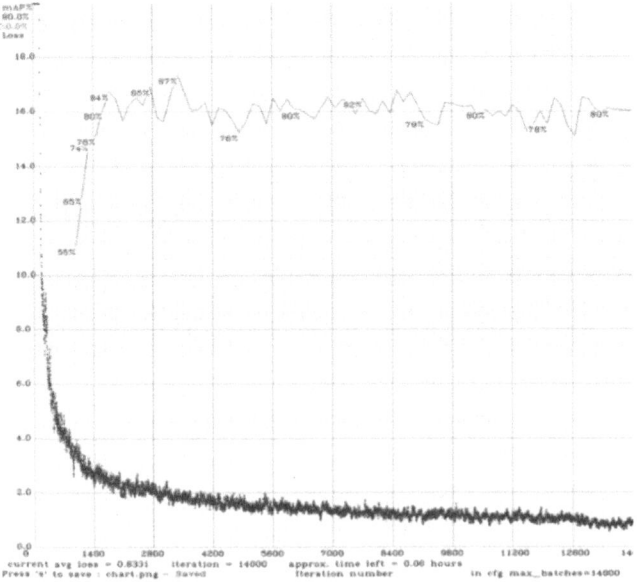

Fig4. Accuracy of each class

Mean Average Precision (mAP): Table 3 compares the model's mAP for all object classes with an existing model. The proposed approach achieved a 30% improvement in mAP, demonstrating its superior performance.

Computational Resources: The entire YOLOv4 model was trained and run on an NVIDIA GeForce RTX 3080 Ti GPU paired with an AMD Ryzen 5 800H CPU (Figs. 5, 6, 7, 8, 9 and 10; Table 4).

Fig. 5. Training chart of YOLO V4

Table 4. Comparison of results with existing [14] A Real-Time Object Detector for Autonomous Vehicles Based on YOLOv4.

S.No	Precision	Classes	Yolov3 (%)	Yolov4 (%)	Our Model (Yolov4 (%))
1	MAP	Overall	80.52	53.74%	80.01
2	AP	Car	79.49	90.50%	81.38
3	AP	Bike	83.07	43%	75.95
4	AP	Bus	-	49.3%	66.21
5	AP	Truck	-	55.7%	74.91
6	AP	Ambulance	-	-	85.14
7	AP	Auto	-	-	96.43
		Cluster			

Fig. 6. YOLO v4 detection and classification in 416x416 image

3.3 Counting Vehicles Using YOLO v4

Unlike vehicle detection, counting is a completely different task. It required various other libraries for this task. Counting is done using tensor-flow platform. A new set of libraries TENSOR FLOW, OPEN CV, LXML, TQDM ABSL-PY, EASYDICT, PILLOW and PYTESSERACT should be installed. The versions of tensor flow and OPEN CV must match with the CUDA DNN version. The best weights out of 14000 iterations are present in dark-net format. So, these weights should be converted into tensor flow format. The counting is carried out for both images and video. It can also be implemented using a webcam.

Fig. 7. YOLO v4 bike detection in 416x416 image

Fig. 8. YOLO v4 lorry detection in 416*416 image

Fig. 9. Vehicle Detection and classification in 64x64 image

Since the same weights are converted to tensor flow format the classes of vehicles should also be same. Hence, the classes should be configured according to the training weights taken for vehicle detection. There are 2 kinds of custom functions used for counting. One is for total vehicle count and the other is vehicle count per class. These 2 functions are used to count and keep track of the number of vehicles detected at the

Fig. 10. YOLO v4 bus Detection in 64x64 image

given moment. Now, a new flag "count" should be added to the "detect" command. The outputs of total count of vehicles and number of vehicles can be observed in fig__ and fig__. These are outputs for images (Figs. 11, 12, 13, 15, 16, 17).

There is an important parameter that needs to be considered while executing count to videos. That parameter is speed (frames per second). The detection and count speed of the model completely depends on the GPU and CUDA DNN versions. For our model, as mentioned in "training and results" the same NVIDIA GEFORCE RTX3080ti GPU and CUDA DNN version 11.6 is used. With this equipment and software, the model has achieved a speed of 14 to 15 frames per second. The results of the command window for video execution can be noted in Fig. 14.

Fig. 11. Count for Total Number of Vehicles in 416x416 image

Fig. 12. Count for Total Number of Vehicles in 416x416 image

Fig. 13. Count for Total Number of Vehicles in 416x416 image

lorry: 0.51
car: 0.58
car: 0.92
car: 0.77
car: 0.70
car: 0.87
car: 0.73
car: 0.77
car: 0.72
car: 0.78
car: 0.62

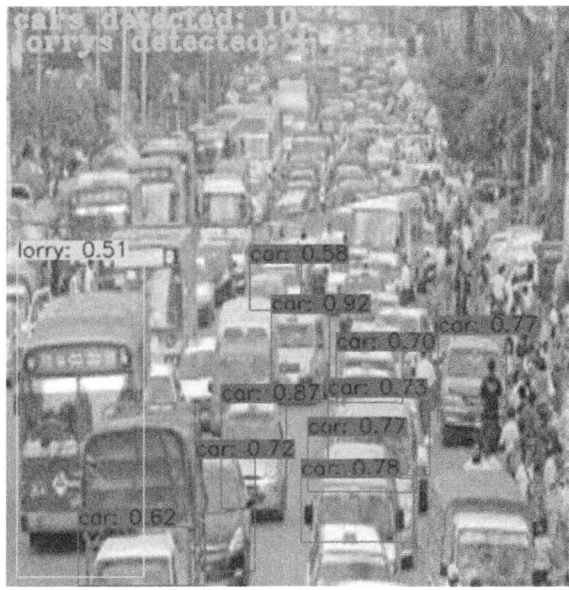

Fig. 14. Count for Total number of vehicles in Command Prompt

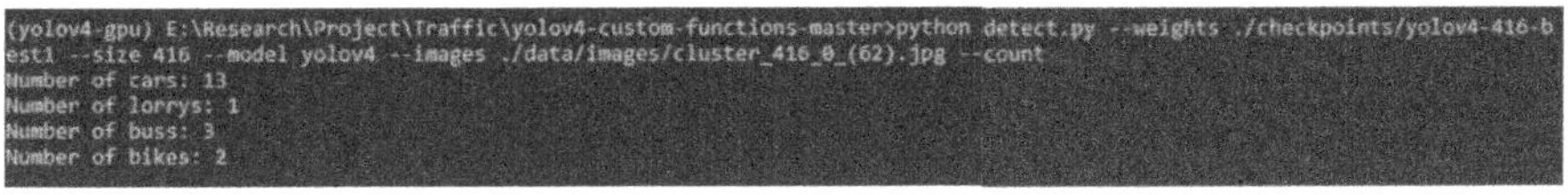

(yolov4-gpu) E:\Research\Project\Traffic\yolov4-custom-functions-master>python detect.py --weights ./checkpoints/yolov4-416-b
est1 --size 416 --model yolov4 --images ./data/images/cluster_416_0_(62).jpg --count
Number of cars: 13
Number of lorrys: 1
Number of buss: 3
Number of bikes: 2

Fig. 15. Count for Total Number of Vehicles per class in 416x416 image

Fig. 16. Count for Total Number of Vehicles per class in 416x416 image

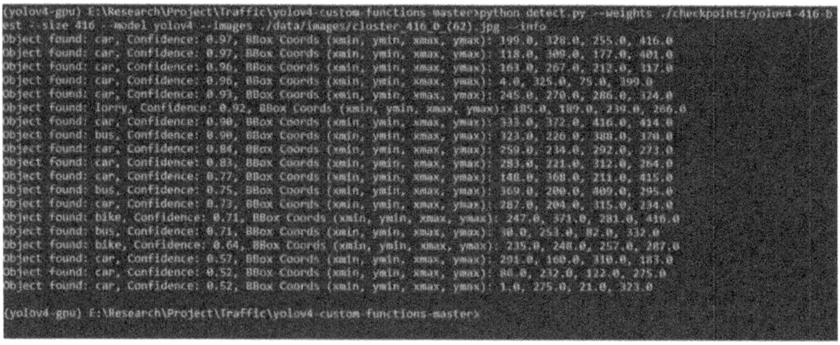

Fig. 17. Count for Total Number of Vehicles per Class in Command Prompt

4 Conclusion

This paper proposes a framework that uses YOLO V4 for the detection, classification of vehicles and total count of vehicles per frame in traffic images. The YOLO v4 model is trained using the transfer learning approach using pre trained weights. Using the transfer learning approach helped to add more accuracy to the model. Since YOLOv4 is a single stage object detector, selecting that model resulted in higher speeds (nearly 15 fps). With both accuracy and high-speed object detection, this model will be a better choice for real world implementations. Based on the count of vehicles, the total time estimation can be done at each traffic signal. This model gives two types of counting output, one is the total count of vehicles in the frame while the other is the class wise count of vehicles in the frame. Hence this makes this model much more viable to use when we need the count of particular type of vehicles like ambulances. This YOLOv4-based framework effectively detects, classifies, and counts vehicles in traffic videos. Transfer learning boosted accuracy (80% mAP), while the single-stage architecture delivered real-time performance (14–15 fps). The model not only provides total vehicle counts but also counts by class, enabling applications like prioritizing emergency vehicles. This framework has promising potential for improving traffic flow through density-based signal control.

References

1. Tahmid, T., Hossain, E.: Density based smart traffic control system using canny edge detection algorithm for congregating traffic information. In: 3rd International Conference on Electrical Information and Communication Technology, EICT 2017, vol. 2018-January, pp. 1–5. Institute of Electrical and Electronics Engineers Inc (2018). https://doi.org/10.1109/EICT.2017. 8275131

2. Prakash, U.E., Thankappan, A., Vishnupriya, K.T., Balakrishnan, A.A.: Density based traffic control system using image processing. In: 2018 International Conference on Emerging Trends and Innovations In Engineering And Technological Research, ICETIETR 2018. Institute of Electrical and Electronics Engineers Inc (2018). https://doi.org/10.1109/ICETIETR. 2018.8529111

3. Prakash, D., Devi, B.S., Kumar, R.N., Thiyagarajan, S., Shabarinath, P.: Density Based Traffic Light Control System, 1994–2000 (2017). https://doi.org/10.15662/IJAREEIE.2017.0603142

4. Tian, Z., Shen, C., Chen, H., He, T.: FCOS: Fully convolutional one-stage object detection. In: Proceedings of the IEEE International Conference on Computer Vision, vol. 2019-October, pp. 9626–9635. Institute of Electrical and Electronics Engineers Inc (2019). https://doi.org/ 10.1109/ICCV.2019.00972

5. Adarsh, P., Rathi, P., Kumar, M.:. YOLO v3-Tiny: Object Detection and Recognition using one stage improved model. In: 2020 6th International Conference on Advanced Computing and Communication Systems, ICACCS 2020, pp. 687–694. Institute of Electrical and Electronics Engineers Inc (2020). https://doi.org/10.1109/ICACCS48705.2020.9074315

6. Lin, T.Y., Dollár, P., Girshick, R., He, K., Hariharan, B., Belongie, S.: Feature pyramid networks for object detection. In: Proceedings—30th IEEE Conference on Computer Vision and Pattern Recognition, CVPR 2017, vol. 2017-January, pp. 936–944. Institute of Electrical and Electronics Engineers Inc (2017). https://doi.org/10.1109/CVPR.2017.106

7. Manish Kumar Singh, M.K.S., Krishna Deep Mishra, K.D.M., Subrata Sahana, S.S.: An intelligent realtime traffic control based on vehicle density. Int. J. Eng. Technol. Manage. Sci. 24–29 (2021). https://doi.org/10.46647/ijetms.2021.v05i03.004

8. Liu, W., Anguelov, D., Erhan, D., Szegedy, C., Reed, S., Fu, C.Y., Berg, A.C.: SSD: Single shot multibox detector. In: Lecture Notes in Computer Science (including subseries Lecture Notes in Artificial Intelligence and Lecture Notes in Bioinformatics, vol. 9905 LNCS, pp. 21–37. Springer Verlag (2016). https://doi.org/10.1007/978-3-319-46448-0_2

9. Kim, H., Lee, Y., Yim, B., Park, E., Kim, H.: On-road object detection using deep neural network. In: 2016 IEEE International Conference on Consumer Electronics-Asia, ICCE-Asia 2016. Institute of Electrical and Electronics Engineers Inc (2017). https://doi.org/10.1109/ ICCE-Asia.2016.7804765

10. Cao, J., Cholakkal, H., Anwer, R.M., Khan, F.S., Pang, Y., Shao, L.: D2Det: towards high quality object detection and instance segmentation. In: 2020 IEEE/CVF Conference on Computer Vision and Pattern Recognition (CVPR), Seattle, WA, USA, 2020, pp. 11482–11491. https://doi.org/10.1109/CVPR42600.2020.01150
11. Zhang, S., Wu, G., Costeira, J., Moura, J.: Understanding Traffic Density from Large-Scale Web Camera Data, pp. 4264–4273 (2017). https://doi.org/10.1109/CVPR.2017.454
12. Oñoro, D., López-Sastre, R.: Towards Perspective-Free Object Counting with Deep Learning, p. 9911 (2016). https://doi.org/10.1007/978-3-319-46478-7_38
13. Adarsh, P., Rathi, P., Kumar, M.: YOLO v3-Tiny: object Detection and Recognition using one stage improved model. In: 2020 6th International Conference on Advanced Computing and Communication Systems, ICACCS 2020, pp. 687–694. Institute of Electrical and Electronics Engineers Inc (2020). https://doi.org/10.1109/ICACCS48705.2020.9074315
14. Meel, V.: YOLOv3: Real-Time Object Detection Algorithm (What's New?). Viso.ai, 25 Feb. 2021. viso.ai/deep-learning/yolov3-overview/
15. Guy, T.A.I.: TheAIGuysCode/Yolov4-Custom-Functions. GitHub, 7 June 2021. github.com/theAIGuysCode/yolov4-custom-functions
16. Alexey.: AlexeyAB/Darknet. GitHub, 21 Aug. 2020. github.com/AlexeyAB/darknet
17. Sein, M.M., Htet, K.S., Murata, K.T., Phon-Amnuaisuk, S.: Object detection, classification and counting for analysis of visual events. In: 2020 IEEE 9th Global Conference on Consumer Electronics (GCCE), Kobe, Japan, 2020, pp. 274–275, https://doi.org/10.1109/GCCE50665.2020.9292058
18. Wang, R., Wang, Z., Xu, Z., Wang, C., Li, Q., Zhang, Y., Li, H.: A real-time object detector for autonomous vehicles based on YOLOv4. Comput. Intell. Neurosci. (2021). https://doi.org/10.1155/2021/9218137
19. vehicle detection | Kaggle. (n.d.). Retrieved from https://www.kaggle.com/datasets/rohan300557/vehicle-detection
20. Indian Vehicle Dataset | Kaggle. (n.d.). Retrieved from https://www.kaggle.com/datasets/radhesyam/indian-vehicle-dataset
21. Bike Detection Dataset | Kaggle. (n.d.). Retrieved from https://www.kaggle.com/datasets/zwartfreak/bike-images?select=1570811000981
22. TRANCOS Dataset | Kaggle. (n.d.). Retrieved from https://gram.web.uah.es/data/datasets/trancos/index.html
23. Albumentations documentation—bounding boxes augmentation for object detection (no date) Bounding boxes augmentation for object detection—Albumentations Documentation. Available at: https://albumentations.ai/docs/getting_started/bounding_boxes_augmentation/#:~:text=322%2C%20117%5D%20.-,yolo,x%2D%20and%20y%2Daxis. Accessed: 04 October 2023
24. Rajput, V.: Yolo V4 explained in full detail, Medium (2022). Available at: https://medium.com/aiguys/yolo-v4-explained-in-full-detail-5200b77aa825. Accessed: 04 October 2023
25. Praharsha, V.: Yolov4 model architecture, OpenGenus IQ: Computing Expertise & Legacy (2022). Available at: https://iq.opengenus.org/yolov4-model-architecture/. Accessed: 04 October 2023
26. Valli, S., Kumar, K.N.S., Nath, K.K., Prabhakaran, K.M.: Detecting and classifying the vehicles in traffic signal using transfer learning. In: Ray, K.P., Dixit, A., Adhikari, D., Mathew, R. (eds.) Proceedings of the 2nd International Conference on Signal and Data Processing. CSDP 2022. Lecture Notes in Electrical Engineering, vol 1026. Springer, Singapore (2023). https://doi.org/10.1007/978-981-99-1410-4_36

27. Prabhakaran, K.M., Debebe, F.T., Kamalakannan, M.: Identification of fish species and grading in fish market using transfer learning. In: 2023 IEEE World Conference on Applied
Intelligence and Computing (AIC), Sonbhadra, India, pp. 715–719 (2023). https://doi.org/10.
1109/AIC57670.2023.10263937
28. Aishwarya, N., Manoj Prabhakaran, K., Tsegaye Debebe, F., Sai Sree Akshitha Reddy, M.,
Pranavee, P.: Skin Cancer diagnosis with Yolo deep neural network. Proc. Comput. Sci. **220**,
651–658 (2023). ISSN 1877–0509. https://doi.org/10.1016/j.procs.2023.03.083

Ensemble Model of VGG16, ResNet50, and DenseNet121 for Human Identification Through Gait Features

Aswin Asok[1]([✉]) and Cinu C. Kiliroor[2]

[1] Mar Athanasios College for Advanced Studies Tiruvalla, Tiruvalla, India
aswinasok333@gmail.com
[2] Indian Institute of Information Technology, Kottayam, India

Abstract. Human Gait Recognition is a type of behavioral biometric authentication based on walking pattern of an individual. Every individual has a unique way of walking making authentication based on gait features difficult to masquerade. It is non-intrusive in nature as it does not require any active participation from the subject making it an apt identification technique. In the past, techniques used in this field required significant amount of expert knowledge for feature identification and also lacked the ability to capture all the complex gait patterns resulting in low accuracy of the predictions made. The paper presents an ensemble model for gait recognition, combining knowledge of multiple Convoluted Neural Network (CNN) models namely VGG16, ResNet50 and DenseNet121. The individual models were fine-tuned on the Casia-B dataset and an ensemble model was created to exploit the individual strengths of the models making this proposed model, a powerful one in terms of accuracy.

Keywords: Human gait recognition · Non-Intrusive · Ensemble Model · CNN · VGG16 · ResNet50 · DenseNet121 · Fine-tune · Casia-B

1 Introduction

Human Identification by extraction and analysis of gait features has gained huge popularity over the years owing to its advantages such as non-intrusiveness, capability to identify individuals from a distance making it suitable for security and surveillance. The identification systems developed for this purpose use deep learning and computer vision based algorithms to extract features from the gait data which may in the form of silhouettes or gait energy images. The extracted features may include variation in stride length, height, hip angle, knee angle etc. The most significant advancement in the field of gait-based human identification is the use of deep learning architectures to extract distinctive features from the gait sequences as the sequences of the same subject can lead to ambiguity due to variations in clothing style or illumination.

However, the complexity in human walking patterns is such that it demands efficient models to make predictions with high accuracy. To address this challenge, an ensemble

H. K. et al. (Eds.): AIKP 2023, CCIS 2127, pp. 276–283, 2024.
https://doi.org/10.1007/978-3-031-68617-7_20

model integrating three powerful deep learning architectures, VGG16, ResNet50, and DenseNet121, can be synergistically combined to exploit their complementary strengths and mitigate individual weaknesses. The proposed ensemble model choice is adopted in such a way to leverage the individual strengths of VGG16, ResNet50 and DenseNet121. VGG16 has a simple architecture which is easy to implement. ResNet50 make use of residual connections to mitigate the vanishing gradient problem and thus provides high accuracy. DenseNet121 consist of dense connections in which each layer receives input from all the previous layers thus enabling the model to learn highly complex features. Together, the ensemble combines the distinct feature extraction capabilities of the individual models, enhancing the overall performance and robustness of the gait recognition system.

2   Related Works

Extensive research has been conducted over the years to develop reliable, efficient and accurate gait recognition systems. Various techniques for gait feature extraction and representation have been explored, including various algorithms, silhouette detection and correlation, measuring pressure variations in floors with the help of sensors, using popular CNN architectures and combination of the formers to develop a robust mechanism for human gait recognition.

2.1   Traditional Methods

Traditional methods of gait recognition involved model-based techniques which constructed an articulated structure of human body using various pose estimation and key points detection algorithms[1, 2] and model-free approaches that do not required an explicit model for extraction of gait features. The Model based methods consists of acquiring the gait data, constructing a statistical or mathematical model, applying dimensionality reduction techniques like Principal Components Analysis (PCA) or by comparing gate sequences by Dynamic Time Warping (DTW) followed by extraction of distinct features which in turn represents the unique features of individuals for identification. The model-free approaches captured gait features directly from the data and hence were computationally efficient.

The traditional methods have been widely used in gait recognition due to their simplicity and ability to work with limited training data. However, these methods are prone to degradation under variations in clothing, walking conditions, occlusions and view angles.

2.2   Deep Learning Methods

The recent advances in deep learning have caused researchers to adapt neural network-based methods, such as CNNs, RNNs, and siamese networks, which can automatically learn relevant features from gait data, outperforming handcrafted methods. These methods serve as a powerful tool to automatically extract complex but distinct features from the gait data. Wang et al. [3] proposed a multi-channel CNN model to process a set of consecutive images in parallel and had the ability to extract the features simultaneously. Arshad et al. [4] applied two pre-trained CNN models to learn the gait features and features were fused and best features were selected. Zhang et al. [5] in 2022 proposed a system for gait recognition using densenet and spatial transformer network. In 2023 Jashila Nair Mogan et al. [6] presented a gait recognition system by utilizing CNNs and vision transformer.

Gait recognition can be challenging due to variations in clothing, viewpoint, and walking conditions, and ensemble models help address these issues. Leveraging complementary information and handling uncertainty, ensemble models provide more accurate and reliable predictions. The advancements in transfer learning enabled the integration of efficient architectures like ResNet, DenseNet, and VGG, enhancing the performance of the ensemble model.

3 Proposed Ensemble Model

The proposed ensemble model [Fig. 1] combines the predictions of three CNN architectures namely VGG16, ResNet50, and DenseNet. The proposed model leverages the strengths of these individual models to make a final prediction using average voting. The ensemble model architecture which is implemented using a custom ensemble model class is designed to incorporate the predictions from the three individual models.

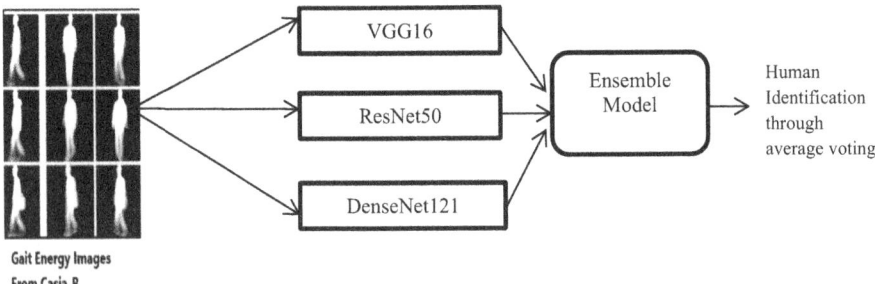

Fig. 1. Workflow of the proposed Model

4 Experiment and Methodology

4.1 Experimental Setup

The experiment is implemented using Google Colab which is a Jupyter notebook environment that runs entirely in the cloud, the premium version of which provided access to an NVIDIA A100 GPU with 40GB GPU RAM which accelerated the training of the models on the dataset. The experiment involved fine-tuning the VGG16, ResNet50, and DenseNet models on gait energy images from the Casia-B dataset using the fastai library. It is built on top of PyTorch and provides a higher level of abstraction. The Casia-B dataset consists of gait data captured from 124 human subjects, with each subject recorded from 11 different views.

4.2 Dataset

The experiment employed a dataset known as CASIA-B [Fig. 2], comprising Gait Energy Images (GEIs) captured from 124 human subjects observed from 11 different views. CASIA-B is a widely utilized gait dataset which contains gait data with three variations namely view angle, carrying condition and clothing. The format of the image filename in the Dataset is 'aaa-bb-cc-ddd.png', where

   aaa: subject id, from 001 to 124.
   bb: walking status can be 'nm' (normal), 'cl' (in a coat) or 'bg' (with a bag).
   cc: sequence number.
   ddd: view angle, can be '000', '018', …., '180'.

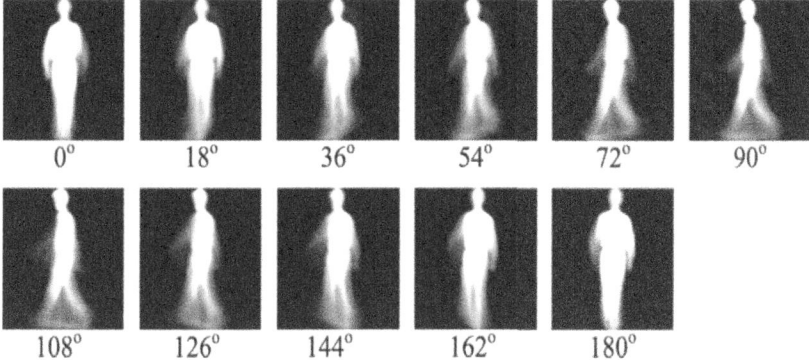

Fig. 2. Sample GEIs from the CASIA-B dataset [7]

4.3 Methodology

The Casia-B dataset is accessed via Google drive, loaded and preprocessed using the data loader of fastai library known as the ImageDataLoaders. The dataset is partitioned into training and testing sets with a validation percentage of 20%. Training involved three distinct models, namely VGG16, ResNet50, and DenseNet, all fine-tuned on Casia-B dataset using the Fastai library. The ensemble model is constructed by combining the predictions of the three trained models using average voting. For a given test image, each individual model provided a probability distribution over the classes. The ensemble model fused these distributions by averaging the probabilities and selecting the class with the highest average probability. The performance of the ensemble model is evaluated using a validation image from the Casia-B dataset. Various evaluation metrics are used to compare the performance of individual models and the proposed ensemble model such as F1 score and Gain & Lift charts. In summary, the study employed a deep learning-based approach, incorporating an ensemble model formed through the averaging technique, to accomplish human gait recognition.

5   Results and Discussion

The experimental results show that the ensemble model outperformed the individual models in terms of reliable predictions and recognition accuracy [refer Table 1]. The average voting mechanism in the ensemble model helped to mitigate errors and uncertainties present in the individual models, leading to improved performance. The F1 Scores of individual models and the Ensemble Model were calculated [refer Table 2] and the results highlighted the importance of the ensemble mechanism as a reliable source of prediction.

Table 1. Accuracy of the Trained Models

Model	Accuracy (%)
VGG-16	89.796
ResNet50	89.155
DenseNet121	89.017
Proposed Ensemble Model	89.990

Table 2. Comparison of F1 Scores of Individual Models and Ensemble Model

Model	True Label	Predicted Label	F1 Score obtained
VGG-16	bg-01	bg-02	0.0
ResNet50	bg-01	bg-01	1.0
DenseNet121	bg-01	bg-01	1.0
Proposed Ensemble Model	bg-01	bg-01	1.0

The Gain & Lift Charts were generated using the following label mapping:
{'bg-01': 0, 'bg-02': 1, 'cl-01': 2, 'cl-02': 3, 'nm-01': 4, 'nm-02': 5,'nm-03': 6, 'nm-04': 7, 'nm-05': 8, 'nm-06': 9},where bg-01,bg-02,cl-01,cl-02,nm-01,nm-02,nm-03,nm-04,nm-05,nm-06 represent the walking status subclasses inside each of the 124 classes inside the Casia-B dataset.

The Gain and Lift Charts for VGG16 model demonstrate that it is effective in identifying humans based on gait features for all nine classes (walking statuses). The gain [Fig. 3] steadily increases for each class. The lift values [Fig. 4] being greater than 1 for most classes indicate that the performance of the model is better than random chance, with a few classes having significantly better performance than random. The ResNet50 model performs well for most classes, with varying levels of accuracy improvement as more data points are considered. Classes 0, 2, and 3 demonstrate particularly good performance, with high lift values [Fig. 4] indicating the importance in classification capability of the model. The DenseNet model appears to perform relatively well for most classes, with varying levels of accuracy improvement with more data points. Classes 3 and 6 demonstrate particularly good performance with relatively high lift values [Fig. 4], indicating the importance in classification capability of the model.

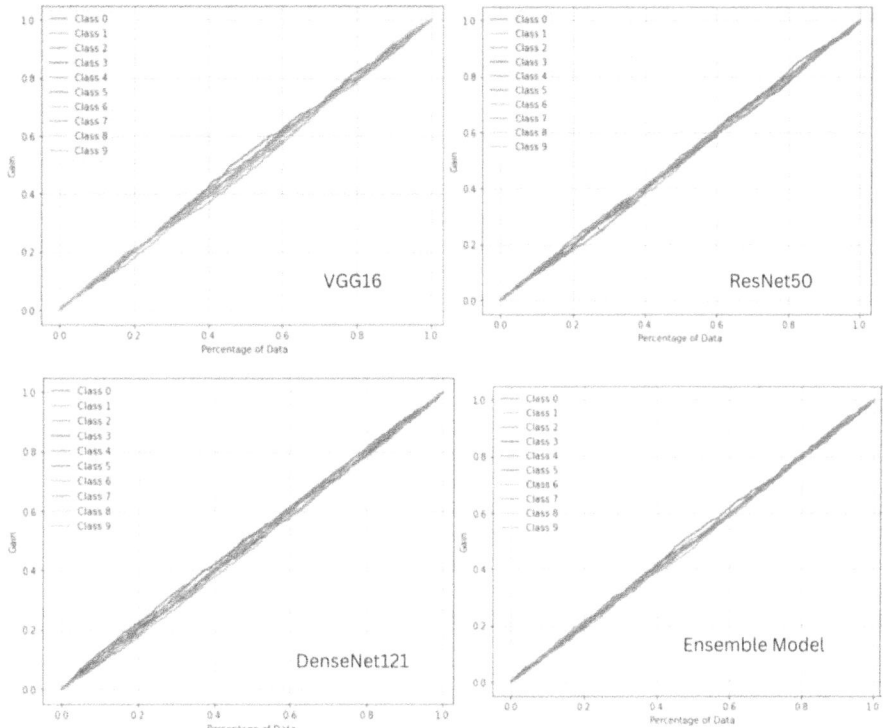

Fig. 3. Gain charts for different models

The Gain and Lift Charts for the Ensemble model [Fig. 3,Fig. 4] of VGG16, ResNet50, and DenseNet show that the model is capable of identifying humans based on gait features for all classes (walking statuses).The gain values increase steadily as the ranked samples increase, indicating that the model performs well in capturing true positive instances for most classes. The lift values suggest that the performance of the ensemble model for most classes is comparable to random chance, with a few exceptions (Class 2, Class 4, Class 5, Class 6), where the model performs significantly better than random.

The Ensemble model demonstrates an advantage over individual models regarding model consistency and robustness. It effectively captures true positive instances for all classes with a relatively consistent lift value close to 1, indicating balanced performance across the classes. In contrast, individual models show variations in performance across classes, with a few achieving slightly better lift values than others (e.g., ResNet50 having higher lift for a few classes). The consistent performance of the ensemble model suggests that it mitigates any potential weaknesses or biases that individual models might exhibit.

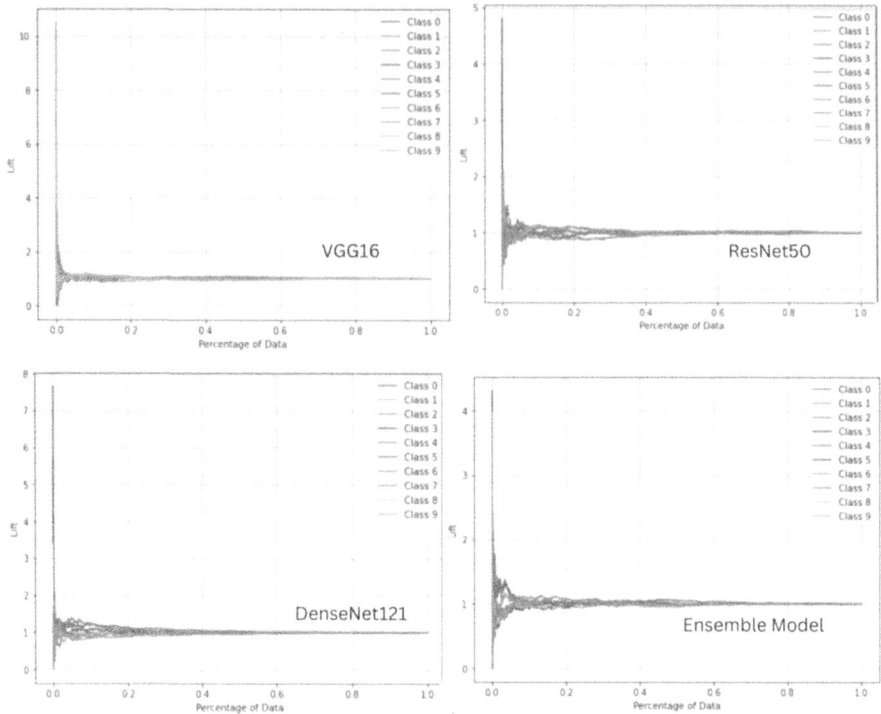

Fig. 4. Lift charts for different models

6 Conclusion

The proposed ensemble model for human gait recognition utilized the strengths of deep learning architectures. The ensemble model leveraged the strengths of VGG16, ResNet50, and DenseNet to achieve enhanced recognition accuracy. The experimental results highlight the benefits of using an ensemble model for human gait recognition. By combining the strengths of multiple models, the ensemble approach achieves improved accuracy compared to individual models alone. The enhanced performance can be attributed to the complementary capabilities of the different models within the ensemble, resulting in more robust and reliable predictions.

The ensemble model performed exceptionally well on the dataset used but may not generalize well to new and diverse gait data. Training ensemble of 3 large networks named VGG16,ResNet50 and DenseNet121 is computationally intensive and could limit the practicality of the model in real-time applications. Future prospects of the work include work on optimizing the model for real-time processing and reducing computational requirements.

References

1. Lima, V.C.d., Melo, V.H.C., Schwartz, W.R.: Simple and efficient pose-based gait recognition method for challenging environments. Pattern Anal. Applic. **24**, 497–507 (2021)
2. Choi, S., Kim, J., Kim, W., Kim, C.: Skeleton-based gait recognition via robust frame-level matching. IEEE Trans. Inf. Forensics Secur. **14**(10), 2577–2592 (2019). https://doi.org/10.1109/TIFS.2019.2901823
3. Wang, X., Zhang, J., Yan, W.Q.: Gait recognition using multichannel convolution neural networks. Neural Comput. Applic. **32**, 14275–14285 (2020). https://doi.org/10.1007/s00521-019-04524-y
4. Arshad, H., et al.: A multilevel paradigm for deep convolutional neural network features selection with an application to human gait recognition (2020). https://doi.org/10.1111/exsy.12541
5. Zhang, J., Zhang, C., Jiang, J.: Gait feature extraction using DenseNet and spatial transformer network. In: Proceedings of the 18th International Conference on Control, Automation, Robotics, and Vision (ICARCV) (2022)
6. Jashila Nair, M., Lee, C.P., Lim, K.M., Ali, M., Alqahtani, A.: Multi-Model Gait Recognition with Convolutional Neural Networks and Vision Transformer (2023).https://doi.org/10.3390/s23083809
7. Xing, X., Wang, K., Yan, T., Lv, Z.: Complete canonical correlation analysis with application to multi-view gait recognition (2016). https://doi.org/10.1016/j.patcog.2015.08

Natural Language Processing

Performance of Sentiment Analysis APIs on Political Opinion Polling

Colton Johnson[✉] and Manjeet Rege

University of St. Thomas, St Paul, MN 55105, USA
crjohnson09@ole.augie.edu

Abstract. Social media, due to its deep use throughout the United States, has the potential to supply accurate opinion polling. This study aims to replicate job approval polls conducted by professional pollsters through the utilization of sentiment analysis. A Kaggle dataset of Twitter messages from the end of the 2020 United States Election was selected and prepared. The sentiment of each tweet within this dataset was classified by language models created by cloud providers and accessed through APIs. We used two evaluation methods: hypothesis testing and confusion matrix accuracy. Regarding the hypothesis testing, the sentiment classification proportions were evaluated against job approval data aggregated from professional pollsters and did not perform well enough to accept the null hypothesis of no independence. Regarding the confusion matrix accuracy, the classifiers were evaluated against two sets of manually labeled tweets: general sentiment and political sentiment. The classifiers performed reasonably with general sentiment but poorly for political sentiment.

Keywords: politics · polling · social media · sentiment analysis · commercial language model API

1 Introduction

One of the hallmarks of the 2016 and 2020 United States Presidential elections were the inaccuracy of political polling at the local level. Local level congressperson races were sometimes off double digits from the predicted difference ratio. This was attributed to several factors, including the non-response bias [11]. A typical poll will either use telephone interviews, online opt-in portals, or recruited focus groups or panels to first collect raw opinion data. Part of this collection process will include core demographics and other variables to properly apply weighting techniques that will correct for over or underrepresentation [12]. The cost and time needed to conduct these active surveys, particularly on collection, leaves an open desire for innovative approaches. One approach that has received consistent attention is sentiment analysis: the use of Natural Language Processing techniques to extract, transform, and interpret opinions or attitudes from a text and classify them as positive, neutral, or negative [2]. Many of the large cloud providers in recent years have created language models that offer sentiment analysis and are available through simple, web-based Application Programming Interfaces or APIs.

© The Author(s), under exclusive license to Springer Nature Switzerland AG 2024
H. K. et al. (Eds.): AIKP 2023, CCIS 2127, pp. 287–300, 2024.
https://doi.org/10.1007/978-3-031-68617-7_21

One can apply these techniques to publicly available data such as social media. As many as 72% of Americans use social media in some way [14]. Because the depth of social media use is remarkably high, a sentiment analysis approach promises to tap into vast amounts of opinion information.

This paper will investigate two questions: is the use of sentiment analysis language models a viable substitute for professional polling; and what is the performance difference between the selected models in this task? The language models selected are Azure's Cognitive Service (Azure), Google's Cloud Language API (Google), and Amazon Web Service's Comprehend (AWS). We will refer to these models and their interfaces as APIs to highlight their professional quality and ease of use.

Moving away from human surveys to algorithm-assisted observational studies may address the biases and polling issues found in the former, but such a move will risk introducing new biases and issues. One glaring issue with a social media approach is the lack of core demographic information. Without demographic information, the results of a social media study cannot be readily weighted to address overrepresentation. We admit that we do not have sufficient data to perform this weighting process. Therefore, we will conditionally test the relative improvements between the selected sentiment analysis models against "source of truth" traditional polls. In addition, we have opted to use job-approval polls as they are more analogous to sentiment analysis results and are not subject to the election-day participation bias otherwise subject to any poll.

1.1 Background of Political Polling Using Social Media Data

Studies using social media for political opinion include a range of simple to sophisticated features. Early studies used the count of candidate mentions. In a systematic random sampling review of studies involving sentiment analysis between 2014 and 2019, it was found that each study used either a lexicon approach or a vectorization approach [8]. We will introduce the approaches and note recent studies that cover the topic of using social media sentiment analysis against polling data.

Count: The user-mentioned count approach is the earliest and simplest feature method. The Twitter API includes methods to readily extract this feature. The features constructed are typically the sum of candidate-user mentions, such as #candidate's name. This is the method used in Tumasjan et al. [15] and Coletto et al. [7]. Critics attempted to replicate the results from Tumasjan et al. in Gayo-Avello et al. [9] and found the method to perform worse than traditional polling. It should be noted that the United States was not the country studied in these user-mentioned count studies and that the United States has a different culture for both Twitter and politics.

Lexiconic: The lexiconic approach to sentiment analysis entails the use of a pre-labeled corpus of specific sentiment terms. These terms are assigned a value such as the positive, neutral, and negative classes. The sentiment value of a text is then derived from the proportion or ratio of sentiment terms. This is the method used in O'Connor et al. [13]. The lexicon approach can also determine a sentiment score by a magnitude, rather than being restricted to classes. Cody et al. [6] uses the "hedonic" lexicon, which labels individual words on a scale of one (least happy) to nine (most happy). In this case, the mean happiness score is used instead of proportion or ratio. In terms of weaknesses, this method relies upon a representative lexicon and the aggregate of sentiment terms heuristic. A lexicon intended for formal speech will perform poorly for social media posts. There is also the basic heuristic that specific words that amount to only a subset of the entire text can sufficiently represent the text's sentiment. Adjectives, adverbs, or contextual phrases not in the lexicon may modify the meaning of sentiment terms. The critics in Gayo-Avello et al. [9] also attempted to replicate the results from O'Connor et al. [13] and again found the method to perform worse than traditional polling.

Natural Language Processing Vectorization: The machine learning approach entails conversion of the entire corpus into a map of vectors. "Word Vectorization" is the blanket term used for the numerous methods to achieve this. In the most basic approach is known as one-hot encoding, a count vector is constructed by creating a class dictionary and then counting each instance of class for each observation. No contextual information is acquired, the words within each record in the corpus are treated as a "bag of words." The vocabulary is the list of all unique class terms. This is the method used in Bermingham et al. [3] and Joyce, B., & Deng, J [10]. In both cases, the extracted tokens were then used in a machine learning classifier model; the Adaboost MNB classifier and Navies Bayes Algorithm respectively. The word count vector is then used as the independent variable with the class being the dependent variable. More recent approaches have incorporated embedding to encode even contextual information [1]. The vectorization methods of the APIs used in this study are not explicitly documented.

From here, the studies range from a variety of feature transformation and evaluation methods. Some studies used a direct comparison, namely the user-mentioned count studies. Others transformed the features into a sentiment ratio, that is the positive sentiment divided by negative sentiment. Finally, others used sentiment proportion, which is the sentiment class divided by the sum of observations, for each class. We have also listed their evaluation methods, which are: Mean Absolute Error, Root Mean Squared Error, Mean Rank Match, and Correlation. The Table 1 below is a list of the reviewed studies, their feature method, their inference, their final extracted feature, and their evaluation method.

Table 1. List of Studies

Feature Method	Study	Inference	Model	Evaluation
Count of @ Candidate	Tumasjan et al. [15]	Mere number of tweets mentioning a political party can be considered a plausible reflection of the vote share and its predictive power even comes close to traditional election polls	Direct Comparison	MAE

(continued)

Table 1. (*continued*)

Feature Method	Study	Inference	Model	Evaluation
Normalized Count @ Candidate	Coletto et al. [7]	Model produces high correlation for consumer confidence presidential approval to Twitter sentiment	Linear Regression	MAE, RMSE, MRM
Count & Lexiconic (OpinionFinder)	Gayo-Avello et al. [9]	Attempted method used in Tumasjan et al. & O'Connor. Found using Twitter to predict elections is not better than chance	Direct Comparison & Sentiment Ratio of Lexicon predicted labels	MAE
Lexiconic (OpinionFinder)	O'Connor et al. [13]	Moving average of Twitter sentiment highly correlates for consumer confidence and presidential approval	Sentiment Ratio of Lexicon predicted labels	Correlation
Lexiconic (labMT hedonometer)	Cody et al. [6]	Appropriately filtered Twitter sentiment predicts President's job approval three months in advance, and correlates well with surveyed consumer sentiment	Average Positive Sentiment of Lexicon predicted score	Correlation
Lexiconic (OpinionFinder) & Navie Bayes	Joyce, B., & Deng, J [10]	Correlations to polling data were as high as 94% when using a moving average smoothing technique on tweets 43 days from the election	Sentiment Ratio of Lexicon and ML predicted labels	Correlation

(*continued*)

Table 1. (*continued*)

Feature Method	Study	Inference	Model	Evaluation
Vectorization	Bermingham et al. [3]	While Tweets have some predictive quality that is augmented by sentiment analysis, they do not perform well when compared to traditional polling	Sentiment Proportion of ML predicted labels	MAE

2 Methodology

2.1 Data Collection and Pre-processing

For the privacy concerns of this project, only publicly available datasets from Kaggle, with appropriate licenses or use agreements, will be used as the source of conversations or comments. Discussion on the content of tweets will be described in general terms, such as "this tweet requires context to score." The dataset used was collected using the Twitter API "statuses_lookup "and "snsscrape" and using the keywords #DonaldTrump and #Trump. The dataset was collected between 10-15-2020 to 11-07-2020.

Tweet pre-processing includes the following steps:

1. The difference between the tweet created at date and the user created at date is calculated. Accounts younger than 30 days are removed from the sample. This is to remove potentially abusive accounts.
2. One tweet was randomly selected per user to establish independence as tweets per user wildly varies. The Pew Research Center had found that as much as eighty percent of tweets come from ten percent of users [17].
3. Incomplete tweet records were removed.
4. Regular expressions were used to clean the text. They: removed line breaks, removed "@username", removed URLs, and finally removed special characters. Regarding the hashtag, (a word or spaceless phrase preceded by the "#" symbol and is to identify content) the hashtag character was removed but the text was preserved as a single word.
5. To give all the APIs even footing, only tweets in English were used. The library selected to aid in language detection was spaCy [16], an open-source library for natural language processing. The Language Detector function evaluates sample text and assigns language class and confidence. Upon review, we determined that the tweets classified as non-English but had a low confidence rating (below 90%) should be classified as English. The tweets labeled non-English at the end of this process were not used in the evaluations.
6. The tweet text (string) was then sent to each of the three APIs for sentiment classification. The vectorization process was handled by the API.

7. One of the issues with comparing the APIs is that the Google API returns a continuous sentiment score between 1 and -1 rather than a class. After experimenting with the data, we opted to use a value from zero (exclusive) as the demarcation between the neutral class and the positive and negative classes. This demarcation value was seventy percent of one standard deviation, or $0.7 * 0.4487 = 0.314$.

8. Another issue arises with the AWS API, which incorporates a mixed sentiment class. As a solution, tweets falling into this category will be reclassified as neutral.

9. To facilitate further comparisons and experimentation, we devised an additional classifier and dataset.

   a. In the case of the new classifier, the class provided by each API was aggregated to create an ensemble classifier. For each tweet, the sum of negative, positive, and neutral classes was found, and the highest class was selected. Tweets with evenly split classes were classified as "neutral."

   b. In the case of the new dataset, each tweet was replicated for the number of likes and retweets. This was done to augment the predictive power of our methodology using lower or "less effort" types of Twitter engagement data, liking and retweeting. While it is possible to retrieve the list of liking and retweeting users, tweets older than a week cannot be retrieved using the twitter API. Therefore, the effect of prolific and nonprolific users cannot be controlled and independence cannot be assumed. We adjusted our evaluations to accommodate a comparison which is discussed in the evaluation section. The original dataset will be called Normal Dataset and the replicated dataset will be called the Replicated Dataset.

10. A group-by function was used to place each tweet into a date group to create daily counts of each tweet class. Date Groups are the sequential days from 10-15-2020 to 11-06-2020; ergo 10-15-2020 is 0 and 11-06-2020 is 23.

11. Three daily aggregations, for each API, were created for evaluation: daily negative proportion, daily positive proportion, and sentiment score.

   a. Daily negative proportion is the sum of negative class tweets divided by the total daily tweets.

   b. Daily positive proportion is the sum of positive and neutral class tweets divided by the total of daily tweets. Justification for combining the positive and neutral class is discussed in the next section.

   c. Sentiment score is the ratio of the sum of positive and neutral class tweets divided by the sum of negative class tweets. This is done to replicate the evaluation method used in O'Connor et al. [13] and Joyce, B., & Deng, J [10].

12. Finally, each of the daily aggregations for the two datasets produced noisy data. To smooth out each dataset, the LOWESS smoothing method was performed. In the original paper, LOWESS is defined as "[r]obust locally weighted regression is a method for smoothing a scatterplot, (xi, yi), i = 1, $\cdots$, n, in which the fitted value at xk is the value of a polynomial fit to the data using weighted least squares, where the weight for (xi, yi) is large if xi is close to xk and small if it is not." [5] This method was selected to replicate the smoothing function using the poll data, discussed in the next section. Upon testing, we found that the best smoothing results occurred using the entire dataset.

13. Finally, due to the low tweet rate of the average Twitter use, an additional dataset was created to capture the lower or the "least effort" type of social media engagement,

liking and retweeting. Each tweet was replicated for the number of likes and retweets. However, while it is possible to retrieve the list of liking and retweeting users, tweets older than a week cannot be retrieved using the twitter API. Therefore, the effect of prolific and nonprolific users cannot be controlled and independence cannot be assumed. We adjusted our evaluations to accommodate a comparison which is discussed in the evaluation section. The original dataset will be called Normal Dataset and the replicated dataset will be called the Replicated Dataset.

The polls used to evaluate the API classification data are sourced from FiveThirtyEight [4]. This dataset provides daily weighted estimates of polling data. Polls are weighted based upon methodological standards, historical accuracy, "house effect" or consistent difference from aggregated poll data. Finally, data was smoothed using local area regression. This study does not have the means to replicate this weighting method. Therefore, our evaluation methods will account for some error. The following are the data categories for each day used in evaluation:

1. The dataset is divided into subgroups. "All polls" is the subgroup that will be used.
2. The dataset supplied approval and disapproval estimates as well as confidence ranges. Only the estimates will be used.
3. Dates missing from the dataset were imputed using the mean of the dataset.

In summary, two sample datasets of tweets were prepared. The datasets will include daily positive proportion, daily negative proportion, and sentiment score. These proportions and scores are based on the classifications provided by four APIs: Azure, Google, AWS, and the ensemble classifier. These two sample datasets will then be evaluated against the polling dataset. This can be seen in Figs. 1, 2. Additionally, the distribution and sum of observations of sentiment classifications for each dataset can be seen in Figs. 3, 4.

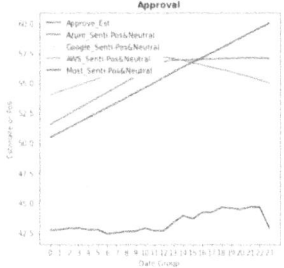 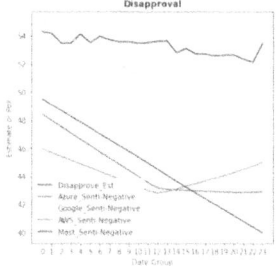 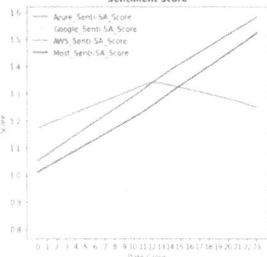

Fig. 1. Normal Dataset

2.2 Evaluation Methods

2.2.1 Manual Review of API Classification Data

An initial review of the API classification data found that the classifiers were heavily biased towards the neutral class and against the positive class. These results warranted a

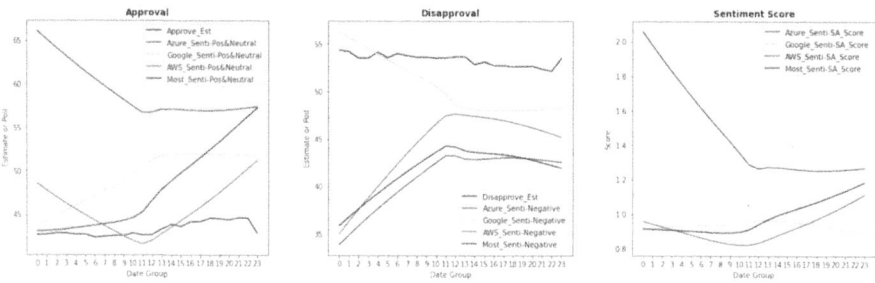

Fig. 2. Replicated Dataset

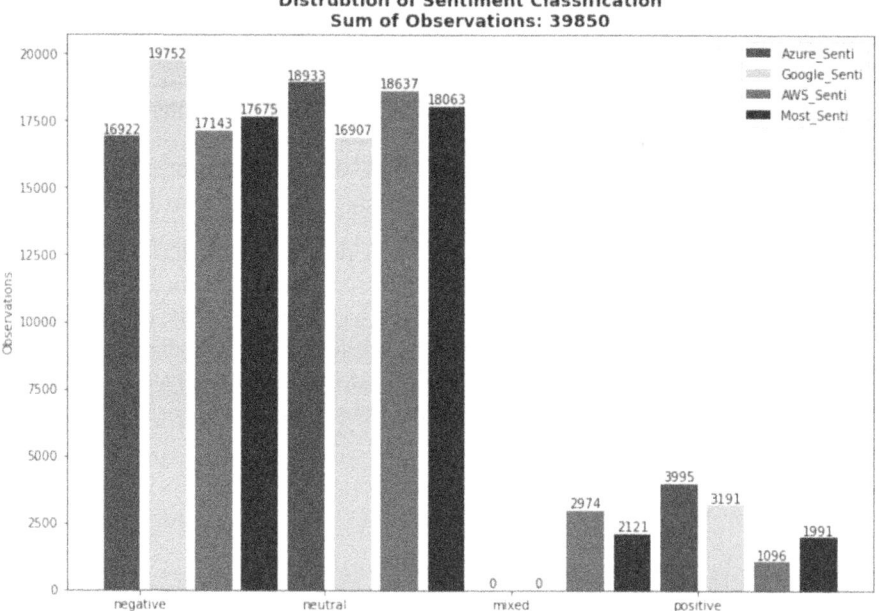

Fig. 3. Class Distribution for Normal Dataset

closer inspection of the tweets against their class. 435 records were randomly selected for manual classification. We have opted to review, and label based on two perspectives: based generic sentiment and "political" sentiment. Generic sentiment will match the typical classification into positive, neutral, and negative abstractions. Political sentiment will be classified based on the following criteria:

Tweets were classified as positive based on:

- Statements of praise or approval towards the candidate
- Disparaging remarks towards the opponent
- Disparaging remarks towards both candidates but with a clear statement of final support for the candidate

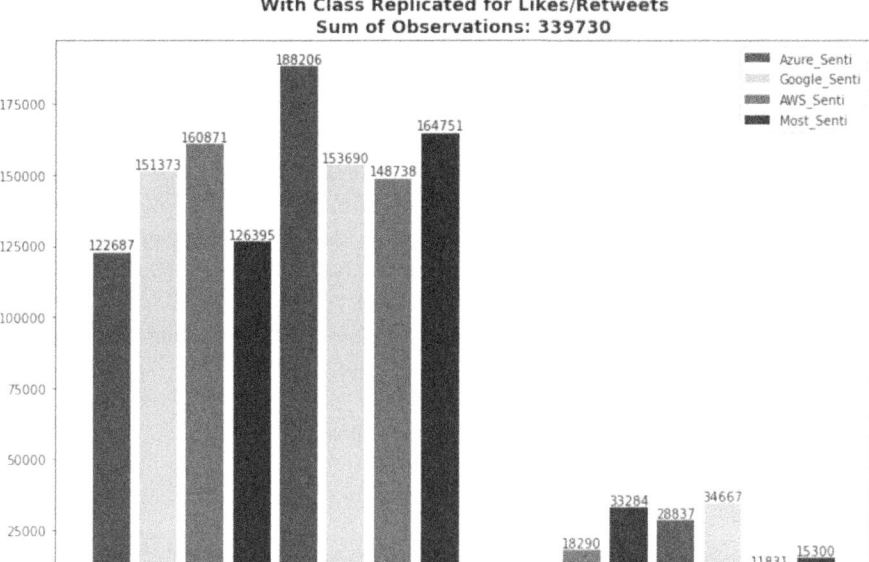

Fig. 4. Class Distribution for Replicated Dataset

- Statements of fact which are favorable for the candidate
- Candidate/campaign talking points
- Stating only the candidate's name

Tweets were classified as negative based on (inverse above):

- Statements of disdain or disapproval towards the candidate
- Approving remarks towards the opponent
- Disparaging remarks towards both candidates but with a clear statement of final support for the opponent
- Statements of fact which are favorable for the opponent
- Opponent/opposing campaign talking points
- Stating only the opponent's name

Tweets were classified as neutral based on:

- Disparaging remarks towards both candidates and with no clear statement of final support
- Statements of fact favorable to neither candidate
- Off-topic statements

Once manually labeled, the results will be used to construct a confusion matrix and accuracy scores for evaluation.

2.2.2 Hypothesis and Correlation Testing of API Classification Data Against Poll Data

Two statistical tests were selected to evaluate each dataset. These tests are as follows:

The Welch's t-Test for Independence is the primary evaluation method used for comparing the proportional dataset against the polling dataset. Unlike many other studies, this study seeks to disprove independence and prove replication of professional polling. We adopted the typical .05 significance level for independence. The Welch's t-Test was chosen over the Student's t-Test as the sample data is small, noisy, and with different variances when compared to the polling data. The test is defined as:

$$t = \frac{x_1 - x_2 - d}{\sqrt{\frac{s_1^2}{n_1} + \frac{s_2^2}{n_2}}} \text{ as the test statistic}$$

$$df = \frac{\left(\frac{s_1^2}{n_1} + \frac{s_2^2}{n_2}\right)^2}{\frac{s_1^4}{n_1^2(n_1-1)} + \frac{s_2^4}{n_2^2(n_2-1)}} \text{ as the degrees of freedom}$$

Spearman Correlation is used as a supplement evaluation method. Again, this was chosen over the Pearson Correlation as the sample data is small, noisy, and with different variances when compared to the polling data. Additionally, since the Replicated Tweets dataset does not check and control for individual users like the Normal Dataset, a non-parametric method is a better evaluation method. The correlation is defined as:

$r = 1 - \frac{6\sum d_i^2}{N(N^2-1)}$ where d is the difference between i observations and N is the number of observations.

3 Results

3.1 Manual Review Sample of API Classification Data

After the manual review, a confusion matrix comparing the predicted classes against the manually labeled classes for each API was generated. The outcomes are presented in Fig. 5.

Remarkably, the classification by the APIs exhibited a pronounced bias towards the neutral class, while displaying a bias against the positive class. Across all the classifiers, the negative class showed the least confusion. Also note the absolute difference between the two confusion matrices. This section demonstrates a strong disconnect between generic and political sentiment. Indeed, the political sentiment accuracy of tweets in the review sample is 42% for the Azure API, 40% for the Google API, and 39% for the AWS API. However, the accuracy of just the generic sentiment was found to be

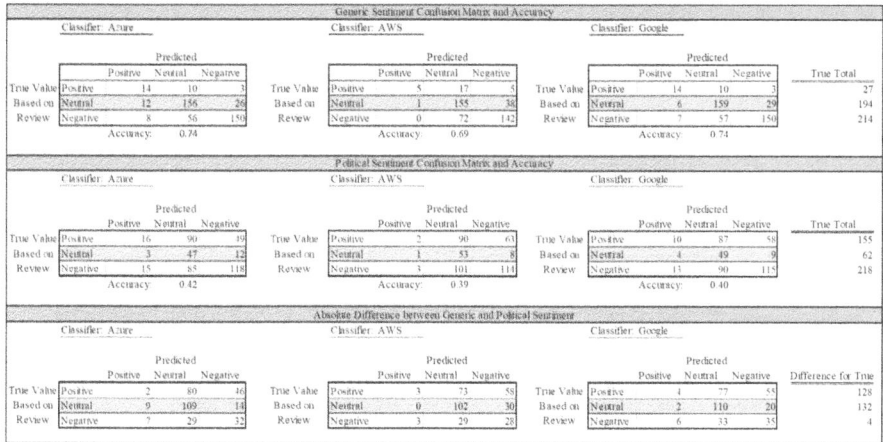

Fig. 5. Confusion Matrix Results from Manual Review

74% for the Azure API, 69% for the Google API, and 74% for the AWS API. It is worth observing that the disconnection exists primarily between generic and political sentiment for the positive and neutral classes, while the negative class remains less affected by this divergence. This supports the hypothesis that people write differently based on context for things they like or are neutral to, but not when they are discussing things they dislike.

3.2 Overall, API Performance and Feasibility: Hypothesis and Correlation Testing of API Classification Data Against Poll Data

The objective of accepting the null hypothesis was not reached by any classifier None of the classifiers achieved the objective of accepting the null hypothesis. The results can be seen in Fig. 6. P-values are displayed in exponential (E) notation. The positive proportion produced stronger independence p-values but had weaker correlations. Some of the t-tests achieved the goal of rejecting independence with weaker data smoothing. However, this would weaken the sentiment score correlation. With stronger data smoothing, most of the sentiment scores were found to have strong correlations, 50% to 80%, and to be statistically significant. We have opted to report the results when using stronger smoothing as that method produces data that is more readily comparable to the poll data. Finally, the p-values for each of the tests had enormous variance. The top performing API can be 10 or more significant figures apart from the worst performing. Across the two datasets, the APIs typically performed best with the Replicated dataset. The improvement is on average 10 significant levels. However, the Replicated dataset has a mixed correlation of positive and negative coefficients. Since the poll data changes only a small amount, this further supports that the Replicated dataset had a better performance.

The ensemble classifier emerged as the top performer across various evaluation categories, which is to be expected. Ensemble models are typically more powerful than their constituent parts. The ensemble classifier produced the strongest correlation with the sentiment score but had mixed results with the proportion data. In terms of individual APIs, the Google API exhibited the strongest performance. The API had the top results with the proportion data but had mixed results with the sentiment score data. In reviewing our process, this makes sense. We had selected a hyperparameter to determine the Google API's demarcation between the neutral class and the positive and negative classes. This provides additional evidence that there is an issue with the neutral class.

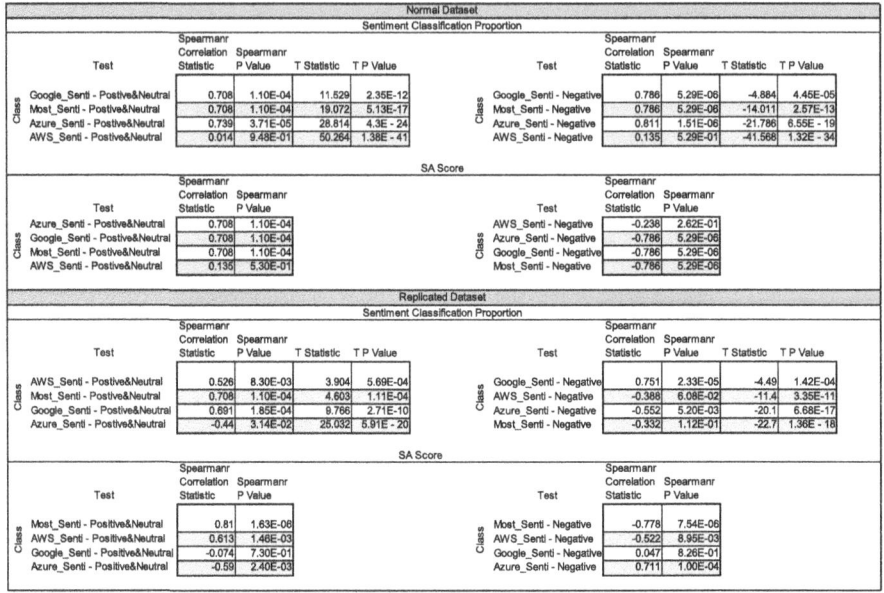

Fig. 6. Hypothesis and Correlation Testing Results

4 Discussion

After scrutinizing the result, the first question we had to ask ourselves was: "What happened?" Despite the state-of-the-art machine learning techniques underpinning the APIs, the less advanced classifiers employed in previous studies exhibited more robust correlations. Indeed, our results affirm the findings in Gayo-Avello et al. [9], and Bermingham et al. [3], studies critical of or found results against the use of social media in election prediction and polling. In an important distinction, both studies used sentiment proportions. We observed that the methodology in Joyce, B., & Deng, J [10] and O'Connor et al. [13] used a lexiconic, ratio-based sentiment score. This method may have suppressed the neutral class by assigning low confidence sentiments into an equal split of the positive and negative classifications. This is akin to using binary to two class classifiers where three or more classes would be more appropriate. So, while the correlations between their sentiment score and elections or polls may be strong, translating into multi-class proportional data robustly emulating those tangible results is unlikely.

This further underscores the challenge associated with the neutral class. We surmise that the heavy neutral class was a result of several issues. One issue may have been our preprocessing method, particularly hashtag handling. During the manual review, it was often observed that crucial sentiment-related information was embedded within hashtag text. Due to the absence of spaces in hashtag phrases, the API's vectorization process likely interpreted them as single words. The API's model is unlikely to recognize that word, as it was trained on a distinct corpus. This explains much of the inaccuracy found in both generic and political sentiment reviews. The studies that performed best used a lexiconic method or trained their own classifier model upon these hashtag terms and thus likely adapted to this expanded vocabulary. A technique to disassemble these phrases may help improve accuracy on models lacking the hashtags in the training corpus. Unfortunately, we were unable to find an acceptable approach for disassembling hashtags. Another issue is the existence of mixed sentiment tweets. That is, tweets that have negative and positive sentiment phrases. This is more readily addressable as entity-level sentiment analysis techniques have been developed. Indeed, some of the API's used in this study include entity-level sentiment models, though they were not reviewed. Entity-level classifiers will first identify entities within a sentence, and then a sentiment is calculated for each entity. This method may also address the issue of off-topic discussions as unrelated entities may be dropped. A more complicated issue to tackle is the change in writing patterns noted in the manual review. For example, many statements of fact were often classified as neutral yet contained a candidate's talking points or campaign platform. These were labeled positive in the manual review for political sentiment. Classifying these often requires context outside of the text itself. This can be addressed by constructing new supervised models but would require close attention to social media topic trends and rapid model development, which are outside the scope of this study. However, negative sentiment was found to be similar regardless of the discussion context. This suggests that a single-class classifier for the negative class may be ready for demographic bias weighting and final evaluation and then implementation for public consumption.

5   Conclusion

In conclusion, we have provided: a brief overview of the current sentiment analysis approaches for political opinion, an examination of the accuracy of the APIs classification, a discussion on the disconnect between the sentiment class and political support (political sentiment), and an examination the performance of the sentiment analysis APIs against professional polls. Overall, the results based on our procedures do not produce a robust method that can emulate traditional polling practices. Various measures have been identified to enhance accuracy, including the integration of likes and retweets, population-based weighting, refined handling of hashtags, adoption of targeted sentiment analysis, and regular or cyclical model development. With these steps, sentiment analysis of social media may approach the quality of professional pollsters.

References

1. Almeida, F., Xexéo, G.: Word embeddings: A survey. arXiv preprint arXiv:1901.09069 (2019)

2. Agarwal, B., Mittal, N., Bansal, P., Garg, S.: Sentiment analysis using common-sense and context information. J. Comput. Intell. Neurosci. **9** (2015)

3. Bermingham, A., Smeaton, A.: On using Twitter to monitor political sentiment and predict election results. In: Proceedings of the Workshop on Sentiment Analysis where AI meets Psychology (SAAIP 2011), pp. 2–10 (2011, November)

4. Bycoffe, A., Mehta, D., Silver, N.: How popular is Donald Trump? FiveThirtyEight. Retrieved July 26, 2022 (2021, January 20). https://projects.fivethirtyeight.com/trump-approval-ratings/

5. Cleveland, W.S.: Robust locally weighted regression and smoothing scatterplots. J. Am. Stat. Assoc. **74**(368), 829–836 (1979)

6. Cody, E.M., Reagan, A.J., Dodds, P.S., Danforth, C.M.: Public opinion polling with Twitter. arXiv preprint arXiv:1608.02024 (2016)

7. Coletto, M., Lucchese, C., Orlando, S., Perego, R.: Electoral predictions with Twitter: a machine-learning approach. IIR (2015)

8. Drus, Z., Khalid, H.: Sentiment analysis in social media and its application: Systematic literature review. Proc. Comput. Sci. **161**, 707–714 (2019)

9. Gayo-Avello, D., Metaxas, P., Mustafaraj, E.: Limits of electoral predictions using twitter. In: Proceedings of the International AAAI Conference on Web and Social Media, vol. 5, No. 1, pp. 490–493 (2011)

10. Joyce, B., Deng, J.: Sentiment analysis of tweets for the 2016 US presidential election. In: 2017 IEEE MIT Undergraduate Research Technology Conference (URTC) (2017). https://doi.org/10.1109/urtc.2017.8284176

11. Kennedy, C.: Key Things to Know About Election Polling in the United States. Pew Research Center, Washington, D.C (2022). https://www.pewresearch.org/fact-tank/2020/08/05/key-things-to-know-about-election-polling-in-the-united-states/

12. Kennedy, C., Lopez, J.L., Keeter, S., Lau, A., Hatley, N., Bertoni, N.: Confronting 2016 and 2020 Polling Limitations. Pew Research Center, Washington, D.C (2021). https://www.pewresearch.org/methods/2021/04/08/confronting-2016-and-2020-polling-limitations/

13. O'Connor, B., Balasubramanyan, R., Routledge, B. R., Smith, N.A.: From tweets to polls: linking text sentiment to public opinion time series. In: Fourth international AAAI conference on weblogs and social media (2010, May)

14. Social Media Fact Sheet. Pew Research Center, Washington, D.C (2021). https://www.pewresearch.org/internet/fact-sheet/social-media/

15. Tumasjan, A., Sprenger, T., Sandner, P., Welpe, I.: Predicting elections with twitter: What 140 characters reveal about political sentiment. In: Proceedings of the International AAAI Conference on Web and Social Media, vol. 4, No. 1, pp. 178–185 (2010, May)

16. Virtanen, P., et al.: SciPy 1.0: fundamental algorithms for scientific computing in Python. Nat Methods **17**(3), 261–272 (2020)

17. Wojcik, S., Hughes, A.: Sizing Up Twitter Users. Pew Research Center, Washington, D.C (2019). https://www.pewresearch.org/internet/2019/04/24/sizing-up-twitter-users/

Summarization of Telugu Text Discourses

K. Bhuvaneshwari[✉], S. A. JyothiRani, and V. V. Haragopal

Department of Statistics, Osmania University, Hyderabad, India
k.bhuvaneshwari7@gmail.com

Abstract. A text summary is a condensed version of the original text that high-lights the key points. Most of the Natural Language processing applications are widely used on text data which is readily available in English language. Limited research is being carried out on Telugu language textual data. Manual text summarization necessitates a large group of talented, unbiased persons, a substantial financial investment, and a considerable amount of time. In this study, we proposed an investigative approach for extractive text summarization that uses essential features such as order of the sentences in the given document, sentence similarities with title, word-frequencies, and document centrality of Telugu language to summarize the text data in Telugu. To rank the sentences, an improved sentence scoring approach is used. The event and named entity scores are used in this sentence scoring method. Applying statistical measures to the events and named entities that have been obtained is how sentence scoring is done. The word frequency wf score is determined by counting the instances of the event or named entity. The inverse sentence frequency isf can be calculated using the number of sentences in which the events and named entities occurred. The wf isf score of term t is calculated as the product of word frequency and inverse sentence frequency. Finally, based on the wf isf score, it determines the terms significance and includes it in the summary. The sentences were then ranked based on the scores calculated for each and every phrase while taking into account all of the given features. For this research study, we collected Telugu speech transcripts of a proficient Indian speaker Chaganti Koteswara Rao, recognized for his talks on Sanatana Dharma.

Keywords: Text summarization · Telugu · sentence similarity · word frequency · inverse sentence frequency · Natural language processing

1 Introduction

Text mining is the process of analyzing large amounts of text available on the internet or in documents. Finding the opinion in the dense text is the main challenge. Systems for text summarization assist in analyzing the extensive content to produce useful summary. The process of creating a condensed version of a certain text is known as text summarization. Since the advent of online information, the field of Natural Language Processing (NLP) has received a lot of attention. Information extraction is one example of the technique that uses human-generated language in either form to help the user. Several issues are presented in this area, including those related to the understanding and creation of human

H. K. et al. (Eds.): AIKP 2023, CCIS 2127, pp. 301–309, 2024.
https://doi.org/10.1007/978-3-031-68617-7_22

languages. These are the difficulties associated with the task of text summarization. There are several NLP tools available, including stemmers, PoS taggers, named entity recognition systems, parsers, etc., to make human languages comprehensible.

In general, extractive summarization and abstractive summarization are the two categories into which text summarization tasks can be divided [1]. Extractive summarization retrieves the most appropriate sentences as they appear in the text, whereas abstractive summarization uses natural language generation tools to produce new sentences from the set of concepts or topics contained in the document [2]. Textual data Summarization is a sub discipline of NLP that is used to consolidate the original text into a concise summary while retaining the source text's meaning [3]. This type of automatic text summarization is common in the English language. However, because of the variations in morphology and structure of the dialects, this technique is not likely to apply for Indian language summarization. Dealing with the constant flow of text data on the internet in India, there is a growing need for text summarization techniques in Indian languages to extract key information and communicate it effectively.

These techniques seek to extract essential information and efficiently convey relevant content from the source text in a concise manner. However, the wide range of morphological and structural features found in Indian dialects makes it difficult to apply this approach for summarizing them. The increasing amount of textual data on the internet in India necessitates the development of text summarization techniques in Indian languages. The grammatical rules and sentence structures in Indian languages pose a notable challenge due to their distinctiveness. Therefore, in order to develop effective text summarization techniques for Indian languages, it is necessary to have a thorough understanding of their linguistic intricacies and cultural context.

In this study, as The Telugu language lacks the necessary annotated corpora, effective morphological analyzers, name dictionaries, POS taggers, etc. Despite the long and rich literary heritage of Indian languages, technological advancements are rather recent. We proposed an analytical approach for extractive text summarization that uses essential features like sentences order in the given document, sentence similarities with title, word-frequencies, and centrality of Telugu documents to summarize the articles in Telugu. For this work, we collected Telugu speech transcripts of a proficient Indian speaker Chaganti Koteswara Rao, His lectures on puranams are frequently seen and livestream on tv channels such as Bhakti TV and TTD. He is a well-known Telugu speaker all over the world recognized for his talks on "Sanatana Dharma". Here we gathered 21 episodes speech transcripts of his discourses on "Sanatana Dharma".

2 Literature Review

Text summarization generates an automatic summary that includes all relevant information from the original text [4]. People are becoming increasingly overwhelmed by the volume of information and documents available online due to the expansion of the internet and big data. This motivates the aim of many researchers to create a technical method that can automatically summarize texts [5]. Text summarization research has been explored since the mid-twentieth century, when [6] first discussed it openly using a statistical technique called word frequency diagrams. In the area of NLP, text summarizing is a hard challenge since it involves accurate text analysis, such as lexical and semantic analysis, to produce an effective summary [7]. Additionally, a good summary needs to be brief, contain key details, and take readability, non-redundancy, relevancy, coverage, and coherence into account [8]. The problem of how to include all these elements in a summary is really difficult.

In [9] authors suggested a way for summarizing Punjabi text. Based on nine weighted text features, including named entities, title words, and keywords, it determines the sentences. To identify the Punjabi terms associated with text attributes, they utilized rule-based and dictionary-based techniques. To summarize the material in Bengali text, [10] concentrated on identifying text feature scores. Using K-means clustering, [11] suggested a Bengali summarizer. In [12] they proposed a latent semantic analysis-based kannad text summarizer. They used LSA to determine the semantic link between sentences in their work. Additionally, the SVD idea is used to create document summaries.

A Marathi text summarizer proposed by [13] based on the text rank technique suggested by [14]. The "Pagerank" algorithm has been utilized in a graph-based technique to determine the importance of sentences. Additionally, it has two unsupervised methods for extracting keywords and sentences. [15] rule-based Marathi text summarizing technique in which questions are created for each phrase based on noun terms. The answers to the top-ranked questions are then extracted after each question has been ranked in order of priority. The compilation of these questions' responses is regarded as the document's summary.

A diversity-centric extractive text summarization framework for the Telugu language, incorporating k-means clustering, has been put forth by Sravani and Humera [16]. During the pre-processing phase, the Telugu language text undergoes a series of operations such as tokenization, tagging, and the elimination of stop words. Subsequent to the initial processing, the frequency of the lexical units is calculated, and subsequently, clusters are generated based on the syntactic structure of the sentences. The sentences are ranked and subsequently pruned based on their frequency, with the elimination of low-frequency sentences. The generation of a summary is based on the application of a ranking mechanism. The current extractive textual data summarization techniques have not adequately addressed the issue of redundancy elimination within summary sentences.

A novel extractive text summarization approach utilizing the Text-Rank algorithm has been proposed in [17]. The proposed methodology employs the technique of extractive text summarization on a corpus consisting of multiple Telugu text documents. The utilization of a "Continuous Bag-Of-Words (CBOW)" model has been employed for the purpose of word embedding. Next, a similarity matrix is generated using the cosine similarity method. The generation of a graph is facilitated through the utilization of a similarity matrix. Subsequently, the Text-Rank algorithm is employed to assign rankings to the sentences.

In [18], a comprehensive analysis of various techniques for text summarization in the Telugu language has been presented. During the pre-processing phase, the Telugu text undergoes tokenization, wherein it is divided into smaller units called tokens. Additionally, parts of speech are assigned to these tokens, enabling a deeper understanding of the grammatical structure. Furthermore, any stop words present in the text are eliminated, as they typically do not contribute significantly to the overall meaning. The TFIDF method is employed to extract the keywords. The selection of significant sentences is determined by their respective scores. The summary, which consists of extracted sentences from the text, undergoes post-processing through techniques such as summary refinement and rephrasing.

A novel approach for multi-document abstractive text summarization in the Telugu language has been proposed by the authors in reference [19]. The proposed method utilizes a semantic similarity matrix to enhance the summarization process. The calculation of similarity involves the utilization of various techniques such as Recurrent Neural Networks (RNN), Jiang similarity, and the incorporation of semantic concepts. The performance of this specific method is evaluated using the ROUGE score. The observed ROUGE score exhibits a lower value when employing this particular approach.

In this paper, we presented an investigative method for text summarization that summarizes Telugu articles using key features such as sentence order of appearance in the given document, sentence similarities with title, word-frequencies, and Telugu document centrality. To rank the sentences, an improved sentence scoring approach is used. The event and named entity scores are used in this sentence scoring method. The identification and extraction of named entities are accomplished through the utilization of a sophisticated computational technique known as the Hidden Markov Model (HMM).The sentences were then ranked by calculating scores for each sentence while taking into account all of the given features.

3 Research Methodology

Text Summarization in Telugu is an important application of Natural Language Processing (NLP). This section proposes a heuristic method for automatically summarizing the Telugu documents. To rank the sentences, an improved sentence scoring method is used. The proposed framework for text summarization is detailed in Fig. 1.

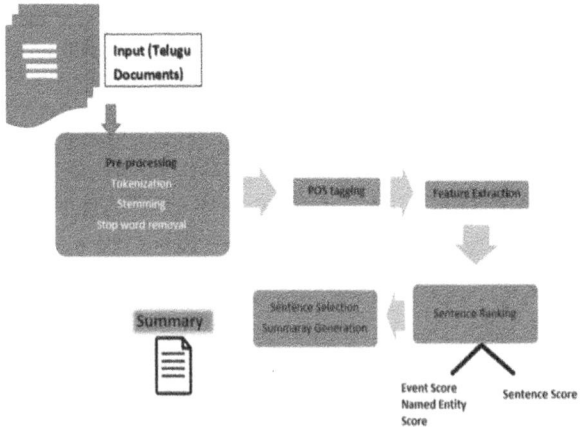

Fig. 1. Frame work for Text summarization of Telugu documents

3.1 Data Collection

For this study, 21 episodes of Telugu speech transcripts on "Sanathana Dharma", discourses of a proficient Indian speaker Chaganti Koteswara Rao were collected.

3.2 Pre-processing

Data pre-processing is an important step in any study because it converts raw data into a usable and convenient format for analysis [20]. Multiple Telugu text documents are given as input for summarization. The input document is to be pre-processed as it contains lot of noise. To retrieve hidden information, the text data must be cleaned. Stop words, numerical values, punctuation, stemming, and lemmatization are all removed during pre-processing. For this purpose, python programming language is used as it has various text processing tools and other NLP libraries.

Initially by installing "indic nlp" and its dependencies, which is a python package, a corpus of different text files is being created. The Indic NLP Library aims to develop Python-based tools for Natural Language Processing and ordinary text processing in Indian languages [21]. The script, pronunciation, language grammar, and other aspects of Indian languages are highly similar, and this library aims to offer a universal answer to very frequently used toolkits for Indian language text.

After completion of pre-processing tasks such as sentence tokenization, removing numbers and punctuation, word tokenization, and stemming with porterStemmer. Porter stemming is a technique for getting rid of words which has more typical morphological and inflexional endings. Its primary application is as part of the term normalization process. Indic NLP library includes built-in stop words in Telugu, and a custom file was created to remove stop words found in the current text data.

3.3 Text Summarization

The Textual Data Summarization involves condensing the source text into brief documents while maintaining its original meaning, typically used in the field of NLP. [22]. This automatic textual summarization is extensively utilized in the English language. Yet, this technique is not considered applicable for Indian language summarization because of the differences in dialects in terms of their structure and morphological characteristics. When dealing with the constant influx of text data on the web in India, the demand for text summarization tools in Indian languages has risen. These tools play a crucial role in identifying the key facts and conveying relevant details from the source material.

The suggested method makes use of the language properties "Events" and "Named Entities." Events are words used to describe actual occurrences. The actions are described by the verbs in the text. They play a crucial part in determining if a statement is relevant for a summary. The name of a person, place, thing, or animal involved in the occurrence of this action is referred to as a Named Entity. In the language, nouns are the POS associated with such words. The feature extraction phase of the suggested method retrieves the events and named entities that are present in each sentence and sends them for statistical analysis.

The named entities are captured by employing Hidden Markov Model (HMM). It is a ML technique that was originally developed for Speech Recognition practices. However, it has since been adapted for the task of NER in NLP tasks [23].

HMMs can be mathematically described using a set of three parameters denoted as $\lambda = (A, B, \Pi)$.

The three fundamental components of a probabilistic model are

I. Start Probability (Π), refers to the likelihood of a specific tag appearing as the first tag in a sentence.

II. Transition Probability ($A = aij$), refers to the likelihood of the next tag 'j' appearing in a sentence, given the current occurrence of a specific tag 'i' and

III. Emission Probability ($B = bj(O)$) refers to the likelihood of occurrence of output sequence for given a state 'j'

The above probabilities are computed through python by using "pomegranate" package which offers efficient and adaptable implementations of probabilistic mod-els from single probability distributions to more complex compositional models like Bayesian networks and HMMs through which Named Entities are captured.

Applying statistical metrics to events and named entities is how sentence scoring is done. The word frequency score is determined by counting the instances of the event or named thing. The word frequency score calculated by computing the correlation between the concentration of events/named entities in the document and the total number of events/named entities. The word frequency score (wfs) is calculated by using Eq. 1. The inverse sentence frequency (isf) can be calculated using the number of sentences in which the event/named entity occurred. The calculation of the inverse sentence frequency of events and named entities is explained by Eq. 2. The term that appears in the most sentences is given the least weight in the summary. The word's wf isf score is calculated as the product of word frequency (wf) and inverse sentence (isf) frequency. Based on the wf isf score, Eq. 3 determines that the term's relevance should be included in the summary.

$$Wf_{w(D)w \in \{Event/NamedEntity\}} = \frac{\text{Occurences of word w in document D}}{\text{Total number of words w in document D}} \quad (1)$$

$$ISf_{w(D)w \in Event/NamedEntity} = \log_e \frac{\text{Total number of sentenc es in document D}}{\text{Number of Sentences containing term t}} \quad (2)$$

$$WF\_ISf_{w(D)w \in Event/NamedEntity} = WFtD * ISFt(D) \quad (3)$$

In the sentence, the sum of each event's or named entity's "wf isf" score is calculated. Further, the correlation between this value and the number of events and named entities in the entire sentence gives the sentence score.

The calculation of sentence score is shown in Eq. 4.

$$Sentence\ Score = \frac{\sum WF\_ISF}{\text{Total number of efevents and named entities in Sentence Si}} \quad (4)$$

The sentences are arranged in chronological order of sentence scores in the sentence ranking stage. The threshold for sentence selection is set using the average score of these sentence scores. Only sentences that score higher than the threshold in the suggested method are chosen for summary.

4   Results and Discussion

The study's comprehensive findings are presented in this section. Initially we collected the Telugu transcripts of all the 21 episodes of "Sanatana Dharma" prophecies by Sri.Chaganti Koteswar Rao.

By using Indic NLP library in python a corpus was built and performed the pre-processing and cleaning of the raw Telugu text (Fig. 2).

Fig. 2. Corpus of "Sanatana Dharma" Episodes

By applying Statistical metrics to events and named entities sentence scores were calculated. A threshold for sentence selection is set using the average score of these sentence scores. Then only the sentences that have highest score than the threshold chosen for summary.

Figure 3, shows one of the episodes of Sanathana Dharma with sentence scores.

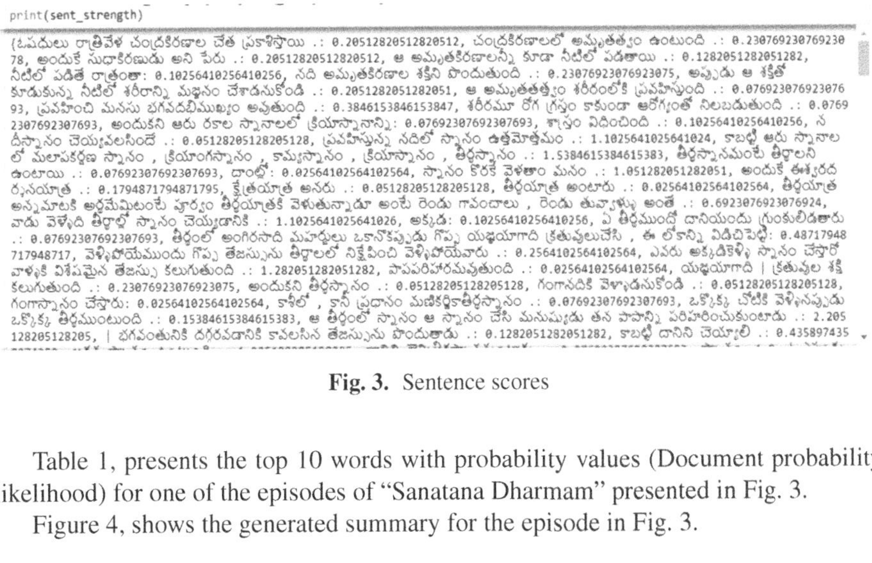

Fig. 3. Sentence scores

Table 1, presents the top 10 words with probability values (Document probability likelihood) for one of the episodes of "Sanatana Dharmam" presented in Fig. 3.

Figure 4, shows the generated summary for the episode in Fig. 3.

Table 1. Top 10 words with corresponding probabilities

S.No	Word	Probablity
1	స్నానం	0.9085
2	మనసు	0.4827
3	శౌచం	0.4139
4	తపస్సు	0.3448
5	తేజస్సు	0.2414
6	శక్తి	0.2068
7	నీళ్ళు	0.2069
8	శాస్త్రం	0.1724
9	గోవిందా	0.1578
10	బంగారు	0.1379

బలశ్చ శౌచం అపారమైన తేజస్సు ఉద్భవిస్తుంది సుక్రమమైన స్నానం వల్ల .. బలం - ప్రతిరోజూ నియమంగా , చక్కగా స్నానం చేసే వాడి శరీరంలో ఉన్న నాడీమండలం బాగా పనిచేస్తుంది . శుష్క సశాస్త్రియంగా , భగవద్గీతతో కనీసం గోవిందా , గోవిందా , గోవిందా అంటూ స్నానం చేస్తే చాలు , నీకు పది రకాలైన ప్రయోజనాలను స్నానం ముళ్ళిచెప్పగలదు . కానీ కాలంతో నిమిత్తం లేకుండా ఎప్పుడైనా చేసే స్నానం ఒక్కచే నైమెత్తిక స్నానం అంటారు .

Fig. 4. Sample Summary Output

5 Conclusion and Future Scope

This research proposes an extractive text summarization approach based on enhanced sentence scoring mechanism for Textual data in Telugu language. In order to determine the important phrases in the text for generating the summary, linguistic criteria such as events and named things are considered. Using events and named entity occurrences in the text, sentence score is calculated. To create the summary that best describes the whole text content, the unique sentences with the highest rankings are chosen. If future, our research interest is to assess the quality of the summaries generated by this method by comparing with manual generated summaries.

In this work, the extractive summarization approach is used and implemented. The next approach named as abstractive approach of automatic text summarization on Telugu language could be the upcoming challenge.

References

1. Verma, P., Om, H.: A variable dimension optimization approach for text summarization. In: Harmony Search and Nature Inspired Optimization Algorithms, pp. 687–696. Springer, Singapore (2019)
2. Kadam, D.P., Patil, N., Gulathi, A.: A comparative study of Hindi text summarization techniques: genetic algorithm and neural network. Int. J. Innov. Adv. Comput. Sci, **4**, 541–548 (2015)

3. Chen, F., Han, K., Chen, G.: An approach to sentence-selection based text summarization. In: TENCON'02. Proceedings. 2002 IEEE Region 10 Conference on Computers, Communications, Control and Power Engineering, vol. 1. IEEE, pp. 489–493 (2002)
4. Adhika Pramita, W., Supriadi, R., Guruh F,S., Edi, N., Abdul, S., Affandy, A., De Rosal, I.M.S,: Review of automatic text summarization techniques & methods. J. King Saud Univ. Comput. Inf. Sci. **34**(4) (2002)
5. Allahyari, M., Pouriyeh, S., Assefi, M., Safaei, S., Trippe, E.D., Gutierrez, J.B., Kochut, K.: Text summarization techniques: a brief survey. Int. J. Adv. Comput. Sci. Appl. **8** (2017)
6. Lun, H.P.: The automatic creation of literature abstracts. IBM J. 159–165 (1958)
7. Rane, N., Govilkar, S.: Recent trends in deep learning based abstractive text summarization. Int. J. Recent Technol. Eng. **8**, 3108–3115 (2019)
8. Verma, P., Pal, S., Om, H.: A comparative analysis on Hindi and English extractive text summarization. ACM Trans Asian Low-Resource Lang. Inf. Process. **18**, 30–39 (2019)
9. Gupta, V., Lehal, G.S.: Automatic Punjabi text extractive summarization system. In: Proceedings of COLING 2012: Demonstration Papers 2012 Dec, pp. 191–198
10. Efat, M.I., Ibrahim, M., Kayesh, H.: Automated Bangla text summarization by sentence scoring and ranking. In: 2013 International Conference on Informatics, Electronics and Vision (ICIEV) 2013 May 17, pp. 1–5. IEEE
11. Sumya, A., Aysa, S.A., Md Palash, U., Md Delowar, H., Shikhor Kumer, R., Masud Ibn, A.: An extractive text summarization technique for Bengali document (s) using K-means clustering algorithm. In: Imaging, Vision & Pattern Recognition (icIVPR), 2017 IEEE International Conference on. IEEE, 1–6 (2017)
12. Geetha, J.K., Deepamala, N.: Kannada text summarization using Latent Semantic Analysis. In: Advances in Computing, Communications and Informatics (ICACCI), 2015 International Conference on. IEEE, pp. 1508–1512 (2015)
13. Yogeshwari, V.: Rathod. 2018. Extractive Text Summarization of Marathi News Articles (2018)
14. Mihalcea, R., Tarau, P.: Textrank bringing order into text. In: Proceedings of the 2004 Conference on Empirical Methods in Natural Language Processing 2004 Jul, pp. 404–411
15. Deepali Kailash, G.: Rule based text summarization for Marathi text. J. Glob. Res. Comput. Sci. **9**(5), 19–21 (2018)
16. Khanam, M.H., Sravani, S.: Text summarization for Telugu document. IOSR J. Comput. Eng. (IOSR-JCE). **18**(6), 25–28 (2016)
17. Manjari, K.U.: Extractive summarization of Telugu documents using TextRank algorithm. In:2020 Fourth International Conference on I-SMAC (IoT in social, mobile, analytics and cloud)(I-SMAC) 2020 Oct 7, pp. 678–683. IEEE
18. Kallimani, J.S., Srinivasa, K.G.: Information extraction by an abstractive text summarization for an Indian regional language. In:2011 7th International Conference on Natural Language Processing and Knowledge Engineering 2011 Nov 27, pp. 319–322. IEEE
19. Sudha, D.N., Latha, Y.M.: Multi-document abstractive text summarization through semantic similarity matrix for Telugu language. Int. J. Adv. Sci. Technol. 513–521 (2020)
20. Vijayarani, S., Ilamathi, M.J., Nithya, M.: Preprocessing techniques for text mining-an overview. Int. J. Comput. Sci. Commun. Netw. **5**(1), 7–16 (2015)
21. Ramesh, G., et al.: The largest publicly available parallel corpora collection for 11 indic languages. Trans. Assoc. Comput. Linguist. **9**(10), 145–162 (2022)
22. Srivastava, R., Singh, P., Rana, K.P., Kumar, V.: A topic modelled unsupervised approach to single document extractive text summarization. Knowl.-Based Syst. **21**(246), 108636 (2022)
23. Nasar, Z., Jaffry, S.W., Malik, M.K.: Named entity recognition and relation extraction: state-of-the-art. ACM Comput. Surv. (CSUR) **54**(1), 1–39 (2021)

Summarizing Students' Text-Only Answer Sheet Using SBERT and K-Means Clustering and Evaluating It Using Semantic Search

Namita Kiran$^{(\boxtimes)}$, Leena Ragha, and Tushar Ghorpade

Department of Computer Engineering, Ramrao Adik Institute of Technology, D Y Patil Deemed to be University, Nerul, Navi Mumbai, India
namitakiran20@gmail.com, {leena.ragha, tushar.ghorpade}@rait.ac.in

Abstract. Covid-19 pandemic has forced the education system to move online. Online classes and examinations have become norm of the day. Reading long article on screen is a tedious and time-consuming task. The current solutions have limitations as a tool for examination in terms of text size, vocabulary, and efficiency in the evaluation. An automatic evaluation system that evaluates students' text-only answers can reduce the burden of teachers. In his work, we first perform extractive summarization of students' answer using SBERT and K-means clustering for summary creation. To extract diversity from text, sentences from each cluster are picked based on similarity score. If two sentences have similarity score > 0.8, only one of them is picked for summary generation. The generated summary is evaluated based on results obtained through semantic search based on similarity with the reference summary. The results are promising as the marks obtained by the student using proposed solution is very close to that allotted by teacher after manual evaluation.

Keywords: SBERT · Transformer · K-Means and cosine similarity

1 Introduction

Text Summarization [1, 25] refers to rewriting the text into a shorter, concise form, less than the original size. The aim is to identify and remove all out of context and repeated texts and produce a semantically correct summary of the article. Summarization of an article can be abstractive or extractive in nature. Abstractive summarization [2] rewrites the text using new words whereas extractive [2] picks relevant sentences "as it is". Such a summarization solution is required by numerous applications namely research analysis, abstract generation, news summary etc. Automating the manual process of assessment of an article is a challenging task. In the manual process, an evaluator who is an expert in the domain of the article reads the article, ignores all irrelevant details, spelling mistakes, few grammatical mistakes, etc., and looks for those key sentences for their semantic correctness, looks for the use of important key words and the sentence or paragraph context as per the question. The final marks are the cumulative impact of all the above observations.

© The Author(s), under exclusive license to Springer Nature Switzerland AG 2024
H. K. et al. (Eds.): AIKP 2023, CCIS 2127, pp. 310–323, 2024.
https://doi.org/10.1007/978-3-031-68617-7_23

The answers may be in soft text form or may be in the handwritten image form. With the advancement in the image processing tools, the same assessment tool can evaluate the images of handwritten answers as well. Such solutions, not only speed the assessment process, they also overcome the manual errors, bias and malpractices and will bring a new paradigm in the education system. However, the automation of the assessment is a very complex and challenging research domain. In this paper we propose a framework for the assessment of an article that can also grade the article for its quality. The research adopts a novel approach in summarization as well as evaluation technique. In generating an extractive summary, the cosine similarity method is used to compare sentences with each other. Sentence that is very similar to another is removed and distinct one preserved. This approach provides us a comprehensive summary. This keeps in consideration that even outliers that hold necessary information are preserved while similar sentences are removed. By adjusting the similarity threshold, the length of summary can be controlled by the user. For evaluation, semantic search based on cosine similarity score is used which is a better evaluation parameter than ROUGE. This is a very simple approach. Only one standard answer is needed to evaluate the answer of the entire class. Also, it outputs the total marks obtained without teacher's intervention.

The paper is organized with Sect. 2 concentrating on the literature survey of the research work. Section 3 consists of the proposed method. Section 4 discusses the Experiment and results and finally the conclusive remarks and the references.

2   Related Works

Towards this, we surveyed various technologies used in research works by various researchers and analysed the technologies for their capabilities, limitations, and the summarization accuracy. Various deep-learning models like seq2seq [15], seq2seq with attention are used for text summarization. Addition of Attention [12, 13, 16, 22] module in plain seq2seq helped concentrate on relevant words. They produce satisfactory results, however, they are not always reliable and suited to only short and informal texts like product review, sentiment analysis. Also, they suffer from vanishing and exploding gradient problems. BERT (Bi-directional Encoder Representations from Transformers) [9, 11, 14, 19] used to create sentence embedding, is an advancement over deep-learning models because it keeps in consideration the context of the word. The transformer architecture was first introduced by Google in a paper titled "Attention is all you need" [4]. The paper demonstrates the architecture and inner workings of the transformer. Transformer is the basic architecture based on which BERT, T5, GPT, RoBERTA, DistilBERT and various other models are built. It is a stack of 6 encoders and 6 decoders. The input embedding of 512 dimensions is fed to the first encoder. Each encoder consists of a Multi-head self-attention layer and a position-wise fully connected feed forward layer. The output of the encoder is fed to the decoder. Decoders are a stack 6 layers. Each layer has three sub-layers. In addition to multi-head self-attention and Feed Forward Network, there is a masked multi-head attention layer. The purpose of the attention layer is to map a query and set of key-value pairs to the output, where, query, key, value and output are vectors. The output is obtained as a weighted sum of the values. The weight is computed by correlation between the query and the corresponding key. The authors of the paper "Fine-tune BERT for Extractive Summarization" [2] uses BERTSUM, a variant of BERT on CNN/Dailymail dataset to generate summary. It uses BERTSUM with a label y with values 0 or 1 depending on whether the sentence is important or not and should be included in summary. The model outperformed the previous best on ROUGE. Leveraging BERT for Extractive Text Summarization on Lectures [1] prepares lecture summarization service. The paper uses a transformer based model BERT for text vectorization. It outputs a learned embedding which is a leap ahead of all the previous techniques. The paper demonstrates BERT as a modified version of a basic transformer. Like humans, BERT looks at all the words in a sentence, left or right at the same time to predict the next word. It is an encoder-only model trained on two tasks-Masked language model and Next sentence Prediction. There are two standard configurations of BERT:

- BERT-base- It consists of 12 transformer blocks, 12 self-attention heads, 768 hidden layers and is trained on 110 million parameters.
- BERT-large-It contains 24 transformer blocks, 16 self-attention heads, 1024 hidden layers and is trained on 340 million parameters.

Besides there are other configurations namely BERT-tiny, BERT-mini, BERT-medium. These can be used in case of resource constraints. BERT-base and BERT-large are widely used. BERT handles out-of-vocabulary words using the tool *Wordpiece* tokenizer. Original transformer consisted of six blocks of encoder and decoder. Each encoder has self-attention heads. Multi-headed transformer consists of more than 1 head. Self-attention helps to focus on relevant words in a sentence and draw out insignificant words. These are trained on huge corpus and thus yield state-of-the-art results. The output of BERT is a high-quality learned embedding. Gokul P.P Student, Akhil BK Student, Shiva Kumar K.M in paper Sentence Similarity Detection in Malayalam Language using cosine similarity [6] used cosine similarity for paraphrasing Text in Malayalam language i.e. the text rewritten using similar words that convey the same meaning. The proposed approach consisted of two tasks. Task 1 categorized data into Paraphrase (P) and Non-Paraphrase (NP). Task 2 consisted of a Semi Paraphrase (SP). The training data was tokenized and *POS* tagged. Cosine similarity was used to detect similarity between original and paraphrased text. In testing phase 900 sentence pairs for task1 and 1400 sentence pairs for task2 were used which yielded an accuracy of 0.8 and 0.59 respectively. The drawback of the model is that it requires a good number of training data. In the paper Essay Test Based E-Testing Using Cosine Similarity Vector Space Model [7] by Wahyudi, Ricky Akbar, Teguh Nurhadi Suharsono and Ahmad Syafruddin Indrapriyatna used essay paper for computer-based evaluation. Conventionally computers could evaluate only multiple choice or true/false based questions. Lecturers' answers were matched with students using a vector space model. The document and query were converted into vectors and then matched by angle between them. Smaller the angle, higher the cosine value and thus greater the similarity. Five sample answers are taken as reference to evaluate one question each having the same truth value. TF-IDF is used for text vectorizing. TF-IDF (Term Frequency-Inverse Document Frequency) takes into account frequency of word to weigh its importance. In TF most frequently occurring words in a sentence are given higher weightage, on the other hand IDF neutralizes the importance of commonly used words in a document i.e. if a word occurs in every sentence its value will be 0. Hence, IDF prioritizes least frequently occurring words. TF-IDF is a product of Term Frequency and Inverse Document frequency. The biggest drawback of using TF-IDF in text summarization is that it neglects the semantics of the word. Also the sequence of words in a sentence is not important. If a term is frequently occurring throughout the document its DF will be low. This may be undesirable for applications like text summarization where certain words relating to the central idea of the topic will be frequently occurring and is expected. The proposed algorithm uses BERT that take into account the importance of words rather than frequency of occurrence of any word. The paper Automatic Thai Subjective Examination using Cosine [8] by Pongsakorn Saipech and Pusadee Seresang-takul uses a slightly different approach. It tries to incorporate synonyms of the word or phrase while comparing the text. The text is preprocessed and tokenized into words or phrases. Reference answer is matched with the student's subjective answer. Synonyms of the words were also compared. Semantic similarity of Indonesian sentences using natural language processing and cosine similarity by Reza Fauzan et al. [9] calculated sentence similarity using cosine method. Word similarity was obtained using Wu Palmer and WordNet Bahasa. The result yielded an accuracy of 86,67%. A Descriptive Answer Evaluation System Using Cosine Similarity Technique [10] by Dr. Meenakshi A. Thalor uses keyword extraction from text. The teacher's answer is the standard answer with which the answer of student1 and student2 is matched. All the unique words in the three documents (teacher and two students) are used as features and TF-IDF of each word is calculated. The result shows that marks allotted by the system are close to that of the teacher evaluating manually. Authors K. Ampili and S. Kanakala in Tweet Summarization Using Clustering Mechanisms [20] classifies twitter posts as relevant/irrelevant. It uses the BERT paradigm and DBSCAN as a clustering mechanism. M. Xia, Y. Zhao, R. Cui and G. Jin in the paper Research on unsupervised MDS technology based on graph structure [21] generates a multi-document summary. It first uses pre-trained BERT for sentence representation and then centroid and Maximum Marginal Correlation algorithm (MMR) to identify redundant sentences in candidate summary.

Some of the above approaches uses TF-IDF for text vectorization which has a drawback that it assigns low values to commonly used words that may be important. The proposed algorithm uses BERT that overcomes this problem. Clusters obtained using BERT encodings are more semantically distinct compared to TF-IDF. This work is inspired by BERTSUM approach and it goes a step ahead to include diversity in summary. Above approaches uses ROUGE for evaluation. Here cosine similarity is used which is a better scale to measure quality of summary.

3   Proposed Method

The proposed method tries to overcome the loopholes in existing system. The flow of the algorithm is depicted in Fig. 1. Extractive summarization is used because we want to evaluate students' answers as she/he has written. For the experiment, a sample question is taken for which students' answer is evaluated.

The reference text is the standard answer prepared by the teacher. The students' answers is encoded using BERT. A general architecture of BERT is depicted in Fig. 2. It consists of 12 layers of encoders. The output is a contextualized embedding. These embeddings are learned i.e. words are contextually identified in a sentence. BERT embeddings are used to create cluster.

314   N. Kiran et al.

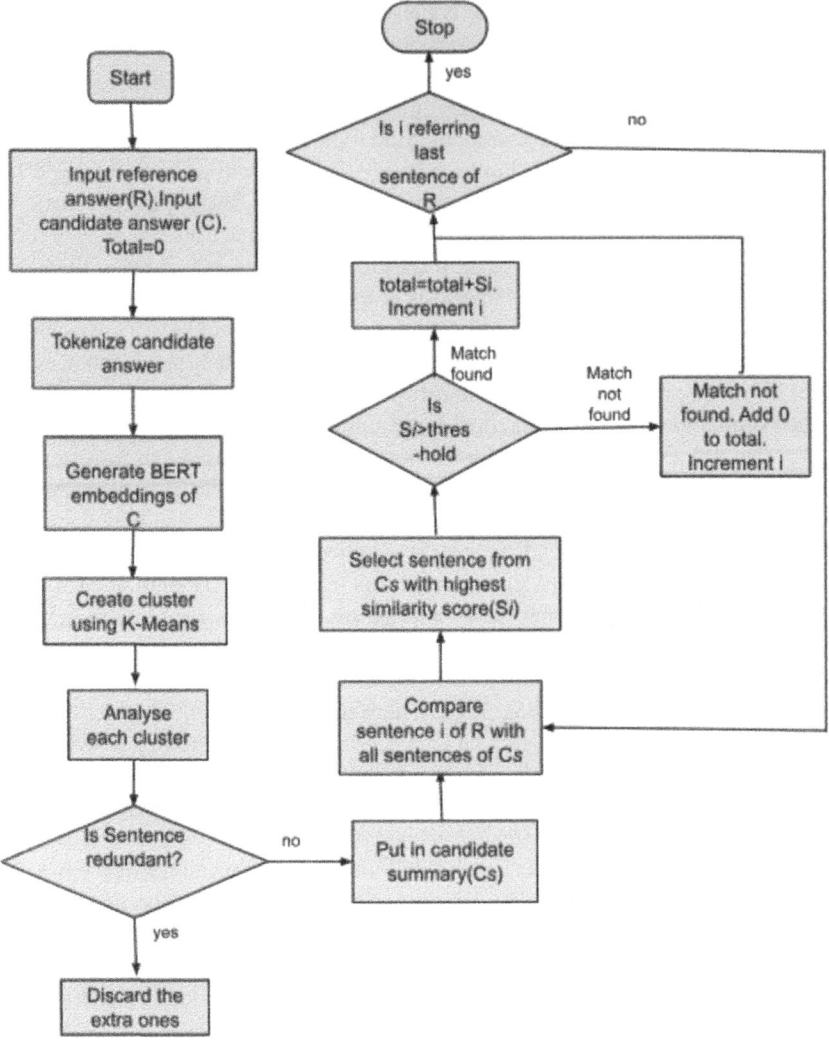

Fig. 1. Framework of summarization and assessment

BERT model used for the experiment is all-MiniLM-L6-v2. This is a sentence-transformer. It maps sentences to a 384 dimension vector space. This particular model is used for the experiment as we deal with sentences instead of words. It is used as sentences or short paragraph encoders. It has been trained on a very large sentence level dataset. It is fine-tuned on a 1B sentence pairs dataset. Training method known as contrastive learning objective is used in which a sample sentence is given and the model is trained to predict the most suitable pair out of randomly given sample sentences. Applications where sentence encoder is used are semantic search, information retrieval and clustering. The student's answer undergoes further processing. Summary generation

Generate contexualized Embeddings

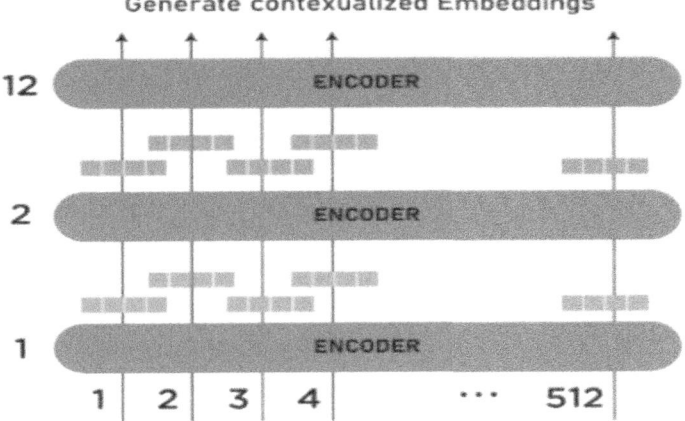

Fig. 2. General architecture of BERT [11]

is done using K-means clustering [17, 24]. Similar data points in encoded text form a cluster. Earlier approaches directly chose a cluster as summary. In this work, a summary is generated by picking sentences from each cluster. An intermediate level of filtering based on cosine similarity [5] is applied to each cluster to pick only unique sentences and remove redundant ones. Sentences that are similar to another above a certain threshold (t1 = 0.8) are discarded. Threshold can be set as per requirement. Dissimilar sentences from each cluster are aggregated to form a comprehensive summary. The purpose is to drop repeated sentences as much as possible and pick diverse ones. Further, the work evaluates the students performance using the generated summary. The encoded reference is a learned representation and is used for semantic search. The final summary obtained is semantically matched [18] with reference summary. If similarity between reference summary and student's summary is found to be above threshold (t2 = 0.5),the search is successful i.e. that particular text is in students answer and cosine similarity score is added to marks, else 0 is added. The semantic search evaluation system used in this work is better than ROUGE (Recall Oriented Understanding of Gisting Evaluation) [3, 23]. ROUGE compares n-gram without taking into consideration the contextual meaning of the word. E.g 'bank' in the phrase 'river bank' or 'money bank' is the same for ROUGE.

4   Experiment and Result

The student while answering should follow certain instructions. The student should write answers in the sequence demanded by the question. The flow of answer is crucial to obtain good score.

The students' answer may have following flaws:-

- Logically incorrect sentences
- Redundancy
- Lengthy answers
- Sentences irrelevant to question

Also, it is expected that student touch diverse aspects of the topic. The answer should be wholesome. Even outliers hold necessary information. And the summarized version should reflect the same. It should avoid contextually repeated lines and capture diversity. In the experiment we create summarized text free of above flaws.

The sample question taken for evaluation is:

"What is cryptography. What are threats to information security? Explain crypt-analysis."

Candidate answer (C) used for evaluation is:

"Cryptography is the art and science of converting plaintext into cipher-text. Cipher-text is the encoded text. In cryptography plain-text is converted into cipher-text. Cipher-text is an encrypted form of plain-text. The purpose of cryptography is to secure the text. Security goals to be achieved are-confidentiality, integrity and availability. Encoded text cannot be easily read by humans. So, cannot be interrupted by adversaries who can use the information to gain illegal benefits. There are various threats to information security. The threats to information security are attacks threatening confidentiality e.g traffic analysis and snooping. Attacks threatening Integrity are masquerading and replaying. Repudiation- Sender or receiver fraudulently repudiates or denies that the message was sent or received. Notarisation can avoid repudiation. Attacks threatening availability are Denial of Service attacks. Adversaries send thousands of requests to the same server at a time. Either from the same source or multiple sources. Cryptanalysis is an attempt to decode cryptographic algorithms. It is performed by ethical hackers or researchers to harm the target for bonafide reasons. In cryptanalysis the hackers try to break the code and get information. Hackers try to safeguard the information by finding the loopholes in the security system."

The Reference answer (R) is:

"Cryptography is the art and science of converting plaintext into ciphertext. The purpose of cryptography is to secure the text. Security goals to be achieved are-confidentiality, integrity and availability. Attacks threatening confidentiality are traffic analysis and snooping. Attacks threatening integrity are masquerading, modification and repudiation. In masquerading, the interceptor impersonates somebody else to whom the receiver of mail may trust. Denial of service attack is attack on availability. Cryptanalysis is an attempt to decode cryptographic algorithms by ethical hackers or researchers to find loopholes in the security system."

The experiment can be performed in following steps:

Step 1: Tokenization- Tokenize the candidate answer using *nltk* sentence tokenizer. It converts sentences into input tokens. Length of the tokenized sentence is 20.

Step 2: Encoding- Input is fed to BERT. The model used is all-MiniLM-L6-v2 from module SentenceTransformer. The output is 2-D text embedding of shape (20,384). The output is normalized. Figure 3 shows scatter plot of sentence embedding.

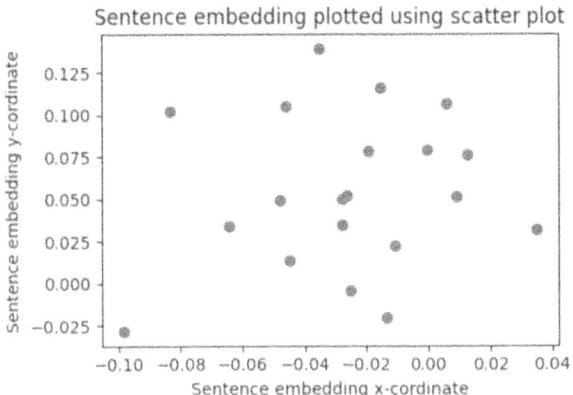

Fig. 3. Scatter plot of sentence embedding

Step 3: Clustering-The text embeddings obtained from step 3 are clustered using K-Means algorithm. The question can be of various types. It can be one single question or may have subparts. The number of clusters to be formed through K-Means is decided by the demand of question e.g. if the question has two subparts, parameter n_clusters = 2. n_clusters = 3 is taken for the experiment as question expects answer in three subparts. Cluster 1, cluster 2 and cluster 3 are formed as shown in Fig. 4.

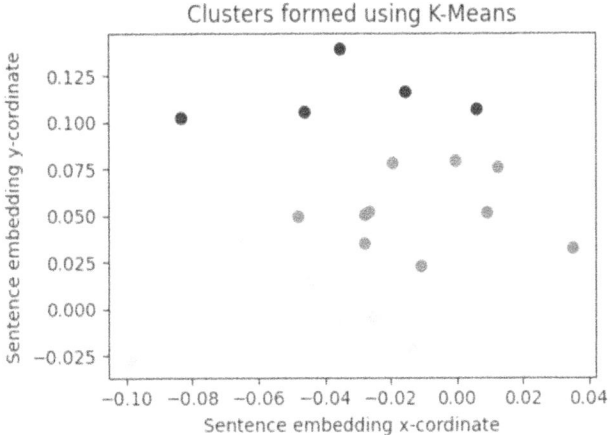

Fig. 4. Text labelled into 3 cluster

Each cluster is analyzed one by one. First cluster 1 is taken for consideration. To choose relevant sentences, each sentence is matched with all following sentences on cosine similarity scale.

$$\text{Cosine similarity}(A, B) = \frac{A \cdot B}{\|A\|\|B\|} = \frac{\sum_{i=1}^{n} A_i B_i}{\sqrt{\sum_{i=1}^{n} A_i^2} \sqrt{\sum_{i=1}^{n} B_i^2}} \tag{1}$$

Equation 1 is a cosine similarity formula between A and B. It is basically angle between A and B. If the similarity(cos) is more than 0.8, the second sentence is dropped from the summary list. The step is repeated for cluster 2 and cluster 3. The Table 1 shows clusters and the picked up sentences from each cluster.

Table 1. Table containing clusters

Cluster number	Text in cluster	Sentences chosen for summary creation
1	Cryptography is the art and science of converting plaintext into cipher-text. In cryptography plain-text is converted into cipher-text. The purpose of cryptography is to secure the text. Security goals to be achieved are-confidentiality, integrity and availability. Cryptanalysis is an attempt to decode cryptographic algorithms	Cryptography is the art and science of converting plaintext into cipher-text. The purpose of cryptography is to secure the text. Security goals to be achieved are-confidentiality, integrity and availability. Cryptanalysis is an attempt to decode cryptographic algorithms
	Number of sentences: 5	No. of sentences: 4
2	Cipher-text is the encoded text. Cipher-text is an encrypted form of plain-text. Encoded text cannot be easily read by humans. So, cannot be interrupted by adversaries who can use the information to gain illegal benefits. There are various threats to information security. The threats to information security are attacks threatening confidentiality e.g. traffic analysis and snooping. Attacks threatening Integrity are masquerading and replaying. Notarisation can avoid repudiation. It is performed by ethical hackers or researchers to harm the target for bonafide reasons. Hackers try to safeguard the information by finding the loopholes in the security system	Cipher-text is the encoded text. Encoded text cannot be easily read by humans. So, cannot be interrupted by adversaries who can use the information to gain illegal benefits. There are various threats to information security. The threats to information security are attacks threatening confidentiality e.g. traffic analysis and snooping. Attacks threatening Integrity are masquerading and replaying. Notarisation can avoid repudiation. It is performed by ethical hackers or researchers to harm the target for bonafide reasons. Hackers try to safeguard the information by finding the loopholes in the security system
	Number of sentences: 10	Number of sentences: 9

(continued)

Table 1. (*continued*)

Cluster number	Text in cluster	Sentences chosen for summary creation
3	Repudiation- Sender or receiver fraudulently repudiates or denies that the message was sent or received. Attacks threatening availability are Denial of Service attacks. Adversaries send thousands of requests to the same server at a time. Either from the same source or multiple sources. In cryptanalysis the hackers try to break the code and get information	Repudiation- Sender or receiver fraudulently repudiates or denies that the message was sent or received. Attacks threatening availability are Denial of Service attacks. Adversaries send thousands of requests to the same server at a time. Either from the same source or multiple sources. In cryptanalysis the hackers try to break the code and get information
	Number of sentences: 5	Number of sentences: 5

All the sentences in the cluster 3 are picked because their similarity score is less than 0.8. It conveys that the student's answer is not repetitive and the intention of the summary creation is to preserve distinct informative sentences expelling only the repetitive ones. This important task cannot afford to lose any informative sentence relevant to the question. If the lines were repeated, the summary would have been smaller. If the evaluator needs less number of sentences in summary it can decrease the threshold(t1) value.

The final summarized text is

> *"Cryptography is the art and science of converting plaintext into cipher-text. The purpose of cryptography is to secure the text. Security goals to be achieved are-confidentiality, integrity and availability. Cryptanalysis is an attempt to decode cryptographic algorithms. Cipher-text is the encoded text. Encoded text cannot be easily read by humans. So, cannot be interrupted by adversaries who can use the information to gain illegal benefits. There are various threats to information security. The threats to information security are attacks threatening confidentiality e.g traffic analysis and snooping. Attacks threatening Integrity are masquerading and replaying. Notarisation can avoid repudiation. It is performed by ethical hackers or researchers to harm the target for bonafide reasons. Hackers try to safeguard the information by finding the loopholes in the security system. Repudiation- Sender or receiver fraudulently repudiates or denies that the message was sent or received. Attacks threatening availability are Denial of Service attacks. Adversaries send thousands of requests to the same server at a time. Either from the same source or multiple sources. In cryptanalysis the hackers try to break the code and get information."*

Length of students summary is 18. The length of the summary is less than the original summary. However, here length is 18 because the student's answer is less repetitive and relevant to the topic.

Step 4: Evaluation-Each sentence in the reference summary is compared with each sentence in summarized text obtained in step 3. Length of reference summary is 8. The Table 2 shows the most similar sentence in the students' summary and its respective score. Threshold(t2) is 0.5 and similarity score is calculated as in Eq. 1. The thresholds for similarity score are to be adjusted by the evaluator depending on whether the evaluator wants the paper to be strictly or leniently checked.

Table 2. Semantic search of reference summary in students summary

Sr. no.	Sentence in Reference summary	Similar sentence in students summary	Similarity score
1	Cryptography is the art and science of converting plaintext into ciphertext	Cryptography is the art and science of converting plaintext into cipher-text	0.96
2	The purpose of cryptography is to secure the text	The purpose of cryptography is to secure the text	0.98
3	Security goals to be achieved are-confidentiality, integrity and availability	Security goals to be achieved are-confidentiality, integrity and availability	0.97
4	Attacks threatening confidentiality are traffic analysis and snooping	The threats to information security are attacks threatening confidentiality e.g. traffic analysis and snooping	0.87
5	Attacks threatening Integrity are masquerading, modification, repudiation	Attacks threatening Integrity are masquerading, replaying	0.85
6	In masquerading, the interceptor impersonates somebody else to whom the receiver of mail may trust	-	0.0
7	Denial of service attack is attack on availability	Attacks threatening availability are Denial of Service attacks	0.89
8	Cryptanalysis is an attempt to decode cryptographic algorithms by ethical hackers or researchers to find loopholes in the security system	Cryptanalysis is an attempt to decode cryptographic algorithms	0.90

As per the observation the students answer is very close to the teacher's reference answer. The student has mentioned all the points except that in row 6. None of the lines in students' answers match the teacher's summary above the threshold of 0.5. Thus 0 point is allotted. In the above answer students scored 6.42 out of 8 or 8 out of 10 as the total marks for the question is 10. Thus, the answer is of good quality. The experiment was repeated with some average and poor quality answers too. The marks obtained were almost same as allotted by the teacher through manual evaluation.

Table 3. Change in marks obtained with change in threshold

Sr. no.	Threshold(t2)	Similarity score	Marks obtained
1	0.4	6.88	8.6
2	0.5	6.42	8
3	0.6	6.42	8
4	0.7	6.42	8
5	0.9	3.81	4.75

Table 3 shows change in marks obtained with change in threshold (t2). Threshold below 0.4 indicates the paper is leniently evaluated 0.9 means it is strictly evaluated.

$$\text{Marks obtained} \propto \frac{1}{t2} \tag{2}$$

As the threshold increase or decrease, the marks obtained behave accordingly. Here, average threshold of 0.5 is taken which is an optimum for most cases.

Thus, this approach is comparatively simple to use. It can help evaluators save time and effort. Results will be automatically generated within minutes. Students and teachers do not have to wait for days to complete manual evaluation. Thus helping in the growth of students. Even students can self-evaluate themselves. It can also be used independently for summarization task. The use of BERT provides more contextualized embeddings compared to TF-IDF and results are reliable and can be used for practical purposes. The query search method looks for semantic similarity instead of common n-grams. The method is more evolved and gives better result compared to previous techniques.

5 Conclusion and Future Scope

The approach can be used to design an automatic evaluation system. With advancement in technology it can even be used for handwritten notes. The results are very encouraging. The limitations are that it can evaluate text-based answers only. Figures and tables cannot be evaluated. Further, work is needed in this area. Also, student and teacher can take different examples to elaborate the same concept. It fails to evaluate the example if it varies from that of reference even if the student's example is correct. Thus, although the algorithm shows promising results but improvements need to be done. The approach is good to be used for text-based answers. With the inclusion of examples and figures, it can be used for all practical purposes.

References

1. Miller, D.: Leveraging BERT for extractive text summarization on lectures. arXiv preprint arXiv:1906.04165 (2019)
2. Liu, Y.: Fine-tune BERT for extractive summarization. arXiv preprint arXiv:1903.10318 (2019)
3. Rouge, L.C.Y.: A package for automatic evaluation of summaries. In: Proceedings of Workshop on Text Summarization of ACL, Spain (2004)
4. Vaswani, A., et al.: Attention is all you need. In: Advances in Neural Information Processing Systems 30 (2017)
5. Sun, X., et al.: Sentence similarity based on contexts. Trans. Assoc. Comput. Linguist. (2022)
6. Gokul, P.P., Akhil, B.K., Shiva, K.K.M.: Sentence similarity detection in Malayalam language using cosine similarity. In: 2017 2nd IEEE International Conference on Recent Trends in Electronics, Information & Communication Technology (RTEICT). IEEE (2017)
7. Akbar, R., Suharsono, T.N., Indrapriyatna, A.S.: Essay test based E-testing using cosine similarity vector space model. In: 2022 International Symposium on Information Technology and Digital Innovation (ISITDI). IEEE (2022)
8. Saipech, P., Seresangtakul, P.: Automatic Thai subjective examination using cosine similarity. In: 2018 5th International Conference on Advanced Informatics: Concept Theory and Applications (ICAICTA). IEEE (2018)
9. Fauzan, R., et al.: Semantic similarity of Indonesian sentences using natural language processing and cosine similarity. In: 2022 4th International Conference on Cybernetics and Intelligent System (ICORIS). IEEE (2022)
10. Thalor, M.A.: A descriptive answer evaluation system using cosine similarity technique. In: 2021 International Conference on Communication information and Computing Technology (ICCICT). IEEE (2021)
11. Devlin, J., et al.: BERT: pre-training of deep bidirectional transformers for language understanding. arXiv preprintarXiv:1810.04805 (2018)
12. Khanna, U., Ghodratnama, S., Beheshti, A.: Transformer-based models for long document summarisation in financial domain. In: Proceedings of the 4th Financial Narrative Processing Workshop@ LREC 2022 (2022)
13. Kieuvongngam, V., Tan, B., Niu, Y.: Automatic text summarization of covid-19 medical research articles using BERT and GPT-2. arXiv preprintarXiv:2006.01997 (2020)
14. Wang, C., Cho, K., Gu, J.: Neural machine translation with byte-level subwords. In: Proceedings of the AAAI Conference on Artificial Intelligence, vol. 34, no. 05 (2020)
15. Sennrich, R., Haddow, B., Birch, A.: Neural machine translation of rare words with subword units. arXiv preprintarXiv:1508.07909 (2015)
16. Clark, K., Khandelwal, U., Levy, O., Manning, C.D.: What does BERT look at? An analysis of BERT's attention. arXiv preprintarXiv:1906.04341. (2019)
17. Sinaga, K.P., Yang, M.-S.: Unsupervised K-means clustering algorithm. IEEE Access 8 (2020)
18. Wu, C., Yan, M.: Learning Deep Semantic Model for Code Search Using CodeSearchNet Corpus. arXiv preprint arXiv:2201.11313 (2022)
19. Adwani, S., Shelke, P.P.: A novel approach to text summarization of document using BERT embedding. In: 2023 Third International Conference on Advances in Electrical, Computing, Communication and Sustainable Technologies (ICAECT), Bhilai, India (2023)
20. Ampili, K., Kanakala, S.: Tweet summarization using clustering mechanisms. In: 2022 4th International Conference on Advances in Computing, Communication Control and Networking (ICAC3N), Greater Noida, India (2022)
21. Xia, M., Zhao, Y., Cui, R., Jin, G.: Research on unsupervised MDS technology based on graph structure. In: 2023 3rd Asia-Pacific Conference on Communications Technology and Computer Science (ACCTCS), Shenyang, China (2023)

22. Thiruthuvaraj, R., Jo, A.A., Raj, E.D.: Explainability to business: demystify transformer models with attention-based explanations. In: 2023 2nd International Conference on Applied Artificial Intelligence and Computing (ICAAIC), Salem, India (2023)
23. Narrain, J.M., Taneja, V., Atrey, S.B., Sivaram, J., Singh, D.: Extractive summarization - a comparison of pre-trained language models and proposing a hybrid approach. In: 2023 Winter Summit on Smart Computing and Networks (WiSSCoN), Chennai, India (2023)
24. Dutulescu, A.N., Dascalu, M., Ruseti, S.: Unsupervised extractive summarization with BERT. In: 24th International Symposium on Symbolic and Numeric Algorithms for Scientific Computing (SYNASC), Hagenberg/Linz, Austria (2022)
25. Srividya, K., Bommuluri, S.K., Asapu, V.V.V.K., Illa, T.R., Basa, V.R., Chatradi, R.V.S.: A hybrid approach for automatic text summarization and translation based On Luhn, Pegasus, and Textrank algorithms. In: 2022 International Conference on Smart Generation Computing, Communication and Networking (SMART GENCON), Bangalore, India (2022)

Measuring Business Model Disclosure Quality in Integrated Reports Using NLP Techniques

Aneetha Sukhari[1]([✉]) [ⓘ], Abejide Ade-Ibijola[2] [ⓘ], and Daniël Coetsee[1] [ⓘ]

[1] School of Accounting, University of Johannesburg, Johannesburg, South Africa
sukhaar@unisa.ac.za
[2] Johannesburg Business School, University of Johannesburg, Johannesburg, South Africa

Abstract. Corporate disclosure has significantly evolved in recent years, providing stakeholders with a wealth of information in diverse formats. This information is unstructured data, which cannot be easily retrieved and analysed. Consequently, there is a need to transform information in corporate reports into structured data to facilitate in-depth analysis by users of corporate reports. As a starting point to analysing unstructured data in corporate disclosure, we selected the business model aspect of integrated reports. This paper investigates the quality of business model disclosure in 370 integrated reports of JSE-listed companies and compares the evolution of business model disclosure quality over a period of five years. In doing so, we designed a multi-dimensional disclosure index to measure business model disclosure quality based on dimensions such as quantity, dispersion, coverage, and depth. The content analysis was automated by incorporating the multi-dimensional disclosure index into a newly designed text analysis software tool, called Business Model Analysis Tool (BMAT). BMAT uses algorithms based on natural language processing (NLP) techniques. The results from BMAT depict an increase in dispersion, coverage, and depth of disclosure of all components of business models, indicating an enhancement in the quality of business model disclosure. An overall adherence to the International Integrated Reporting Framework was noted.

Keywords: Integrated reporting · business model disclosure · content analysis · algorithms · NLP techniques

1 Introduction

The increase in corporate disclosure has resulted in capital market participants having access to substantial amounts of data in varying formats (Dyer et al. 2017; Lewis and Young 2019). The information contained within corporate reports is unstructured. Unstructured data lacks a standardised format and cannot be easily retrieved consistently using automated techniques (Köseoğlu 2022; Lewis and Young 2019). This complicates the analysis of corporate reports of multiple companies and industries over time (Türegün 2019). Lewis and Young (2019) highlight the importance of transforming the information in corporate reports into structured data to enable meaningful analysis. NLP techniques make it possible to defragment and analyse unstructured data in corporate reports.

© The Author(s), under exclusive license to Springer Nature Switzerland AG 2024
H. K. et al. (Eds.): AIKP 2023, CCIS 2127, pp. 324–343, 2024.
https://doi.org/10.1007/978-3-031-68617-7_24

Recent research advocates for more qualitative content analysis of integrated reports using technology (Dumay and de Villiers 2019) and raises the importance of developing suitable proxies for integrated reporting quality (de Villiers et al. 2017). Beattie et al. (2004) suggests that the quality of non-financial disclosure has different dimensions which should be considered. This paper proposes that a proxy for each content element of the integrated report be designed, tested, and automated. The proxy should take into consideration the different dimensions of disclosure. As a starting point, in this paper, a multi-dimensional disclosure index is designed to assess the quality of business model disclosure. The multi-dimensional disclosure index designed in this paper is based on the principles of the multi-dimensional disclosure indices designed in previous studies, which assessed the quality of environmental disclosure (Helfaya and Whittington 2019) and forward-looking disclosure (Beretta and Bozzolan 2008). The reason for choosing business model disclosure is that the business model is at the core of the business and is used to transform capitals and deliver value to society.

The business model consists of a few components: inputs, business activities, outputs, and outcomes on capitals (IIRC 2021). Furthermore, there is no standardised format for presenting business models in integrated reports, which results in companies using a combination of diagrams, tables, and words. The lack of structure of business model disclosure in integrated reports poses a challenge for in-depth analysis because the information relating to inputs, business activities, outputs and outcomes on capitals cannot be easily accessed, analysed and contrasted across companies and time periods, which diminishes its usefulness for decision-making. A rigorous approach to assessing business model disclosure would be to design a multi-dimensional disclosure index using algorithms based on NLP techniques to facilitate the content analysis of business model disclosure. Therefore, the research question explored in this paper is – Could a disclosure index measuring the different dimensions of quality using algorithms based on NLP techniques be designed to assess the quality of business model disclosure?

The paper is structured as follows. Section 2 provides an overview of prior literature exploring business model disclosure, multi-dimensional disclosure indices and NLP techniques. Section 3 sets out the methodology. The design of the multi-dimensional disclosure index is explained in Sect. 4. In Sect. 5, the design of Business Model Analysis Tool (BMAT) and its functionality is demonstrated. Section 6 provides the findings. Finally, Sect. 7 concludes the study.

2   Literature Review

According to the International Integrated Reporting Framework ("The Framework"), "the aim of an integrated report is to describe the company's value-creation process" (IIRC 2021; 2013a). Value created, preserved or destroyed by a company over time manifests itself in increases, decreases or transformations of the capitals caused by the company's business activities and outputs (IIRC 2021; 2013a). Business model disclosure gives the user a better understanding of which critical external factors impact the company, what the company does to create value for its stakeholders, the company's desired outcomes, which capitals the company relies on, the company's positioning in the value chain and the markets in which it operates (IIRC 2021; 2013b). The business model consists of a few components: inputs, business activities, outputs, and outcomes on capitals (IIRC 2021; 2013a).

Inputs are defined as "the capitals (resources and relationships) that the company draws upon for its business activities" (IIRC 2013a). Business activities are the actions that take place to convert inputs into outputs (IIRC 2013b). Outputs are the "key products and services and any by-products or waste produced by the company" (IIRC 2021; 2013b). Outcomes are the internal and external consequences for capitals as a result of business activities and outputs and can be positive or negative (IIRC 2021; 2013a). Value-creation manifests itself in outcomes on capitals (IIRC 2013c, 2021). Recently, there has been a shift from the financial value created, which focuses on financial capital, towards the creation, preservation, or erosion of value in each of the six capitals (IIRC 2021; 2013c).

Prior research has explored the quality of business model disclosure in integrated reports using manual content analysis (Bek-Gaik and Surowiec 2022; Truant et al. 2020; Sukhari and de Villiers 2019). Sukhari and de Villiers (2019) proposed a framework for assessing the business model disclosure using the criteria in the Framework and Background Paper on Business Models. Bek-Gaik and Surowiec (2022) and Truant et al. (2020) assessed companies' business model disclosure based on the disclosure index proposed by Sukhari and de Villiers (2019). The criteria in the framework comprised descriptions of inputs, business activities, outputs, outcomes, effectiveness, and readability of the business models (Sukhari and de Villiers 2019). In conclusion, the quality of business model disclosure was evaluated using single-dimensional models and manual scoring systems based on identified questions for each of the components of the business model disclosure.

Prior studies designed and applied multi-dimensional disclosure indices to assess the quality of environmental reporting (Helfaya and Whittington 2019) and forward-looking disclosure (Beretta and Bozzolan 2008). These studies found that single-dimensional models were insufficient to appraise the quality of non-financial information (Beretta and Bozzolan 2008; Helfaya and Whittington 2019). A multi-dimensional disclosure index was designed to measure the quality of forward-looking disclosure in annual reports (Beretta and Bozzolan 2008). The dimensions assessed were quantity, dispersion, coverage, and depth. The authors found that the model captured information used by analysts in decision-making, and the multiple dimensions in the model were more valuable than a simple disclosure index. However, applying multi-dimensional disclosure indices to large samples manually is challenging.

To aleviate this problem, studies used qualitative data analysis software, such as NVivo and Non-numerical Unstructured Data Indexing Searching & Theorizing, to analyse non-financial information, but this software was confined to word and sentence counts (Abed et al. 2016; Hussainey 2004). A recent development is the application of NLP techniques to evaluate the quality of non-financial disclosure in corporate reports (El-Haj et al. 2020, 2019; Miura et al. 2021; Nakagawa et al. 2020; Türegün 2019). NLP techniques is a subset of artificial intelligence that uses computational techniques to extract meaning from structured or unstructured text (Chowdhary 2020; Kao and Poteet 2007). Text mining makes extensive use of NLP techniques. Text mining is a systematic process of discovering and extracting knowledge from text, using information retrieval, text classification and clustering, entity, relation, and event extraction (Kao and Poteet 2007).

Prior studies assessed the quality of integrated reports using text mining techniques (Miura et al. 2021; Nakagawa et al. 2020). Nakagawa et al. (2020) evaluated a sample of Japanese listed companies' integrated reports. In the first step, high-quality integrated reports were analysed to identify and extract the descriptive words, topics and terms associated with environmental, social and governance disclosure. Thereafter, a disclosure index was developed based on the identified words, topics, and terms which was then used to analyse the sample of integrated reports. The sample of integrated reports were assessed for the occurrence of these words, terms, and topics. Miura et al. (2021) used text mining techniques to identify the occurrence of specific words to evaluate the quality of integrated reports from Japanese universities. A word cloud was generated to identify the sample's most frequent words and the topics were organised by word clustering.

3   Research Method

The evaluation of business model disclosure is achieved in two steps. Firstly, a multi-dimensional disclosure index is created and incorporated into a new text analysis software, called the Business Model Analysis Tool (BMAT), which uses algorithms based on NLP techniques to evaluate the quality of business model disclosure in integrated reports. Secondly, the results generated from BMAT are interpreted using descriptive statistics to assess whether the quality of business model disclosure improved.

3.1   Sample and Data Collection

Table 1 depicts the sample selection. The sample selection starts with the top one hundred JSE-listed companies based on market capitalisation. Fourteen companies had no business models from 2016 to 2020 and were removed from the sample. Ten companies were eliminated from the sample due to incomplete listings from 2016 to 2020. One company traded two types of shares, and one company had a dual listing and was removed from the sample. The final sample is, therefore, 370 reports for 74 companies and ranges for five years from 2016 to 2020. South Africa was one of the first countries to mandate the King Report for listed companies in 2013, making South African listed companies the ideal setting for research on integrated reporting (de Villiers et al. 2014). Therefore, the companies would have had time to implement the Framework's requirements since 2013.

Information on business model disclosure was obtained from companies' integrated reports, which were obtained from Equity RT or company websites. Information from interactive or encrypted reports were extracted using Optical Character Recognition (OCR) software. In cases where the components of the business model disclosure were not clearly labelled, the aspects disclosed in the business model section were categorised into the component it best described. In instances where the business model disclosure was not clearly identified, the report was searched for disclosure on inputs, business activities, outputs, and outcomes on capitals. The components of the business model disclosure were identified, classified under one of the components of the business models, and thereafter, copied and pasted into the BMAT software in the respective block.

Table 1. Sample – Quality of business model disclosure

	No. of companies	No. of observations
Sample size	100	500
Companies with no business models	(14)	(70)
Incomplete listings in 2016, 2017, 2018, 2019 and 2020	(10)	(50)
Dual listed companies	(1)	(5)
Companies trading two types of shares	(1)	(5)
Final sample	**74**	**370**

3.2 Measurement of Business Model Disclosure

Stemler (2001) defines content analysis as "a systematic, replicable technique for compressing many words of text into fewer content categories based on explicit coding rules". This research method enables researchers to "make replicable and valid inferences from texts, or other meaningful matter to the contexts of their use" (Krippendorff 2004: 18). By establishing guidelines for coding, it facilitates the identification and analysis of patterns in large datasets (Stemler 2001; Weber 1990). Krippendorf (2004) states that content analysis can be performed using a computer and the resulting data should provide information that can be interpreted to answer the research questions. In this paper, we applied the steps set out by Weber (1990) for content analysis.

Firstly, the recording units were all text in integrated reports relating to the components of the business models, namely the inputs in the form of the six capitals (financial, human, intellectual, manufactured, natural, and social and relationship), business activities, outputs, and outcomes on each of the six capitals. Secondly, the quality dimensions assessed were quantity, dispersion, coverage, and depth of business model disclosure. These dimensions are detailed in Sect. 4. The third step was to define the coding rules for each assessed dimension. A scoring index for business model disclosure quality was designed in Sect. 4. The final score was called business model disclosure quality, abbreviated to BMQ_i. The fourth step was to manually evaluate the integrated reports of a sample of twenty companies using the criteria in Sect. 4. Thereafter, the software developers designed BMAT, which is explained in Sect. 5. The reliability of the software was evaluated by comparing to the manual results to the results generated from BMAT. Thereafter, the final version of BMAT was designed. Finally, the sample of 370 business models was coded, and the scores were generated by BMAT and exported to Excel. The scores were merged into one spreadsheet for all five years for further analysis, which is discussed in Sect. 6.

4 Design of the Multi-dimensional Disclosure Index

The quality of business model disclosure is evaluated by designing and applying a multi-dimensional disclosure index, adapted from prior studies of Beretta and Bozzolan (2008) and Helfaya and Whittington (2019). The multi-dimensional model designed in this paper differs from the models discussed in Beretta and Bozzolan (2008) and Helfaya and Whittington (2019) by being re-named to Business Model Quality Index (BMQ_i). Its primary purpose is to evaluate the quantity, dispersion, coverage, and depth of business model disclosure, whereas the above-mentioned prior studies assessed environmental disclosure and forward-looking disclosure. The dimensions in Helfaya and Whittington (2019) and Beretta and Bozzolan (2008) were allocated as follows: 50% quantity, 12.5% dispersion, 12.5% coverage and 25% depth. In this paper, the percentage allocation of each dimension was changed to calculate the final score based on 20% quantity, 20% dispersion, 20% coverage and 40% depth. The allocation was made to reduce the effect of quantity on the overall score, to create an more average allocation to each dimension, but keeping depth as twice the values of dispersion and coverage. Business model quality (BMQ_i) is calculated as 20% of the Relative Quantity Index (RQN_i) and 80% of the Richness Index (RCN_i).

The figure https://bit.ly/3Os9Sk1 depicts the dimensions of quality in the multi-dimensional disclosure index to evaluate the quality of business model disclosure. The multi-dimensional disclosure index comprises the Relative Quantity Index and the Richness Index. The Richness Index is the average sum of the Width Index and Depth Index. The Width Index encompasses the Dispersion Index and Coverage Index. Each aspect of BMQ_i score is discussed below and a summary of the calculations for BMQ_i is available: https://tinyurl.com/57tcpyrm.

4.1   Business Model Quality Index

BMQ_i is calculated as 20% of the Relative Quantity Index (RQN_i) and 80% of the Richness Index (RCN_i). BMQ_i is calculated as:

$$BMQ_i = 0.8 * (RCN_i) + 0.2 * (RQN_i) \tag{1}$$

where:

BMQ_i = business model quality index comprising of the richness index and quantity index,

RQN_i = percentage of business model information within the integrated report relative to the sample,

RCN_i = richness score computed as the average of the width and depth scores.

4.1.1   Quantity of Business Model Disclosure

The Relative Quantity Index (RQN_i) is calculated by counting the number of words that relate to the business model disclosure in the integrated report and dividing it by the highest number of words in the sample. The Relative Quantity Index in this paper differs from Helfaya and Whittington (2019) and Beretta and Bozzolan (2008) in that word count was used. These prior studies used the number of pages as a measure. The RQN_i provides an indication of the number of words pertaining to business models relative to the sample. RQN_i is calculated as follows:

$$RQN_i = \frac{total\ number\ of\ words\ of\ business\ model\ information}{highest\ number\ of\ words\ of\ business\ model\ information\ in\ the\ sample}$$

$$\tag{2}$$

where:

RQN_i = percentage of business model information within the integrated report relative to the highest number of words in the sample.

4.1.2 Richness Index

The richness index (RCN_i) is the average of the width and depth scores. It provides an indication of what information is disclosed and how it is disclosed (Beretta and Bozzolan 2008). RCN_i is calculated as follows:

$$RCN_i = \frac{1}{2}(WID_i + DEP_i) \tag{3}$$

where:

RCN_i = richness score computed as the average of the width and depth scores.

4.1.2.1 Width of Business Model Disclosure

The width index (WID_i) is the average of the coverage and dispersion scores. WID_i provides an assessment of whether the different components of business models are disclosed. WID_i is calculated as follows:

$$WID_i = \frac{1}{2}(COV_i + DIS_i) \tag{4}$$

The way in which coverage and dispersion are calculated is discussed below.

4.1.2.1.1 Coverage of Business Model Disclosure

The coverage index (COV_i) measures whether each sub-topic on the disclosure index have been disclosed in the business model. COV_i is measured as the percentage of components disclosed out of the total number of components expected to be in the business model. The aspects being evaluated are the business model's components: financial capital, human capital, intellectual capital, manufactured capital, natural capital, social and relationship capital, business activities, outputs, and outcomes for each of the six capitals. Therefore, the total number of aspects being evaluated is 14. A yes is awarded if the item is disclosed, and a no otherwise. The number of yeses for each company is added and divided by 14. Helfaya and Whittington (2019) and Beretta and Bozzolan (2008) calculated COV_i by awarding a 0 or 1 for the presence or absence of sub-topics in environmental disclosure and forward-looking disclosure, whereas this paper awards a percentage considering all components of the business model. COV_i is calculated as:

$$COV_i = \frac{number\ of\ aspects\ disclosed}{total\ number\ of\ aspects\ being\ evaluated} \tag{5}$$

4.1.2.1.2 Dispersion of Business Model Disclosure

The dispersion index (DIS_i) measures the spread of words disclosed across each sub-topics on the disclosure index relative to the total number of words in the business model disclosure. It indicates how the number of words in each sub-topic is spread across the business model. In this case, the sub-topics are each of the six capitals, business activities, outputs, outcomes on the six capitals and other information. DIS_i is calculated similarly to Helfaya and Whittington (2019), and Beretta and Bozzolan (2008) but has been modified for the components of business models. DIS_i is calculated as:

$$DIS_i = \frac{the\ number\ of\ words\ in\ each\ sub\text{-}topic}{total\ number\ of\ words\ that\ pertain\ to\ the\ business\ model} \tag{6}$$

4.1.2.2 Depth of Business Model Disclosure

Depth is assessed by designing and applying a disclosure index. The disclosure index was designed from the Framework, IIRC Business Models Background Paper, a review of twenty business models and prior studies which were discussed in Sect. 2 (IIRC 2013a, 2013b, 2021). Depth assesses the presence of specific keywords, quantitative information, industry-specific terminology and indicators of value creation, preservation, or erosion. Keywords are identified for each of the fourteen aspects of business model disclosure from the Framework, IIRC Business Models Background Paper, a review of twenty business models, and prior studies. The keywords selected give the reader information about each business model component. An overall score for DEP_i is calculated using the formulae in Eqs. (7) and (8). DEP_i is calculated as:

$$DEP_i = \frac{Quality\ score\ based\ on\ scoring\ index\ table}{Maximum\ quality\ score} \tag{7}$$

Maximum quality score is calculated as:

$$Number\ of\ items\ on\ disclosure\ index\ \times\ Maximum\ score \tag{8}$$

The criteria used to assess each component of the business model disclosure is explained below.

Inputs

The keywords and scoring criteria for inputs are available at: financial capital: https://bit.ly/3V2DPtd; human capital: https://bit.ly/3gxDLmw; intellectual capital: https://bit.ly/3Xq2LMS; manufactured capital: https://bit.ly/3GEOaHv; natural capital: https://bit.ly/3i8PE2J; and social and relationship capital: https://bit.ly/3AG6j3Q.

Business activities

Herein, the business model disclosure is examined for the activities, processes, or operations of the company. The business activities are assessed manually to identify the number of industry-specific business activities. The number of industry-specific business activities is inserted into the software under "Number of industry-specific keywords". Industry-specific keywords relating to business activities are identified by words that pertain to a particular industry, which are identified from other companies in the same industry. The keywords and scoring criteria for business activities are available at https://bit.ly/3GFvwPW.

Outputs

In this part of the analysis, the products and services of the company are identified. Next, the outputs are assessed manually to identify if the description of outputs is industry-specific or generic. Industry-specific keywords for outputs are identified by words that pertain to a particular industry, which were identified from other companies in the same industry. The score for industry-specific keywords is selected on the software from 0 to 4, under "Disclosed outputs". The keywords and scoring criteria for outputs are available at https://bit.ly/3U25WYq.

Outcomes on capitals

The outcomes on each of the capitals are assessed manually to identify if the creation, preservation, or erosion of value for each of the six capitals are disclosed. The value creation, preservation, or erosion of value are indicated by an increase, decrease, or neutral in the respective column for each of the six capitals. A yes or no is selected on the software under "Indication of creation". This is applied to each of the six capitals individually. The keywords and scoring criteria for outcomes on capitals are available at https://drive.google.com/file/d/1mLvUrhZcX3T2PqpKd7tdbQscb1_OGCm0/view.

5   Development of Software

A software named BMAT was designed to calculate BMQ_i. BMAT was designed in Microsoft's Visual Studio using C/# programming language. Regular expression libraries were used for text processing. The criteria and calculations described in Sect. 4 were programmed into the software. BMAT analyses the business model disclosure using algorithms based on NLP techniques. Using BMAT allowed textual data from integrated reports to be processed reliably and removed the bias of manually evaluating large amounts of text. BMAT facilitated the search for character strings, texts, and computation of scores for the assessment of BMQ_i. The functionality of the software is discussed next.

The first screen after installation prompts the user to select the company and the year being evaluated from the drop-down boxes. Figure 1 provides the user with the option to paste the information individually in each of the text boxes. The information required is the inputs, namely, financial capital, human capital, intellectual capital, manufactured capital, natural capital and social and relationship capital, business activities, outputs, outcomes on each of the six capitals, and other information. This information, company name, and evaluation year is stored in a text file for the user's future reference. Before proceeding to the next section, a prompt asks the user to confirm that all relevant text has been pasted. If No is selected, the software takes the user back to the screen to paste the text. If yes is selected, the software takes the user to the next screen in Fig. 2.

On the next screen (Fig. 2), the user must indicate the number of industry-specific business activities disclosed in the textbox "Number of industry-specific keywords". The user must then select the number of industry-specific outputs disclosed in the "Disclosed outputs" textbox. Under "outcomes" for each of the six capitals, the user would select yes or no under "Indication of creation" to indicate if the company disclosed the creation, preservation, or erosion of value under outcomes on capitals. Then the user would click on "Estimate", which then takes the user to the next screen (Fig. 3).

The screen (Fig. 3) provides the word count calculations. The software bases all word count calculations using the System.Text.RegularExpressions namespace of the Microsoft's.Net Framework Library (a library that supports the development of programs/software applications). This namespace identifies patterns in text and various operations can be performed by matching the input string to the pattern. This screen calculates the quantity score (RQN_i) (Fig. 3). The software calculates the business model

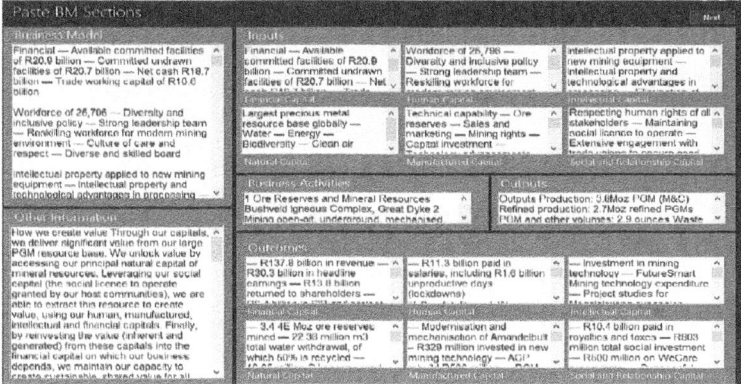

Fig. 1. Screenshot of BMAT - Paste sections

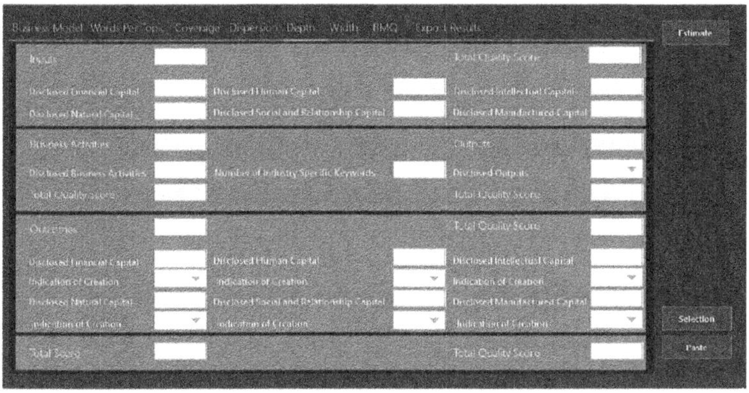

Fig. 2. Screenshot of BMAT – Depth RQN_i

word count using a function called WordCount. A regex pattern that any alphanumeric character that constitutes a word was used, and the count was returned as the business model word count. The software calculated the quantity score by finding the quotient of the business model word count and the highest business model word count in the sample, as described in Sect. 4.1.1.

The screen (Fig. 4) provides the word count for each sub-topic in the business model. A control total is built in, which identifies differences between the sum of the word counts for inputs, outputs, business activities, outcomes on capitals, other information and the total business model word count. This helps to identify whether words were counted twice or not. The software calculates the word count in each sub-topic using the WordCount function. The control total is a sum of the inputs, business activities, outputs, and outcomes. The difference is calculated by finding the difference between the control total and the business model word count calculated under the business model tab.

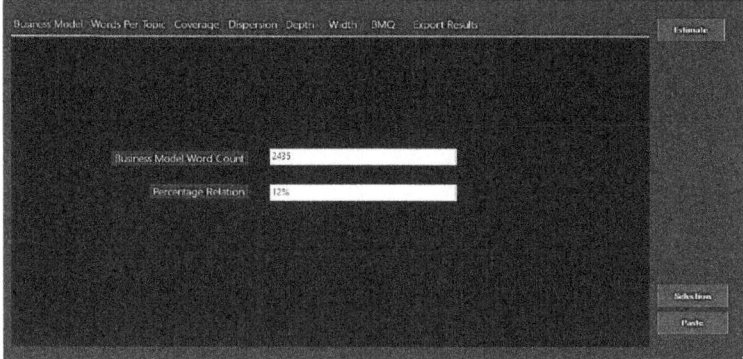

Fig. 3. Screenshot of BMAT - Word count

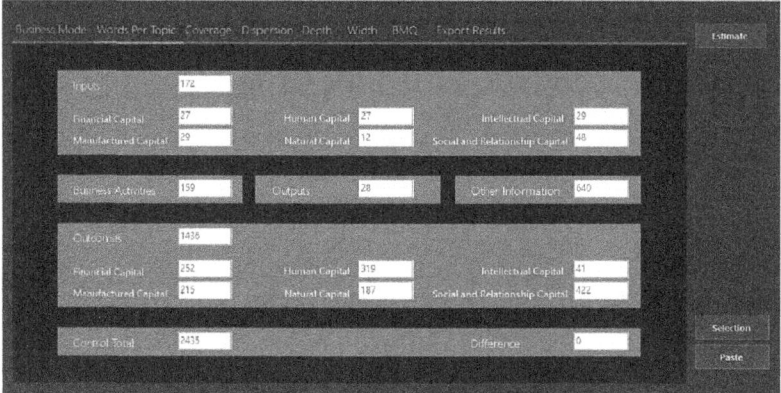

Fig. 4. Screenshot of BMAT - Words per topic DIS_i

The screen (Fig. 5) displays the calculation of dispersion (DIS_i) which has the parameters: words per sub-topic and business model word count. The Dispersion function makes use of the dispersion calculation, described in Sect. 4.1.2.1.2, and returns the result. The function is called for each sub-topic and the relative result is displayed.

The screen (Fig. 6) provides the calculation of coverage (COV_i). The software makes use of the Coverage function which has the parameters textbox and sub-topic word count. An if-statement is used to decide whether the coverage should be "Yes" (provided that the textbox is not null) or "No" (provided that the textbox is null). The coverage function makes use of the coverage calculation described in Sect. 4.1.2.1.1 and return the result. The result is displayed in the relevant textbox.

Figure 7 provides a calculation of width (WID_i) for each component of the business model. The software uses the function called WidthFunc with the parameters: coverage and dispersion. The parameters are then used to calculate the width according to the width formula discussed in Sect. 4.1.2.1 and the result is then returned. The function is called for each component of the business model and displayed.

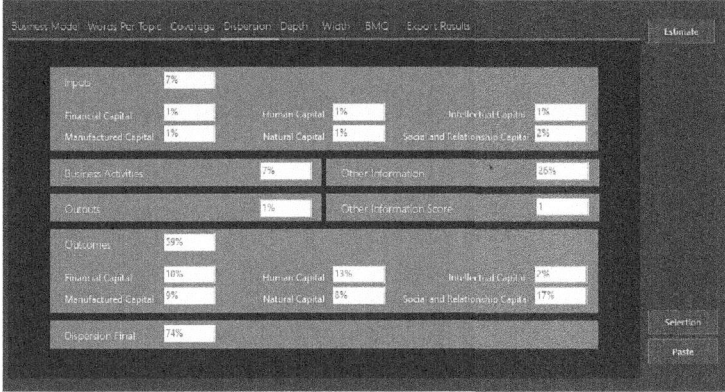

Fig. 5. Screenshot of BMAT - Dispersion

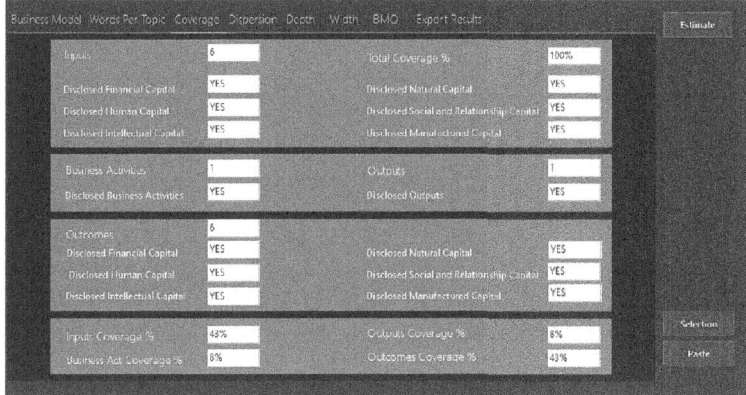

Fig. 6. Screenshot of BMAT - Coverage

The screen (Fig. 8) displays the DEP_i score for inputs, business activities, outputs, and outcomes on each of the six capitals according to the scoring criteria discussed in Sect. 4.1.2.2.

The screen (Fig. 9) provides the scores for all the variables making up the final calculation of BMQ_i. The software uses the total depth result from the depth tab page, the quantity score from the business model tab page and the total width result from the width tab page. The final calculations of BMQ_i are calculated with the formula described in Sect. 4.1. Thereafter the user can select "Export" and the scores will be exported to Excel.

6   Empirical Analysis and Results

The results and interpretation of the overall business model disclosure quality and each dimension of BMQ_i being quantity, coverage, dispersion, and depth are presented below.

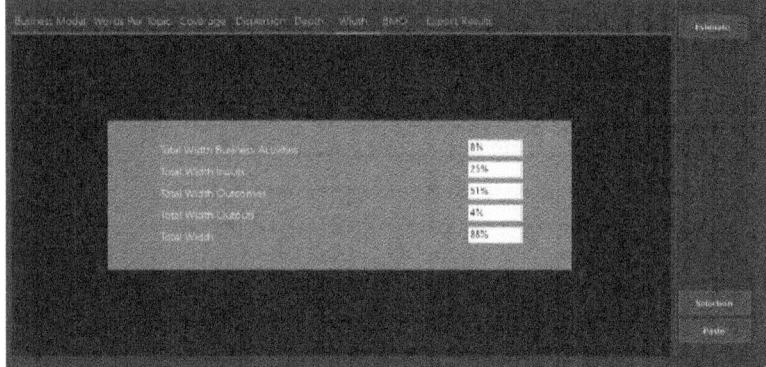

Fig. 7. Screenshot of BMAT - Width

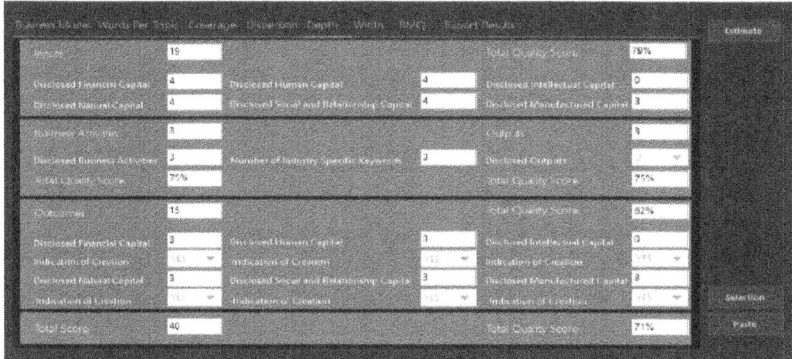

Fig. 8. Screenshot of BMAT - Depth

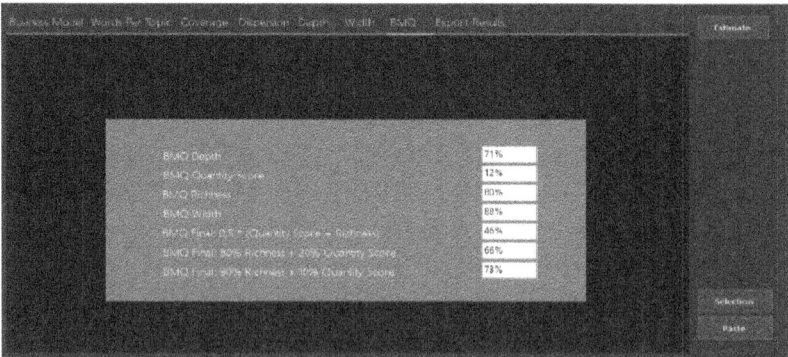

Fig. 9. Screenshot of BMAT - All scores

6.1 Business Model Disclosure Quality

Table 2 provides the descriptive statistics for BMQ_i.

Table 2. Descriptive statistics for BMQ_i

	2016	2017	2018	2019	2020
Number of observations (n)	74	74	74	74	74
Mean	52.9	55.9	59.1	60.3	62.6
Median	54.3	58.6	61.4	62.8	64.8
Standard deviation	15.6	14.1	11.9	12.4	11.5
Minimum	17.9	25.1	24.4	28.9	24.1
Maximum	80.6	80.7	88.9	85.1	89.1

Table 2 indicates that the mean and median for BMQ_i increased by 10% points, indicating an improvement in business model disclosure quality over the five years. However, a mean score increasing from 52 to 62.6 over the sample period suggests room for improvement in business model disclosure that are interpreted under each dimension below. The median exceeds the mean in all five years, indicating that the average is skewed toward higher values. The minimum score is 17.9, and the maximum score is 89.09. The maximum and minimum scores increased, confirming an increase in the quality of business model information over the five years. The standard deviation decreased, indicating that the spread and deviation reduced over time, meaning more consistency was achieved. Companies with higher scores presented well-structured business models in which the components were clearly labelled with adequate information disclosed under each component. The lower scores were due to companies needing to identify the six capitals, resulting in an unstructured business model with scattered information which did not cover all the six capitals. In some cases, companies with lower scores also needed to identify the four components of the business model, making it difficult to differentiate between them and resulting in low scores. In conclusion, business model disclosure quality increased over the five years, and these findings corroborate with Sukhari and de Villiers (2019), Truant et al. (2020) and Bek-Gaik and Surowiec (2022), who also noted an improvement in the quality of business model disclosure.

6.2 Quantity

Table 3 provides the descriptive statistics for RQN_i.

According to Table 3, the mean for RQN_i decreased 4% points, indicating that the quantity of business model disclosure decreased over the five years. The median for RQN_i also decreased from 2016 to 2020 by 1% points. The median fluctuated and the standard deviation decreased over the five years. The decrease is due to how the relative quantity was calculated. The maximum score was 100 and the mean reduced from approximately 12 to 8 over the sample period, indicating that the maximum scores were outliers. The

Table 3. Descriptive statistics for RQN_i

	2016	2017	2018	2019	2020
Number of observations (n)	74	74	74	74	74
Mean	12.2	10.5	11.9	11.1	8.0
Median	5.0	5.7	6.7	6.9	4.2
Standard deviation	20.3	16.1	16.7	16.0	14.1
Minimum	0.9	0.4	1.4	1.8	0.5
Maximum	100	100	100	100	100

mean is lower indicating that the concentration of the scores is even below the lowest average score.

The good low average score for quantity is mainly attributed to how the quantity index was calculated by following previous research (Helfaya and Whittington 2019; Beretta and Bozzolan 2008). The issue is that the index is based on the company with the highest word count. The low average score for quantity reduces and reduces overall, creating a false impression that BMQ_i improvement is needed in the quality of business model disclosure. The low average score further substantiates our decision to reduce the RQN_i from 50% to 20%. Further research is needed to evaluate whether quantity should be a factor to be considered in evaluating the overall quality of disclosures. Alternatively, other means could be designed to calculate the quantity dimension if included in the multi-dimensional disclosure index.

6.3 Coverage

Table 4 provides the descriptive statistics for the coverage of business model disclosure.

Table 4. Descriptive statistics for COV_i

	2016	2017	2018	2019	2020
Number of observations (n)	74	74	74	74	74
Mean	74.1	79.0	86.4	87.2	90.2
Median	85.8	89.3	92.9	92.9	100
Standard deviation	27.3	25.7	18.7	15.6	16.1
Minimum	14.3	7.1	14.3	42.9	14.3
Maximum	100	100	100	100	100

According to Table 4, the mean and median for COV_i increased significantly, indicating that the business model disclosure required by the Framework has improved considerably. The median exceeds the mean in all five years, indicating that the average is skewed toward higher values. The median increased to 100, also being the maximum, confirming that companies are increasingly adhering to the requirements of the Framework. The minimum score of below 15 indicates that some companies require improvement. Companies with low scores should have disclosed all the sub-topics of the business model whereas,companies with higher scores covered most of the sub-topics in their business models.

6.4 Dispersion

Table 5 provides the descriptive statistics for the dispersion of business model disclosure.

Table 5. Descriptive statistics for DIS_i

	2016	2017	2018	2019	2020
Number of observations (n)	74	74	74	74	74
Mean	85.8	85.3	85.8	84.8	87.5
Median	92.5	89.4	89.5	90.3	90.9
Standard deviation	16.4	14.1	13.7	14.9	11.0
Minimum	36.9	42.0	39.0	44.4	41.6
Maximum	100	100	100	100	100

According to Table 5, the mean for DIS_i increased slightly, indicating that dispersion of business model disclosure has generally improved over the five years. The relatively high average score of over 80 indicates that most entities adhere to the Framework's requirements and that companies disclosed each of the various components of the business model, namely inputs on capitals, business activities, outputs, and outcomes on capitals. The mean above 90 confirms excellent dispersion, with some entities scoring the maximum. The standard deviation is relatively low, indicating that most entities are concentrating on the excellent score. The minimum score increased from 36.9 to 41.6, indicating that outlier entities on the lower scale need improvement. Companies with lower scores disclosed some components of the business model.

6.5 Depth

Table 6 provides the descriptive statistics for DEP_i of business model disclosure.

According to Table 6, the mean and median for DEP_i increased by 17%, signalling that the depth of business model disclosure was enhanced over the five years. The median exceeds the mean in all five years, indicating that the average is skewed toward higher values. The mean increasing to a score of 63.6 and the median increasing to 67 indicates that improvements could still be made in the depth of the business model disclosure by most of the companies. While most entities adhere to the requirements of the Framework, dispersion and coverage improvements could still be made in deeper explanation and

Table 6. Descriptive statistics for DEP_i

	2016	2017	2018	2019	2020
Number of observations (n)	74	74	74	74	74
Mean	46.4	52.4	55.7	59.3	63.6
Median	50.0	57.1	57.0	62.0	67.0
Standard deviation	21.2	20.7	17.0	17.4	17.7
Minimum	5.4	5.4	9.0	21.0	11.0
Maximum	89.3	83.9	86.0	86.0	88.0

interpretation of the business model information. The decrease in the standard deviation further indicates that companies are moving closer to the average, which is increasing. The minimum score ranging from 5.4 to 21 identifies inconsistencies and that some companies require greater improvements.

Companies with high scores made good disclosure using appropriate wording from the list of keywords and disclosed quantitative information for each component of their business models. However, further analyses of the results indicate that the disclosure of the inputs to the capitals could improve. Some companies needed to identify the six capitals, which meant that their business models were not structured around the six capitals, resulting in lower scores. In addition, some companies combined human and intellectual capital, making it difficult to differentiate between the two capitals. Combining human and intellectual capitals also impacted the scores for outcomes on the six capitals. Low scores were also attributable to the need for more quantitative information relating to the six capitals.

Overall, the business activities disclosure clearly and concisely depicted the business processes, business operations and operating models, making it easy to identify the core business activities. For example, some companies used diagrams and flow charts to demonstrate their core business functions. Some companies, however, did not articulate their business activities clearly. Regarding outputs, companies with high scores provided their industry-specific products and services, quantitative information on these products and services, and waste products. High scores were attributable to the products and services being easily identifiable and described adequately. Conversely, companies with low scores did not identify their key products and services, and some needed to provide quantitative information about their outputs. Finally, regarding outcomes, companies with higher scores had a separate section dedicated to value creation. They addressed value creation, preservation, and erosion for each of the six capitals together with a quantitative assessment of value creation, preservation, and erosion. Companies with lower scores did not identify the six capitals and could not disclose any indication of creation, preservation, or erosion of value.

6.6   Pearson Correlation Between BMQ_i, RQN_i, $DISi$, $COVi$ and $DEPi$

A strong and significant correlation was identified between BMQ_i and COV_i while DEP_i being the indicator of whether an entity adheres to the requirements of the Framework, provides relevant and valuable information. However, the correlation with DIS_i could be more consistent and has a significantly narrow range. Hence further research is needed regarding the reasons and whether DIS_i is a good measure to assess the quality of disclosure. Lastly, the correlation with RQN_i is below 50%, which is expected based on our previous comments regarding our concern about including the quantity measure. These findings show evidence that BMQ_i is influenced by quality measures and not quantity measures. In addition, the findings corroborate with Beretta and Bozzolan (2008), in which the overall quality of forward-looking information was significantly positively correlated with width.

7   Conclusion

The objective of the paper was to design an innovative tool to assess the different dimensions of business model disclosure. The multi-dimensional disclosure index provides a holistic assessment of the business model disclosure quality. The quantity, dispersion, coverage, and depth were assessed, and a final score was calculated. The multi-dimensional disclosure index also considered other factors such as the absence or presence of specific keywords for each of the components of business models, disclosure of quantitative information, disclosure of industry-specific words, and indicators of value-creation.

The BMAT tool was developed to automate the application of the multidimensional disclosure index. BMAT uses algorithms based on NLP techniques to expedite the content analysis of business model disclosure. In addition, the use of the BMAT resulted in consistency in applying the multi-dimensional disclosure index. The results from BMAT showed an improvement in the quality of business model disclosure over the five years, with a marked increase in the quality of disclosure in all business model components. The results showed that most companies adhere to the requirements of the Framework but that aspects of the depth of business model disclosure could be improved regarding the inputs, outcomes and outputs, and the related link to each capital. Companies with high depth scores made disclosure using specific keywords, quantitative information for each capital, industry-specific products and services, and indicators of value-creation, preservation, or erosion. The high score but lower correlation of DIS_i to the BMQ_i raises some issues regarding the use of dispersion of the business model information to assess the quality of business model information, which could be researched further. The low score for RQN_i and lower correlation with BMQ_i questions the use of quantity as a measure of quality. These findings support the results of prior work of Bek-Gaik and Surowiec (2022), Sukhari and de Villiers (2019) and Truant et al. (2020). In addition, these findings were consistent with Beretta and Bozzolan (2008) findings.

This paper has a few limitations. Firstly, the sample was limited to 370 integrated reports of 74 South African listed companies over five years. Secondly, South Africa has a mandatory integrated reporting requirement and results may differ in other countries. Thirdly, BMAT was specifically designed for the intended purpose and, therefore, cannot be applied to other reporting aspects but would need to be modified to include different aspects of integrated reporting.

The increase in non-financial disclosure provides opportunities for future research. First, the method to assess business model disclosure could be improved; for example, machine learning techniques could be incorporated into BMAT to enhance its functionality further. Also, the multi-dimensional disclosure index could be augmented; for example, the list of keywords used to assess the components of the business model could be refined, and additional measures could be added, such as the link from business model disclosure to key performance indicators, risks, and strategy. Furthermore, more complex measures of semantic units, such as phrases, sentences, and the tone of business model disclosure, could be assessed. In addition, new measures of value-creation, preservation, and erosion could be designed. Finally, the research could explore the possibility of using artificial intelligence to design an information architecture that would gather, assimilate, and report information on business models to ensure that reporting encompasses all relevant information.

References

Abed, S., Al-Najjar, B., Roberts, C.: Measuring annual report narratives disclosure: Empirical evidence from forward-looking information in the UK prior the financial crisis. Manag. Audit. J. **31**(4–5), 338–361 (2016)

Beattie, V., McInnes, B., Fearnley, S.: A methodology for analysing and evaluating narratives in annual reports: A comprehensive descriptive profile and metrics for disclosure quality attributes. Account. Forum **28**(3), 205–236 (2004)

Bek-Gaik, B., Surowiec, A.: The quality of business model disclosure in integrated reporting: Evidence from Poland. Eur. Res. Stud. J. **XXV**(1), 3–26 (2022)

Beretta, S., Bozzolan, S.: Quality versus quantity: The case of forward-looking disclosure. J. Account. Audit. Finance **23**(3), 333–375 (2008)

Chowdhary, K.R.: Fundamentals of Artificial Intelligence. Springer, New Delhi (2020). https://doi.org/10.1007/978-81-322-3972-7

de Villiers, C., Rinaldi, L., Unerman, J.: Integrated reporting: Insights, gaps and an agenda for future research. Account. Audit. Account. J. **27**(7), 1042–1067 (2014)

de Villiers, C., Venter, E., Hsiao, P.: Integrated reporting: Background, measurement issues, approaches and an agenda for future research. Account. Finance **57**(4), 937–959 (2017)

Dumay, J., de Villiers, C.: Qualitative accounting research: Special issue introduction. Account. Finance **59**(3), 1447–1890 (2019)

Dyer, T., Lang, M., Stice-Lawrence, L.: The evolution of 10-K textual disclosure: evidence from Latent Dirichlet Allocation. J. Account. Econ. **64**(2–3), 221–245 (2017)

El-Haj, M., Rayson, P., Walker, M., Young, S., Simaki, V.: In search of meaning: lessons, resources and next steps for computational analysis of financial discourse. J. Bus. Finance Account. **46**(3–4), 265–306 (2019)

El-Haj, M., Alves, P., Rayson, P., Walker, M., Young, S.: Retrieving, classifying and analysing narrative commentary in unstructured (glossy) annual reports published as PDF files. Account. Bus. Res. **50**(1), 6–34 (2020)

Helfaya, A., Whittington, M.: Does designing environmental sustainability disclosure quality measures make a difference? Bus. Strategy Environ. **28**(4), 525–541 (2019)

Hussainey, K.: A study of the ability of (partially) automated disclosure scores to explain the information content of annual report narratives for future earnings. PhD (Social Science and Law) Thesis. University of Manchester, Manchester (2004)

IIRC: International Integrated Reporting Framework. International Integrated Reporting Council, London, UK (2013a)

IIRC: Business Model Background Paper for Integrated Reporting. International Integrated Reporting Council, London, UK (2013b)

IIRC: Value Creation Background Paper for Integrated Reporting. International Integrated Reporting Council, London, UK (2013c)

IIRC: The International Integrated Reporting Framework. International Integrated Reporting Council, London, UK (2021)

Kao, A., Poteet, S.R.: Natural Language Processing and Text Mining. Springer, London (2007). https://doi.org/10.1007/978-1-84628-754-1

Köseoğlu, S.D.: Financial Data Analytics. Contributions to Finance and Accounting. Springer, Cham (2022). https://doi.org/10.1007/978-3-030-83799-0

Krippendorff, K.: Content Analysis: An Introduction to Its Methodology, 2nd edn. Sage Publications, Thousand Oaks (2004)

Lewis, C., Young, S.: Fad or future? Automated analysis of financial text and its implications for corporate reporting. Account. Bus. Res. **49**(5), 587–615 (2019)

Miura, T., Furukawa, T., Harada, J., Hirano, Y., Hashimoto, T.: Evaluation of universities' integrated reports using text mining technique. In: 2021 IEEE International Conference on Service Operations and Logistics, and Informatics, SOLI 2021, pp. 1–6. IEEE (2021)

Nakagawa, K., Sashida, S., Kitajima, R., Sakai, H.: What do good integrated reports tell us?: An empirical study of Japanese companies using text-mining. In: Proceedings - 2020 9th International Congress on Advanced Applied Informatics, IIAI-AAI 2020, pp. 516–521 (2020)

Stemler, S.: An overview of content analysis. Pract. Assess. Res. Eval. **7**(17) (2001)

Sukhari, A., de Villiers, C.: The influence of integrated reporting on business model and strategy disclosures. Aust. Account. Rev. **29**(4), 708–725 (2019)

Truant, E., Culasso, F., Argento, D.: Disclosing strategies and business models in the integrated report. Symphonya Emerg. Issues Manag. **1**, 108–128 (2020)

Türegün, N.: Text mining in financial information. Curr. Anal. Econ. Finance **1**(647), 18–26 (2019)

Weber, R.P.: Basic Content Analysis, 2nd edn. Sage Publications, Thousand Oaks (1990)

Machine Learning and NLP Approach to Predict Hospitalization Upon Adverse Drug Reaction Symptoms of Covid-19 Vaccine Administration

Anubhav Tiwari[1,2], Bharath Kumar Bolla[3(✉)], and Sridevi Bonthu[4]

[1] Upgrad Education Pvt Ltd, Mumbai, India
[2] Liverpool John Moores University, London, UK
[3] Salesforce, Hyderabad, India
`bolla111@gmail.com`
[4] Vishnu Institute of Technology, Bhimavaram, India

Abstract. The COVID-19 pandemic has persisted for over one year and nine months. Identifying vaccines with higher-than-average rates of adverse reactions (ADRs) is crucial to take appropriate measures. This paper proposes leveraging machine learning and artificial intelligence advancements to develop a computer-based decision system to provide a more proactive approach to identifying and treating vaccine-associated ADRs, potentially mitigating hospital overcrowding during critical periods. To this end, we aim to create a predictive model that can identify the requirement for hospitalization by examining symptom notes of individuals who suffered from adverse reactions after receiving the COVID-19 vaccine. Our findings demonstrate that character and word embedding techniques offer superior results to domain-based embeddings (BioBERT) and SentenceBert. Implementing this model in hospitals could expedite decision-making for Covid-19 vaccine adverse reactions, potentially mitigating hospital overcrowding during critical period.

Keywords: Covid-19 · Vaccine · Adverse Reactions · VAERS · Covid-19 vaccine · BioBert · SentenceBert

1 Introduction

The COVID-19 pandemic emerged in November 2019 and has persisted for over one year and nine months. By April 2021, approximately 140 million individuals worldwide had contracted the virus, and its mortality rate had reached 3 million. Despite extensive scientific efforts to develop a cure, a concrete course of treatment has not yet been established. Many countries have implemented stringent lockdown measures to prevent the highly contagious respiratory disease from spreading. The pandemic has resulted in incalculable losses, including significant human casualties and widespread economic instability. This situation makes us reconsider our claims of possessing a highly sophisticated and advanced research mechanism.

H. K. et al. (Eds.): AIKP 2023, CCIS 2127, pp. 344–358, 2024.
https://doi.org/10.1007/978-3-031-68617-7_25

Upon perusing the annals of history, it becomes apparent that the current pandemic is not a unique occurrence in human history. Throughout history, humanity has faced numerous pandemics, such as the Spanish Flu (1918–1920), which resulted in approximately 100 million deaths; the Asian Flu (1957–1958), which caused roughly 1.1 million deaths; and the Swine Flu (2009–2010), which generated approximately 575,400 deaths [1]. In response to these pandemics, humanity has continuously strived to develop drugs and vaccines with immediate effects to combat the viruses and for future generations to mitigate the effects of such viruses [2]. However, it is essential to note that every drug or vaccine has side effects.

The administration of drugs and vaccines is intended to enhance the immune system and prevent the occurrence of illness. However, there have been instances where they have caused adverse effects [3]. While most of these are mild to moderate, a small percentage of individuals may experience severe reactions, and some may even be fatal [4]. In the case of smallpox vaccines, mild to moderate side effects included rashes, swollen lymph nodes, and fever [5]. At the same time, severe reactions ranged from eye infections, rashes covering the entire body, encephalitis, severe infections, and death. The development of adverse drug reactions (ADRs) following immunization can vary from sudden onset to several days. Identifying vaccines with higher-than-average rates of ADRs is crucial to take appropriate measures. The US FDA reports that 6.7% of patients experience severe ADRs, with a fatality rate of 0.32% [6]. During the COVID-19 pandemic, the primary focus was to develop vaccines quickly. While several vaccines have been developed and are currently in use, none have efficacy rates greater than 85%, and the World Health Organization has not recognized some. This situation underscores the need for studies on the ADRs associated with these vaccines [7].

Earlier identification of ADR severity following vaccination is a significant challenge. People who exhibit ADRs require immediate attention, and critical cases necessitate hospitalization. Hospitals struggled with bed shortages during the pandemic, and healthcare workers are under enormous pressure. On top of that, due to the ongoing vaccination campaign, more and more vaccinated individuals reported adverse symptoms, further straining the healthcare system. Therefore, there is a need to develop a system that can predict the severity of ADRs.

To this end, we propose leveraging machine learning and artificial intelligence advancements to develop a computer-based decision system. This system will analyze the regular symptom text of patients and predict if the adverse reactions require priority treatment and hospitalization. The Vaccine Adverse Event Reporting System (VAERS), established in 1990 by the FDA and CDC, collects reports of vaccine-related adverse events [8]. However, VAERS is a self-reporting system; only a small fraction of adverse events may be reported. Our proposed system aims to provide a more proactive approach to identifying and treating vaccine-associated ADRs.

This research aims to create a predictive model that can identify the requirement for hospitalization by examining symptom notes of individuals who suffered from adverse reactions after receiving the COVID-19 vaccine. The research objectives are as follows:

- To build a machine learning model that can predict hospitalization based on demographic features of vaccine-administered patients

- To evaluate classification models that can accurately predict the need for hospitalization by utilizing the data from VAERS.
- To determine the ideal combination of term embeddings of VAERS and demographic data to build a hybrid model to predict hospitalization due to vaccine ADRs

2 Literature Review

The literature review delves into several sections, exploring the utilization of natural language processing in electronic health records and clinical notes to address diverse scenarios.

2.1 Application of NLP on Electronic Health Records

Computing technology has played a pivotal role in facilitating clinical decision-making, with its inception traced back to 1987 when the concept of clinical decision support was introduced. This concept aimed to aid healthcare professionals in making clinical decisions by utilizing medical data about patients and the necessary medical knowledge to interpret such data [9]. The evolution of research during the 1990s brought about the emergence of a specialized field within Data Science known as Natural Language Processing (NLP). NLP involves teaching computers to comprehend human language statements or phrases. The focal point of NLP lies in understanding the intricate interactions between computers and human languages [10].

The work presented by Afzal et al. [11] developed a technique to detect critical limb ischemia (CLI) using natural language processing (NLP) on clinical notes of a community-based peripheral arterial disease (PAD). The NLP algorithm achieved high accuracy, making it a promising tool for patient care and clinical decision support systems. The automated CLI-NLP system for identifying CLI instances from clinical notes is expected to improve research and patient care quality for CLI. NLP has significantly expanded electronic health record (EHR) usage by facilitating symptom science and discovering new disease symptoms. NLP has been extensively used for extracting symptom information from free-text narratives in EHRs, as reviewed by Koleck et al. [12], which studied twenty-seven papers published between 1997 and 2017. Furthermore, symptom science has been employed for disease classification tasks to benefit medical science.

2.2 Text Embeddings for Semantic Analysis

The use of word embeddings has become increasingly popular in natural language processing (NLP) tasks, with Word2Vec [13] being a widely adopted shallow neural network technique for learning these embeddings. The Continuous Bag of Words and Skip-gram approaches are the two proposed models for Word2Vec, with the former predicting the current word based on the context and the latter predicting the context based on the current word. GloVe [14] learns word embeddings from a co-occurrence matrix and uses vector embeddings to match predicted and global co-occurrence statistics in the training corpus, unlike Word2Vec. ELMo [15] is a contextualized embedding at the word and character level that considers the complete phrase when assigning an embedding to each word using a bi-directional RNN trained on a specific task. FastText [16], an extension of Word2Vec, is another robust and fast framework that treats each word as a Bag of Character n-gram, allowing for the consideration of the morphological structure of words. Fasttext has shown to outperform Word2Vec in many scenarios [17].

Doc2Vec [18], an extension of Word2Vec, is used to build a numeric representation of a document by incorporating another vector (paragraph) because records do not come in logical structures like words. BioSentVec [19] is a medical domain-specific embedding algorithm that incorporated the sentence embedding technique and was shown to capture sentence semantics better than other alternatives. A study comparing word embeddings derived from various corpora found that embeddings inferred from clinical notes and biomedical research papers mimic medical keywords better [20]. Additionally, character embeddings and Elmo embeddings can be combined to tackle the problem of missing embeddings for OOV words, misspelled words, and varied noun and verb forms [21].

Finally, the training of word embeddings poses challenges such as the training data's size and domain, the embedding model's characteristics, and the resulting model's quality, which must be considered.

2.3 Transformer Models

Pretrained language models (PLMs) based on transformers have revolutionized natural language processing by combining the power of transformers, transfer learning, and self-supervised learning. This paper focuses on a groundbreaking study by Devlin et al. [22] from Google AI Language that introduces BERT (Bidirectional Encoder Representations from Transformers), which has generated significant interest in the machine learning community for its cutting-edge results in various NLP tasks. The key technical breakthrough of BERT is using bidirectional training of the Transformer model for language modeling, which enables a better understanding of language context and flow compared to previous models that relied on left-to-right or a combination of left-to-right and right-to-left training. BERT's innovative MLM methodology enables bidirectional training in previously untrainable models by masking input tokens and training the model to predict the masked tokens. BERT has paved the way for several in-domain PLMs in the biomedical research community, including BioBERT [23], Clinical BERT [24], BioMegatron [25], and CodeBERT [26], which are optimized for specific biomedical text mining applications. In the study conducted by Alsentzer et al., Clinical BERT [24] was trained using clinical text from the MIMIC-III database, which contains approximately two million notes. The study describes different variations of Clinical BERT, including Clinical BERT, which uses all note types and starts with BERT-Base, and Clinical BioBERT, which incorporates text from all note formats and is based on BioBERT. Additionally, the study discusses Discharge Summary BERT, which is based on BERT-Base and uses only discharge summaries, and Discharge Summary BioBERT, which is based on BioBERT and uses only discharge summaries. A study by Symeonidou et al. (2019) demonstrates that transfer learning based on BioBERT can significantly outperform existing ADR recognition methods, while Huang et al. (2019) show that ClinicalBERT outperforms Bag of Words, Bi-LSTM, and BERT in predicting patient readmission using discharge summaries.

3   Research Methodology

3.1   Dataset

The dataset is taken from VAERS (Table 1). This data is given voluntarily by the family members of the patients [8]. Some fields are well structured and can be directly used to train the models, and some are unstructured (e.g., symptom_text, which is the symptom notes provided by the patient). The adopted dataset is divided into structured and unstructured parts to complete the experiment. Out of 37,000 records, hospitalization is labeled for only 4000 (10%), indicating data imbalance, which was resolved by using SMOTE algorithm [27]. SMOTE works by selecting instances in the feature space that are close together, drawing a line in the feature space between the examples, and drawing a new sample at a location along that line.

Table 1. Dataset and features description

Header	Description of Contents
VAERS_ID	Sequential Unique ID
RECVDATE	This is the VAERS that received the information/form
STATE	Two Letters from the US Postal Service State Code where the vaccine was given
AGE_YRS	The age of the vaccine recipient in years
CAGE_YR	Calculated age of vaccine recipient in years [date of vaccine – date of birth]
CAGE_MO	Calculated age of vaccine recipient in months
SEX	Sex (M - Male, F - Female, Unknown - Blank)
RPT_DATE	The reporter's date of completion of the form
SYMPTOM_TEXT	Reported symptom text – This is the symptom notes or the text reported by the patient
DIED	A "Y" is used if the vaccine recipient died; otherwise, the field is left blank
DATEDIED	Date of Death
L_THREAT	Life-Threatening Illness - A "Y" is put if the vaccine patient experienced a life-threatening incident as a result of the vaccination
ER_VISIT	Emergency Room or Doctor Visit – If emergency room or doctor visit was needed a 'Y' is put
HOSPITAL	Hospitalized - A "Y" is used if the vaccine recipient was hospitalised as a result of the injection

(*continued*)

Table 1. (*continued*)

Header	Description of Contents
HOSPDAYS	Number of days Hospitalized - If the vaccine recipient was hospitalised, a space is given in this field for the number of days the vaccine recipient was hospitalised
X_STAY	Prolongation of Existing Hospitalization - A "Y" would be put in this area if a patient's hospitalisation is extended as a result of an adverse event related to the vaccine
DISABLE	Disability - A "Y" is put in this field if the vaccine recipient was disabled as a result of the vaccination
RECOVD	Recovered - If the vaccine recipient healed from the adverse incident, a "Y" is entered in the field. The vaccinee has not recovered from the adverse incident, as shown by the letter "N." The state of the vaccine recipient's recovery is indicated by the letter "U" or "blank."
VAX_DATE	Vaccination Date - The date of vaccination, as entered in the form's designated area
ONSET_DATE	Adverse Event Onset Date - The date on which adverse event symptoms associated with the vaccine first appeared, as reported in the form's stated area
NUMDAYS	Number of days (Onset date - Vax. Date) - The calculated time between the vaccine date and the onset date (in days)
LAB_DATA	Diagnostic laboratory data - This text field includes a narrative of any specific medical tests or laboratory findings that were entered in the form's designated field
V_ADMINBY	Type of facility where vaccine was administered -The type of facility delivering the vaccine may be noted on the VAERS form by the reporter. Depending on the form version, the choices are different. The abbreviations stand for: PUB – Public; PVT – Private; MIL – Military; PHM – Pharmacy or store, SCH – School or Student health Clinic; SEN – Nursing home or senior living facility; WRK – Workplace clinic; OTH – Other; UNK - Unknown
V_FUNDBY	Type of funds used to purchase vaccines - In Box 16 of the VAERS form, the reporter should indicate the type of funds used to purchase the vaccines administered in Box 13. The abbreviations stand for: PUB – Public; PVT – Private; MIL – Military; OTH – Other/Unknown
OTHER_MEDS	Other Medications - This text field provides a narrative of any prescription or non-prescription drugs taken by the vaccine recipient at the time of vaccination, as reported in the form's stated field

(*continued*)

Table 1. (*continued*)

Header	Description of Contents
CUR_ILL	Illnesses at time of vaccination - This text field includes a narrative of any diseases that were present at the time of vaccination, as stated on the form's designated field
HISTORY	Chronic or long-standing health conditions - This text field provides a narrative of any pre-existing physician-diagnosed birth defects or medical conditions that occurred at the time of vaccination, as stated on the form's designated field; it also includes pre-existing physician-diagnosed allergies
PRIOR_VAX	Prior Vaccination Event information - This field contains details about previous vaccine events that was registered in the form's listed field
SPLTTYPE	Manufacturer/Immunization Project Report
TODAYS_DATE	Date Form Completed
BIRTH_DEFECT	Congenital anomaly or birth defect - A "Y" is used if the vaccine recipient has a congenital disorder or birth defect as a result of the vaccination; otherwise, the area is left unmarked
OFC_VISIT	Doctor or other healthcare provider office/clinic visit - A "Y" is used if the vaccine patient had an office/clinic appointment with a doctor or other healthcare provider involved with the vaccination
ER_ED_VISIT	Emergency room/department or urgent care - A "Y" is used if the vaccine patient has an emergency room/department or urgent care visit as a result of the vaccination
ALLERGIES	Allergies to medications - This text field includes information regarding any pre-existing physician-diagnosed allergies that were present at the time of vaccination and were reported in the form's designated field

3.2 Data Cleaning

The structured data contains all the fields except symptom_text. All the other text columns (other_meds, cur_ill, history, allergies) are normalized to simple Yes or No based on their responses. Various pre-processing techniques applied to text are lower casing, removing punctuation characters, tokenization, stop-word removal, stemming, and lemmatization. Later, the symptom_text is transformed into embedding vectors.

3.3 Data Transformation

The unstructured data, Symptom_text, must be converted into vectors for modeling. This work employed four embedding strategies viz., Word2Vec, FastText, SBERT, and BioBERT.

The Word2Vec algorithm generates a dense, high-dimensional vector for each unique word in the corpus, ensuring high similarity between the word and a similar context [13]. FastText embeddings are an improvement over the Word2Vec technique [16]. It assigns a vector to every word by ignoring the morphology of words. SBERT is a pre-trained model that employs Siamese and triple network architectures to generate sentence embeddings that are semantically relevant [28]. These embeddings can be compared by using cosine similarity. BioBERT is a pre-trained BERT trained on the biomedical text [23]. The embeddings created by this model can be employed in applications like medical Named Entity Recognition (NER), relation extraction, etc.

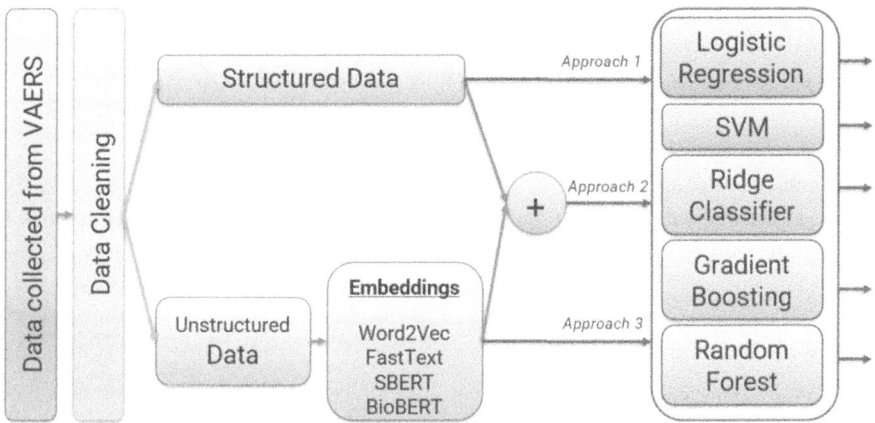

Fig. 1. Experimental design for the three modeling approaches.

3.4 Modelling Approaches

We trained five different classification algorithms, viz., Logistic Regression, Support Vector Machines (SVM), Ridge Classifier, Gradient Boosting, and Random Forest, by following three different approaches, as shown in Fig. 1.

Approach 1: In this approach, the classification algorithms are trained using only structured data. Age, gender, number of days, other medications, history, allergies, and current illness are considered structured data columns (Fig. 2).

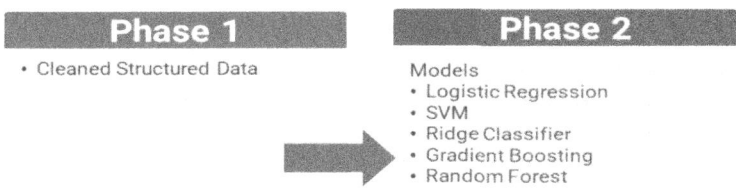

Fig. 2. Approach 1-Classification models on Structured Input

Approach 2: In this approach, only unstructured data (symptom_text) is used to train the models. The symptom_text is vectorized with the help of 4 embedding techniques

(Word2Vec, FastText, SBERT, and BioBERT). All five models are trained with all the adopted embedding techniques (Fig. 3).

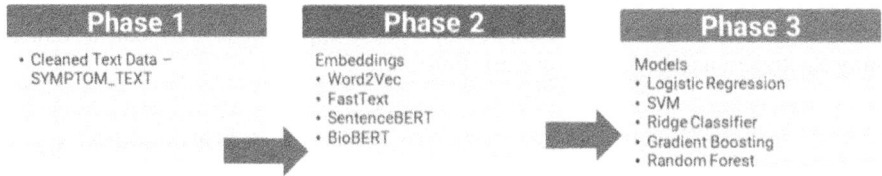

Fig. 3. Approach -Classification models on embeddings of SYMPTOM_TEXT

Approach 3: This approach utilizes the multimodel aspect of the data. To train the models, structured data and unstructured data embeddings are combined. This approach trains five models for every embedding technique (Fig. 4).

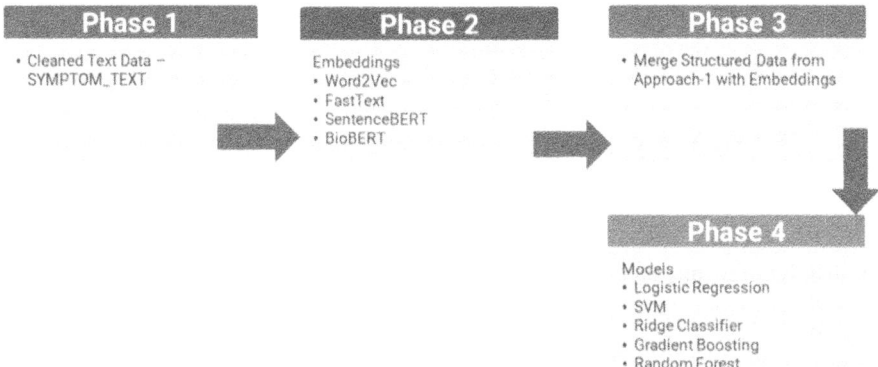

Fig. 4. Approach 3-Classification models on embeddings of SYMPTOM_TEXT and structured Data

3.5 Data Split

All the models in all the approaches are trained with a uniform data split. 70% of the data is utilized as training data, and the remaining 30% is used as test data.

3.6 Evaluation Metrics

Evaluation Metrics Evaluation metrics are used to interpret the reliability and consistency of the algorithms. We used Precision, Recall, Accuracy F1-Score, and ROC-AUC for evaluating the model performance in all three approaches.

4 Results

The central aim of this investigation revolves around predicting hospitalization necessity for individuals exhibiting adversarial symptoms. An erroneous non-hospitalization prediction for a person requiring medical care could have severe consequences. Consequently, the minimization of False Negatives is imperative from a programmatic perspective. Recall is the primary evaluation metric of utmost significance in light of this concern.

Additionally, a pivotal consideration is to ensure that the model does not exhibit redundancy, implying that it does not incorrectly classify a substantial portion of non-hospitalized instances as requiring hospitalization. This could hinder the model's practical deployment and undermine its effectiveness in efficiently allocating beds for critical cases. Thus, the imperative is minimizing False Positives, a notion that Precision encapsulates. To strike a balance between the competing demands of Recall and Precision, the F1-score, serving as a harmonic amalgamation of Recall and Precision, emerges as the secondary evaluation criterion of paramount importance.

4.1 Approach-1: Classification Models on Structured Data

Results for approach-1, where we use only vaccine recipient demographic and medical history data to predict the hospitalization, are depicted in Table 2. The Random Forest Classifier and Gradient Boosting Classifier outperform other models in accuracy, with 85.52% and 84.26%, respectively. However, the Gradient Boosting Classifier has a higher AUC score of 79.87% and an F1 score, indicating better overall performance in classification. All the linear models, Logistic Regression, Ridge Regression, and SVMs, seem to optimize Recall, whereas nonlinear model Random Forest and Gradient Boosting optimize towards Precision. However, gradient boosting is the best model owing to its superior performance on the F1 score.

Table 2. Approach-1 Results

Model	Accuracy %	AUC%	Recall%	Prec.%	F1%
Logistic Regression	71.31	76.06	68.28	21.84	33.08
SVM - Linear Kernel	71.01	0	68.28	21.69	32.89
Ridge Classifier	71.68	0	67.77	22	33.21
Gradient Boosting Classifier	84.26	79.87	58.14	34.69	43.43
Random Forest Classifier	85.52	72.41	35.81	32.33	33.97

4.2 Approach-2: Identifying Hospitalization Based on Symptom Text

For approach 2, embeddings were generated from the SYMPTOM_TEXT column using four distinct techniques: Word2Vec Embeddings, FastText Embeddings, Sentence BERT

Embeddings, and BioBERT Embeddings. Twenty models were created for this approach, resulting from combining five models and four embedding methods. The findings presented in Table 3 are organized based on recall percentages for each embedding technique. FastText embedding emerged as the most effective, closely followed by Word2Vec. Notably, the FastText-SVM combination exhibited the highest recall rate at 87.14%. Among the top ten performing models, there were four instances of Fast-Text, four of Word2Vec, and two of BioBERT.of FastText and Random Forest Classifier has the highest F1 score of 72%. FastText embeddings consistently show higher recall and F1 scores than other embeddings, indicating their better performance in correctly identifying positive cases and achieving a balance between precision and recall. Among the machine learning models, the Random Forest classifier consistently performs better regarding both recall and F1 score across various embeddings. FastText embeddings combined with the Random Forest classifier emerge as the most effective combination for achieving high recall and F1 scores.

Table 3. Approach-2 Results

Embeddings	Model	Accuracy %	AUC%	Recall%	Prec.%	F1%
Word2Vec	SVM	88.11	NA	86.92	46.31	60.5
	Ridge Classifier	88.24	NA	86.62	46.51	60.5
	Logistic Regression	89.79	94.76	86.58	50.53	63.8
	Gradient Boosting	90.58	94.95	84.13	52.99	65
	Random Forest	94.25	95.26	70.81	73.03	71.9
FastText	SVM	88.08	NA	**87.14**	46.23	60.41
	Logistic Regression	89.7	94.89	86.96	50.24	63.7
	Ridge Classifier	88.29	NA	86.52	46.59	60.6
	Gradient Boosting	90.89	95	84.5	53.94	65.8
	Random Forest	**94.37**	**95.44**	69.65	**74.48**	**72**
Sentence BERT	Ridge Classifier	79.97	NA	82.18	31.98	46.04
	Logistic Regression	81.75	88.97	80.27	33.99	47.75
	SVM	81.87	NA	80.2	34.24	47.93
	Gradient Boosting	84.02	89.2	76.96	37.05	50.01
	Random Forest	90.84	89.98	53.57	56.25	54.83
BioBERT	Ridge Classifier	83.24	NA	83.03	36.57	50.75
	SVM	84.18	NA	82.08	38.24	52.06
	Logistic Regression	84.69	91.22	81.94	38.82	52.67
	Gradient Boosting	86.05	90.79	79.04	41.14	54.1
	Random Forest	92.33	91.35	56.27	65.2	60.36

4.3 Approach-3: Classification Using Symptom Text and Patient Demographic Data

The embeddings derived from the SYMPTOM_TEXT column were combined with the eight structured data features. This approach resulted in 20 models—5 models multiplied by four embeddings. Table 4 presents the metrics for the combination of embeddings and model. The combination of FastText and SVM achieved the highest recall at 88.05%. Four FastText models and four Word2Vec models made it to the top ten, along with two models of BioBERT.

Table 4. Approach-3 Results

Embeddings	Model	Accuracy %	AUC %	Recall %	Prec %	F1%
Word2Vec	Logistic Regression	91.12	95.57	86.92	54.6	67.05
	SVM	89.46	NA	86.28	53.58	64.48
	Ridge Classifier	89.34	NA	86.38	49.30	62.75
	Gradient Boosting	92.50	95.67	82.62	60.18	69.61
	Random Forest Classifier	**94.31**	95.46	70.06	**73.93**	71.90
FastText	SVM - Linear Kernel	88.87	NA	**88.05**	49.31	62.73
	Logistic Regression	90.50	95.67	86.99	52.61	65.56
	Ridge Classifier	89.52	NA	85.76	49.77	62.97
	Gradient Boosting Classifier	92.04	95.77	83.31	58.21	68.50
	Random Forest Classifier	94.26	**95.82**	73.13	72.09	**72.59**
Sentence BERT	Ridge Classifier	81.97	NA	81.97	34.55	48.6
	SVM	82.43	NA	81.05	35.15	48.99
	Logistic Regression	83.09	90.16	80.44	36	49.73
	Gradient Boosting	84.74	89.68	76.99	38.34	51.18
	Random Forest Classifier	89.97	88.82	53.74	58.71	56.07
BioBERT	Ridge Classifier	83.8	NA	83.1	37.42	51.59
	Logistic Regression	85.2	91.75	82.52	39.8	53.68
	SVM	84.63	NA	82.52	38.99	52.88
	Gradient Boosting	86.23	90.81	77.26	41.33	53.84
	Random Forest Classifier	92.38	91.64	55.34	65.88	60.11

Comparing the results of approaches 2 and 3, it is evident that FastText embeddings yielded approximately 5% higher average recall values than BioBERT. This observation aligns with the nature of the data. The report system (VAERS) allows non-medical individuals to submit data in simple English rather than using medical terminology. Consequently, FastText and Word2Vec techniques outperformed Sentence BERT and BioBERT pre-trained embeddings, focusing on easy-to-understand language. The better performance by FastText and Word2Vec over transformer modelks is also observed on sarcasm detection in headlines [29]. Approach 3 displayed the most favorable results by combining embeddings and structured data. While the improvement in evaluation parameters was not hugely different, the consistency of the outcomes was noteworthy.

5 Conclusion

The study's findings demonstrate the effectiveness of non-medical individuals' data in predicting hospitalization post-COVID-19 vaccine administration. The outcomes highlight that character and word embedding techniques offer superior results to domain-based embeddings (BioBERT) and SentenceBert. The optimal model, "FastText-Random Forest," was selected for its reasonable recall, precision, and satisfactory F1 score. Additionally, the research underscores that incorporating additional features like age, gender, and medical conditions marginally enhances prediction rates. Implementing this model in hospitals could expedite decision-making for Covid-19 vaccine adverse reactions, potentially mitigating hospital overcrowding during critical periods.

Further enhancements can be made to the study by integrating cutting-edge machine learning and natural language processing techniques, such as "data augmentation," to generate new text from existing data, addressing the data quality limitation. Future research avenues include exploring more complex deep learning models for improved performance.

6 Limitations and Future Recommendations

We encountered numerous challenges and surmounted them to attain the research's ultimate findings. The constrained availability of system memory or RAM resources emerged as a significant hurdle, particularly when managing extensive embedding datasets featuring extended vector lengths: this predicament, a common limitation across projects employing similar techniques, significantly constrained progress. Beyond technical limits, the research also encountered the issue of insufficient high-quality data for effectively training and evaluating the models. To enhance research outcomes, we posit that augmenting data by introducing fresh text or leveraging alternative ML and NLP methodologies for text generation from existing data may hold promise.

Further enhancement of the study conducted as part of this research could involve integrating cutting-edge machine learning and natural language processing techniques, including 'Data Augmentation,' to produce new text from pre-existing data. Such an approach could potentially address one of the research's vulnerabilities: the deficiency of high-quality data. Another avenue for future exploration is adopting advanced deep learning models such as Long Short-Term Memory (LSTM) networks and Transformer models.

References

1. A Brief History of Vaccination. https://www.who.int/news-room/spotlight/history-of-vaccin ation/a-brief-history-of-vaccination. Accessed 24 June 2023
2. Greenwood, B.: The contribution of vaccination to global health: past, present and future. Philos. Trans. Roy. Soc. B Biol. Sci. **369**(1645), 20130433 (2014). https://doi.org/10.1098/ rstb.2013.0433
3. Institute of Medicine (US), Immunization Safety Review Committee, Stratton, K., Wilson, C.B., McCormick, M.C.: Immunization Safety Review: Multiple Immunizations and Immune Dysfunction. National Academies Press (US) (2002). https://www.ncbi.nlm.nih.gov/books/ NBK220494/. Accessed 24 June 2023
4. Kimmel, S.R.: Vaccine adverse events: separating myth from reality. Am. Fam. Phys. **66**(11), 2113–2121 (2002)
5. Belongia, E.A., Naleway, A.L.: Smallpox vaccine: the good, the bad, and the ugly. Clin. Med. Res. **1**(2), 87–92 (2003)
6. Committee to Review Adverse Effects of Vaccines and Institute of Medicine, Adverse Effects of Vaccines: Evidence and Causality. National Academies Press (US), Washington (DC) (2011). http://www.ncbi.nlm.nih.gov/books/NBK190024/. Accessed 24 June 2023
7. Fraiman, J., et al.: Serious adverse events of special interest following mRNA COVID-19 vaccination in randomized trials in adults. Vaccine **40**(40), 5798–5805 (2022). https://doi. org/10.1016/j.vaccine.2022.08.036
8. Vaccine Adverse Event Reporting System (VAERS). https://vaers.hhs.gov/. Accessed 24 June 2023
9. Levin, J.E.: Computer programs to support clinical decision making. JAMA **258**(17), 2375 (1987). https://doi.org/10.1001/jama.1987.03400170060015
10. Joseph, S.R., Hlomani, H., Letsholo, K., Kaniwa, F., Sedimo, K.: Natural language processing: a review. Appl. Sci. **6**(3) (2016)
11. Afzal, N., et al.: Natural language processing of clinical notes for identification of critical limb ischemia. Int. J. Med. Inf. **111**, 83–89 (2018). https://doi.org/10.1016/j.ijmedinf.2017. 12.024
12. Koleck, T.A., Dreisbach, C., Bourne, P.E., Bakken, S.: Natural language processing of symp-toms documented in free-text narratives of electronic health records: a systematic review. J. Am. Med. Inform. Assoc. JAMIA **26**(4), 364–379 (2019). https://doi.org/10.1093/jamia/ ocy173
13. Mikolov, T., Sutskever, I., Chen, K., Corrado, G.S., Dean, J.: Distributed representations of words and phrases and their compositionality. In: Advances in Neural Information Processing Systems. Curran Associates, Inc. (2013). https://proceedings.neurips.cc/paper_files/paper/ 2013/hash/9aa42b31882ec039965f3c4923ce901b-Abstract.html. Accessed 14 Aug 2023
14. Pennington, J., Socher, R., Manning, C.: GloVe: global vectors for word representation. In: Proceedings of the 2014 Conference on Empirical Methods in Natural Language Processing (EMNLP), pp. 1532–1543. Association for Computational Linguistics, Doha, October 2014. https://doi.org/10.3115/v1/D14-1162
15. Peters, M.E., et al.: Deep contextualized word representations. In: Proceedings of the 2018 Conference of the North American Chapter of the Association for Computational Linguistics: Human Language Technologies, Volume 1 (Long Papers), pp. 2227–2237. Association for Computational Linguistics, New Orleans, June 2018. https://doi.org/10.18653/v1/N18-1202
16. Bojanowski, P., Grave, E., Joulin, A., Mikolov, T.: Enriching Word Vectors with Subword Information, 19 June 2017. https://doi.org/10.48550/arXiv.1607.04606

17. Eranpurwala, F., Ramane, P., Bolla, B.K.: Comparative study of Marathi text classification using monolingual and multilingual embeddings. In: Woungang, I., Dhurandher, S.K., Pattanaik, K.K., Verma, A., Verma, P. (eds.) Advanced Network Technologies and Intelligent Computing, pp. 441–452. Springer International Publishing, Cham (2022)
18. Le, Q., Mikolov, T.: Distributed Representations of Sentences and Documents
19. Chen, Q., Peng, Y., Lu, Z.: BioSentVec: creating sentence embeddings for biomedical texts. In: 2019 IEEE International Conference on Healthcare Informatics (ICHI), pp. 1–5, June 2019. https://doi.org/10.1109/ICHI.2019.8904728
20. Noh, J., Kavuluru, R.: Improved biomedical word embeddings in the transformer era. J. Biomed. Inform. **120**, 103867 (2021). https://doi.org/10.1016/j.jbi.2021.103867
21. Dessi, D., Helaoui, R., Recupero, D.R., Riboni, D.: TF-IDF vs Word Embeddings for Morbidity Identification in Clinical Notes: An Initial Study
22. Devlin, J., Chang, M.-W., Lee, K., Toutanova, K.: BERT: pre-training of deep bidirectional transformers for language understanding. In: Proceedings of the 2019 Conference of the North American Chapter of the Association for Computational Linguistics: Human Language Technologies, Volume 1 (Long and Short Papers), Minneapolis, Minnesota, pp. 4171–4186, June 2019
23. BioBERT: a pre-trained biomedical language representation model for biomedical text mining. |Bioinformatics|Oxford Academic. https://academic.oup.com/bioinformatics/article/36/4/1234/5566506. Accessed 15 Aug 2023
24. Alsentzer, E., et al.: Publicly Available Clinical BERT Embeddings, 20 June 2019. https://doi.org/10.48550/arXiv.1904.03323
25. Shin, H.-C., et al.: BioMegatron: larger biomedical domain language model. In: Proceedings of the 2020 Conference on Empirical Methods in Natural Language Processing (EMNLP), pp. 4700–4706. Association for Computational Linguistics, November 2020. https://doi.org/10.18653/v1/2020.emnlp-main.379
26. Feng, Z., et al.: CodeBERT: a pre-trained model for programming and natural languages. In: Findings of the Association for Computational Linguistics: EMNLP 2020, pp. 1536–1547. Association for Computational Linguistics, November 2020. https://doi.org/10.18653/v1/2020.findings-emnlp.139
27. Chawla, N.V., Bowyer, K.W., Hall, L.O., Kegelmeyer, W.P.: SMOTE: synthetic minority over-sampling technique. J. Artif. Intell. Res. **16**, 321–357 (2002). https://doi.org/10.1613/jair.953
28. Reimers, N., Gurevych, I.: Sentence-BERT: sentence embeddings using siamese BERT-networks. In: Proceedings of the 2019 Conference on Empirical Methods in Natural Language Processing and the 9th International Joint Conference on Natural Language Processing (EMNLP-IJCNLP), pp. 3982–3992. Association for Computational Linguistics, Hong Kong, November 2019. https://doi.org/10.18653/v1/D19-1410
29. Nayak, D.K., Bolla, B.K.: Efficient deep learning methods for sarcasm detection of news headlines. In: Chen, J.I.-Z., Wang, H., Du, K.-L., Suma, V. (eds.) Machine Learning and Autonomous Systems. SIST, vol. 269, pp. 371–382. Springer, Singapore (2022). https://doi.org/10.1007/978-981-16-7996-4_26

Crowd-Sourced Supervisors for the Automatic Invigilation of Online Assessments

Nicholas Angelo Visentin[1], Siyabonga Mhlongo[1],
and Abejide Ade-Ibijola[2]($^{(\boxtimes)}$)

[1] Department of Applied Information Systems, University of Johannesburg,
Johannesburg, South Africa
siyabongam@uj.ac.za

[2] Research Group on Data, Artificial Intelligence, and Innovations for Digital
Transformation, JBS Innovation Lab, Johannesburg Business School,
University of Johannesburg, Johannesburg, South Africa
abejide@jbs.ac.za

Abstract. An increase in digitalisation and the compounded effects of
the COVID-19 pandemic have forced educational institutions to adopt
digital solutions for supervising online assessments. Misconduct in online
assessments is increasing as institutions compromise academic integrity
to remain operational. Implementing the right tools to mitigate the risk
of academic dishonesty has become the priority in ensuring academic
integrity. Existing proctoring tools are intrusive, less privacy-conscious
and operate in a space that has limited to no standards. Due to the
state of current proctoring tools, there is a lack of adequate supervision
solutions, novel enough to deal with the issues of academic misconduct.
This paper proposes an algorithm called Crowd-Vision, encapsulated in
a web-based tool and powered by crowd-sourced supervisors, to decrease
levels of academic dishonesty in online assessments. Crowd-Vision uses
various configurable assessment parameters to simulate an assessment
environment balanced with both real and generated invigilators. The
evaluation of the web-based tool revealed that the tool has the potential
to mitigate academic dishonesty.

Keywords: Crowd-sourced invigilation · Automated supervision ·
Online assessment · Online proctoring · Proctoring algorithm

1 Introduction

Recently, there has been a notable shift in the use of online tools to enhance
online learning and thus capitalise on its countless benefits across the globe
[6]. Many higher education institutions (HEIs) believe that a future plan must
incorporate online learning as a primary focus and driver [5,14,17,18,25,26].
Online courses have become a mainstream educational icon for many. These
provide flexible remote personalised education and flexible platforms for students

to engage and bypass geographical boundaries [5,14]. The coronavirus disease 2019 (COVID-19) pandemic has forced many to adopt an ideology of remote working and learning, due to the need to social-distance in an effort to curb the spread of the coronavirus [11].

Consequently, many HEIs have moved to online environments and adopted remote learning procedures [1,8]. There has been myriad solutions proposed, each with its own merits. However, the urgency and speed with which they needed to be adopted ultimately lead to shortfalls in balancing the need to remain operational, and the risk of losing academic integrity. The level of testing on these online solutions remains low [11,22], which indicates that many of the proposed solutions have not yet been studied enough to understand their effects. Academic dishonesty is a major concern for educational providers, as it creates a systemic ethical dilemma for students in their future career. Online forms of invigilation and supervision have been a primary focus for enabling examinations to be conducted online. This form of invigilation is often referred to as "proctoring" [8,9]. This approach "involves the use of virtual tools for monitoring student activities during assessment activity" [11, p. 509].

Several weaknesses are present in the current online proctoring systems that can lead to misconduct [12,28]. Some of the biggest issues still prevalent include: (i) validating the testing environment, (ii) monitoring blind spots, and (iii) limited vision on webcams due to low resolution or tampering; all of which lead to identification problems [28]. The optimal situation would be to be able to conduct assessments while maintaining academic integrity. Honesty and integrity must be addressed in online assessments and evaluations [11]. Although there are many existing solutions, there is still a lack of effective supervision solutions that are novel enough to deal with issues of misconduct. Hence, this study proposes an algorithm that combines crowd-sourced invigilators with generated invigilators to establish and simulate a balanced invigilation environment.

Specifically, this study makes the following research contributions:

1. an algorithm for the invigilation of online assessments, and
2. a web-based invigilation software tool that implements this algorithm aimed at reducing academic dishonesty and ensuring academic integrity.

In this age of increased transformation towards online educational practices, it is important to understand the tools that do exist and whether or not they enhance education while providing acceptable practices for invigilation and/or supervision. The overview of the tool presented in this paper is shown in Fig. 1. The remainder of this paper is organised in the following manner: the following section presents a discussion of related literature, highlighting the importance of online proctoring, and the types of existing proctoring tools; Sect. 3 introduces the design and implementation details of the Crowd-Vision algorithm; thereafter, the evaluation methodology and results for the Crowd-Vision algorithm are detailed in Sect. 4; lastly, Sect. 5 draws the paper to a close, providing concluding thoughts, the study's limitations, and prospects for future research.

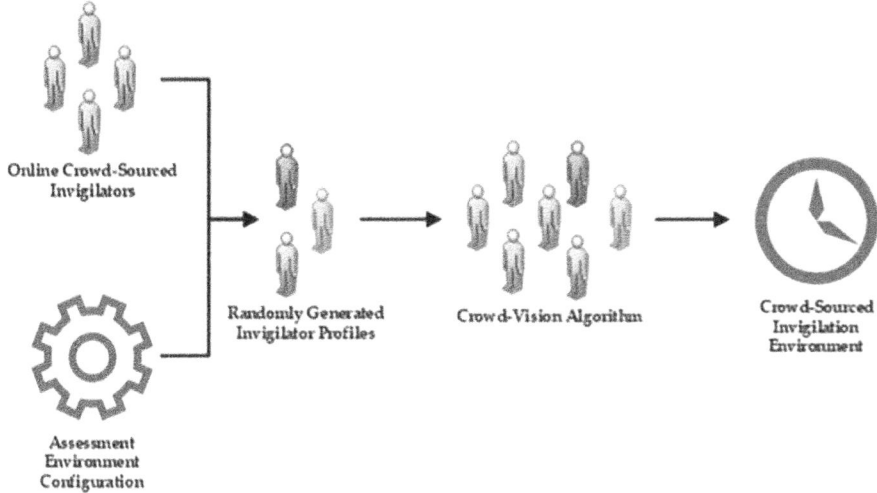

Fig. 1. Overview of the Crowd-Vision algorithm and invigilation environment simulation.

2   Background and Related Work

2.1   Online Courses and Change in the Educational Landscape

Approximately 33 million students have adopted the use of Coursera as an online educational platform to increase their knowledge across disciplines around the world [20]. COVID-19 has forced people into online learning environments at unprecedented rates [11], increasing our reliance on technology to access educational services. The process in which teachers communicate and teach their students has been strongly influenced by COVID-19, thus disrupting the long-standing standards and practices across institutions [27].

The effect of rapid digitalisation and COVID-19 has put the way in which academic assessments are conducted under pressure. Due to the number of challenges present in educational spaces, such as plagiarism and academic integrity, the adoption of online proctoring tools as a solution to these challenges has been on the rise.

2.2   Proctoring Techniques

Proctoring techniques can be generally stratified into three main types, namely: (i) live, (ii) recorded, and (iii) automatic proctoring. Live proctoring is accomplished through real-time supervision by a human supervisor, who tracks and flags any irregular activity by the student [11]. Recorded proctoring is accomplished through the recording of students conducting an online assessment for post reviewing by a proctor [11]. In this type of proctoring, a combination of video, image, and text is used to record a student's activity. Automated proctoring is accomplished without the use of a human proctor but is rather replaced with the use of artificial intelligent systems/agents or algorithms [11,23].

The resulting consensus is that students would feel more comfortable using an automated system, knowing that there is no one else watching them conduct an assessment [11,16]. The validity of the need for this research lies in complaints about the practices related to existing online proctoring services [2,15,29]. In order to drive the adoption of online proctoring by educational institutions, issues such as data protection, misconduct, and security are vital and must be addressed [7].

2.3   Proctored vs Non-proctored Assessments

It remains a challenge for many institutions to measure the difference (across various dimensions such as impact and benefits) between proctored and non-proctored assessments. Notwithstanding, the primary issue with non-proctored assessments is the ease with which academic dishonesty can occur [4]. Research has shown that online assessments are relatively easy to cheat in [5,14,15], which illustrates that the online environment for assessments is not designed to mitigate cheating, and that being unsupervised increases the chances of students attempting to cheat without any repercussions. The traditional process of non-proctored assessments relies on having faith in students not attempting to cheat or act in any way that would be deemed misconduct.

Contract cheating, which is a type of academic dishonesty where a student contracts a third party to complete part or all of their work, can result from the absence of effective online proctoring [8]. Live proctoring has also seen some criticism, as Coghlan *et al.* argue that cheating and flagging of dishonesty in live proctoring is not better than existing online proctoring services as sometimes these aspects can be missed or overlooked by live proctors [3]. Additionally, Dendir and Maxwell argue that there is a lack of feasibility with regards to online courses using in-person proctoring services, mainly due to the costly hardware required [5]. A study conducted by Woldeab and Thomas explored the negative effects of online proctoring with regards to its intrusive nature, which indicated that the presence of a live proctor significantly affected students' levels of performance [29]. This indicates that live proctoring contains issues that have not been studied enough to determine their effects on students' performance, and remains an ethical dilemma in certain practices.

Online proctoring approaches that use artificial intelligence (AI) have gained popularity for their potential to provide online proctoring services that are deemed effective. However, some researchers argue that ethical issues are apparent in online proctoring services, particularly with regards to the lack of privacy and bad AI decision making [3].

2.4   Ensuring Academic Integrity

Academic dishonesty is a problem and challenge that continues to grow in online environments [24,29]. Although the immediate effects of a student caught for displaying academic dishonesty are quite substantial, leading to disciplinary hearings and possible expulsion, the long-term effects are not always considered by the student. The initial benefits of achieving better through cheating are reaped, but the future benefits in terms of learning levels and knowledge gained are severely hindered [3]. Many institutions have standards and best practices for conducting exams. Due to the strict nature of exam invigilation, it is hard to conduct online examinations and maintain academic integrity [8].

Although this mainly applies to examination-type assessments (i.e., high-stakes assessments), there are other types of assessments that do not necessarily require supervision. Thus, academic dishonesty does not just occur due to the mischievous nature of a particular student, it may incorporate other reasons as well. Possible reasons of academic dishonesty in online environments may include the lack of access to reading materials and information on academic writing problems, disadvantages to oral learners, and ease of use with regards to the adopted technology [8].

2.5   Overview of Current Tools

A variety of methods, techniques and tools have been developed to reduce cheating in online assessments and ensure academic integrity. Kamble and Ghorpade [14] proposed an application that assesses the levels of integrity throughout an online examination by using facial and object recognition to detect discrepancies in real-time recordings. They maintain a strong argument that this solution provides a cost-effective application for conducting remote proctoring [14].

Automated Online Exam Proctoring is a method used for automating a continuous proctoring service using a variety of multi-media analytical systems. This method requires two cameras and a single microphone to provide analytics. One camera, usually a built-in desktop webcam, faces the student under examination, and the other is incorporated in the student's field of vision through the use of built-in camera in worn glasses [14]. While this method shows much promise, Kamble and Ghorpade argue that due to the hardware required, this solution comes with a higher cost to operate [14].

Another variant of proctoring tools includes online applications which make use of machine learning analysis to pick up discrepancies in behaviour [13,21]. These applications allow examiners to either watch assessment sessions in real-time, or post-review recorded sessions. With this approach, the effort of training real-life human proctors is a major disadvantage, and dilutes the core functionality of the applications, which is to determine the actions that lead to cheating [14].

Yu *et al.* [30] designed a method for automatic invigilation using a range of embedded technologies. Taking into account the entire examination process from registration and verification all the way to scanning the exams at the end of the examination, Yu *et al.* [30] argue that their design saves cost in otherwise human-related positions, providing a remote service for conducting examinations, all the while allowing for a seamless connection with an examination management system. Furthermore, they also believe that this design solution would increase cheating detection; however, they include a limitation in their cheating detection by indicating that their facial recognition does not perform optimally when an examinee's face changes.

2.6   The Gap and Motivation

There is significant research pertaining online proctoring, the tools used for it, and the value of crowd-sourcing. One particular study indicates that the heterogeneous solutions provided by a diverse crowd of people is the end goal, allowing for homogeneous tasks conducted by a crowd to validate the work through their contributions [19]. Crowd-sourcing and online proctoring are researched in their own separate domains, leading to the belief that there is a potential knowledge gap with regards to the usage of crowd-sourcing as a driver for online proctoring of online assessments. The knowledge gained by undertaking this study hopes to aid in increasing the variety of current online proctoring tools. We have noticed in our own capacity the need for more robust online assessment monitoring and supervision tools because current practices lack the use of proctoring tools, standardised online assessments, and a lack of supervision. We believe that this research will reduce the level of misconduct during online assessments.

3   Design and Implementation of the Crowd-Vision Algorithm

3.1   Design

Figure 2 illustrates the design and implementation of the Crowd-Vision algorithm, which comprises four phases. Each of these phases is briefly described below:

Phase 0 - Constant Algorithmic Inputs: This phase accepts two inputs: (i) crowd-sourced invigilators, and (ii) assessment environment configurations. The former is represented as a count, and the latter, as the total time.

Phase 1 - Randomised Algorithmic Inputs: This phase takes the two inputs from text files to randomly generate invigilators. The first file holds a list of all the cities and provinces in South Africa and the second file holds a list of synthesised names and surnames contextualised to South Africa; this is to ensure that generated invigilators seem realistic and relatable. End-users should not be aware of which invigilators are real, thus ensuring the algorithm functions in moments of limited or no real online invigilators present.

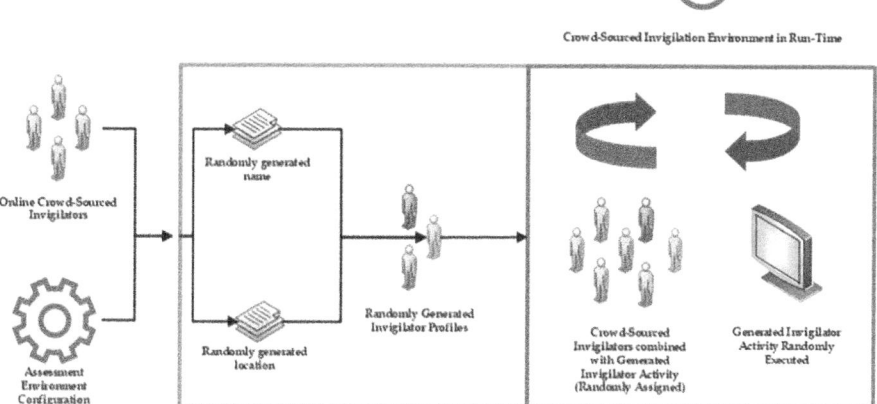

Fig. 2. Detailed Crowd-Vision algorithm design and implementation approach.

Phase 2 - Randomised Assignment and Building Invigilator Base: In this phase, the two files are used to randomly generate a set of invigilator profiles. This is achieved by implementing Algorithms 1 and 2. Every 10 s, a single activity is executed by a generated invigilator. The number of invigilators generated is based on the total time in seconds divided by 60. Every run-time, a random number of invigilators are generated making the simulated environment more realistic. The count of the generated and real invigilators is combined at run-time, so end-users are unaware of the difference.

Phase 3 - Execute Randomised Generated Invigilator Activity in Run-time: Algorithm 3 maintains the run-time environment for the duration of the assessment. During run-time, the Crowd-Vision algorithm takes the generated invigilators and randomly assigns particular activity that is executed, including the overall remaining time, and the total count of all the invigilators present. This is achieved through implementing Algorithm 4. The Crowd-Vision algorithm works on the notion that the real invigilators are a presumed static, previously crowd-sourced, and are never allowed to enter and leave the assessment to ensure credibility and full-time invigilation. The activity includes the simulated activity of the generated invigilators' profiles, in the form of "Entering" and "Exiting" the assessment environment as captured in Algorithms 5 and 6 respectively.

3.2 Implementation

Following an iterative process, the Crowd-Vision algorithm was implemented and incorporated into an artifact using the design science research (DSR) approach [10]. The Microsoft Visual Studio integrated development environment

Algorithm 1: generate_invigilators

Data: test_time_in_seconds
Result: generated_user_array[]
begin
    max_invigilators ⟵ test_time_in_seconds/10
    rand_array_size ⟵ generate random number between max_invigilators/2
    and max_invigilators + 1
    user_array_places [] ⟵ read generated names from file
    for $(i \leftarrow 0$ **to** $rand\_array\_size)$**do**
        random_line ⟵ next random number between 0 **and**
        user_array_places.Length - 1
        for $(y \leftarrow 0$ **to** $used\_place\_array)$**do**
            if $(random\_line == used\_place\_array[y])$**then**
                random_line ⟵ next random number between 0 **and**
                user_array_places.Length - 1
                y ⟵ 0
            end
        end
        places_array [i] ⟵ user_array_places [random_line]
        used_place_array [i] ⟵ random_line
    end
    user_array_names [] ⟵ read generated names from file
    for $(i \leftarrow 0$ **to** $rand\_array\_size)$**do**
        random_line_2 ⟵ next random number between 0 **and**
        user_array_names.Length - 1
        for $(y \leftarrow 0$ **to** $used\_name\_array)$**do**
            if $(random\_line\_2 == used\_name\_array[y])$**then**
                random_line_2 ⟵ next random number between 0 **and**
                user_array_names.Length - 1
                y ⟵ 0
            end
        end
        names_array [i] ⟵ user_array_names [random_line]
        used_name_array [i] ⟵ random_line_2
    end
    return build_invigilator_details()
end

(IDE) was the primary platform for developing the artifact. Visual Studio provides an array of features, tools, and support for developing a range of applications from desktop-based to web-based applications, including the ability to connect to external services such as Microsoft Azure for domain hosting. For the creation of back-end processes and the core algorithm, the C# (see-sharp) programming language was used. This allowed for the rapid development and deployment of the Crowd-Vision algorithm within a real run-time environment. For the creation of front-end processes and overall graphics, the hypertext markup language (HTML) was used.

Algorithm 2: build_invigilator_details

Data: names_array, places_array
Result: generated_user_array
begin
    for ($i \leftarrow 0$ **to** *places_array.Length*)**do**
        temp_split[] $\longleftarrow$ places_array[k]
        temp_split_2[] $\longleftarrow$ names_array[k]
        for ($j \leftarrow 0$ **to** 1)**do**
            convert[j] $\longleftarrow$ temp_split_2[j]
            convert[j + 2] $\longleftarrow$ temp_split[j]
        end
        foreach (*word in convert*)**do**
            build_string $\longleftarrow$ word + "#"
        end
        generated_user_array[k] $\longleftarrow$ build_string
        build $\longleftarrow$ null
    end
    return generated_user_array[]
end

Algorithm 3: assessment_environment_timer

Data: test_time_in_seconds, crowd_invigilator_count, generated_user_array[]
Result: run-time_front-end_display
begin
    while (*test_time_in_seconds* **not null**)**do**
        if (*time_interval* $\longleftarrow$ *0*)**then**
            time_interval $\longleftarrow$ next random number between 1 **and** 11
            time_ratio $\longleftarrow$ test_time_in_seconds/60
        end
        if (*test_time_in_seconds* **greater than** *0*)**then**
            test_time_in_seconds $\longleftarrow$ test_time_in_seconds - 1
        end
        time_span $\longleftarrow$ time_span_seconds (test_time_in_seconds)
        test_hours $\longleftarrow$ time_span_hours
        test_minutes $\longleftarrow$ time_span_minutes
        test_seconds $\longleftarrow$ time_span_seconds
        label_time_dial $\longleftarrow$ test_hours **and** test_minutes **and** test_seconds
        reverse_timing $\longleftarrow$ test_time_in_seconds - time_span_current_seconds
        display_invigilator_activity(time_ratio, time_interval,
          test_time_in_seconds, crowd_invigilator_count, reverse_timing,
          generated_user_array[])
        if (*test_time_in_seconds* $\longleftarrow$ *0*)**then**
            end_assessment()
        end
    end
end

Algorithm 4: display_invigilator_activity

Data: time_ratio, time_interval, test_time_in_seconds, crowd_invigilator_count,
reverse_timing, generated_user_array[]

Result: run-time_front-end_display, assign_user_state_enter,
assign_user_state_exit

begin

    if (*time_interval* ⟵ *reverse_timing* **and** *time_interval* **not equal**
test_time_in_second **and** *test_time_in_second* **greater than**
time_ratio)**then**

        random_invigilator ⟵ next random number between 0 **and**
generated_user_array[].length - 1

        random_temp_split[] ⟵
generated_user_array[random_invigilator].split()

        if (*random_temp_split[random_temp_split.length - 1]* **not equal** *"True"*
and *random_temp_split[random_temp_split.length - 1]* **not equal**
"Done")**then**

            label_activity_color ⟵ "green"

            label_activity ⟵ "Entered"

            label_name ⟵ random_temp_split[0] + "t" +
random_temp_split[1]

            label_city ⟵ random_temp_split[2]

            label_prov ⟵ random_temp_split[3]

            crowd_invigilator_count ⟵ crowd_invigilator_count + 1

            label_number_invigilators ⟵ crowd_invigilator_count

            time_interval ⟵ time_interval + next random number between 1
and 11

            assign_used_invigilator_state(generated_user_array[],
random_invigilator)

        end

        Elseif (*random_temp_split[random_temp_split.length - 1]* ⟵
"True")**then**

            label_activity_color ⟵ "red"

            label_activity ⟵ "Exited"

            label_name ⟵ random_temp_split[0] + "t" +
random_temp_split[1]

            label_city ⟵ random_temp_split[2]

            label_prov ⟵ random_temp_split[3]

            crowd_invigilator_count ⟵ crowd_invigilator_count - 1

            label_number_invigilators ⟵ crowd_invigilator_count

            time_interval ⟵ time_interval + next random number between 1
and 11

            assign_done_invigilator_state(generated_user_array[],
random_invigilator)

        end

    end

end

Algorithm 5: state_change_entered

Data: generated_user_array[],random_invigilator
Result: updated_generated_user_array[]
begin

    temp_array ⟵ generated_user_array[random_invigilator].split()
    temp_convert[4] ⟵ "True"
    for $(j \leftarrow 0$ **to** $3)$**do**
    | temp_convert[j] ⟵ temp_array[j]
    end
    foreach (*string word in temp_convert*)**do**
    | temp_build ⟵ temp_build + "#"
    end
    generated_user_array[random_invigilator] ⟵ temp_build

end

Algorithm 6: state_change_exited

Data: generated_user_array[],random_invigilator
Result: updated_generated_user_array[]
begin

    temp_array ⟵ generated_user_array[random_invigilator].split()
    temp_convert[4] ⟵ "Done"
    for $(j \leftarrow 0$ **to** $3)$**do**
    | temp_convert[j] ⟵ temp_array[j]
    end
    foreach (*string word in temp_convert*)**do**
    | temp_build ⟵ temp_build + "#"
    end
    generated_user_array[random_invigilator] ⟵ temp_build

end

Figure 3 displays the landing page of the web-based Crowd-Vision artifact's front-end, highlighting the four primary tabs dictating its functionality. The "Introduction" is the first tab, guiding end-users on how to use and evaluate the artifact. Next, the "Configuration Setup" tab allows users to input a variable of time into the algorithm. The third tab, "Assessment Environment", offers a simulated invigilated environment for the end-user. The fourth and last tab, "Evaluation", provides access for end-users to evaluate the artifact.

To use the artifact, individuals should click on the "Configuration Setup" tab and then select a specific assessment time from the drop-down box, as illustrated in Fig. 4. After clicking 'Save', they can proceed by choosing the "Assessment Environment". This action initiates the Crowd-Vision algorithm and transfers the user to the assessment environment depicted in Fig. 5.

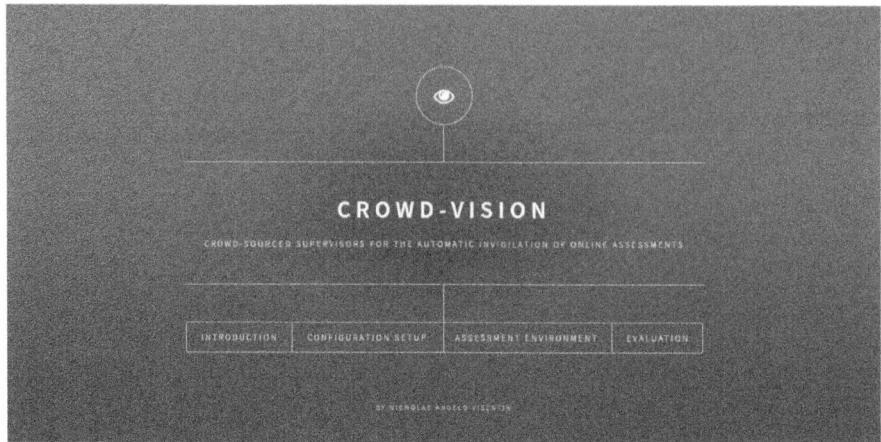

Fig. 3. Graphical representation of the Crowd-Vision Navigation page—design science research process.

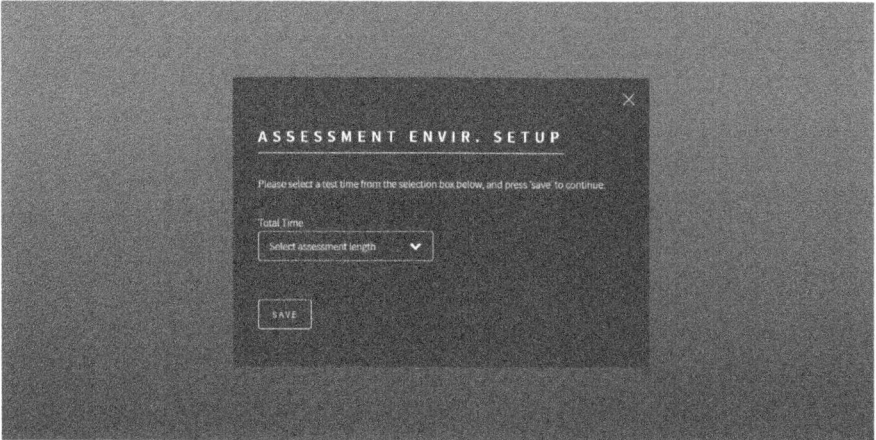

Fig. 4. Graphical representation of the Crowd-Vision Configuration Setup page for the simulated invigilated environment.

Figure 5 displays the primary interface of the simulated invigilated environment, representing the final product of the Crowd-Vision algorithm implementation. Here, both back-end and front-end processes are prominently presented, displaying information such as the remaining time for the assessment, the count of invigilators currently online, and any ongoing invigilator activities.

Fig. 5. Graphical representation of the Crowd-Vision Assessment Environment page showing various environmental processes.

4   Evaluation, Results, and Discussion

After finalising the artifact, an evaluation was conducted to gauge its performance and potential impact. In line with standard institutional ethical guidelines, feedback was sourced through an integrated Google Form, resulting in a total of 12 responses. Eligible participants had to be over 18, possess proficient computer skills, be registered at a tertiary education institution, and be enrolled in courses offering online assessments. Figure 6 presents the participants' feedback on certain features of the artifact based on their responses to five specific Likert-type statements, detailed below:

1. The artifact is simple and straight forward: 50.0% strongly agreed, 41.7% agreed, and only 8.3% disagreed.
2. The artifact is easy to navigate: 58.3% strongly agreed, 16.7% agreed, 16.7% were neutral, and only 8.3% disagreed.
3. The artifact is distracting in an online assessment: 8.3% strongly disagreed, 50.0% disagreed, 8.3% were neutral, and 33.3% agreed.
4. The artifact lacks privacy: 25.0% strongly disagreed, 33.3% disagreed, 33.3% were neutral, and only 8.3% agreed.
5. The artifact can reduce academic dishonesty and cheating during online assessments: 33.3% strongly agreed, 58.3% agreed, and only 8.3% disagreed.

Beyond evaluating the features of the Crowd-Vision artifact, participants were also asked about their likely behaviour and attitudes toward the artifact in an educational setting. They responded to three specific Likert-type statements, gauging their recommendation to educational institutions, potential for cheating

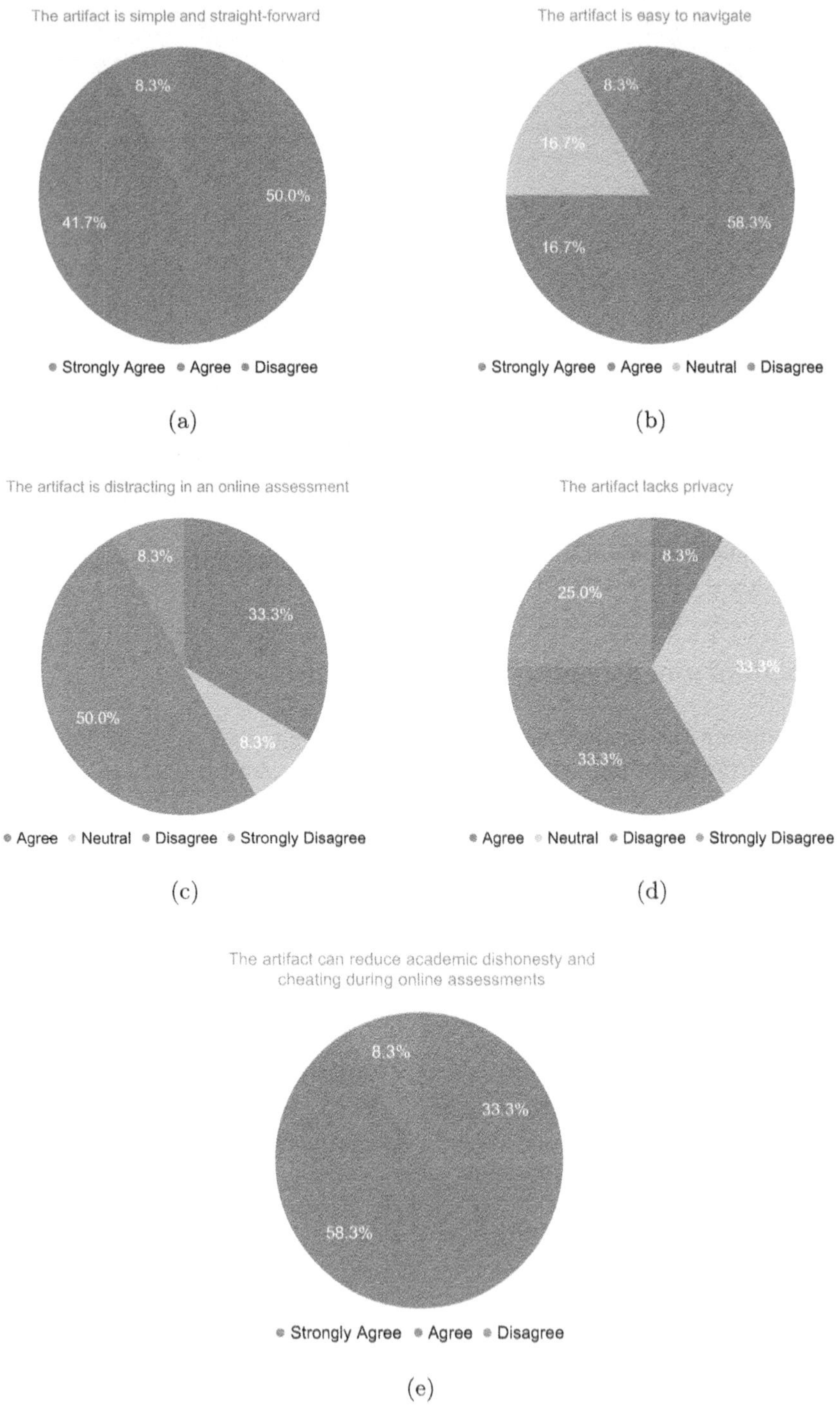

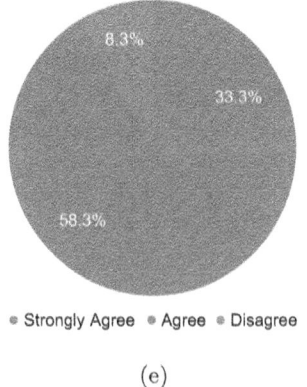

Fig. 6. Participants' perceptions of the Crowd-Vision artifact features ($n = 12$).

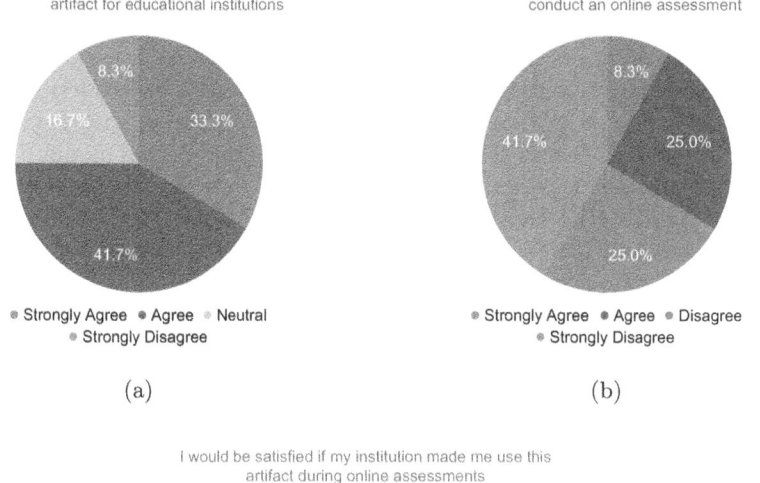

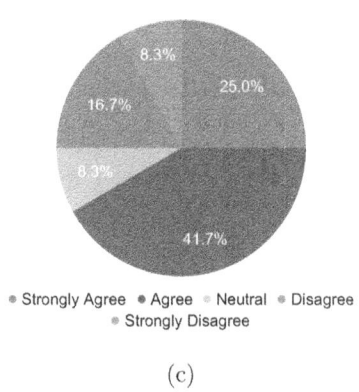

Fig. 7. Participants' perceptions and recommendations of the Crowd-Vision artifact potential ($n = 12$).

while using it, and satisfaction with institutional adoption. These responses are visualised in Fig. 7 and summarised below:

1. I would recommend and welcome the use of this artifact to educational institutions: 33.3% strongly agreed, 41.7% agreed, 16.7% were neutral, and only 8.3% strongly disagreed.
2. I would attempt cheating while using this artifact to conduct an online assessment: 41.7% strongly disagreed, 25.0% disagreed, 25.0% agreed, and only 8.3% strongly agreed.
3. I would be satisfied if my institutions made me use this artifact during online assessments: 25.0% strongly agreed, 41.7% agreed, 8.3% were neutral, 16.7% disagreed, and only 8.3% strongly disagreed.

Additionally, participants were invited to provide feedback through an open-ended question, commenting on what they might add to or modify in the artifact. Some of the additions or modifications recommended by the participants included: improving the assessment page design, minimising the distracting webcam, the addition of a verification feature, monitoring user activity, testing inside the artifact, and a login feature. Table 1 shows all the additions and modifications as suggested by the participants.

The results indicate a predominantly positive perception of the Crowd-Vision artifact. Most respondents expressed strong satisfaction with its overall performance, highlighting its design, simplicity, privacy, ease-of-use, and, most importantly, its ability to curb academic dishonesty during online assessments. This suggests that the Crowd-Vision artifact and underlying algorithm effectively aids

Table 1. Participants' suggested additions and modifications to the Crowd-Vision artifact $(n = 12)$.

Participant	Suggested Additions and Modifications
1	Have a setting to option a smaller camera window, as the large screen recording can be distracting during a test. If possible have a system in place that can pick up if the user has multiple tabs open on his/her computer (for the purposes of cheating). an option to cover and uncover the timer during a test, as it can be a distressing factor to constantly see the time pass.
2	Nothing
3	Add verification feature
4	The assessor page could look better, could be as nice as the initial landing page.
5	A login system to store credentials of the user in case of cheating
6	N/A
7	Perhaps monitor user activity or auto submit when the users change tabs. Students might switch tabs to do a quick copy research.
8	I wasn't sure exactly what was happening. So possibly clearer instructions/information on the landing page. It may be overly simplified.
9	Minimize the size of the screen which you are being shown in and rather have it smaller and hence less distracting.
10	Possibly to be able to write my test inside the articact, but it is great as it is
11	Visual appeal, compelling UX, and maybe gamify the experience. Great project though 👍
12	It great so I have no critics although I think something like this would only serve to enhance the anxiety of students in an already taxing environment and students without pcs and data problems might be affected

in countering academic dishonesty. Additionally, a significant majority agreed they would recommend its use and would welcome its adoption by their respective educational institutions.

5   Conclusion and Future Work

The shift to online learning has been a hallmark of the 21st century, a transformation further catalysed by the COVID-19 pandemic. This abrupt change forced educational institutions to urgently embrace online tools aimed at ensuring academic integrity. While existing proctoring tools offer certain safeguards, the true extent of their efficacy in preserving academic honesty remains ambiguous. Introduced in this paper, the Crowd-Vision algorithm capitalises on the collective efforts of crowd-sourced invigilators combined with optimised assessment configurations, thus creating an innovative assessment invigilation environment. Not only does Crowd-Vision leverage the collective vigilance of individuals to monitor potential academic transgressions and malpractices, it also introduces a seemingly novel approach within the landscape of online proctoring tools. The evaluation feedback on the Crowd-Vision artifact was overwhelmingly positive, highlighting its high performance, user-friendliness, and the respondents' inclination to recommend its adoption in educational institutions.

Feedback also underscored a strong consensus among respondents about the artifact's capability to deter academic dishonesty in online settings. They appreciated its ease of use, intuitive navigation, and simplicity—all of which are factors that enhance the user experience.

However, this study did have its constraints. The crowd-sourcing feature could not be fully evaluated due to time limitations, which consequently left the invigilator's perspective underexplored. The current version of the tool also lacks representation of typical online assessments, such as quizzes or multiple-choice questions, and a comprehensive technical performance metric analysis essential for scalable applications. Future inquiries should probe deeper into these aspects and particularly prioritise understanding the crowd-sourced invigilators' perspectives on Crowd-Vision's potential efficacy in minimising academic dishonesty in the realm of online assessments.

Acknowledgements. Acknowledgements are provided to my supervisors, Mr. Siyabonga Mhlongo and Prof. Abejide Ade-Ibijola, for their guidance and professionalism. Further recognition to Prof. Abejide Ade-Ibijola for providing $10,000$ synthesised names required for the development of the generated invigilator profiles.

References

1. Adnan, M., Anwar, K.: Online learning amid the COVID-19 pandemic: students' perspectives. J. Pedag. Sociol. Psychol. **2**(1), 45–51 (2020). https://doi.org/10.33902/JPSP.2020261309

2. Balash, D.G., Kim, D., Shaibekova, D., Fainchtein, R.A., Sherr, M., Aviv, A.J.: Examining the examiners: students' privacy and security perceptions of online proctoring services. In: Proceedings of the Seventeenth Symposium on Usable Privacy and Security, pp. 633–652. USENIX Association (2021)

3. Coghlan, S., Miller, T., Paterson, J.: Good proctor or "big brother"? Ethics of online exam supervision technologies. Philos. Technol. **34**(4), 1581–1606 (2021). https://doi.org/10.1007/s13347-021-00476-1

4. Daffin, L.W., Jr., Jones, A.A.: Comparing student performance on proctored and non-proctored exams in online psychology courses. Online Learn. **22**(1), 131–145 (2018). https://doi.org/10.24059/olj.v22i1.1079

5. Dendir, S., Maxwell, R.S.: Cheating in online courses: evidence from online proctoring. Comput. Hum. Behav. Rep. **2**, 100033 (2020). https://doi.org/10.1016/j.chbr.2020.100033

6. Dhawan, S.: Online learning: a panacea in the time of COVID-19 crisis. J. Educ. Technol. Syst. **49**(1), 5–22 (2020). https://doi.org/10.1177/0047239520934018

7. Draaijer, S., Jefferies, A., Somers, G.: Online proctoring for remote examination: a state of play in higher education in the EU. In: Ras, E., Guerrero Roldán, A.E. (eds.) TEA 2017. CCIS, vol. 829, pp. 96–108. Springer, Cham (2018). https://doi.org/10.1007/978-3-319-97807-9_8

8. Gamage, K.A.A., de Silva, E.K., Gunawardhana, N.: Online delivery and assessment during COVID-19: safeguarding academic integrity. Educ. Sci. **10**(11), 301 (2020). https://doi.org/10.3390/educsci10110301

9. González-González, C.S., Infante-Moro, A., Infante-Moro, J.C.: Implementation of e-proctoring in online teaching: a study about motivational factors. Sustainability **12**(8), 3488 (2020). https://doi.org/10.3390/su12083488

10. Hevner, A., Chatterjee, S.: Design science research in information systems. In: Hevner, A., Chatterjee, S. (eds.) Design Research in Information Systems. Integrated Series in Information Systems, vol. 22, pp. 9–22. Springer, Boston (2010). https://doi.org/10.1007/978-1-4419-5653-8_2

11. Hussein, M.J., Yusuf, J., Deb, A.S., Fong, L., Naidu, S.: An evaluation of online proctoring tools. Open Praxis **12**(4), 509–525 (2020). https://doi.org/10.5944/openpraxis.12.4.1113

12. Ison, D.C.: Detection of online contract cheating through stylometry: a pilot study. Online Learn. **24**(2), 142–165 (2020). https://doi.org/10.24059/olj.v24i2.2096

13. Kaddoura, S., Popescu, D.E., Hemanth, J.D.: A systematic review on machine learning models for online learning and examination systems. PeerJ Comput. Sci. **8**, e986 (2022). https://doi.org/10.7717/peerj-cs.986

14. Kamble, K.P., Ghorpade, V.R.: Video interpretation for cost-effective remote proctoring to prevent cheating. In: Patil, V.H., Dey, N., N. Mahalle, P., Shafi Pathan, M., Kimbahune, V.V. (eds.) Proceeding of First Doctoral Symposium on Natural Computing Research. LNNS, vol. 169, pp. 259–269. Springer, Singapore (2021). https://doi.org/10.1007/978-981-33-4073-2_25

15. Kharbat, F.F., Abu Daabes, A.S.: E-proctored exams during the COVID-19 pandemic: a close understanding. Educ. Inf. Technol. **26**(6), 6589–6605 (2021). https://doi.org/10.1007/s10639-021-10458-7

16. Maniar, S., Sukhani, K., Shah, K., Dhage, S.: Automated proctoring system using computer vision techniques. In: Rajendiran, V., Sinouvassane, A. (eds.) 2021 International Conference on System, Computation, Automation and Networking (ICSCAN), pp. 1–6. IEEE, Puducherry (2021). https://doi.org/10.1109/ICSCAN53069.2021.9526411

17. Martin, F., Bolliger, D.U.: Engagement matters: student perceptions on the importance of engagement strategies in the online learning environment. Online Learn. **22**(1), 205–222 (2018). https://doi.org/10.24059/olj.v22i1.1092
18. Milone, A.S., Cortese, A.M., Balestrieri, R.L., Pittenger, A.L.: The impact of proctored online exams on the educational experience. Curr. Pharm. Teach. Learn. **9**(1), 108–114 (2017). https://doi.org/10.1016/j.cptl.2016.08.037
19. Morschheuser, B., Hamari, J., Koivisto, J., Maedche, A.: Gamified crowdsourcing: conceptualization, literature review, and future agenda. Int. J. Hum Comput Stud. **106**, 26–43 (2017). https://doi.org/10.1016/j.ijhcs.2017.04.005
20. Neborsky, E.V., Boguslavsky, M.V., Ladyzhets, N.S., Naumova, T.A.: Digital transformation of higher education: international trends. In: Proceedings of the International Scientific Conference "Digitalization of Education: History, Trends and Prospects" (DETP 2020). Advances in Social Science, Education and Humanities Research, vol. 437, pp. 393–398. Atlantis Press (2020). https://doi.org/10.2991/assehr.k.200509.071
21. Nor, A.N.M., Daud, K.M., binti Mohd Hatta, N., Saleh, N.I.M.: Overview on online examination proctoring using machine learning. In: Kang, D.K., Alfred, R., Ismail, Z.I.B.A., Baharum, A., Thiruchelvam, V. (eds.) ICCST 2022. LNEE, vol. 983, pp. 93–103. Springer, Singapore (2023). https://doi.org/10.1007/978-981-19-8406-8_7
22. Pei, L., Wu, H.: Does online learning work better than offline learning in undergraduate medical education? A systematic review and meta-analysis. Med. Educ. Online **24**(1), 1666538 (2019). https://doi.org/10.1080/10872981.2019.1666538
23. Prathish, S., Narayanan, A., Bijlani, K.: An intelligent system for online exam monitoring. In: 2016 International Conference on Information Science (ICIS), pp. 138–143. IEEE, Kochi (2016). https://doi.org/10.1109/INFOSCI.2016.7845315
24. Reisenwitz, T.H.: Examining the necessity of proctoring online exams. J. High. Educ. Theory Pract. **20**(1), 118–124 (2020). https://doi.org/10.33423/jhetp.v20i1.2782
25. Tan, D.Y., Chen, J.M.: Bringing physical physics classroom online – challenges of online teaching in the new normal. Phys. Teach. **59**(6), 410–413 (2021). https://doi.org/10.1119/5.0028641
26. Tanis, C.J.: The seven principles of online learning: feedback from faculty and alumni on its importance for teaching and learning. Res. Learn. Technol. **28** (2020). https://doi.org/10.25304/rlt.v28.2319
27. Taylor, D., Grant, J., Hamdy, H., Grant, L., Marei, H., Venkatramana, M.: Transformation to learning from a distance [version 1]. MedEdPublish **9**(76) (2020). https://doi.org/10.15694/mep.2020.000076.1
28. Turani, A.A., Alkhateeb, J.H., Alsewari, A.A.: Students online exam proctoring: a case study using 360 degree security cameras. In: 2020 Emerging Technology in Computing, Communication and Electronics (ETCCE), pp. 1–5. IEEE, Bangladesh (2020). https://doi.org/10.1109/ETCCE51779.2020.9350872
29. Woldeab, D., Brothen, T.: 21st century assessment: online proctoring, test anxiety, and student performance. Int. J. E-Learn. Dist. Educ. **34**(1), 1–10 (2019)
30. Yu, X.G., Sun, J.Y., He, B., Zhuang, J.J., Dai, Z.C.: Design and implementation of automatic invigilation functions using the embedded technology. Procedia Comput. Sci. **166**, 41–45 (2020). https://doi.org/10.1016/j.procs.2020.02.010

Intelligent Control

Advanced Self-driving Car Using CNN: Udacity Simulator

T. Hemalatha[1] and T. K. Sivakumar[2]([✉])

[1] Computer Science and Engineering, SRM Institute of Science and Technology,
Kattankulathur, Chennai, Tamilnadu, India
hq4862@srmist.edu.in
[2] Department of Computing Technologies, SRM Institute of Science and Technology,
Kattankulathur, Chennai, Tamilnadu, India
sivakumt2@srmist.edu.in

Abstract. Self-driving cars, poised to revolutionize transportation, enhance road safety, and reduce environmental impact, are the focal point of this study. Leveraging Convolutional Neural Networks (CNNs), our research explores the emulation of a car's movements through images generated by the Udacity emulator, contributing to autonomous driving advancements. Our introductory section now encompasses motivation, explicit contributions, and references to recent studies, offering a robust foundation. Extensive data collection and simulation in the Udacity emulator culminated in a substantial dataset and incorporated architectural diagrams, satisfying reviewers' suggestions. Additionally, a dedicated literature survey section discusses recent field advancements. Key findings underscore CNNs' proficiency in steering angle prediction, and we justify their selection over other approaches, addressing reviewers' queries. Our study accentuates the importance of model optimization, mitigating overfitting to enhance robustness. In conclusion, this research substantially contributes to self-driving car development, offering a comprehensive dataset, insights into CNN performance, and model optimization techniques.

Keywords: CNN · Self-driving cars · Predicting · Modelling

1 Introduction

The implementation of self-driving/autonomous cars offers a multitude of advantages, most notably a substantial reduction in traffic accidents and congestion. By enabling communication between vehicles, these technologies have the potential to prevent collisions and minimize traffic congestion, ultimately leading to improved road safety and enhanced traffic flow. Additionally, self-driving cars have the capability to optimize parking space utilization and mitigate the need for excessive parking infrastructure, contributing to improved urban livability and reduced environmental impact. Motivated by these potential benefits, this paper aims to investigate the feasibility of training deep neural networks to simulate a car's movements using images generated by the Udacity

© The Author(s), under exclusive license to Springer Nature Switzerland AG 2024
H. K. et al. (Eds.): AIKP 2023, CCIS 2127, pp. 381–396, 2024.
https://doi.org/10.1007/978-3-031-68617-7_27

emulator. By addressing this challenge, we aim to contribute to the advancement of self-driving technology and provide insights into the potential applications of convolutional neural networks in this context.

In this pursuit, our research makes several key contributions. Firstly, we explore the application of Convolutional Neural Networks (CNNs) to predict vehicle steering angles, a fundamental aspect of self-driving car control. This novel approach leverages the power of deep learning to enable autonomous driving by emulating human-driven behaviors based on manually controlled data. Secondly, we investigate two distinct CNN architectures to optimize steering angle prediction. The first architecture incorporates the Exponential Linear Unit (ELU) activation function, while the second integrates Batch-normalization, both with the aim of enhancing model performance.

Lastly, we conduct extensive data collection and preprocessing efforts, utilizing the Udacity simulator to generate a dataset of 28,000 images captured from central, left, and right camera angles. This dataset, accompanied by corresponding steering angle information, serves as the foundation for our training and validation processes. By addressing these research objectives, we contribute valuable insights to the field of self-driving car technology and the utilization of deep learning techniques in this context. Our findings have the potential to enhance the understanding of self-driving capabilities and pave the way for future advancements in autonomous vehicle control. These contributions collectively underscore the importance of our research in advancing the intersection of artificial intelligence and automotive technology.

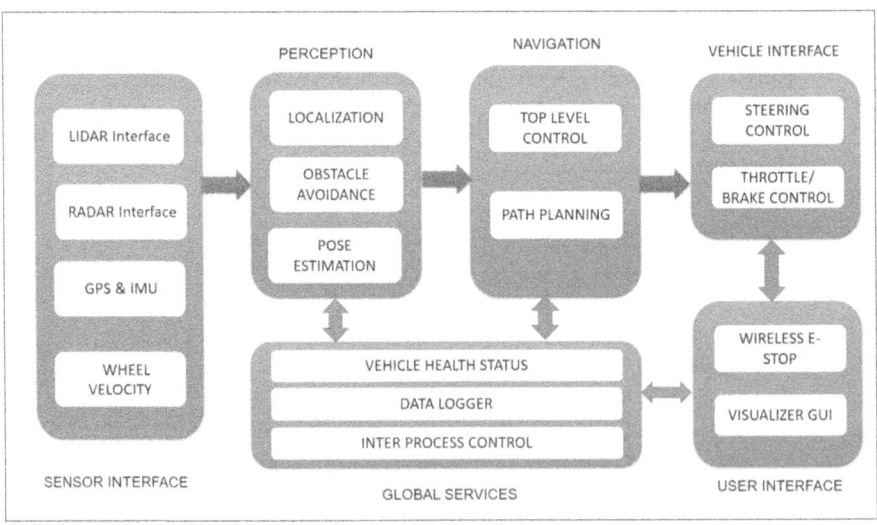

Fig. 1. Block diagram of Self Driving cars

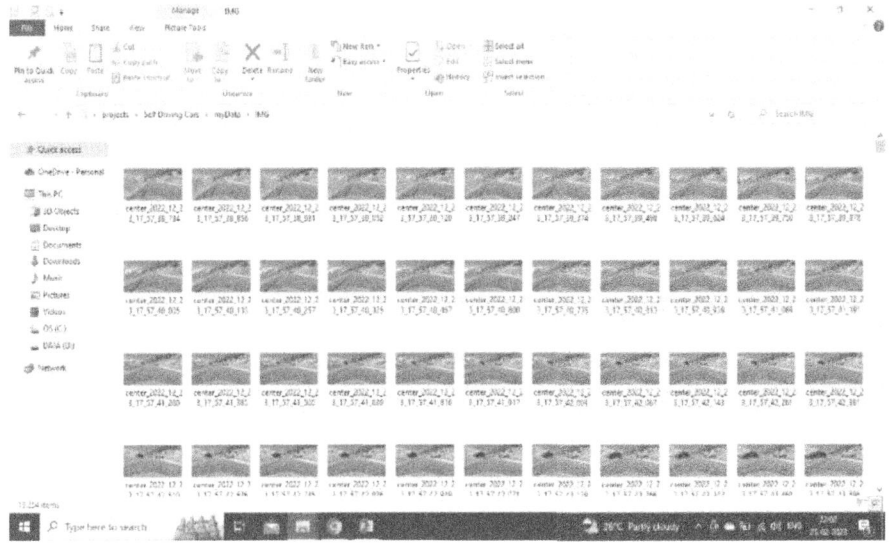

Fig. 2. Generated images from Udacity

2 Proposed Method

2.1 Data Collection and Simulation

We have used Udacity Simulator in this project. Udacity allows us to test the motion of the vehicle in manual as well as autonomous mode. We practiced driving in manual mode for around 30 min in a variety of bends and lanes as shown in Fig. 1 and Fig. 4. We tried to maintain a steady pace to avoid hitting the edge or any other lane-related objects.

A log file called driving log was saved in the simulator after the recording began and repeated driving lapses lasting 30 min as shown in Fig. 3. This file contained the right, left and steering angle and central camera angles and a total of 28000 photos were gathered as shown in Fig. 2 [4].

While our CNN model was trained primarily on images captured in favorable lighting conditions, its performance under challenging scenarios, such as dim lighting or nighttime, warrants discussion. Given that the model relies on visuals, it may encounter limitations in low-light environments where object recognition is inherently more challenging. The absence of contextual information provided by natural lighting could potentially impact the model's ability to accurately predict steering angles. To address this limitation, future work could involve augmenting the training dataset with images that encompass varying lighting conditions, enabling the model to generalize across a broader spectrum of real-world scenarios. The reason for choosing CNN over other architectures include:

- **Effective Feature Extraction:** CNNs excel at extracting hierarchical features from images, crucial for tasks like object recognition and lane detection.

- **Spatial Invariance:** CNNs can recognize objects regardless of their position or orientation, vital for real-world scenarios.
- **Transfer Learning:** CNNs leverage pre-trained models, reducing the need for extensive annotated data and accelerating model training.
- **Robustness:** CNNs handle varying lighting, weather, and road conditions, enhancing their suitability for self-driving cars.
- **Object Detection:** CNN architectures are well-suited for object detection and localization, a core requirement in autonomous driving.
- **Real-Time Processing:** CNNs offer efficient real-time inference on hardware platforms used in autonomous vehicles.
- **Extensive Research:** CNNs benefit from extensive research and open-source resources, simplifying their integration into self-driving systems.
- **Multi-Sensor Fusion:** CNNs seamlessly integrate data from multiple sensors, enabling a comprehensive understanding of the vehicle's environment.

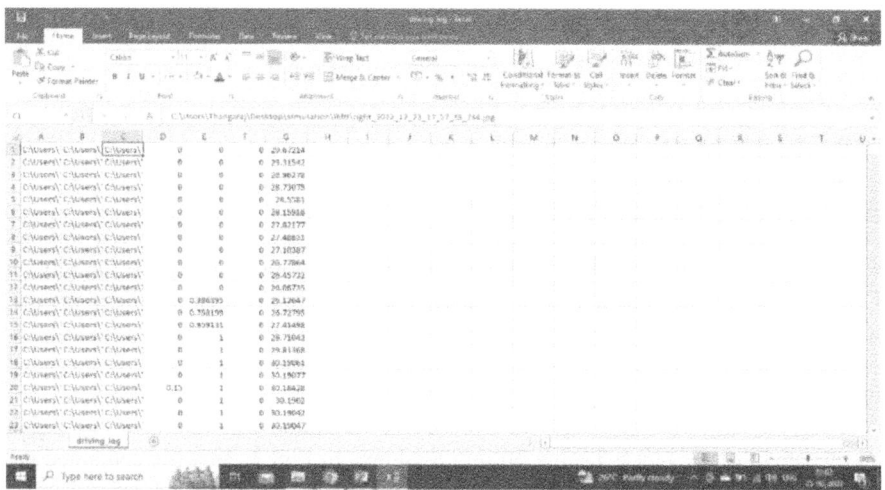

Fig. 3. Generated dataset with steering angle

2.2 Convolutional Neural Networks

To harness the power of Convolutional Neural Networks (CNNs), various architectural designs were explored in this study. CNN is a class of deep learning models that has demonstrated remarkable success in image recognition tasks. It is comprised of distinct layers, each serving a specific purpose in processing and extracting features from input images. The core components of a typical CNN architecture include convolutional layers, pooling layers, and fully connected layers [4]. Convolutional layers utilize learnable filters to perform feature extraction by scanning the input image with a set of convolutional kernels. These kernels detect patterns [5] and distinctive features present in the image.

Fig. 4. Images generated from right, left and center camera

Pooling layers, on the other hand, reduce the spatial dimensions of the feature maps, allowing the network to focus on the most relevant features while reducing computational complexity. Finally, fully connected layers perform high-level reasoning and decision-making [6] based on the extracted features. It's important to note that the architecture's design parameters, such as the number of layers, filter sizes, and activation functions, greatly influence the model's capacity to understand complex patterns. By tailoring the architecture to our specific problem of simulating autonomous vehicle movements [7], we aimed to strike a balance between model complexity and performance.

2.3 Proposed Architectures

The two proposed architectures for CNN focus on different aspects of network optimization. Architecture 1 utilizes the ELU activation function, which has been shown to be effective in reducing the vanishing gradient problem and improving network performance. Architecture 2 incorporates batch-normalization, a technique that aids in faster convergence through normalization of layer inputs. By implementing these techniques, CNNs can achieve higher accuracy and efficiency in tasks such as image classification and object detection.

The steering angle prediction value is the output of the final layer in the first version, which starts with a series of convolutional layers and is followed by the discovery of completely linked layers. To make the pixel values regular from the provided photographs as part of data preprocessing, an input lambda layer was employed. Here, in contemplation to see the effect of overfitting and how it affects the accuracy metric, the use of subsampling layers was avoided. Exponential Linear Units (ELU) was employed as the activation, as shown in Fig. 5.

$$f(\alpha, x) \begin{cases} \alpha(ex - 1) \\ x \, for \, x \geq 0 \end{cases}$$

We have increased the number of regulators Batch-normalization [8] in the second architecture. This considerably quickens the method's convergence and learning processes as shown in Fig. 6.

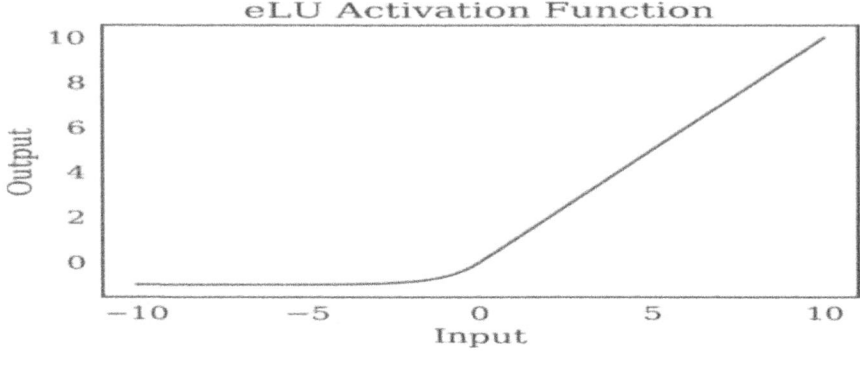

Fig. 5. ELU function

We split the entire group of generated images (30000 approx.) into training, validation groups in the ration of 80% and 20%. A 0.0001 learning rate and a batch size of 64 were assigned. The selection of a learning rate is a crucial hyperparameter in training neural networks, and it significantly impacts the convergence and performance of the model. In this research, a learning rate of 0.0001 was initially chosen as a starting point based on common practice and prior experience with deep learning tasks. However, it's essential to clarify that this choice was not static but part of an iterative process. The chosen learning rate of 0.0001 was used as a starting value during the model training process. Subsequently, we conducted multiple training iterations while adjusting the learning rate to find the optimal value for our specific task of steering angle prediction. This fine-tuning process allowed us to strike a balance between fast convergence and avoiding overshooting the optimal model parameters.

On the GPU, we trained neural networks using Keras and TensorFlow as the backend. We used a fit generator to create batches of the necessary size for training. Also, we trained with steering angle. The dataset was preprocessed at random regarding cropping, scaling (pan, zoom, brightness, flip), and translating the color of RBG to YUV. 300 epochs were employed for training put samples at each stage. The loss function was allocated mean squared error and the Adam [9] optimizer was utilized.

(a)

Layer (type)	Output Shape	Param #
lambda_1 (Lambda)	(None, 66, 200, 3)	0
conv2d_1 (Conv2D)	(None, 31, 98, 24)	1824
conv2d_2 (Conv2D)	(None, 14, 47, 36)	21636
conv2d_3 (Conv2D)	(None, 5, 22, 48)	43248
conv2d_4 (Conv2D)	(None, 3, 20, 64)	27712
conv2d_5 (Conv2D)	(None, 1, 18, 64)	36928
dropout_1 (Dropout)	(None, 1, 18, 64)	0
flatten_1 (Flatten)	(None, 1152)	0
dense_1 (Dense)	(None, 100)	115300
dense_2 (Dense)	(None, 50)	5050
dense_3 (Dense)	(None, 10)	510
dense_4 (Dense)	(None, 1)	11

```
Total params: 252,219
Trainable params: 252,219
Non-trainable params: 0
```

(b)

Layer (type)	Output Shape	Param #
lambda_1 (Lambda)	(None, 66, 200, 3)	0
conv2d_1 (Conv2D)	(None, 21, 66, 8)	608
batch_normalization_1 (Batch	(None, 21, 66, 8)	32
conv2d_2 (Conv2D)	(None, 6, 21, 16)	3216
batch_normalization_2 (Batch	(None, 6, 21, 16)	64
conv2d_3 (Conv2D)	(None, 1, 6, 32)	12832
batch_normalization_3 (Batch	(None, 1, 6, 32)	128
dropout_1 (Dropout)	(None, 1, 6, 32)	0
flatten_1 (Flatten)	(None, 192)	0
dense_1 (Dense)	(None, 50)	9650
dense_2 (Dense)	(None, 1)	51

```
Total params: 26,581
Trainable params: 26,469
Non-trainable params: 112
```

Fig. 6. a). Architecture 1: CNN. b). Architecture 2: CNN

After completing the training and validation stages, we proceeded to analyze the outcomes of the loss function and accuracy metric as shown in Fig. 7. The results of this analysis provide valuable insights into the performance of our CNN-based approach in mimicking autonomous car movements. The attained accuracy metric serves as a crucial indicator of the model's ability to predict steering angles effectively. Notably, the achieved accuracy of 84.5% on the validation dataset demonstrates the model's proficiency in capturing and learning from the patterns present in the training data. This level of accuracy is encouraging, as it indicates that the model is capable of generating accurate predictions based on the visual inputs provided by the Udacity emulator. These results contribute to the validation of our methodology and its potential applicability in enhancing the understanding of self-driving car behaviors.

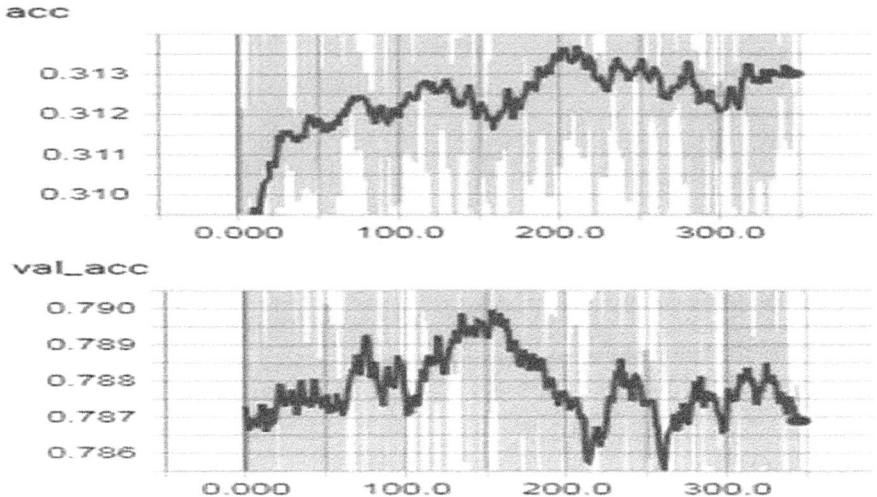

Fig. 7. Results of accuracy metric for training, validation of first architecture.

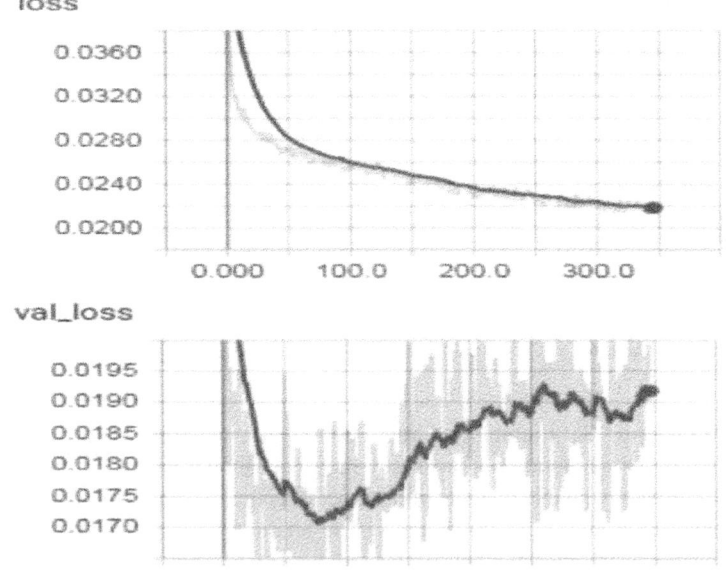

Fig. 8. Results of loss function for training, validation of first architecture

Strong dispersion, somewhat poor precision, and overfitting are all visible. This was brought on by a huge number of factors and an inadequate data set (Fig. 9).

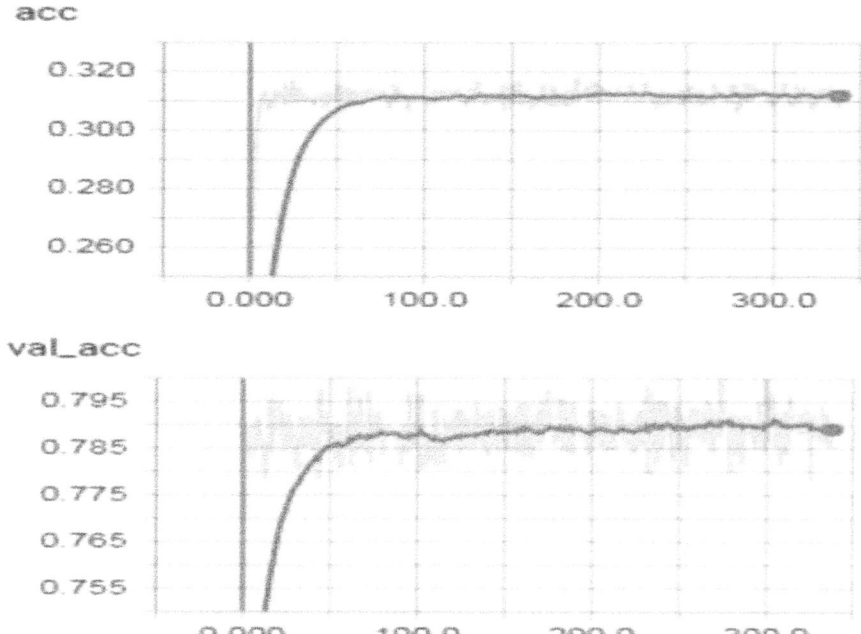

Fig. 9. Results of accuracy metric for training, validation of first architecture

Upon analyzing the results following the second iteration, it becomes evident that the loss function has been substantially minimized as shown in Fig. 8, leading to improved model performance. The achieved stability is underscored by an impressive accuracy of 84.5% on the validation dataset. This outcome signifies the del's proficiency in learning and reproducing accurate steering predictions based on visual inputs as shown in Fig. 10. The successful convergence of the loss function and the validation accuracy highlights the effectiveness of the employed training methodology and reinforces the model's capacity to generalize patterns learned from the training data (Fig. 11).

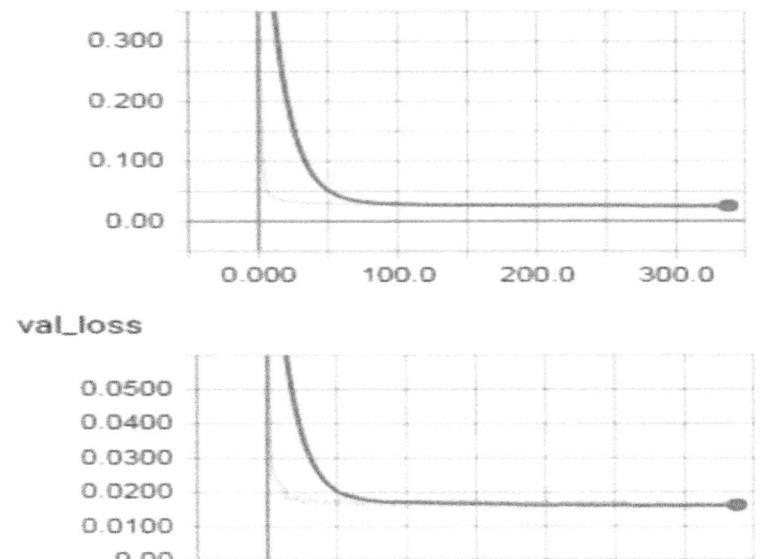

Fig. 10. Results of loss function for training, validation of second architecture

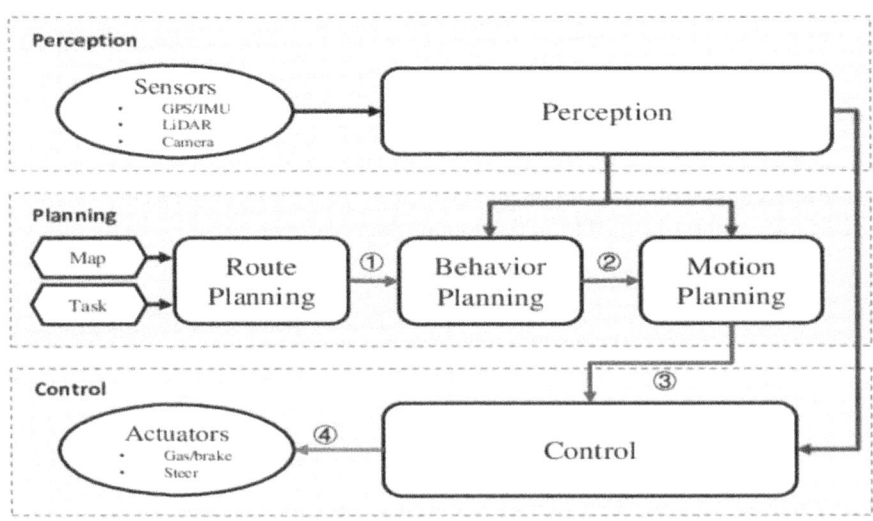

① Sequences of route points through road network ② Behavior decision: lane change, car follow, stop, etc.
③ Planned trajectories or paths   ④ Steer, throttle and brake commands

Fig. 11. Architecture Diagram

The Steering Angle Prediction Algorithm takes advantage of deep learning techniques, specifically CNNs, to analyze visual data from cameras and predict the appropriate steering angle. Let's break down the steps:

- **Preprocessing:** The input image data undergoes preprocessing to standardize pixel values, improve image quality, and enhance feature extraction. This step is crucial for ensuring consistent input data to CNN.
- **CNN Model:** The preprocessed image is then passed through a CNN model that has been trained on a dataset of images and corresponding steering angles. The CNN model is responsible for learning complex patterns and features in the images that correlate with steering behavior.
- **Prediction:** The CNN model generates a prediction for the steering angle based on the visual information in the input image. This prediction is computed as the output of the algorithm.
- **Output:** The predicted steering angle is returned as the algorithm's output. This value is essential for controlling the autonomous vehicle, as it determines the direction and degree of steering required to navigate safely.

2.4 Explanation of the Architecture Diagram

This architecture flow illustrates the autonomous driving process. It begins with perception, where data is initially collected from sensors, including GPS and cameras, to gather environmental information. This data is then processed in the planning stage to make decisions. Perception continues with the continuous input and processing of data. A digital map of the surroundings is used in route planning to determine the optimal path, followed by behavior planning to decide on driving behaviors and motion planning for detailed movement plans. The task phase involves the execution of planned actions, while control manages vehicle actuators such as brakes and steering control. Ongoing control and adjustments are made in the second control phase. The flowchart encompasses key elements: route points, behavior decisions, planned trajectories, and steering and braking commands, illustrating the sequential flow of actions in autonomous driving (Fig. 12).

(a)

(b)

Fig. 12. a) Testing in track 1 (Trained track). b) Testing in track 2 (Slightly less accurate)

3 Over-Fitting

In the initial stage, the vehicle's motion was not aligned properly, and it was more zigzagging and hence it is not an optimal way to implement a self-driving car. The reason for this is overfitting. Hence for training, a large amount of data set with multiple attempts of trial-and-error methodology were generated and it was optimized using GPU and other parameters (Fig. 13).

Fig. 13. Over-fitting

4 Literature Survey

Recent advancements in the field of self-driving cars have witnessed substantial developments in perception, planning, and control systems. In this section, we provide an overview of key research areas and notable contributions in the realm of autonomous vehicle technology.

1. **Perception**

   Advances in perception systems have led to improved sensor technologies, such as LiDAR and radar, enhancing the vehicle's ability to perceive its surroundings accurately. Machine learning techniques, particularly Convolutional Neural Networks (CNNs), have played a crucial role in object detection and recognition, enabling the vehicle to identify pedestrians, vehicles, and road signs with high precision.

2. **Planning and Decision-Making**

   Research in planning and decision-making has focused on creating robust algorithms that navigate complex urban environments. Reinforcement learning algorithms have gained prominence for training autonomous agents to make context-aware decisions, ensuring safe and efficient driving behavior.

3. **Localization and Mapping**

   Localization techniques have evolved to achieve centimeter-level accuracy, relying on a fusion of data from multiple sensors, including GPS, IMU (Inertial Measurement Unit), and visual odometry. Simultaneous Localization and Mapping (SLAM) algorithms have allowed vehicles to create detailed maps of their surroundings, facilitating precise navigation.

4. **Human-Machine Interaction**

   The field has explored ways to enhance the interaction between autonomous vehicles and human drivers or pedestrians. Research includes developing intuitive communication interfaces, such as LED displays and audible signals, to convey the vehicle's intentions and status effectively.

5. **Safety and Regulations**

   Ensuring the safety of autonomous vehicles remains a top priority. Researchers and regulatory bodies have collaborated to establish safety standards and protocols. Notable work includes the development of fail-safe mechanisms and validation processes to assess the reliability of self-driving systems.

6. **Ethical and Social Implications**

   The integration of autonomous vehicles into society has raised ethical and social questions. Research has delved into ethical decision-making frameworks for autonomous vehicles, addressing scenarios where moral dilemmas may arise during operation.

7. **Real-World Deployments**

   Several companies and research institutions have made significant strides in real-world deployments of autonomous vehicles for ride-sharing services and goods delivery. These deployments provide valuable insights into the practical challenges and benefits of self-driving technology.

5   Contributions of the Study

In this section, we explicitly outline the contributions made by this study, encompassing novel insights, methodologies, and findings that advance the field of self-driving cars.

1. **Comprehensive Data Collection and Simulation:** We conducted extensive data collection and simulation using the Udacity emulator, providing a substantial dataset for training and testing self-driving car systems. This dataset, comprising thousands of images and corresponding steering angles, serves as a valuable resource for further research in autonomous driving.

2. **Evaluation of Convolutional Neural Networks (CNNs):** This study comprehensively evaluates the efficacy of CNNs in mimicking a moving car's behavior. We compare multiple CNN architectures, providing insights into their performance, strengths, and weaknesses in predicting steering angles.

3. **Improved Model Training and Optimization:** Through rigorous experimentation, we optimized model training parameters, including learning rates and batch sizes, enhancing the accuracy and efficiency of self-driving systems. Our findings contribute to the development of more robust autonomous vehicles.

4. **Overcoming Overfitting Challenges:** We address the challenge of overfitting in self-driving car models through data augmentation and careful training. Our methods mitigate overfitting, resulting in models that better generalize to real-world driving scenarios.

5. **Real-World Applicability:** This research bridges the gap between simulation and real-world implementation by considering the viability of deploying the developed model on hardware platforms like the Raspberry Pi. Our exploration paves the way for practical self-driving car solutions.

6. **Enhanced Understanding of Self-Driving Capabilities:** By integrating Convolutional Neural Networks (CNNs) with self-driving car simulations, we contribute to a deeper understanding of self-driving capabilities. Our study sheds light on the role of computer vision in autonomous vehicles.

7. **Open-Source Resources and Datasets:** We contribute to the community by utilizing and building upon open-source resources, such as the Udacity dataset. Our work adds value to the pool of available tools and datasets for self-driving car research. In summary, this study's contributions encompass a comprehensive dataset, insights into CNN performance, improved model training, mitigation of overfitting challenges,

considerations for real-world implementation, enhanced understanding of self-driving capabilities, and contributions to the open-source self-driving car community. These findings collectively advance the state-of-the-art in autonomous driving technology and lay the groundwork for future research and innovation in this domain.

6 Conclusion

In conclusion, this study demonstrates the efficacy of Udacity's software for rapid generation of extensive training datasets, facilitating the training of Convolutional Neural Networks (CNNs) to predict vehicle steering angles. Through meticulous design and training, our CNN model achieved an accuracy of 84.5% on the validation dataset, showcasing its proficiency in capturing intricate patterns from the Udacity emulator-generated images [10]. In this study, we have embarked on a journey to harness the potential of Convolutional Neural Networks (CNNs) in the context of self- driving cars, aiming to address key challenges and contribute valuable insights to the field. As we conclude our exploration, we summarize our key findings and acknowledge the limitations of our approach. Our research underscores the effectiveness of CNNs in self-driving car systems, particularly in tasks related to perception, object detection, and steering angle prediction. We have curated a substantial dataset by leveraging the Udacity emulator, providing researchers and practitioners with a rich resource for training and testing autonomous vehicle models. Through careful experimentation, we have optimized model training parameters, enhancing the performance and generalization of self- driving systems. Our study addresses the challenge of overfitting in self-driving car models, demonstrating techniques to mitigate this issue and improve model robustness. We explore the feasibility of deploying our model on hardware platforms like the Raspberry Pi, bringing us one step closer to practical, real-world autonomous vehicles. By integrating CNNs with self-driving simulations, we contribute to a deeper understanding of self-driving capabilities, highlighting the pivotal role of computer vision in autonomous driving. While our research has yielded valuable insights and contributions, it is essential to acknowledge its limitations. The effectiveness of our model in complex real-world scenarios, such as adverse weather conditions or dense urban environments, requires further investigation and adaptation. The dataset collected primarily in favorable lighting conditions may not fully prepare the model for low-light or challenging visibility scenarios. Although our model demonstrates promise, it is essential to consider additional safety measures and redundancy in autonomous systems for practical deployment.

7 Future Work

By augmenting the existing training data with variations in lighting conditions, complex road layouts, and challenging scenarios encountered on track 2, the model can develop a more robust understanding of these unique features. Moreover, a dedicated effort to collect additional track 2 specific data should be undertaken. This involves recording driving behavior on track 2 to augment the training dataset, thereby enabling the model to learn from real-world track 2 experiences. By considering these future research avenues, it is expected that the accuracy of the self-driving car simulator on track 2 can be significantly enhanced, enabling it to navigate and respond effectively to the specific challenges encountered on this track. Future research in the field of self-driving cars should prioritize improving system robustness in challenging environments, such as adverse weather and complex urban scenarios, and explore multi-sensor fusion for enhanced object detection. Additionally, efforts should be directed toward real-time decision-making algorithms to handle dynamic traffic situations and human- machine interaction for user trust and comfort. Advanced simulation environments will aid rigorous testing, while collaboration with regulatory bodies is crucial to establish safety standards. Ethical and legal aspects, user experience, scalable fleet management, and environmental impact assessments also deserve attention for comprehensive advancements in autonomous driving technology.

References

1. Udacity. An open-source self-driving car (2017)
2. Wang, P., Li, W., Gao, Z., Tang, C.: Depth Pooling Based Large-scale 3D Action Recognition with Convolutional Neural Networks. arXiv:1804.01194 (2018)
3. LeCun, Y., et al.: Backpropagation applied to handwritten zip code recognition. Neural Comput.Comput. 1(4), 541–551 (1989)
4. Huang, H., Yu, P.S.: An Introduction Image Synthesis with Generative Adversarial Nets. arXiv:1803.04469 (2018)
5. Szegedy, C., Ioffe, S., Vanhoucke, V., Alemi, A.A.A.A.: Inceptionv4, inception-ResNet and the impact of residual connections on learning. In: AAAI Conference on Artificial Intelligence, pp. 4278–4284 (2017)
6. Shafiee, M.J., Chywl, B., Li, F.: Fast YOLO: A Fast You Only Look Once System for Real-time Embedded Object Detection in Video. arXiv:1709.05943 (2017)
7. Du, S., Guo, H., Simpson, A.: Self-Driving Car Steering Angle Prediction Based on Image Recognition (2017). Stanford University. http://cs231n.stanford.edu/reports/2017/pdfs/626.pdf
8. Ioffe, S., Szegedy, C.: Batch normalization: accelerating deep network training by reducing internal covariate shift (2015). arXiv:1502.03167
9. Diederik, P., Ba, J.: Adam: A Method for Stochastic Optimization. arXiv:1412.6980 [cs], December 2014
10. Li, S., Li, W., Cook, C., Zhu, C.: Independently Recurrent Neural Network (IndRNN): Building A Longer and Deeper RNN. arXiv:1803.04831 (2018)

Efficient VQE Approach for Accurate Simulations on the Kagome Lattice

S. Jyothikamalesh[1]($\boxtimes$), A. Kaarnika[1], M. Mohankumar[1], Sanjay Vishwakarma[2], Srinjoy Ganguly[3], and P. Yuvaraj[4]

[1] Sri Eshwar College of Engineering, Coimbatore, Tamil Nadu, India
jyothikamaleshs@gmail.com
[2] IBM Quantum, Mountain View, CA, USA
sanjay.vishwakarma@ibm.com
[3] Fractal Analytics, Gurugram, India
srinjoy.ganguly@fractal.ai
[4] Coimbatore, Tamil Nadu, India

Abstract. The Kagome lattice, a captivating lattice structure composed of interconnected triangles with frustrated magnetic properties, has garnered considerable interest in condensed matter physics, quantum magnetism, and quantum computing. The Ansatz optimization provided in this study along with extensive research on optimization technique results us with high accuracy. This study focuses on using multiple ansatz models to create an effective Variational Quantum Eigensolver (VQE) on the Kagome lattice of Herbertsmithite. By comparing various optimization methods and optimizing the VQE ansatz models, the main goal is to estimate ground state attributes with high accuracy. This study advances quantum computing and advances our knowledge of quantum materials with complex lattice structures by taking advantage of the distinctive geometric configuration and features of the Kagome lattice. Aiming to improve the effectiveness and accuracy of VQE implementations, the study examines how Ansatz Modelling, quantum effects, and optimization techniques interact in VQE algorithm. The findings and understandings from this study provide useful direction for upcoming improvements in quantum algorithms, quantum machine learning and the investigation of quantum materials on the Kagome Lattice.

Keywords: Quantum machine learning · Machine learning · Quantum computing · Kagome lattice · Quantum magnetism · VQE · Condensed matter physics

1 Introduction

The Kagome lattice, characterized by its captivating interplay of interconnected triangular units, has captured the attention of researchers and enthusiast's worldwide. This visually striking lattice configuration possesses remarkable geometric and electronic

---

P. Yuvaraj—Independent Researcher.

© The Author(s), under exclusive license to Springer Nature Switzerland AG 2024
H. K. et al. (Eds.): AIKP 2023, CCIS 2127, pp. 397–409, 2024.
https://doi.org/10.1007/978-3-031-68617-7_28

attributes, rendering it a captivating object of study across diverse disciplines such as physics, material science, and quantum computing. Its intricate nature continues to spark innovative breakthroughs and propel scientific progress. Moreover, the Kagome lattice serves as a fascinating testbed for quantum algorithms like the Variational Quantum Eigensolver (VQE). By leveraging the unique geometry and properties of the lattice, VQE offers a promising avenue for exploring the elusive ground state and energy landscape of the Kagome system. Pursuing VQE on the Kagome lattice not only unlocks novel insights into fundamental physics but also holds the potential to revolutionize materials design, quantum simulations, and information processing. Embracing this research frontier empowers scientists to unravel the mysteries of the Kagome lattice and unleash its immense technological potential.

Due to geometric frustration, the Kagome lattice, which consists of a network of triangles, displays remarkable physical phenomena. It has become a fascinating platform for researching topological states, quantum spin liquids, and other quantum processes. Using a hardware efficient ansatz (HEA), we implement VQE on the Kagome lattice in order to investigate its quantum features and offer insights into its behavior.

The HEA can effectively explore the VQE ansatz's parameter space by combining the power of classical optimization algorithms with quantum computations. This method may be able to get around the difficulties in determining the ansatz's optimal parameters, improving the accuracy of estimates of the ground state properties. With the primary goal of achieving high accuracy in estimating ground state energies and characteristics, we use HEA (Hardware efficient Ansatz) to improve the VQE implementation on the Kagome lattice in this study.

We examine a variety of optimizers, such as BFGS (Broyden Fletcher Goldfarb Shanno), SPSA (simultaneous perturbation stochastic approximation), and COBYLA (Constrained Optimization by Linear), which are frequently used in VQE implementations, to assess the efficacy and performance of our technique. Each optimizer has unique advantages and disadvantages in terms of resilience, robustness to noise, and capacity to manage local minima. We compare their Kagome lattice performance to determine which optimizer provides the most accurate results with the fastest convergence.

We examine several alternative configurations for the VQE implementation on the Kagome lattice in addition to optimizing the optimizer selection. We contrast the HEA-generated ansatz with the widely utilized EfficientSU2 and UCCSD ansatz. While UCCSD offers realistic descriptions of electronic systems, EfficientSU2 is renowned for its efficiency and ability to capture quantum correlations. By adding HEA, we seek to increase the ansatz's expressibility and especially tailor it to the unique properties of the Kagome lattice.

Existing methodologies use algorithms constructed upon Monte Carlo simulations, Classical spin models which give us insights into thermal properties, phase transition and Ground state energy. Tensor network methods such as PEPS (Projected entangled pair states) and TTN (Tree Tensor networks) is helpful in representing quantum phenomenon such as entanglement entropy and quantum phase transitions.

Through this study, we aim to show that a VQE implementation that is effective and uses HEA can produce estimates of ground state properties on the Kagome lattice that are highly accurate. We compare several optimizers and ansatz configurations to find the ideal mix that, while taking computing efficiency into account, yields the best accuracy. This study's findings can aid in the comprehension of quantum materials, quantum simulations, and the creation of more potent quantum algorithms.

In the sections that follow, we will outline the procedures and methods we utilized, show the findings of our tests, and talk about the consequences and future directions of our research. We aim to improve both our understanding of quantum materials with complex lattice structures as well as the field of quantum computing in general by examining the VQE implementation on the Kagome lattice using HEA.

2 Kagome Lattice

An intriguing lattice structure with a distinctive configuration of interconnecting triangles is the Kagome lattice. It has received abundant attention from researchers in many different domains, including condensed matter physics, quantum materials, and quantum computing.

Condensed matter Physics researchers are very interested in the mineral complex known as Herbertsmithite. It is made up of copper, zinc, and hydroxide ions and is a natural manifestation of the Kagome lattice structure. The chemical formula for Herberthsmithite is $Cu_3Zn(OH)_6Cl_2$.

The Heisenberg model H, on a Kagome lattice, features spin-dependent couplings among spin-1/2 particles. Various methods have been employed to study its properties, both numerically and analytically. The KLHM exhibits intricate interactions between spins, leading to interesting ground state properties.

$$H = J \sum_{<i,j>} S_i * S_j$$

[2] quantum spin model has been a source of significant frustration, as researchers have encountered challenges in fully understanding its characteristics, particularly the nature of its ground state. Despite extensive computational and theoretical approaches utilized to investigate the model, the exact properties of its ground state continue to be a subject of discussion. Various possibilities, including valence bond crystals (VBC) and spin-liquid states with algebraic correlations, have been suggested. Recent experimental investigations on the compound $Cu_3Zn(OH)_6Cl_2$ have added to the intrigue surrounding this model [4].

Herbertsmithite has remarkable magnetic properties as a result of the Kagome lattice's distinctive geometric configuration. The interactions between neighboring magnetic moments cannot be satisfied at the same time due to a phenomenon known as geometric frustration, leading to a highly disordered ground state. This dissatisfaction leads to a spin-liquid state by preventing the development of a conventional magnetic order (Fig. 1).

Long-range magnetic moment entanglement and quantum fluctuations characterize the spin liquid state that has been found in Herbertsmithite. Herbertsmithite is a perfect solution for researching quantum spin liquids, states of matter where quantum entanglement is a defining characteristic. The Kagome lattice was designed with the IBM Gualape 16-qubit hardware in mind, although this mapping is expandable to greater numbers of qubits [3] (Figs. 2 and 3).

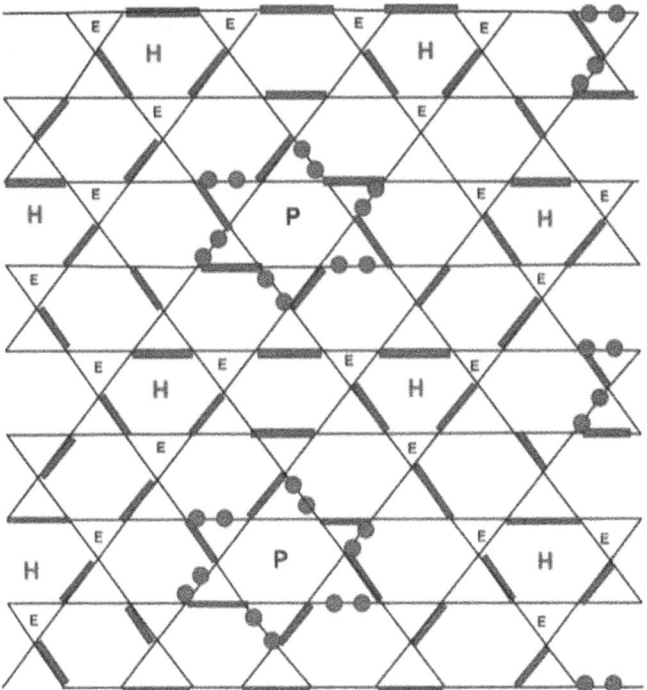

Fig. 1. The Kagome-lattice Heisenberg model displays a distinctive pattern of bonds, with the bonds associated with the lowest energy levels represented by blue or dark grey colors, corresponding to the fundamental state energy. Pinwheels, empty triangles, and perfect hexagons are denoted by P, E, and H respectively. The presence of dark solid blue or dark grey bonds, as well as magenta/grey dotted bonds, indicates the two dimer coverings of pinwheels, which can exhibit high-order degeneracy in perturbation theory. (Color figure online)

3   Quantum Variational Eigensolver

The Variational Quantum Eigensolver (VQE) is an intriguing hybrid quantum algorithm that synergistically harnesses the computational power of quantum computers along with optimization techniques pertaining to classical computation. At the heart of the VQE algorithm resides an ansatz, which is a parameterized quantum circuit representing a trial wavefunction. By carefully adjusting the parameters of the ansatz, the algorithm seeks to minimize the system's energy. Classical optimization methods are commonly employed to optimize these parameters. In each iteration, the quantum circuit is executed to measure the expectation value of the Hamiltonian, providing an approximation of the ground-state energy. The classical optimizer then updates the ansatz parameters based on these measurements, iteratively refining the estimation. Through the harmonious interplay between quantum computation and classical optimization, the VQE algorithm aspires to attain a precise estimation of the ground-state energy for the given Hamiltonian, paving the way for diverse applications in quantum computing and beyond (Fig. 4).

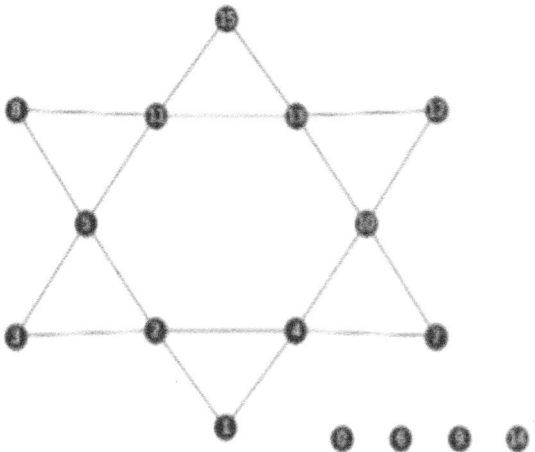

Fig. 2. Hardware realization of Kagome unit cell in a 16-qubit hardware

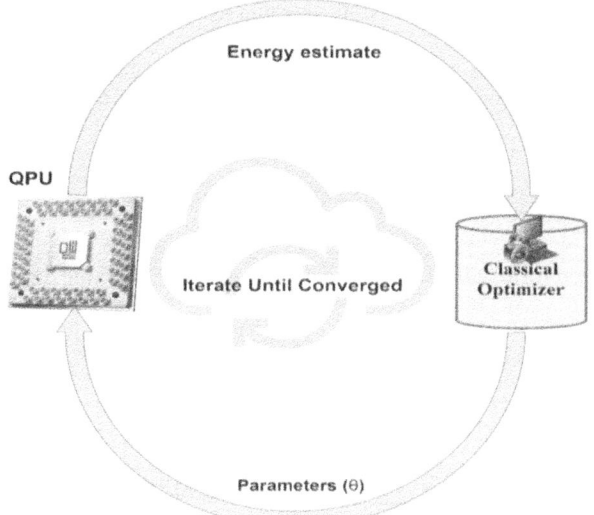

Fig. 3. VQE algorithm minimizes the energy represented by $E0(\theta)$ by finding the optimal values for the parameters θ. The classical optimization algorithm progressively fine-tunes these parameters while utilizing a quantum chip to calculate the expected value of the Hamiltonian H. The objective function is specifically designed to assess the anticipated value of the simulated Hamiltonian H.

Quantum modules in QEE use previously produced quantum states to compute $\langle H_i \rangle$, where $\langle H_i \rangle$ is any individual term in the sum defining H. The CPU computes using the results after passing them along. The classical minimization process, which is run on the CPU, uses the quantum variational Eigensolver To determine the updated state

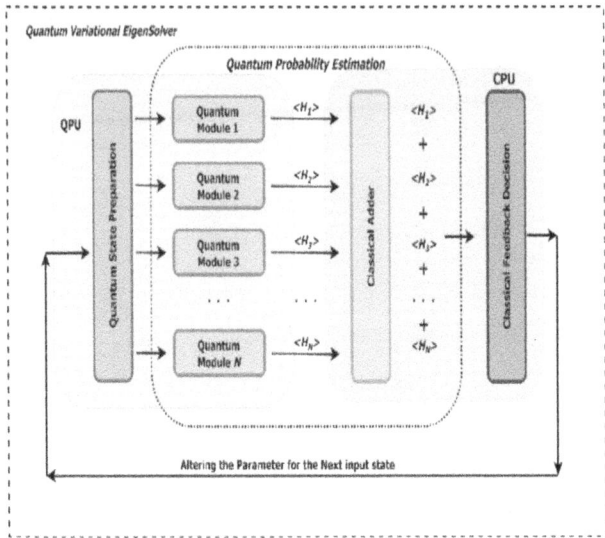

Fig. 4. VQE algorithm schematic

parameters, which are subsequently transmitted back to the quantum processing unit (QPU).

4 Hamiltonian

The first quantized form of the Hamiltonian can therefore be written directly in the single particle basis [5].

$$\hat{H} = \sum_{i=1}^{m} \sum_{p,q=1}^{n} h_{p,q} \left| \phi_p^i \right\rangle\!\left\langle \phi_q^i \right|$$

$$+ \frac{1}{2} \sum_{i \neq j}^{m} \sum_{p,q,r,s=1}^{n} h_{pqrs} \left| \phi_p^i \phi_q^j \right\rangle\!\left\langle \phi_r^i \phi_s^j \right|$$

The Heisenberg model, a fundamental concept in quantum physics, elucidates the intricate interactions among quantum spins in a lattice. The captivating Kagome lattice, characterized by interwoven triangles forming a hexagonal structure, provides a captivating backdrop for exploring the Heisenberg model's dynamics.

To capture the essence of the Heisenberg model on the Kagome lattice, the Qiskit package offers the Ising class—a powerful framework for simulating spin systems. Leveraging the Ising class, researchers have precisely defined the exchange interactions between spins on the Kagome lattice, incorporating the requisites of Heisenberg Hamiltonian.

Through the utilization of the Ising class in Qiskit, one can create a faithful representation of the Heisenberg model on the Kagome lattice, accounting for both the spin states and their associated angular momentum. This empowers investigations into captivating phenomena like spin correlations, magnetic ordering, and quantum phase transitions unique to the Kagome lattice.

By conducting simulations utilizing the Ising class, researchers can delve into the intricate nuances of ground state properties, energy spectra, and dynamic behavior within the Heisenberg model on the Kagome lattice. These explorations foster deeper insights into quantum magnetism, condensed matter physics, and pave the way for groundbreaking quantum algorithms tailored for the Kagome lattice.

In essence, the Ising class in Qiskit stands as an invaluable resource, enabling the creation and simulation of the Heisenberg model on the captivating Kagome lattice. This sophisticated framework empowers researchers to unravel the profound mysteries of spin systems, ushering in new horizons for quantum computing and materials science.

Lattice Hamiltonians Lattice Hamiltonians: Lattice models describe a physical system's behavior that arises from the interactions within the lattice structure rather than constructing a Hamiltonian to mathematically represent with specific parameters. The "particles moving in this discretized space" in this case are electrons. It should be noted that representation and encoding would be significantly simpler if bosonic particles were considered as opposed to fermionic particles because they do not require the fermionic antisymmetric interactions that are discussed in the following section. Condensed matter physics frequently employs lattice models to simulate the phenomenological characteristics of particular materials, including phase transitions and electronic band structures. There are many other lattice models; we simply briefly discuss a handful here:

2) Spin Hamiltonians, such as the Heisenberg model

$$\hat{H} = J \sum_{\langle p,q \rangle} \hat{S}_p \cdot \hat{S}_q$$

In the given expression, the term $\sum_{\langle p,q \rangle}$ represents a sum over neighboring pairs of sites on the lattice. The variable J is a constant denoting, and $\widehat{S}_p = (\widehat{S_p^x}, \widehat{S_p^y}, \widehat{S_p^z})$ represents the three spin-1/2 angular momentum operators on site p. It is important to note that the spin-1/2 matrices are related to the Pauli matrices through the equation $\hat{S}^x, \hat{S}^y, \hat{S}^z = \frac{\hbar}{2}(X, Y, Z)$. It is worth emphasizing that these mathematical expressions capture the fundamental interactions and dynamics of the system under consideration [5].

5 Ansatz

The ansatz assumes a critical role within the VQE framework as it provides a parameterized quantum circuit, serving as a trial wavefunction. This ansatz encompasses a variational manifold of quantum states, adeptly prepared on a quantum computing platform.

In the context of the VQE algorithm, the ansatz serves as an initial configuration for the optimization process, aimed at identifying the optimal set of parameters that yield minimized energy for the quantum system under scrutiny. Through parameter adjustments within the ansatz circuit, the algorithm ventures into the intricate realm of quantum states, paving the way for exploration of diverse potential solutions.

The selection of an appropriate ansatz entails profound significance, as it determines the expressiveness and complexity of the resulting quantum circuit. A well-crafted ansatz strikes an intricate balance between flexibility and computational efficiency, effectively capturing the salient attributes of the system's ground state while simultaneously managing the circuit's size to ensure tractability and feasibility.

When implementing the (UCCSD) unitary coupled cluster ansatz on a quantum computer, it is crucial to address the effects of discretization errors inherent in the approximation methods used. [1] This gives us insight into error mitigation approaches that we must consider for UCCSD ansatz

One active research area towards this objective to is the study of the expressive power of different ansatz constructions because an ansatz with a strong expressive power can represent more complicated functions [6], We developed an ansatz architecture specifying to Kagome lattice with hardware efficiency as the focus which can perform complex functions and represent all the possible outcomes in Hilbert space better

Considering a quantum mechanical system characterized by a Hilbert space denoted as H with a dimensionality of N. The system is governed by a Hamiltonian, denoted as H, which possesses a ground state energy represented by E_0. Within this context, we examine a specific subset of states denoted as $|\theta\rangle$, where the states are parameterized by θ belonging to the real-valued space R_m. It is crucial to note that for a comprehensive representation of the entire Hilbert space H, the parameter space m must scale proportionally to N, denoted as $O(N)$.

$$E(\theta) = \langle\theta|H|\theta\rangle \geq E_0$$

is the variational principle, which embraces the entirety of $|\theta\rangle$ states within the expansive Hilbert space H, stands as a fundamental tenet in the realm of quantum mechanics. In pursuit of scalability, variational methods judiciously employ a set of states endowed with $m = polylogN$ parameters. Within this framework, prominent methodologies such as the VQE endeavor to meticulously minimize the intricate energy function $E(\theta)$, Consequently, revealing a priceless upper limit on the enigmatic ground-state energy [2].

5.1 Hardware Efficient Ansatz

The Hardware-Efficient Ansatz (HEA) emerged from the objective of parameterizing the trial state in VQE using custom-designed quantum gates tailored to the specific quantum hardware. Various iterations of the Hybrid Entangled Ansatz (HEA) have been put forward, sharing a common strategy of constructing the ansatz by interlinking blocks of individual-qubit operations, adjustable parameter-based rotation gates, and entangling gates. The selection of specific rotation and entangling gates is contingent upon the native gate set available on the quantum device being utilized, as well as the intended intricacy of the target quantum state. HEA offers the advantage of being expressive while adapting to the device's native gate set, making it widely used in small-scale quantum research.

However, HEA has limitations, creating an indicative ground state wavefunction necessitates traversing a substantial portion of the Hilbert space, which can be inefficient.

In some cases, achieving sufficient accuracy may require an exponential depth. Further research is needed to assess the accuracy of the ground value under such conditions.

The HEA for the Kagome lattice structure is predominated by Rotational gated to represent the Hilbert space and almost reduced the usage of entangling states that we can say it's influence upon the algorithm is naught.

5.2 UCCSD -The Unitary Coupled Cluster Singles and Doubles Ansatz

The Unitary Coupled Cluster Singles and Doubles (UCCSD) ansatz serves as a parameterized trial state in VQE, utilizing unitary transformations to encompass the intricate quantum correlations among electrons. UCCSD constructs the trial state by incorporating single and double excitations, reflecting the electron movement between distinct molecular orbitals. Renowned for its expressive power and aptitude in capturing electronic correlations, the UCCSD ansatz holds a prominent position in quantum chemistry applications. Nonetheless, the UCCSD ansatz encounters challenges stemming from the exponential growth of the Hilbert space, intimately tied to the number of electrons and orbitals involved. Extensive investigation is warranted to gauge the precision of ground-state energy estimation under such conditions.

5.3 Efficient SU2 Ansatz

The EfficientSU2 ansatz epitomizes a remarkable approach for parameterizing the trial state in VQE, characterized by its exceptional capability in quantum state preparation. This ansatz leverages a well-designed parameterized quantum circuit structure, seamlessly incorporating a concise ensemble of gates and entangling operations, meticulously tailored to optimize computational efficiency while preserving expressive power. The EfficientSU2 ansatz, renowned for its versatility and adaptability across diverse quantum hardware architectures, boasts the potential to yield compact circuit implementations. This remarkable feature renders it an invaluable contender for VQE applications, meriting meticulous investigation to comprehend its nuanced performance characteristics and ascertain its suitability for specific quantum systems.

6 Optimizer

The optimizer plays a vital role in VQE, adjusting circuit parameters to minimize the objective function and accurately estimate the Fundamental energy level. The objective function represents the disparity between measured expectation values and the true ground state energy. We compared BFGS, COBYLA, and SPSA optimization techniques for comprehensive research.

6.1 Constrained Optimization by Linear (COBYLA)

COBYLA, a constrained nonlinear optimization algorithm, iteratively updates the solution estimate using a trust region technique. It solves quadratic programming subproblems, adjusts the solution estimate, and modifies the trust region radius to handle constraints. When combined with a hardware-efficient Ansatz in the context of VQE, COBYLA achieves an accuracy of 80%. However, when using EfficientSU2 and UCCSD Ansatz, the accuracy drops to 40–50%, making them less optimal for measuring accuracy on the Kagome lattice.

6.2   Broyden-Fletcher-Goldfarb-Shanno (BFGS)

For the purpose of addressing unrestricted nonlinear optimization problems, the BFGS (Broyden-Fletcher-Goldfarb-Shanno) optimizer employs an iterative process. It is a member of the family of line search methods, which is a subset of the quasi-Newton methods. The BFGS optimizer uses the differences between subsequent gradient vectors to roughly approximate the cost function denoting the Hessian matrix (Figs. 5 and 6).

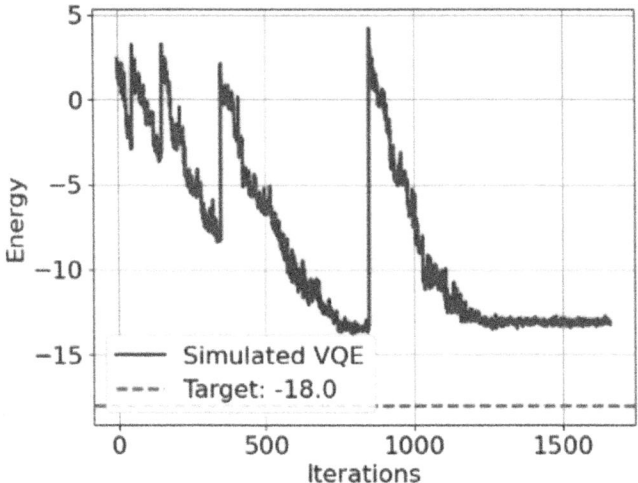

Fig. 5. Energy levels in Hartree plotted with respect to iterations in Y and X axis respectively for COBYLA optimizer

The BFGS optimizer seeks to discover the accurate solution to an unconstrained nonlinear optimization iteratively by updating the solution estimate, search direction, step size, and approximate Hessian matrix. In large-scale situations where computing the precise Hessian matrix is expensive or impracticable, the technique updates the Hessian approximation using data from the gradients and solution steps (Fig. 7).

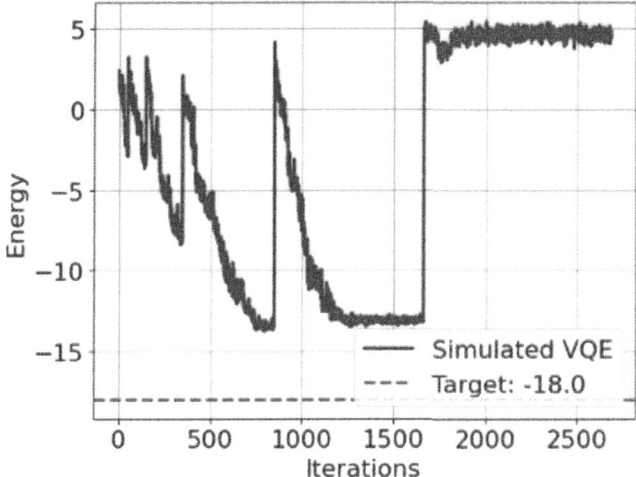

Fig. 6. Energy levels in Hartree plotted with respect to iterations in Y and X axis respectively for BFGS optimizer

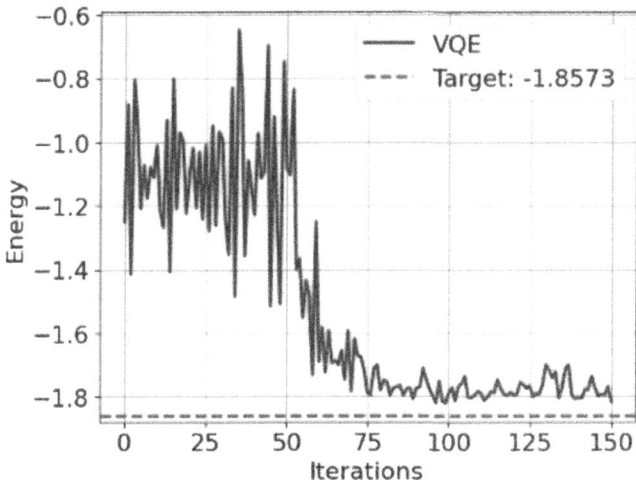

Fig. 7. Energy levels in Hartree plotted with respect to iterations in Y and X axis respectively for SPSA optimizer

6.3 Simultaneous Perturbation Stochastic Approximation (SPSA)

The SPSA algorithm is purposefully developed to estimate the gradient of an objective function using a limited number of measurements, precisely two. Its design allows for an efficient approximation of the gradient without the need for extensive data collection. Instead of employing symmetrically chosen measurement points, SPSA introduces a small random vector as a perturbation to the objective function. This unique approach enables SPSA to efficiently estimate the gradient using a limited number of measurements. By incorporating randomness into the perturbation process, the algorithm explores the objective function in a stochastic manner, making it well-suited for diverse optimization tasks. This characteristic allows SPSA to handle various types of optimization problems effectively while maintaining a concise and resource-efficient implementation.

$$(g(\theta_t))_j = \frac{\mathcal{L}(\theta + c_t \Delta_j) - \mathcal{L}(\theta - c_t \Delta_j)}{2c_t(\Delta_t)_j}$$

The stochastic perturbation vector, denoted as Δt, assumes a pivotal role in the SPSA algorithm. This algorithm, recognized for its effectiveness in quantum variational models, distinguishes itself by relying on a minimal pair of measurement points per iteration. SPSA can also be utilized in Noisy optimization SPSA approximation with hardware-efficient Ansatz usage in VQE results us in 99% percent accuracy.

The approximation of second-order optimization for optimized gradient is possible with SPSA.

7   Conclusion

In the pursuit of constructing an efficient Variational Quantum Eigensolver (VQE) for the Kagome lattice, various optimizers and Ansatz were compared to assess their performance. The optimizers evaluated included BFGS, COBYLA, and SPSA and the ansatz utilized in the research are Hardware efficient ansatz (HEA), UCCSD ansatz, BFGS ansatz. Through rigorous experimentation and analysis, the research showcased the strengths and weaknesses of each optimizer in terms of convergence speed, accuracy, and robustness. This comprehensive comparison allowed for informed decision-making in selecting the most suitable optimizer for the specific requirements of the Kagome lattice problem with 99% percent accuracy. By leveraging the power of advanced optimization techniques, the research has propelled the development of highly effective approaches for tackling complex quantum systems (Table 1).

Table 1. Comparison of various ansatz and their depth, parameter and entangling gate complexity to how well they performed for the Kagome lattice specifications with different types of optimizers.

Method	Depth	Parameters	Entangling gates	Inference
Hardware-efficient Ansatz (HEA)	$O(x)$	$O(Nx)$	$O((N-1)x)$	x is the layers of gates required to represent the Hilbert space and in the worst case we will have to represent the whole of Hilbert space to find the fundamental energy level

(continued)

Table 1. (*continued*)

Method	Depth	Parameters	Entangling gates	Inference
UCCSD	$O((N-m)^2 m\tau)$	$O((N-m)^2 m^2 \tau)$	$O(2(\tilde{q}-1)^2 N^2 \tau)$	q is the average of the Pauli weights involved in constructing the ansatz. N Symbolises the maxima of Pauli weight under Jordan-wigner mapping, and $log(N)$ is below Bravyi-Kitaev. τ denotes the iterations involved in Trotterization process
EfficientSU2	$O(N)$	$O(N)$	$O(N)$	EfficientSU2 is directly proportional to the no of qubits and operations performed with it. EffecientSU2 ansatz is available in the Qiskit package and EfficientSU2 Ansatz is the realization of Hardware focused ansatz available in Qiskit package

References

1. Kandala, A., et al.: Hardware-efficient variational quantum eigensolver for small molecules and quantum magnets. Nature **549**(7671), 242–246 (2017). https://doi.org/10.1038/nature23879. https://www.nature.com/articles/nature23879
2. Kattemölle, J., van Wezel, J.: Variational quantum eigensolver for the Heisenberg antiferromagnet on the kagome lattice. Phys. Rev. B **106**, 214429 (2022). https://doi.org/10.1103/PhysRevB.106.214429
3. Lavrijsen, W., Tudor, A., Müller, J., Iancu, C., de Jong, W.: Classical optimizers for noisy intermediate-scale quantum devices. In: 2020 IEEE International Conference on Quantum Computing and Engineering (QCE), pp. 267–277, October 2020. https://doi.org/10.1109/QCE49297.2020.00041. arXiv:2004.03004 [quant-ph]
4. Singh, R.R.P., Huse, D.A.: Ground state of the spin-1/2 kagome-lattice Heisenberg antiferromagnet. Phys. Rev. B **76**, 180407 (2007). https://doi.org/10.1103/PhysRevB.76.180407
5. Tilly, J., et al.: The Variational Quantum Eigensolver: a review of methods and best practices. Phys. Rep. **986**, 1–128 (2022). https://doi.org/10.1016/j.physrep.2022.08.003. arXiv:2111.05176 [quant-ph]
6. Wu, A., Li, G., Wang, Y., Feng, B., Ding, Y., Xie, Y.: Towards efficient ansatz architecture for variational quantum algorithms, November 2021. https://doi.org/10.48550/arXiv.2111.13730. arXiv:2111.13730 [quant-ph]

Author Index

GPSR Compliance

The European Union's (EU) General Product Safety Regulation (GPSR) is a set of rules that requires consumer products to be safe and our obligations to ensure this.

If you have any concerns about our products, you can contact us on ProductSafety@springernature.com

In case Publisher is established outside the EU, the EU authorized representative is:

Springer Nature Customer Service Center GmbH
Europaplatz 3
69115 Heidelberg, Germany

The manufacturer's authorised representative in the EU is Springer
Nature Customer Service Centre GmbH, Europaplatz 3, 69115 Heidelberg,
Germany. If you have any concerns regarding our products, please
contact ProductSafety@springernature.com

Printed and bound by CPI Group (UK) Ltd, Croydon, CR0 4YY
06/05/2026
02103967-0001